Larry
Merry Christmas
2006!
Love,
Janis

GARDENING IN THE TROPICS

R.E. Holttum
Ivan Enoch

TIMBER PRESS
Portland, Oregon

GARDENING IN THE TROPICS

© 1991 Times Editions Pte Ltd
© 2002 Times Media Private Limited

Published in North America by
Timber Press, Inc.
The Haseltine Building
133 S.W. Second Avenue, Suite 450
Portland, Oregon 97204, U.S.A.

Reprinted 1995, 1997, 1999, 2002

Designed by Octogram Design, Singapore
Typeset by Superskill, Singapore
Colour separation by United Graphic, Singapore
Printed by Times Offset, Malaysia

ISBN 0-88192-309-5

CONTENTS

Introduction   *vii*

The Tropical Climate   *1*

Garden Planning   *9*

Soils, Cultivation and Manuring   *29*

Propagation and Pruning   *40*

Herbaceous Plants and Dwarf Shrubs   *53*

Ornamental Shrubs and Climbers   *89*

Hedges   *141*

Trees and Palms   *153*

Lawns   *195*

Foliage Plants   *203*

Orchids   *247*

Other Kinds of Gardens   *275*

Vegetables   *313*

Fruits and Fruit Trees   *331*

Pests, Diseases and Weeds   *351*

Appendices   *367*

INTRODUCTION

Since the first production of this book there have been a great many changes affecting gardening in the tropics, although the basic methods of cultivation and management remain the same. The range and number of plants available to gardeners in this region has increased enormously and new ornamentals appear each year. There has been a considerable increase also in the range and effectiveness of many garden chemicals such as fertilizers and pesticides which are marketed under different trade names in different parts of the world, though the active chemical is the same in each product. A list of ingredients should be given on the container of each product and the gardener should read this to ensure that the chemical he requires is present. The use of some of the newer chemicals has been banned in many countries because of their effect on the environment, and some of these are, in any case, highly dangerous unless used with extreme caution. Consequently, in the chapter on pests and diseases, there are descriptions only of those chemicals which are regarded as safe and easy to use by the home gardener.

In all parts of the tropics there has been a great increase in the rate of house building and, because of the demand for lower-priced accommodation, many of these new houses are small, with very little or no space available for gardening. Flats or apartment buildings are more common, and, despite the lack of space in each unit, it is still possible to do a little gardening, especially if there is a small balcony where a few pots or a small trough can be accommodated. Some houses have no outdoor space, but it still may be possible to create miniature gardens in pots which can be kept on window-sills or, with the right choice of plants, entirely indoors. Suggestions for several kinds of miniature gardens have been given, together with lists of suitable plants to be used.

The original chapters have been retained and some have been increased considerably because of the greater number of plants now available. Brief descriptions of all plants are given, together with a note on the method of propagation and suggestions on how they may be planted to give the most decorative effect. Lists of plants suitable for various conditions are provided but there is no reason why the species mentioned should not be tried in other situations, provided the cultural conditions are adjusted accordingly. Many of the plant names in the original edition have been retained, but in some cases their Latin names have been changed and this has been mentioned where possible. Unfortunately, many of the additional plants described in this revised edition have no common name, although gardeners may be familiar with their Latin names, such as 'Philodendron'. Technical names for all these plants are those used in *Hortus Third*, a dictionary of cultivated plants published by the staff of the L.H. Bailey Hortorum at Cornell University. The plant descriptions are arranged alphabetically, regardless of whether they appear under their common or Latin name.

Many of the long-established ornamental plants grown in Singapore and Malaysia and other parts of the tropics originated from tropical America, and there has been relatively little breeding or selection work done with them in order to produce new varieties. New species have been brought into cultivation and there is scope, therefore, for home gardeners to try a little artificial hybridizing, as the production of new plants from seeds offers a better opportunity for the appearance of new forms or colour varieties. Most of the cultivated tropical ornamental plants have relatively few, if any, cultivars when compared with those of temperate regions, and in a number of cases the cultivars available were produced originally in the heated greenhouses of temperate countries and from there they were redistributed to the tropics. It is possible now that this situation may change because the increased building of new houses, together with a greater interest in house plants, has created a larger demand and this has resulted in a much larger commercial production of many plants. In addition, the increased interest in garden ornamentals and house plants has been stimulated now by the easy availability of information on their culture, and by the fact that such items as pots, fertilizers, pesticides and garden equipment are available in forms which are more convenient to use in small gardens or where space is very limited.

Most of the plants described here are available quite easily from nurseries, or they can be obtained by exchange with other gardeners, especially if there is a local Gardening Society which organizes various kinds of meetings.

When visiting nurseries, it is important to allow plenty of time for looking in every corner as it is sometimes possible to find a single neglected specimen of a desirable plant set aside and almost hidden from view. Small nurseries which are slightly untidy and muddly offer the most excitement for such exploration, whereas tidy, well kept nurseries may not yield such delights.

The ornamental plants which have been described have been considered from their decorative value only in any kind of garden and no account has been taken of any superstitions which may be associated with any particular species. Should there be any such connection, then the plants concerned can be avoided and substituted with others in order to give a similar kind of effect in a planting scheme.

At the present time, very many of the plants described here are grown commonly as house plants in most temperate countries, though they may be smaller in size there than when they are grown in the tropics. However, if they are grown in heated greenhouses, they may attain a comparable size to those grown out of doors in the tropics. Many of these tropical plants will tolerate a much wider range of temperatures than is usually imagined and will grow luxuriantly in centrally heated houses where the day and night temperatures show a wide difference. It should be remembered that in the wet tropics the high humidity will keep the temperature much lower during the day than in a dry tropical area. Consequently, many plants of the wet tropics are almost ideally suited for culture in the centrally heated buildings of temperate countries. In these places, potting mixtures, fertilizers and pesticides are made up and used in exactly the same way, but burnt earth will not be available and can be replaced by various kinds of potting mixtures produced, some of which are sterilized; all are suitable for growing house plants. The potting mixture can be altered by the addition of sand or peat to suit the needs of the plants.

Good drainage is essential and plants should be positioned in the house to receive as much light as possible for good growth; in fact, they often thrive so well that they need to be kept under strict control. In these centrally heated houses, pot plants are often kept near radiators where the temperature is higher, but they will then become very dry. This can be counteracted by standing the pots in a container with a layer of moist peat at the bottom. It makes the air around the plants more humid and they should grow rapidly. Fumes from coal or gas fires will stop the growth of some of these tropical plants, for example Begonia, but others, such as some palms or Philodendron, are not affected. Some of the tropical plants grown in centrally heated rooms are treated with chemicals to prevent them from growing too tall, for example Hibiscus, and there is no reason why this treatment should not be used also in the tropics for pot plants to adapt them to small rooms.

Many of the ornamental garden plants from the tropical lowlands will grow very well up to about one thousand metres above sea level, and sometimes above this, as the daytime temperature at these altitudes is often almost as high as in the lowlands. However, the night temperature will be much lower and for some plants this is beneficial. Often these plants will show better leaf and flower colour at the higher elevations than they do in the lowlands and frequently the flowers remain open for a longer period.

Although the book focusses on gardening in Malaysia and Singapore, many of the plants mentioned are available everywhere in the tropics. In other parts of the world, however, different cultivars may be available and where possible these variations have been mentioned. Some new varieties have appeared since this revision was initiated and are rapidly becoming as well known as the originals. A few species of wild plants are described as suitable garden plants, but in other parts of the tropics there are wild plants also, especially trees, which can be used as ornamentals. When selecting wild plants for use in the garden, some features to be sought are shape and size; size, form and colour of flowers; colour and form of foliage; and the method of propagation. A wild plant in the garden may grow extremely vigorous because of lack of competition from other plants, and it may therefore need strict control to prevent it from spreading too rapidly.

It is hoped this book will provide some help for gardeners in many parts of the wet tropics, as well as in temperate regions.

1 THE TROPICAL CLIMATE

Compared with other parts of the world, the Malaysian climate is very uniform. This is especially true as regards temperature, the daily range of which varies little throughout the year, the mean (in the lowlands) being somewhere near 27 degrees Centigrade. Rainfall varies more, and there are quite regular seasonal changes in some parts of the country. In other parts, especially the south, rainfall distribution varies much from year to year and there is no dry season. But in all parts of the country, except the extreme north, the dry seasons are far less marked than in most tropical places, and the average yearly rainfall is high. These high and uniform conditions of temperature and rainfall have very profound effects on the growth and flowering of plants. Some of the effects are direct, and some indirect, through the soil. We will consider briefly these effects in the following paragraphs, because they limit the activities of Malaysian gardeners. It is true that by the use of different kinds of soils, by careful cultivation, and by glass or other roofing, the gardener can mitigate to some extent the effects of excessive rainfall, but without control of humidity and temperature, the gardener is at the mercy of the climate and must make the best he can of it.

Apart from the direct effects of uniform high temperature and rainfall, there is a negative effect which is very important. Many plants live in seasonal climates, and are adapted to seasonal change. They rest in cold or dry seasons and grow in warm or wet weather. But it is flowering and fruiting that are of most interest to the gardener, and these are usually related to climatic change. Some plants flower before leaf growth begins; some flower on the leafy shoots; and some when leaf growth is complete. In many, the formation of flower buds takes place only in dry weather. In some, length of day is important; they will flower only in the long days of summer, or only in the short days of autumn. But in almost all cases flowering (and therefore fruiting) is related to a definite stage in the annual series of climatic changes. In short, most plants flower when they receive a definite climate stimulus, and that stimulus is a *change* of climate.

Now in Malaysia, we have very little climatic change, and therefore many plants native of other countries will not flower here, or in some cases they flower very little. Judged from the present standpoint, there are two kinds of garden plants that are successful in Malaysia: first, those that will flower all the year, needing no stimulus of change; and second, those that will respond to the rather small climatic changes occurring in Malaysia. There is a third class, comprising only certain trees (such as the Flame of the Forest); these go through their cycles of leaf-renewal, flowering and leaf fall independent of climate. Our dry weather is not dry enough or regular enough to make them drop their leaves; they appear to keep their leaves until they have become inefficient, and then drop them (whatever the weather), renewing them almost immediately.

Of plants that flower throughout the year, the following are examples: the Buttercup tree (Cochlospermum), Allamanda, *Bougainvillea glabra* and its varieties, the Peacock Flower (Caesalpinia), several shrubby species of Cassia, most kinds of Clerodendron, Duranta, Galphimia, Gardenia, Hibiscus, Ixora, Lantana, Oleander (*Nerium indicum*), Frangipanni (Plumeria), the Potato tree (*Solanum macranthum*), several kinds of Thunbergia. It is interesting to note that many of these plants are definitely seasonal in flowering in a climate on the borders of the tropics, such as Hong Kong. Often, too, they never flower as profusely in Malaysia as they do in a seasonal climate; as we have flowers all the year round, we have to be content with fewer at one time. Some indeed are so grudging of flowers that they are hardly worth growing in Malaysia.

Plants that flower in response to climatic change vary much in the kind of stimulus to which they will respond. Some need only a few days of rainless weather, especially if this follows a wet period. Others need so much dry weather that they will not flower every year; and so we get a gradation to those that will not flower at all. Of course, a plant may behave differently in different parts of the country. Many shrubs and trees which need a dry season as a stimulus to flowering are much more successful in the north than in the south. Dadap trees (Erythrina) lose their leaves and are covered with a mass of scarlet flowers every year about February in the north of the Malaysian peninsula, but in the south there is not enough dry weather to make them do this, and flowering is irregular and scanty. Some shrubs that need only a small stimulus will flower several times in the year (e.g. Petrea) though in seasonal climates they flower only once. The same applies to bulbs such as Zephyranthes and Crinum.

There is another kind of climatic stimulus that we have in Malaysia, namely a sudden fall of temperature. When a great storm sweeps over the country, as it often does on a hot day, the air temperature will fall ten degrees or more in a very few minutes. Some kinds of plants are sensitive to this sort of change. The most remarkable example is the Pigeon Orchid, which is found on almost all old trees in the open countryside; this flowers nine days after such a storm. But there are also shrubs and trees which are sensitive to this stimulus. Of course, their flower buds must be ready; they grow to a certain stage, and then wait for the fall of temperature, which starts them all on their final growth. Coffee is one example, and the great Angsana tree (Pterocarpus) is another.

The above remarks apply chiefly to trees, shrubs, climbers and other permanent woody plants. As regards herbaceous plants, these are normally divided into annuals and perennials. An annual plant, in a seasonal climate, passes through its whole life in one growing season. It starts from a seed, grows up, flowers, fruits and dies, leaving seeds which rest until the next season.

In temperate climates there is only one growing season a year, and so such plants are called annuals. But in Malaysia the growing season is continuous. We can plant an annual at any time, and in three months or so it will produce seeds, which we can plant again; so we can have three generations or even more in a year, and the term 'annual' becomes meaningless. It is useful, however, as a name for those shortlived plants which normally behave as annuals. But we find that there is not a very sharp line between annuals and more permanent plants. Some plants which are treated as annuals become rather woody at the base and go on flowering longer than the normal annual, and from these we pass on to dwarf shrubs.

Herbaceous perennials are usually adapted to rest in the non-growing season, often by means of an underground rootstock, corm or bulb. As with woody plants, many of them need a rest between growing seasons, or a certain amount of drought or cool temperature to form their flower buds. In most such cases, they will not grow in Malaysia. It is only a few which will go on growing and flowering all the time – or will rest in spite of our climate, or can be rested artificially at our temperatures – which will succeed. Michaelmas Daisies and Golden Rod come into the first category, though they are always dwarfed, flowering prematurely. Dahlias and Gladiolus are perennials which can be rested. This should be done until they begin to grow again, which may perhaps be in three months, and this new growth can start at any time of the year.

The above remarks apply primarily to the lowlands of Malaysia, but the same general principles hold for our hill stations, though the kinds of plants concerned are largely different. There is the same limitation due to the absence of strong climatic change. Plants from temperate regions with a similar mean temperature to that of our hill stations will often not thrive, or not flower, in Malaysia because they do not have the stimulus of change to which they are adapted to respond.

Another uniformity of our climate, in lowlands and highlands alike, is the length of daylight, which varies little from twelve hours throughout the year. The variation may be, at most, only half an hour, but this is sufficient stimulus to cause flowering in some plants. There are some plants which will flower only in days longer than this; many of these plants cannot be grown successfully here. On the other hand, we can grow successfully many autumn-flowering (i.e. short day) plants of northern latitudes, such as Michaelmas Daisies and Dahlias; but these will flower at all times in Malaysia; and so they tend to be precocious, and must have intensive manuring to make them grow as large as possible before the flowers appear.

The uniform high temperature of Malaysia has a direct effect, making rapid plant growth possible, *providing other necessary conditions are also fulfilled*. This proviso is of the greatest importance. It is no use expecting a plant to grow fast if its roots are starved of water or air or the other things they need. The better adapted a plant is to respond to higher temperatures by making more rapid growth, the more efficient must be our methods of cultivation; that is, of course, if we wish to get the best results.

But high temperature has a direct effect on other things also. It accelerates physical and chemical processes taking place in the soil. Humus and organic manures decompose more rapidly, thus the effect of manuring is more transient. It is best not to give too much manure at a time, and to apply it frequently. Though little is known of these matters, it is probable that nitrogen-fixing bacteria are active in Malaysian soils, and that these are stimulated also by the high temperature; but they need humus if they are to work efficiently. Another point to remember is that the bare soil of a garden bed, exposed to the full sun, attains a much higher temperature than the air, or than soil which is shaded from the sun. This is another cause of active decomposition of humus in garden beds. In passing, we may also note that the roots of some plants will not stand the high temperature of such exposed soil, though their leaves will stand full exposure to the sun. Such plants need shelter until they are large enough to shade their own roots.

The evenly distributed and copious rainfall of Malaysia and the high average humidity of the air also make for rapid plant growth – again, if other necessary conditions are fulfilled. The most important of these conditions, so far as most plants are concerned, is adequate aeration of the soil. For roots need air; they must breathe, or they cannot live. Now, one of the effects of heavy rain is to compact the surface soil, especially if it inclines to have a high clay content; this results in reduced aeration. Simultaneously, the high temperature is causing decomposition of the organic matter which helps to keep the soil open; and so the two climatic factors of high rainfall and high temperature work together to spoil the tilth of the soil and make it a less healthy place for root growth. Thus any soil inclined to be heavy (as many of our soils are) needs frequent cultivation and organic manure to keep it in good order. Another consideration immediately arises. A small garden bed of good soil is of no use if it lies in a heavy clay. Such a bed allows the rain to pass through it, but if the rain is held up by the clay underneath, the bed may remain waterlogged for hours or even days. Healthy root growth of most plants is impossible in such conditions. Either deep digging or subsoil drainage is necessary to carry the rain water below the level occupied by the roots. This is, of course, not necessary in light soils.

Thus, to take full advantage of the benefits of high temperature and frequent rain enjoyed in Malaysia, our methods of cultivation must be careful and thorough, and also frequent throughout the year. Manures are also needed, and are dealt with in a chapter of this book; but without satisfactory cultivation manures are wasted. If we manure a plant, and see no benefit from the treatment, we may infer that the roots are not happy; they have not enough air and perhaps too much water (too much water is a more common complaint in Malaysia than too little). All our cultivation is aimed at the roots of the plant; and the great difficulty of gardening is that we cannot see those roots.

In any garden the growing conditions will seldom be even throughout the whole area and some parts of the garden will have a totally different climate from other parts. For instance, trees, walls or buildings will cast shade continuously or for part of each day only and they will also give some protection from the effect of wind. The changing position of the sun throughout the year will alter the amount and position of shade in a garden so that some parts will be in full sun for several months but will be shaded for the remainder of the year. This variation in shade will affect the choice of plants which can be grown in different positions. Shade-loving plants in positions which would become exposed to full sun for several months of the year would develop severe leaf scorch and growth would become slow or might even stop completely. The soil, and consequently the plant roots, would also be affected by changes in temperature caused by alteration in shade position. Plants near walls or buildings can suffer severely from this change in temperature and the situation may be aggravated by reflected heat and light especially, for example, from concrete or plaster surfaces.

In small gardens, this kind of situation can be a problem but in larger gardens where there may be trees of reasonable size, shade-loving plants can be positioned so that they benefit from the shade cast by trees and buildings. A garden of ornamentals is a small ecological unit in which plants with different growing requirements can be raised together to their mutual benefit. Such an arrangement can be accomplished easily in an informal garden so that sun-lovers and shade-lovers can be grown together quite happily. But in a formal garden, this kind of combination of plants may not be possible and fewer species may be grown.

History of Gardening in Malaysia

A garden is an unnatural place in Malaysia. It is, of course, unnatural in any country, being a place where plants are grown and tended which would otherwise not survive in competition with the natural flora of the country. But in Malaysia this is particularly so since the natural vegetation of the country is a high forest, and a garden is essentially an open place. One result of this is that few native Malaysian species are suitable for Malaysian gardens, with the further consequence that most of our garden

plants have been brought from other countries. Indeed, most of the commonly grown ornamental plants in the country at the present time came from South America and a much smaller number came from tropical Africa. The vegetables grown here are mostly of extra-Malaysian origin.

The earliest Malaysian gardens no doubt consisted of the native fruit trees of the country (Durian, Mangosteen, Rambutan and the rest) and vegetables of Asiatic origin, such as Keladi, true Yam, Long Bean and Cucumber. But at a very early date a number of plants were brought from the American tropics, both by the Spaniards across the Pacific and by the Portuguese round the Cape. These were chiefly useful plants, such as Papaya, Chiku, Pineapple, Sweet Potato and Chilli; but some ornamentals were also brought, chief of them being the Frangipanni, which had become a common plant in many parts of the eastern tropics by the middle of the 17th century, though there is no doubt that its original home was Mexico.

The 18th century saw an increasing introduction of ornamental plants from the West Indies and South America to the hothouses in Europe, and a few of these were taken to the East, notably Caesalpinia (Peacock Flower or Pride of Barbados) and Lantana. But we had to wait till the 19th century before we found systematic introductions of this kind, chiefly through the Botanic Gardens which were established at Calcutta, Buitenzorg, Peradeniya, Singapore and Penang. It is unnecessary to make lists of such introductions, but it may be of interest to indicate the origin of a few of the most striking of our garden plants, and also to indicate progress made in recent years.

Of all our flowering trees, none is more brilliant than the Flame of the Forest or Flame Tree (well known under the name Poinciana, though more correctly called Delonix). Trees of this kind are now planted in all the warmer parts of the world, and it is strange to think that only just over a century ago the species was confined to a part of its native Madagascar. It was given a prominent place in the *Botanical Magazine* of 1839, as a recent discovery of great horticultural promise. It must have been distributed rapidly to many countries soon after that time. We do not know when it first arrived in Malaysia, but it would be perhaps about 1850. At any rate it was not known at the time Raffles founded Singapore.

Among flowering shrubs Bougainvilleas probably take first place. The first Bougainvillea seen by a European botanist was at Rio de Janeiro, during Bougainville's great voyage in the 1760s. Plants were apparently not brought alive to Europe before 1800 and first flowered in Paris about 1830. It was some ten years later that they first flowered in England, and their travels to the Eastern tropics perhaps began about this time. The earliest kinds in cultivation were the varieties of *Bougainvillea spectabilis*, which are seasonal in flowering, and so not well suited to Malaysia, and it is unlikely that these were ever much grown here. The perpetual-flowering *B. glabra* was not known in cultivation until about 1860 and probably did not reach Malaysia before 1870. The crimson Mrs. Butt was not known outside of South America before 1910, and did not reach Malaysia until 1923. Its orange form, Mrs. McLean, arrived some ten years later. Since that time artificial hybrids have been made and many are in cultivation in Malaysia at the present time. Bougainvilleas, like Poinciana, are (with few exceptions) still just as nature gave them to us.

The story of Cannas, which give more colour in gardens than any other group of herbaceous plants, is quite different. The original wild species of Cannas were never popular garden plants. It was not until they had been hybridized that the modern large-flowered forms appeared. The original wild plants came chiefly from South America, but the hybridization was done in Europe, first in France and then in Italy, where the type of Canna we now know appeared about 1890.

In the case of all the plants mentioned above, we have been indebted to other parts of the world for supplying beauty of colour to our gardens. Let us finally take a case of local production. The commonest cut flower in Malaysia used to be Vanda Miss Joaquim. This is a hybrid, but it is one raised in Singapore, and one of the parent species is a native Malaysian plant (*Vanda hookeriana*), the other introduced from Burma (*V. teres*). The hybrid first flowered in the garden of Miss Joaquim in Singapore in 1893, and from that one plant were propagated, by cuttings, the countless thousands that are still grown at the present time. Vanda Miss Joaquim was chosen to be Singapore's national flower in 1981.

This brings us to recent developments and future prospects. Every year a large number of different plants are introduced for trial at the Botanic Gardens in Singapore and Penang, and by many individual gardeners also. The most useful of these soon become generally known and cultivated. Out of many trials, few new plants of general utility result; but looking back over the last fifty years, we can see a big change, and a considerable improvement in variety of local plants, as a result of this continuous effort of new introduction. Many of the new plants are still in their native condition, wild species from Malaysia or some other part of the world. But some are hybrids, such as the Canna mentioned above, and many fine kinds of Hibiscus. Some of these hybrids are not suited to Malaysian conditions, which is not surprising if we remember the peculiar nature of our climate, and the fact that hybrids raised in other parts of the world are naturally selected for their suitability to the climates there.

It is becoming more and more clear that the way to more and better new garden plants in Malaysia is through local hybridizing and selection. We must use as parents those kinds of plants which are really well suited to our climate, flowering freely and growing strongly, and mate them with related species or varieties which have other good qualities, but are perhaps less well adapted to our climate. We have seen the result of this process with orchids. Vanda Miss Joaquim was a finger post showing the way. Now we have many other generations of hybrids raised from it by mating it with other Vandas; we also have hybrids of the Scorpion Orchids, Dendrobiums, Spathoglottis and many other orchids. The same process should be applied to other plants, especially the group of flowering shrubs. Sometimes hybridization is impossible, for reasons which we do not understand. Often it is difficult, and skill and ingenuity are needed to find a suitable technique, and patience to carry the matter through to the production of results. But there is no doubt of the possibility of using the many plants we have already introduced to Malaysian gardens to produce a wealth of new and finer forms which would transform our tropical gardens as the gardens of temperate regions have been transformed by the plant breeder during the last half century.

There are a number of native Malaysian species which should be tried as ornamental garden plants so that the cultivation and propagation techniques can be established. This should not be a difficult task and subsequently the plants could be used for hybridizing with related imported species so that varieties with different forms and flower colours could be obtained.

As regards garden technique, there have been no distinctive local developments except for the burnt earth technique of the Chinese gardeners which is so valuable for the cultivation of the more difficult pot plants. As indicated above, we have to adapt our methods to the local climate, but the methods are essentially the same as in temperate regions. Other directions in which technique might be improved are the drainage for garden beds in heavy soils and the use of special soil mixtures for different purposes such as seed germination or for rooting of cuttings. Modern techniques in propagation, such as the use of mist sprays and of rooting hormones, should be tried with many of the plants in which vegetative propagation is difficult, so that a higher percentage of new young plants can be obtained.

In the matter of garden design, Malaysia has shown little progress. A short chapter is included in this book on the subject, indicating the difficulties under local conditions, and making some suggestions. There is no doubt that few gardens in Malaysia are planned, as they might be, with thought of unity and harmony of design, and very little is made, in any garden, of minor architectural features such as low walls, well planned steps and paved paths. These things cost money; but compared with the cost of the average house the expense is not great, and can add immensely to the beauty of a garden and help to bring it into harmony with the lines of the house. Design is all-important in tiny gardens of town houses, or in flats or apartments where only pots or troughs are available for planting.

Names of Garden Plants

The names of plants are always a difficulty to the gardener. And yet they are of great importance; for if plants had no established names, we should have great confusion, and seedsmen's lists would be impossible. Some names are certainly difficult; but few are more difficult than Rhododendron, Chrysanthemum and Scindapsus, which are familiar to everybody. The fact is that the names of tropical plants are mostly new to the person coming from another country and the residents of the country often know a plant only by a vernacular name or by some conspicuous feature which can be mentioned. It is therefore confusing to be confronted with a large number of new names. From the gardener's point of view it is more important to be able to recognise his plants, and to learn their habits so that he can use them to the best advantage, than to know their names. But it is not really difficult to learn the names one by one as we learn the look of the plants and their ways. Nobody ever yet made a good garden without mental as well as physical effort, and the small extra mental effort necessary to learn the correct names of the plants is well worthwhile.

Broadly speaking, plants have two kinds of names: botanical and popular. It is the botanical names that present the greatest difficulty to the beginner, so we will deal with them first and at greater length; but it should be emphasized that popular names, though often easier to remember and more pleasant in common use, may yet be misleading because they are often local in their application. We have the Flame Tree in Malaysia, but there are other Flame Trees in other countries. We often call our Flame Tree the Flame of the Forest; but in Burma a quite different tree has that name. In general, if you go to another country, you find a new set of popular names for the same plants; but the botanical names are universal, and that is their great value. They are the keys to all the information written about the different kinds of plants. If we do not know the correct botanical name of a plant, this information is denied to us; and if we have the wrong name, we may find a whole lot of wrong information. So we see the importance of the correct naming of a plant, and of the maintenance of a stable system of botanical nomenclature.

Botanical names are based on the idea of a **genus**, which is a group of different kinds of plants which are yet similar to each other in various ways. For example, there are several kinds of Ixora, and yet they are so similar in their general appearance that anyone would recognize them as a natural group, even without a detailed examination of their structure. Ixora is a genus; and to distinguish the different kinds of Ixora, the botanist gives each a special adjective, in Latinized form, following the name of the genus. Thus the large-headed Ixora is *Ixora javanica*, because it was first known from Java; and the red Ixora with smaller heads of flowers and smaller unstalked leaves is *Ixora coccinea*. This method of binomial nomenclature was systematized by Linnaeus in the 18th century, and Latin was chosen because it was the universal language of learned men. Each binomial represents a **species**. Sometimes we have two kinds of plants resembling each other exactly except in the colour of the flowers; in such cases it is customary to call them varieties or cultivars. Thus there is a yellow variety of the red *Ixora coccinea*. Sometimes different varieties of the same species may differ in other minor characteristics besides colour. Botanists differ in their views of the status of species and varieties, and there is no known method of defining these exactly.

Botanical names apply primarily to wild plants. But garden plants are often different from wild plants and many can only be perpetuated by vegetative propagation so that there is now a separate set of rules governing the naming of such plants. They are often given 'fancy' horticultural names which are not Latinized. If the garden plant is clearly a variety of a natural species, we use the species name, and after it the 'fancy' name, e.g. *Ixora coccinea* 'Sunkist'; but if the garden plant is a hybrid (that is, derived by the mating of two or more botanical species), we use only the generic name and then the fancy name. Thus the common garden Vanda is a hybrid produced by crossing *Vanda hookeriana* and *Vanda teres*; the hybrid is called Vanda Miss Joaquim. The small pink Bougainvillea is probably a hybrid; it is at any rate of garden origin, and it is called Bougainvillea Rosa Catalina. Hybrids can now be registered to avoid duplication of names and also to try and prevent the name of a good hybrid being used for an inferior one.

Many tropical garden plants have no well recognized English name. In such cases it is useful to adopt the botanical generic name, and this has been done in a great many cases. Thus the generic names Begonia, Dahlia, Petunia, Bougainvillea, Gardenia, Hibiscus, Gloriosa, Hydrangea, Aster, Canna, Plumbago and Philodendron are all well known. Where there are many species or varieties in a genus, we must have a distinguishing name for each, and for this purpose we can if we like invent a name for local use. In practice this has not often been done, and there is some scope for someone with imagination to devise suitable names. As an indication of the possibilities, the reader is advised to consult Mr Corner's book, *Wayside Trees of Malaya*. In this book, names are given in English and Bahasa Malaysia for almost all the trees (and some tall shrubs are now included).

There are, of course, popular names for plants in other languages besides English, and in Malaysia we ought always to find out whether there are Malay names for our garden plants. In many cases there are not, for, as indicated above, the majority of garden plants are not native to the country, and many have only been introduced within the last few years. But a number of commonly introduced as well as native plants have been given names by Malays, and they are often very appropriate and interesting as well as euphonious. There are a large number of interesting examples in Mr Corner's book.

But though the common names in living languages are pleasant to use, the gardener who pursues his subject very far, or who aspires to collect a number of different species or varieties in any one genus, will find that he is driven to botanical names, both for exactness and for brevity. Who, for example, would invent popular names for all the different species of Begonia or Dendrobium that are worth cultivating?

2 GARDEN

PLANNING

The planning of a garden depends on many things. First on the site, its orientation, shape and contours, and probably on the position of the house and its entrances, and on the position of any existing trees. It depends further on how much time, materials and labour we are prepared to put into the making of the garden. Next, on what plants are available, and finally, on our particular taste or any special purpose we may have for the garden, or for any part of it. All of these factors operate in any country, but the factor which is specially controlled by local conditions is the nature of the plants available. The peculiar problems of garden planning in Malaysia are to adapt locally cultivated plants to our ideas of design, and to adapt our design to make use of the peculiar characters of local plants.

To design a garden effectively one must have a good knowledge of the plants available and their behaviour. It is hoped that some of the chapters in this book will help Malaysian gardeners to know some of their plants, and it should be remembered that many of these plants are grown also in other parts of the tropics where there may be slight differences in climatic conditions which would cause small changes in the behaviour of the plants. At the present time a number of these species are grown extensively in temperate countries as house plants, and although the growing conditions are different, the principles of management will be the same, so that anyone with some knowledge of tropical gardening should be able to grow these plants easily in those countries. However, one must live with plants and watch them grow to have a proper understanding of them, and as we do this our ideas about them and their possibilities will grow and develop, and we shall see new ways of using them. The present chapter is an attempt to give, briefly, some points that need to be considered in garden design and of the bearing of them on local conditions.

Compared with those of temperate countries, garden plants in Malaysia lack some useful features but excel in others. The great lack is of small plants of a size comparable to the rock garden plants of temperate regions. Next we have a comparative lack of variety in our herbaceous plants, many of which are short-lived; also a lack of plants that give a really massed effect of flowers. On the other side of the picture, we have a growing season that extends throughout the year, so that, with proper cultivation and manuring, we can make a new garden effective in a comparatively short time. And though we never have massed flowerings, we can have a considerable variety of flowers in moderate quantities throughout the year, set off by the perennial green of trees and grass. It is not a good idea to try and create a temperate-style garden in the tropics because the plants spread rapidly and would need constant attention in order to keep them to size, otherwise the garden would soon become a small jungle. It is much better, therefore, in the hot, wet climate of Malaysia, to make a careful choice of plants in order to avoid too much dense growth and the continuous attention which would be needed. But we can have a change of aspect in the garden, as in temperate countries, because some of the tropical trees are partly or completely deciduous and when the leaves have dropped the appearance of the garden is altered completely.

Many people never have the opportunity of designing an entirely new garden; but it is often possible to redesign old gardens, or at least parts of them. Everyone who is really interested in his garden thinks of changes that would improve it, or comes across new plants which can be used to add variety, or to produce new effects. But when one is making a new garden from bare ground, one has a different problem, with much greater possibilities. Unfortunately, it too often happens that such an opportunity is wasted through lack of thought or knowledge, both of which are needed for the production of an effective design.

In the tropics, many older houses had large gardens, sometimes of one or two acres in extent, and when labour was plentiful the maintenance of these gardens presented no problems. However, today, when there is far less labour available and wages are much higher, it would be expensive to maintain such a garden in first-class condition throughout the year. From this point of view, an informal arrangement would be best, using plants which need relatively little attention. Trees and shrubs with grass would be one solution to the problem, especially as large areas of grass can be cut quite easily and rapidly with a motor mower. Borders and beds need much more maintenance work to prevent them from becoming overgrown and untidy. The number of pot plants should be controlled because the attention they need daily could become laboursome instead of being a pleasure, and this might reduce the gardener's enthusiasm.

In recent years, large numbers of new houses have been built in and around towns and cities, and as many of these are grouped together in housing estates, the individual plots of land are often very small. Detached and semi-detached houses may be set on a total area of five to fifteen hundred square metres of land, most of which would be taken up by the building itself, so that very little space is left over for gardening. Terrace or link-houses usually have a much smaller area available for planting, and this may be entirely at the front or back of the house. If terrace houses have a larger area of land, it is likely to be long and narrow in shape, and this restricts the choice of plants which can be grown.

Many new apartment buildings have been built and the individual flats vary considerably in size and design. They range from very small places, sometimes without a balcony, to spacious, luxury flats with a floor area equal to that of a house, and with plenty of room for indoor plants and balcony gardening. In smaller flats it is possible to create tiny gardens of several kinds and these can form part of the interior decoration. Miniature gardens, bottle gardens, aquarium gardens and bonsai culture are all suitable for such situations and are mentioned later in the book.

In small houses or flats there may be troughs of varying size provided and these are easily used to make a small garden or they can be filled with an arrangement of pot plants. Troughs are very useful when space is limited because they are easier to maintain than pot plants and leave more space which can be used for other purposes.

Some houses have small indoor areas which are shaded but can be used as a garden and special consideration is needed for this because the number of plants which will grow successfully under these conditions is a little restricted. Window-boxes fitted on the outside wall of houses or flats provide another method of creating a small garden in a limited space. Here again, the choice of plants must be made carefully.

Large Gardens

The ideal situation is to have a new plot of land and to plan the house site and garden together. Often the house designer does not think of the garden, but from both practical and aesthetic standpoints, the two are complementary, and thought should be given to the garden when the position of the house on the site is decided; planned together, they will jointly make the best use of the land. One is controlled, of course, by practical considerations such as the position of main roads from which entrances must be made; the aspect and contours of the land; and the topography of the surrounding ground and the buildings upon it. But these are considerations which must be used to maximum advantage in order to give the house the best possible position and orientation, so that the garden, or parts of it, will be secluded, if required, and will have convenient access and other such considerations.

For example, if trees are desired for screening part of the house, or for shading part of the garden, then space must be allowed for them. An essential adjunct to any large garden is a small nursery where young plants can be propagated and pot plants can be grown until they are fit for display; it is convenient to combine this with the vegetable garden, and perhaps also with a small area devoted to growing flowers for cutting. Careful thought is necessary for the siting of such an area, so that while kept separate from the ornamental part of the garden, it will still have a suitable aspect and convenience of access for manure, potting materials and other garden equipment.

In a garden of sufficient size, there may be a tennis court and the orientation of this needs some consideration as it is best if its length lies from north to south, which may affect the possible arrangements of the other parts of the garden. If trees are desired to give lateral shade to the court, there must be sufficient room for these.

In many modern, large gardens a swimming pool is often constructed and this may be set into the ground or raised above it. In the latter arrangement the sides of the pool will need to be screened and this can be done by using pot plants or by planting flowering shrubs around it. A swimming pool set into the ground should be planned and sited so that it forms an integral

Above: Formal planting: Junipers, clipped shrubs

Right: Layout of plants around pond

Small pond surrounded by rocks and shrubs

part of the garden; such a pool needs a surrounding paved area as well as space for filtering and pumping equipment. Suitable flowering shrubs and trees can be grown near by so the whole area is linked to the remainder of the garden in a natural way.

No large trees should be grown near any kind of swimming pool as they will eventually overhang the water and the falling leaves and flowers will cause a great deal of trouble because they will clog the filters and will also sink to the bottom of the pool from where they are difficult to remove. Large tree roots may also damage the walls of a swimming pool so that small cracks will develop and the water will seep away slowly. The siting of a new house will therefore need very careful thought if there are plans for a tennis court or a swimming pool in the garden.

Drives and Paths

Having decided the main division of the ground between house, garage and (if they are to be provided), kitchen garden and nursery, ornamental garden, and tennis court or swimming pool, the next problem is the position of drives and paths. These serve not only useful purposes in giving access to house and garden, but also divide the ground into a definite pattern which must be the basis for planting design. Some thought must be given, therefore, to the aesthetic as well as the practical aspects of drives and paths, so that they may

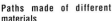
Paths made of different materials

add to the beauty of the garden, and give space for the planting of trees, shrubs or borders, as well as serve their immediate useful purpose. Another practical consideration of importance in the wet tropics is surface wash from heavy rain, and the provision of drains to carry away storm water. A sloping drive or path becomes a stream of water during a tropical shower and its surface can be washed away if it is not stabilized in some way, such as with asphalt or cement. Red laterite roads, at one time common in Malaysia, make a pleasing contrast of colour to the green of grass and garden plants, but on sloping ground they are not practical, at least not for drives.

For paths on sloping ground, the problem may be solved by having steps at intervals, the parts of the path between each step being quite level. Wash is thereby reduced to a minimum, and laterite gravel can be used safely. The siting of the steps can be used with considerable effect to give a distinctive note to the design of the garden. Their construction should be planned carefully, as ugly steps can spoil the whole effect completely. Naturally, such a stepped path cannot be used for a wheelbarrow or other vehicle but when there is plenty of space available, a narrow strip of pathway immediately adjacent to the steps (provided these are not too high) can be arranged as a gentle, smooth slope covered with grass so that a wheelbarrow can be moved up and down easily.

Another possible scheme for paths is to make them of bricks or concrete slabs flush with the grass level. Though naturally more expensive than gravel paths, they are practical and can be very effective. A still further possible treatment is to use concrete slabs (or flat stones, if available) as stepping stones. These enable one to walk dry-shod across grass in rainy weather or when the grass is wet with morning dew; they are quite attractive and need little maintenance except to see that they do not become overgrown with grass. One disadvantage of a path made either of bricks, stone or concrete slabs, is that in a shaded place where the air remains moist continuously, these materials can become covered with a layer of green algae, which could make them very slippery. In dry weather, it looks charming, but after the shortest of rainstorms, the algae becomes very

Courtyard planting: Cinnamomum,
Cyrtostachys, Manihot

Courtyard planting: Cinnamomum,
Cyrtostachys, Licuala

Path border: Dwarf Ixora and
Coreopsis tinctoria

a good deal of maintenance is necessary to keep the plants in satisfactory condition for distant viewing.

It is often appropriate to have beds or low borders beside paths and in this way they emphasize the patterns made by the paths and are also easy of access. Paths through the middle of a garden should not have tall borders beside them that obstruct the view of the remainder of the garden. Shorter plants in borders or a series of beds are more appropriate and the monotony may be relieved, in the case of a border, by the inclusion of a few taller shrubs; or if there is a row of beds, single tall shrubs or conifers may alternate with long beds of shorter plants, or a single tall shrub may stand at each end of the row. The positioning and planting of beds and borders give scope for the gardener to use imagination and produce a whole variety of ideas.

One often sees a row of uniform small round beds for single shrubs beside a path but shrubs rarely grow so well when planted singly as they do in a border, where they have more room to spread their roots. However, there are occasions on which separate planting is desirable. A mixed set of shrubs in such a row looks most incongruous. Although a uniform series may seem to lack variety, it can be used with effect to give a formal treatment; and in that case the shrubs must be tended very carefully to keep them in good condition and of uniform size, or the defects will detract entirely from the essential formality of the scheme. Conifers (Chinese Juniper or Thuja) are much better than flowering shrubs for such formal treatment. Ixoras can be used if they are really well tended, pruned and sprayed. Randias can also be effective, but are difficult to maintain in uniform condition. Even the smaller Bougainvilleas can be used, if they are carefully trained to shape by tying in their long branches. Climbers of other kinds can be used also if they are grown on a uniform series of supports.

Low beds may be planted with one species only, or a group of mixed species can be used. In the former case it is better to use chiefly the perennials and dwarf shrubs because annuals last such a short time only. In mixed planting, use may be made of Zephyranthes or other such small plants for the edge. A row of pink or cream Zephyranthes all along the front of a row of beds gives a beautiful display of colour at fairly frequent intervals. Annuals may be interspersed in mixed planting of long borders or medium-sized beds and it is best to grow them in pots to about half their full size before planting them out.

Beds or borders beside a central walk, or which may for other reasons be seen from both sides, should be planned accordingly, with smaller plants along both sides and taller plants in the middle. Such borders can be rather wider than those designed to be viewed from one side only, but their width depends also on the size of the plants which are to be used. One-sided borders are best usually at the back of a lawn, often near the boundary of the garden, or part of it, and, as with all floral effects, they need a background in order to show to greatest advantage. This is usually provided by hedges or trees, or both. Hedges may be formal or informal, and in either case they can be brought into the design of the garden if thought is given to the matter before planting. Probably the formal trimmed green hedge makes the most satisfying background for most purposes, but the flowering hedge also has its uses.

A mixed border of shrubs and smaller plants near the boundary of a garden may have a straight edge in front, parallel to the boundary, or there may be an irregular curving edge which is less formal in appearance. The treatment depends on the lie of the ground and the relation of the border to other planting in the garden. The straight front gives a formal effect which will be suitable in a more or less symmetrical scheme, but may be quite out of place if the ground is of irregular shape. A curved edge may be used deliberately to break up the straight edge of a rectangular piece of ground and so fit it for an informal planting scheme.

Borders can become overgrown very quickly in this climate and therefore they need continuous gentle attention. If they are allowed to become very badly overgrown, then the hard pruning which is necessary will result in a mass of bare stems and twigs which will be unsightly for a long time until the plants have recovered and made new growth. The soil will be exposed to the hot sun and may dry out; so watering will be necessary until the plants have grown again. Some care is also needed because many plants do not survive very hard pruning, or may recover from it only very slowly. When a considerable variety of the smaller bedding plants are used then a good deal of maintenance is needed and consequently it is not wise to make more borders than can be maintained easily. However, the larger shrubs, in general, require less attention, though all must be inspected at intervals for pests, which must be controlled, and all need occasional manuring and pruning to keep them in good order. Therefore, a mixed planting of the more floriferous larger shrubs is often useful for boundary purposes and the smaller plants are better placed nearer the house. Such planting must be bold to be effective. Unfortunately, few shrubs are really covered with flowers in Malaysia, but enough of them produce a moderate and continuous flowering to make such a group quite colourful. All shrubs grow better in a continuous area of cultivated ground than in small single beds and

the mixed planting, therefore, makes for more vigorous growth. Shrubs of different heights can be used, the smaller being planted in front and the taller behind. Scandent or climbing shrubs such as Bougainvilleas do not fit into such a mixed planting. However, it is possible to have a mixed planting of scandent shrubs only, though it tends to become a thicket which is difficult to manage. Not all Bougainvilleas are suitable for this treatment, as some only flower well when their root growth is restricted. Further notes on this subject are found elsewhere in this book.

Two practical points must be remembered always when siting the borders or long beds. Owing to the excessive wash of heavy rain in Malaysia it is wise to keep the beds as level as possible so that in undulating ground they should follow the contours approximately. The other point is exposure to sun. Most of the best flowering plants need full sun, or almost full sun to be really successful. Failing this, they are usually best with full morning sun, and, if possible, borders should be located on the east side of trees or buildings – though this is by no means essential, except for those plants which produce flowers during the morning hours only. If a border is seen especially in the morning, it is pleasant to grow plants which flower best at that time as they are not showy during the later part of the day. Similarly, a border seen in the evening may have flowers which open at that time, such as Cestrum, Moonflower, Hymenocallis and other night-flowering species.

Walls

Reference has been made already to the possibilities of walls at the change of level between two terraces; these are useful as they prevent erosion and soilslip during periods of heavy rainfall. They can be used also to separate dif-

Trees planted close to walls give a shady effect

ferent areas of the garden, or to surround a loggia and similar outdoor areas where one may sit and relax at different times of the day. Many large modern buildings and houses have walls of various sizes and with different kinds of surfaces as part of their overall design, and, if desired, these can be used to support climbing plants to help cut down the amount of glare and heat reflected from the surfaces.

In a garden, different materials can be used for making a wall and the choice will depend on the final effect and function desired. Quarry stones, bricks in a variety of finishes, pre-cast concrete bricks in a range of designs, and similar ready-made structures, often used for preventing erosion, can all be used. It is worthwhile making enquiries about all sorts of materials when any garden construction is contemplated.

An informal wall can be made very decorative by growing trailing plants such as Verbena and Russelia, or such herbaceous perennials as Coreopsis, or some of the hardier ferns and Begonias, in the crevices of its face, as well as along its top. Alternatively, if a wall the full height of the terrace is impracticable then a low, skirting wall up to 30 cm or more high, along the foot of the bank, can be used to hold pockets of earth for similar plants. Under these conditions, they will have excellent drainage so that any of the usual bedding or pot plants will succeed. It is, however, necessary to replace any soil which may be washed away during heavy rain and to give regular applications of fertilizer.

When there are terraces, there must be steps to lead from one level to another, and the design of these must be in keeping with that of the wall (if any) in which they are set. The width of the flight of steps will depend on the size of the garden and must harmonize with the general design. Steps should not be too steep and the length of each tread should not be less than that of an average human foot. Where there is plenty of space, very wide treads can be built, and if the paving stones are arranged so that there are narrow gaps at different points, then small creeping plants can be grown in these for an attractive and natural appearance. At the top and bottom of a flight of steps in a formal wall, capitals may be placed, and it may be appropriate to set shrubs or conifers, in large pots or jars of suitable shape, on the tops of these capitals, to give contrast to the level line of the wall. In such an arrangement, the plants should be of formal shape, and the pots or other containers can be designed to accord with the structure of the wall and the steps. Carefully designed features of this kind can add immensely to the beauty of a garden, but bad or incongruous ones can bring disharmony that will detract from the general appearance.

Paving, Paths and Patios

Crazy paving is mentioned in another chapter. Some small plants grow better in it than elsewhere so that an area of such paving can be useful and also very decorative. It may take the form of paths, such as ordinary garden paths, or it may be arranged as part of a wide flight of steps, or part of a more or less formally planned area. Such an area may also contain Waterlily pools, formal plants in pots, seats or ornaments of various kinds. Crazy paving must have a good solid foundation and also good drainage, with a minimum of 30 cm of rubble and sand. Planting in such paths is best kept to the sides or they will be of little use for walking upon, but there are some tough, low-growing plants which will survive a great deal of trampling, and are ideal for this kind of situation. Crazy paving looks best if it is fairly wide and it may surround a central bed in a lawn, with branches leading to the sides where they join up with paths to other parts of the garden. If a considerable number of plants are to be used in a paved area then it is best positioned where it is independent of paths, for instance in the middle of a terrace, or in the middle of a lawn instead of a flower bed. In the last instance, narrow flower beds can be arranged around the paved area and can be planted with very short plants, but one or two very small shrubs could be used also to give a little height to the arrangement and to provide a little contrast with the small plants.

A paved area at one side of a house is always pleasant if it can be arranged. It may be a raised terrace, or on the same level as the neighbouring parts of the garden. If used frequently, such an area is best paved completely with no gaps between the materials used. Bricks, tiles, stones or precast concrete slabs can be used alone or in combination. If the

Planting of low walls

**Plants grown on a high wall:
Epipremnum with Coleus and
Codiaeum in front**

Group against wall:
Monstera and
Asplenium nidus

area is large enough, then one or two spaces may be left so that single flowering shrubs can be planted, and this can be most effective. Such an area should always be planned to harmonize with the house, both in size and materials. It is very useful for sitting out of doors at different times of day, and can be decorated in various ways to make it part of the general garden design. Potted plants can be arranged in different ways upon it; borders may be made all around it and these can contain plants of varying height to act as a screen if necessary; a low wall with entrances and capitals or a low trough can be built around it, and it is possible to make sunken beds in a definite pattern or for single shrubs; a small pool with Waterlilies and a fountain can also be very effective in such an area.

The amount of such elaboration naturally depends on the size of the paved area and also upon the amount of space which is to be kept clear for chairs or other garden furniture. The treatment can be kept formal and not more planting should be attempted than can be kept in good order easily. A terrace of this kind is usually best situated facing east, but it can be placed in any other part of the garden and if necessary can be shaded with climbing plants supported on wooden trellis work or on brick or stone pillars.

Garden Ornaments

These may be used in any kind of garden and can be varied to suit personal taste. A few well chosen pots or jars, stone figures, lanterns or fountains can add interest to the design of a garden, but the use of too many should be avoided at all costs. Ornaments must be in keeping with other constructional materials of the formal part of the garden, such as paving, walls or steps. Elaborate Chinese jars or large pots and stands, though beautiful in their own

Group planting in trough: Rhapis and Dieffenbachia

right, do not always tone in with a severe paving scheme such as may be chosen for a terrace; in such a place well proportioned pots of good shape and simple design are more appropriate. Good concrete pots are not easy to obtain, and a clumsy or badly proportioned one will spoil the appearance of a well designed terrace, but plain brown or green Chinese jars look much better. The more elaborate type of Chinese pot with matching pedestal does not look well against a background of brickwork and is much better against weathered stone. Large rectangular plastic containers can be used and the sides can be made to look more attractive by covering them with a special mixture which looks like stone when it has hardened.

Pergolas and Arches

There are so many beautiful climbers in the tropics that a pergola is almost an essential feature of a large garden. It is possible, of course, to support climbing plants in other ways, but for the larger ones a pergola is the most satisfactory method both as regards utility and appearance. It may be used to divide one part of the garden from another, or to lead from the house to some part of the garden. It is, after all, a place for walking underneath plants and should lead somewhere even though the beauty of the flowers it bears may best be seen from outside. If a pergola is built on a lower terrace then the flowers which appear on the top of it will be seen most effectively from some higher point in the garden. There are some climbers, such as Thunbergia and Mucuna, which have long, hanging inflorescences and these are seen best when walking through the pergola. Alternatively, a pergola may be built one-sided, like a cloister, along the side of the house where it will give some shade, or it may form two or three sides of a rectangular formal garden.

The best height for a pergola is about 2½ m, although for some special reasons it may be taller than this. Its pillars may be of any desired materials to conform with the house or surroundings. If it is made of brick then the most satisfactory kind are small ones, if these can be obtained. The cross-pieces at the top should be bold enough to be in proportion to the pillars and should project a little on each side. They can be made of concrete or hard timber, but soft timber is not worth using as it lasts for a short time only. There must be room to plant climbers so that their roots can grow strongly, and large pots or tubs are not really big enough to allow for sufficiently vigorous growth, especially of the bigger climbers such as Chonemorpha, Beaumontia and Odontadenia. Such plants are best placed in a well dug bed just adjacent to the paved area.

An arch is like a short pergola, but may be of more varied design. Usually, the simplest design is best and it should be of such size and proportions as will fit the surroundings. Wood, bricks, concrete or steel tubing may make the main supports. An arch looks best at some definite point on a path: at a junction; at the top of a short flight of steps; or where the path leads from one part of the garden to another. An arch without any relation to its surroundings looks incongruous and some other form of support would be better. In general, arches are better for the lighter climbers and pergolas for the heavy, strong-growing kinds.

Vegetable Garden and Nursery

Some sort of nursery is an essential adjunct to a large garden. A small shed would be useful, with a bench for potting and a place to keep pots and burnt earth; also an area for making compost, a bench or two for pot plants (one preferably in the shade and one in the sun), and a few beds for the propagation of cuttings and perennials. Such a place could be increased in size as much as necessary at any time. If required, beds or boxes for salad vegetables, larger vegetables and cut flowers can be provided as and when needed so that there would be no necessity for growing them in the ornamental part of the garden whose appearance they would mar. A nursery garden of this kind need not be ugly but even if kept neat and tidy it will be quite different in appearance from the ornamental garden and best, therefore, kept separate. An interesting gate in the hedge, or a suitable arch, are possible features at the boundary. A nursery garden should not be shut in too much by trees or buildings, otherwise many plants will not thrive. In order to keep it in suitable proportion to the main part of the garden, it would have to be considered when the original site plan of the whole garden is made. Fitting it in afterwards is difficult, to say the least, because this will mean making changes to the original garden design after some planting has been done.

Small Gardens

Small gardens are those of about one quarter of an acre or less in area and in many modern detached and semi-detached houses the amount of land available around the actual building varies considerably, sometimes being only the bare minimum which is allowed under municipal bye-laws. Frequently, at the present time, houses are grouped together in small estates and the buyer has no choice in the siting of the house on the building plot or in the position of the driveway which is usually fixed also. Given these circumstances, some planning is essential before planting because the choice of plants will depend on the amount of space available, the amount and position of shade throughout the year and also on the position of underground drains, septic tanks, water and gas pipes, electricity and telephone conduits, and finally the storm drains around the house. It is important to find out the position of all the underground services before any deep digging is attempted.

When the space available for planting is very small, there may be room for one or two shrubs or pot plants only, but even then, with a little ingenuity and imagination, it is possible to create a small landscape. If there is sufficient space a trough could be built and this is a good way of gardening on a small scale; and though the space is severely limited, it is possible to grow a few vegetable or spice plants and some ornamentals at the same time. The choice of any of these plants will be limited by the aspect of the house and the position of the trough in relation to it. Small terrace houses often have a short drive of concrete, and this, together with the walls of the house, can become very hot during the middle of the day as well as reflect a great deal of heat and glare. The amount and position of shade cast by the house will vary during each day and will also alter throughout the year as the position of the sun changes. This will affect the choice of plants which are to be grown.

When gardening is limited to a few pot plants, it should be remembered that, in general, those plants which are grown for their flowers will need plenty of sunlight, whereas many of the plants grown for their foliage only will tolerate a good deal of shade. Pot plants which are kept for long periods inside a house may eventually suffer from insufficient light, so that their growth will be very slow and the foliage may become dry and dusty. Whenever possible, these plants should be placed outside during a shower of rain which will freshen them; they will benefit also from being left outside during the night – as often as can be arranged. Some pot plants are kept in airconditioned rooms or offices for long periods where the air is constantly dried and the temperature is lower, and although a number of foliage plants are robust enough to tolerate these conditions, they must eventually be taken outside for several months to recover. However, if these plants are sprayed with water once or twice each week, or if the leaves are wiped over with a wet cloth, they will tolerate the drier air in such rooms for a much longer time.

When there is space enough for trees to be planted in a small garden, careful choice of species is necessary because size of trees should complement size of house, and their position in the garden must be considered carefully. With very limited space, it may not be possible to grow a tree because of the position of underground drains or because of overhead electricity or telephone cables, but it is possible to grow shrubs in such situations.

Trees should not be grown where their branches would eventually touch overhead electricity cables as a great deal of damage could be done during high winds or heavy rain and it would be dangerous if cables were broken by moving branches. When trees are planted, they should not be placed too close to a fence because the trunk will enlarge and damage it and the crown will spread and shade the garden of the neighbouring house, which may cause some annoyance to the owners. Also, it is unwise to grow large species in a small area as the roots will damage the drains and septic tanks, and if the crown is spreading then the fallen leaves may clog gutters and storm drains, resulting in puddles of water which make good breeding places for mosquitoes. It is very important, therefore, in the planning of a small garden, to choose suitable plants and to position them well.

If the gardener wishes to create the effect of a small landscape in such a limited area, it is wise to plant trees as far away from the house as possible and shorter plants nearer to it. In this way the crowns of the trees will not block the view from windows and their shade will not darken the rooms in the house, but they will act as a screen from neighbouring houses or any unsightly features outside the garden. Small gardens can be formal or informal in the same way as larger ones, but because of the restricted space, fewer plants can be used so that the maintenance of a formal arrangement is much easier and less laboursome.

If pot plants only are used to create a garden in a small area, the gardener must think carefully about the number which can be used, because some of the space will be needed for a few pots in which to germinate seeds, or to root cuttings. Also, the management of too many pot plants could become burdensome if the gardener must spend all his spare time watering them; this applies especially to times when there is no rain because the pots will then dry out much faster and need to be watered two or three times a day. Pot plants can be used to make a formal or informal arrangement, or they can be grouped satisfactorily into a small landscape, but the choice of plants must be done with a little care for any of these arrangements.

Groups of pot plants can be very effective. If the pots are, for any reason, a little unsightly, they can be concealed with small rocks of various sizes arranged as a border around the group, or smaller pots with trailing or very dense, bushy plants can be placed to make a low screen around the whole group. Pot plants in groups derive mutual benefit from the intermingling of the foliage which prevents the heat of the sun from drying out the soil too quickly, and the atmosphere around these plants remains very much more moist than it does around single plants. Watering will be needed less frequently and can be done more easily by using a watering can fitted with a fine rose, which means the two jobs of wetting soil and damping foliage can be done simultaneously. Should the foliage in such a group become very dense, it is important to make sure sufficient water falls on the soil in the pots because the leaves deflect a great deal of water and, as the pots are not visible, the gardener may not realise what is happening until some of the plants wilt suddenly or die.

A combination of small shrubs grown directly in the ground with pot plants can be very effective also. Often in a garden there are concrete or metal covers to drains or septic tanks and these can be concealed conveniently and easily, if required, by an arrangement of pot plants. If there is sufficient space, some dwarf shrubs can be planted near by to hide them, or trailing plants can be allowed to grow over them. Whichever method is used, it is important that the plants can be moved aside easily when it is necessary to remove the covers for maintenance work.

Climbing plants can be used effectively in small gardens and may be grown on a fence, on trellises, or over a small pergola. They are useful as a screen or for providing some shade, and can be grown also directly on the wall of a house – although this is not always a good idea as they can harbour insects which eventually find their way into the house. A wall which receives full sunlight for the whole day may become too hot for some kinds of climbing plants because the roots are killed before they can attach themselves to the wall. Plants grown on, or close to a hot wall are liable to become very dry and are almost always subject to attack by red spider. If this is not controlled, the leaves will soon become discoloured and drop very quickly so the plant becomes unsightly. Climbing plants grown where plenty of air can circulate around them will suffer less from this pest and may even remain free from it.

Although space may be very limited, it is best, if possible, to grow climbing plants directly in the ground as they will be larger and more vigorous than if planted in pots. If pots are used they should be as large as possible and when the climbing plant has made good growth the surface of the soil in the pot can be covered with some small herbaceous plants, though regular application of fertilizer will be neces-

Garden nook with small pool

Roof garden: Dracaena, Codiaeum, Coleus

sary in order to maintain all of the plants in good condition.

A small patio can be shaded quite easily with a climbing plant supported on wooden slats and pot plants needing shade for good growth can be kept underneath, thus increasing the variety of plants which can be grown. A patio arranged in this way cannot be used for a short time after a rainstorm as water will continue to drip from the leaves for an hour or so; also, if dead leaves accumulate above the slats they will remain wet and will decay there because they cannot be blown away. Rotting leaves will harbour many insects and will eventually cause the slats to rot, but this situation can be avoided by spacing the slats at very wide intervals so dead leaves may fall through to the floor where they can be swept up easily.

Detail of a crimson Morning Glory

In slightly larger gardens, where trees or shrubs can be grown, it should be remembered that these will create shaded areas which can be used for growing other plants suited to such conditions, thus increasing considerably the choice of plants available to the gardener. Sun-loving and shade-loving plants can be combined in any garden in this way so that the whole area can be used to the best advantage.

The space in front of terrace houses is often very small but can be used in various ways. If it is paved completely, groups of pot plants or some potted shrubs can be used for decoration. There may be sufficient space for a small border along one side where several kinds of plants could be grown, or perhaps a tiny lawn could be made using one of the fine-leaved grasses and this could include one or two suitably placed, well grown small shrubs. Alternatively, when the whole area is paved, it might be possible to build a trough of suitable size and if this is filled with earth, a considerable number of plants could be grown much more successfully than in pots. One advantage of a trough is that it is neat in appearance, takes up relatively little space so that the remainder of the area can be cleaned easily and quickly and be used for other activities. Plants grow better in a trough because there is room for the roots to spread; if the rim is wide enough it can be used as a seat. On balconies or verandas where there is sufficient space, a trough provides a most suitable and efficient way of doing a little gardening and can give great enjoyment.

Garden Equipment

There are many tools for a variety of purposes in the garden currently available but one can manage quite easily with very few kinds. Tools intended for very specific purposes may be used very infrequently and in a small garden would be unnecessary. For a small garden, the basic equipment needed for general cultivation would be:

1 Cangkul
1 Assam fork
1 Pair of secateurs
1 Garden rake
1 Hand trowel
1 Hand fork
1 Watering can with a fine rose

In addition, a few pots are needed for raising seeds and rooting cuttings, and a small basket would be useful for carrying rubbish, prunings or soil. As the garden becomes more established, a few more items of equipment can be added and these could include:

1 Long-handled hoe, to make weeding less laborious
1 Long length of garden hose for watering (the reinforced rubber kind is a little expensive but lasts for very much longer than the plastic type which often becomes kinked unless stored properly, and then frequently develops many small holes)
1 Small saw with coarse teeth (for cutting larger branches)
1 Long-handled pruner (for trimming bushes without the aid of a step-ladder)
1 Hard brush or broom for sweeping leaves and grass trimmings
1 Wheelbarrow (in a larger garden, this makes transport of materials much easier)

Stakes of various sizes, small plant labels, string and thin wire are other items which are used frequently in an established garden.

Sprayers are available in a range of sizes and small hand models are excellent for applying plain water, insecticides or pesticides in small quantities. They are easy to manipulate and produce a very fine mist which covers all parts of a plant efficiently and easily. It is a good idea to keep separate sprayers for water and pesticides so that no accidental application of chemicals can be done. The smallest hand sprayers are inexpensive and are excellent for use on all pot plants but in a larger garden where it may be necessary to spray trees or shrubs or large numbers of pot plants, a knapsack sprayer would be better because the spray can be projected to a greater distance than with a hand spray.

The largest item of equipment needed would be a mower for cutting grass and there are very many different kinds available with a great range of prices. The simplest kinds are hand machines but others are powered by electricity or by small petrol-driven motors. In very small gardens the hand machines are adequate, and provided the grass is never allowed to grow too high, they are easy to use and trouble-free. Powered machines are useful in larger gardens where bigger areas can be mowed quickly and easily, but they must be cleaned and oiled regularly otherwise they will soon need many small repairs. Powered lawn mowers are of two kinds: the cylinder type, in which several horizontal blades are arranged around a central axis, and the rotary type in which two blades are held parallel to the ground and spin around horizontally. Both kinds are efficient and the choice will depend on personal taste.

All cylinder lawn mowers have a removable metal box which collects the cut grass and avoids the necessity of sweeping up trimmings after mowing, but only some of the rotary kinds have such a collecting box. When using a rotary machine without a box, grass should be mown more frequently and because it never then grows very tall, the trimmings can be allowed to remain where they fall and will quickly rot down to form plant food without affecting the appearance of the lawn. If grass is allowed to grow tall then a rotary machine of this kind can still be used but the amount of trimmings will be so large that they must be swept up and put on the compost heap. If they are allowed to lie on the lawn they will be so thick in some areas that the grass underneath will yellow and the lawn will appear very patchy. If cylinder type machines are used frequently there will be no need to attach the collecting box because the quantity of trimmings will be relatively small and they can be allowed to remain where they fall. If, after mowing, there are small heaps of trimmings left lying on the lawn, these should be broken up and scattered widely over the surface of the lawn with a broom. Electrically powered machines must be used with great care in order to avoid cutting the cable which can cause serious personal accidents, and the gardener must therefore be constantly alert when using this type of machine.

Pots and Containers

Earthenware pots used to be the only kind used for growing plants, but these have been replaced very largely by plastic pots and saucers. Earthenware pots and saucers are heavy and bulky to store whereas the plastic kinds are very light and store in a much smaller space. Earthenware pots are porous so water can pass slowly through the sides and evaporate. This helps to cool them a little and allows some air to penetrate the soil, causing plant roots to concentrate in the soil immediately next to the wall of the pot. Plastic pots are not porous and the soil takes much longer to dry out, so a little care is necessary with watering in order to avoid waterlogging. The walls of these pots are also very thin so that changes of temperature will occur much more rapidly than with earthenware pots. Plant roots tend to be more evenly spread through the soil in plastic pots.

Round plastic pots are not usually available in very large sizes but it is possible to get plastic containers in rectangular shapes and these appear to be made of much thicker and stronger material. They are useful for growing groups of plants and take up relatively little room, although the shiny, smooth appearance of many may not be acceptable to gardeners if they are needed inside a house. These containers are available in different colours and some are made to resemble stone of different kinds. Larger rectangular containers could be used inside troughs so that replacement of plants and soil could be done more easily.

Round earthenware pots can be obtained in a wide variety of sizes from very tiny thumb pots to very large ones about 40 cm in diameter and these will have from one to five drainage holes in the base. Special pots are available for orchid growing and these have very large holes in the sides so air can circulate freely around the orchid roots. There are also shallow pots about 15 cm high which are used as seed pans or for rooting cuttings and these are available with or without drainage holes in the base. They are often glazed on the inner surface so water cannot seep through the sides.

For permanent decoration, either inside a house or on a veranda or patio, very large earthenware jars are obtainable, ranging from about 45 to 60 cm in diameter. These usually have one or two drainage holes in the base, are glazed on the inner surface, and often have a broad, flattened rim. They are excellent for growing small shrubs or groups of plants because there is plenty of root room, and if the drainage holes are closed the pots can be used with great effect as small water gardens with ornamental fish and water plants. When they are filled with earth these pots are very heavy so it is important to decide on their permanent position before they are filled. If possible, they should be raised slightly on some small stones or pieces of brick so that water can drain away freely from underneath. If they stand directly on the ground or a flat surface – and this applies to ordinary flower pots also – water will not run off easily and some will be trapped underneath the pot where it will remain for a long time. Eventually the soil will become

waterlogged. When this happens, earthworms can enter the pot and will soon spoil the soil mixture.

The large Chinese dragon jars which are often seen for sale may be used but they have no drainage holes. They are thick-walled and glazed inside as they are used for importing preserved food but they can be used as ornamental containers for potted plants which should be raised on a layer of gravel or small stones placed at the bottom of the jar. These large jars should not be used for a water garden as there appears to be some sort of residue from the food and its preservative which is difficult or impossible to remove, however much scouring and cleaning is done. The growth of water plants is likely to be affected and fish will die within twenty-four hours.

Ornamental earthenware containers of various shapes, sizes and colours are made and these are often glazed both inside and outside so water cannot pass through. Some are made without drainage holes and potted plants are merely placed inside them and are treated in the usual way so that the container is really used to conceal the actual flower pot. Some of the containers have a drainage hole in the base and these are often sold with a matching saucer to be placed underneath. However, it is important that the saucer is glazed on both sides, otherwise water will pass through it and the surface on which the pot is standing, especially if it is wood, can be stained very badly. Other kinds of ornamental containers are made to be hung up as decoration and these need a small pot of trailing plants placed inside. They should be turned around each day so that the trailing stems grow evenly on all sides.

Unglazed earthenware pots which have had plants growing in them for a long time may become unsightly because fertilizer which is placed on the soil reacts with the clay of the pot. This can sometimes be remedied by scrubbing the outside with a hard brush, but the trouble will recur and scrubbing is necessary at regular intervals; such pots can be relegated to the nursery. For this reason, earthenware pots should not be placed on a floor covered with mosaic tiles or terrazo because the dissolved fertilizer which comes through the pot in the excess water will stain or damage the surface very badly. Such stains are almost impossible to remove from these surfaces and if there is some damage also to the surface, it is rather expensive to have it repaired. Pots should always, therefore, be placed on glazed saucers on such surfaces and these will also prevent the water from spreading all over the floor.

Urns of various shapes are available, with or without pedestals, and these are usually stone-coloured or white. They can be used on veran-

The soil is the medium in which the roots live, from which they obtain water and food needed by the plant. Successful gardening is based on good soil management, and to manage the soil effectively we must know something about the roots and their needs. Unfortunately, the soil is not a simple substance; it is extremely complex in physical and chemical structure, and different soils vary much in these respects. In addition to this, the soil contains a vast flora and fauna of microscopic organisms which play their part in its economy and in providing for the needs of the roots. It may also contain harmful organisms, which can injure or destroy roots.

The needs of the roots can be stated briefly. They are firstly water, secondly certain simple chemical substances dissolved in that water, and thirdly air. It is easy to arrange for the roots to have enough water, and not difficult to provide the right substances dissolved in the water. But to provide simultaneously a balanced supply of both water and air is a much more difficult matter, and yet a good garden soil must do this; and the aim of a large amount of garden work is to maintain the soil in such a condition that it will do so.

The soil is composed in part of the mineral substances of the earth, and in part of organic substances, the decaying remains of plants and animals. The mineral substances may be defined, according to the size of the particles which compose them, as stones, coarse or fine sand, gravel, silt and clay. Every soil particle has the power of holding a film of water on its surface. The smaller the particles, the more of them there are in a given volume, and also the greater their surface area. Therefore a clay soil, with very small particles, can hold more water than a sandy soil. But at the same time the smaller particles can pack more closely together, and the passage of water through such a soil must be slow. Equally, the passage of air through a clay soil, especially if it is wet, is also slow. On the other hand, the sandy soil that holds less water has larger spaces between the particles and so allows a freer passage for water and air. Thus we see that a clay soil has good water-holding properties but does not afford adequate air supply for roots, while a sandy soil does not hold much water but does provide a satisfactory flow of air. If we could combine the good points of both, we should

have a good soil; for example, if we could break the clay into pieces, each piece consisting of many particles holding water between them, but with good air spaces between the pieces, we should achieve our object. This is where the organic part of the soil plays its part.

Decaying organic matter in the soil is called humus. It is derived from dead leaves, dead roots, animal dung and other waste substances produced by animals and plants. The decay of humus is brought about by the bacteria and other microscopic organisms in the soil, of which there are millions in every handful. The bacteria feed on the humus, and ultimately some of them decompose it into simple soluble substances which the roots can absorb; and so the dead leaf that falls to the ground eventually provides material for the building of another leaf. It is clear, therefore, that decaying organic matter makes plant food. It is probable also that some of the organisms that are nourished by the humus absorb nitrogen from the air, and thus add to the stock of combined nitrogen in the soil that will ultimately be available to roots of plants.

But apart from providing an important part of the food needed by roots, the organic matter helps greatly to maintain a satisfactory physical state in the soil. The addition of organic matter to clay has just that necessary effect of breaking it up so that it will give free passage for air. As mentioned in the introductory chapter, our uniformly warm and wet climate exaggerates the bad qualities of a heavy soil, and therefore the need for organic matter is even greater than in cooler or drier climates; and at the same time, owing to the high temperature, the humus decays very rapidly, so that it needs frequent renewal. Sandy soils in our climate do not dry out as fast as in some countries, owing to the frequent rain; and in fact some plants (like Oleanders), which need the stimulus of a little drought to make them flower, are best in sandy soils. But for most plants sandy soils are improved by the addition of plenty of organic matter, which greatly improves its water-holding powers as well as provides plant foods. Thus we see that organic matter improves both heavy and light soils, making the one more pervious to air and giving the other a better water-holding capacity, at the same time adding plant food to both. But before we deal with the sources of organic matter available to the gardener, let us consider the chemical side of plant nutrition.

As already remarked, roots take up plant food with the water from the soil. The food is not what we should consider food; it consists of fairly simple salts in dilute solution. The other part of the food of plants comes from the air entering the leaves, and is the gas called carbon dioxide. By means of the energy of sunlight, the green parts of plants are able to manufacture sugars and starch from water and carbon dioxide; and with the addition of the salts absorbed by the roots, the plant cells can make all the complex substances needed for the production and structure of new stems, leaves, flowers and seeds. These manufacturing processes have never been achieved so efficiently in laboratories, and so we are still dependent on plants to supply us with all our food, either directly, or through animals; ultimately the source of it all is the green plant cell and its power of absorbing the sun's energy.

It is thus evident that, in addition to supplying a proper amount of water and air to the roots of plants, the gardener must also supply some of the things dissolved in the water. The majority of these things are needed in such minute quantities that almost all soils provide them; the quantities are indeed so small that it is only in recent years that the need for some of them has been demonstrated. In practice, there are only two things that we need to worry much about; these are nitrogen and phosphorus. There is a third substance that comes next in importance, and is always considered in questions of manuring, and that is potassium. But Malaysian soils mostly contain enough potassium, and a certain amount more is always added when we dig organic matter into the soil, so that for most purposes the question of adding extra potassium to the soil does not arise. Nitrogen however is of great importance, as it is the next most important element after carbon, hydrogen and oxygen in the structure of the living parts of plants. Organic matter in the soil provides nitrogen, but rather slowly, and if we want rapid growth we usually have to add extra nitrogen in some way. Phosphorus is not needed in such large amounts, but it is a very important element, and a plant cannot make proper use of extra nitrogen unless it has enough phosphorus, so it is important to see that it is added. The ways in which we can provide these necessary elements are discussed below, under manuring.

There is still another important element that is present only in small amounts in Malaysian soils, namely calcium (commonly included in the name lime, which is calcium oxide or hydroxide). Lime, like humus, has the power of making clay soils more porous; it also reduces acidity. Though present in small amounts, lime is usually adequate for plant growth, but in black valley soils the addition of lime, probably to counteract acidity, is certainly valuable and is practised regularly by Chinese market gardeners, who grow green crops on such soil. On most hill soils, only a small amount of lime, at intervals of say one year, is needed, and many gardens which receive none appear to be none the worse. Lime may also help to liberate other substances from the soil, making them available for absorption by roots; but in that case the loss of those other substances must sometimes be made good by manuring.

Cultivation

By cultivation we mean manipulating the soil in various ways to improve its texture, increase its content of plant food, and destroy weeds. The texture of soil is improved merely by breaking it up in the process of digging, but when we dig we generally add organic matter, which, as noted above, must be present if the soil is to be satisfactory, and needs frequent renewal. Forking is next done, to break up the surface soil more finely and mix it more thoroughly with the compost or manure; if a fine surface is needed, as for a seed bed, raking completes the process. Later, hoeing may be necessary to destroy weeds, and also to break up the surface of the soil if it should become caked.

The local tool for digging is the cangkul, which takes the place of the spade used in temperate countries. For forking, a cangkul fork (Assam fork) is very effective, but too frequently a gardener uses a cangkul when he should use a fork. Often it is necessary to apply manure to growing plants, and for this to be effective the manure should be mixed with the surface soil. If this mixing is done with a cangkul, many of the

When destroying weeds with a hoe, one should be careful not to damage the roots of the plant

Lush greenery of a tropical garden

roots of the plant will be cut, and this may have a serious effect on growth, or may even kill some of the plants; this injury can be avoided by the use of a fork.

When opening up new ground for planting, whether it be flower bed, border, a tree or a vegetable patch, it is advisable to dig fairly deeply. If the soil is at all heavy, deep digging is essential, as undisturbed clay becomes very compacted, and most plants will not grow in it; deep digging of such ground is also necessary to secure the drainage of surplus water after heavy rain, failing which the surface soil will become waterlogged. The smaller the area dug, the greater the need for this deep cultivation of a heavy soil. A heavy soil should not be dug in wet weather, as this will only increase its stickiness; but such a soil will benefit very much by being broken up and exposed to the sun in dry weather. Red lateritic soils are very hard when dry and digging should be done a short time after a little shower of rain but not immediately after heavy rain. The texture of such soil improves very quickly after organic matter has been added. A light soil is not so much in need of deep digging, but will benefit by it if a liberal amount of organic matter is available.

If only a small bed is being dug, it is necessary first to dig out all the earth, and then to mix it with the compost or manure as it is returned. If a large area is to be dug, as for a vegetable garden, a trench is first made at one end, to the full depth required, and say 60 cm wide, the earth removed being carried to the other end of the plot. The trench is then filled with the broken up earth of the next 60 cm of ground, duly mixed as required with organic matter, and the process repeated throughout the plot. In the case of heavy soil, it is good to mix as much undecayed or half-decayed vegetable refuse (dead leaves, etc.) as possible with the lower layers, as this will help to maintain an open texture. With a light soil, the compost which has been well decayed (see below) is better, as it has good water-holding properties and provides more readily available plant food.

When an area of ground has been deeply dug, and has had plants growing in it, no further deep digging should be necessary for some time (say two or three years), as the roots will help to keep it open. Subsequent cultivation need only be concerned with the top 15–30 cm, whether it be between successive crops of vegetables or for the manuring of permanent shrubs or other woody plants.

Hoeing to destroy weeds needs to be done carefully, so as not to damage the roots of the cultivated plants. Annual or shortlived weeds are controlled by hoeing at an early stage, before flowering; but there are some very troublesome perennial weeds which are difficult to destroy even by repeated hoeing or forking. One in particular, commonly called nutgrass, is very troublesome and almost impossible to eradicate; care should be taken to avoid earth in which it has been growing.

Composting

The word 'compost' is used for a prepared mixture of rotted organic matter, ready to add to the soil. In recent years, much research has been carried out in both temperate and tropical countries, including Malaysia, on the preparation of compost, with the object of using available waste organic matter to the best advantage. The essentials of the process are to pile the waste matter in a heap, made so that it is both well aerated and moist. Under these conditions, the micro-organisms which bring about rotting of the material have the best conditions for growth, always provided that they have enough nitrogenous matter to feed them. Most garden refuse, especially leaf sweepings, is too poor in nitrogen to rot quickly. It is therefore necessary to add a richer source of nitrogen, and this is best provided by cattle dung. It is not always easily available and instead a small quantity of sulphate of ammonia can be mixed with a little soil and the mixture sprinkled in between the layers of compost material. The addition of wood ashes, to provide potash and also to make the mixture less acid, is also advisable. When the heap is properly made, and a sufficient amount of nitrogenous matter added, decomposition soon becomes so rapid that the interior of the heap becomes quite hot, and remains so for a fortnight or more; under such conditions, seeds of weeds, and also many harmful organisms, are destroyed. For this reason, the process has been used for the disposal of human excreta, any parasitic organisms in which are destroyed by the high temperature.

The Department of Agriculture in Malaysia issues information on the making of compost and the quantities of ingredients to be used are given but these need not be exact and an approximation to the stated proportions can be used.

The garden materials which form the basis of compost are cut grass, leaf sweepings, clippings or prunings from hedges and shrubs (especially when these are young and succulent), dead weeds and other plants which have been pulled up from the garden. It is best to mix the greener materials (such as grass) with the harsher dead leaves, as the former decays more rapidly and assists in the decomposition of the tougher material. The size of the compost heap to be made will be governed by the amount of space available and in large gardens a heap about 3 m long and 2 m wide can be made, but it should not be more than $1\frac{1}{3}$ m high. If it is higher, the pressure at the bottom will be so great that there will be insufficient aeration. The heap is made in layers of about 15–20 cm thick, and on top of each layer is placed a thin layer of cattle dung, and on to the mixture also is sprinkled a liquid made from cattle dung and wood ashes in water. The proportions advised are 200–300 kg of garden refuse, 25 kg of cattle dung, and 1 kg of fine dry wood ash. The liquid mentioned above is made from 33 litres of water, 4 kg of cattle dung and 250 g of wood ash; the remainder of the dung and ashes are added as described, a little on top of each layer of garden refuse.

It is also possible to use domestic refuse, such as waste food of all kinds, fruit rinds, rotten fruit, old leaf vegetables and other such material, and this is often a convenient way of disposing of such refuse. It must, however, be covered over immediately so that flies cannot use it as a breeding place. Urine may be added also to the heap; and as this is a better source of nitrogen than cattle dung, it may largely take the place of dung.

If cattle dung or urine are not available then bacterial action in the compost heap can be encouraged by adding a little sulphate of ammonia, as mentioned previously, or commercially prepared activators which should be used according to the directions on the packet.

In small gardens a compost heap of one half or one third of this size can be made and can be kept tidy by surrounding it with a length of galvanized chicken wire mesh which will prevent the material from falling about.

The temperature of the heap rises quickly and should reach maximum after about two days. This may be tested by pushing a smooth dry stick into the heap, leaving it there for a minute or two, then testing it with the hand. It should be both hot and moist, but not too wet. Moisture is usually sufficiently maintained in the heap by rain, but in dry weather it may be necessary to add water. When the weather is very wet it is wise to cover the heap with material such as polythene sheeting in order to prevent the compost from becoming too wet and also to prevent the decayed material from being washed away. If the heap becomes too dry, decomposition will be very slow or may even stop altogether.

After about fifteen days, under normal conditions, the temperature usually falls almost to atmospheric temperature, and the heap should be turned and remade; it will then start again in active decomposition and rise in temperature. The process of remaking the heap is repeated a second and, if necessary, a third and fourth time. Usually the rotted material is in a sufficiently decomposed state after six to eight weeks from the beginning of the operation.

Another method of composting involves the turning of the heaps every four weeks. It consists in making a row of four compartments (of a rough wooden framework), each about one metre cube. One of these is filled every week, and after the fourth week the first compartment is cleared and refilled, the original material being turned and repiled in a heap in front. After two turnings each lot of material is ready for use. The system has the advantage of ensuring regular periodic handling of each lot of material, a week being an easier interval to remember than a fortnight.

Well made compost has a nitrogen content rather higher than that of cattle dung, and it should have comparable amounts of the other essential materials for plant growth. As mentioned above, it is necessary to add organic matter to garden soils to maintain them in good physical condition. There is little doubt also that from a chemical standpoint compost and other organic manures add other things to the soil besides the mineral elements needed by the plant roots. In recent years much information has been obtained about growth-promoting substances, minute quantities of which have a great effect on plants, and it is likely, though not yet sufficiently demonstrated, that part of the value of organic matter in the soil consists in the provision of such substances.

Well rotted compost is easy to mix with garden soil, and its further decomposition in the soil, to provide plant food, is rapid. It is possible to use compost that is not completely rotted and this is especially suitable in heavy soils, as it has a more lasting effect in keeping the soils well aerated; but presumably such incompletely rotted compost is less quickly converted into plant food.

In addition to the use of compost to mix with the soil when preparing beds for planting, it may be forked into the surface soil around growing plants at a later stage, or it may be used as a mulch on the surface. This mulch provides plant food by decomposition, and also protects the surface soil, and roots in it, from the more drastic effects of direct sunlight and heavy rain. But decomposition of such a mulch is rapid and its use may not always be economic.

A compost heap should be made as far away as possible from the house and should not be located near a tree, otherwise the roots of the tree will grow into the compost and will remove all of the plant nutrients as they are formed.

Fresh grass clippings can be used immediately as a mulch on flower beds, vegetable plots or around shrubs and young trees. However, the clippings should not be placed in direct contact with the plants because they become closely packed and a great deal of heat is generated. This, together with the large amount of moisture in the grass clippings, will encourage the development of fungi and bacteria which could attack and damage the plants. Such a mulch should be kept 10–15 cm away from the plant stems and will still afford adequate protection to the soil as well as decompose slowly to provide plant food. Leaves from trees are satisfactory for this purpose but have the disadvantage that, until they are partly decayed, they are easily blown about in high winds unless covered with a thin sprinkling of soil. A mulch of leaves or grass clippings will help to retain a surprising amount of moisture in the soil and has considerable value from this point of view during spells of dry weather.

Manures

A manure is anything added to the soil to increase its fertility for plant growth. Manures are usually divided into two classes, organic and inorganic (or artificial). Organic manures are derived from decaying material of plant or animal origin; that is, they are derived from living organisms. Inorganic or artificial manures (often called fertilizers in a general way) are made by some chemical process, and not from decaying organic matter. Organic manures provide most of the chemical substances necessary for plant growth. Inorganic manures, on the other hand, may only provide one of the many substances needed by the plant. Organic manures are therefore much safer to use; inorganic manures must be used with care or the result may be an unbalanced diet for the plants.

Organic Manures

Almost any kind of organic matter may be used as manure, but some kinds are better than others, and some are more easily available; and it is not economic to use as manure materials which can be used as food for men and animals, though rotten food, such as decayed fish or prawns, is often good as manure.

Organic manures vary a great deal in the amount of plant food they contain. Some are very concentrated, some much less so. Compost, prepared as described above, is one of the less concentrated organic manures, but is very valuable, as already indicated, in improving the physical texture of the soil. However, we often need a manure which provides a more rapid supply of food to the roots, and that is when we must use one of the other organic manures or an artificial fertilizer.

The roots of plants can take up only fairly simple chemical substances, and these must be in dilute solution. Organic materials are for the most part complex and insoluble, and must be decomposed before they can·be taken up by the roots. An organic manure which will decompose quickly is therefore more effective than one which decays slowly. The rate of decay is dependent partly on temperature, and under Malaysian conditions is much more rapid than in cooler climates. This is useful in making the manure more quickly available, but at the same time it means that the manure disappears more rapidly. A practical result is that we should not apply too much manure at once, as much of it may decompose and be lost before the plants can use it. Small applications of manure at frequent intervals are much more efficient; and still greater efficiency is attained if the manures can be decomposed to a soluble condition, immediately assimilable by the roots, before they are applied. This latter practice is that adopted by most Chinese gardeners; together with their technique for attaining a well aerated soil, it explains the success of their pot culture.

Cattle Dung

This used to be the commonest organic manure used in Malaysia, but at the present time, in most areas, it is in short supply and can be expensive to buy. Gardeners living in more rural areas probably could obtain a reasonable supply much more easily than those in suburban areas. (Some fortunate gardeners may have access to a supply of horse dung and this can be used in the same way as cattle dung and has the same effect.) Either kind of manure can be mixed directly with the soil, or used in making compost, or mixed, when fresh, with water and the liquid applied to the soil around the plants, or it may be dried and used for mixing with potting soil. Probably some nitrogen is lost in the drying process. Fresh dung contains a certain amount of soluble material which is almost immediately available to roots, and so the liquid obtained by soaking fresh manure for a short time in water makes an efficient fertilizer. But cattle dung does not contain a high proportion of plant food.

Urine

Whether this is derived from animals or man, it is a valuable manure as it contains a much greater proportion of the excreted nitrogen than dung; its whole content is in solution, almost immediately available for use by plants. It should not be used fresh and undiluted on many plants but is best kept for a few days and then diluted with about four times its bulk of water; it may then be watered directly on to the ground around the plants. It may also be used, as noted above, as a source of added nitrogen in the preparation of compost. It is an excellent manure for orchids. Probably part of its value lies in the growth-promoting substances it is known to contain. If it is stored for some time before use, the container should be kept away from the house as it can become a little odorous and it should be kept covered to prevent dilution by rain water and also to prevent mosquitoes from breeding in it.

Prawn Dust

Vegetable gardeners often use a great deal of this product and it is a very valuable manure of fairly concentrated nature. It may be used direct, by mixing it with the soil in preparing a bed; but often ants are troublesome as they carry away a great quantity of the prawn dust. A more effective method, therefore, is to mix it with ten times its bulk of water, let it rot for two days, and then apply the liquid. This is done, of course, after the plants have begun to grow. As the liquid becomes very strong smelling, the container should be kept well away from the house, and this is easily done in the country, but in towns and cities, where space is more limited, it could cause annoyance to the neighbours and might also bring the gardener into conflict with the Municipal Health Authorities. For green crops such as Chinese cabbage, which must grow very rapidly, Chinese market gardeners often dig a good deal of prawn dust into the bed before planting; they claim that ants are not troublesome in the rather wet valley soils where the green vegetables are often grown. However, in some parts of the country the use of prawn dust encourages the appearance of very large numbers of flies which are exceedingly unpleasant and could be a health hazard. Prawn dust should be used therefore with a little care, but if it

were covered with soil there would be no trouble from flies and the strong smell would be reduced considerably.

Groundnut Cake and Soybean Cake

Both products are the residue left after milling of the seed for extraction of the oil, and they can be used for feeding cattle as they have a high nutritive content. Groundnut cake is also one of the most concentrated organic manures, the nitrogen content being particularly high. The cake may be broken up into small pieces and mixed with the soil; but it is better to soak it in water for one or two days, stir well, and then pour the mixture on the soil round the plants. Chinese gardeners usually soak the cake in water in large jars for three or four weeks, by which time it becomes very foul-smelling, but the liquid so obtained contains nitrogenous material which is immediately available to roots, and it is a very efficient manure, though not pleasant to use.

The proportions used are about ½ kg cake to about 5 litres water; the jar must be kept covered, and stirred from time to time. Only the liquid is used. It is diluted with several times its bulk of water before being poured on the soil around the plants; some plants will tolerate a more concentrated solution than others. Once the jar is in use, it can be maintained indefinitely by adding a little more cake and water as required. This method would not be possible in towns as the strong smell would annoy neighbours. However, the method is particularly suitable for pot plants which require special feeding, but must naturally be combined with careful soil management to give the roots proper physical conditions for growth.

Poultry Manure

This is obtained from chickens and ducks and is a valuable manure, more concentrated than cattle dung. It may be used either direct or in liquid form after rotting for a short time in water. It has a high nitrogen content and can be used on plants requiring a great deal of this substance at a particular stage of their growth. Poultry manure which is stored should be kept covered as it is strong-smelling and can become a centre for fly-breeding.

Guano

This is the name given to deposits found in limestone caves which are inhabited by bats, and consists of the rotted bat dung. Owing to variation in local conditions, there is much variation in the composition of guano, even from the same cave. It is usually a better source of phosphorus than of nitrogen. Some guanos have a high manurial value. The material is usually available in the limestone districts of Malaysia, and is worth the attention of people residing in those districts, but only guano of high grade would be worth the expense of long distance transport.

Bone Meal

The product is made from the bones of animals which have been used as food. It contains some nitrogen, but is particularly useful as a source of phosphorus and calcium. Coarsely ground bone meal provides a source of phosphorus over a long period but finely ground material gives a quick source of supply of this element.

Dried Blood

A concentrated organic manure which is sometimes used in mixed fertilizers as well as on its own. It has a high nitrogen content as well as other plant foods and should be kept in an airtight container as it absorbs water very easily and when this happens some of the nitrogen content is lost. However, when combined with bone meal it makes an excellent mixture for pot plants.

Fish Meal

When available, this is a good fertilizer but should be dug into the soil immediately as it can be very strong-smelling. Fish waste from markets can also be used but, again, must be covered with soil immediately because of the smell and because it will attract flies. Fish products give a good supply of nitrogen and some phosphorus.

Seaweed

In coastal areas, seaweed may be available in some quantity and is an excellent source of calcium and potash. In some seasons of the year, large amounts of seaweed can be collected, but before use it must be washed thoroughly or should be allowed to stand in heavy rain for some time to remove all traces of salt water. It can be dug into the soil directly or used for making compost.

Sludge

This is available as a dried product from sewage farms and is safe to use as well as being odourless. It can be dug into the soil directly, or it can be used for making compost. Sludge helps to improve the texture of the soil and also provides plant food.

Green Manure

Growing plants may be dug into the ground and will decay there, thus providing humus. Weeds and grass may be used in this way provided they are well covered with soil to prevent their regrowth. Alternatively, plants may be grown specially as green manure and are dug into the soil as soon as they have become sufficiently large and leafy. During the time of decomposition, some nitrogen is lost and a little sulphate of ammonia should be applied to counteract this depletion. Plants which can be used for this purpose are Vigna (Mung beans, Long beans and Cowpeas), Centrosema, Pueraria and Calopogonium, which are cover crops, Amaranthus or any other quick growing leafy plants. Green manuring can be practised on flower beds or vegetable plots, and is very useful on land which has not previously been cultivated, especially if the soil is heavy, as it gives an immediate improvement in soil texture and provides an initial amount of plant food for the first crop which is grown.

Many commercially prepared organic fertilizers are available which are convenient to use and especially suitable for pot plant work.

Inorganic or Artificial Manures

These are either of mineral origin, or are products or by-products of large-scale chemical processes, some of them being made from atmospheric nitrogen. They are relatively simple in chemical structure, and each provides only a few of the many elements necessary for plant growth. Therefore, while almost any organic manure may be used alone with satisfactory results, it is generally necessary to use a mixture of inorganic manures to provide a balanced ration for roots of plants. Such mixtures are prepared by manufacturers of fertilizers, and are commonly sold as 'Complete Fertilizers'. The composition of such mixtures varies, some having a higher nitrogen content or phosphorus or potash content than others. Some manufacturers also make mixtures containing both organic and inorganic manures, the idea being that the inorganic part will be more immediately available to roots while the organic part decomposes later and provides plant food over a longer period of time.

Some artificial manures are soluble, some not, or only slightly soluble. The former are usually washed out of the soil by rain if given in excess. They should therefore be given in small quantities only at a time when the roots can make the most use of them; that is, they should be applied to plants which are in active growth but not to those which are in a resting phase. They are most easily given in the form of a dilute solution which is watered on to the bed or pot. The less soluble artificial manures are naturally more durable, as they decompose slowly, and larger amounts may be applied safely at relatively long intervals.

Artificial manures are slightly expensive but they are concentrated, convenient to handle and to apply, and are therefore worth the expense involved as they can be stored for a long time without deterioration. They are cleaner in use than organic manures, and more pleasant to apply to plants which are close to or inside the house. For plants in the open ground, they are a most valuable supplement to a basic dressing of compost or dung, but can never take the place of the organic material in maintaining a satisfactory physical texture in the soil.

Artificial manures must be stored carefully under dry conditions, otherwise they will deteriorate and may become useless. Small quantities in tins, bottles or polythene bags are usually safe enough, but larger quantities may be in thick paper bags or sacks and these should be raised from the floor on boards or stood on a thick layer of polythene sheeting. If the bags or sacks are placed directly on a concrete floor, any spilled fertilizer may react with the concrete and cause it to break up. Floors of brick, stone or concrete will allow water to pass through slowly and a wet patch will appear underneath any articles left on such surfaces. Consequently, the moisture which rises through such floors would cause rapid disintegration of paper bags placed directly on them and the fertilizer would become useless. Polythene sheeting placed over the floor or a layer of wooden planks raised on blocks will prevent any trouble from moisture rising through the floor. Mosaic tiles or a terrazo surface on a floor will prevent water from passing through but should be protected from spilled fertilizer which will discolour or damage the surface.

Storerooms or garden sheds should be kept locked so that small children and domestic pets have no access to the fertilizers or other garden chemicals such as pesticides and insecticides. All chemicals should be clearly labelled so that there can be no possibility of error when they are needed. No garden chemicals of any kind should be kept near food. Some fertilizers absorb water from the air and either become very wet or may be completely liquefied, so that they should be kept in closed polythene bags or plastic containers. Thick paper bags or cardboard boxes should not be used for storing such fertilizers as they would soon disintegrate.

Old and useless fertilizers should not be thrown away haphazardly but should be disposed of carefully. It is probably best to dig a deep hole in some unused corner of the garden and to bury the material thoroughly.

On no account should it be thrown into storm drains or into a lavatory as it could damage the concrete of the drainpipes or the septic tanks.

Many different mixtures of inorganic fertilizers are produced and their composition is usually expressed by the amount of nitrogen, phosphorus and potash which they contain (this is usually referred to as the percentage of N, P and K). Varying combinations of these elements are made and often other substances, such as calcium (Ca), magnesium (Mg), boron (B) and manganese (Mn), may be included to suit various kinds of soils. N, P and K are always the basic ingredients and are combined in different proportions for different kinds of plants as well as for different stages of plant growth. Nitrogen is needed for normal healthy growth of plant tissues but an excess of this element will cause rapid growth and soft tissues which are more susceptible to attack by pests and diseases. Phosphorus is essential in the early stages of plant growth as it encourages good root development, enhances disease resistance and is important for fruit production. Potassium is necessary for the formation of protoplasm in the plant cells and helps to promote resistance to some kinds of plant disease. It is also necessary in the food manufacturing process which occurs in leaves as well as for higher fruit yield in trees.

Some of the more commonly available fertilizers are listed below.

Ammonium Sulphate

This is a soluble salt which provides a valuable source of nitrogen. It is particularly useful for green leaf vegetables, such as Lettuces, Spinach and Cabbages, as nitrogen is needed most for the growth of leaves. If the ground has had a good dressing of compost, and preferably also some phosphorus (see below), a solution of ammonium sulphate is one of the best manures for the rapid development of leafy growth. An excess of nitrogen, however, is not good for most plants, and it is better to use a mixed fertilizer which can provide other elements besides nitrogen. Ammonium sulphate is also good for lawns, but here again, it must from time to time be supplemented by the addition of phosphate. Ammonium sulphate must never be mixed with lime. When using ammonium sulphate or other soluble fertilizers, a dilution of 30 g to 4½ litres of water is usually satisfactory. More concentrated solutions may damage roots and do more harm than good.

Ammonium Nitrate

This is not used a great deal on its own as

a fertilizer as it very quickly absorbs moisture from the air, but it does not increase the acidity of the soil and is therefore suitable for use on acid soils.

Nitro-chalk

This is a mixture of ammonium nitrate and limestone and does not absorb moisture from the air very readily so that it is much easier to store. The nitrogen is easily available to plant roots and the limestone content prevents the soil from becoming acid or sour. Nitro-chalk is therefore very useful as a top dressing on acid soils.

Calcium Cyanamide

In addition to nitrogen, this compound also contains lime and does not make the soil acid but it must be used carefully as it may kill young plants. If it is applied about two weeks before planting it is perfectly safe.

Urea

This is a good source of nitrogen but absorbs moisture very easily and consequently storage can be difficult. The nitrogen is available very quickly to plants and the urea is more easily handled if it is mixed with limestone.

Other fertilizers which will supply nitrogen are calcium nitrate, potassium nitrate and sodium nitrate, but all of these absorb water very easily and can be difficult to store.

Rock phosphate

A naturally occurring product, this is ground finely for use as a fertilizer. It is best used on acid soils because on these it is broken down faster into the soluble form which can be absorbed by the roots. It is also good on soils with a high content of organic matter, but it is not so good on sandy or neutral soils as it does not decompose. It is not soluble in water and is held by the soil for a considerable period, though it becomes available slowly for roots. Roots, however, need only a very little phosphate, and they appear to be able to procure it as rapidly as they need it when given in this way. It is thus only necessary to apply rock phosphate at long intervals of six months or even one year; about 60 g per square metre is sufficient. For woody plants such as trees and flowering shrubs, a good quantity of compost with the soil at planting, and some rock phosphate, are all that is needed to secure good strong growth. It is a good idea to use phosphate on all cultivated ground as all local soils are deficient in phosphorous. It is especially important in the case of vegetables as every harvest removes a large amount of phosphorus from the soil.

Basic Slag

This is a finely ground powder which is insoluble in water but is useful on acidic soils as it contains other minerals which are needed by plants for healthy growth. It breaks down in the soil into a form which can be absorbed by the plant roots.

Fused Magnesium Phosphate

Similar in properties to rock phosphate, this contains a small quantity of magnesium which is deficient in some Malaysian soils. Magnesium is an essential ingredient of the green colouring matter in plants and is therefore necessary for healthy growth.

Superphosphate

This is partly soluble in water and the phosphate is available to plants fairly quickly and easily.

Potassium

Fertilizers containing potassium are used in all the 'complete' mixtures sold by manufacturers. Potassium is not deficient in our Malaysian soils, but it is seriously deficient in poor sandy and quartzite soils. However, in most cases the ordinary gardener can provide all the potassium he needs by using some wood ashes in preparing his compost.

Muriate of potash and sulphate of potash are available and can be used as a basic dressing or as a top dressing. On acid soils the effect of both is improved if a little lime is also applied at the same time.

Calcium

An essential element for most plants, it is usually applied to the soil in the form of lime. Lime is an extremely useful addition to the soil as it neutralizes acidity and releases many of the plant nutrients which would otherwise remain in a form unavailable to the plants. Too much lime should not be applied as it could cause a deficiency of trace elements (which are needed by plants in very small quantities only), and other manures or fertilizers would then have to be applied to counteract this effect. However, application of a little lime is always beneficial. Lime is available in several forms. Quicklime is calcium oxide and should be handled carefully because when water is mixed with it great heat develops and it can burn. It must be kept away from the eyes and should be stored out of the reach of children. Hydrated lime is quicklime after water has been added and this is quite safe to use. Ground chalk or ground limestone are forms of calcium carbonate and easy to handle. Also available are magnesium lime and ground magnesium limestone, the latter being the easiest to use.

Lime is best raked into the top 5 cm of soil and can be applied at the rate of ½ kg to 30 square metres of ground; this should be sufficient to last for about three years. It should not be mixed with any nitrogenous fertilizer as there will be some interaction and ammonia will be lost. Basic slag should not be mixed with lime for the same reason. When using lime and a nitrogenous fertilizer, the lime should be applied about two weeks before the latter. Continuous application of ammonium sulphate will cause a loss of calcium carbonate from the soil which will become acidic and this will need correcting by the application of lime in some form.

All of these manures and fertilizers are used as top dressings or are incorporated into the soil, but there are available at the present time liquid preparations which are sprayed on to the plants and are absorbed by the leaves. These are known as foliar sprays and are of some use for many kinds of pot plants. Foliar sprays are ready-mixed and the instructions on the container should be read thoroughly before the spray is applied. Fertilizer of any kind, if too concentrated, will severely damage or kill a plant.

Many 'balanced' fertilizers are available commercially in liquid or solid form and these are convenient for the small gardener, especially if there is little storage space around the house. These fertilizers are very suitable for people living in flats or apartments where space is limited and only a few pot plants may be grown. They keep quite well, so if some storage space is available, it is cheaper to buy as large a container as possible, rather than the very small packaged quantities which are often available in shops. The latter are of use when only one or two pot plants are grown and, because only small quantities of fertilizer are used, these little packets may then be adequate.

Town dwellers may not have access to soil, and if they wish to grow pot plants there are sometimes available dry potting mixtures, composts or peat; these are easy to use but some storage space will be needed, especially as artificial fertilizers must be added to them.

4 PROPAGATION AND PRUNING

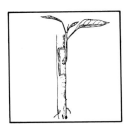

Bud grafting

Plants may be propagated from seeds, or from parts of an existing plant. The latter method is called vegetative propagation because it is concerned only with dividing the vegetative body of a plant, and has nothing to do with the flowers. New plants raised by vegetative propagation, by cuttings, marcots or grafts, are really still parts of the mother plant from which they came, and have exactly the same characters. But seeds are only produced by flowers, and the embryo or young plant in the seed is the result of a mating between male and female cells in the ovary of a flower. The male cells are derived from pollen grains, often brought by insects from other flowers. Thus a seed is not like a cutting; it is derived from two parents and receives part of its nature from each. If the two parents differ in any way, the seedling will reflect the differences. Thus vegetative propagation is a method of securing absolute uniformity, whereas propagation by seeds introduces the possibility of difference. In practice, carefully bred annuals are near enough to being identical, and so differences among seedlings are negligible. But in carefully bred plants there may be differences, which may be desirable or undesirable, between one individual and another. We may use the method of seed production to combine the good characters of different plants, but having effected such a combination, we maintain it by vegetative propagation.

One plant will probably produce many seeds, so that propagation by seeds is often the quickest way of increasing our stock. In the case of annuals there is usually no other way, though a number of annuals (such as African Marigolds and certain Cabbages) may be grown from cuttings. If there is any variation among the annuals of which we want seeds (as, for example, frequently occurs in Celosia), we ought always to select the best plants from which to take seeds. Even then we are not sure of the pollen parent, and so there is some chance of variation, but the more we select, the purer our strain will become. It should be remembered that when two plants showing desirable characters are crossed and the resulting seed is germinated, then only some of the seedlings will show the expected combination of characters and many will be inferior to both parents. It is essential, therefore, to grow as many seedlings as possible and then to select rigorously: the plant showing the best characters may be slower or weaker in growth than the others. Any attempts at crossing will be attended by many disappointments but success, with the appearance of one or two good plants only, is exhilarating.

In view of these remarks on the crossing of plants, it might be useful to give here a very brief outline of a simplified technique which could be used by those wishing to make an attempt in this aspect of garden plants.

There are some limitations to the crossing of plants and it should be remembered that those chosen to be the parents should be somewhat related. This means that varieties within a species or species within a genus could be used, but plants which are widely separated from each other, such as those in the Rubber family and those in the Palm family, could not be crossed. The combination of plants from two different genera is not usually possible except in very few cases and the orchids provide a good example of this, as some of the garden forms are a combination of two, three or sometimes four different genera.

Simple crossing work can be attempted with a very small amount of equipment. All that is needed are:

1 small watercolour paintbrush
    for transferring pollen
1 pair of small scissors
    (nail scissors are adequate)
1 sharp blade, preferably with
    a good pointed tip
A number of small, waterproof paper
    bags
Several small labels
1 small bottle of methylated spirit
    or rectified spirit (available from any
    pharmacy store)

The procedure is quite simple but care must be taken not to damage the flowers which are selected, otherwise disease may destroy the young fruit before it is ripe. After selecting the plants to be used as parents it is wise to make several similar crosses so that there will be a greater chance of success. On each plant choose several flowers which are almost ready to open. Each one should be covered with one of the small paper bags in order to prevent any pollen from other plants reaching them. Reciprocal crosses should be made, which means that if plant A is used for pollen and plant B is the female parent then you should make another cross using plant A as the female parent and plant B as the pollen parent.

The flowers to be used as the female parent should have the petals and the stamens removed to prevent self-pollination but care should be taken to avoid damaging the stigma which is the receptive point situated at the tip of a little stalk on the top of the ovary. When it ripens, it usually becomes sticky and will then hold the pollen. As soon as it is ripe the transfer of pollen can be made. The paintbrush should be dipped into the alcohol and allowed to dry for one or two minutes. This is important otherwise the alcohol will kill the pollen. Remove the paper bag from the flower to be used as the male parent and pick up some of the pollen from the stamens with the paintbrush. Transfer this to the stigma of the 'female' flower, using the brush lightly so as to cause no damage. Re-cover each flower with a small paper bag and tie on one of the labels which should have the date and the kind of cross made written upon it. Use two other flowers to make the reciprocal cross. If the stamens are large enough, they can be picked off with the forceps and gently touched to the stigma of the 'female' flower. Brush or forceps should be dipped in alcohol and allowed to dry after each use to prevent any contamination.

The 'female' flower should be looked at each day until the young fruit begins to enlarge. At this stage the paper bag can be removed although the label must remain. The young fruit will develop much better when it is uncovered and there will be no danger of further pollination. When it ripens the seeds can be extracted and planted in the usual way.

This is the basic method for cross-pollination and it would be best to try out the technique first on large flowers which are easily manipulated. With small flowers the technique must be modified by the person doing the crossing in order to suit the situation. It is very important to prevent pollen from any unknown source reaching the stigma of the flower you are using as the female parent.

There are modifications and refinements of this technique for crossing plants but these are not relevant to this book. The outline just given is sufficient for anyone wishing to make a first attempt at this method of plant propagation. It is a slow job and needs a great deal of patience but could be a most rewarding hobby.

Some plants never produce seeds in Malaysia. To propagate these we must make cuttings. Sometimes these are easy to strike, sometimes difficult. Some plants have a rootstock which grows rapidly and is easily divided (e.g. Cannas), and these are easily increased by vegetative means. Plants which produce no seeds and are difficult to grow from cuttings are naturally less common than those easily propagated, and are therefore much prized. The beautiful climber Odontadenia is one of these.

In the case of shrubs and other large plants, a cutting or marcot will often produce a new individual more quickly than a seed. This is another reason why vegetative propagation may sometimes be preferable to the sowing of seeds.

Thus the choice between seeds and cuttings depends on many factors; and sometimes there is no choice. In any case, propagation is one of the gardener's most important duties, and should be carried out with care. Otherwise seeds, plants and time may be easily lost. In the chapters which follow, the usual method of propagation for each kind of plant is indicated. In this chapter, the methods are described.

Seeds

Seeds are in part a device of nature for allowing a plant to rest over a period when growth is impossible; that is, over a cold or dry season. But in Malaysia growth is always possible. Therefore, the seeds of most local plants do not need to rest, and in fact many of them will not remain alive very long in storage. Seeds brought here from other countries also will not keep long in good condition, especially if they are not kept dry. Small seeds will often keep for some months if carefully dried and then stored in tightly stoppered bottles or airtight tins, but if left in paper packets they will hardly keep more than two or three weeks. Storage of seeds is therefore important, and the stock should be renewed as often as possible.

In the case of seeds imported from other countries, it is best to import in small quantities as required. A gardener may easily be self-supporting as regards seeds of plants that seed freely in Malaysia, but he must regularly collect a new stock, keeping one or two plants of each sowing for this purpose. If necessary, these can be kept in a nursery bed, so as not to spoil the ornamental garden by having to keep untidy old plants. The need for selecting good plants as seed bearers must be remembered. Those plants which produce very few or no seeds in Malaysia must be grown from cuttings or seed must be imported.

Sowing Seeds

This is usually reckoned a simple operation, but for best results must be done with care. Seeds are usually sown in pots or pans, though some large vegetable seeds (e.g. Beans and Maize) are sown directly in the ground. Large seeds need much less care than small ones; they have a plentiful reserve of food to start the young plant in life, and they are usually less liable to troubles such as damping-off than small seeds. On the other hand, some large seeds (as, for example, many palms) are very slow to germinate, and may take months before they show signs of life.

Pots for seedlings must be clean. If we use an old pot it should be thoroughly scrubbed and dried before use. This will help to get rid of undesirable microscopic organisms that might harm the seedlings. Cover the drainage holes with some clean crocks and then some coarse dead leaves to keep the earth from washing through. Next comes the potting soil. This must be light in texture so as to be well aerated. It is best to sterilize the soil or to use burnt earth. Soil may be effectively sterilized either by spreading it on a piece of corrugated iron and putting this over a fire, stirring the soil occasionally, or by putting it into a large shallow iron pan with a little water and bringing it to a boil. In the latter case, the soil should be spread out to dry before using, or it may be too wet. A mixed potting soil should contain some sand and some well rotted compost; the proportion 1 part sand, 1 part compost and 2 parts sterilized soil is satisfactory.

The pot should be about two-thirds filled with this mixture, and then to within 2½ cm of the top with the same mixture but more finely sifted. The surface should be pressed down evenly with a piece of wood. The seeds are then distributed on this surface, and covered with a thin layer of the same sifted soil; the thickness of this layer should be about equal to the thickness of the seeds. The top-soil is then pressed down again and the pot watered with a fine rose. The seeds should not be sown too thickly. Small seeds, such as Petunia, can be mixed with sand (the mixing must be thorough); this will help to distribute them evenly. Larger seeds may be planted separately. Pots should be placed on a bench protected from ants, which often carry away small seeds before germination begins.

Very small seeds such as those of Begonia and Gloxinias, (now called Sinningia), should not be covered, but left scattered on the surface of the potting soil. They are best watered from below, by plunging the pot (not too deeply) into water until the surface is just moist. Watering with a watering-can will wash such small seeds away.

Seeds that are just germinating need to be kept just moist, but not too wet. If they are too dry, growth will stop and the seeds may be killed; if too wet, they will not have enough air, and damping off fungi will be encouraged. Pots containing seeds should, therefore, be put in a sheltered place, and watered lightly often enough to keep the surface soil moist. Small seeds on or near the surface of the soil are much more in danger of drying than larger ones which are safely covered. Therefore, it is usual to put a piece of glass over the pots containing small seeds, leaving a little room for ventilation, until the seeds germinate, or even for a few days after that. Some seeds germinate better in the dark. In such cases, dark paper over the glass is useful. Young seedlings should not be exposed to the force of a tropical rainstorm otherwise they will be broken or beaten to the ground and the soil can be washed out of the pot, taking many of the seeds with it.

As soon as the seeds germinate they should be brought into good light and protected from heavy rain for the reasons just mentioned. As they grow they should be hardened off if possible to stand full sun, but shade-loving plants naturally will not stand this. If seedlings are kept in too weak a light they become too tall and thin, and are difficult to handle at transplanting; also they are not so hardy. Seedlings in the open may be protected from rain by glass screens, if available. Otherwise, attap covers or polythene sheeting may be put over them during rainstorms.

Transplanting

Seedlings should be transplanted as soon as they are big enough to handle. If they are to be grown as pot plants, the move may be a final one. They are then planted in a good burnt earth mixture (see Chapter 5) and sheltered from sun and rain until they have begun new growth, when they are gradually hardened off to full exposure and manured from time to time as required.

Plants for bedding out may first need to be

put into other pots or boxes to grow them to a larger size before they are exposed to full sun and rain in a garden bed. In this case, a burnt earth mixture in the boxes is most satisfactory, or failing that a mixed soil that has been sterilized. The boxes should be quite shallow, and should have good drainage at the bottom. The seedlings are best removed from their original pot with a small, flat, pointed piece of wood; care should be taken to disturb the roots as little as possible. A hole is made in the soil in the box with a round stick and the seedling placed in it; then the earth around the seedling is pressed down firmly with the fingers, care being taken not to damage the plant. At this first transplanting the seedlings may be 20–60 cm apart, according to their size. After transplanting, the boxes are put into a sheltered place, or covered with attaps, to protect the young plants from sun and rain until they have recovered from the shock. Then they should be hardened off to full exposure, or to as much as the plants will eventually stand. As soon as they are large enough, they are put out into beds.

As mentioned above, flowering pot plants may be transplanted in most cases into their final pots from the seed pans if a good burnt earth mixture is used. This mixture is not liable (within a reasonable time) to become sour and waterlogged, so that overpotting does not matter. It is otherwise, however, if a burnt earth mixture is not used. In that case, it is much safer to pot off the seedlings first in small pots, and then move to larger pots when their roots have filled the small ones. The reason is that if a small seedling is planted directly into a large pot of ordinary soil, the rain will usually spoil the texture of the soil before the roots have time to grow through it. Small seedlings, such as those of Petunia, will of course need two transplantings in any case.

Tree Seedlings

Many trees are most conveniently propagated from seeds, though it is better to marcot certain kinds, and others are usually grown from cuttings. Some tree seeds are fairly large, and give little trouble in handling. They are best grown in pots, unless a large number are required, in which case they may be raised in a nursery bed. Small seeds, like those of Casuarina and Lagerstroemia, need handling much as seeds of herbaceous plants, and the seedlings must have two transplantings.

The seedlings may be transplanted straight from the pots to their final site, in which case details of treatment are as described in Chapter 8. It may be desired to grow the tree on to a larger size before planting out. This is possible if the young tree is put into a nursery bed, staked and pruned carefully (see section on pruning at the end of this chapter), and also pruned at the roots. The roots halfway round the young tree should be cut about 30 cm from its base, and the disturbed earth replaced. Then a month later, when it has got over the shock and begun to grow new roots, the other half is similarly treated. This process is carried out every few months up to the time of transplanting the tree. The object is to keep the roots in a compact mass, so that when the time for transplanting comes, most of the roots can be moved without cutting. In practice, it is not possible to move a tree without some damage to the roots. Pruning of the leaves is also necessary at the time of moving to reduce the loss of water which the damaged roots cannot make good.

Vegetative Propagation

This is sometimes called asexual propagation, because it results in the multiplication of plants without the sexual union necessary for the formation of seeds. In strongly seasonal climates, vegetative propagation, like seed-sowing, must be done at a definite season of the year (which may differ according to the kind of plant concerned), but in Malaysia such propagation may be carried out at any time. The methods of vegetative propagation with which we will deal are: cuttings, layering, marcottage, etiolation, budding and grafting.

Cuttings

These are portions cut off a plant, of such a kind that they will grow into complete new plants; they may be of stems, leaves or roots. Stem cuttings are most commonly used, and there are two kinds, called hardwood and softwood cuttings. There are also special cases, such as cacti and orchids, which come into neither category. As regards orchids, their propagation is so different in many ways that the subject is deferred to the special chapter on orchids.

Hardwood Cuttings

These are made from branches of which the wood is firm, and usually the original green skin of the branch has been replaced by a thin layer of brown bark. Generally speaking, parts of branches which have newly matured (that is, the parts immediately behind the green parts) are used as cuttings, but sometimes (see below) cuttings of older and thicker branches may be used.

The cutting to be used should be 15–40 cm long, and both ends should be cut cleanly with a sharp knife, the basal cut being just below a bud. A clean cut does not injure tissues except the cells actually severed, and it allows the plant to build up a barrier against the invasion of fungi which might cause a rot before the cutting is able to begin growth. Cuttings should be placed in a pot or bed of sand or light sandy soil. Soil with too much organic matter in it encourages the growth of harmful fungi. About one-third of the cutting should be buried in the sand. A cutting so placed begins after a time to form roots, without which it must eventually die. Some kinds of cuttings produce roots quickly, some slowly, and some will rarely produce roots at all. The slow rooting kinds need special treatment and we will refer to them later. The soil around the stem can be gently pressed to make sure the cutting is firmly set in. The container of cuttings should be kept in a sheltered place as strong winds will cause movement and this will prevent roots from developing.

If the cuttings are in a pot, they are best inserted around the edge. The pot should be placed in a position sheltered from strong sunlight and the sand should be kept moist. Leaf buds may soon begin to grow. This is not necessarily an indication that roots have developed, but if the leafy shoots persist and increase in vigour, roots have probably been formed. The sand and its cuttings may then be carefully tipped out of the pot, and it will be seen which have rooted. The cuttings must be handled very carefully to prevent injury to the delicate new roots. Those which have rooted should each be put in a separate pot containing a potting mixture, like the one described for seedlings. The rooted cutting should be placed in the pot when the latter is half full of soil, and the rest of the soil is then put around it and gently pressed down. Or if the cuttings are strongly rooted and of a hardy kind, they can be put straight out into their final position in the open ground.

Some kinds of cuttings are very hardy, and can be put straight into beds in the open ground from the beginning, even with full exposure to the sun; such are Hibiscus, Barleria, Ixora, and some kinds of Bougainvillea.

Certain trees may be propagated from large woody cuttings, notably the Dadap (*Erythrina indica*), Angsana (*Pterocarpus indicus*) and Gliricidia. The cuttings may be 1–2 m long, and 5 cm or more thick. They may be planted in the position where the trees are to grow, or rooted first in a nursery bed. Such large cuttings have a big reserve of food in them, and grow rapidly; but not all trees can be propagated in this way.

Softwood Cuttings

These are made from the green ends of branches and include what are known as tip-cuttings. Most will not stand much exposure, though a few kinds (such as Sweet Potato cuttings) which root quickly will stand full sun. Softwood cuttings must retain most of their leaves; leaves lose water rapidly and this cannot be made good until roots have been formed. Hence the need for shelter from sun and drying winds. The cuttings may be put into a pot of sand, like hardwood cuttings, and the pot kept in a sheltered place and watered regularly. But cuttings which are at all slow to root are best with different treatment, and this method can be used also for woody cuttings which are slow in rooting.

This treatment is to place the cuttings in a closed frame, with a rooting bed made of coir dust, or a mixture of coir dust and sand. Coir dust holds moisture and air, and it does not become mouldy if it is kept continuously moist. Before use, it should be thoroughly washed in two changes of water and then spread out to dry. For cuttings, it should be thoroughly moist, but loose and not sodden. Overhead watering makes it sodden, but if the frame is kept closed, overhead watering is not necessary. The air in a closed frame containing moist coir dust is saturated with moisture, and so the cuttings do not wilt. It is possible to keep unrooted but still leafy cuttings of some kinds in such conditions for months, whereas if fully exposed they would wither and die. In this way slow rooting cuttings may be kept alive long enough to allow them to form roots. If only a few cuttings are to be rooted, they can be put into a large pot half filled with coir dust (or sand) and covered with glass, the pot standing in a saucer of water. Several annuals, including African Marigolds, Celosia and Melampodium, may be grown from cuttings by this method.

Another method is to use a large glass jar – the kind used by hawkers for ice-water is very suitable; or old carboys which are used for transporting acid can be cut down for this purpose. These large bottles need to have the neck and shoulder cut away before they can be used for rooting cuttings. Broken bricks to a depth of 5 cm are placed in the bottom, and water with them; then 10 cm of coir dust. The top of the jar is covered with a piece of glass.

For gardeners with plenty of space, there are available small mist propagation outfits, but these are slightly expensive and need to be placed in a permanent position as they require a fixed water supply as well as a waterproof electricity cable and fittings. Although the equipment may be set in the ground, it is much better to place it in a raised bed surrounded by a very low brick wall as this will ensure that the drainage will be very good. The rooting medium can be sand and the very fine spray of water is controlled by a time switch and also by means of special metal 'leaves' held on short supports above the

Propagation chamber

rooting medium. While these 'leaves' remain wet, the supply of water is automatically cut off, but as soon as they become dry the water supply is turned on, producing a very fine spray which keeps the air around the cuttings continuously moist. The effect is the same as in the large glass jars.

Root formation in stem cuttings may be encouraged by the use of growth regulators (growth hormones), which are available as liquids or as powders. These substances are particularly useful for cuttings which root only with difficulty as they encourage the early formation of roots and increase the number and quality of roots which are produced. They can be used on cuttings which root easily but this is probably a waste of material, although a more uniform development of roots is obtained.

If liquid preparations are used, the solutions are made up to the recommended concentration and the cuttings are soaked in this for twenty-four hours before planting in the rooting medium in the usual way. If powdered preparations are used, then the ends of the cuttings only need to be sufficiently damp for the powder to stick to them when dipped into it. Excess powder is removed by gently tapping the cuttings on the edge of the container. The cutting is then inserted in a hole made in the planting medium with a small stick. This prevents too much loss of powder as the cutting is pushed into the soil. After treatment with either kind of preparation, the cuttings are planted and cared for in the usual way. When using proprietary preparations, follow the directions for use very carefully, as some brands are meant for certain types of cuttings only.

Sometimes difficult subjects root best from heel cuttings. These are made from side branches which are removed by pulling them backwards away from the parent stem; the result is that the side branch breaks away with a downward pointing piece (or heel) of the main stem at its base. A heel cutting made from a small side branch which is not in active growth is sometimes useful for propagating difficult woody plants. Treatment of such cuttings with hormone powder is also helpful.

Root Cuttings

This method is not often used in Malaysia, but there are certain plants, such as Guava, Breadfruit and some kinds of Citrus, which are best propagated in this way. Vigorous roots, not too young nor too old, should be selected, and cut into lengths of about 10 cm. They are placed horizontally in a pot in sandy soil, covered to a depth equal to their own thickness. One or more buds should form on each cutting, and each bud will produce shoots and

roots of its own. When these new plants are well established, the root cutting should be carefully removed from its pot and severed so as to separate the daughter plants, each of which can then be put into its own pot. Dracaenas can be propagated from stem cuttings which are buried horizontally in the same way as root cuttings.

Leaf Cuttings

A severed leaf of most plants cannot be used for propagation, but a few kinds of leaves will form buds if suitably treated. The chief garden plants propagated in this way are Begonias, African Violets (Saintpaulia), Bryophyllum, Sansevieria, Crassula, Peperomia and Kalanchoe.

The long, fleshy leaves of Sansevieria should be cut into pieces about 20 cm long. These can be inserted into the planting medium and will produce roots and a new shoot from the basal portion. The cuttings can also be kept in water until they produce roots and can then be potted as usual. The water should be changed every two or three days to stop the development of mosquito larvae.

Of the Begonias, those called the Rex varieties are often propagated by leaf cuttings. A large leaf is laid flat and the main veins are cut through with a very sharp knife. The leaf is then laid, with its upper surface upwards, on the surface of the sand, and is held down lightly by putting several very small stones on it. Buds with roots form at the places where the veins have been cut and these can be removed, as soon as they are large enough, and planted up in separate pots. Alternatively, the leaf may be cut into several pieces which are then inserted at a slight angle into the sand. Buds and roots will form at the ends of the cut veins below the sand surface. In both methods the sand must never become too wet, otherwise the leaf cuttings will rot away. It is better to keep the rooting medium a little on the dry side in order to avoid any disappointment.

Other Begonias, African Violets, Peperomia, Kalanchoe and Crassula can be propagated by inserting the leaf stalk into sand and after some time one or more shoots will develop at the ends of the stalks and the young plants can be potted, separately. Again, it is better to keep the rooting medium slightly dry, otherwise the cuttings will rot before they have rooted.

Some leaves will produce roots but not shoots and in such cases it is sometimes possible to use what are called leaf-bud cuttings. These include the leaf, its stalk and a small piece of the parent stem. At the base of the leaf stalk there should be a well-formed bud and this should be positioned about one centimetre below the surface of the rooting medium. After roots develop the bud will grow out to form the shoot. Hormone powder can be used to encourage rooting in this case.

Cuttings of Succulents

Succulent plants, such as Cacti, are adapted to dry climates, and their cuttings need special care in the damp climate of Malaysia. As a general rule, cuttings of succulents should be rooted in pure sand, and the sand should not be watered until new roots have begun to form; protection from rain is of course essential. The larger members of the Cactus family (Cereus and Opuntia), and also the larger species of Euphorbia which have a similar habit of growth, may be grown from quite large cuttings (up to one metre long). A cutting should be laid down in a sheltered place to dry off for two or three days. It should then be placed erect, with its base resting on the surface of the sand, and tied to a supporting stake. It must not be watered until it has begun to form roots, when a little water may be given. Cuttings of Frangipanni (Plumeria) also need protection from too much moisture. They should be inserted a short distance only into the sand, which must be kept just moist; if too wet, the cuttings may rot before they root.

Layering and Marcotting

In these two processes, branches still attached to the parent plant are induced to form roots and only when the roots are formed are the branches severed. In general, these methods are used for plants which are difficult to root from cuttings, or in order to have a larger and more shapely plant than could be obtained from a cutting in a similar time. The *marcotte* is the French equivalent for the English 'layer'. For some reason, the French word has come to have a special meaning in Malaysia, and is now used here for the process which is sometimes called air-layering.

In layering, a low branch is pegged down to the ground and then covered with earth. In marcotting, a ball of earth is bound round a branch at some distance above the ground and kept moist. In both cases, the intention is to cause rooting where the branch is covered with earth. Often it is necessary to treat the branch in some way to induce roots to develop; this is nearly always the case with marcotting, but some plants will root when layered without other treatment than covering the branch with earth; in fact, some plants will form roots wherever their branches touch the earth.

Layering can only be used for plants with low branches, or for climbers with flexible stems which can be bent down to the ground. If a layered branch does not form roots, a very oblique cut may be made to the middle of the stem, or a ring of wire may be twisted tightly

round the branch and the part so treated covered with earth.

With some plants, such as Philodendron, the long stems may be laid on the ground and covered at intervals with soil. Roots will develop on the covered portions and eventually the stem can be cut into pieces, each having its own roots and a shoot.

For marcotting, a branch must be girdled by removing a complete band of bark with a sharp knife. This is easily done by making two cuts through the bark right round the branch. The distance between the cuts should be about twice the thickness of the stem. The bark is easily removed from between the two cuts and the bare surface of the stem can be dusted with hormone powder. The barkless portion is then covered with a soil mixture to make a ball about 8 cm in diameter. The soil mixture should be slightly moist so that it can be moulded around the stem. It is covered with coconut fibre or moss to hold it in place and the whole is then covered with polythene sheeting which must be firmly tied around the stem and soil mixture. The soil mixture must be kept continuously moist by daily watering if there is no rain, but care must be taken not to allow rain water to gather inside the polythene covering, otherwise the stem tissues may begin to rot.

The main difficulty in marcotting is keeping the soil continuously moist; consequently, daily observation is needed. If the marcot is exposed to full sunshine for most of the day then it could be covered with several sheets of paper for a time to prevent it from drying out quickly. After a few weeks, or sometimes as much as three months, roots will be seen in the soil ball. When they appear strong enough, the branch may be cut below the marcot, and potted (without disturbing the root-filled ball of soil) in a sufficiently large pot of earth. It should be kept in a sheltered place until it has recovered from the shock of cutting. Some plants such as Amherstia are difficult and may not stand the shock of having the branch cut straight through, even though plenty of roots are visible. In such cases it is better to cut partly through the branch below the marcot a week or so before the final cut is made, or the process of cutting may be made in two or more stages.

Most shrubs and trees may be propagated by this method. In the case of certain trees, quite large branches may be rooted, and the use of these may provide young plants of a size which would take several years to develop from seeds; examples are *Cassia fistula* and *Cassia javanica*. For a large marcot, a strong, straight branch must be selected (usually one growing upright); it should be marcotted as described above. When the roots begin to

Marcotting

a

b

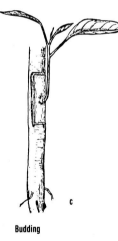

c

Budding

show through the ball of earth, more earth is added outside it, and again held in place by coconut fibre, or by a piece of sacking. For a large branch (which may be up to 3½ m long), the operation must be repeated two or three times, and it will be six months before the branch can be severed. But in six months we may have a young tree which would take several years to grow from seed, and also one which will flower earlier than a seedling. Other trees which may be easily rooted by this method are Tembusu, wild Cinnamon and some common species of Eugenia.

In cases where roots do not form readily, constriction of the branch by placing a ring of wire around it, and twisting the wire, may help to induce root formation. Another method which is useful in some cases is to make a longitudinal slit in the bark, lift the bark a little on each side of the slit, and insert a small stone to hold the slit open. The stem is then covered with soil mixture as described before.

Etiolation

If a plant is kept in darkness, it loses colour and often grows spindly; such a plant is said to be etiolated. It has been found that etiolated branches form roots more readily than branches normally exposed to light, and this behaviour has been used for propagation. Etiolation has been especially used in Britain for propagating stocks for fruit trees. Formerly seedling stocks were used, but these varied much in their effect on the scions grafted upon them, and for greater uniformity it was necessary to propagate stocks vegetatively. The etiolation method has been found suitable for a number of garden shrubs and trees in Malaysia.

The plant to be propagated is planted in a very oblique position in a shallow trench, with its main stem at an angle of only 20–30° to the ground. When it is established, the main stem and branches are pegged to the bottom of the trench and covered with a layer of sandy soil. Many buds on the branches will then begin to develop and will produce shoots growing vertically upwards. When these buds begin to grow, more earth, to a depth of 20–25 cm, is added. In some cases the young shoots will soon produce roots at the base, where they are etiolated; in other cases it is necessary to remove the earth when they are well grown and twist a ring of wire round the base of each, just above its junction with the buried branch, and replace the earth. When roots have formed near the base of an etiolated shoot, it may be severed and planted in a pot or bed; it should be protected from the sun until new growth is established. After one lot of rooted shoots have been cut off, the buried plant

should produce another batch of shoots. The advantage of this method is the number of plants which can be propagated simultaneously from one parent plant.

Budding and Grafting

These are methods by which part of one plant (called the *scion*) is made to unite with the rooting base of another plant (the *stock*). In budding, the scion is applied to the stock in the form of a single bud; in grafting, the scion is a small branch which is attached to the stock. These methods are used when other types of vegetative propagation fail, or when the scion is found to grow or yield fruit more satisfactorily on a stock rather than on its own roots. The stock has considerable influence on the scion, and success in budding and grafting may depend on the choice of a suitable stock. This question has been intensively investigated in England in connection with the grafting of a number of different kinds of fruit trees, including Apples, Pears and Plums, but it has not received much attention in Malaysia. Some stocks make the scion more, some less, vigorous in growth. Dwarfing stocks may be of value for very vigorous scions, and may promote flowering and fruiting.

Budding is chiefly used in Malaysia for propagation of high-yielding varieties of rubber, and for superior varieties of fruit trees. A form of grafting is also used for some fruit trees, and both budding and grafting can be used for certain kinds of ornamental plants, notably some of the finer varieties of Hibiscus which are not vigorous on their own roots.

The operations of budding and grafting must be done quickly, and with a minimum of handling, so that the delicate growing tissues which are to be united may not be injured. Quickness and neatness are only achieved by practice, and the beginner should not be discouraged if his first efforts are not all successful.

Budding

The stocks to be used are usually seedlings, but in the case of Hisbiscus, rooted cuttings of strong varieties are used. The stock plants must be in vigorous growth if budding is to be successful, and it is usually best to have the plants in nursery beds rather than in pots. The bud to be used as scion is taken from a branch which is slightly woody and has lost its leaves. However, buds can be taken from any suitable stem, provided the bark can be removed easily and cleanly. The essential implements are a sharp knife and some raffia for tying the bud firmly to the stock.

A horizontal cut is made in the bark of the stock round about a quarter of its circumference, and a short, vertical, downward cut at each end of the horizontal one. The cuts should penetrate right through the bark, but not into the wood. The bark below the horizontal cut is gently pulled away from the wood, and then pulled downwards; this will expose part of the cambium, which is the actively growing tissue between the wood and the bark. If the stock is in vigorous growth the bark will peel away easily from the cambium. About three-quarters of the flap of bark is then cut off horizontally, leaving a small free flap at the base of the wound.

A bud must now be cut from the scion, with an area of bark around it about equal in size to the bare patch of cambium on the stock. If there is a small core of wood behind the bud when it is cut off, this wood should be removed, so that the delicate tissue at the base of the bud may be in contact with the cambium of the stock. The patch of bark around the bud should be carefully trimmed if necessary, and then placed in contact with the exposed cambium of the stock, the lower edge of the bud-patch being placed behind the small free flap of bark left on the stock. Once so placed, the bud-patch must not be moved; it should be tied in position immediately with raffia, successive windings of which will be above and below the bud itself, which is left free. Finally, a bunch of leaves is tied to the stock just above the bud, to protect it from the sun.

After a fortnight or so, it will be seen whether the bud and stock have united. If they have done so, the bud should soon commence growth, and when this begins the stock should be cut off a little way above the bud. When the bud has grown into a strong new shoot, the top of the stock above it should be trimmed away carefully so that the wound will be covered by a new growth of bark.

Instead of peeling off a rectangle of bark from the stock, incisions in the form of a T may be made, and a triangle of bark on either side of the T lifted, thus making room for the bud and its patch of bark.

Grafting

In this case, a branch of the scion of about the same thickness as the stock should be used. The ends of the stock and scion are then cut in such a way that they will fit together exactly, with the cambium of each in contact with the other. There are various ways of cutting the stock and scion; they are known as cleft graft, saddle graft and side graft, the words indicating the kind of cut made. The cutting must be done quickly and neatly, and the stock and scion fitted together without any lateral motion which would damage the cambium. After the junction is made, it must be tied firmly with raffia. The graft should then be

Approach grafting

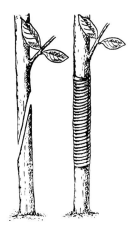

Side graft

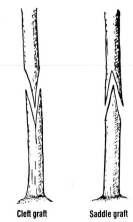

Cleft graft   **Saddle graft**

shaded until the scion has begun to make new growth.

A modified method is approach grafting. A seedling stock is placed beside the branch which is to be grafted upon it (while the branch is still attached to the tree). Adjacent parts of the stock and scion are then pared of their bark, and part of their wood also, the two cut surfaces of equal shape and size being placed in contact and bound together. When they have united, the scion branch is severed from its tree and the top of the stock is also cut off. The result is a grafted plant, but the graft is not so neat as that achieved by other methods. Approach grafting is, however, a successful method, and can be used for propagating a number of shrubs and trees.

Tubers

Plants which form underground resting tubers can usually be propagated from these. Among ornamental plants, the following have tubers: Gloriosa, Caladium, Dahlia; among edible plants: Yam, Artichoke, Keladi, Sweet Potato. For practical purposes, the corms of Gladiolus may be classed here as stem tubers.

It is often possible to grow a new plant from part of a tuber (e.g. the top of a Yam). If a tuber is cut for propagation purposes, the cut surfaces should be covered with powdered charcoal before planting; this helps to keep rotting fungi from attacking the cut surfaces. Tubers should usually be kept in a cool, dry place until they show signs of growing, and then planted. Though Dahlias have tubers, it is usually best in Malaysia to propagate them from young green cuttings; the tubers do not rest well here. Sweet Potatoes are also commonly grown from cuttings, as this is a quicker method than planting tubers. Some kinds of plants, however, can only be propagated from tubers; such are Caladium and Gloriosa.

Tubers which are dug up for propagation purposes must of course be fully mature. Maturity of the tubers may usually be judged by the dying of the aerial stems.

Suckers

Suckers are young shoots arising from the base of the plant. They are produced by some trees and shrubs at the base of the main stem, or from roots well away from the base of the stem. In the former case, the suckers are not always rooted at the base, but may be induced to form roots by the methods used in layering; when rooted, the suckers may be removed for propagation. Root suckers may be dug up with part of the root bearing them; they are commonly produced by the West Indian 'Cherry' (Muntingia), some Ixoras, the African Tulip tree and Randia (Angels Trumpets).

Other perennial plants have underground stems called rhizomes, which in some species are enlarged because they contain a great deal of stored food material. Pieces of the rhizomes can be used for propagation, or alternatively older plants may be divided into several parts, each containing a number of rhizomes. Plants which can be propagated in this way are Cannas, Bananas, Heliconias and Michaelmas Daisies, Gingers and Bamboos. With larger plants, such as Bananas, a single sucker can be removed from the parent plant as soon as it has produced some roots of its own. In seasonal climates, perennial plants of this nature rest in the dry or cool season, but in Malaysia most of them grow continuously and may be propagated at any time.

Some plants grow from bulbs and those with small bulbs, such as Zephyranthes, usually increase themselves quite well on their own. However, those plants with large bulbs, such as Hippeastrum, may be very slow in this respect, but it is sometimes possible to increase your stock by vegetative means. Select a large, well grown bulb which has not developed flowers and cut it into four pieces longitudinally (i.e. from top to bottom). Be sure that each piece has a portion of the very short, flat stem concealed within the base of the bulb. The segments are placed in damp sand with only the basal portions covered, and after some time one or more shoots will develop which will eventually form bulbs. The sand must not be kept too wet, otherwise the bulb segments will rot.

Pruning

The subject of pruning requires great care as well as knowledge of the particular plants to be pruned. There is a right and a wrong way to prune and it is hoped that the following remarks will be of some help.

There are a number of reasons why we prune plants. Some plants have to be pruned in order to establish a good shape, others are pruned so that they are given the fullest opportunity of producing flowers and consequently fruit. Many plants are pruned because of their dense growth and their need for air. In a number of plants, such as Bougainvilleas and Ixoras, a proportion of the central shoots die because of this lack of air and these have to be cut off; but it is better to thin the plant out before any of these shoots start to die back. When a plant becomes leggy, it will usually form a bushy growth just below the cut if pruned back; this will give it strength as well as shape. There are some plants which require cutting back almost as one cuts a hedge in order to produce the best show of flowers.

Notable in this respect is *Plumbago auriculata*. If this is planted in a bed, it is beneficial to prune it back to within 30 cm of the ground after each flowering. In some countries Plumbago is treated as a climber, but in Malaysia its treatment has to be totally different in order to produce the maximum amount of flowers.

Young trees of Poinciana, Angsana, Jacaranda, Acacia and a number of others, if not pruned, become leggy and misshapen and seldom form a good crown. The object of pruning these trees is to promote a more bushy growth. If a shoot of any of the above trees is cut back, immediately below the cut numerous new shoots will commence to grow and so cause the plant to become bushy. Most of these trees should be allowed to develop their original seedling shoot up to a height of approximately 3 m. In order to form a crown, the top 60 cm should be pruned back, and from immediately below this cut, as already mentioned, a number of new shoots will form.

These shoots in their turn will also need pruning to within 1½ m of the main trunk after sufficient growth has been made. The tree may then be allowed to develop naturally, with the exception of any particular long growth which should be pruned back when noticed. Small trees which are intended for screening purposes need to develop a main trunk of 60–100 cm high only in order that the branches may originate from as low down as possible. Bixa and Thevetia can be treated in this way and, if they become too tall, can be pruned back very hard which will result in dense new bushy growth.

There are a number of plants which flower on the new shoots and in this category we have Bougainvilleas, Caesalpinia, Duranta, Jatropha and quite a number of others. Most of these plants are inclined to get rather straggly and the flowers are almost invariably at the ends of the shoots. If they are periodically pruned back, new shoots are formed and the flowering will be freer. This also keeps these tall and sometimes leggy shrubs within bounds and of a better shape than when they are left to their own devices.

The thinning out of fruit trees allows a better circulation of air through the plant, and the reduction of shoots and leaves, particularly in a tree which is producing a luxuriant abundance of leaves, encourages it to flower and so produce more fruit. When pruning fruit trees with the idea of air circulation and greater fruit productivity, it is best to try and prune away the central shoots and branches, thus allowing the sun and air to penetrate and so ripen the wood prior to bud forming.

There are a number of general rules which should be followed when pruning. In the actual cutting, a sharp knife must be used in order to ensure a clean cut. If the cut is clean, fungus pests are less liable to cause damage to the wound. The cut should always be in an upright direction in order to prevent water settling on the surface and so causing a rot to start. If a shoot or branch is too large for a knife, a saw should be used and the rough surface cleaned off with a knife or plane.

When pruning large lateral branches, the cut should be made flush with the trunk; if a short stump is left, this will only die back to the trunk and the rot will then injure the healthy part of the tree. A short stump would look unsightly, but if the branch is cut off flush with the trunk, the bark of the latter will eventually cover the wound and the final appearance would be much improved. After the branches have been pruned back, a further precaution against the entrance of parasitic fungi is that of painting over the wound with white paint or any of the suitable preparations which are now available for the purpose. This not only prevents the surface of the wood from splitting due to the sun, but will exclude water and air. Coal tar is often used for this purpose but has the disadvantage of becoming very hot when exposed to the sun.

Another form of pruning is called pollarding. There are a few trees in Malaysia which warrant this type of pruning, but it has one disadvantage. The principle is to cut a large tree which has got out of hand, right back to the main trunk and from here new branches will form. Angsanas respond well to this type of treatment and usually old trees which have started to die back at various points show remarkable improvement. This may prolong the life of the tree considerably. Tembusu reacts to pollarding, but more slowly than Angsana. The disadvantage of this type of pruning is that a number of new branches growing from one section of the trunk may weaken the tree at the point of cutting. However, if the number of branches is limited to two or three, it is definitely a worthwhile process. The new branches produced by this method of pruning are often somewhat soft at first and are liable to be snapped off by strong winds; consequently, they should be pruned lightly to encourage the growth of more woody tissue, which will prevent any weather damage.

Root Pruning

This type of pruning is practised chiefly in temperate countries and usually on fruit trees. However, root pruning of certain plants in Malaysia is often beneficial. The object of root pruning is to counteract the growth of certain trees in order to induce them to produce more flowers. In some countries, plants naturally receive a check in their growth by perhaps a period of drought or a spell of cold weather. In Malaysia, or at least in the southern part, there are no such periods and artificial means must be devised. The practice is to cut a trench 60–100 cm deep around the tree to be treated, at a minimum distance of 1½ m from the trunk. All the roots which are met with should be cleanly severed, and, if large, painted over with coal tar. With a fairly large tree, this distance would be as much as 3 m away from the trunk. This treatment will restrict the amount of food absorbed by the plant and so cause a check. More experiments in root pruning are desirable. The reaction of many garden plants to this practice in Malaysia is unknown.

This method is used when large trees are to be moved, but it must be done at least one year before the move is made. The pruning will encourage the development of more small roots near the base of the main trunk so that when the tree is finally removed with a large earth ball around the roots it will take less harm than if it had been moved with a few large roots only. When trees of any size are moved in this way they are usually a little slow in growth for one or two seasons and need regular watering until they are well established.

More recently, another method of propagation, known as tissue culture, is being used increasingly, especially with horticultural plants. By this method a small portion of plant tissue is grown under controlled conditions until it produces a number of small plantlets which can eventually be grown in pots. By this means a large number of plants exactly similar in all characters to the parent plants can be produced in a relatively short time. It has considerable application for commercial growers but is not suitable for amateur gardeners. The method is a form of vegetative propagation, and tiny pieces of plant tissue are grown on special culture media in sterile conditions until a suitable number of small plantlets have been produced. When these have developed sufficient roots, they are potted up and hardened off very carefully until they can be transplanted and grown under normal conditions.

5 HERBACEOUS PLANTS AND DWARF SHRUBS

In this chapter are included all small to medium-size bedding plants, some being herbaceous, some bulbous and some woody, but not the larger flowering shrubs which are dealt with in a later chapter. There is of course no sharp line of distinction between the two groups, and in making mixed borders some of the larger shrubs may, sometimes, be included; but broadly speaking, the most useful plants for mixed planting will be found here. Some species are also included which are not very successful as bedding plants, but can be grown in pots. A good many others are also very useful as pot plants, and with skill can be made into much finer specimens in this form of culture than in beds. Ferns and other foliage pot plants are dealt with in a separate chapter.

In the chapter on raising plants from seeds, there are directions for preparing beds and for the handling of seedlings, so these need not be repeated here. A note on the preparation of borders may, however, be useful. The size of the border depends on the way you plan your garden; if there is plenty of space available it should be not less than 1½ m wide, and preferably 2 m. If some of the taller shrubs are to be planted, the border should be even wider. Deep digging is the first essential; 60 cm is usually about right, but if the soil is very heavy the first digging may profitably be even deeper, to ensure good drainage. When returning the soil, mix it with a liberal amount of compost, or of half-rotted or even fresh grass cuttings, leaf sweepings and other such materials; also, in the middle layers, some cattle dung if it is available. The effect of a deep digging of this kind will last several years. When the soil is all returned, it will be some centimetres higher than the surrounding earth and it should be allowed to settle a little before planting is begun.

In planting a mixed border, some thought should be given to the final size of the plants and to the grouping of colours. The tallest plants should be at the back, and the smallest ones in front if the border is at the side of the garden; but if it is positioned in the centre of a lawn where it can be viewed from all sides, then the tallest plants should be in the centre. If several flower beds are fairly close together then they may be treated as separate units or they may be planned as a single unit. As separate units, it would be best to use plants of medium or short height and this method lends itself easily to formal planting; but if the group of beds is treated as one unit, then taller plants can be used and may be positioned in such a way as to create a small landscape with the smaller plants arranged around them. The shape, size and arrangement of the flower beds will determine the positioning of the taller plants in such a plan.

The question of annuals will also have to be considered. These are shortlived and best used in small groups among the more permanent plants, so that the border never looks bare. If annuals can be raised to moderate size in pots before planting out, a quicker display of flowers will be obtained, but this involves more work and a place for a pot plant nursery. A mixed border of this kind is often improved by the addition of a few taller shrubs, which breaks the uniformity of its lines. For example, Ixora, standard Hibiscus, Brunfelsia, Crotons and Jatropha are suitable.

As soon as new plants are well established in growth, they can be brought on more rapidly by the application of manures or fertilizers. There is a chapter in this book on the subject. Here it may suffice to say that the best results are obtained by application of manure in liquid form, as this does not disturb the roots. Probably manuring in this way once a fortnight at first, and then less frequently, will suffice. Most of the plants listed here, except the annuals, will go on flowering for some months, but they will require pruning. Plants vary in the extent to which they will stand pruning, but most of those mentioned here will stand it

quite successfully. A general pruning is a good opportunity for undertaking further cultivation and manuring. In this case it is a good thing to add more organic material to the soil (compost or cattle dung); this is best forked in, as a fork does less damage than a cangkul. The average gardener often does much damage to bedding plants by needlessly cutting their roots with a cangkul when applying manure. If all the young growing roots are cut, the plant cannot make use of the manure until it has grown some more.

Plants in Pots

The special value of growing flowering plants in pots is that the soil conditions can be controlled more effectively, and therefore it is possible to supply more perfect conditions for healthy root growth: it is also possible to control water supply and manure, and thus to control flowering of certain woody shrubs. But to take full advantage of pot culture, it is necessary to use suitable soil, and to control water and manure carefully; otherwise results may be no better than in the open ground. The Chinese gardeners of Malaysia have developed a method of using burnt earth in pot culture which is very efficient, and we therefore attempt to give the essentials of this method here. But it should be emphasized that every kind of plant is different in its behaviour, and there can be no rule of thumb that will cover all occasions. Careful observation of the behaviour of plants is the first necessity for all gardeners; it is the result of this kind of observation over a period of years that gives some people an apparently instinctive knowledge of how to handle plants.

Earth for burning should be on the heavy side. Ordinary red earth that is distinctly sticky when wet is satisfactory; but some gardeners say that black earth from low-lying situations is preferable. The earth is broken up into fairly large pieces, and piled up on top of some old wood and other refuse, into a heap some 1½ m high and 2 m across. A cover to keep off the rain is necessary. The stacking of the pile is a matter requiring skill. It must allow just enough circulation of air to keep a slow fire burning. The fire is allowed to burn for about two days, sometimes longer. When the opera-

tion is finished, the earth is changed from its original condition of clay to a porous granular state. It will consist of a fair proportion of large pieces, which should not be broken up too small, grading down to dust. The dust is not good for plants that require a particularly well aerated soil, and can be removed if necessary by the use of a fine sieve. The essential qualities of burnt earth are that it will absorb water without becoming sticky, the lumps readily breaking down when the soil is watered; and that it is sterilized, all pests and diseases being destroyed. A small amount of burnt earth can be made quickly by spreading lumps of clay on a piece of small mesh expanded metal and lighting a good fire beneath it. Very small quantities can be made by baking a few lumps of clay in an oven.

Burnt earth is usually not used alone. For potting plants, the usual method is to take three parts of burnt earth to one part of dried cattle dung, which supplies the organic matter necessary in any good soil. But for most plants it is possible to use compost instead of cattle dung. When preparing for potting, the burnt earth should be graded in size. Crocks are placed at the bottom of the pot and on top of these some of the larger pieces of burnt earth, to fill say one-third of the pot; the remainder of the pot is then filled with the mixture of burnt earth and dry dung or compost, and is ready for planting. Or in some cases it may be best to have a top layer of small size burnt earth only.

After the plants are well started in growth, they are given liquid manure (cattle dung water, urine, the liquid from rotting groundnut cake, or artificial fertilizers) every few days; this promotes rapid growth. The fact that the burnt earth absorbs water, and yet provides a very open soil, gives a perfectly balanced condition of air and water supply for the roots of plants. In fine weather the plants will not suffer from excess of water, as they will with most kinds of untreated earth. Plants that need a particularly well aerated soil, or that will not stand too much water, may be potted with the coarser lumps of burnt earth only, with less organic matter; if they are then kept sheltered from rain, watering can be controlled and any desired condition of moisture maintained. In this way it is possible to grow difficult plants that defy ordinary potting methods.

It might be thought that sand could be used just as well as burnt earth, but this is not so. Each grain of sand is quite impervious to water and the amount of water it will hold on its surface is very small. But a piece of burnt earth is like a sponge. It holds a considerable amount of water, can give this up again slowly, maintaining a moist atmosphere in the soil for some time. Sand and a varying amount of compost may be used for succulent plants that need very dry conditions, but it dries out too quickly for most plants.

Another advantage of burnt earth is that it prevents the usual dangers of overpotting. If soil is inclined to become sodden, overpotting is fatal; the soil will become useless before the roots of a small plant have had time to grow into it. But burnt earth maintains its open condition for some time, so that a small seedling may be planted in a large pot, saving the trouble of repotting it several times. There does come a time, however, when the burnt earth loses its fresh condition. It is always desirable to repot with fresh burnt earth, not to use the old potting mixture again; but such soil may be very useful to lighten the earth in flower beds; it usually has the disadvantage that it contains many seeds.

In addition to the materials just mentioned there are a number of other organic and inorganic products available which can be used in potting mixtures or in the garden to help improve the soil texture. The organic products are peat, sphagnum moss and shredded bark, sawdust or wood shavings, and the inorganic materials are sand, vermiculite and perlite.

Peat is partly decomposed plant remains and will vary considerably in composition and acidity depending on the vegetation from which it originated. The most usual kind available to gardeners is dark brown or black and is fibrous in texture. It has a high water holding capacity but is low in plant nutrients and should not be allowed to dry out completely as it is very difficult to moisten it again. This is especially important when a high proportion of peat is used in potting mixtures. Peat can be bought in bags of different sizes and can be stored conveniently in these indefinitely. If, after long storage, it seems very dry, then it should be soaked in water for one day so that it becomes quite sodden. It should not be used in this very wet state but when needed, the excess water can be squeezed out very easily by hand and the peat can be used immediately in a potting mixture.

Sphagnum moss is available in many places and is very light in weight but has a high water holding capacity. It contains very few plant nutrients but is relatively sterile and is good for

Asystasia chelonoides (l)

Asystasia gangetica (mauve form)
(r)

Asystasia gangetica (cream form) (l)

Alcaea rosea (r)

germinating seeds as it contains substances which inhibit damping-off fungi.

Shredded bark, sawdust and wood shavings are by-products of timber mills and can be used for the same purpose as peat. They decompose slowly and if used in quantity some sulphate of ammonia should be added to counteract the loss of nitrogen during decomposition. Sawdust can be used on its own for rooting cuttings or germinating seeds but a little care is necessary because some timbers contain substances which inhibit these processes and sawdust from them should be washed several times in warm water before it can be used safely.

Any of these organic products will hold a great quantity of moisture and when they are used in potting mixtures it may be necessary to water less frequently otherwise they soon become waterlogged and the plants will not grow.

Vermiculite is a heat treated mica-like material having the ability to absorb large quantities of water with dissolved plant nutrients and these are readily available to plant roots. The expanded vermiculite can be obtained in various grades but only the horticultural type should be used as the insulation types are not suitable.

Perlite is a material of volcanic origin and is heat treated so that the particles become expanded into sponge-like granules. Although it

can absorb water only, this is readily available to plant roots. Perlite contains no plant nutrients and cannot absorb any which are dissolved in water so that if it is used on its own then regular application of fertilizer will be necessary for plants to make adequate growth.

Vermiculite and perlite are available under various trade names and can be bought in small quantities when required but both are somewhat expensive. They are used extensively by commercial growers.

These organic and inorganic materials can be mixed with garden soil or sand to make suitable potting mixtures for growing almost any kind of plant. Different proportions will be needed to suit the requirements of the plants which are to be grown. Gardeners can make up their own mixtures but the number of bags of material needed can occupy a considerable amount of storage space and this may not be practical in a small house or flat.

However, ready-made potting mixtures are available which are either soil-based or peat-based and these can be used directly. They can be bought in bags of different sizes so that storage is much easier when space is limited and they can be used immediately for growing plants in pots, troughs or in very small town gardens.

These potting mixtures come in various

grades suitable for seed germination, growing of young plants or for growing mature plants. Regular application of fertilizer is advisable after the plants have been growing in these mixtures for about six to eight weeks. The advantage of using these mixtures is that they are free from weed seeds and pests, and they are extremely convenient for gardeners living in apartment buildings where it is often difficult to obtain soil and other materials for growing pot plants.

Crazy Paving

A certain number of small flowering plants will grow better in the crevices of crazy paving than in ordinary garden beds. If the paving is laid with a good free-draining base of sand, the plants will have drainage as good as if they were in a pot, their roots are largely protected from heavy rain, and they have full exposure to the heat of the sun. Cuphea, Hymenanthe-rum, the small Verbena and *Zinnia linearis* are useful plants for this position; but almost any of the smaller herbaceous plants or smallest shrubs might be used.

Full sun is necessary. The soil in the crevices can be renewed as required, and occasional manuring with liquid manure is desirable. A small area of such paving, combined with suitable flower beds, may be used as a decorative feature, as part of a path system, or as an area around a seat or other garden furniture. When a paved area is a single feature, it may be given variety by planting one or more small shrubs or larger herbaceous plants along with the small ones. The restricted area available in front of many small terrace houses could easily be planted in this way and maintenance would not be difficult.

House Plants

Many of the plants mentioned in this chapter and the one on foliage plants (Chapter 10) are grown very commonly in temperate countries in greenhouses, conservatories and sunrooms, but in addition, they have become very popular as house plants for room decoration in homes and offices, and are used also in the public areas of many large buildings which are centrally heated. Many of these tropical plants are naturally small and others can be kept to a suitable size quite easily so that they make excellent decoration for small rooms or restricted spaces. The larger kinds are not suitable for this purpose but may be used effectively in large buildings. There are, very often, troughs or other kinds of containers in which these plants can be grown in groups, so that they will present a more satisfactory appear-

ance and will be much more suitable for the space available and the size of the building. A number of these plants, such as varieties of Begonia, Asparagus and some ferns, have been grown for many years in heated greenhouses by enthusiasts in these countries. At present some of the smaller species such as Saintpaulia and some Peperomias are very popular for growing in very restricted spaces, whereas the larger kinds such as Philo-dendrons and Monstera are used frequently in bigger rooms and small conservatories because of their size and imposing appearance; in fact, before they grow too large, they can be used very effectively also in smaller rooms in conjunction with some kinds of contemporary furniture.

A few of the species which have been described are frequently planted outside in many temperate countries during the summer months only, though they must be lifted, of course, and brought inside again before there is any likelihood of very low temperatures and frost. Most of the species described in these two chapters are freely available in temperate countries where they are produced in quantity by nurseries which specialize in this type of plant and which supply stock for sale in many stores and Garden Centres.

The increased interest in these plants at the present time is due largely to the wider use of central heating in homes, offices and large buildings where the temperature can often be as high as in many of the tropical humid areas. The night temperature is often much lower than the day temperature, but many of the tropical plants make excellent growth despite this variation. The air in centrally heated rooms can become very dry and this does not suit all kinds of tropical plants, though many of them do grow quite well under such conditions and the more sensitive kinds could be kept in bottle gardens or terraria in which the air would be humid continuously. Such small gardens, if well positioned and illuminated, can be very decorative and need less frequent attention than plants in pots. If several tropical plants are grown together in a suitable ornamental container they will often thrive much better than a single plant grown on its own. This is because the close planting which is necessary results in the leaves being more closely pressed together so that the air around them remains more humid; they are then less affected by the dry atmosphere of the room than the leaves of single plants, which would be much more exposed to it and would dry out more quickly. In dry air the leaves of some of these tropical plants will roll up and often the margins will become brown and shrivelled. Groups of tropical plants grown to a good size in ornamental containers are sold very often and can be used immediately as room decoration.

Plants such as Maranta, which need more humid air, can be managed in a slightly different way. The pots can be put inside some kind of ornamental container in which a layer of peat or small gravel chips has been placed at the bottom. These materials can be kept moist, though any standing water must not be allowed to come above the bottom of the pot otherwise the plant roots will rot very quickly. As the water evaporates it will provide sufficient humidity around the leaves of the plant and its growth will be much improved.

The leaves of house plants will eventually become very dusty as they are never exposed to rain, but this can be avoided by spraying with a very fine mist of water from a hand sprayer. When this is done the pots should be placed in a wash basin or a kitchen sink so that the excess water falling from the foliage will not damage table-tops and window-sills. If the plants have large leaves these may be wiped over individually with a soft, clean, damp cloth.

Aerosol sprays are available for use on the leaves of foliage plants and make them shiny. Sprays, however, should be used with some care as the foliage of many plants is not usually very glossy and they could look a little unnatural if such sprays are used on them.

Practically all plants grown for flowers or coloured foliage will need as much light as possible and to this end should receive sunlight for as long as can be arranged throughout each day. Without this, few flowers will develop and leaves will not colour well, especially as the light intensity is less than in tropical areas, and in the winter months the days are very much shorter. In temperate countries therefore, the positioning of such plants will be of the greatest importance. On the other hand, for shady places or those out of direct sunlight there is a wide range of other tropical plants that can be used with great effect, and some of which, like Saintpaulia or Sinningia, will in addition flower well under such conditions, while others, such as many of the foliage plants, thrive so well with good treatment that they grow rapidly and need some control at frequent intervals. Some of the foliage plants seem able to tolerate a much wider range of growing conditions than may be expected, and consequently they will often survive a considerable amount of neglect. However, such plants cannot be put outside to recover, as would be done in the tropics, but should be repotted and given good growing conditions; recovery is likely to be very slow.

In temperate countries tropical house plants can be grown well in any of the good potting mixtures that are produced commercially and these may be soil-based or peat-based. There are different mixtures available for different purposes such as seed germination, seedling growth, or growth of adult plants, and in addition there are 'grow-bags' on sale which are made of very thick polythene and contain a soil mixture with some added fertilizer. These are used for growing a few ornamental or vegetable plants for one season only, after which they are discarded. These bags are very useful in confined spaces and must be cut open before plants are placed in the soil mixture, but watering must be carefully controlled as there is no provision for drainage. Peat-based potting mixtures hold moisture for a longer time than soil-based ones and watering, therefore, needs to be less frequent otherwise there is some danger of waterlogging. Any of these mixtures can be modified by the addition of fine gravel, sand or peat, to suit the requirements of the plants which are to be grown.

Balanced fertilizers in solid or liquid form are also available commercially and are convenient to use for house plants. The slow release fertilizers are a little expensive but are useful because they are applied two or three times a year only. The liquid fertilizers are also very convenient to use as they are clean and odourless and need only the correct dilution with water before application. If this kind of fertilizer is given regularly in place of a normal watering, the plants will make much better growth than if the solid kind is used, as so often happens, at irregular and infrequent intervals.

House plants are sometimes troubled with pests but in most cases they can be controlled easily by the use of a systemic insecticide or fungicide, and some preparations contain a mixture of both, so that less frequent spraying will be necessary. Greenhouse or conservatory plants may sometimes require more complicated methods of control which are not usually necessary for the average house plant gardener.

Growing conditions for the different kinds of plants are outlined in the appropriate chapters with a brief mention also under some of the individual plant descriptions. Although these conditions apply to the tropics, and the growing of plants there in and around houses and other buildings, they will serve also as a guide for the general management of these plants in temperate countries, so that their requirements for temperature, humidity, amount of water and sunlight or shade may be met as closely as can be arranged. It should be remembered that many plants will have a definite requirement for one particular growing condition, such as temperature, humidity or shade, and if this requirement is supplied, then very often, the plants will tolerate a greater variation in

Browallia elata

Begonia (light green foliage)

Begonia (coloured foliage)

Capsicum annuum

the accompanying growing conditions than may be expected.

Notes on the Most Useful Plants

Agapanthus orientalis (African Lily)

These plants have thick rhizomes with long strap-shaped leaves and the flowers are held in large, almost globular heads at the top of long, leafless stalks. Blue-flowered and white-flowered forms are available and both kinds grow well in large tubs or pots. The plants do well in the highlands, where they can be planted out in beds or grown in pots, and they flower for a long period. Hybrid seed is available in other parts of the world and should be imported for trial in the Malaysian climate as some forms are more suited to a warmer climate than others. The species would be useful in the garden as it has good blue flowers and this colour is uncommon in tropical lowland plants.

In temperate countries these plants are grown outside in large wooden tubs or pots during the summer months, but most varieties must be brought inside before the first frost. They make excellent plants for a conservatory but are too large for small rooms.

Ageratum (Flossflower)

Herbaceous plants with small, fluffy, blue-mauve flowers often in compact heads. Several varieties, tall and dwarf, are offered by seedsmen in temperate countries, but few of these flower at all well in the lowlands of Malaysia. A dwarf variety which flowers well has been selected and is propagated by cuttings in Singapore. The plants need a light soil, full sun, and must not have too much water or manure, which makes them leafy at the expense of flowers. These plants seem best in crazy paving, or in a rock garden, and will flower for several weeks. Seeds germinate easily and seedlings need a good, bright light from an early stage.

One species, *A. conyzoides,* is common as a weed throughout the lowlands and under suitable conditions can produce large heads of flowers. If these plants were brought into cultivation, and some selection were done, it is possible that some acceptable garden plants could be obtained and these would have the advantage of being adapted to the climate. This species also grows wild in the highlands where it produces much larger flowering heads with flowers of a better colour. The flower colour ranges from the typical blue-mauve to white.

Ageratum is often seen as a flowering house plant in temperate countries and some varieties are used outside as bedding plants during the summer months.

Ageratum conyzoides

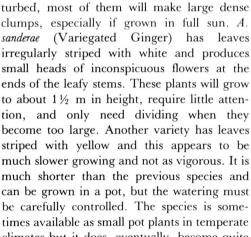

Coleus x hybridus (r)
Coleus x hybridus (r)
Coleus x hybridus (l)
Coleus x hybridus (l)

Alternanthera ficoidea

Alpinia

Several species of Alpinia are grown and some have attractive variegated foliage. If left undisturbed, most of them will make large dense clumps, especially if grown in full sun. *A. sanderae* (Variegated Ginger) has leaves irregularly striped with white and produces small heads of inconspicuous flowers at the ends of the leafy stems. These plants will grow to about 1½ m in height, require little attention, and only need dividing when they become too large. Another variety has leaves striped with yellow and this appears to be much slower growing and not as vigorous. It is much shorter than the previous species and can be grown in a pot, but the watering must be carefully controlled. The species is sometimes available as small pot plants in temperate climates but it does, eventually, become quite large and is not suitable then for small rooms.

A. purpurata (Red Ginger) is an attractive species which has entirely green leaves and long inflorescences at the ends of the stems. These carry red bracts but the flowers are small and white. The flowering heads remain on the plant for a long time and retain their colour for almost the entire period. These plants will grow up to 1¾ m high, but if growing conditions are suitable they can become

taller than this. Propagation of all kinds is easy kinds is easy by means of division. There is a variety of this species in which the bracts and flower stalks are rose pink.

Alternanthera (Joseph's Coat, Calico Plant)

An edging plant about 15-20 cm high with small leaves and inconspicuous flowers. The species most commonly grown is *A. ficoidea* and there are a number of forms which differ in the colour of their leaves. These may be red, pink, yellow, red and green, red and yellow, copper or tricoloured. The plants need full sun in order to develop their colour properly, and although they will grow very well in some shade, the leaves will remain green. It is easily propagated by cuttings or by division of old plants. It must be trimmed regularly to keep it neat and can be kept to 15-20 cm high. If allowed to become too tall before trimming, recovery may be irregular as some of the weaker plants may die instead of producing new shoots. Some cultivars are available as house plants in temperate countries and are useful for very small spaces or in groups of plants, but good light is essential.

Alternanthera dentata cv. rubiginosa

A foliage plant with dark red or purple leaves,

useful as an edging to mixed borders or as a ground cover. Young plants should be pinched out to encourage branching and full sun is required for leaf colour to develop well. Propagation is by means of cuttings.

Ananas comosus cv. variegatus (Pineapple)

There are several varieties of pineapple in which the leaves are variegated and the plants are very decorative. Usually the variegation is in the form of longitudinal yellow or ivory stripes and there is sometimes a little pink coloration near the base of the leaf. The flowering head is short and stout, and supplies additional colour as the flowers are violet. The plants are relatively short and can be grown in full sun near the edge of a border, or they may be grown in pots or troughs. Well drained soil is essential: they need plenty of water but must not become waterlogged or they will rot very quickly. Propagation is by means of suckers which grow from between the leaves below the inflorescence, or by using the crown of leaves from above the inflorescence. The variegated forms are frequently grown as house plants in temperate countries.

Angelonia salicariifolia

Dwarf shrubs with numerous erect shoots bearing small leaves and very many small flowers which are violet-blue, pink, white or particoloured. A very useful bedding plant, flowering continuously, standing drastic pruning, and easily divided. When dividing for replanting, cut back the stems to half their length, and after planting shelter them for a week or so in sunny weather. For full flowering, a sunny place is essential and a light soil is best. If the plants are allowed to become too tall, the stems tend to fall over and although they still produce flowers the whole plant will become straggly in appearance. This can be avoided for a short time by appropriate staking, but it is probably better to prune the plants hard and wait for a new crop of shoots and flowers. It grows equally well in the highlands and the flowers develop a better colour.

Aphelandra squarrosa (Zebra Plant)

This plant has variegated leaves and striking heads of flowers. The leaves are dark green and shiny with the veins bordered in white. Each inflorescence carries many large yellow or orange-yellow bracts and from between these the long yellow flowers protrude. There are several varieties available which show differences in the amount and distribution of the white markings, as well as some differences in the habit of the plant. Propagation is by cuttings of half-ripe wood or from soft young growth. Seeds are sometimes available. Two or three other species are also grown as ornamentals but are not as common.

This is available often as a house plant in temperate countries but needs plenty of sunlight in order to flower and develop well coloured leaves.

Artemisia lactiflora (White Mugwort)

This herbaceous perennial has erect tufted stems 60–100 cm high bearing little heads of fluffy white flowers – not very showy but produced freely. The plant is easily propagated by division and the tall shoots should be cut back when this is done. It is useful in a border to give variety, and can be used also to give lightness in some mixtures of cut flowers. Another species of Artemisia is also grown frequently and this has dark green finely divided leaves. It makes a mound of foliage with a soft mossy appearance if it is trimmed at intervals. If it is not trimmed the stems become tall and produce flowers and the plant is not then so attractive. Propagation is easy by cuttings.

Asparagus

Two species with a number of varieties are commonly grown in pots although some of them do very well when planted in beds or troughs. *A. densiflorus* is a plant with tuberous roots and erect or slightly drooping stems. The normal leaves are reduced to tiny white scales and the narrow leaflike structures on the stem are in fact small modified branches called cladophylls. The cultivar 'Myers' (sometimes called *A. Myersii*) has erect stems with a large number of closely arranged short side branches which give the whole structure a very dense appearance. The stems may reach 60 cm in length but are usually much shorter, and the side branches are about 3–5 cm long. The cladophylls are a bright green and when well grown this is one of the most attractive pot plants as it is neat in appearance, trouble-free and can be grown satisfactorily in light shade. Propagation is by seeds or by division of old plants. Small quantities of liquid manure or artificial fertilizer at regular intervals, and not too much water keep the plants in good condition.

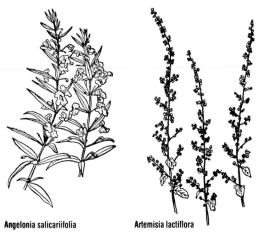

Angelonia salicariifolia   Artemisia lactiflora

Aster (perennial)

Asystasia gangetica

Impatiens balsamina

The cultivar 'Sprengeri' is very commonly grown as an ornamental pot plant but it grows remarkably well also in beds, provided there is good drainage. The stems and branches are longer than in the last-mentioned variety, and the appearance is very much more open. The stems become drooping and the plants are therefore excellent in pots kept in hanging baskets, or in troughs where they can droop over the sides. If grown directly in the ground, the stems are shorter and arch outwards from the centre of the plant, needing no support of any kind. Propagation is by seeds or by division.

A. setaceus, formerly A. plumosus (Asparagus Fern)

This is a well known and commonly grown species with tall, slender, tough, climbing stems. It is well known to florists as the branches are cut and mixed with small sprays of flowers and is usually called 'Asparagus Fern'. The whole plant is dark green with tiny needle-like cladophylls and the stems may reach 1½–2 m or more in length with many side branches which are held horizontally so that the plant has a layered appearance. It is best grown in pots or troughs where the watering can be controlled and it is not so successful in beds. Careful watering and application of small regular quantities of fertilizer are all the attention needed, and propagation is by seeds or by division. The long twining stems can be cut to keep them short and this will cause many more side branches to develop so that the plants will eventually become rather bushy in appearance. This is probably the best treatment for plants in pots although a small framework can be fixed into a pot and the twining stems can be trained onto it – but this arrangement is not always very tidy in appearance. There are several varieties of this species but they are less common in cultivation although they need exactly the same treatment.

Both species and their cultivars have been grown as house plants in temperate countries for a very long time.

Aster, Annual

Asters listed by European seed firms are often not very strong in the lowlands of Malaysia, but several strong and free-flowering strains have been selected by local gardeners. These seed freely, and are grown in pots in a burnt earth mixture; with less intensive methods, they are poor.

Aster, Perennial (Michaelmas Daisies)

A large variety of these herbaceous autumn flowers are grown in temperate regions, including some very fine colours in blue, violet, lilac and pink. Some good varieties tried in Singapore were unsuccessful, and blues did not produce their true colour; more trials are needed. All varieties flower continuously here, and need intensive manuring to induce them to grow to a good size. Several lilac-mauve varieties (one very dwarf) are fairly successful. After flowering, dig up the plants and divide them, manure the bed and replant. Mixed hybrid seeds would be worth trying on the chance of finding a new variety suited to Malaysia.

Asystasia chelonoides

A dwarf shrub, bushy, with small leaves and numerous rather small, dull purple flowers with lighter markings which are carried in short sprays. It is useful in borders or pots; stands hard pruning and needs full sun. Too much fertilizer results in a great deal of leafy growth and no flowers. Propagation is by means of cuttings.

Asystasia coromandeliana (A. gangetica)

A scrambling plant which can be induced to make a bushy form by pruning. The flowers are large and are produced almost continuously throughout the year. There is a range of flower colour from cream through pale purple to deep purple. Full sun is best and more flowers are produced if the soil is poor. The plants can be allowed to scramble through other shrubs or small trees or they can be encouraged to grow over a fence. Little fertilizer need be applied, otherwise the plants grow very strongly and can smother neighbouring plants.

Balsam (Impatiens balsamina)

Several varieties of the common Balsam are grown and may be single-flowered or double-flowered. The colours range from white through pink and red to mauve. For really fine plants Balsams are best grown in pots by the burnt earth method and should be intensively manured. Good plants can also be produced in fresh garden soil in troughs where there is more root room, and provided manuring is generous. Seeds are produced freely but some of the double-flowered varieties do not come true from seed. The flowers do not last very long but a succession of buds are produced for several weeks. The red-flowered Impatiens wallerana hybrids, which need a little shade, do well in pots or borders, flowering for a few months, after which they can be propagated by cuttings to produce a new crop of flowers. Both of these species are common house plants in temperate countries. Several species are native to Malaysia. Of these I. oncidroides, which has large yellow flowers and grows in the highlands, should be used for hybridization to increase the colour range of lowland forms.

Crinum jagus
Crinum latifolium

Crinum asiaticum

Begonia x sempeflorens-cultorum

Begonia (tall variety)

Begonia, Bedding
(B. x semperflorens-cultorum)

There are a number of varieties of this small-leaved, small-flowered Begonia that are very successful in beds and flower continuously for many months with little attention. They make good pot plants also and are quite accommodating. The flowers are pink or white and the foliage of some varieties is a deep bronze. Propagation is by means of cuttings; which should be rooted in sand in a sheltered place, and new varieties can be raised from seed, which is very small.

Many varieties, both single and double-flowered forms, are grown as house plants in temperate areas and some of them are used extensively as summer bedding plants in the garden.

Begonia, Tall Varieties
(B. coccinea, B. corallina, B. maculata)

These are normally grown as pot plants and require plenty of light, without full exposure to sun, as well as good drainage and regular manuring. Some forms can be grown in beds or troughs, provided they are lightly shaded, and when they become old the stems can be pruned back almost to ground level and the plants will, after a short time, produce new shoots from the base. There are a number of varieties and hybrids, some needing protection from rain, and some more light than others; the flowers are white, pink or red. When well grown, they make very fine plants but they do very much better in the highlands at about one thousand metres altitude. Propagation is from cuttings placed in sand in a shady place.

With potted plants, the soil can be allowed to dry out completely, after which it can be thoroughly moistened and may then be left until it is dry again. Although the plants may wilt a little, this treatment seems to do them no harm and is better than giving a little water every day which keeps the soil continuously moist and can easily lead to rotting of the stems at the base.

Many of the cultivars of these species are grown as house plants in temperate countries but they will eventually become too tall and large and should be replaced with young plants obtained from cuttings. Careful management is necessary, but the young leaves spotted with white or silver are very decorative and some forms bear magnificent hanging clusters of flowers.

Beloperone guttata (Shrimp Plant, Justicia brandegeana)

This is a small shrub with numerous erect shoots, each bearing at its tip an elongated head of dull red bracts with small white flowers like teardrops between the bracts. It can be

Crossandra infundibuliformis
Cuphea hyssopifolia

Carex morrowii
Dianella ensifolia (variegated)

green cuttings taken from old plants which have been cut back after flowering. The plants produce suckers that have their own roots and these may be separated and used for propagation also. Growing plants must be carefully pinched back to induce shapely branching, except in the case of the small 'button' varieties. Full sun is essential.

Coleus x hybridus (Flame Nettle)

Herbaceous foliage plants with leaves variously coloured red, bronze, crimson or purple. and small blue flowers at the ends of the branches. The plants are easily propagated from green cuttings and may be grown in pots or borders. Full sun is essential for complete development of colour in the leaves, and adequate manuring to ensure strong growth. Small caterpillars are sometimes troublesome but are controlled quite easily by hand-picking. New varieties may be grown from seeds obtained from locally grown plants, or they may be imported.

Most garden Coleus are hybrids, and so give mixed offspring from seeds. Young seedlings all show a similar colour pattern on the first three or four leaves and should be grown on until they have five or six leaves, when the leaf colour of the adult plant will begin to appear and selection for the best kinds can be done. Often the plants which show the better colour patterns are not quite as vigorous as the remainder and may be lost because of slower or weaker growth.

These plants are among the more common house plants in temperate countries but need as much light as possible to develop full colour.

Coleus x hybridus

Coreopsis basalis (Tickseed)

Annual plants with daisy-like flowers having brown centres and yellow rays and remaining in flower longer than most annuals. It can be grown in beds or pots, and seeds are produced freely but can also be bought from most seed merchants.

Coreopsis tinctoria

This is another annual plant but is more slender than the previous species. There are tall and dwarf forms, some of which have entirely bronze-coloured flowers. All forms are easy to grow in beds and are useful as cut flowers. Seeds are produced in fair quantity and may be saved for growing another crop.

Coreopsis tinctoria

Coreopsis, Perennial

A very strong growing plant with a low bushy tuft of leaves from between which grow solitary yellow flowers on long, slender stems. The plant needs full sun and should not be given too much manure or it will not produce flowers. It is easily propagated by division and

Dianthus hybrid

Gerbera jamesonii (double)

Gerbera jamesonii (double)

Gerbera jamesonii (single)

Gynura aurantiaca

Helianthus annuus

Cosmos sulphureus

Cleome speciosa

Cosmos grandiflora

Gomphrena globosa

it is better to use the locally established variety than to grow from imported seeds.

Cosmos, orange (variety Klondyke)
This is a tall strong growing annual with brilliant orange flowers which produce seeds freely, and it can be grown in beds, but does not last very long. A fine yellow variety is also sometimes grown.

Cosmos, purple and white (*C. bipinnatus*)
Although this is less vigorous than the last species, it is a useful plant for cut flowers and is best grown from imported seeds. The plants need full sun, good cultivation and regular manuring.

Costus speciosus (Crepe Ginger)
Although this plant is frequently grown in gardens, it also occurs wild in Malaysia. The stems can grow 2–3 m high and eventually a dense group of them will be formed. Each stem carries large, broad, oval leaves which are arranged spirally, and the younger parts of the stems grow in a strong spiral, giving the plant a slightly unusual appearance. Flowers are produced in short, dense spikes at the tip of the stems, and they open in series over a period of several weeks. Single flowers are large, white and shortlived. Propagation is by means of division and the plant may be grown in full sun, but does much better in light shade.

Crinum
Bulbous plants of several species, with lily-like flowers borne several together at the top of a leafless stalk. The finest has large white flowers and is sometimes called the Java Lily (*C. jagus*); this grows best in slightly wet ground, under a little shade, and flowers frequently, with heads of about six flowers, each lasting two days and heavily scented at night. If buds are cut when they are full size, they will open the same evening and make excellent decoration in the house. Flowers kept in water will last for two or sometimes three days.

Sometimes the plants are attacked by caterpillars and may be completely destroyed as the insects eat all the leaves and chew their way down into the bulb. Fortunately, these attacks seem to be very irregular and similar plants only a short distance away can be unharmed. Spraying with an insecticide will give control but must be done before the insects have reached the bulb, and a repeat spraying should be done after about five or seven days to destroy any other individuals which may have developed after the first spraying.

The other good species, *C. amabile*, needs full sun and is a much larger plant with very

| Crinum jagus | Crossandra infundibuliformis | Cuphea ignea |

broad leaves. Its large heads of flowers have white petals with a broad band of pink along the centre.

The local *C. asiaticum* makes a good garden plant and can become very large. It has very broad, long leaves and produces long-stalked inflorescences of white flowers which have narrow petals and a strong fragrance. Each inflorescence will last for about two weeks and a new one will then develop from near the base of another leaf. The whole inflorescence or single flowers can be used for table decoration. The plant grows well in full sun or in a little shade and, if it is given regular fertilizer applications, will flower almost continuously. A well grown plant may grow to 1½ m high and wide, and makes a very striking addition to a garden. Seeds are produced freely and will germinate easily.

There is another species of Crinum very similar to *C. asiaticum,* but having broader leaves and inflorescences with many more flowers which are deep pink on the outer surface. This can be grown in the same way and in the same kind of places as *C. asiaticum.*

Crossandra infundibuliformis (Firecracker Flower)

Dwarf shrubs of compact, bushy habit with erect heads of flowers. Two colour forms are available, one with pale orange flowers, the other with apricot-orange flowers. It is a most useful plant, not too rapid in growth, and flowering continuously for months. The pale orange variety seems more vigorous as a bedding plant and both kinds need full sun in order to produce the largest number of flowers. The soil should be well drained and well manured and propagation is by means of half-woody cuttings. The plants are sometimes attacked by scale insects which can be controlled by spraying; if this is not done, they will become unsightly very quickly.

This plant is often seen as a house plant in temperate countries but may become too large for smaller pots used in restricted spaces. Good light is needed.

Cuphea

A few species and varieties are in cultivation. One of the commonest is *C. ignea* (Cigar Flower), a small herbaceous plant up to 60 cm in height, with small leaves and bright red flowers which are freely produced for a long time. *C. x purpurea* is another herbaceous species growing to about 45 cm in height and with larger flowers in shades of mauve, pink and violet. In the lowlands, these species have a tendency to become a little straggly, but this can be concealed by suitable staking or by growing them in between other plants which will give them some support. Both are easily grown from seeds or cuttings and do well in pots or borders, on sun rockeries or in crazy paving, where they will remain in flower for several weeks. Both species grow more strongly in the highlands and *C. ignea* may often be found there as self-sown plants.

A third species, *C. hyssopifolia* (False Heather), is commonly grown as a bedding plant or in pots. It is a small, much branched shrub, growing to 60 cm in height, and has very small dark green leaves. The branches tend to be held upwards at a fairly sharp angle so that each plant is somewhat funnel-shaped while it is young. The small flowers are white, pink or purple and are produced continuously over several months. The basal parts of these plants can become bare after some time but if they are planted in beds this may be concealed by growing some short ground cover plants around them. Often used as a house plant in temperate countries.

Cyperus alternifolius (Umbrella Plant)

Herbs with short rhizomes making a dense clump up to one metre or a little more in height. The triangular stems have reddish

Dianthus chinensis

brown sheaths at the base and at the tips there are a large number of long, narrow, leaf-like bracts arranged very close together. Small sprays of tiny flowers develop from between the bracts but are not conspicuous. When grown in beds, it makes a shapely plant and only needs removal of old stems to keep it tidy. In soil which tends to dry out the plant is best grown in light shade. It can be grown in pots for a short time, but eventually becomes too big and vigorous. Propagation is easily done by means of division.

Cyperus alternifolius cv. gracilis (Dwarf Umbrella Plant)

A small tufted perennial herbaceous plant growing to about 50 cm in height and easily grown in pots or troughs. It makes small clumps of triangular green stems which carry a group of very narrow, short bracts at their tips. Propagation is by division of old plants.

Both forms are commonly available as house plants in temperate countries and will tolerate a little shade. The potting mixture should be kept moist at all times when the plants are grown in this manner.

Dahlia

Most kinds of Dahlia grow reasonably well in the lowlands of Malaysia, though they are not so strong or free-flowering nor so brightly coloured as at the hill stations. They need full sun, very good drainage, and rather intensive manuring for good growth. In pots they only flower for a short time, but some varieties (perhaps most) may be placed in raised beds (surrounded by a low wall), which combines good drainage with more root room than in pots; plants in such beds will flower for several weeks. After the plants have begun to die back, the tubers may be dug up and rested in a dry place, and may be replanted when they begin new growth; it is also possible to propagate from small green cuttings taken from a sprouting tuber; these root easily in moist sand, in a shady place.

Dianella ensifolia

A tufted herbaceous plant which will reach about 60 cm in height and is wild in this country. The flowers are small, pale blue or white, with yellow stamens, and are followed by bright blue berries which are very attractive. The normal form is not grown very much although it could be used as a ground cover under trees. There is a form with variegated leaves which can be grown in beds or troughs but this is not as robust in growth as the normal form. The leaves have a broad cream or white border and the plants do best in light shade, so that it is possible to combine them with taller plants in a border. Propagation is by division or by seeds, but the latter may not come true.

Dianthus

A small double Dianthus which behaves as a perennial is easy to grow in pots or beds. Full sun and well drained soil are essential; propagation by division of old plants is not difficult. *Dianthus chinensis* of many varieties may be grown easily from imported seeds, and remains in flower for a few months; it is successful in beds in not too wet weather. True carnations may be grown in pots, but flower rather poorly. They are a little more vigorous in the highlands but do not flower very freely. More experimention with varieties of carnation is needed.

Dissotis plumosa (Osbeckia)

A low, creeping plant with small, opposite, light green leaves and red stems which root as they grow over the soil. Large mauve-pink flowers are produced continuously and these have long, conspicuous yellow stamens. The plant is very useful in hanging baskets or troughs where the stems can trail over the

Heliconia

Episcia cupreata

Heliconia psittacorum

Heliconia humilis

sides, but it can be used also as an edging in borders, provided it does not become shaded by other plants, as it must have full sun in order to flower best. It can be used also in sun rockeries. Propagation is by means of cuttings. This is an attractive plant which deserves much greater use in the garden.

Drimiopsis saundersiae

Although this small bulbous plant is not easily available, it is worth growing as it makes an attractive small foliage plant in pots and needs very little space. The long, thick leaves are grey-green with dark green blotches over the whole surface and small white flowers are produced in short spikes. The plants will grow in a little shade and if they are kept inside a house for a long period, they should be sprayed with water every week or they can be put outside during a shower of rain.

Episcia (Flame Violet)

A pretty creeping plant with soft partly dark red leaves and crimson flowers. Some varieties have leaves which are coloured in two shades of green. These plants may be grown over rocks, or in hanging pots or baskets, and flower continuously. They are also very successful grown as ground cover in large troughs which are protected from rainfall as they completely cover the soil surface and will then trail over the sides of the trough. Other plants can be allowed to grow up through the Episcia and this makes a very attractive arrangement. The two commonest species are *E. cupreata* which has dark red, bronze or bronze and green leaves, and *E. reptans* which has dark green leaves with light green markings. Both are propagated easily from rooted portions of the creeping stem. Both species grow best in continuous light shade. They are available as house plants in temperate countries and should be cared for in the same way as Saintpaulia. Good light is necessary but not direct sunlight.

Helianthus angustifolius

If planted outside in the garden it is often exceedingly difficult to prevent damage by snails.

Gaillardia (Blanket Flower)

Herbaceous annuals or perennials, growing easily and flowering well in pots or beds in full sun. Perennial kinds will flower for many months and may be propagated by division of old plants. Annual plants will produce seeds, but to maintain a good strain, occasional renewal from imported seeds is desirable.

Galphimia glauca

A small bushy shrub up to one metre in height with erect heads of small yellow flowers, and very useful in beds or large pots as it flowers

Eranthemum wattii

A low perennial herbaceous plant or dwarf shrub with pretty violet-purple flowers, useful in a border or sun rockery but will also stand a little shade. It has thick fleshy roots and is propagated from cuttings.

Eucharis grandiflora (Amazon Lily)

A bulbous plant with short, broad, dark green leaves and large white flowers held in a small group at the top of a tall leafless stalk. The flowers resemble a large Narcissus in shape. The plant needs shade and can be grown in the ground, in troughs or in pots. Snails will completely destroy this plant and must be strictly controlled.

Eurycles amboinensis

This is an excellent foliage plant with almost round, dark green leaves on long stalks arising from ground level. Heads of white flowers are produced on long stalks at 2–3 month intervals and are an added attraction. The plant grows best in light shade, but is very susceptible to damage by snails, though it makes an attractive pot plant and is very successful in troughs.

Hippeastrum

Hemigraphis alternata

Eranthemum wattii

Hemerocallis fulva

Eucharis grandiflora

Gaillardia x grandiflora

continuously for many months. It needs full sun and a well drained soil, otherwise it becomes subject to attack by a bacterial disease. It is easily propagated from seeds which are produced freely.

Gerbera jamesonii (Barberton Daisy)

These perennials, with mauve, pink, orange, yellow or white flowers, are admirable for cutting. Though best suited to cooler conditions, they will grow well in the lowlands, and several varieties flower fairly freely. A well drained soil, which must not be too dry, frequent liquid manure after the plants are well established, and full sun (or almost full) are needed.

Transplanting must be done with care and the crowns of the plants not buried too deep (correct depth may be judged by examining established plants). Well grown plants produce many side shoots, which may be separated for propagation, or new plants may be grown from imported seeds. No seeds are produced in Singapore, but should be looked for in the drier parts of Malaysia as they may yield new varieties. Imported seeds should be planted immediately as they do not keep well. Some fine varieties have been produced in Bangkok, and these will flower quite well in Malaysia.

Gladiolus

These well known plants, of many varieties and colours, are grown from corms in pots, beds, or troughs. All kinds will grow in the lowlands but are not so strong or compact as in the hills. If new corms for further planting are desired, the plants must be regularly manured,

even after the flower is completed, until the leaves begin to turn brown, then the corms are taken up and dried off under cover from rain and sun. When dry they may be stored in boxes under cover, until they begin to show signs of new growth; then they are best put into sand beds, and watered, until new growth has well begun, when they may be planted out.

They are most useful as cut flowers. Plants usually produce a number of very small corms as well as one or two large ones; these small corms may be used for propagation like the large ones, but they will not produce flowers in their first growth and several growing seasons may pass before they reach flowering size. If the plants are not manured well while growing, then the new corms which are produced will be successively smaller and no flowers will appear.

Gomphrena globosa (Batchelor's Buttons)

Herbaceous annuals with globular heads of flowers in various shades of purple, mauve and white; easy to grow in borders and flowering longer than most annuals. If they become too tall, the plants look a little untidy. Seeds are produced freely and germinate readily.

Gynandropsis speciosa (*Cleome speciosa*, Cat's Whiskers)

This annual is often called Cleome, but this name properly belongs to a related genus. It is one of the easiest annuals to grow and can attain one metre in height. Each plant is sparingly branched and each branch terminates in a mass of white or pink-mauve

Galphimia glauca   Gerbera jamesonii   Gomphrena globosa   Gynandropsis

flowers which are shortlived, but there is a long succession of blooms produced on each stem for two to three weeks. This is a fine tall bedding plant; hardly worth growing in pots, and produces seed freely.

Gynura aurantiaca (Purple Velvet Plant)

This is a perennial herb with some erect stems and some long scrambling ones. The leaves and stems are covered with soft purple hair and the small flower heads carry little orange flowers. The species tends to be low growing here and by pruning the longer stems it can be encouraged to become more bushy in habit. It needs full sun for the purple colour to develop fully and should have well drained soil with careful watering. Propagation is by means of cuttings. It can be grown in troughs or as an edging plant around borders and beds.

This is often available as a house plant in temperate countries but must receive as much light as possible.

Hedychium coronarium (Ginger Lily)

This plant of the Ginger family grows in the same way as Cannas and has white, very fragrant flowers in compact heads at the ends of the leafy stems. Like Cannas, it has a creeping rootstock, from which it may be propagated by division. The flowering stem carries a number of green bracts, each concealing several flower buds which open in succession so that only one flower appears from each bract every day for four or five days. Consequently, the whole inflorescence will carry from one to four flowers each evening and this may continue for about three weeks.

The plants are sometimes attacked by a stem borer and this can only be kept in check by destroying affected stems early. There are red-flowered species of Hedychium but they do not flower well in the lowlands of Malaysia.

This species is sold as a house plant in temperate countries.

Helianthus annuus, Annual Sunflower

Besides the tall, large-flowered kinds, which grow and flower well, there are several varieties of the smaller type, grown from imported seeds, which produce bushy plants with many flowers; these are excellent bedding or pot plants, flowering for many weeks and some produce a fair number of seeds which can be used for propagation. Full sun is essential. Tall kinds may need staking to prevent damage in strong winds or heavy rain.

Helianthus, Perennial (H. angustifolius)

This is one of the most useful herbaceous perennials. It has narrow leaves and stems one metre or more in height, carrying yellow

flowers like small sunflowers on short or long side stalks; it is easy to grow, is propagated by division of the old plants and is good in borders or pots, and for cut flowers. It needs replanting about once a year and is very susceptible to attacks by snails. These will devour all part of the plants including the buds on the rootstock and whole plants can be destroyed within two or three days. Continuous attention combined with trapping or poisoning of snails is the best method of control.

Helichrysum bracteatum (Strawflower)

A perennial plant usually grown as an annual and developing many branches, each terminating in a flower head with many stiff bracts surrounding it. These may be yellow, orange, red or white and the whole head may be dried and used as an 'everlasting flower'. In the lowlands, growth is not strong and protection from rain is necessary, but in the highlands the species grows quite well in beds or pots. Propagation is by seeds.

Heliconia humilis (Lobster Claw)

These plants have stems up to 1½ m high carrying large leaves which can be 1½ m long and 25 cm wide. The conspicuous part of the plant is the inflorescence which is flat and carries two rows of large, stiff, pointed, bright red bracts having green tips and margins. The flowers are relatively inconspicuous and have green-tipped white petals. The plants will form well shaped clumps eventually and young shoots need protection from snails. They grow well in full sun and good soil and benefit from regular manuring; they will also tolerate some shade but will become a little taller and may not flower so well.

Division of the rootstock is the best method of propagation and after replanting watering should be frequent until the new plants are established. Only the young leaves are damaged by snails; as soon as they reach a certain stage of maturity the snails will leave them untouched. However, when young leaves are eaten by snails, they show rows of ragged holes across the leaf blade and this will make the plant untidy in appearance.

Heliconia pendula

A tall plant up to 2 m high with leaves about 1 m long and 30 cm wide. The flowers are produced on long pendulous inflorescences which carry six to ten red bracts. Growing conditions are the same as for the Lobster Claw plant.

Heliconia psittacorum
(often called Japanese Canna)

Despite the common name, this plant is

Hedychium coronarium

Helianthus angustifolius

Catharanthus roseus: white and pink flowers

Iresine herbstii

Impatiens balsamina

Impatiens balsamina

Hymenocallis littoralis

Jacobinia

neither a Canna nor Japanese. It is a perennial plant of the Banana family, growing in the same way as a Canna, with erect flower stalks bearing stiff orange bracts (the showy part of the plant) with small flowers in their axils. It needs rather wet ground to grow strongly, or plenty of humus, and full sun. If left undisturbed, it will form a dense thicket 1–1½ m high, and under such circumstances it should be uprooted and replanted as it can harbour a great number of weeds which are not easily removed from between the stems. Both leaves and flowers are constantly used in modern flower arrangements. It can be used for screening unsightly spots in the garden or in a wet area where few other plants would grow, but it should be used with care in a bed as it can become very invasive.

Heliconia sp.

The correct botanical name for this species is in some doubt but the plants are commonly grown for their foliage. They are relatively short plants, about one metre or more in height and have variegated foliage which may be green and yellow, green and white, green and bronze or entirely bronze. They can be grown in pots, beds, or troughs and make neat, dense clumps which are rather slow growing. Flowers are rarely produced and the plants need full sun in order to develop the best leaf colour. The colour shows to best effect against a background of dark green foliage.

Hemerocallis fulva (Day Lily)

These plants grow best in the highlands where the temperature is slightly lower. Each plant has a tuberous rootstock which produces narrow, flat leaves and tall stems carrying several large yellow or orange fragrant flowers. Propagation is by means of division and the plants are easy to establish.

Hemigraphis alternata (Red Ivy)

A prostrate perennial plant rooting at the nodes and very good as a ground cover. The opposite leaves will reach 10 cm in length and are purple on the undersurface, and grey with an almost metallic appearance on the upper surface. Small white flowers are produced but they are relatively inconspicuous. It needs full sun in order to develop the colour properly and can be grown in beds, troughs or hanging baskets. Propagation is by means of cuttings.

Hippeastrum (Red Lily)

Bulbous plants with narrow strap-shaped leaves that produce large red or parti-coloured flowers at the end of a long leafless stem. Two other kinds are also commonly grown, one having salmon-coloured flowers and the other having white petals with pink veins. All kinds

will flower at least once a year and even a short period of dry weather seems to stimulate flowering. Bulbs may be dug up and dried off to induce flowering and, as a result of this treatment, they make very handsome pot plants or cut flowers. Some of the finer larger kinds, with flowers of many shades, only bloom after they have been rested in cool storage (a month in the bottom of the refrigerator).

Crossing the large-flowered kinds with the more free-flowering smaller ones might produce new varieties with larger flowers and a more free-flowering habit. Cross-pollination is easy, as the stamens are large and the three-lobed stigmas are conspicuous. The fruits take about one month to ripen and contain thin black seeds which will germinate very quickly if they are viable. Seedlings should flower soon after they are two years old.

The breeding of fine Hippeastrums suited to the Malaysian climate would be a worthwhile hobby. Bulbs of good large-flowered varieties may be obtained from Hong Kong and Europe and sometimes from Singapore. If imported at the resting stage, they will flower soon after arrival. Some kinds do not flower again unless chilled or grown in the hills.

Alcea rosea (Hollyhocks)

Some kinds of Hollyhocks grow and flower well in the lowlands but they are best in pots, grown from seed and treated as annuals. Burnt earth is best as a potting mixture. More trials are needed to select kinds best suited to the Malaysian climate. If good kinds are found, seed should be saved. The plants can be grown very successfully also in the highlands. Single- and double-flowered forms are available.

Hydrangea macrophylla

A few varieties of the common garden Hydrangea grow and flower well in Malaysia; they were probably imported direct from

Hippeastrum

Hydrangea macrophylla

Impatiens balsamina (double)

white flowers appears over a long period of time. Propagation is by means of cuttings and the plants can be grown in pots or in beds, but must have full sun if flowering is to be satisfactory. Regular manuring will help to prevent the lower leaves from dropping, which would spoil the appearance of the plants. However, should they become a little bare, then some ground cover plants grown around the base of these shrubs would conceal this fault until new plants have been raised.

Often available as a house plant in temperate countries and it flowers for a long time, but needs reasonably strong light.

Pedilanthus tithymaloides (Japanese Poinsettia or Slipper Flower)

This is a much branched succulent plant which can be grown in pots, troughs or beds and will tolerate a great deal of harsh treatment. There are two or three varieties which differ in size of plant, closeness of leaf arrangement, and colour. In all varieties, when they are fully established, small sprays of flowers are produced on short stems at the ends of the branches.

There is a dwarf form with leaves arranged very close together in two rows and this will grow to about 35 cm in height. Another form is twice as tall, with more widely spaced leaves which can be up to 10 cm long, and with stems one metre or more in length. A third form is variegated and the whole plant is irregularly marked with white, pink and green.

For best development, the plants need full sun, a well drained soil, limited watering and very little fertilizer. Some of the shorter forms can be used to make a very effective edging around beds, or for formal planting in beds surrounded by concrete or paving stones.

Pruning several times while the plants are young will encourage many branches to develop, which will give a very dense, bushy appearance eventually. The variegated forms treated in this way can be unusual in appearance and are very suitable for planting in troughs or beds around buildings where there is a great deal of heat and reflected light. Plants which are not pruned can become straggly very quickly, especially the taller varieties. Propagation is very easy by means of cuttings, and almost any short piece of stem will root if it is pushed into the soil.

Pentas lanceolata (formerly *P. carnea*)

Dwarf or medium bushy shrubs with mauve, pink or white flowers in small heads, much as in Ixora. Useful for bedding or in mixed borders, needing full sun to flower well and standing hard pruning. Propagation is easy from green cuttings. Seeds are often produced, but plants from these show some variation in flower colour and the best of these should be preserved by cuttings.

Flowers are of two forms. In one, the stigma projects from the mouth of the flower and the stamens are hidden in the tube. In the other form, the stamens protrude from the tube and the stigma is hidden. Each plant has one flower form only, but if seeds are required, both kinds must be grown together to ensure cross-pollination.

Oxalis corymbosa

Pedilanthus tithymaloides (dwarf form)

Pentas bussei
(formerly *P. coccinea*, Red Pentas)

This differs from the previous species in its bright red flowers, in preferring light shade, and in being subject to attack by beetles at night. It will do well in a sunny border, provided other plants shade its roots. If beetle attacks are prevented, it grows strongly and flowers freely and continuously, but does not produce seeds in Singapore. Here it has only one flower form, that with the projecting stigma. It would be necessary probably to have the second flower form before seeds could be obtained. It is propagated easily from cuttings and is useful as a cut flower. Hybrids between this and *P. lanceolata* occur in Sri Lanka, but are not yet grown in Malaysia.

Peristrophe

A shade-loving herbaceous plant with some medicinal uses, and easily grown from cuttings. It has small, strongly two-lipped flowers of mauve or purple. One species grows wild in Malaysia, but has rather small flowers, and another has larger leaves and large flowers and makes a good ground cover under the shade of trees. It needs to be cut back a little at intervals to prevent it from becoming too tall and straggly.

Petunia x hybrida

There are many varieties, but the large and double-flowered kinds are not strong in the lowlands, and it is best to keep to the small-flowered kinds which grow strongly and freely. There are many colour forms, and flowers may be white, pink, red, mauve, purple or blue, in various shades, and many have bicoloured petals. A group of pots with plants all of one colour variety makes a very fine show and is highly suitable for small gardens or where space is restricted. It may be possible to grow on a second batch of plants of a different colour variety which would give an extended display of flowers and would provide a change of mood in the garden when the first plants have finished flowering.

Seeds are very small, and need careful handling. Plants must be grown in pots or in hanging baskets, in a burnt earth mixture, and, if properly tended, will flower for weeks or even

Pentas bussei

Pedilanthus tithymaloides (variegated form)

Platycodon grandiflorus   Plumbago auriculata   Rudbeckia hirta

months. Good drainage, not too much water and occasional manuring are desirable. The plants produce seeds freely but these may not come true. Experimentation with new varieties of imported seeds is always worth trying.

Phlox drummondii (Annual Phlox)

These are small, weak-stemmed herbaceous plants up to about 15–20 cm high. They have small, oval, light green leaves, and flowers in a wide range of colours. They may be red, pink, purple, mauve, white or bicoloured. In some forms the petals are entire and in other forms they are cut or fringed to varying degrees. Best grown in pots or troughs where watering can be controlled, and regular manuring is necessary. Staking may be needed unless the plants are grouped together, so that the stems intermingle and provide mutual support. The plants are easily grown from seeds and need full sun; but they must have a little protection from heavy rain which will spoil the flowers and may beat the plants to the ground. Seeds are produced and imported seeds are always available.

Platycodon grandiflorus (Balloon Flower)

These are short erect or semi-prostrate plants which are grown in pots or in well drained troughs or rockeries. Good drainage and full sun are essential in order to produce good flowers. Several flowers are developed in series along each stem and the buds are very large and balloon-like, hence the common name of the plant. Regular manuring is necessary and older seedlings may need to be stopped in order to encourage branching. There are several colour varieties and the flowers may be deep blue, pale blue, lilac or white. The plants tend to be small in this climate but flowering is almost continuous. Propagation is from seeds or by division of old plants.

Plumbago auriculata, formerly P. capensis (Blue Plumbago)

This is best treated as a dwarf shrub (in beds or pots) and pruned hard back, with manuring, after each flowering; in this way it will give solid displays of bloom. Propagate from green cuttings in coir dust in a closed frame, or by division of old plants; in the latter case prune before lifting, and handle carefully to avoid damage to roots. Full sun is desirable for free flowering, but the plants will grow quite well and flower a little in light shade.

Sometimes seen as a house plant in small pots, in temperate countries, but it is often grown as a scandent shrub on a wall in conservatories where it flowers freely and is extremely attractive. It needs full light for as long as possible. It is usually planted in large wooden tubs, or directly in the ground.

Plumbago indica, formerly P. rosea

This is a sprawling shrub with small flowers of a peculiar deep pink on elongating sprays, and is best pruned hard back after flowering to keep it in shape. It flowers best in full sun, and is subject to attack from thrips and beetles, but spraying with insecticide ensures a good display of flowers. This plant is poisonous.

Pseuderanthemum reticulatum

Included here although it could also be used as a foliage plant. It is a short shrub which can be grown well in pots or beds, provided it receives full sun. Relatively few branches are produced but they carry large, closely arranged, oval leaves which are dark green with yellow-bordered veins. The young leaves are entirely yellow so that a plant with several young shoots is very conspicuous. Each branch terminates in a large inflorescence of many flowers, which are white with fine red spots on the petals, and these also are very attractive.

The plant will tolerate a range of growing conditions but regular manuring is necessary. It can be very effective for a massed display but the appearance can be a little overwhelming unless it is combined with plants having plain green foliage. Propagation is from cuttings.

Roses (Rosa)

It is impossible to grow really fine roses in the plains of Malaysia, but reasonably good

Russelia equisetiformis

Russelia sarmentosa

Saintpaulia ionantha

Salvia splendens

blooms can be secured, especially in the neighbourhood of hills, where rather cooler nights are the rule. Roses need well dug and manured beds, and occasional manuring during growth; they flower continuously and may be pruned as desired. After a time the plants become too old and must be replaced. Propagation is from cuttings or marcots.

The chief pests are beetles which eat the leaves at night; these are difficult to control and in small gardens hand-picking at night can be done or frequent spraying with insecticide carried out. Spraying will need to be repeated after rain.

Several varieties of roses have long been grown here and may be obtained from nurseries. There is scope for breeding new varieties better suited to lowland conditions in Malaysia; for this purpose it would be well to import roses grown in southern China rather than from cooler countries. At the hill stations, good roses of a great variety can be grown and hybrid tea forms and ramblers seem to do best. Among the newly imported varieties, some grow quite well while others are very weak. Selection from the stronger growing varieties would help to establish forms which are better suited to the climate.

Rudbeckia
(Black-eyed Susan)

R. hirta flowers well and continuously. It is a perennial herbaceous plant similar in habit to the perennial Coreopsis but not so vigorous nor so easy to transplant; the flowers are deep yellow with a prominent black centre. *R. laciniata,* which should be tall, sometimes flowers fairly well at about 45 cm high, but most plants from imported seeds fail to flower, though they go on growing indefinitely. The mauve-pink *R. purpurea* (now called *Echinacea purpurea*) flowers fairly well but the plants are not vigorous. Some hybrid Rudbeckias offered by seedsmen in Britain are fairly successful, but inferior to Gaillardia which they resemble.

Ruellia ciliosa

A perennial herb with stems which become prostrate as they elongate. The whole plant is covered with short, soft hair. Small groups of flowers are produced in the axils of the dull green, narrow, oval leaves. The petals are lavender or blue-mauve and the flowers are produced almost continuously when the plants are well established.

It is excellent in pots or troughs where the stems can be allowed to trail over the sides. Snails will completely destroy it very quickly and must be rigidly controlled. Propagation is quite easy from cuttings but these must not be allowed to become too wet, otherwise they will rot before they develop any roots.

Russelia equisetiformis, formerly *R. juncea* (Coral Plant)

A shrub with long, slender stems carrying tiny leaves and numerous small, bright red flowers on the smaller branches; useful for bedding if given some support or can be allowed to trail over a wall, or in a pot or basket from which it can droop. It is easily propagated by division of old plants (which must be pruned back), or from cuttings.

In full sun, it flowers freely and continuously, and prefers dry conditions when the stems are shorter and the whole plant develops a pleasing, graceful shape, with arching, self-supporting stems. Under wetter conditions, the stems grow longer and then fall over on to the soil so that they need staking to prevent the plant from looking untidy. The plants are excellent in a sun rockery or on the edge of a mixed border where they receive plenty of sunshine, and small plants are very decorative in pots on sunny window sills. They will grow happily in a small pot for a long time before they need repotting, and will not object to a few days without water.

Russelia sarmentosa

An erect shrubby plant with close tufts of red flowers which are smaller than those of *R. equisetiformis*; useful for borders, flowering freely and continuously and easily managed, but not so showy on account of its smaller flowers. It has much larger leaves than the previous species which makes it quite distinct in appearance. It is propagated from cuttings.

Saintpaulia ionantha (African Violet)

A small herbaceous plant from East Africa, with a rosette of soft grey-green or dark green leaves and sprays of small violet-blue flowers. It is easy to manage as a pot plant in light shade, especially if protected from heavy rain. It can be propagated from leaf cuttings and by division of old plants. In recent years, many new varieties have been produced and a number of these are available here. They may have double or single flowers which are in shades of violet, mauve, purple, pink or white. It must not be overwatered or it will quickly rot and it is better therefore to keep it slightly dry. These plants are now among the most commonly grown house plants in many parts of the world.

Salvia (Sage)

Several kinds of Salvia, either the herbaceous annuals or the perennials, may be grown in Malaysia. The brilliant red *Salvia splendens* is best grown as a pot plant in the lowlands. It will not attain the size to which it grows in cooler conditions, but it is very showy and well worth growing. In the hill stations, it can be planted in beds and will reach one metre in

Tropaeolum majus

Wedelia triloba

Tagetes patula (French Marigolds)

Salvia farinacea

Tagetes erecta (African Marigolds)

Salvia splendens

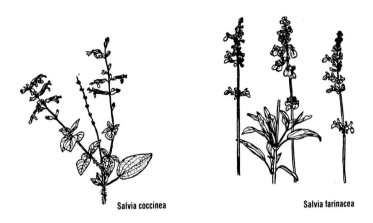

Salvia coccinea

Salvia farinacea

Sinningia (Gloxinia perennis)

Sinningia speciosa

height, flowering continuously for many months.

Imported seeds are used. There is a variety with a white calyx and a form with purple flowers, both of which are attractive but not as popular as the original scarlet form. *Salvia coccinea* has much less showy red flowers, but is a much hardier plant in the lowlands, growing easily in beds or borders and flowering for a considerable time; its slender stems give it an attractive light habit and it produces seeds freely. *Salvia farinacea* has pale blue or white flowers and grey-green foliage; it is a dwarf woody plant that grows well if not in a soil which is too wet, and it will flower freely and continuously. It may be propagated from cuttings, and plants will live for about one year if carefully tended.

Sinningia (Gloxinia is now included under this name)

Herbaceous plants with succulent stems, rather fleshy leaves and attractive lilac-mauve bell-shaped flowers on the stem above the leaves. It is grown in pots in light shade or in a rock garden and may be kept in flower for a considerable period. It will reach about 60 cm in height and is propagated from cuttings.

S. speciosa (Gloxinia) is a tuberous perennial plant, with large, waxy, bell-shaped flowers of many colours, often with striking patterning. The flowers may be white, or various shades of pink, red, mauve, lilac, blue or purple, some of which are very intense. Many varieties have bicoloured flowers. They are not easy to grow to perfection in the lowlands and are best grown from seed which is very small and must be under cover from rain, throughout the day, with sun up to about ten o'clock in the morning only.

A burnt earth mixture, containing dried cattle dung or compost, is satisfactory. After flowering, the plants die down, and the tubers rest; this is the difficult stage, as the tubers often rot. Some varieties do not rest but make new growth from the tubers as soon as the old flowering stems are cut off. Water carefully at this stage, or again the tubers will rot. New plants may be grown from leaves, as for Begonia.

Gloxinias have been grown for a long time as house plants in temperate countries and need a porous potting mixture with careful watering. A humid atmosphere around the plants is best and a peat-based potting mixture gives good results.

Solidago virgaurea (*S. brachystachys*, Golden Rod)

Although these perennial plants will grow and flower in the lowland tropics, they are never as robust as they are in a cooler temperature.

Zinnia elegans, **Large-flowered**

These are best grown from imported seeds. They are usually grown in pots by the burnt earth method, and need extensive manuring for best results. In beds, they are susceptible to bacterial wilt which is common in old garden soils; there is no effective large-scale control for this, and if the soil is infected then sensitive plants cannot be grown. Flowering of Zinnias begins about two months from seed planting and continues for about three weeks. Leaf curl is a common disease, probably best controlled by sulphur dust.

Zinnia angustifolia, **formerly** *Z. linearis*

This is a dwarf, free-flowering annual with small narrow leaves and orange-yellow flowers. It lasts longer than most annuals, and is especially useful in pots or in crazy paving. It is liable to get too wet in ordinary flower beds, but is satisfactory in light soils; and in dry weather in heavier ones. It is one of the few really good dwarf flowering plants that we have. Small quantities of seed are produced and should be carefully saved.

Zinnia angustifolia

6 ORNAMENTAL SHRUBS AND CLIMBERS

Shrubs are erect bushy plants and climbers are those which are not strong enough to stand alone but must have support of some kind. The two kinds are usually quite distinct from each other but there are some plants which can be treated either as shrubs or as climbers, depending on the management they receive as they grow. It is convenient, therefore, at the outset to define four classes of plants which will be dealt with in this chapter.

Shrubs are woody plants of moderate size which need no support and have no adaptation for climbing. Usually they have several main stems arising from ground level but by careful pruning many of them can be kept to a single stem and these, if allowed to grow unchecked, can become very large and may even become small trees.

Scandent Shrubs are plants with long woody stems which grow through and over neighbouring plants and in a garden these may be supported on pergolas and archways. However, these plants can be pruned to prevent them from producing very long stems and, kept to a bush form in this way, they can be used either as shrubs or climbers. Bougainvilleas are a good example of such plants.

Woody Climbers are plants with thick woody stems which need support and they cannot, as a rule, be kept to a bushy form by pruning.

Slender Climbers are plants with much more slender stems but the distinction between these and woody climbers is not a sharp one, although it is convenient.

Some of the plants in each of these groups are grown frequently as house plants in temperate countries where, with suitable management, they are easily maintained.

Shrubs

Acalypha

Two species are commonly grown as ornamentals and there are a number of different forms, all having large leaves and small flowers carried in spikes. They are best planted in small groups in a mixed border, or they can be used with great effect as an informal hedge. All forms can be grown very easily from cuttings.

Both species may be grown in pots as house

Acalypha hispida

plants in cooler countries and it is important that the forms with variegated leaves receive as much light as possible in order to develop their full colour. The soil in the pots should not be allowed to dry out completely otherwise any of these plants drop their lower leaves and will not be as attractive in appearance.

A. hispida (Red Cat's Tails) has large plain green leaves and produces great quantities of branched, hanging inflorescences, from 36 to 50 cm in length, carrying very many small, fluffy flowers; the appearance has therefore given rise to the common name of Cat's Tails. The most usually grown form has dark red flowers but two other kinds are available, one having deep purple flowers and one having white flowers.

The plants tend to be rather open in habit and are best grown in a mixed border, although a group of them in the centre of a flower bed surrounded by shorter flowering plants can be effective also. The stems can be cut back almost to ground level and a new crop of shoots will be produced within a few months. Flowering is continuous but the stems tend to become leafless at the base and then the plants may look untidy. Pruning should be done before this stage is reached, or low growing plants may be positioned to conceal the stems of the Acalypha.

A. wilkesiana is a commonly grown species with numerous cultivars, all having variegated leaves. These may be green and white or green and yellow, or various combinations of dark red, bronze, reddish brown and brown. The leaves of some forms are flat but in others they are strongly undulate and the variegation may be in the form of a simple coloured margin or it may appear as an irregular patterning which is different on every leaf.

The flowers of this species are inconspicuous and are greenish or tinged with pink. All cultivars make dense bushes when well managed and can be grown as single specimens, in groups, or as informal hedges. Full sun is necessary for the best colour development, and in shade the leaves of these plants become almost entirely green. When pruning, use a pair of secateurs. Large-leaved plants such as these do not look well if cut with garden shears as many of the leaves are cut in half, spoiling the general appearance of the whole bush.

When used as an informal hedge, the plants can be kept to 1–1½ m in height, but single specimens can sometimes be allowed to grow a little taller than this. A mixture of cultivars can be planted to give very interesting formal or informal colour patterns, and these can be very effective on banks or sunken areas where they will appear to great advantage. This kind of planting is best done on a large scale because the size of the plants and their strong colours give an exceedingly striking and bold effect. These plants can be grown also at the hill stations, and the red-leaved forms especially are very much more intensely coloured there.

Aglaia odorata (Mock Lime)

A shrub of quiet appearance with dark green compound leaves. At intervals throughout the year, it produces short inflorescences of small globular yellow flowers which are very fragrant. The plant may grow to 2 m high and usually needs no pruning as it shapes itself. It may be grown singly, in groups or in a mixed border.

Baphia nitida

This large shrub or small tree is a legume and has dark green foliage which makes it an admirable background for other flowering plants. It may be grown singly or in groups, and it makes an excellent hedge as it tolerates clipping very well, but this should be done with secateurs because the leaves are large and many would be cut in half if pruning were done with garden shears. This would spoil the appearance of the hedge until new leaves developed. Sufficient space should be allowed when the plants are grown as a hedge as it should be at least one metre wide in order to look well. Small, white, bean-type flowers are produced and are followed by fruits with good seeds which may be used for propagation.

Barleria cristata

These easily grown shrubs may be established quickly from cuttings, which can be planted directly in the ground where they will root in about two weeks. The young plants should be pinched out to encourage dense, bushy growth because if this is not done they tend to produce many long unbranched stems and the whole bush will be a little thin in appearance. The

Barleria cristata (2 varieties)

plants are best grown in a group or as a low informal hedge and will flower for several weeks two or three times each year. Too much pruning will prevent flowering.

The long tubular flowers are two-lipped and there are several colour forms available. Two or three forms with flowers in various shades of mauve are commonly seen and those with the darker coloured flowers are the most desirable. There is also a variety with bicoloured flowers conspicuously striped with mauve and white. A white-flowered form is also available, but the flowers are slightly smaller than in the other forms and the plant has a different habit, being more upright in growth, with stiffer branches. The flowers are held in denser clusters and after the petals have fallen the bracts and sepals remain and turn brown so that they can make the plant a little untidy in appearance. The mauve and bicoloured forms are the most satisfactory ones in the garden.

Barleria needs full sun and, when established, the plants will tolerate dry conditions. In full bloom, the bushes appear to be covered in a haze of soft colour which is most pleasing. After flowering, the plants can be trimmed and in a short time new shoots will develop and will produce another crop of flowers. When used as a formal hedge, more frequent trimming is needed, so that no flowers are produced. And because there is a tendency for the lower parts of the plants to become bare, it is better to keep it to a height of about one metre or less and it should then remain leafy almost to ground level, especially if it is given a little fertilizer about three or four times a year.

Barleria lupulina

A medium-sized, open bush with long, narrow, dark green leaves having red veins. If it is pruned regularly to encourage branching it will become more dense, and can be used effectively as a low hedge, either on its own or in combination with other suitable plants of similar habit. If it is planted singly it must be given regular applications of fertilizer and should be pruned to encourage branching. Without this treatment it will become very open with long, straggling branches.

Orange flowers are produced in series on short, spindle-shaped inflorescences and flowering occurs over several weeks. Propagation is from seeds or cuttings.

Acalypha hispida

Acalypha wilkesiana

Acalypha wilkesiana

Bixa orellana

Barleria cristata

Bixa orellana (fruit)

Acalypha wilkesiana

Aglaia odorata

Brunfelsia pauciflora

Baphia nitida

Acalypha wilkesiana

Acalypha wilkesiana

Barleria cristata

Caesalpinia pulcherrima (yellow form)

Barleria prionitis

Caesalpinia pulcherrima

Bauhinia acuminata

Brunfelsia americana

Caesalpinia pulcherrima (cerise form)

Caesalpinia pulcherrima (normal red form)

Barleria lupulina

Calliandra surinamensis

Calliandra surinamensis

Calliandra surinamensis (avenue)

Calliandra haematocephala

Clerodendron macrosiphon

Cestrum nocturnum

Clerodendron fragrans

Carissa carrandas (fruit)

Clerodendron macrosiphon

Clerodendron macrosiphon

it can become very dense and will grow to 2 m or more in height. Propagation is by means of seeds which germinate easily, provided they are sown immediately after the fruit has ripened. The seedlings are a little slow in growth and must not be given too much water.

Cassia

Several yellow-flowered shrubby species of this genus can be obtained, all being easily propagated from seeds, and they can be planted singly, in groups, or in mixed borders. Most of the species will shape themselves, but they will tolerate pruning and this may be necessary for older plants, or those which have become misshapen.

Cassia auriculata is a bush growing to 1½ m in height, flowering freely and continuously. *C. biflora* is also a bushy, free-flowering species with a somewhat hemispherical shape and bright yellow flowers. It can be pruned very hard when necessary. Both of these species do better in the north of the country than in Singapore.

C. fruticosa is an erect, slightly branched small tree, with leaves having a few large leaflets and producing continuously a number of

Cassia biflora

Cassia fruticosa

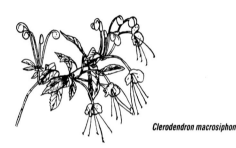

Clerodendron macrosiphon

Above: *Clerodendron paniculatum*
Right: *Clerodendron paniculatum*
Below: *Clerodendron paniculatum*

pale yellow flowers. When well grown, this plant is very attractive as the drooping branches give it a distinctive appearance.

C. laevigata and *C. didymocarpas* are very decorative in the hills, but do not grow strongly in the lowlands. *C. splendida* is a very sprawling shrub, with scattered large flowers of a deep yellow.

Cassia alata (Candlestick Cassia), a wild species, can be used very effectively as a garden plant and is a sparingly branched shrub or small tree growing to 2 m high. It has very large pinnate leaves, with attractive oval leaflets which fold upwards at night so that the plant has a totally different appearance at that time. The long inflorescences carry bright yellow flowers which are protected by brownish orange bracts before they open. Many fruits are produced and these are green at first, becoming black when ripe, and are very distinctive in appearance. Propagation is easy from seeds so that old plants, which can be gaunt in appearance, are best removed and replaced with seedlings. Pruning can be done, but the plants are liable to become misshapen and are best grown in a mixed border where the lower parts of the stem are concealed. This species will grow in somewhat wet soil and can be useful for planting at the sides of streams and ponds.

The leaves and stems have some medicinal use and are said to cure ringworm and other skin diseases.

Cestrum

Cestrum (Jessamine)

In the lowlands, the only Cestrum which grows well is *C. nocturnum*, 'the lady of the night'. This is a tall bush producing large panicles of long, narrow, greenish flowers at the ends of the branches, and at night these become very fragrant. It grows best in a light soil and is susceptible to a root disease if too wet. It grows equally well in the hills and two other species are grown there: *C. elegans* with red-purple flowers, and *C. aurantiacum* with yellow flowers. They bloom almost continuously and all species can be propagated from cuttings.

Citrus

Some of the citrus species which are usually grown for their fruit can be used also as ornamentals, especially the smaller kinds. They may be grown in large pots or in a border and they have been described in another chapter. In temperate countries the small fruited kinds are often grown as house plants and seeds of any of the forms germinate easily there, making very attractive indoor plants.

Clerodendron

To this genus belong several small trees and shrubs which are associated by Malays with magic properties. An English name suggested for them is 'Witches' Tongues' because of the characteristic protruding stamens. One species commonly used in gardens is the Pagoda Flower (*C. paniculatum*) which has large, deeply lobed, dark green leaves and stems which are sparingly branched. The red flowers are produced in a large, terminal, rather conical inflorescence which is very conspicuous and during good weather will retain its attractive appearance for two or three weeks while the flower buds open in series.

The lower part of the stem quickly becomes leafless and the plants will look a little ungainly, but if they are placed at the back of a border, or behind some low growing plants, the bare portions can be concealed so that only the flowering parts are visible. After flowering, the branches should be cut back and new ones will develop very quickly after two or three weeks. When treated in this way, the plants can be kept to a height of about 1½–2 m, and the first new leaves to develop will often be very large so that the shrub is very bold in appearance and makes a striking addition to a mixed border. The species can be planted in small groups or in a mixed border, or it may be used in a shrubbery. Less commonly seen is another cultivar which is exactly similar in appearance and differs only in having cream-coloured flowers.

Clerodendron fallax (*speciosissimum*) is a related species with shorter stems, larger bright red flowers in smaller heads, and is less robust in

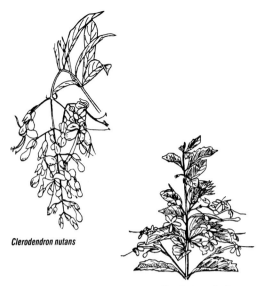

Clerodendron nutans

Clerodendron calamitosum

growth in the lowlands. *C. macrosiphon* is a small shrub with dull green leaves, but periodically throughout the year the whole bush becomes covered with large numbers of very long-tubed white flowers which are striking in appearance both before they open as well as afterwards.

Clerodendron nutans is a native Malaysian shrub growing to 1½ m or more in height, sparingly branched and producing pendulous groups of pure white flowers. It is best grown on good soil with the roots shaded, but is probably best managed as a pot plant so that growing conditions are more easily controlled. *C. ugandense* is a scandent shrub, with flowers of two shades of blue, but it is not very vigorous in Malaysia and does not flower profusely.

Clerodendron fragrans (*philippinum*) is a sparingly branched shrub, sometimes a little untidy in appearance. It has large, slightly lobed leaves and produces terminal heads of very fragrant white flowers which are often tinged with pink. The flowers are semi-double or double and are excellent for cutting and for use in small flower arrangements. This plant is worth growing for the fragrance only, despite the fact that it does not always develop a good shape. *C. calamitosum* makes a useful plant for pots and borders and is compact in growth with bunches of small, fragrant, white flowers. Most Clerodendrons are easily propagated from cuttings.

Codiaeum variegatum (Croton)

All plants of this species are classed as shrubs but they show a considerable range of size from less than 1 m high to about 2½ m high, and practically all of them have variegated leaves. The plants may be grown in pots, in a border, or as a hedge. They need well drained soil and benefit from occasional application of liquid manure. Full sun is essential at all times, otherwise the lower leaves will drop and the young leaves will remain greenish and will not develop their full colour.

There is great variation in the shape of the leaves and in their colour combinations. In Malaysia, the most commonly grown varieties show at least six quite distinct leaf shapes but there are others to be found, although they are not so frequently seen because, very often, they are more difficult to grow. Leaves may be large or small, long and very narrow, short and broad, short and narrow, simple or lobed and some varieties have leaves in which the blade is interrupted at one point along the midrib. The leaf blade may be flat or twisted and the edges may be undulating, upturned or downturned.

The varieties show wide differences in the number of colours and the patterning of their leaves so that some may have a two-coloured leaf with a fairly simple pattern of spots while others may show several colours displayed in irregular patterns which are different on every leaf of the plant. However, it is essential in all cases for the plants to receive sunshine all through the day so that the colour develops its full intensity.

If these shrubs are not supplied with fertilizer occasionally many of the lower leaves will drop away and the plant will look ungainly as the branches will retain a few leaves only near their tips. Crotons can be propagated by marcotting or by means of half-woody cuttings. Young shoots can often be rooted by keeping them in a jar of water for some time; the water should be changed at intervals to prevent the development of mosquito larvae.

Crotons should be used with care in a garden or a landscape arrangement as their strong colours can be very dominant and can lead to a feeling of unrest. Also, some of the leaf patternings are very gaudy and can be tiring to the eye when seen in a large mass. When crotons are grown in pots it is essential that they are given regular application of fertilizer so that they will hold all of their leaves for as long as possible. Although these plants appear to have thick, tough leaves, they cannot

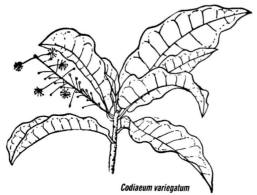

Codiaeum variegatum

be kept in airconditioned rooms for any length of time and when grown in pots they are really best out of doors.

A number of the forms are used as house plants in cooler countries but plenty of light and fertilizer are essential.

Cordyline

This group of shrubby plants is often included in the genus Dracaena. The leaves are narrow or lanceolate, usually leathery in texture, and are often crowded towards the end of the branches. The leaf colour shows a great deal of variation, and combinations of purple, red, pink and yellow are frequent. The flowers are borne in terminal branched panicles and may be greenish, yellowish or pink in colour, but some cultivars rarely produce any blossom.

Most of these plants need full sun in order to develop the leaf colouring to its fullest extent but some of the forms will tolerate a little shade without too much disadvantage. Seedling plants do not show the brilliant colours seen in older specimens, but if new plants are obtained by using older stems as cuttings, then the adult leaf coloration will show as soon as the new shoots have developed three or four leaves.

Practically all of the forms available in Malaysia belong to *C. terminalis* and this species is usually a shrub up to 3½ m high with purple or purplish green leaves. The young leaves are bright rose pink while they are still growing and the flowers as well as the stems of the inflorescences are a paler shade of pink. This plant will tolerate a great deal of mistreatment and, although it develops its best colour in full sun, the leaves will retain a good deal of their purple colour in light shade but the plants will appear a little sombre in such situations. Small specimens can be grown in pots for some time and are useful as decoration around buildings, but they will eventually become too large for the pots and should be planted out in the ground. The dark foliage of this shrub in a mixed border provides an excellent background and contrast for the bright flowers and green foliage of other shrubs.

The species has produced a number of different forms which differ in leaf shape and colour, as well as the amount of branching which occurs. Some of these forms have been given special names and these are always propagated vegetatively. The leaves may be long and narrow or very broad and spear-shaped and will show various combinations of red, pink, cream, white and green. The majority of these highly coloured forms are sparingly branched and look best when grown as young pot plants, but if they are planted out in a border they will eventually become tall and the lower parts of the stem will be bare so that they need to be screened with other plants. As

Codiaeum variegatum

Codiaeum variegatum

Codiaeum variegatum

Codiaeum variegatum

Codiaeum variegatum

Codiaeum variegatum

Codiaeum variegatum

Codiaeum variegatum

Codiaeum variegatum

Codiaeum variegatum

Codiaeum variegatum

Cordyline terminalis

Dracaena cincta (centre), *Dracaena fragrans* (left), *Pleomele reflexa* (foreground)

Dracaena fragrans cv. Victoria

Dracaena deremensis cv. warneckii

Dillenia suffruticosa

Dillenia suffruticosa

Dillenia suffruticosa

Dracaena surculosa

Dracaena goldieana

young pot plants, they make a striking display because the colours of the new leaves are so brilliant.

Some forms are grown as house plants in other countries and are quite easy to manage as they will tolerate drier air than some other indoor plants. Good light and regular applications of fertilizer are essential for house plants.

Dracaena

This genus contains both large and small shrubs, many of which are grown for ornamental purposes, especially as a number of them have strikingly coloured leaves. Some species have very slender stems and others have large, thick, tree-like stems, but all are grown for their foliage. Most of the species will tolerate shade and for this reason they can be grown underneath large trees or in quite heavily shaded areas around buildings. All kinds can be easily propagated from stem cuttings or by marcotting and all are a little slow in growth. Occasionally, the growing points of the stems are destroyed by beetles which can be controlled by using an appropriate spray. But even without such treatment the beetles will eventually leave the plant and as the older parts of the stems remain undamaged, new shoots will form very quickly. All species and forms mentioned are available as house plants in temperate countries and they require no special treatment.

The most commonly grown species are *D. fragrans* and *D. reflexa,* the former having long strap-shaped leaves and the latter having much shorter and narrower leaves. *D. fragrans* can become very tall and the stems may not branch until the tips are removed. However, if these long stems are allowed to continue growing unchecked, they will eventually arch over and, later, side branches will develop from their middle sections so that very interesting shapes are obtained. Unfortunately, the leafy side branches are very heavy and during strong winds or heavy rain the main stem can break very easily. When the stems of these plants are cut back, new buds develop just below the cut surface and if the main stem is small it may be too weak to support several strong branches growing near its tip. It is better, therefore, to cut the main stem back to about 30–60 cm above ground level where it will be larger and stronger and better able to support the new branches. These plants are slow growing and often retain their leaves along the whole length of the stem, even after they have grown to 3–4 m in length.

Pieces of stem 1–3 m long can be used as large cuttings and if these are pushed vertically into the ground, they will eventually form roots and shoots, but several months will pass before signs of growth appear. Propagation is

easy by means of cuttings of any length and in order to produce pot plants pieces of stem about 30–60 cm long can be used. These are partly buried in good soil and will produce one or two new shoots, after which the plants should be transferred to fairly large pots for further growth. Short pieces of stem 10–15 cm long are often placed in a bowl of gravel chips with water only and these will produce one or more shoots which will remain attractive for a very long time, especially if a little liquid artificial fertilizer is added to the water occasionally. But if these plants are to be kept permanently, they must at some time be planted in soil.

D. fragrans is often grown as a pot plant as it will tolerate a great deal of bad treatment and consequently it is used frequently for decoration outside buildings as well as inside in large areas used for public functions. If the plants are given regular applications of fertilizer, practically all of the leaves will be retained for a long period of time and many of them will reach one metre in length. The plants can be kept for considerable periods of time in airconditioned rooms, but eventually must be taken outside to recover; recovery may take several months.

There are five cultivated forms which have variegated leaves and of these, the most easily available are var. *lindenii* which has the leaves margined with greenish yellow; var. *Victoria* in which the leaves are broadly margined with cream or golden yellow; and var. *Massangeana* in which the leaves show a broad central yellow band with wide green margins. The yellow or cream coloration is seen best in the young leaves; as they become older the colour changes to green. Consequently, young potted plants from short cuttings will show good colour and are best for indoor decoration but plants which are grown outside in the garden will only show the colour near the branch tips where it may be hardly noticeable, especially if the plants are very tall.

Dracaena deremensis

This species is usually grown as a pot plant and can reach one metre or slightly more in height. It has closely arranged, broad, dark green leaves, with narrow longitudinal silver or white stripes, and there are a few cultivars which differ in the amount and distribution of the colour. The most commonly grown form is the cultivar *Warneckii* which has several longitudinal white bands near the margins and a central pale green or whitish green portion near the midrib. This plant is easily grown from cuttings and in a pot can be kept to a good shape with little effort. In the cultivar *Bauseii*, the leaves have a broad green margin and the central portion is silvery in colour.

Cordyline terminalis

Dracaena godseffiana (D. surculosa)

A shrubby species which makes an excellent pot plant but is equally at home when planted out in a border. It has medium-sized, oval or elliptic leaves which are pointed at the apex, and they are arranged in pairs or in whorls of three. The thin, wiry stems grow in length for some time, and although they appear leafless, they do carry small scale-leaves, but their growth suddenly becomes very slow and two or more normal leaves are produced close together near the tip of the stem. This habit of growth may be repeated two or three times before side branches develop, so that young plants may appear a little thin at first until more leaves have expanded. The leaves are dark glossy green with densely arranged cream or yellow spots.

One or two cultivars are available and differ only in the density of spotting so that in the most extreme case the leaves are almost completely covered with creamy white blotching, and at the other extreme the leaves show a very little pale green mottling or a few pale green spots only.

Dracaena goldieana

A very striking species with large spear-shaped leaves boldly patterned with pale green and dark green. It makes an excellent pot plant as it is slow growing and retains its leaves along the whole length of the stem. If grown in a border outside the house some care is needed to prevent it from being smothered by neighbouring plants. The leaves are dark glossy green with broad, irregularly-shaped transverse bands of pale green which become silvery in colour as the leaf ages. The young leaves are tinged with pink while they are unfolding.

Dracaena marginata

The name of this species is the one commonly used by horticulturalists, but in some catalogues it may appear under the names D. cincta or D. concinna. The plants can grow to 5 m in height and have a most distinct appearance because the stems are bare and carry numerous leaves closely arranged near their tips. The leaves are flat, up to 60 cm long, and are very narrow; they are olive green with red or purple margins. The stems tend to remain unbranched until the terminal part is cut off or is damaged in some way, and afterwards two or three branches will develop. With this in mind, it is possible to produce plants of striking and interesting shapes which are very suitable for indoor decoration or for use in courtyards within large buildings.

Propagation is from large stem cuttings which should not be kept too moist until they have rooted. Old stems can be cut back almost to ground level and will soon produce a number of new shoots. The plants appear to grow better with less water than some other species of Dracaena. Small plants make good pot specimens provided they receive regular applications of fertilizer. Tall specimens in very large pots can be kept in this way almost indefinitely and are excellent for permanent decoration, especially if they are manured regularly and if the leaves are sprayed with water frequently to keep them free of dust.

Dracaena reflexa (also known as Pleomele reflexa, Pride of India)

This plant can grow to 9 m in height but can also be grown as a pot plant when the size can be controlled very easily. The leaves are short and narrow with wavy margins and on potted plants are held on the stems almost down to ground level, but if the plants are grown in an outside border and are allowed to become very tall, then the lower parts of the stems will become bare. The normal form of this species has dark green leaves and branches fairly freely, so that it can be used very effectively as a screen up to 3 m high. Pruning should be done occasionally with secateurs to encourage the growth of young leafy branches. This form can be used also as a pot plant and will withstand a great deal of harsh treatment.

There are a number of cultivars and one of the most attractive is called 'Song of India'. Its leaves have very broad yellow margins, but this form is slower in growth than those with entirely green leaves. Most other cultivars have completely green leaves of varying shape and size and these grow as well as the normal form. The plants are propagated easily from cuttings which must not be kept too wet until they have rooted.

Dracaena sanderiana

A plant with slender stems holding leaves along their whole length for a long time. The leaves are of medium length, narrow with wavy margins and dark green with a broad white marginal stripe. The species makes a good pot plant and can be propagated easily from cuttings. Older plants will develop branches from near the base.

Duranta repens (D. plumierii, Golden Dewdrop)

This well known plant is a tall shrub with small leaves and stems often carrying spines. The plants can grow to 6 m in height but are usually kept much shorter than this by pruning. The branches are often drooping and carry inflorescences at the tips of practically all the shoots. The flowers are small, lilac-blue or white, and are followed by bright orange berries so that the bushes are attractive when flowering and fruiting. There is also a form which has variegated leaves and this needs full sun in order to develop the full coloration; it is slightly different in shape to the forms with green leaves.

Duranta needs careful pruning otherwise the basal parts of the stems become bare of leaves and the shrubs will look untidy. It will flower and fruit almost continuously but if flowers only are desired, the inflorescences must be removed as soon as the flowers have faded. There will be an interval of several weeks before a new crop of flowers appears.

Duranta can be used as an informal hedge but, because of its somewhat spreading and drooping habit, it will need considerable space. In this case pruning will serve two purposes: the removal of faded flowers and the cutting back of stems to encourage the growth of more leafy branches which will produce another crop of flowers. The plants can be used as a formal hedge which is clipped frequently, but under these circumstances they will not flower and unless great care is exercised there is a tendency for the lower parts of the hedge to become thin and bare. Propagation of all forms can be done by means of cuttings or from seeds.

Eranthemum nervosum
(E. pulchellum)

This small shrub has simple hairy leaves and erect spikes of blue flowers. It grows best under light shade and although it is not really showy it is worth cultivating as one of the few truly blue-flowered shrubs. It is easily propagated from cuttings.

Eugenia uniflora
(E. michelii, Surinam Cherry)

A very attractive evergreen shrub with small, dark green, shiny leaves which are bright red when very young and change through pink to green as they mature. The flowers are small with white petals and are borne singly in the axils of the leaves. They are followed by attractive bright red, round fruits which are deeply grooved and look like small lanterns hanging along the branches. This plant is most attractive when grown singly, and with a little pruning it will become very dense, but it needs full sun otherwise it will become thin and will not produce flowers. It can be used also as a very decorative hedge. The fruits can be used for making jam or jelly but as the seeds are a little large they should be removed after cooking. Propagation is done from seeds which are a little slow in germination and several weeks may pass before the seedlings appear.

Euphorbia antiquorum

A large spiny shrub, eventually growing to 4 m high, with thick, succulent, dark green

Ervatamia coronaria flora pleno

Ervatamia coronaria

Galphimia glauca

Duranta repens

Euphorbia pulcherrima

Duranta repens

Duranta repens (variegated)

Exoecaria bicolor

Euphorbia tirucalli

Euphorbia antiquorum

Euphorbia pulcherrima

Eranthemum tricolor

Pseuderanthemum reticulatum

Euphorbia cotinifolia

Evodia

Strobilanthes

Strobilanthes

stems which are three- or four-angled. The leaves are small and are seen only on the younger parts of the stems. Under normal conditions they remain on the plant for a short time, but in dry conditions the leaves will drop very soon after they have grown to full size. The plant looks good when grown singly but may also be placed at the back of a border so that the basal parts can be screened by other plants. This Euphorbia will make a dense rounded bush with many branches which are held vertically, giving the plant a very stiff and characteristic appearance. A well grown plant gives an impression of great strength and solidity.

The best growth is obtained in full sun and propagation is easy from cuttings of any size. Flowers are produced occasionally but they are small, yellow or yellowish green in colour, and are shortlived. This plant could be used to form a hedge which would be somewhat massive in appearance and could be kept from 1 to 3 m in height. However, pruning would be necessary, at infrequent intervals only, but should be done carefully because the branches are thick and when removed they will leave a very large scar which could be unsightly. The stems of this plant become very hard and woody so that when used as a hedge, the close-packed stems with their short, sharp spines will keep out all intruders.

Euphorbia cotinifolia

This plant can be very handsome as it has small dark red leaves arranged in whorls of three around the stems and provides some intense colour when there are no flowers on neighbouring plants. It is easily grown from cuttings but needs full sun to develop the full colour of the leaves. Young plants must be pruned to encourage bushy growth, and regular application of fertilizer is necessary so that new leaves will be large and well coloured. These plants will tolerate quite dry conditions but on poor soil the growth will be straggly and the leaves will be small; but the response to an application of fertilizer is rapid, and new leaves of good size are soon produced.

It is possible to keep these plants in pots but they are best planted out in a mixed border or as single specimens. In a mixed border, the plants may not develop a good shape but this is of no consequence because the branches become long and appear between the foliage of other plants, where their tips hold a cluster of the red leaves in the sunlight, providing useful spots of bright colour in the border. Small plants can be kept in pots for some time, and provided they receive some fertilizer and full sunlight, they are very effective on a window sill, with light shining through the leaves.

Sometimes available as a house plant in other countries but needs plenty of light and regular application of fertilizer.

Euphorbia pulcherrima (Poinsettia)

Shrubs with bright red leaves (bracts) on the flowering shoots. The plants are usually grown in pots, or as shrubs planted out in the garden, and must be pruned at intervals to encourage the growth of new shoots and also to keep them to any required size. If left unpruned, these plants become tall and rather straggly in appearance, with bare stems, and leaves near the tips of the branches only. Flowering is seasonal but in the Malaysian climate a plant will often have a few stems with flowers at all times of the year. A good crop of flowers is produced after a short dry spell and the coloured bracts are retained on the plants for several weeks. After flowering it is best to prune the plant and when new shoots have developed these will produce more flowers after the next period of dry weather.

Plants in pots may have the amount of water reduced and this will encourage the production of flowers whenever required. The plants can be grown in the lowlands and the highlands but the colour is much better in the latter areas. There are forms available which have pink, white or cream-coloured bracts, and these grow just as easily as the normal form. Propagation is from cuttings. A commonly available house plant in temperate countries.

Euphorbia pulcherrima

Euphorbia tirucalli
(Milkbush, Bone Bush)

This is another plant with succulent stems and very small leaves which drop from the plant very quickly after they have matured. The stems are round and the smaller ones are closely arranged near the ends of the main branches. It makes an interesting plant in a garden and can be grown singly or in a border. If left undisturbed, it will grow to 10 m in height. At first it will be columnar in shape but will become much broader and more rounded in outline as it becomes older. Flowers are not produced very often in Malaysia but the plant is easily propagated from cuttings of various sizes. The stems contain a great deal of white latex which is said to be used for curing skin diseases, but it should not be used indiscriminately for this purpose.

Evodia sp. (Euodia)

A small to medium-sized shrub which can be grown in pots for some time but is best planted outside where it may be grown in groups or in a mixed border. The leaves have three to six long, narrow leaflets with very wavy margins and they are light green or yellowish green in colour. The shrub is round or oval in shape and is conspicuous because of the leaf colour so that it looks especially good if positioned where it can be viewed with the sunlight shining through the foliage. Large numbers of small, greenish yellow flowers are produced on short branched inflorescences and these are followed by many small brown fruits which can make the bush look a little untidy but are easily removed with secateurs. Quantities of seeds are produced and germinate easily but propagation can also be done from cuttings.

If the plants are allowed to flower and fruit continuously, they will become a little thin but this can be avoided by judicious pruning to encourage the production of new leafy shoots. Young plants in pots are very attractive because of their dense appearance and conical shape so that they can be used very effectively for decoration around buildings in full sun. However, as soon as the pots become full of roots the plants will drop many of their leaves and new plants will be needed.

Although the foliage of these shrubs is a pleasing colour they should be planted in moderation because the effect of large groups of plants with pale green or yellow foliage can give a feeling of unrest in the strong tropical sunlight. Single specimens or small groups interspersed with plants having darker foliage are much more effective.

Gardenia jasminoides

Ficus deltoidea

This is a small shrub with slender branches and can be grown in a pot or on a tree branch where it does not become very large and the foliage never becomes dense enough to cause leaf-fall on the supporting branch. There are several forms available which differ mainly in the shape and size of the leaves. It makes an attractive pot plant because of the neat, well-spaced leaves on the slender stems and the very open habit. The plant will tolerate fairly dry conditions and can make effective bonsai trees as it is easily managed in this form. In a border or bed it should not be near strong growing or densely leafy plants that would soon overwhelm it. It is probably best on its own with a short ground cover plant, or against a background of dark foliage to show up its shape and branching. Often grown as a house plant in other countries where, in a suitable pot, it will grow to about 1 m in height.

Fuschia

A few cultivars of this genus are grown successfully in the highlands and flower well. Propagation is by means of cuttings which root easily. In the lowlands the plants make weak growth and will survive for some time but are never very happy and will not produce flowers. Some success is gained in airconditioning but these plants drop many leaves and are slow to recover in not entirely suitable conditions.

Gardenia

Gardenia jasminoides is a shrub with dark green shiny leaves and will grow to 2 m in height. It does best in full sun but will tolerate a little shade for part of each day, although it will not then flower as freely. There are several cultivated forms but the one most commonly grown in Malaysia is *G. jasminoides* var. *fortuniana*. This has pure white double flowers which have a very strong sweet scent and the leaves are either opposite in arrangement or in whorls of three. When grown in full sun a bush will produce a few flowers continuously but will never develop a great mass of bloom. The plant is often troubled by mealy bugs and this leads to the leaves becoming black with a covering of sooty mould, but spraying with an appropriate insecticide will cure this trouble. Propagation can be done from woody cuttings or by marcotting. Often available as a house plant in temperate countries.

Hemigraphis alternata

In recent years a shrub under this name has been grown increasingly in gardens as it can be used singly or in groups, and can be planted also as a hedge. It responds well to clipping and makes an excellent formal hedge up to 2 m high and 1 m thick. The plant has very narrow leaves with red veins and inconspicuous white flowers produced in short dense inflorescences, but frequent clipping will prevent the formation of flowers.

Single bushes can be trimmed to various simple shapes and are useful then in a formal garden. The stems may become bare at the base unless the plants are trimmed regularly while they are very young. Propagation is very easy by means of cuttings and the plants do best in full sun. The leaves are often light green in colour so that the general effect is not too dark and overpowering when the plant is grown as a hedge or screen. The name of this plant is in some doubt and it is possibly a species of Strobilanthes.

Hibiscus

This is one of the best known of all tropical flowering shrubs, the most commonly grown species being *H. rosa-sinensis* and its hybrids. When grown unchecked, these plants can reach 2–3 m in height but they may be used also to make a useful hedge. The normal form has large, bright red flowers carried singly in the axils of the leaves and they last for one day only, but a succession of blooms is produced so that each day there will be a new crop of flowers. In the lowlands the flowers begin to close up at about noon but in the highlands they remain open the whole day. There are numerous hybrids obtained by crossing *H. rosa-sinensis* with other species and they have

Hibiscus mutabilis   *Hibiscus mutabilis* (double)   *Hibiscus rosa-sinensis*

Hibiscus rosa-sinensis   *Hibiscus rosa-sinensis*   *Hibiscus rosa-sinensis*

Hibiscus rosa-sinensis   *Hibiscus rosa-sinensis* (double)   *Hibiscus schizopetalus*

Hibiscus rosa-sinensis cv. cooperi

Ixora coccinea cultivar

Ixora coccinea

Ixora coccinea cultivar

Ixora coccinea (white form)

Ixora javanica

Ixora coccinea (pink form)

Ixora chinensis

Ixora coccinea (dwarf)

Ixora javanica

flowers ranging from white through yellow and orange to pink and red. There are both single and double-flowered forms and the latter remain open throughout the day.

Propagation is easy by means of cuttings or marcots. Budding can be done and two or three varieties may be grown on one stock. Weaker varieties may be budded on to the ordinary hedge Hibiscus. Seeds have been produced in the northern part of Peninsular Malaysia although they are not usually developed in the middle and southern parts of the country. This is probably due to the more seasonal climate of the northern areas. Cross-pollination could be attempted in order to produce new colour varieties suited to the Malaysian climate. There are many more forms available in other parts of the tropics and subtropics and if some of these could be tried out in this country, it would be possible to begin a small breeding programme. The varieties available at present do show marked differences in the habit and size of the plant as well as in the form, colour and size of both leaves and flowers.

Hibiscus needs full sun in order to flower well but the plants can tolerate a little shade, although they will not then produce many flowers. When used as a formal hedge the frequent clipping which is necessary will prevent flowering but as an informal hedge which is trimmed at long intervals only, the plants will flower almost continuously and make a most attractive sight. When grown as an informal hedge the basal parts of the shrubs may become bare, but if desired, low growing perennials could be grown near by to conceal the base of the Hibiscus plants. The plants will grow on most soils and respond well to application of fertilizer but it will be found that some varieties flower much more freely than others. Usually Hibiscus is untroubled by pests and diseases; mealy bugs can sometimes become a nuisance but are easily controlled by spraying with an appropriate insecticide. Some varieties of Hibiscus are available as house plants in cooler countries and often these plants have been treated with chemicals to keep their growth short and, therefore, to make them more suitable as decoration in smaller rooms.

Hibiscus mutabilis (Rose of Sharon)

This shrub is totally different in appearance from the previous species as it makes a broad bush up to 5 m in height and has hairy, greyish green leaves. The flowers are pure white when they first open and are slightly cup-shaped, but as they age during the day the colour changes to deep pink or almost red before they finally close up. There are single and double-flowered forms which will grow

equally well in the lowlands and the highlands. This species does best on well drained soil and needs some pruning to prevent the branches from becoming too long and straggly. It is easily grown from cuttings which must not be kept too wet, or it can be grown from seed which is produced abundantly.

Hibiscus schizopetalus

A shrub with bright red hanging flowers having deeply divided petals which curve backwards towards the stem, and a very long, flexible stamen tube. This species is about the same size as Hibiscus rosa-sinensis and can be used in exactly the same way and in similar situations, but the flowers are smaller and not quite as showy.

Hibiscus syriacus
(Blue Hibiscus)

Although this is not well suited to growth in the humid tropics, it can be managed quite well as a pot plant. There are single and double-flowered forms but they do not flower as freely as in more seasonal climates.

There is also another species of Hibiscus which has very small pink flowers and this is easy to grow although not commonly seen. It is easily propagated from cuttings and makes an excellent pot plant, but it should be tried for bonsai culture as the flowers, resembling miniature Hibiscus flowers, would be most appealing.

Hibiscus schizopetalus

Honckenya ficifolia
(Clappertonia ficifolia)

This less well known shrub will grow to 2–3 m high and can be planted singly, in a mixed border, or it may be used as a low screen. It has large lobed leaves and short sprays of flowers which have white or pinkish mauve petals. Propagation is by means of seeds or from cuttings and the plants need full sun for best growth.

Ixora

There are many varieties of Ixora which are grown in Malaysia, and their flowers are white, yellow, pink or red.

Ixora finlaysoniana is a native of Thailand and will grow into a small tree if left unpruned. It has fragrant white flowers and produces some seeds which may be used for propagation although germination is slow. Often the roots of this plant are near the soil surface and if these are damaged they will produce young leafy shoots from the cut surface. When these shoots are large enough, they can be detached with a portion of the root and then may be planted in a pot or in a permanent position in the garden where they can remain until well established.

Honckenya ficifolia

The other Ixoras, with coloured flowers, are divided into two main groups: *Ixora coccinea* in which the leaves are stalkless and have broad bases which almost clasp the stem; and *Ixora javanica* in which the leaves are larger with a conspicuous stalk and narrow base. Between these two is the *Ixora chinensis* group which is somewhat intermediate in character, having leaves with short stalks and bases which do not clasp the stem. Some forms of these two species are used as house plants in other countries and appreciate fairly high humidity.

Ixora coccinea is a much branched shrub 1–1½ m high with dark green shining leaves and flowers held in dense terminal inflorescences. Each flower has a tube up to 3 cm long and although the normal colour is bright red there are several forms available with colours ranging from yellow to deep orange and orange-red. The plants are slow in growth and need full sun.

Ixora chinensis is a shrub up to one metre in height with dense terminal heads of flowers. The corolla tube will reach 2½ cm in length and there are forms with white, pink, yellow or orange flowers. These plants also are slow in growth and need full sun.

Ixora javanica is a larger shrub, more upright in habit, and will grow to 1½–4 m in height. Growth is quicker than the previous species and it produces much larger heads of orange-red flowers 15–18 cm in diameter. The plants will grow and flower equally well in full sun or in light shade.

A dwarf form of *Ixora coccinea* is available which is a small, very dense shrub growing to ½–⅔ m in height only. The leaves and flower heads are smaller than the normal form but when well grown the entire bush is covered with flowers and is extremely decorative. This variety is very useful for formal planting or it may be grown as a low hedge. It needs little trimming to keep it in shape and can be grown also in pots very successfully. There are forms with bright red, orange-red or pink flowers.

All Ixoras flower continuously, are easy to grow, and need little pruning unless they are to be kept to any particular height. Propagation is by means of cuttings or marcots but some forms produce many seeds and these should be germinated as there would be a possibility of obtaining new colour forms. Ixoras are relatively free from pests and diseases but caterpillars can sometimes ruin new flower heads and should be controlled by spraying with an insecticide.

Jatropha

Three species of this genus are grown in Malaysia and are useful for planting in beds and borders; two of them make attractive pot plants while they are small.

Ixora coccinea

Jatropha pandurifolia

Jatropha multifida (leaf)

Jatropha gossypifolia

This plant is often found growing wild in dry areas and poor soil. It makes a good subject for rockeries as it is slow in growth and can provide a little height to the rockery landscape. The plant is a small shrub with very thick stems and attractive lobed leaves which are purple when young and become dark, shiny green when mature. The flowers are produced in short inflorescences and although they are small, they are attractive because of their blood-red petals. Small, bright green oval fruits are produced which are conspicuous and add to the decorative appeal. The plants are grown easily from seeds or from cuttings but the young plants must not be overwatered or they will rot very quickly. This species is best grown in rockeries, in pots, or in hot, dry areas where it will thrive with the minimum of attention.

Jatropha pandurifolia

This is a medium-sized bush with dull, dark green leaves which are often tinged with purple; the inflorescences carry small bright red flowers. The plants flower continuously but tend to be straggly in habit when grown singly. For this reason they are best grown in a group or in a mixed border so that the lower parts of the plants are screened with other species. This Jatropha should not be allowed to grow too tall as the stems tend to become long and straggly, with leaves near the tips only. It is best to prune regularly in order to encourage the growth of new shoots. If fertilizer is applied regularly, the plants will retain the older leaves for much longer and the overall appearance will be much improved. The leaves show a little variation and although most of them are simple in shape there will be some which show slight lobing of the margins. There is a cultivar which produces pink flowers but this does not seem to flower as freely as the red-flowered form. Propagation is easy by means of cuttings and marcots.

Jatropha multifida
(Coral Plant)

This is a tall, sparingly branched shrub which will grow to 3 m in height. It has large, decorative, palmately lobed leaves with very narrow lobes, and these are light green in colour. The small bright red flowers are carried in large, broad inflorescences with red stems so that the whole structure is extremely conspicuous. The plants grow best in full sun and can be propagated from seeds which germinate easily. Young plants are very attractive in pots but must be planted out when they become taller; the best position for them is at the back of a bed or border where the lower parts of the stems can be concealed.

Jatropha podagrica (Tartogo)

This is a much smaller plant growing to about 50 cm in height and having a swollen stem which gives it a very characteristic appearance. The plant has large, somewhat round, dark green leaves which are deeply lobed and have long stalks. The small red flowers are borne in large terminal inflorescences which have red stems so that the whole structure is very striking in appearance. Fruits are produced freely and when young they are pale green, making a pleasing contrast with the red stems of the inflorescence.

This plant can be grown for a long time in a pot and will tolerate quite dry conditions, but it can be grown also in a border and should be placed near the front. With regular application of fertilizer, the leaves may grow to 30–40 cm in diameter and will be very dark green in colour, but the margins may then curl upwards so that the plants may appear unhealthy; it is best, therefore, to apply fertilizer at infrequent intervals. The leaves will not then grow quite as large but will remain flat and the appearance of the plant will be improved. Seeds are produced freely and are easy to germinate.

Justicia betonicaefolia

A perennial, shrub-like plant producing many conspicuous long inflorescences with large green and white bracts subtending the white flowers. The plant can be grown as a low informal hedge or in a mixed border, but it should be pruned after flowering so that new shoots will develop and produce another crop of flowers. Propagation can be done easily by means of cuttings. The plant flowers best in full sun but it will grow quite well in a little shade although fewer flowers will be produced.

Kopsia

These plants are large, slow growing shrubs which will reach 6 m in height and can be used as single specimens, in groups or in borders.

Kopsia fruticosa has large, light green, spear-shaped leaves and terminal inflorescences of pink and white flowers with long, slender corolla tubes. If left unpruned, it will make a rather open bush which is very attractive. If it is pruned while young, many more shoots will develop and although a dense bush can be produced, the general appearance is not as good. The method of treatment will depend on the final effect which is needed. No seeds are developed and propagation is from cuttings or marcots. The bark of this species is attractive as it is pale grey or light brown.

Kopsia singaporensis is another bush of similar size to the previous species but the bark is dark and sometimes almost black. The branches are not as angular in their growth as in the previ-

Juniperus (prostrate form)

Jatropha pandurifolia

Kopsia singaporensis

Justicia betonicaefolia

Kopsia fruticosa

Kopsia fruticosa

Jatropha podagrica

Kopsia fruticosa

Lantana camara (yellow form)

Lantana camara (white form)

Lantana camara (red form)

Lantana montevidensis

Lantana montevidensis

Lagerstroemia indica

Manihot dulcis

Murraya paniculata

Malvaviscus arboreus

Manihot esculenta (variegated)

Murraya paniculata

plants can become a little ungainly. The short, terminal inflorescences carry small, very fragrant orange and white flowers which open in the evening and fall the next day. Fruits are produced freely and should be removed because they make the plant look untidy. Propagation is best done from cuttings of half-ripe wood.

Ochna serrulata (Mickey Mouse Plant)

A small shrub with very attractive flowers and fruits, which will grow to 2 m in height, although in Malaysian gardens it is usually only about half this size. The plants have shiny green leaves, large, bright yellow flowers, and fruits with a number of black fruitlets set on an enlarged brilliant red receptacle. The bushes need some pruning in order to develop a good shape and they grow best in full sun. Propagation can be done from seeds or from half-ripe woody cuttings. Small groups of these plants look best but they can also be planted in a border with low-growing species around them.

Pandanus (Screw Pine)

Although these plants may be classified as shrubs for ordinary garden purposes, some of the species can grow very large and may then be thought of as trees. Several species are grown as ornamentals. All have long, relatively narrow leaves with short spines along the margin and the midrib so they should not be planted too close to a path. Some forms are used as pot plants in other countries and are easy to manage as they will tolerate quite a wide range of growing conditions.

Pandanus dubius (P. pacificus) has broad, dark green leaves with the midrib set in a deep, broad V-shaped groove. While young, the plants can be grown in pots, but when they become larger, the prickly leaves make them difficult to handle. They will, however, quickly outgrow a pot and must then be planted out in the garden where they will reach 2–3 m in height with leaves up to 1½ m long and 10–20 cm broad. Leaves of young plants in pots are usually much less than one metre long. Many side shoots will develop and the plants then have a very bold appearance and look effective planted singly, or in a small group of plants where their form will show to advantage without being obscured by too many other plants. Propagation can be done by detaching some of the side shoots which have one or more short roots at the base; these can be planted in pots until they have made a good root system.

Pandanus sanderi is commonly grown in gardens and can become very large if allowed to grow unchecked. Such plants can reach a height of 6–8 m and spread, but small plants can be grown in pots for a long time until they become too large, when they are difficult to handle because of the prickly leaves, and are best planted out in the ground. The leaves have longitudinal yellow stripes and a large plant is very striking in appearance. Many side shoots form and some of these may have entirely green leaves. The latter should be removed and destroyed as they will never develop the yellow stripes. Side shoots which have grown one or two roots can be detached and used for propagation.

Pandanus veitchii is very similar in appearance to the last species but has slightly larger leaves which are striped with white, and requires similar management.

Pandanus pygmaeus is a very small species growing to about 50 cm high. It has very narrow leaves with deep yellow longitudinal stripes. It makes an excellent pot plant because of its size, but can be used also at the edge of a border, although it does not produce as many side shoots as the large species and does not, therefore, become very dense.

All of the Pandanus species are sometimes spoilt by attacks of beetle larvae which destroy the growing point. The presence of these pests remains undetected until the group of young leaves in the centre of the plant suddenly falls over; if these are removed, it will be seen that they have been completely eaten through at the base by the larvae. It is sometimes possible to remove these pests by hand, but if this cannot be done then the plant should be sprayed with an insecticide. If the stem below the growing point is undamaged, new side shoots will develop within a few weeks, and after several months the plant will be restored to its former glory. The new shoots should be sprayed at intervals as a precautionary measure. This trouble from beetle larvae does not seem to occur in all parts of the country. The larvae are very similar in appearance to those which damage palm trees.

Petraea

Two species of this genus are grown as ornamentals. One is a scandent shrub which is described later, and the other is *Petraea rugosa* which is a slow growing bushy shrub having shorter sprays of flowers than the other species. The sepals and petals are broader, giving a better display of the lilac and violet colours. This plant can grow to 2½ m high but is usually much shorter than this and can be kept to any required height by pruning. The shrubs can be grown singly or in a mixed border and they flower frequently after short spells of dry weather. Propagation is from marcots or cuttings which are slow to root.

Phaleria blumei

A bushy shrub of medium size, with simple leaves and clusters of pure white flowers at intervals on the old wood. The flowers are shortlived but very beautiful and the plants will grow in light shade. Propagation is by means of seeds or cuttings.

Phyllanthus myrtifolius

This is a useful low growing shrub which develops a rounded shape up to 1 m high and 2 m wide. It has many slender branches carrying tiny, narrow leaves 1½ cm long, which makes it appropriate for some kinds of rockery or as a ground cover. The branches which touch the ground will often develop roots and these portions can be used for propagation. Large cuttings of old wood can also be used for propagation but the results may sometimes be disappointing.

The plant can be pruned and kept to any definite size. When well established it will tolerate a great deal of harsh treatment but the lower parts of the branches may become bare and unsightly. The only remedy for this is to prune hard, and if a little fertilizer is applied at the same time, this will help the plant to recover and new shoots will be produced very quickly. Because of its somewhat prostrate habit, small potted specimens are very useful for surrounding groups of pot plants arranged for decoration inside buildings or in courtyards; they conceal the pots very effectively.

Plumeria (Frangipanni)

Although these plants can be grown as shrubs for some time, they will eventually become small trees up to 10 m high. The common Frangipanni (P. rubra) has pointed leaves, smallish white flowers with a yellow eye, and some pinkish coloration on the outside. There are also several very handsome varieties with larger flowers which are variously coloured with pink and yellow, and a large white-flowered form (Plumeria obtusa) which has blunt-ended leaves.

All are easy to grow in well drained soil and a sunny position; they flower freely but in the northern parts of the country, however, flowering tends to be more seasonal, though not entirely so. Leaves are dropped about once each year but the plants are never totally bare of leaves at any time except in strongly seasonal areas where they are completely deciduous. The fragrant flowers are useful for cutting. Propagation can be from cuttings or marcots which must not be kept too wet before roots have formed. New forms can be raised from seed which is produced frequently by some varieties and germinates easily. Seedlings do better if kept slightly dry and will rot very quickly if overwatered.

Polyscias (Panax)

These are useful plants which will survive much poor treatment. They are grown for their foliage and to keep them in good condition they must be pruned and given applications of fertilizer – both on a regular basis. Several species and cultivars are grown, all having compound leaves, and in many instances these are variegated.

P. balfouriana has one to three broad round or oval leaflets which are normally dark green and shiny, but there are several cultivars available. In some of these, the leaflets are variegated with yellow or white.

P. filicifolia has pinnate leaves in which many of the long leaflets have very deeply lobed margins, but this is a variable character and a single plant may also show leaflets with entire margins as well as many intermediate kinds. Some cultivars have variegated leaflets but others have pale yellow or yellowish green young leaves at the stem tips which make the plants very conspicuous. In order to maintain this appearance, pruning must be done regularly to encourage the development of new shoots so that the plants always have some of these new, brightly coloured young leaves. The species may be grown in pots as a 'Ming tree'.

P. fruticosa has leaves which may be long or short, bipinnate or tripinnate, and green or variegated. The leaflets of many forms are deeply lobed.

P. guilfoylei is available in a number of

Petraea rugosa   *Phaleria blumei*   *Plumeria obtusa*   *Polyscias*

Plumeria obtusa   *Plumeria rubra*

Plumeria obtusa   *Plumeria rubra*   *Plumeria rubra*

Plumeria rubra   *Plumeria rubra*   *Plumeria rubra*

Plumeria rubra   *Plumeria rubra*   *Plumeria rubra*

forms, most of which have variegated pinnate or bipinnate leaves. The leaflets are of various shapes and have unequally lobed margins; the variegation often appears as a white margin.

All of the plants just mentioned grow easily from cuttings but must not be overwatered while they are rooting. When established in pots, they will tolerate complete drying of the soil for short periods and will recover easily when watered again. They make good foliage pot plants but can also be used as single shrubs outside in the garden, or they may be planted in groups; some of the cultivars can be grown as a very attractive low hedge. When used for this purpose, the plants must be pruned regularly and given fertilizer, otherwise the lower leaves will drop and the appearance will be spoilt. Some of the cultivars are excellent for bonsai culture as the branches are easily trained in various ways and if this is done in conjunction with careful pruning, whole plants can be encouraged to form a variety of interesting shapes.

All forms are available as house plants in temperate countries. They should not be allowed to dry out and appreciate a weekly spray with water. Cuttings should be kept warm until rooted and afterwards will tolerate lower temperatures.

Portlandia grandiflora

This excellent shrub is not easily available, which is unfortunate as it is a most desirable garden plant producing large trumpet-shaped flowers. The shrub grows to 1–1½ m in height and has very dark green, glossy leaves. Propagation is by means of cuttings. The plants are suitable for gardens of any size and can be grown singly or in a border of mixed shrubs.

Pseuderanthemum atropurpureum

A shrubby plant with deep purple leaves which often show variegations of paler purple and red. It is easily grown from cuttings but needs pruning when young to encourage bushy growth. If this is not done, the stems tend to become tall and the plants will develop a small, bushy, oval or rounded crown while the lower parts of the stems will be bare. It needs full sun to develop a good colour and is probably best in a mixed border so that other plants can screen the bare lower parts. It is possible to use this plant as a very low hedge, but it must be pruned frequently after planting out so that many branches develop as low down as possible.

Pseuderanthemum reticulatum

Frequently this plant is used as a highly decorative foliage pot plant because of its brightly coloured young leaves. In addition, however, it does produce large sprays of attractive white flowers at the ends of the branches. The plant can be kept to an easily manageable size in pots but if planted out it can grow to 3 m or more in height and may become a little gaunt in appearance. It is better therefore to keep it fairly short by pruning which will encourage new leafy shoots to develop. These are the ones which show the brightest colour. Young leaves are bright yellow and as they become older they change to dark green with yellow veins. The white flowers are heavily spotted with crimson near the throat of the corolla tube. This plant can be most effective in a mixed border on account of its coloured leaves and showy flowers.

Both species of Pseuderanthemum are grown as house plants in cooler countries, but need careful pruning so that they develop a good shape.

Randia

The Malaysian species of Randia do not flower freely enough to be good garden plants. However, *Randia macrantha* (Angels' Trumpets), which originated in West Africa, is used often as a garden shrub and flowers more frequently. After a short period of dry weather, these plants will drop their leaves and two or three weeks later a new crop of leaves develops at the same time as a large number of flowers. The bush becomes quite spectacular as it is covered with sweetly scented flowers which are very large, white and trumpet-shaped. Some of the buds open later than others, so that this lovely appearance is maintained for about two weeks. Propagation is by means of cuttings. The plants thrive best in light shade but will grow in full sun, although the leaves will then be more wrinkled in appearance.

Rhododendron indicum (Azalea indica)

In lowlands, this grows into a small shrub, kept easily in a large pot, but it thrives, flowering almost continuously, in the highlands. Flowering is more sporadic in the lowlands but well worth the effort as large, funnel-shaped, lilac-pink flowers are produced in small attractive clusters.

In the Malaysian highlands there are a few wild species of Rhododendron that should be tried as garden plants. Some grow on the ground and others as epiphytes on tree branches. Under cultivation, where growing conditions can be controlled, they could probably be induced to flower more frequently, a great advantage as it would extend the range of flowering plants available, especially in the highlands. Hybridization could be attempted as some of the species produce large trusses of attractive strikingly-coloured flowers. Hybridization has been done between highland and

Randia macrantha

Strophanthus grata

Randia macrantha

Rhododendron indicum (Azalea)

Reevesia thyrsoidea

Sanchezia nobilis

Solandra longiflora

Solandra longiflora

Sambucus javanica

Reevesia thrysoidea

Tecoma stans

Tecoma stans

lowland species with some degree of success but this work needs to be continued.

Rhodomyrtus tomentosa (Rose Myrtle, Kemunting)

This plant is found wild on sandy sea coasts, especially on the eastern side of Peninsular Malaysia. It has grey-green leaves and large pink flowers which blend well with the soft leaf colour. Small fruits are produced containing a purple pulp and this can be eaten raw or used for making jam. The plants grow into very dense bushes up to 1½ m high and, in coastal areas especially, they would make a good, thick hedge resistant to sea winds. Full sun is necessary with fairly dry growing conditions and the plants will then flower almost continuously.

Ricinus communis (Castor Oil Plant)

Although this plant is grown commercially in some parts of the world for the production of oil, there are many cultivars, and a number of these are grown as ornamentals because of their attractive, almost round, deeply-lobed leaves. It is easily grown from seeds and there are tall and short forms available which are suitable for different situations. Tall forms look good in a mixed border and short forms can be grown for some time, with great effect, as single specimens. Some varieties have pale bronze or dark purple-bronze leaves and are useful in a mixed border as they provide colour and bold leaf shapes. All forms seed freely but the purple-leaved kinds may not come true from seed. Although the plants will persist for two or three years, it is best to re-place older ones with new seedlings as they tend to become a little straggly in appearance. Some forms are used as house plants in temperate countries and may also be planted outside during the warmer parts of the year.

Sambucus (Javanese Elder)

This is a true Elder, growing into a tall spreading shrub or small tree and flowering fairly freely and continuously in a sunny place. It produces small white flowers in large flat-topped heads which are very striking in appearance and have a strong, sweet smell. The plants grow best in good soil and can be pruned to develop a good shape, but on poor soil they often become straggly and will not flower well.

Propagation is very easy from cuttings and the plants need little attention, but they do benefit from the application of a little fertilizer three or four times each year. Although the plants are best grown singly or in small groups, the lower parts of the stems often become bare and may be unsightly. However, these plants will withstand very hard pruning

so if they are cut back to about 20–30 cm above the ground, new leafy shoots will soon grow and the appearance of the plant will be improved. This species appears to grow equally well in the highlands and the lowlands.

Solandra longiflora (Chalice Vine)

This short, scandent woody shrub grows well in sun or light shade. It has oval shiny leaves and very large white or creamy-white flowers which are shaped like goblets and very striking. Good flowering occurs two or three times each year but one or two flowers are produced in the remainder of the year also. Propagation is by means of cuttings. The plant may be grown successfully in a very large pot or jar, but does best when planted out in the ground and is most satisfactory in a mixed group of species.

Solanum macranthum (Potato Tree)

This tall, spreading shrub or small tree grows very rapidly, especially when planted in good, deep soil and given regular manuring. It will then flower freely and continuously, producing clusters of large flowers which are deep violet when they open and fade to white in a few days. New flowers are produced in each cluster for about two or three weeks and consequently each group will show a mixture of various shades of violet and white simultaneously. Many fruits are produced and these resemble Tomatoes in size and shape. They become orange when fully ripe and contain many seeds which germinate easily, providing a convenient means of propagation.

These plants are best grown singly and will shape themselves without any pruning. If allowed to grow into a small tree, the crown will be hemispherical or round in shape and, being rather open, will give light shade only. When grown as a bush, pruning will be necessary at intervals to keep the plant to the size required. If flowers are needed, the branches must be allowed to grow unchecked for some time, otherwise no blooms will be produced. With this method of treatment, then, after pruning, there will be an interval of two or three months before flowers develop on the resulting new shoots. If, however, a continuous display of flowers is needed, half the branches can be pruned back and the remainder allowed to go on flowering; then, when new shoots have developed and are about to flower, the older flowering stems can be cut back. This procedure can be carried out indefinitely, especially if the plants are manured regularly.

When grown as shrubs, the plants can be used to provide a striking display of leaves in a border. The normal leaves are large and lobed, with a few prickles on each surface, but

Sambucus javanica

Solanum macranthum

Tecoma stans

Thevetia peruviana

Thunbergia erecta

when new shoots are produced after pruning, the young leaves are very large and can be 30–50 cm long, thus providing a very bold contrast of form in a border. Such large leaves are only produced on young shoots so that the plants must be hard pruned at intervals in order to encourage the continuous development of new leafy shoots.

Tabernaemontana (Susun Kelapa)

Several species of this genus are native to Malaysia and some are grown as ornamentals in gardens. The most common one resembles Gardenia in habit but has smaller flowers which are not fragrant. Flowers are semi-double and pure white and they are produced almost continuously throughout the year. The plant may be grown singly or in a mixed border where its large, shiny leaves make a useful permanent display. Propagation is by means of cuttings. Well grown plants can also be used to make an attractive low hedge.

Tecoma stans (*Stenolobium stans*, Yellow Bells)

This is a tall, rather open shrub with a pleasant light green foliage and compact erect bunches of bell-shaped, yellow flowers, produced frequently throughout the year. Many fruits will develop, each containing numerous small winged seeds, and although these germinate easily, the growth of the seedlings is a little slow and propagation is therefore better done by means of cuttings.

The shrub grows quickly and a well shaped plant will develop within a few months. After flowering, all shoots should be cut back and this will result in the development of another crop of leafy shoots which will flower after five to eight weeks. If fruits are allowed to ripen, the plant will not flower again until these have dropped away and new shoots have developed. This shrub can be planted singly, in groups, or in a mixed border, and can be used as a light screen which is most effective when in full flower.

Thevetia (Yellow Oleander)

This bushy shrub has leaves resembling those of the Oleander but the general appearance of the plant is less stiff. If left unpruned, it will grow into a small tree and can then be useful as a light screen. The most common form has

Tabernaemontana

yellow funnel-shaped flowers but there are varieties which have white or orange flowers. The plants need full sun and flower best in slightly dry soil and so can be used in a large rockery quite effectively. Flowering occurs throughout the year and many fruits are produced, but these are poisonous and children should not be allowed to play with them. Propagation is by means of cuttings or by seeds which are a little slow in germinating.

Thunbergia

Several species of this genus are grown as garden plants and some of them are shrubby in habit. These flower well and can be grown singly, in groups, in mixed borders, or as low hedges. They flower at intervals throughout the year and can be grown in full sun or light shade, but if used as a hedge then the frequent trimming will result in fewer flowers.

T. affinis is a dense, bushy shrub of medium size with neat small leaves and large flowers of a rich violet colour with a long white corolla tube. *T. erecta* is similar in habit but has smaller flowers of less vivid colouring, and there is also a form with pale flowers, sometimes almost white. *T. kirkii* has attractive lobed leaves and small mauve-blue flowers, but these are not produced very freely. All species can be propagated from cuttings and need the same cultural treatment.

Thysanolaena maxima

Although this is a grass, it is included here because it makes a dense clump of leafy stems and can be used in the garden in exactly the same way as the usual flowering shrubs. Each stem produces a large inflorescence with many very slender branches which give it a delicate appearance and can be used very effectively in floral arrangements. The plant will grow to 2 m in height and the stems carry large, spear-shaped leaves along their whole length. As the stems are produced very close together, the whole clump eventually becomes very dense and the plant could be used as an informal hedge in certain situations.

It grows best in light shade though it can be planted also in full sun, but in either situation it likes plenty of moisture in the soil. In full sun during a prolonged dry spell, the leaves will roll up during the day and this spoils the appearance of the plant, but they will recover during the night or after watering. Propagation is by division of old rootstocks. This plant can be grown in both lowlands and highlands and is most effective when planted singly because it makes a neat, shapely bush. It is useful also on steep banks, provided there is sufficient water, as the root system is very tough and helps to prevent erosion and soil slip.

Tithonia

The shrubby species of Tithonia is a sprawling plant of medium height with attractive yellow flowers which look like small sunflowers. In the lowlands, this species does not flower well but in the highlands it flowers freely and continuously so that it is an excellent garden plant in places above 600 m. In the lowlands, it is best grown for its foliage as it produces light green lobed leaves which are very decorative, but the stems should not be allowed to grow too tall because they become bare at the base and look untidy. In the highlands the plants can be grown effectively in a mixed border where other plants will hide the lower parts of the stems. The flowers are good for cutting and last for a long time in water. Propagation is by means of woody cuttings.

Vitex

Several species of this genus are found wild in Malaysia but only one shows sufficient distinction to be of use as a garden plant. This is a form of *V. negundo* which has compound leaves with three to five leaflets. The undersurfaces

Thunbergia erecta

Thunbergia erecta

Allamanda cathartica

Allamanda cathartica

Tithonia

Allamanda violacea

Thevetia peruviana

Bougainvillea (double)

Bougainvillea (double)

Bougainvillea (double)

Bougainvillea formosa

Bougainvillea magnifica

Bougainvillea

Bougainvillea (white)

Bougainvillea Mrs Palmer

Bougainvillea

Bougainvillea (orange)

Bougainvillea formosa (standard)

Bougainvillea

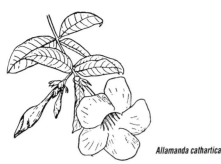
Allamanda cathartica

Bignonia magnifica

Bougainvillea hybrid

and the young stems are a bright purple. The flowers are carried in short sprays at the ends of the branches and although individually they are small, they are most attractive as they are blue. Grown as a bush, the plant is very decorative because when the wind blows through the foliage, the underside of the leaves shows up conspicuously and the whole plant appears to change colour.

It will tolerate very hard pruning and even a thick stem can be cut back to 30–60 cm high and will soon produce a crop of new shoots. If pruning is not done the plant will grow into a small tree which is equally attractive. Propagation is best from cuttings of mature wood. The species can be planted singly, or in a mixed border, or it can be used to make a light screen.

Wrightia religiosa

This is an attractive bush which can be planted in the garden in the usual way or it may be used for topiary work and bonsai culture. It makes an excellent pot plant and can be grown almost indefinitely in this way, provided it is manured regularly. The plant has slender stems with small, oval, dark green leaves which have a very neat appearance. Pendulous clusters of small, white, fragrant flowers are produced at intervals throughout the year and have a delicate appearance.

The plant will grow in full sun or light shade and tends to produce tall, upright stems which become more or less horizontal at the tip. It is best to shorten these and the side branches which develop afterwards will grow horizontally, giving the plant a layered appearance. By careful pruning, the shape of the plant can be changed so that it becomes more bushy. Propagation is by means of mature woody cuttings but these are very slow in rooting and marcotting would be more reliable.

Scandent Shrubs

Allamanda

Four kinds of yellow-flowered Allamanda are common in Malaysia and there is one with mauve or purplish flowers. Three yellow kinds are varieties of *A. cathartica*, the largest flowered one, var. *Hendersonii*, being treated as a woody climber, and the others as scandent

shrubs. The fourth kind, *A. schottii*, is more bushy in character and can be regarded also as a variety of *A. cathartica*. All Allamandas are easy to grow and will flower continuously in a sunny position with very little attention. The flowers are useful for cutting and will last several days in water. The mauve-flowered species, *A. violacea*, flowers better in the northern parts of the country and can be kept to a bush form by pruning. All kinds can be propagated easily from cuttings and var. *schottii* produces seeds regularly.

Sometimes available as house plants in cooler climates but needs careful management as it can become very large.

Bignonia magnifica (Arrabidaea magnifica, Saritaea magnifica)

A very vigorous shrub or climber with large, bell-shaped, mauve-pink flowers produced in frequent flushes throughout the year. It is best planted singly and may be kept as a bush by pruning, or it may be allowed to grow over a pergola, or into a tree. It requires full sun and occasional applications of fertilizer will keep it in good condition. Propagation is from woody cuttings.

Bougainvillea

Bougainvilleas are among the best decorative shrubs in Malaysian gardens and a number of different kinds have been introduced. All are typical scandent shrubs and may be grown as thick bushes, or on supports. Some kinds flower best if they are kept to a single stem at the base and must then be grown with a strong central support, or must be fastened to a tripod. There are three groups of varieties; (1) the *glabra* group which are perpetual flowering in Malaysia; (2) the *spectabilis* group, including hybrids between these and the *glabra* group, which flower only as a response to dry seasons; and (3) the group of Mrs. Butt, which are seasonal but can be made to flower very successfully in pots.

The *glabra* group all have purple or magenta bracts, of varying size and depth of colour. The best variety, of rich, bright colour and very large bracts, is the variety *magnifica*. The variety *formosa* has almost equally large bracts but they are paler. These large forms are very vigorous if well treated, but in order to obtain a free display of flowers it is essential that they make new growth all the time, and this means a good, deep soil, manured at intervals. A white variety is also available. There is also a form with purple, white and bicoloured flowers carried in one inflorescence. This is very vigorous and striking and is named 'Mrs. Palmer'.

The *spectabilis* group shows much more variation in colour. The old varieties are a very large magenta kind and the light brick red *laterita*. There is also a very fine large pink variety known as var. *thomasii*. These three, and others, have been hybridized together, and in some cases also with varieties of the *glabra* group, and a considerable series of shades of orange, red, pink and mauve have resulted. In Malaysia some of these flower more freely than others. All do better in the north, where the climate is more seasonal, than they do in Singapore, but some are well worth growing in the south, even though they do not give quite such fine or regular displays. Among the best is one of the first, Rosa Catalina, a small mauve-pink form that flowers freely and makes an attractive pot plant; Lord Willingdon, with a brighter colour, is also very good.

B. x Buttiana is thought to be a hybrid of *B. glabra* and *B. peruviana* and is very vigorous in growth with crimson or orange bracts fading to purple or mauve. There are a number of cultivars available such as 'Golden Glow' with pale yellow bracts fading to apricot; 'Louis Wathen' with orange bracts and imperfect flowers; 'Mrs. McLean' with orange bracts and perfect flowers; and 'Mrs. Butt' with scarlet bracts and perfect flowers. The plants flower only after dry weather, and most freely in sandy soils. Pot plants can be made to flower by controlling the watering. The general principle is that feeding and watering encourage leafy growth; starving and shortage of water encourage flowering.

Most Bougainvilleas are quite easy to propagate from woody cuttings but some forms, especially *laterita*, are a little difficult. Experiments in budding and grafting might yield some useful information on the management of these plants. When grown in pots, Bougainvilleas should be pruned after flowering, and then manured regularly to produce new growth. Some kinds will only flower when manuring is stopped and watering restricted. The varieties of Bougainvillea show some differences in habit of growth and may need slightly different methods of pruning to produce the greatest number of flowers.

Bougainvilleas are grown in many other parts of the world and do well in subtropical climates. They grow very successfully in the Mediterranean region and are often used as house plants in temperate countries. Some forms are better than others as house plants as they can be kept to a reasonable, manageable size and will flower well if watering is controlled carefully.

Congea

A species native in southern Thailand and northern Malaysia produces, very freely, small sprays of flowers in groups, each group being surrounded by four spreading mauve-pink bracts which are the showy part of the plant. It is a most useful garden plant and the flowers last well in water after cutting. When possible, it can be allowed to grow into a tree and then it makes a very fine sight when in flower. It can be pruned to keep it to a bush form but should not be pruned too frequently as this will prevent flowering. With this treatment, it makes a rather sprawling bush. Its correct name is *Congea velutina*.

There is another species which is commonly grown as a garden plant and is much more vigorous. This is *Congea tomentosa* which has larger leaves and flowers and the bracts around the groups of flowers are white or silvery white. When in full flower it is very striking and is especially so if allowed to grow into a tree. This species can also be kept to a bush form by pruning but the stems must be allowed to produce flowers between each pruning. The plant can be grown over a pergola or allowed to trail down over a bank where it is most effective and will help to prevent erosion. Both species grow easily from woody cuttings and young plants need shade for their roots until they are well established.

Holmskioldia sanguinea

This is a scandent shrub with slender stems and opposite leaves. The numerous small, orange-scarlet flowers have a curved, trumpet-shaded corolla which rises from a shallow, saucer-shaped calyx about 15 mm wide. Flowering is seasonal after dry weather and the colour of the flowers is much more brilliant in the highlands where the plants are also much more vigorous. It is best to prune hard each year after flowering, otherwise the plants may become straggly. Propagation is easy by means of woody cuttings. This plant is best grown over some kind of support and does not make

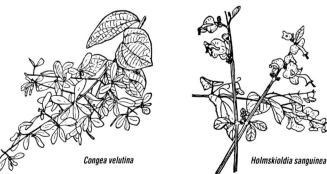

Congea velutina *Holmskioldia sanguinea*

Beaumontia multiflora

Congea tomentosa

Beaumontia multiflora

Congea rubra

Holmskioldia sanguinea

Ipomoea carnea

Ipomoea carnea

Jasminum sambac

Tecomaria capensis

Tecomaria capensis

130

Clerodendron thomsonae

Clerodendron thomsonae

Lonicera japonica

Ipomoea carnea

Jacquemontia pentanthe

Acacia mangium

Mussaenda erythrophylla

a very satisfactory bush shape, even with careful pruning.

Ipomoea carnea

A Morning Glory with rather stout woody stems and large, soft flowers of very pale pink. In full sun it flowers very freely but the soft corolla tube tends to collapse at about midday when it is very hot and sunny. On cooler days the flowers will remain in good condition much longer. The plant may be trained over a pergola, or by careful pruning it may be grown into a bush. It can be propagated from woody cuttings.

Jasmine

One of the Malaysian species of Jasmine is a woody climber which forms a reasonable bush if pruned occasionally. It has star-shaped white flowers which are very fragrant in the heat of the day.

Mussaenda

A group of woody climbers, some of which are native to Malaysia. The best garden plants are the red *Mussaenda erythrophylla* from West Africa, and the cream-coloured *M. glabra*. The red species somewhat resembles Poinsettia because of the large, red, leaf-like sepals on some of the flowers, but the habit is that of a scandent shrub and the crimson sepals are softly hairy. Both species flower well and continuously in full sun and can be kept as bushes by careful pruning. If not pruned they can be allowed to scramble into an old tree and are then most effective. Propagation is by means of woody cuttings.

Petraea volubilis

The climbing Petraea with its graceful sprays of lilac flowers is one of the best known of Malaysian garden plants and was introduced from South America. It may be treated as a sprawling bush kept in shape by pruning, or it can be grown on a support, or over an archway. Flowering occurs in flushes after dry weather several times in the year. There is a white-flowered form available in Central America. Propagation is by means of woody cuttings.

Roupellia grata
(Strophanthus gratus)

A vigorous plant with shiny, dark green leaves and close clusters of large, fragrant, pink flowers produced at the ends of the branches. The flower buds are dark crimson, waxy in appearance and most decorative. In full sun, it can be kept in flower almost continuously by regular pruning and will make a shapely bush, but if not pruned it will produce very long stems growing through and over neighbouring plants. These will not produce many flowers, but if they are trained over a support in a fairly horizontal position many side shoots will develop and each of these will produce a cluster of flowers. The flowers are excellent for cutting and last a long time in water. Propagation is from woody cuttings.

Tecomaria capensis

Usually this plant is grown as a shrub, but if it is not pruned it will, when it is well established, produce very long trailing stems which can be tied to a fence or some other kind of support. Side shoots on these long stems produce flowers; when grown in this way the plants would be very useful in a mixed collection of climbers for a screen.

Petraea volubilis

Vernonia elliptica

This vigorous woody climber produces quantities of long leafy stems which are useful for covering walls and fences. The plant does not appear to flower in Malaysia but propagation is easy from cuttings of old wood or from pieces of stem which have rooted where they touch the ground. The plant will eventually make a dense cover but must be trimmed from time to time to keep it tidy. It is very useful for covering large retaining walls in full sun as the stems trail downwards over the stones and seem to be unaffected by the heat. When the plant has grown sufficiently dense, it reduces considerably the amount of heat and light reflected from stones or concrete.

Woody Climbers

Afgekia

A strong and quick growing climber with attractive foliage and large trusses of cream and pink pea-shaped flowers with pink bracts. Each inflorescence continues flowering for several weeks. The plants can be grown over a pergola and are easily propagated from seeds.

Allamanda

The large-flowered form, *A. cathartica* var.

Hendersonii, cannot be treated as a shrub in the same manner as the other forms because the stems are relatively thin and grow very quickly so that they need some kind of support constantly. The plants are best grown over an archway or pergola, or on a trellis, and if the long stems are allowed to hang freely, they will flower very well and the plants are then most effective. This climber does not make a dense cover but if it is pruned when young, so that many stems develop, it will make a reasonable thin screen. When possible, it can be allowed to grow up into an old tree and because it does not make dense growth it will not harm the tree and the groups of large yellow flowers will be seen to great advantage.

Argyreia nervosa (Elephant's Ears)

This is an extremely vigorous plant and will cover large areas in a very short time. The whole plant is densely covered with white hairs which give it a silvery appearance. Short clusters of flowers are produced in the axils of the leaves; although they are quite large, the petals are relatively small and not at all conspicuous because of the dense coating of white hairs on them as well as on the sepals. The plant should not be grown on a light fence as it will quickly become too heavy and the fence will collapse. On a strong support it makes a very effective screen and can be used also to shade a patio. At one time it was grown very commonly in many gardens but seems to have fallen out of favour, probably because it is such a strong growing plant and not really suitable for small gardens.

Bauhinia

There are several very fine Malaysian orange-flowered Bauhinias which are woody climbers often seen growing through the crowns of tall forest trees. Most are too large for small gardens but one of the best is *B. bidentata*. Another species, *B. kockiana*, flowers at a moderate size and the large flowers are produced fairly frequently. It is one of the best woody climbers for this country and needs good, deep soil with shade for its roots. It can

Strophanthus gratus

Afgekia

Bauhinia kockiana

be trained over an arch or pergola or allowed to grow into an old mangosteen tree, or some other kind of tree. Propagation is from half-woody or green cuttings in a closed frame and young plants must grow for about three years before they flower freely. Seeds can be used when available.

Beaumontia

This is a group of strong woody climbers with large, cup-shaped, fragrant, white flowers. The finest is *B. murtonii* from Thailand, but *B. multiflora* flowers more freely, especially in the south of Malaysia. *B. jerdoniana* is only successful in the northern areas of the country. All of these plants need very strong supports and can be propagated from woody cuttings. Seeds are produced occasionally and can be germinated.

Bignonia

Many Bignonias native to tropical America are used as garden plants, but few of them flower well in Malaysia. The commonest garden species is *B. magnifica* (*Arrabidaea* or *Saritaea magnifica*), which is mentioned under 'Scandent Shrubs'. *B. rotundata* (*Arrabidaea rotundata*) has small, pale pink flowers produced seasonally in great abundance after the leaves have fallen. *B. venusta* (*Pyrostegia venusta*) has beautiful tubular, orange flowers which are produced abundantly in the highlands but do not develop in the lowlands although the plants will grow there quite easily. In the highlands, this climber is one of the most spectacular plants and if grown over an archway or on a fence it makes a striking display of flowers for most of the year.

B. unguis-cati (*Macfadyena unguis-cati*) has large yellow flowers which are not produced freely. *B. chamberlaynii* (*Anemopaegma chamberlaynii*) has smaller, paler yellow flowers, grows strongly, and flowers freely throughout the year. Although it can be grown over an arch or pergola, it is best on a trellis or supported on the side of a house where the branches can be allowed to hang down so that the flowers can be seen to greater effect. This plant is not spectacular but has a quiet charm which can be enjoyed continuously as there are no strong colours to tire the eye. It can be propagated easily from cuttings.

Camoensia maxima

A handsome woody climber with very large, heavily fragrant flowers, which, unfortunately, are shortlived. The plant is very vigorous and can be grown over an arch or pergola. Propagation is by means of woody cuttings but they are slow in growth.

Chonemorpha fragrans (Getah Gerip Merah)

Three species of this genus, all very similar,

Beaumontia multiflora

Camoensia maxima

are commonly found in Malaysian gardens. All are very large and vigorous and will cover the roof of a good-sized pergola or plant house. They flower freely, producing large, funnel-shaped, white, fragrant flowers. Propagation is by means of woody cuttings which are slow in growth, but marcotting is also possible.

Chonemorpha fragrans

Clerodendron splendens

A handsome climber with medium-sized bunches of showy scarlet flowers, but it does not flower very freely in the southern parts of the country. It is a much larger and more vigorous plant than *C. thomsonae* which is mentioned later.

Ficus pumila (Creeping Fig)

A woody climber which holds to its support by short roots. The dark green leaves are small, and the plant makes a good cover for a bare wall. A form with variegated leaves is available but always looks slightly unhealthy. When the plant reaches the top of its support it develops woody branches with much larger leaves, together with long, oval or oblong, pale green figs which are inedible. These fruiting shoots should be removed to encourage the growth of more shoots which attach themselves closely to the wall. The latter should be trimmed back from doors, windows and the eaves of the house. Propagation is from cuttings which are slow to root, but when well established the plants grow rapidly and may even become rather a nuisance because the stems can invade pots and grow densely in among other plants. This fig should not be allowed to grow up the trunks of trees and onto the main branches as it will make them misshapen and, because of the strong growth, it will shade the smaller branches, causing them to lose their leaves. Both forms are commonly available as house plants in temperate countries.

Ficus pumila

Lonicera (Honeysuckle)

One species of Honeysuckle grows quite well and flowers a little all the time. The plants are not as large or heavy as some of the other climbers mentioned in this section and do not need a large support. They grow best in good soil with regular manuring and full sun.

Lonicera

Odontadenia

Mucuna bennettii

Quisqualis indica

Quisqualis indica

Pyrostegia vanusta

Stephanotis floribunda

Odontadenia

Thunbergia affinis

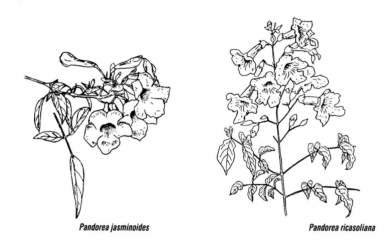

Pandorea jasminoides　　　　　*Pandorea ricasoliana*

Thunbergia grandiflora

Mucuna bennettii (New Guinea Creeper)

A very large woody climber introduced from New Guinea in 1940 and when in flower is one of the most spectacular of all garden plants. For several years it was one of the most popular climbers grown, but it does need a large space and is not really suitable for small gardens. The plant is best grown over a large pergola or over a patio where the long flower trusses can hang freely underneath the foliage and will be seen to the greatest advantage. The brilliant orange-scarlet flowers are large and closely arranged on the stems and make a magnificent display.

Mucuna can also be allowed to grow up into a tall tree such as Tembusu so that when the flowers open the tree appears to have large red lanterns hanging in its crown. Seeds are sometimes produced naturally but can be obtained also by hand pollination and will germinate easily. Marcotting can be done from woody parts of the stem but rooting is slow and handling of the marcots needs some care. If well grown, the plants will flower in about eighteen months, and afterwards should flower once and sometimes twice each year.

Odontadenia

This tropical American species is one of the best woody climbers which can be grown in Malaysia. The flowers, which are large, fragrant and apricot yellow, are produced in groups almost throughout the year. Woody cuttings are slow to root, but marcots can be obtained, and when the plants become established they are vigorous and will need a strong support.

Pandorea

Two species are grown locally, one Malaysian and the other from South Africa. *P. jasminoides* has neat dark green foliage and sprays of flowers which are almost white with a red throat. It needs well drained soil and full sun and although it will grow and flower in the lowlands, it is much more vigorous in the highlands. *P. ricasoliana* (*Podranaea ricasoliana*) is less woody and has light green foliage with trusses of very attractive large, pale pink flowers produced almost continuously. This also needs well drained soil and full sun and does well in the highlands where it is suitable for an archway or a fence. Both species can be propagated from cuttings.

Passiflora

Several Passion Flowers will grow in Malaysia. In the lowlands, the Buah Susu (*P. laurifolia*) is very vigorous but does not flower freely enough to be a good ornamental plant. However, the flowers are large and attractive with a good scent and the plant will make a

Passiflora quadriglandulosa

good screen when grown on a fence. If fruit is needed, two or more plants must be grown so that cross-pollination can occur.

The purple Passion Fruit (*P. edulis*) grows and fruits well in the highlands. Of decorative species, a pink-flowered one with narrow petals (*P. quadriglandulosa*) grows very vigorously and flowers freely in the lowlands, and in the highlands, *P. vitifolia*, with scarlet flowers and rather similar leaves, is very handsome. Some other species are grown but are uncommon.

Pereskia aculeata

This is a member of the Cactus family and needs fairly dry conditions. in order to grow well. It has normal leaves which are bright pink when young and change through pale yellow to light green as they mature. Although these plants can be kept short by pruning and make an excellent ground cover, they do, in addition, produce long trailing stems which will climb through neighbouring bushes. The plants can be used in dry troughs, or allowed to trail over large rocks, or they can be grown against a very hot, sunny wall. The long stems are a little slow in growth and their main disadvantage is that they are very spiny.

Porana paniculata (Bridal Creeper)

A vigorous climber with small, deep green leaves suitable for growing over archways and pergolas, or it can be grown against a wall. Two or three times each year the whole plant becomes covered with short dense inflorescences of small, white, fragrant flowers and is a most attractive sight. It is easily propagated from cuttings.

Quisqualis indica (Drunken Sailors, Rangoon Creeper)

This is a vigorous climber which can cover a large support but is easily kept to a reasonable size by pruning. Several times each year the plant becomes covered with small bunches of fragrant flowers which are white at first and become crimson as they age. Root suckers are produced freely and can be used for propagation, but stem cuttings can be used also.

Stephanotis

A slow-growing climber with beautiful, fragrant, white, wax-like flowers. It needs full sun and a well drained soil but never becomes very dense. Sometimes grown as a house plant in other countries and needs a framework of some kind on which it can climb.

Strongylodon macrobotrys (Jade Vine)

Although this plant has very handsome bluish-green flowers, it is a little temperamental and will not always grow well. It can be grown in the lowlands or in the highlands but seems to be more vigorous in the latter. It should be grown over a pergola or an archway so that the flowering stems can hang freely below the foliage. The inflorescences are up to one metre in length and carry very many flowers for a long period. The plants can be grown from seed and should be tried in various parts of the country in order to find out the conditions which give the strongest growth. If only this plant were a little more vigorous it would be an excellent garden plant because the flowers are of such an unusual colour.

Thunbergia

Two large coarse climbers often grown in gardens are *Thunbergia laurifolia* and *Thunbergia grandiflora*, both of which are extremely vigorous and produce long hanging inflorescences of large white or pale blue flowers. Both plants are best grown on a pergola where the flowering stems can hang below the foliage. The flowers are visited a great deal by large carpenter bees and the inflorescences are covered, especially when they are young, with many small black ants which take the nectar produced from very many tiny glands on the sepals. Both plants can be used on a strong support as an effective screen, and both can be propagated from cuttings.

In the highlands, another species can be grown and this is *Thunbergia mysorensis* (*T.*

Porana paniculata

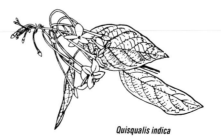

Quisqualis indica

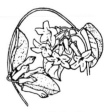

Stephanotis

coccinea). It is fairly vigorous and is best on a pergola where the hanging inflorescences can show effectively. The flowers are medium-sized with yellow and reddish-brown petals of rather unusual shape, giving the inflorescence a distinctive appearance.

Slender Climbers

Antigonon leptopus (Honolulu Creeper or Corallita)

This is a very useful vigorous creeper which can be used as a light screen on low fences. The lower parts of the plants tend to become leafless after some time but if they are pruned hard, new shoots will soon grow to form an effective screen. The flowers are produced in open sprays and may be white, pink or deep pink. They are useful for cutting because they last for some time in water. The stems produce most flowers when they have grown to the top of a fence or a pergola and it is best, therefore, to grow the plants on a low support so that the display of flowers will be more effective. Seeds are produced and can be used for propagation, but those from white-flowered forms do not come true. Cuttings may also be used to produce new plants.

Aristolochia

There are many species of this genus, the flowers always of a curious shape, some being known as Dutchman's Pipe. Some have a very foul smell, including the very large *A. gigas* var. *sturtevantii*, which has flowers nearly 30 cm long. *A. tagala*, commonly grown in Malaysia, has smooth green leaves and cream-coloured flowers with dark purple markings. The fruits are most interesting as they are, at first, oblong in shape, and when they open to release the seeds, they split from the stalk end and open outwards to form a little basket in which the seeds are arranged in neat rows. One or two other species are sometimes seen but are uncommon. All species grow easily from seeds or from cuttings and are best grown

over a low fence where the flowers can be seen easily.

Asparagus setaceus (*A. plumosus*)

Most usually this plant is grown in pots for its fine, dark green, needle-like foliage. The tiny needles are not true leaves but are, in fact, modified stems, so that the plant will tolerate quite dry conditions. Long climbing stems grow from the rootstock, and the plants can be kept in dry troughs where the stems can be arranged to form a light screen. If these stems are tipped, many side branches will develop and a slightly denser screen can be produced.

The side branches are usually held horizontally so that the plant has a layered appearance, and they are used a great deal in florists' shops under the name 'Asparagus Fern' although the plant is not a fern and in fact belongs to the Lily family. Propagation is by means of division and the roots bear a number of small oval tubers. Imported seeds can sometimes be bought and these are easy to germinate. Cuttings can be tried but there is a high failure rate. This species is commonly grown as a pot plant in other parts of the world with cooler climates and, in fact, can be kept outside during the warmer months of the year.

Clematis

In the lowlands, there is a white-flowered species which has been introduced from India and is commonly grown in gardens. It has compound leaves with stalks which twine around twigs for support and the flowers are produced in short branched inflorescences. The plant is suitable for pergolas, archways or trellises and can be grown from cuttings. It is a well behaved plant which flowers freely in full sun. In the highlands, some of the larger-flowered Clematis are successful but are difficult to cultivate in the lowlands where they rarely flower.

Cardiospermum halicacabum (Balloon Vine)

This climber belongs to the Rambutan family

Aristolochia tagala

Thunbergia laurifolia

Antigonon leptopus

Clematis

and makes a very attractive covering for a fence or archway. It has trifoliate leaves with deeply cut leaflets and, although the flowers are small and inconspicuous, the fruits are very attractive as they resemble small inflated balloons. They are pale green when young and become brown and papery when they ripen. Propagation is easy by means of seeds which are produced freely.

Clerodendron thomsonae (Bleeding Heart)

An attractive plant originating from West Africa and often grown in pots where it will flower continuously. If planted in the ground it must have good drainage but in Malaysia it never becomes very large, although it will make a good show of flowers. The flowers are produced in short sprays which are often slightly flattened in shape, and each flower has large white sepals and bright crimson petals, making them very conspicuous.

Very often fruits develop and these are green at first, becoming black when they ripen, and then split open from top to bottom, revealing a bright orange fleshy lining with one to four black seeds embedded in it. The fruits are set on the persistent white sepals so that the whole structure is exceedingly decorative. Propagation can be done from cuttings or seeds (if these can be collected before they are taken by birds).

Clitorea ternatea (Blue Pea)

A slender climber with attractive solitary flowers which last one day only, although the plant produces many buds so that each day there will be several flowers opening. There are single- and double-flowered forms and they may be deep blue or white. The plants make a light screen and are not long-lived, but they seed freely so that replacement plants are available always. The blue flowers are used sometimes to dye cooked rice for local cakes.

Cobaea scandens

Imported seeds of this plant are nearly always available and it grows very well, but may sometimes be a little shy in flowering. It has large purple, bell-like flowers and is suitable for growing on fences or in a trough, provided some support is given.

Antigonon leptopus

Antigonon leptopus

Arrabidaea magnifica (bush form)

Arrabidaea magnifica

Argyreia speciosa

Clerodendron thomsonae

Tristellateia australasiae

Clitorea ternatea

Gloriosa superba

Ipomoea pulchella

Stigmaphyllon ciliatum

Aristolochia tagala

Dioscorea alata (D. bulbifera)

Although normally regarded as a vegetable, this Yam makes an attractive ornamental climber and can be allowed to grow through another woody climber without harm. The leaves are attractively veined, heart-shaped, with very long pointed tips, and frequently a small tuber or bulbil develops in the axil of many leaves. These bulbils can be used for propagation but are slow to germinate.

The plant itself grows from a tuber and the stem dies away completely once or twice each year. The tuber rests for a time and then a new stem develops. The growth of the new stem is very rapid and, as the leaves are usually well spaced along it, other plants are not troubled by shading. If necessary, the tubers can be lifted and stored in a dry place until they begin to sprout again, when they should be planted in the ground.

Gloriosa

A very beautiful climber with narrow leaves ending in tendrils, and flowers with six narrow crinkle-edged red and yellow petals which all turn upwards. The plants grow from tubers and from time to time the stems die down but after a short resting period new stems develop, producing another crop of flowers. If the plants are grown in a bed, there will always be some stems with flowers as they do not all rest at the same time. A good, rich soil and good drainage are necessary, and shade at the roots (provided by low growing plants of another kind) is beneficial. The plants will need support which can be 1½–2 m high. When well-manured, the plants produce new tubers which can be used for propagation.

The species most commonly grown is *G. superba* and the flowers are good for cutting. Another species sometimes seen is *G. rothschildiana* but it is not as vigorous in the lowlands and it has broader petals without the yellow colouring. *G. virescens* with self-coloured flowers grows well in Singapore.

Ipomoea

The deep blue Morning Glory (*I. learii*) grows and flowers well if planted in good soil where it will receive morning sun. It grows strongly in the lowlands and in the highlands, where the flowers last much longer. It is not long-lived and should be renewed each year; this is easily done by propagating from cuttings. The very pale mauve *I. pulchella* with much divided leaves is useful for covering wire netting fences and screens, but it does tend to bunch at the top of the netting, leaving the lower parts open and bare. Many other climbing plants show this tendency and some careful management is necessary.

A more robust species with similar leaves and flowers of a deeper mauve is *I. digitata*, but it is not quite as useful for screening. *Ipomoea horsfalliae* is a very fine species with flowers of a deep wine red but, as it does not usually become very dense, is best grown for ornament only.

The Moon Flower (*Ipomoea bona-nox, I. alba, Calonyction aculeatum*) has a very similar habit to the Morning Glory, but the large, white, fragrant flowers open at dusk and the process is most intriguing to watch. Each flower lasts for one night only and if the plants are in a trough on a patio or veranda, the sight and scent of the flowers can be enjoyed by anyone sitting inside the house.

Plants will bloom for two to three months if they are well grown and, as they are sparingly branched, it is wise to grow three or more of them close together so that a better display of blooms is obtained. Seeds are produced freely and will germinate very easily, especially if sown as soon as they have ripened. The annual Morning Glories, with flowers of many shades of blue, mauve, red and pink, are very beautiful, but shortlived; they are best grown in pots or troughs with supports of split bamboo.

Ipomoea cairica (Railway Creeper)

Originally cultivated as an ornamental, this plant has now gone wild and is found throughout the country as a weed. However, it still has some ornamental use as the flowers are large and a well grown plant can be completely covered with them during the mornings. It is a useful plant for covering awkward fences where little else can be grown but it has a tendency to grow to the top of the fence where it develops a dense mass of stems and leaves which can be unsightly. If the stems are cut back almost to ground level new shoots will soon develop and by pruning can be encouraged to branch so that the lower part of the fence can be hidden. A little fertilizer will help to produce good leafy growth.

The large mauve-pink flowers last for one day only but a succession of bloom is produced over a long period of time. The plants need the minimum of attention and are easily propagated from seeds or cuttings, but they must be kept away from neighbouring bushes which would quickly become covered and would die.

Jacquemontia pentantha

A slender climber with small leaves and sprays of sky-blue flowers, each of which resembles a small Morning Glory. The flowers remain open for almost the whole day and a succession of new blooms is produced for many weeks. The plants are best grown in full sun on a low support as they do not become very dense.

Mixed Acalypha siamea, Erhetia microphylla

A hedge is a living fence or screen, tall or low, formal or informal, for use or ornament, or both. In Malaysia, few kinds of plants are commonly used for hedges, and much more variety might be attempted. It is true that for the normal trimmed hedge of 1½–2 m in height, few shrubs are as suitable as the common Hibiscus; but often an informal untrimmed hedge is as useful as a trimmed one, and for this purpose many flowering shrubs can be used. Much more might also be made of low hedges of shrubs with small foliage, and of tree hedges 6–7 m in height.

The subject of hedges or screens of trees is discussed later in this book. The most useful trees for this purpose are the common Casuarina, the wild Cinnamon, an Acacia, the common Tembusu and the Madras Thorn, all of which respond well to pruning. Naturally, other trees may also be used, the choice depending a good deal on how much space is available. Trees planted as a screen need room to spread on each side or they will not be leafy to the bottom, and the bigger the tree, the greater the thickness required. In a later chapter are notes on the use of some of the tufted palms for planting as screens or tall hedges. The taller kinds of bamboo may be used in a similar way.

Trimmed Hedges of Medium Height

Hibiscus

For planting an ordinary Hibiscus hedge, the procedure is as follows. A trench at least 1½ m wide and 1½ m deep should be dug along the line to be occupied by the hedge, and the earth mixed with a liberal amount of compost as it is returned to the trench. A little rock phosphate, say about 130 g to each 30 cm of trench length, may also be added with advantage. The returned earth will lie about 15 cm above the surrounding ground. Into the earth so prepared, the Hibiscus cuttings should be placed, in two rows 30 cm apart, the cuttings in one row alternating with those in the other, the spacing in each row being also 30 cm. The cuttings should be quite woody (not green), about 40 cm long, one-third being inserted into the ground. It is usual to place them obliquely, to secure several shoots from each.

Pseuderanthemum atropurpureum hedge

If the weather is dry, the ground should be kept moist by watering. In two or three weeks the growth of young shoots from the cuttings should be established; if the weather continues to be dry, watering should be continued, but under normal weather conditions in most parts of Malaysia, this should not be necessary. As soon as young growth is well established, indicating that good roots have formed, a little manure or fertilizer may be forked into the top soil to stimulate more vigorous growth, and this may be repeated at monthly intervals.

The next item of care is to prune the young hedge. It is important to do this in good time or the young shoots will grow straight upwards and not make the spreading bushy growth at the base which is essential for a good hedge. If early pruning is neglected, the result will be a thin hedge which will not provide a good screen. As soon as the young growth is about 60 cm high, it should be trimmed back to about 40 cm; then, when subsequent growth reaches 1 m, it should be cut back again to about 60 cm. This will encourage a spreading bushy growth. The process is repeated at intervals until the hedge attains the desired height. It is most important at this stage to encourage the growth of as many branches as possible from the cuttings so that the base of the hedge will become very thick and dense. Patience is essential as the height of the hedge increases slowly, but this is much better than allowing a

Acalypha siamea hedge (2-3 feet)

Ixora coccinea hedge

Barleria cristata hedge

Hibiscus rosa-sinensis hedge

Bamboo hedge

Ixora coccinea hedge (yellow form)

Sanchezia nobilis hedge

Thunbergia erecta and *Acalypha siamea* hedge

Erhetia microphylla

Hibiscus rosa-sinensis hedge

Strobilanthes hedge

few shoots to grow quickly to the required height with the end result of a poor, thin screen and a hedge which would not be fulfilling its proper function.

The care of a mature hedge is to trim it regularly, to weed out other plants from the bottom (especially tree seedlings), to apply a good mulch of compost and manure about once a year (forking the old soil 30 cm on either side of the hedge), and to watch out for caterpillars or other insect pests. This periodical manuring is essential if the hedge is to be kept in vigorous condition; a starved weak hedge is neither useful nor beautiful.

Dwarf Bamboo

After Hibiscus, probably the commonest kind of trimmed hedge in Malaysia used to be of Dwarf Bamboo, but its popularity has waned over the past few years. The ground is prepared as for a Hibiscus hedge, and then pieces of bamboo are planted at intervals of 30 cm. Bamboo pieces are prepared by dividing the rootstock of clumps from an old hedge, each piece having two or three culms. They must not be planted too deeply, and will need support.

It is not necessary to trim back the young shoots as in a growing Hibiscus hedge, because the bamboo will produce a succession of new shoots from the base, and these will thicken the hedge. The young shoots should be topped as soon as they have reached the height desired for the hedge. Manuring should be carried out as for the Hibiscus hedge, but only after new growth is well established. As new shoots appear from the base, they should be tied in to ensure their upright growth as part of the hedge, and this practice has to be continued throughout to secure a good, thick hedge. About 1½ m is the minimum height for a satisfactory hedge of this kind; the maximum height is about 2½-3 m.

The maintenance of a bamboo hedge is similar to that for a Hibiscus hedge. It is most important to pull out all tree seedlings as soon as they appear, or they will grow up and supplant the bamboo. Grass and other weeds should be removed continuously from around the bases of the bamboo stems, because if they become well established they are extremely difficult to remove, and if they are very dense the lowermost branches of the bamboo may die away and thin places will appear at the base of the hedge.

Regular manuring once a year is very beneficial; compost and a little rock phosphate is sufficient. Sometimes a section of the hedge may die away completely; if this happens, the dead portions should be dug out together with a little of the surrounding soil and burnt. This should destroy any pests or diseases which may

Cordia

have caused the die-back. New soil mixed with a little compost should be used to fill the resulting hole and this left unplanted for three or four months. Then, preferably when the weather is fairly wet, new pieces of bamboo can be planted in order to fill in the gap.

Trimming must be done regularly and evenly if the hedge is to look good; a well trimmed bamboo hedge can make a most effective background to a formal garden, but a badly trimmed hedge is always ugly. It is of course possible to have an untrimmed bamboo hedge, allowed to grow freely without trimming; such a hedge needs pruning every six months to prevent it from becoming too widespread. Some of the larger bamboos may be treated in a similar way, especially the solid bamboo with slender culms and fine foliage; but such taller bamboo hedges are difficult to keep trimmed, as tall step ladders are needed.

One problem with bamboos is that the leaves drop continuously and if the hedge is trimmed this will cause little difficulty except that some of the dead leaves will become caught up amongst the smaller branches and can remain there until they decay. This can easily make the hedge unsightly and the groups of leaves should be removed as far as possible. If the hedge is untrimmed, the leaves fall and eventually form a thick layer for some distance away from the base of the hedge; this will prevent the growth of grass or any other plants. If it is intended that grass should grow as near as possible to the base of the hedge, then dead bamboo leaves must be removed regularly each week. With the larger bamboos this problem can be especially troublesome.

Cordia (String-bush)

A shrub which became very common in Malaysia some years ago is Cordia, the String-bush which makes a good hedge, and can be treated exactly as Hibiscus. It has dull green leaves, very small white flowers and red berries. The berries are eaten by birds, and the seeds are scattered abundantly. Seedlings appear everywhere in the garden and when allowed to persist in hedges Cordia can eventually replace plants such as Hibiscus.

A well kept Cordia hedge is very neat and can be more than 2 m tall. However, during the last three or four years, a great number of Cordia plants have been completely destroyed by the attack of beetles. The beetle larvae eat the leaves and as soon as the plant develops new leaves these also are eaten so that the plant very quickly dies. In some parts of the country the beetle attacks are less severe and it is still possible to grow this plant, but in other parts it is almost impossible to grow it even with regular spraying to destroy the beetles.

Other possible shrubs for trimmed hedges of

medium height are the various species of Acalypha, Bixa, the common purple Bougainvillea, Lantana, the Chinese Privet, various kinds of Panax (Polyscias), a plant named (probably incorrectly) *Hemigraphis alternata*, and a small tree called Streblus. Most of these are dealt with in the chapter on ornamental shrubs and climbers. Their general treatment as hedges is similar to that described for Hibiscus, but each of them has peculiarities, and some notes on these are given below. Other shrubs might also be used. One question always to be considered is that, for a hedge, a considerable amount of planting material is required, and this may not be available in the case of the less common shrubs. An equally important question is the ease of propagation.

Acalyphas

These make quite good hedges, and the bright red-leaved variety gives a distinctive colour, which may or may not be found suitable as a background for other plants. Acalyphas are not so vigorous or so free in branching as Hibiscus, and they need better soil and more frequent manuring to keep them in healthy growth. A really good, deep trench and plenty of compost are needed in the first place, and the subsequent cultivation and manuring at yearly intervals should be done very thoroughly. A weak Acalypha hedge is not ornamental, nor is it useful. Acalyphas all grow easily from cuttings.

In the highlands, some of the Acalyphas, especially those with red leaves, develop much more brilliant colour than they do in the lowlands, and some of them appear to be more vigorous also. Acalyphas with different coloured leaves can be combined to make a very interesting hedge, but the length of such a hedge should be limited as the colour can be so intense it becomes wearisome to the eye. A good combination of Acalyphas for a mixed hedge is to plant *Acalypha siamea* in the front and this should be kept to about ½ m high. Behind this can be grown the red-leaved variety, kept to about 1 m or more in height, and behind this the green- and yellow-leaved variety can be grown to about 2 m high.

Such a mixed hedge needs frequent clipping, so that it remains dense, and frequent manuring to ensure continuous growth with plenty of leaves. This treatment is essential because if the hedge becomes thin with few leaves only, the colour effect will be lost entirely. The coloured leaved Acalyphas are subject to attacks by beetles which eat the leaves. If this occurs, the plants should be sprayed regularly with an insecticide, otherwise the leaves will be eaten away until only a network of veins is left. New leaves would be

Acalypha siamea

eaten as they develop and the plants would eventually be weakened.

Bixa (Anatto)

This can be used as a hedge from 2 m in height, but it is probably best at about 2½ m or more. Its large leaves hang down so that it appears very dense as a hedge and its reddish colour when young is very attractive. Bixa is grown from seeds, which are produced in quantity by old plants. These should be sown first in seedbeds of fine soil, and transplanted when about 15 cm high.

As Bixa is a large shrub, it needs more root room than Hibiscus, and a wider and deeper trench is necessary for satisfactory results – at any rate if a tall hedge is required. Another most important point is regular pruning, as described for Hibiscus, to ensure a good bushy growth spreading on both sides of the line of the hedge; if this is not done, the hedge will soon look thin and the leaves will hardly be enough to make a screen. A Bixa hedge 2½ m high should be at least 1 m thick; if well grown, there are few hedges of this height to equal it in appearance.

If a Bixa hedge has grown a little tall and has become thin, it can often be rejuvenated by cutting back very hard. New young shoots will soon appear on all of the branches and growth can be encouraged by application of fertilizer and regular pruning. Within a few months, a dense new growth will have developed and the hedge will be as good as new.

Bougainvilleas

These do not all make satisfactory trimmed hedges. Some are too rampant and some not bushy enough. The best for a hedge is the common small purple-flowered kind, *B. glabra* var. *sanderiana*. This will make a low trimmed hedge without any support but for a hedge of 1½ m or so high a strong support of posts and wires is needed, the posts preferably of reinforced concrete. Given such a support, the Bougainvillea can be tied to it so as to cover it evenly, and the side shoots trimmed off just as with a Hibiscus hedge. After many years, the hedge will be self-supporting as the branches become densely interwoven and the main stems of the plants grow large and stout.

The preparation of the trench and the planting of cuttings can be carried out as for Hibiscus, except that one cutting per 30 cm is enough. A well grown and well trimmed hedge of this kind looks very fine and is extremely effective, as the plants are tough and prickly. Regular trimming is necessary and will encourage the development of more prickles. A Bougainvillea hedge allowed to spread unchecked is difficult to handle and to restore to a trim condition, but trimming need not be so drastic as to prevent flowering. The colour of the flowers of such a hedge may have to be considered in relation to other garden plants.

Gardenias

These plants can hardly claim a place as a general purpose hedge, but they will form quite a good, thick hedge if they receive plenty of care in the younger stages. They require a rich, well dug bed at the start and frequent applications of cattle dung or compost after growth has commenced. A Gardenia hedge should not be allowed to grow too high as it will become thin at the bottom; a maximum of 1½ m is sufficient. Gardenias are not very rapid growers and require cutting less than most hedges, but it can stand a fair amount if necessary.

Streblus

Lantanas

The better and more free-flowering kinds make attractive flowering hedges, but they do not last in good condition as long as a Hibiscus hedge. It is best to strike the cuttings in a shaded nursery bed, and transplant them to the hedge site when they are rooted. Different kinds of Lantanas differ in habit and vigour of growth, and a hedge of one variety only is best. The plants are very prone to become leafless at the base and will then look very untidy. Hard pruning and fertilizer may remedy this but recovery cannot be guaranteed.

Libocedrus

This is a small Cypress-like conifer with a very neat foliage which may be trimmed without injury. It would make a beautiful hedge. Small cuttings are not difficult to root.

Ligustrum sinense (Chinese Privet)

This is a small tree with small leaves and little clusters of fragrant white flowers. It makes a very good trimmed hedge at the hill stations and although it grows quite well in the lowlands, making a satisfactory hedge, it does not flower as well as in the hills. Cuttings grow very easily.

Panax (Polyscias)

Several kinds of Panax are used as hedges. Those with small foliage look attractive when young, but are apt to become unsightly when old as the base becomes thick and woody and there are not enough branches near the ground. They could probably be kept in better condition if given regular manuring; but too many people forget that a hedge, like other plants, needs cultivation and manure from time to time if it is to grow well.

The form with green and white variegated leaves is usually reliable and there is another vigorous form with large pinnate leaves which are yellow when young but become dark green as they mature. If this form is pruned regularly, it will make a very dense low hedge up to about one metre in height and is very attractive when it shows a large number of the bright yellow young leaves. However, if it is not pruned, the stems can grow up to 5 m high with leaves near the tips only, and then they look very ungainly. All varieties are easily grown from cuttings.

Streblus

Common in Kedah, this is a small tree with small harsh leaves. It is sometimes used in the north of Peninsular Malaysia as a hedge, and could probably be used in the south also. When trimmed, it makes a very dense bushy growth and the small foliage is neat and pleasant, so that it makes a good formal hedge. It is not very fast in growth.

Low Trimmed Hedges

In formal gardens, a low hedge of ½–1½ m high is often useful and effective as part of the design, and there are certain shrubs which adapt themselves well to such planting. A hedge of this kind must have small neat foliage, and must survive close trimming.

Acalypha

One of the best plants for the purpose is a small Acalypha (*A. siamensis*) which looks quite different from the showy variegated Acalyphas already mentioned. It is easily grown from cuttings, and prefers a sandy soil. The more frequently it is trimmed, the smaller the leaves. It makes a very dense hedge which can be kept at about ½ m high as an edging to paths or borders, or it can be grown to about 1½–2 m high as a screen. In the latter case, it can be kept to ½ m in width or grown to 1 m in width. Such a wide hedge can be so dense that one can sit upon the top of it without making any impression. This Acalypha grows very well in full sun or in light shade and can be used for topiary work.

Bougainvillea

The common purple Bougainvillea also makes a good low trimmed hedge; such hedges have been very successful on Penang Hill, where the plant does not grow as vigorously as in the lowlands. The cuttings are planted rather close, and the new growth is trimmed to form a thick bushy hedge about 60 cm high with the top cut level. After this is established, it may be allowed to grow enough to produce a massed flowering before further pruning if desired, but pruning must not be too long deferred or the hedge will become straggly. As

Shaded wall covering

Shaded wall covering

Vernonia elliptica as wall covering

Tristellateia australasiae as wall covering

Lagerstroemia indica, Acalypha wilkesiana, Sanchezia nobilis

Tecoma stans, Lagerstroemia indica, Acalypha wilkesiana

Jasminum sambac as fence cover

Jatropha pandurifolia, Acalypha siamea

Ehretia

Malpighia coccigera

Triphasia

this Bougainvillea is generally very vigorous in growth, except in poor sandy soils, a minimum of manuring only is needed.

Ehretia

During the last few years, a shrub called Ehretia, with pretty, dark green, glossy foliage, like tiny holly leaves, has been used increasingly as a hedge and can be trimmed to a very neat shape. If the hedge is to be self-supporting, then two or three rows of plants would be needed and frequent pruning should be done after the plants have reached 15–20 cm in height so as to encourage the development of a large number of branches. This will make the base of the hedge very dense and, to maintain this condition as the height increases, such pruning must be continued. It means that the hedge will take longer to reach the desired height but this is offset by the fact that it will be very thick.

Often, this plant is grown in a single row close to a wiremesh fence. Such a hedge is usually thin and provides a light screen only. A single row of Ehretia plants will not usually produce a dense hedge but may be sufficient to make a low trimmed hedge at the edge of paths or borders. A great number of small white flowers and little round red fruits are produced so that after its acquisition seedlings will be found everywhere in the garden at all times of the year. Propagation is very easy from seeds or by means of cuttings. This plant will thrive in full sun or light shade.

Malpighia

Another small shrub with miniature holly-like foliage is a species of Malpighia (*M. coccigera*) and it is less frequently grown at the present time. It makes a very attractive hedge up to one metre high, and frequently carries masses of small white star-like flowers. It can be grown easily in pots and trimmed and trained into various shapes. Propagation is easy by means of cuttings and best growth is obtained with well cultivated soil and regular application of manure.

Triphasia (Lime-berry)

A thorny shrub of the Citrus family, Triphasia or the Lime-berry makes a good trimmed hedge to about 1½ m high. It has pleasant small foliage and occasionally flowers, producing small red fruits which yield seeds for propagation. This shrub would appear to thrive best in a sandy soil.

Informal Hedges

Many different shrubs may be used for informal or untrimmed hedges or screens; a border of tall shrubs often serves the latter purpose, but we are here concerned rather with boundary hedges. One advantage of an untrimmed hedge is that it has free scope for flowering, as a trimmed hedge has not; it may therefore be used as part of the colour scheme of the garden. Another advantage is that the shrubs show their distinctive habit, and this may be used to give variety to the landscape. But it must always be remembered that a hedge is essentially a background against which the other plants in the garden will be viewed, and a flowering hedge should be selected with care. For quite formal gardens a plain green, carefully trimmed hedge is usually the most suitable, but elsewhere less formality and more colour may be desirable.

In general, an informal hedge should have a wider trench dug for planting than a formal one, as the shrubs will be more spreading. Some pruning of the young shrubs as they grow will probably be desirable, but less than in a trimmed hedge. The question of periodical cultivation and manuring is again most important; the plants must have vigorous healthy growth or they are unsightly and a prey to insect pests.

Acalyphas

Acalyphas probably make a better informal hedge than a trimmed one, as they can become more bushy, but they need more cultivation and manuring than most shrubs to keep them in good condition. As has been mentioned previously, some are liable to attack by night-flying beetles which disfigure the leaves.

Allamandas

The more bushy Allamandas make a very good informal hedge, but of no great height, and their growth is apt to become a sprawling thicket if not checked. Their cheerful large yellow flowers make a good background to most other plants. They are easily propagated from cuttings, and common enough for a quantity of propagating material to be readily available.

Barleria

Barlerias make useful low, informal hedges, producing occasional flushes of flowers which can last two months or a little longer, but as soon as the stems become too long and the plants look untidy they should be pruned hard back and will produce a crop of new shoots very quickly. A hedge of Barleria grows best in full sun and with careful pruning will remain leafy almost to the base for a long time. It should be well manured from time to time and will then produce plenty of leaves which will keep it dense continuously.

Bougainvillea

The smaller Bougainvilleas make good informal hedges, but again they may become too spreading in growth. They are probably better on some sort of supporting fence, along which the long young shoots can be trained obliquely. The large Bougainvilleas (Mrs. Butt and Mrs. McLean, *B. glabra var. magnifica,* and some of the *spectabilis* hybrids) are successful if supported by a single strong horizontal rail or iron pipe about 1½ m from the ground. They can be pruned much or little as desired.

Crotons

Crotons make a pleasant informal hedge or screen. For this purpose the stronger growing kinds must be selected, and provided with a well dug border one metre wide. A better effect is produced if the plants are not too varied, as a background hedge must have a certain uniformity or it will be too conspicuous and detract from the rest of the garden.

Duranta

When young and vigorous, this makes an attractive informal hedge up to 2 m or more high, and when fruiting is very decorative. It does not, however, last in vigorous condition long enough to be really satisfactory, and soon loses its thickness of growth, thus becoming less effective as a screen. Possibly in the north of Peninsular Malaysia, if well manured, it might be more successful than in the southern part.

Excoecaria bicolor

Here is an attractive shrub with medium-sized simple leaves which are purple on the undersurface. The combination of green and purple is very decorative, especially when the leaves are moved by the wind. The close bushy habit of the shrub makes it useful for screening and little or no pruning is needed. It has a white latex which is poisonous. Propagation is easily done from cuttings.

Hibiscus

Hibiscus mutabilis or the Changeable Rose Hibiscus makes a very good informal hedge, but needs very generous treatment as regards manuring to make it really vigorous. A weak plant of this kind is very unsightly and a prey to insect pests, but a strong plant has a wealth of soft grey-green foliage and a new crop of beautiful large white flowers every morning, changing to deep rose in the evening.

To plant a hedge of this species, a trench one metre wide is needed, and a generous amount of compost and manure is desirable. Cuttings are best rooted in a nursery and transplanted to the hedge (set out at one metre intervals) when well established in growth. Manuring at intervals of three months is desirable. After a year, pruning is usually necessary; this may be repeated twice or three times and then the plants are best rooted up and replaced by new ones.

Ixoras

Either the *javanica* or *coccinea* groups may be used as informal hedges. The stronger growing kinds are the easiest, but some of the slower-growing *coccinea* varieties are perhaps the most attractive. If a good display of flowers is to be maintained, an Ixora hedge needs regular spraying to destroy the caterpillars that frequently eat the flower buds. Otherwise, maintenance of Ixoras is easy, and the hedge will remain in a useful and attractive condition for many years. Occasional cultivation and manuring is however desirable and weeds should be removed from the base of the hedge.

Kopsia

This makes a pretty, informal hedge, flowering most attractively. While young, it is not thickly bushy enough to make a good screen. However, by fairly close planting and judicious pruning, the plants will form a dense screen about 2 m wide after several years. Such a hedge will reach 2–2½ m in height and careful pruning will allow sufficient growth of the twigs to give a good informal shape instead of a very clipped appearance.

Lantanas

Lantanas are probably better as informal than as trimmed hedges, but only the most free-flowering kinds are desirable, and too much mixture of colours is to be avoided. Occasional pruning is desirable, but not excessive manuring.

Calliandra surinamensis avenue

Mixed border or informal hedge (*Acalypha wilkesiana, Sanchezia nobilis, Pseuderanthemum atropurpureum*)

Mixed border or informal hedge (*Acalypha wilkesiana* (2 forms) and *Lagerstroemia indica*)

Alternanthera, Philodendron, Cyperus, Graptophyllum. Partly shaded balcony.

Carpark planting (*Terminalia* and *Peltophorum*)

Polyscias, Graptophyllum, Philodendron

Balcony planting

Balcony planting

Murraya paniculata
(Kemuning)

A very neat shrub with dark green shiny foliage, *Murraya paniculata* makes a good informal hedge but can also be trimmed and kept formal in appearance. It is slow in growth but will reach, eventually, a height of about 2 m. The rather small flowers are white and have a very sweet scent and are often followed by a crop of orange-red fruits which are also attractive.

Pittosporum tobira

This is a shrub or small tree, native of China and Japan, which has attractive, glossy, bright green foliage. It grows well in Singapore, but only in very well cultivated ground. If sufficient care were given, it would make a beautiful informal bushy hedge, but the necessary expenditure of time and work is perhaps hardly justified. The species has also proved very susceptible to attack by a scale insect.

Sanchezia nobilis

Not usually thought of as a hedge plant, but when well grown, *Sanchezia nobilis* makes a somewhat unusual informal hedge up to about 1–1½ m high. It grows easily from cuttings which should be planted fairly close together in a prepared trench. It is probably best to root the cuttings first in a nursery bed and put them into their permanent position as soon as they are well rooted. They should be planted 30–50 cm apart in the hedge and must be pruned a little so that branches will develop near ground level.

The dark green leaves are large and give the hedge a dense appearance. Flowers will be produced on long stalked inflorescences and are unusual in appearance. They are long and tubular, bright yellow, with the stamens just showing at the opening of the tube. As soon as they have died away, the flower stalks should be cut to encourage the development of more branches. Sanchezia can be used also with other shrubs in a mixed hedge.

Tecomaria capensis

This makes a very fine informal hedge of about one metre high. The ground must be well dug, and plants put in about 45 cm apart. When well grown and in full flower, such a hedge is a brilliant sight. A sunny situation is essential.

Thunbergia

The shrubby species of Thunbergia such as *T. affinis* make excellent low hedges. They are very dense and flower at intervals throughout the year but will not grow more than about 1½ m high. Propagation is easy from cuttings

Screening with *Dyera* and *Dillenia*

and the plants can be grown in full sun or very light shade.

Some of the other shrubs mentioned in Chapter 6 can also be used in informal hedges, but it is best to choose those which are easily propagated and which branch fairly freely. Some species have attractive flowers but make good hedges despite the fact that, with regular trimming, very few or no flowers are produced.

Most usually a single species of plant only is used for a hedge of any kind, but it is possible also to use two or more species in various ways to make a hedge. As mentioned earlier, two or three Acalyphas can be grown one behind the other to give a striking formal hedge with a bold and well defined colour pattern. However, in a simple, straight, formal hedge, plants with leaves of different colours can be grown in adjacent blocks, giving a striped effect, although this could be a little wearisome for constant viewing. It is important that all species or varieties used are of about equal vigour and respond well to manuring and pruning.

A 'tapestry' hedge can be grown by using a combination of three or more plant species with leaves of different sizes and colours. They are allowed to grow together so that groups of the different kinds of leaves appear unevenly through the hedge, forming irregular patterns. Such a hedge showing several colours will be of great interest, so it is best situated on its own away from beds or borders of flowering plants. Regular manuring and pruning are necessary to maintain strong growth and plenty of leaves. A hedge of this kind may be of various shades of green, or stronger colours, such as yellow, white, red and purple, can be introduced.

8 TREES AND PALMS

Planting and Care of Young Trees

A tree should live and remain an object of beauty for many years; work spent in giving it a good start is therefore a worthwhile investment, and indeed the failure to take the necessary trouble may result in the production of a weak and misshapen tree that never attains its full stature nor displays its true beauty. A tree cannot be vigorous unless its roots have good conditions for growth; and its trunk and crown will not be shapely unless it has had training and pruning in its early life. The care of a young tree therefore falls into two parts: the treatment of the roots and the treatment of the parts above ground.

The extent of preparation of the ground before planting a tree depends in some measure on the nature of the subsoil. If this is a heavy clay, it is desirable to break it up to as great a depth as possible to give good drainage and consequent aeration for the roots when the tree is planted. In an open and well drained soil, such deep digging may not be necessary. But in any case, a hole at least one metre square should be made in the planting site, and the soil mixed with compost or manure as it is returned; the level of the earth so returned will be 15 cm or more higher than the surrounding ground. If the soil is a heavy clay, it might be well to discard some of it entirely and substitute a lighter soil. A planting hole prepared in this way should give a young tree sufficient root room and nourishment for the first year of its life. After that, it will benefit from a further supply of manure forked into the surface ground around it, or if the ground around the hole is very hard, deep digging and manuring of a circle (or parts of it) 60 cm wide beyond the original hole will be of great benefit.

For most trees, it pays to plant out the seedling as soon as it is big enough to stand in an isolated position; that is at about 50 cm high. Many such trees will attain a height of 3 m, and some even more, in the first year after planting. Of course, it may be possible to procure a young tree 2 m high or more from a nursery, and in this way a few months can be saved; or it may be possible to transplant a young tree growing elsewhere. In the case of transplanting such a tree, it is a good thing to cut its lateral roots, without lifting it, a little while beforehand; then when it is removed the shock will be less severe. A method of propagating trees by large marcots is described earlier, in Chapter 4.

When a young tree is planted, it should be tied to a strong stake to keep it upright, and if it is a seedling from a pot, a shelter (made most easily from a palm leaf) should be placed over it to protect it from the sun until its roots are well established in their new home. It should be watered if the weather is dry during the first few weeks. A transplanted tree of larger size also needs shelter in sunny weather, and usually also needs to have some of the young shoots pruned off, as the roots are damaged in transplanting and cannot supply enough water to maintain the full crown of leaves. The tying of a young tree to the stake is important. It must be firm enough to hold the plant securely and prevent chafing, but it must not be too tight, or it will cause a wound as the tree grows in thickness. Ties should be inspected frequently to see that they are satisfactory.

As the young tree grows it must be pruned to give it the shape desired when it is full grown. This, if neglected, cannot be rectified easily afterwards. In the case of a shade tree, it is usually desirable to have a good, clean trunk to a height of 2 m or more before any branching occurs. Side branches on the young tree must therefore be removed up to the height desired. These branches are best removed with a sharp knife when they are young, and must be cut back flush with the main stem. In this way the scar will be covered quickly with the new bark and later on will be invisible.

If a tree is needed for screening down to ground level, the treatment of course is different. Side branches are encouraged, and if none are produced, the leader may be stopped. In practice it will be found that the kinds of trees chosen for screening usually produce plenty of side branches from an early stage. Such bushy young trees will normally soon be independent of the support of a stake. A tree of which the side shoots are pruned, however, needs support for some time, as its crown, when produced, is some distance above ground and the trunk will not be sufficiently large at this stage to support it properly. Consequently, the crown of such a young tree can be broken or badly damaged by very strong winds or heavy rain. If the first few branches grow long and straggly, without branching again, they are best cut back rather severely; this will make the beginnings of a good bushy crown.

The need for pruning varies considerably with the nature of the tree, but it is not difficult to judge. If a tree is to be grown singly in order to show off its natural shape to the best advantage, then it is not necessary to do any pruning as branches will be shed automatically and the shape will develop without any interference. Such a tree must be planted well away from any others so that good all round development of the crown occurs. If it is shaded, even slightly, by any other trees then the crown will become one-sided or irregular in shape and this condition is almost impossible to correct.

Tree Descriptions

Acacia

For a long time the only species of Acacia grown for ornament in the lowlands of Malaysia was *A. auriculaeformis* but, at the present time, three or four other species are available which grow very successfully and should be more widely used by gardeners and landscape architects. In all of these species the apparent leaves are, in actual fact, the enlarged and flattened leaf stalks. The true leaf form is seen only in seedlings where the first three or four leaves resemble small Mimosa leaves.

A. auriculaeformis makes a bushy tree up to about 10 m in height, and is very rapid in growth. The trees show considerable variation in density of crown but this may be affected partly by the type of soil in which the trees are growing. In some cases the crown is very thin and in others it is very dense and makes an excellent screen. The small, fragrant, yellow, Mimosa-like flowers are produced abundantly throughout the year. Seeds germinate easily and seedlings are ready to plant out in three or four months after sowing. It is better to collect seeds from trees with good dense crowns.

These trees are a little untidy as they drop their leaves continuously throughout the year and constant sweeping is necessary if the grass underneath the trees is to be kept tidy. Many coiled fruits are produced and on thin-crowned trees these can be unsightly as they remain attached to the branches for a long time after the seeds have been shed, giving the tree a very untidy appearance.

Young plants with a trunk of about 4–8 cm in diameter will recover from very hard pruning, but older trees will not do so always. Consequently, young plants can be quite useful in a mixed hedge as they produce a quantity of strong young shoots which make the hedge more dense. Careful pruning will maintain the plants in this condition for a long time, but the new shoots should not be allowed to become too tall and woody otherwise after pruning, new branches may not develop low enough on the main stem to be of use in the hedge. The object should be to keep the main stem much shorter than the hedge itself so that pruning will encourage new young branches to develop in the middle of the hedge where they are needed most.

A. cincinnata is a shorter, much more bushy tree growing to 5–6 m in height and with a very dense crown having a soft, cushion-like appearance because of the long narrow leaves.

Acacia auriculaeformis

Adenanthera pavonina

Many fine branches are developed in the crown, giving it a delicate appearance, and when a few main branches are allowed to grow from just about ground level they become twisted and curved as they enlarge, making the tree most attractive. The relatively small size of this tree, together with the delicate appearance of the crown and the elegant shape of the branches, make this a most desirable plant for the small garden. When the plants are well established, tiny yellow flowers are produced in little round heads, and these are followed by long thin pods containing several small seeds. Fruits are produced almost continuously in the lowlands and the seeds germinate easily and quickly when taken from the pods and sown immediately.

A. mangium is a medium-sized tree with a dense crown up to 10 m in height and with much larger and darker green leaves than *A. auriculaeformis*. It does not drop its leaves as frequently as the latter species and makes an excellent screen. The crown is not wide spreading and the tree is good for lateral shading. Its white fluffy flowers are carried on long spikes which themselves are arranged in clusters on the branches and are very conspicuous when they appear.

A. richii is a commonly grown species easily recognized by its silvery grey leaves. It is a small tree with a rather thin crown and is best grown singly so that the shape of the crown and the leaf colour can be appreciated. The colour shows up best if the tree is grown with a background of plants with dark green foliage, or in a position where the sunlight can fall on it at an angle so that the silvery colour of the leaves is emphasized. Seeds are produced freely and germinate easily. The tree is relatively shortlived and is prone to damage by wind.

Adenanthera pavonina (Saga)

This is a tree of rapid growth, of moderate height and it has a pretty light foliage. It is more bushy in shape than the Rain Tree, but quite spreading enough to be useful for shade. It produces many bright red shiny seeds which are often used by children for games. The flowers are not conspicuous and the trees are deciduous. Propagation is by means of seeds and these germinate in small numbers over a long period of time.

Agathis alba (Damar Minyak)

A native species with a tall, narrow, cylindrical, evergreen crown which can be grown from seed, but the seedlings need shading for about two years and afterwards can tolerate full sun. Growth is rather slow and new shoots and leaves are produced two or three times each year. It is suitable for larger gardens and can

Alstonia

Acacia mangium

Acacia richii

Acacia cincinnata

Araucaria excelsa

Acacia richii

Amherstia nobilis

Cananga odorata

Cananga odorata

Amherstia nobilis

Andira inermis

Baeckia frutescens

Bauhinia monandra

Bauhinia purpurea

Calophyllum inophyllum

Acacia cincinnata

Araucaria

Bertholettia excelsa

Callistemon

be grown singly or in a group of mixed species, or when well grown it could be used for avenue planting. It will grow in the lowlands or the highlands.

Alstonia (Pulai)

Two or three species of this genus are wild in Malaysia and should be used as garden trees as they have an interesting shape when young and are not fussy about soil requirements. They are not suitable for small gardens as they will eventually become very tall. The plants are deciduous and when the new leaves are developing on the branches the trees are very attractive as they have a light and airy appearance when the sun shines through the new foliage. While young, the trees have a layered appearance but as they become older this is lost and the crown becomes oval or cylindrical. Young trees showing the layered shape are very formal and can be used for single planting.

Amherstia nobilis

An introduced, medium-sized, evergreen tree with a dense rounded crown of dark green foliage. The bright red flowers are unusual in shape and are held on long, hanging inflorescences. Seeds are not produced very often and propagation is by means of marcots; consequently the tree is not very common. It is a little too large for small gardens but when there is space it makes an excellent single specimen and gives a little shade. The young leaves are also coloured and appear in a large tassel at the ends of the branches, pink at first, becoming cream and then finally turning green. The young shoots and leaves hang limply at the tips of the branches and as they mature, gradually assume the normal position. Great care must be exercised when cutting a marcotted branch and this should be done in two or three stages as mentioned in the chapter on propagation.

Andira inermis

An introduced tree with a dense round crown of dark green pinnate leaves. The pale pinkish purple flowers are produced very close together in great quantities in inflorescences at the ends of the branches and last for a considerable time. The tree is deciduous and loses all of its leaves about once each year, usually after the dry season. However, new leaves will be produced within a few weeks and these are pale green, giving the tree a light and airy appearance.

Propagation is easy by means of seed. The tree is appropriate planted in a small garden as a single specimen because its roots do not come above the soil surface or damage underground drains.

Araucaria

Three or four species of this introduced genus are grown as ornamentals. They can be kept in pots for some time but eventually must be planted out into the ground as they become too large. All kinds are dark green with evergreen foliage but the leaves are sharply pointed and this makes the handling of the plants a little painful. The plants are formal in appearance with branches arranged in whorls at fairly wide intervals along the trunk, but in older trees the neat appearance may be lost because of the breakage of some of the branches. When grown in pots, especially as they become larger, the plants should receive regular application of fertilizer and will then retain their foliage indefinitely, but if they are starved or kept too dry, then many leaves and some of the branches will drop so that the plants will look untidy.

Plants grown in the ground should be watched carefully as they are very susceptible to attack by white ants and the base of the trunk should be examined frequently so that treatment can be applied promptly at the first sign of damage by these insects. If this is not done the tree can be killed within a month and is liable to fall during a heavy storm or strong wind. *A. bidwilii* and *A. excelsa (columnaris)* are common pot plants and *A. cunninghamii* and *A. hunsteinii* are also used quite frequently.

Arfeuillia arborescens (Hop Tree)

A small, slow growing, evergreen tree, with a dense round crown of light green leaves. It can reach 10 m in height, but by pruning it can be kept much shorter than this for a long time. It can be used in small gardens as single specimens, or in groups in larger gardens, and can also be used for an avenue in which trees of no great size are needed.

Baeckia frutescens (Cucor Atap)

This is a native Malaysian plant which deserves more attention from gardeners. It is suitable for very small gardens and has the appearance of a drooping miniature Casuarina. It will grow in poor soils and in very dry conditions and, although it is slow growing, no pruning is needed. The thin, pendulous branches carry very small needle-like leaves and little white flowers. It can be propagated from seeds or by means of suckers. It makes a shapely plant when grown singly and could be used also for an informal hedge; in a group of other plants it provides a useful contrast in form and foliage.

Bauhinia

There are several species of Bauhinia which form small trees 5–7 m in height, and are very useful for garden purposes, though they do not always flower as freely in Malaysia as in more seasonal climates. They all have rounded, deeply cleft leaves. The best is *B. monandra*, which has beautiful pale pink flowers with one petal marked with crimson. *B. purpurea* has flowers entirely rose-mauve, and the nearly related *B. blakeana* has flowers of a much richer colour. *B. blakeana* is grown from cuttings or marcots, the others from seeds. These trees grow best in full sun and if they become untidy they will tolerate quite hard pruning, after which a crop of new and vigorous young shoots will develop.

Bertholettia excelsa (Brazil Nut)

Although this introduced species will eventually become very large, it is slow growing and has a very shapely and majestic crown. Because of its size it is only suitable for the largest gardens or for parks and can be planted singly or in small groups. It can reach 30 m in height with an oval or cylindrical crown of large, wavy-margined leaves. Flowers are produced after about five to seven years and develop over the top of the crown. They are followed by large, woody, round fruits. The large size of this tree makes it eminently suitable for landscaping in public parks or around large buildings.

Brownea

This is a genus of small spreading trees, rather slow in growth and with beautiful flowers and foliage. The leaves droop in long clusters when young and spread out when they are full grown. The flowers are in large compact clusters of brilliant red hanging among the leaves. To see the flowers to advantage, and also to use the tree for shade purposes, it is well to make some sort of a supporting framework, so that one can stand or sit beneath the branches which usually spread at too low a level to allow for this. *B. ariza* is the most vigorous species, but has smaller heads of flowers and smaller leaves than *B. grandiceps*. Browneas may be grown from marcots or cuttings (slow to root, in a closed frame); seeds are not common.

Callistemon (Bottle-brush Tree)

This small, open-crowned tree originates from Australia and is grown frequently for its light appearance and the bright scarlet flowers which are produced two or three times each year. Flowering occurs on the young twigs which show a peculiar method of growth because leafy sections alternate with flowering sections which have no leaves. The tree grows best and flowers most satisfactorily in dry conditions. Too much rain or wet soil will result in a great deal of leafy growth and flowering will be reduced or may not occur. Young specimens will flower when they are only 1½–2 m high but the slender branches should not be pruned as they will then become drooping and flowers will develop. The scarlet flowers have long stamens and are closely arranged on the stem which then has the appearance of a brush, hence the common name of the tree. Regular pruning will result in a crown which is more dense but flowering will be reduced. The tree is suitable for small gardens because of its size and the open crown which does not cast too much shade. Propagation is by means of cuttings.

Calophyllum inophyllum (Penaga Laut)

A slow growing evergreen tree giving excellent shade when the crown has developed. Although it is best suited to medium or large gardens, it can also be used in smaller ones as it can be kept to size by pruning. In young trees, the crown is very dense but in older ones it can become a little more open and spreading as the main branches enlarge. The leaves are large, oval, flat and dark green, giving the tree a very characteristic appearance. Flowers are produced once or twice each year over the whole crown of the tree. They are white with yellow stamens and have a strong, sweet fragrance. Later the globular pale green fruits develop and hang in small clusters over the crown of the tree. Propagation is easy from seeds and the tree will tolerate quite hard pruning.

Cananga odorata (Kenanga, Ilang-Ilang)

An evergreen tree which can reach 15 m in height and has a slightly drooping appearance because the ends of the branches hang downwards. Clusters of sweet-smelling flowers are produced on the leafy twigs and are green at first, becoming yellow as they mature. There is a dwarf form which grows to about 3 m in height, developing a small, dense, round or oval crown, and is excellent as a single tree in a small garden. The tall form is conical when young but the crown becomes more open when it is older and it is best grown in a group of mixed species. Kenanga flowers are always on sale in the market.

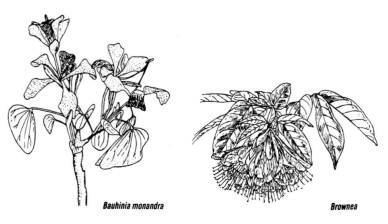

Bauhinia monandra

Brownea

Cassia fistula

Cassia grandis

Cassia grandis

Cassia siamea

Cassia siamea

Cerbera odollam

Cerbera odollam

Cinnamomum iners (with young foliage)

162

Cerbera odollam

Cassia fistula
(Rajah Kayu, Indian Laburnum)

This is one of the finest trees for Malaysian gardens, being of moderate size and producing most beautiful flowers. It is often slow in its early stage, but quite vigorous when growth is well established though it does not normally flower until it is several years old. Old trees lose their foliage gradually about every nine to twelve months (depending on the nature of the individual tree), and when nearly bare produce flowers and young leaves together. The pendulous groups of large yellow flowers are a most beautiful sight against any sort of background.

Propagation is from seed, or large branches may be marcotted. There is a little variation in the yellow colour, some plants having deep yellow flowers while in others they are very pale. Young plants are eaten badly by caterpillars unless regularly sprayed with insecticide. If this is neglected, the plants can be killed as the caterpillars eat all of the leaves, including the new young leaves as they are produced, so that the plants are unable to make sufficient food. Older plants are not troubled in this way and the extra trouble involved in spraying while the plants are small is well worthwhile because the tree is such a lovely sight when it has begun flowering.

Cassia multijuga

Another yellow-flowered Cassia, quite different in habit from the last species as it has a smaller foliage and more open growth, with compact bunches of flowers at the ends of the branches. It is much more rapid in growth (if given good soil conditions), flowers in two years, and at frequent intervals afterwards. When old it is apt to become untidy and needs careful pruning; in any case it is not a long-lived tree, but is very useful on account of its quick growth and frequent flowering. It is propagated by seeds or cuttings.

Cassia siamea (Johar, Kassod Tree)

Very similar to the last species in appearance, but with shorter inflorescences and more closely arranged flowers. It needs the same treatment as the previous species and can be propagated from seeds or from large cuttings about 2 m long. Suitable in very small gardens as it can be kept to size by pruning.

Cassia spectabilis

Another useful tree for the moderate-sized garden, if regularly pruned. It produces large, open inflorescences of pale yellow flowers at the ends of the branches, and these should be cut back after flowering. This will prevent the formation of fruit which can give the tree a very untidy, straggly appearance for several

Crescentia cujete

Cassia fistula

Cassia multijuga

Dyera costulata

months until they are shed. Seeds are produced freely, and seedlings are rapid in growth, flowering in two years.

Cassias, Pink-flowered

These are *C. javanica, C. nodosa, C. renigera,* and *C. grandis.* The most beautiful of these is *C. renigera* but it is rather delicate under Singapore conditions and dies back somewhat at every leaf change; it is best not to prune off the dead parts, as this seems to cause further dying-back. *Cassia nodosa* is common as a wild tree in Pahang, and seems to vary somewhat in the freedom of its flowering. It also seems to be connected by intermediates with *C. javanica.*

Probably *C. javanica* is the more useful tree of the two in Malaysia; it grows rapidly in good ground, makes a pleasant spreading shape, and periodically bears beautiful pink flowers, though never so showy as *C. renigera. C. grandis* (native of South America) is the largest of all the pink Cassias and flowers well in the north of Malaysia, where the climate is more seasonal, but not in Singapore. The large pinnate leaves are a rather sombre dark green and the trunk is also very dark. The tree is too large for very small gardens. Propagation is easy from seeds.

Casuarina (Ru)

In a well drained soil, there are few quicker-growing trees than the common Casuarina, which is therefore often used to produce a screen. For this purpose the trees should be planted fairly close together. When planted 3½ m apart, they give a close screen of a considerable height in three or four years. The foliage is of course light, and does not give as dense a screen as a broad-leaved tree, but it is satisfactory for many purposes. If desired, the trees can be made more bushy by topping them from time to time; in this way a tall hedge can be produced though this is not often attempted in Malaysia. Plants are grown from seeds or marcots. *Casuarina equisetifolia* is variable in habit and if an even row of trees is desired, they should be marcotted from one parent tree.

Two other species of Casuarina are grown commonly as ornamentals, *C. nobilis (sumatrana)* and *C. rumphiana.* The former has stout green twigs held upright and closely bunched at the ends of the twigs while the latter has much thinner green twigs which are slightly pendulous. Both of these species have a formal conical shape when young, but the crown becomes more open in old plants. They are slow-growing and best planted singly so that the shape can be seen to advantage, but are not really suitable for small gardens because, as they get older, the crowns become very spreading and need a great deal of space.

Cerbera odollam (Pong Pong)

This is an excellent tree for screening as it has a dense oval crown up to 10 m in height although it can be kept much shorter than this by pruning. It produces quantities of white flowers almost continuously throughout the year. The large, shiny, dark green leaves are always attractive and the trees often bear many oval green fruits which are about the same size as a tennis ball. The tree can be grown singly or as a screen and is suitable for small and medium-sized gardens. Propagation is from seeds.

Cinnamomum iners (Kayu Manis, Cinnamon)

This small bushy tree is one of the best for screens of moderate height. It reaches a maximum height of about 8 m, is bushy right down to the ground, has a pleasant foliage at all times and particularly beautiful, bright red young leaves. The only disadvantage is its rather slow growth. It takes about three years

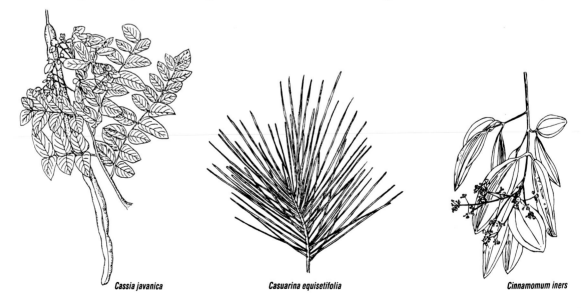

Cassia javanica　　　*Casuarina equisetifolia*　　　*Cinnamomum iners*

to make a plant 3 m high. One way to overcome this is to marcot vigorous branches 2 m long from old Cinnamon trees. Or a Hibiscus hedge may be planted with a young Cinnamon at every 2 m; the Cinnamons will eventually take the place of the hedge. Young trees are grown from seeds, but where the species is common, seedlings are often abundant and may be dug up and transplanted.

Cochlospermum religiosum (Buttercup Tree)

This is a rapid-growing species with an open habit, though not tall, and it produces large, bright yellow flowers continuously. For this reason it is a most useful tree in the garden, although a little pruning is necessary in order to maintain a reasonable shape. Good soil and a sunny position are essential for good growth. Propagation is from seeds or marcots.

Cratoxylon (Mempat, Derum)

This is another Malaysian genus which deserves more attention and might well be planted in gardens though it is hardly used at the present time. The best species is *C. formosum*, a medium-sized tree of upright growth and with a round crown when it is older. It is a deciduous tree and large numbers of small pink flowers are produced all along the slender branches after the leaves have fallen. This occurs at about nine to twelve month intervals and the foliage is pleasant though not distinctive. A tree in full flower is a very beautiful sight and the flowers resemble almond blossom. Propagation is from seed which is produced in quantity and the young trees grow fairly quickly.

Crescentia cujete (Calabash Tree)

A small tree with a dense round or oval crown carrying dark green, shiny leaves. Although the flowers are large, they are relatively inconspicuous because they are green, yet are very attractive under close viewing. The fruits are large, round, green and shiny and grow to about 15–20 cm in diameter. They are very hard and contain a large number of small seeds embedded in a whitish pulp. The plant is suitable for small gardens and can be kept to size by careful pruning. Propagation is from seeds but these are sometimes a little difficult to extract from the fruit as the rind is very tough and not easily broken open.

Cupressus (Cypress)

These are small conical trees useful in a formal garden and rather slow in growth. More rapid-growing kinds have been introduced from Sri Lanka as *C. macrocarpa* but are apparently hybrids between this and another species. These vary considerably in habit, the best being very handsome, but they appear to be shortlived under Malaysian lowland conditions, though good in the highlands. The trees can be propagated by means of small green tip-cuttings.

Dacrydium

There are four species of this genus in Malaysia and all grow in the highlands. Most have densely arranged needle-shaped leaves which give the trees a distinctive appearance. They grow well in the highlands and when young are conical in shape. They will grow in the lowlands but need good care and attention while they are small.

Delonix regia
(Poinciana or Flame of the Forest)

This is the best known flowering tree in Malaysia; its spreading crown makes it a useful shade tree also, but seasonally it is bare of leaves for a month or more. The beautiful scarlet flowers need no description. There is some variation in colour, the two main types being a larger flower of deep red, and a smaller one more orange in colour. Young trees are rapid in growth, slowing down as they begin to form their crown.

Pruning in the early stages of crown production is often useful to produce a good shape. Without pruning, these trees develop several very long arching branches which bend over until they are almost horizontal. New branches rise from the middle of the first ones and these also become long and arched and the process may be repeated several times before the crown begins to take shape. However, if the first branches are pruned hard, new ones will develop near their bases and these also can be pruned in a similar way. If this process is repeated several times, a reasonably dense crown can develop in a much shorter period of time than would be needed if no pruning were done.

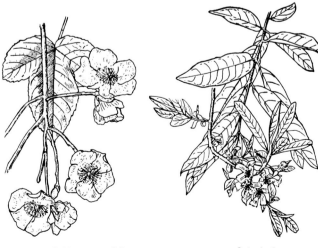

Cochlospermum religiosum   *Cratoxylon formosum*

when viewed from a distance because the neat mounded appearance of the bushes then shows up to very great advantage.

Dyera costulata (Jelutong)

This is a common forest tree in Malaysia and makes an excellent ornamental for large gardens or parks. It will grow to 30 m in height and has a conical to oval crown of dark green, shiny leaves which are shed about once each year. The branching is very regular so that the tree is formal in appearance and is highly suitable for avenue planting. Its growth is relatively slow; consequently it makes a very good single specimen in a large garden as it retains its branches almost to ground level for many years. The flowers are inconspicuous, but the fruits are large curved pods, containing many winged seeds which provide an easy means of propagation.

Elateriospermum tapos (Buah Perah)

This tree is also found wild in Malaysia but is an excellent ornamental as it has a dense round crown of very dark green narrow leaves. New leaves are bright pink or red and when they develop over the whole tree crown it becomes very conspicuous and from a distance appears as though it is in flower. Although it will grow to 30 m in height, it will remain less than half this height under garden conditions and would be best grown in a medium or large-sized garden. It could be planted singly or as an avenue, or in groups of mixed tree species. The flowers are inconspicuous but fruits are produced and propagation is easy from seed.

Enterolobium cyclocarpum

This is a very fine large tree which is deciduous and sheds its leaves once each year. Old trees grown singly have a flattened dome-shaped crown and can be 20–30 m high with a very large trunk. Young trees have crowns which are more irregular in shape. The leaves are bipinnate with very small leaflets and give the tree an appearance of great refinement. The tiny white flowers are produced in small globular heads which are inconspicuous, but the fruits are most decorative as they are broad coiled pods which become dark, shiny brown when ripe. They make excellent decoration if dried and polished. Some trees produce fruits regularly but others seem to produce very few or none at all. Propagation is easy from seeds but if these are not available then marcots can be made. This tree is best planted singly so that its fine shape can be appreciated, but it could be used for avenue planting, provided the plants were set at least 4–5 m from the roadside because the roots come above ground near the trunk and the canopy is very wide-spreading. It is quite unsuitable for small gardens.

Enterolobium saman (Samanea saman, Hujan-hujan, Rain Tree)

This is a fine, large, spreading tree for overhead shade. It is also much favoured by epiphytic ferns and orchids which add a great deal to its beauty. Unfortunately, it is too big for any but rather large gardens or parks. It makes a fine roadside avenue tree but must be planted well away from the roadsides as the main roots tend to come to the surface of the soil and can damage paths made of tarmac or paving stones. It loses its leaves once each year, although it may not become completely bare. New leaves are produced within a few weeks and these are accompanied by large heads of pink and white flowers.

Seeds are produced abundantly and are easy to germinate. The seedlings are ready to be planted out three or four months after germination. A well grown plant should produce a crown of about 10–11 m diameter in five to seven years.

Erythrina variegata (indica) (Dadap, Coral Tree)

In the northern parts of the country where there is a strong seasonal climate, Dadap trees lose their leaves in the dry season and the branches are covered with scarlet flowers. Under such conditions they are most handsome and well worth planting in the garden, more especially as they are quick in growth and easily propagated from large cuttings 2 m or more in length. The stems bear scattered large spines and should be handled carefully.

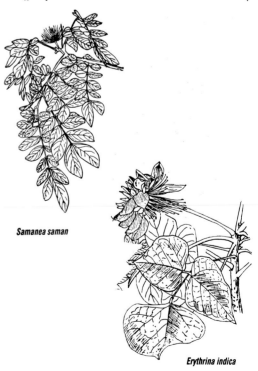

Samanea saman

Erythrina indica

In the south they do not flower well and are not worth planting. However, there is a form with variegated leaves which can be used with some effect in a garden as it is the foliage which is needed rather than the flowers.

Eugenia grandis
(Jambu Laut, now *Syzygium grandis*)

This native species is normally found on sea coasts but grows equally well when planted inland. It is a fine tree for larger gardens and has an oval dense crown of dark green, shiny leaves. It is evergreen and about twice each year produces a crop of flowers. These are formed at the ends of the branches in such large quantities that the whole crown of the tree can be hidden under the trusses of fluffy white flowers. While young it makes a good screen as it holds its branches almost down to ground level; then, as it increases in height, the lower branches are gradually shed. Generally it needs no pruning as it shapes itself. It is also an excellent avenue tree as the roots do not come to the surface of the soil. Propagation is easy from seed which is produced in great quantity.

Fagraea fragrans (Tembusu)

This slow-growing tree is probably the best local species for a tall screen. It is bushy to the ground (if the lower branches are not pruned), has a solid mass of pleasant foliage, moulded in a characteristic way by the branching of the tree, and once a year the crown is covered with great numbers of fragrant flowers. It will grow well in a heavy clay soil and is too large for a small garden, but in one of moderate size it is very useful. If the trees become too large they can be drastically pruned without damage, and afterwards will quickly produce a crop of new shoots. In a smaller garden, a single tree can be kept to a suitable size for many years by careful pruning but may not flower as abundantly as an unpruned specimen. Propagation is from seeds, which are very small, or from marcots. Seedlings can be found near old trees and are easily transplanted. Seeds must be removed from the fruit and washed, otherwise germination will be very slow.

Fagraea fragrans

Ficus benjamina (Waringin, Weeping Fig)

Any Fig tree should be planted well away from storm drains or underground drains as their extensive root systems can cause damage as well as block the drains. *F. benjamina* is a medium-sized tree with a round or oval crown and can be used with excellent effect for landscape planting. However, it does show some variation in the shape and density of the crown so that if even planting is desired, cuttings should be taken from trees with good, well-shaped, dense crowns.

The tree produces large quantities of small orange-red fruits about once each year and these attract very many birds when they are ripe. Seedlings can be grown in pots for a number of years before they finally become too large. The plant will tolerate airconditioning, provided it receives sufficient light. For this reason it is used a great deal for decorating public buildings and has become a very popular house plant in temperate countries. If given regular manuring and a weekly spray with water it will always be attractive in appearance. However, it does produce large quantities of roots which can extend for some distance out of the pot and these should be cut away as soon as they appear. Usually no pruning is needed as the plant will shape itself. Propagation is easy by means of cuttings.

Ficus elastica (India-rubber Plant)

This is a large evergreen tree with a round, open crown and large, oval, leathery, dark green leaves. It can be grown in small gardens where it can be kept to size by regular pruning, but some care must be exercised because of the root system. In larger gardens the crown needs some pruning when it is young, otherwise it is liable to develop a poor shape. Roots may develop from some of the larger branches and when these reach the ground they will enlarge and look like a small tree trunk so that the whole plant would present a very interesting appearance. For this effect, however, a large garden is needed. The species and its varieties are among the most commonly grown house plants in temperate countries.

The new growth of the branches is very attractive as the youngest leaves are covered with bright red, cone-shaped stipules which will drop away as the leaves expand. There are some varieties of this species which have variegated leaves; all of the forms are grown often as pot plants in the tropics and as house plants in temperate countries. As pot plants, they will survive quite adverse conditions and, provided they receive sufficient light, last for a long time in airconditioned rooms. When used as room decoration, the leaves of these plants should be sprayed with water regularly. Propagation is by means of cuttings.

Ficus microcarpa

Similar in appearance to *F. benjamina* but with groups of roots from the branches and twigs. It can be used in exactly the same way as Waringin.

Ficus religiosa (Bo Tree, Peepul)

This is a medium-sized deciduous tree and is suitable for large gardens only. It has heart-shaped leaves with long, narrow tips and when

Ficus elastica

Ficus elastica variegata

Ficus religiosa

Ficus benjamina

Gardenia carinata

Ficus roxburghii

Gardenia carinata

Ficus roxburghii

Gustavia superba

Gustavia superba

Gliricidia sepium

Hevea braziliensis

Hymenaea courbaril

Hibiscus tiliaceus

Hibiscus tiliaceus

young they are pink in colour so that the tree appears as though it is in flower. The leaves fall once each year and the new foliage develops almost immediately so that there is a complete change of aspect in the garden. The tree can be used with great effect in landscape planting as it has a well-shaped crown which is attractive even after the leaves have fallen.

Ficus roxburghii (*F. auriculata*)

This very fine small tree is not suitable for the smallest gardens as it becomes very wide when well grown and covers a great deal of ground. It has thick branches carrying very large, broad, oval leaves which are bronze-green when young and become dark green when they mature. The leaves make the branches very heavy so that they are liable to snap near the base, especially during rainstorms when the weight is increased with the water on them. The tree grows easily from cuttings or marcots and young plants are a little slow to establish.

As far as possible, the lower branches should be retained and the tree will then develop a dome-shaped crown with foliage held down to ground level. In this form it makes an exceedingly handsome addition to the garden as the large leaves make it a strong and eye-catching feature. The tree may be grown singly and will look well in a formal planting scheme. It can be used also in a mixed group of species but the lower branches should then be cut away so that other plants can be grown near by; the Fig will not then develop the dome shape but it will provide useful variation in leaf form and size. Figs are produced at the base of the stem but although they are edible they are rather flavourless.

Filicium decipiens (Kiora Payung)

Although not commonly grown, this tree should be used more as it has attractive foliage, is well shaped and not fussy about growing conditions. It is an evergreen tree which will reach 20 m in height though it may remain about half this size in a garden. It has a somewhat oval to irregular crown of mid-green leaves, flowers and fruits well, and is propagated easily from seeds. The tree is suitable for single or group planting and may be grown in the open or between tall buildings.

Gardenia carinata

This Malaysian tree Gardenia can grow to about 10 m high in about fifteen years. The large, freshly opened flowers are creamy white, becoming bright orange-yellow as they age, and are fragrant. Flowering usually occurs twice each year with a few flowers produced at other times. This is a good garden tree, of upright habit, and not too tall, but is a little slow in growth and will tolerate full sun

Jacaranda obtusifolia

Jacaranda obtusifolia

Juniperus chinensis

Lagerstroemia floribunda

Lagerstroemia floribunda

Melaleuca leucadendron

Mesua ferrea (young, coloured leaves)

Mesua ferrea (conical shape of young tree)

Melia excelsa

Michaelia champaka alba

Mimusops elengi

Michaelia champaka (yellow form)

Whitfordiodendron atropurpureum

Muntingia calabura (layered shape)

the leaves are young and soft. Older leaves which are hard are less troubled by beetles but can be damaged by large grasshoppers.

These trees are also attractive when they are fruiting as they produce large sprays of hard, green, conical fruits which become dark brown when ripe. The fruits are still decorative after they have split open to release the seeds and can be used for dried flower decorative work.

Melaleuca leucadendron (Gelam, Cajeput)

This is a tall tree up to 30 m high with a relatively narrow crown of grey-green leaves. Under natural conditions, it grows in swampy areas but can be planted in dry ground, although it will not then grow as large. Under dry conditions, it can be grown in a small garden as it will be fairly short and the crown will be very narrow. Pruning can be done to encourage more branching and the development of a more rounded crown if this is desired. The bark of these trees is flaky and peels away in short strips. The trees can be used in gardens of any size and when well grown can make a good avenue, but they have a special use in landscape planting where there is wet or swampy ground, as they will thrive under these conditions which would be unsuitable for many other ornamental trees. Seeds are extremely tiny and growth is very slow after germination.

Melia

Two introduced species of Melia are grown commonly in Malaysia: the evergreen *M. indica*, the Nim tree, and the deciduous *M. azederach*, the Persian Lilac. When well grown, *M. indica* (Nim Tree) can make a large tree with a dense light green crown, but often in this country it remains small as it is not really suited to the climate. It grows much better in the northern parts of Malaysia where the climate is more seasonal. It can be grown in small gardens, but needs to be pruned regularly to prevent it from becoming too large. In a larger garden it needs no pruning and is an excellent shade tree. It can be planted singly, in groups or as an avenue.

M. azederach (China Berry, Bead Tree) is a small tree with a thin, open crown of light green leaves. Unless well grown, it can be untidy because the branches are widely spaced and do not develop with any regularity. If young plants are given regular applications of fertilizer and are lightly pruned to encourage more branching, they will develop a reasonably dense crown. This tree can be grown in a small garden but if space is limited, there are many other more decorative trees which can be used.

Both species of Melia are susceptible to attack by white ants which begin their destruction below ground, and the trees may become severely damaged before the white ant tunnels appear at the base of the trunk. As soon as these appear, the ground around the trunk should be thoroughly soaked with a liquid insecticide and the treatment should be repeated several times. This will usually prevent any further damage but the tree may take some time to recover.

Melia excelsa (Sentang)

Although this tree is not commonly available, it makes an excellent ornamental but, because of its size, it is only suitable for large gardens or parks. When well grown, it is very decorative with a broad, oval crown and large, dark green, pinnate leaves which give the plant a very characteristic appearance. It is very effective when grown singly or in small groups of three or five, but it can be used also as the dominant plant in a mixed group of smaller trees. Propagation is by means of seeds.

Mesua ferrea (Ceylon Iron-Wood, Penaga)

This species is native of Malaysia also. Young trees are slow to establish and need to be surrounded with low bushy cover to shelter their roots from the sun. It is best to keep them in some kind of container until they have reached about one metre in height before planting out; but if they are kept too long in a small container, their growth will be stunted and they can become misshapen. The roots will become too large and twisted and if planted out such specimens will take a very long time to recover, or they may remain stunted. If a smaller plant in a container can be transplanted with the minimum of root disturbance, it will begin growth much faster and will develop a better shape. Growth is much more rapid after the trees have reached 1½–2 m in height, and they will then become conical in shape with a very formal appearance, and are periodically covered with new brilliant red foliage. Older trees become more rounded in shape.

Mesua ferrea

A single tree in a lawn will retain its conical shape for many years and is well worth growing for the beauty of its foliage alone. The leaves are dark green on the upper surface and very pale green on the undersurface, so that when the wind blows through the tree startling contrasts of colour are seen. Planted at intervals of 5 m, the trees make a very beautiful screen after about ten years. The flowers appear irregularly in Singapore, but more regularly further north. They are exceedingly fine, being large, pure white and fragrant. Propagation is from seeds, or from cuttings (which are slow to root and should be put into a sand bed in a sheltered spot).

Michelia (Cempaka)

Two species are commonly grown in this country: *M. alba* with white flowers, and *M. champaca*, with yellow or orange flowers. *M. alba* is too large for a small garden as it will grow to 30–40 m high and has a dense oval crown of dark green, shiny leaves. *M. champaca* is much smaller with a more open conical or round crown of rather yellow-green leaves. The flowers of both are very fragrant and are often sold in the markets. *M. alba* seldom fruits in Malaysia but when seeds are produced they will germinate readily and propagation can also be done by marcotting or by cuttings. *M. champaca* fruits readily and produces many seeds which germinate easily, but marcots or cuttings can also be used for propagation. Both kinds can be grown singly or in groups and *M. champaca* is suitable for a small garden.

Millettia atropurpurea (Jenaris)

A slow growing tree with a dense, round crown of dark green, shiny, pinnate leaves. It is most suitable for medium or large-sized gardens and makes an excellent single specimen; it can also be used for avenue planting. Dark purple flowers are produced in large, dense inflorescences after dry weather and are relatively inconspicuous against the dark green

foliage. Many fruits develop and each contains one to four very large seeds which germinate very easily. The species has been renamed *Whitfordiodendron atropurpureum*.

Mimusops elengi (Tanjung)

The flowers of this tree are well known for their sweet fragrance and the tree itself is an excellent slow-growing ornamental plant. It has a very dense, round crown of dark green, shiny leaves which have wavy margins. It is suitable for gardens of any size and in small ones it can be kept to any size by pruning, but in larger ones it will shape itself and no pruning is needed. The small, white, star-like flowers are not easily seen as they are hidden by the leaves, but the fruits are more conspicuous as they are about 2–3 cm long, oval and green at first, becoming red or orange when they ripen. Propagation is easy by means of seed which germinates fairly quickly. The tree can be used for single or group planting and also for avenue planting.

Muntingia calabura (West Indian Cherry)

This is sometimes called the Japanese Cherry, but it is neither a Cherry nor Japanese. It comes from the West Indies, and has small, round fruit containing a large number of very tiny seeds. As a quick growing shade tree of small size, it has no equal. Its chief disadvantage is that bats find the fruits very attractive, and so are frequent unwelcome visitors to neighbouring houses. The bats' excreta also often does some damage to plants beneath the shade of the tree, which is thus not very satisfactory for sheltering pot plants. A young tree of this species will grow rapidly if given good soil, but in poor soil it will remain stunted for a long time. The tree could be used with some success for bonsai culture.

Peltophorum pterocarpum (Batai Laut, Yellow Flame Tree)

There are two local species of this genus, but only one is commonly planted. It is a bushy tree, with foliage quite like the Flame of the Forest, but the flowers are smaller, bright yellow and arranged in close, erect bunches. The trees are deciduous, losing their leaves slowly until they are bare; then the young new growth develops rapidly and finishes with the production of flowers. The whole of the young growth and the flower buds are covered with a thick, dense coating of dark brown, shiny hairs and are very attractive.

After flowering, large numbers of young fruits develop and these are reddish or purple-brown in colour; they are produced in such quantity that the whole crown of the tree may be covered completely, forming an added attraction. A tree in full flower or fruit is very

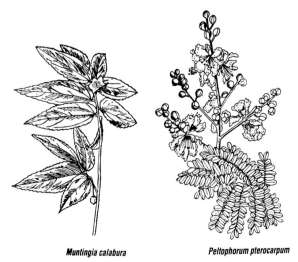

Muntingia calabura   *Peltophorum pterocarpum*

Peltophorum pterocarpum

Podocarpus rumphii

Podocarpus polystachyos (trimmed)

Pterocarpus indicus

Pinus caribaea

Polyalthia longifolia

Pterocarpus indicus

Peltophorum pterocarpum

Pometia pinnata

Pithecellobium jiringa

Salix

handsome and makes a useful specimen tree in a garden. It can also be used for screening purposes, being quick in growth and bushy in shape, but it does not carry branches right down to ground level. Young trees will flower in four or five years and are easily grown from seeds.

Pinus (Pine Tree)

Two or three species of pine are grown in the lowlands but the commonest is probably *P. caribbaea*. It will grow to 30 m in height and good specimens show a formal conical shape. However, some seedlings are irregular in growth with misshapen crowns and unless these fit in with the remainder of the planting scheme they should be uprooted. Pinus is subject to attack by white ants which can kill a tree very quickly. If white ant tunnels are seen at the base of the trunk, then the ground around to a distance of about one metre should be watered with an insecticide and the treatment should be repeated three or four times. Another species which is sometimes available is *P. merkusii* and this needs similar treatment.

Pithecellobium dulce (Madras Thorn)

This species, which forms a medium-sized bushy tree with light foliage, is actually native of tropical America, though it is much cultivated in the drier parts of south India. The climate in Malaysia is not ideal for its growth, but it does very well and the neat, small, grey-green foliage is attractive. The inconspicuous flowers give rise to coiled pods containing large black seeds surrounded by thick pink and white pulp which is eaten greedily by birds.

The seeds germinate very easily but the tree does not grow as fast as Acacia and is longer-lived. Seedlings are often attacked badly by small, green caterpillars and if these are not re-moved, they will destroy the leading shoot, resulting in the production of several new side shoots from the base of the main stem. If all of these are allowed to grow, the plant will look ungainly for some time, but it is best to reduce the number of shoots to one only, or to a group of not more than four stems If a small group of stems are retained, they will develop interesting shapes, especially after they have grown to 20–30 cm in diameter.

The main roots of this tree can appear above ground so it should not be planted too near a paved path. Young seedlings can be planted close together to form a hedge. This is satisfactory if the young plants are pruned early, to make them bushy, and to encourage the growh of a number of branches from near the base. If this is not done, the lower part of the hedge will soon consist of the bare trunks of young trees. Tall shoots which appear above the required level must be cut away as soon as they appear as they will quickly enlarge to form a normal trunk and will spoil the shape of the hedge. With careful management, these trees can make a very pleasant screen. Madras Thorn should be handled with some care as it is very spiny and when used as a hedge it is said to be goat-proof.

Pithecellobium jiringa (Jiring)

A small tree with a dense, well-shaped round or oval crown which becomes conspicuous when a new crop of young leaves is produced as these are bronze-purple for two or three weeks until they mature. The tree can be used in small gardens and gives good shade. In addition, the fruits with their edible seeds are produced once or twice each year. Propagation is easy from seeds.

Podocarpus

Two or three species are grown as ornamentals and all have dark green, shiny foliage which makes a good background for flowering shrubs. *P. polystachyus* has small, narrow leaves and makes a short bushy tree of attractive dark foliage which will stand trimming. It makes an excellent tall clipped hedge if it is allowed to grow thick enough at the base and is comparable to the Yew commonly grown for similar purposes in temperate countries. For planting such a hedge, cuttings are needed, and must be kept in a sand bed for at least three months to root. Growth is slow but the final result is really worthwhile. The plants grow sufficiently densely to be used for simple topiary work, a point mentioned elsewhere in the book.

There is also in cultivation an African species with a smaller bluish foliage, which can be used in the same way. The Japanese *P. macrophyllus* grows well in Singapore and makes compact bushy trees up to 8–9 m tall. It has

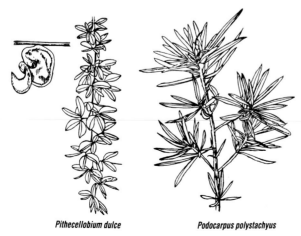

Pithecellobium dulce   *Podocarpus polystachyus*

small, neat foliage, quite similar to that of *P. polystachyus*.

P. rumphii is an excellent, slow growing, evergreen tree for formal planting. The mature foliage is dark green and shiny but young leaves and shoots are a pale, light green and make a pleasing contrast with the older ones. The tree needs no pruning and will eventually reach 20 m in height, but it could be used in smaller gardens as it will tolerate any pruning necessary to keep it to any appropriate size. Young trees retain a conical shape for a long time and afterwards the crown becomes oval or cylindrical. These trees are splendid for single planting or for avenue planting and as the roots do not come above ground they can be planted close to paths or roadsides. The species makes a very good screen as the crown is very dense, and is a good background for smaller flowering trees or shrubs. Propagation is from seeds which are slow to germinate and the initial growth of the seedlings is slow also.

Polyalthia longifolia (Mempisang)

An evergreen tree with long, narrow, dark green leaves having wavy margins. The tree is conical when young and the crown becomes oval as it ages. The species can be grown singly in small gardens, or it may be used for avenue planting, or as a screen. It can be used to great advantage in a formal planting scheme. When established, flowers and fruits are produced freely, and propagation is by means of seeds. No pruning is required as the trees shape themselves.

Pometia pinnata (Kasai)

This is a common wild, riverside tree which should be used more for ornamental purposes as it has bold, dark green foliage of large pinnate leaves. The young leaves are bright red and retain this colour for two or three weeks, making the tree very attractive. It has an open, irregular crown and produces large inflorescences at the ends of the branches, with small flowers which are followed by many black fruits. Propagation is easy by means of seeds. The tree is not suitable for small gardens and is best grown in a group of mixed species where the brightly coloured young leaves will show up to best advantage. It grows very well in wet ground or near a stream and is best suited to larger gardens and parks.

Pongamia pinnata (Mempari)

This tree of medium size grows naturally in coastal areas but is used a great deal as an ornamental as it will grow easily inland and can be kept to size by hard pruning every few years. The pinnate leaves have large, dark green leaflets and the tree crown is usually rounded, especially while the plant is young. This tree is not suitable for very small gardens, but elsewhere it can be planted singly or in a mixed group.

Pterocarpus indicus (Angsana)

This is one of the most well known trees grown as an ornamental and is suitable for medium-sized or large gardens only. It is a large deciduous tree with an oval crown which has a very graceful appearance because of the long hanging young branches. The tree is easily grown from very large cuttings 2 m long and 3-5 cm in diameter. The main roots will appear above ground after some time so it should not be planted near storm drains or fences. The leaves are shed once each year and new ones develop within a few weeks.

Pale yellow flowers are produced in great profusion and in a good season will cover the crown of the tree completely. The fallen petals make a carpet of pale yellow around the base of the tree for several days. Groups of flowers open every few days for a period of about ten days but bad weather will spoil the display. Individual trees show a little variation in the depth of colour of the flowers. Fruits are produced abundantly and the seeds germinate easily but initial growth of the seedlings is slow. Small trees can be kept to a suitable size by pollarding which is done in the same way as for older trees described in an earlier chapter. If such pruning is done regularly, the tree will not flower. When space is available the tree is excellent for avenue planting or for planting in groups to give bold landscape effects. Single trees, when well grown, are also good in parks and very large gardens.

Reevesia thyrsoidea

This is an uncommon small tree which will tolerate some shade and is suitable for a small garden. It produces an open, slightly irregular crown of evergreen foliage and clusters of fragrant, white flowers on the trunk and main branches. These are followed by small, oval, bright red fruits which are very attractive and showy. The tree will grow to 3-4 m in height and can be planted singly or may be used as a light screen. The flowers are partly concealed by the somewhat undistinguished foliage, but this is no disadvantage because in a small garden the tree is viewed at close quarters so that the appearance and scent of the flower is appreciated fully.

Rhodamnia trinerva (Mempoyan, Silver Back)

A small, wild species found throughout the lowlands but excellent for planting in the smallest garden. If pruned, it produces a neat, dense crown which can be kept to any size or shape desired. The rather dull green leaves are

Saraca declinata

Saraca declinata

Swietenia macrophylla (Mahogany)

Stercolia parvifolia

Sterculia parvifolia

Tectona grandis

Tabebuia rosea

Tabebuia rosea

182

Pongamia pinnata

Samanea saman (in playground)

Solanum macranthum

Solanum macranthum

Saraca taipingensis

Saraca taipingensis

Terminalia catappa

Terminalia catappa (leaf colour before falling)

produced on slender branches which tend to droop slightly at the ends so that the general appearance of the crown is very attractive. The undersurface of the leaves is whitish or silvery and shows up conspicuously when the wind blows through the crown. Tiny, inconspicuous flowers are produced in small clusters all along the branches and these are followed by small berries which are eaten very quickly by birds. If the whole crown is cut away, the trunk will soon produce several new shoots. Consequently, the tree can be used as a screen, or it can be planted singly in a small garden, or used in a group of mixed species. Propagation is from seeds or cuttings.

Rhodomyrtus tomentosa
(Rose Myrtle, Kemunting)

The grey-green foliage and the large pink flowers of this tall shrub or small tree make it attractive as a garden plant, especially in dry or sandy areas. It is found wild along the east coast of Peninsular Malaysia and has a dense crown which can be 2 m or more in height, but often is less than this. The species may be planted singly or used as a tall hedge or screen as it withstands the effects of strong winds. The small fruits contain many tiny seeds embedded in a purple pulp which is edible and can be made into jam.

Salix sp.

This small Weeping Willow with narrow leaves is often grown in gardens but the leaves are frequently eaten by caterpillars and some of the branches die back unaccountably, making the tree look untidy. The crown is always thin and although it can be grown in the smallest of gardens, it is never entirely satisfactory. Propagation is from cuttings.

Another species which can be grown is *S. tetrasperma* which is much more robust and is suitable for planting in wet areas or alongside streams and ditches. It is too big for a small garden as it can reach 20–30 m in height. The tree is deciduous, with a round crown, and about once each year it produces a crop of catkins which give it a yellowish green appearance. The tree has little distinction but is useful for wet areas where many other species would not grow. Propagation is from cuttings.

Sandoricum koetjape (Sentol)

A native deciduous Malaysian species with a somewhat oval but irregular crown of dark green trifoliate leaves. The flowers are inconspicuous but the large round fruits about 4–5 cm in diameter remind one of a small peach. The tree grows quite rapidly and will reach 20 m in height. It can be used for planting singly, in groups, or as an avenue or roadside tree. Propagation is from seeds.

Saraca

This genus of the family Leguminosae contains several Malaysian species, all with beautiful flowers, which are produced in large masses on the old wood, among the leaves. All species are forest plants (usually growing beside streams), and none will grow really well in an exposed place. They are best when partially protected by shade from a larger tree and if it is possible to plant them near a stream they will do very well.

S. taipingensis is the best species for gardens, as it is not too tall (about 7 m at most) and has very showy large masses of orange flowers. Young leaves are cream-coloured and develop very rapidly so that they are limp and hang like large tassels from the ends of the branches until they are mature and assume their proper position on the stem. The young pods are large and flat, dark red or purple as they ripen and are another attractive feature of this plant. *S. declinata* is a much taller tree, with smaller bunches of flowers, but very handsome, and suitable for planting in a screen or thicket of trees. Propagation is from seeds and the young trees are rather slow in growth.

S. indica, the Asoka Tree, is sometimes seen in gardens and frequently assumes a very tall, narrow, columnar shape which has definite uses in a formal planting scheme. Trees of this habit may be grown singly, in groups, or in a mixed group with other species to give contrast in form.

Solanum macranthum (Potato Tree)

This is a small evergreen tree of some architectural value because of its very large lobed leaves. It has an open, rounded or dome-shaped crown and the leaves and stems often bear thorns. Large flowers are produced continuously in short inflorescences and are deep violet when they first open but fade to white within a few days. Each inflorescence will therefore have flowers of several shades and is extremely attractive. Fruits are produced freely and propagation is easy from seeds.

Old plants may become a little gaunt in appearance and should be replaced with a well grown seedling which will grow very quickly. By pruning a seedling of about 1–1½ m high, the growth of several side shoots is encouraged and these will carry very large leaves which make an interesting feature in a small garden. As soon as the shoots become too long and begin to branch, they should be cut back so that a new crop of shoots with large leaves will be produced very quickly to retain the general effect in the garden. When treated in this way, no flowers will be produced and the plant is used for the architectural value of its leaves only. The fruits are about the size of a tomato and are yellow or orange when ripe, but inedible as they are full of a large number of small, hard seeds.

Spathodea campanulata (African Tulip Tree)

When planted in good soil, this species is very quick in growth, and has good dense foliage as well as attractive flowers. It is, however, soft-wooded and is liable to be blown down if grown in an exposed place. Trees which have not enough good soil for the active growth of their roots often show a die-back of the crown and unsightly dead branches. The flowers are very handsome but are produced at the top of the crown where they are not seen easily. For this reason, if the garden has a steep slope, it is quite a good idea to plant this tree at the lower end so that the flowers can be viewed from above.

When grown as a single specimen, these trees should not be planted in an exposed position otherwise they are liable to be blown down by strong winds. The trees can be used as a tall screen as they respond very well to pruning and will produce a large number of new shoots carrying large leaves. Under this treatment no flowers will be produced. Propagation is from seed or root suckers. The latter is recommended as seedlings vary in vigour and in bushiness of habit.

Sterculia parvifolia

Although not commonly grown as an ornamental, this tree deserves more attention as it is an attractive deciduous plant up to 4–6 m high with an oval crown of large, light green leaves. It is slow growing and would be suitable for small gardens as it is not wide-spreading. The pink flowers are inconspicuous but when the fruits ripen the tree becomes very striking as the large pods develop in groups and become brilliant scarlet at maturity. They split open so that the large blue-black seeds hang outside around the margins of the pods. The fruits remain on the tree for several weeks before losing their colour.

Flowering and fruiting occur about once each year and because the fruits are partly hidden among the leaves, the effect is never gaudy. Seeds are the easiest means of propagation and germinate easily and quickly. The tree may be used for single or group planting, as a screen, for avenue planting or in a group of mixed species. Seedlings will not fruit until they are about five to seven years of age but will then flower and fruit regularly each year.

Swietenia macrophylla (Mahogany)

This introduced species is a medium-sized deciduous tree with an irregular open crown of dark green, shiny leaves. Small specimens can be grown in a garden but because of the irregular shape of the crown the trees are prob-ably best planted in small groups on their own or in groups of mixed species in a general landscape scheme. The trees will drop their leaves once or twice each year and will remain bare for two or three weeks before the new foliage develops. The inconspicuous flowers are produced at the same time as the new leaves but fruits develop only at the top of the tree crown. When ripe the fruits are large and woody so that the trees should not be planted around car parks.

Each fruit contains many winged seeds which germinate easily, and the seedlings tend to grow to a height of 3–4 m before any branches develop. Many branches develop then almost simultaneously and a narrow oval crown rapidly forms. If a seedling is cut to try and encourage branching, it is likely to produce one shoot which will behave in exactly the same way as the original one, so a little patience is needed and the tree will eventually shape itself. Although such a tall, single-stemmed plant will not look very presentable, it provides the gardener with a conversation piece for some time.

Tabebuia (Trumpet Tree)

An introduced species is sometimes available, but is better suited to a more seasonal climate. It is deciduous and produces flowers while bare of leaves but the trees appear to reach no great size in Malaysia. The large pale pink flowers appear in small clusters and in shape they are very similar to the flowers of Thunbergia. The trees are more definitely deciduous in the northern, more seasonal parts of the country.

In other parts of the tropics, there are yellow-flowered species of Tabebuia which are large trees, completely deciduous, flowering very abundantly while bare of leaves and quite magnificent in appearance.

Tamarindus indicus (Asam Jawa, Tamarind)

Under suitable conditions, this is a very fine, well-shaped deciduous tree with a dense oval crown. It is slow growing and seedlings can be damaged severely by caterpillars so that regular spraying with insecticide is necessary. Older plants seem to be unaffected by these pests. After leaf fall, the new leaves appear within three or four weeks and are pale green, giving the tree a delightful fresh and airy appearance.

Propagation is very easy from seeds which germinate quickly. The tree is best suited to more seasonal climatic conditions when the whole crown of the tree will undergo leaf fall at one time, but in the more southern parts of the country it is less pronounced and leaves may be shed from some of the branches only over a longer period of time.

Chrysalidocarpus lutescens, Ptychosperma macarthuri (tallest plants)　　　　*Caryota mitis*　　　　*Arenga pinnata*

Orange cocos (Cocos nucifera)

Corypha umbraculifera

Tectona grandis (Teak Tree)

In Malaysia, this tree can be grown easily as an ornamental but does not reach any great size. It has very large, broad, oval leaves and in young plants these may be 40–50 cm long and wide so that the effect is very bold and striking. Older plants have leaves which are not quite as large but which still give the tree a distinctive appearance. The tree may grow to 7–10 m in height and will begin flowering after about five years.

The small flowers are produced in long, much-branched inflorescences and later many green, inflated, bladder-like fruits develop. Propagation is by means of seeds. The tree is not suitable for very small gardens, but it can be kept to a smaller size by pruning, and this will result in the production of new shoots with very large leaves which give the plant an architectural quality.

Terminalia catappa
(Ketapang, Sea Almond)

This is a native tree of sandy coasts, and therefore especially useful for planting near the sea, though it will grow almost anywhere. It produces a succession of tiers of horizontally-spreading branches and so forms a useful shade tree, though less spreading and of a different shape from the Rain Tree. A full grown tree reaches a considerable height, and is very handsome. The foliage is changed completely twice each year and before the leaves drop they become a deep, bright red colour, giving the tree a most striking appearance. The colouring of the leaves is better if there has been some dry weather just before leaf-fall.

This is a fine tree for a landscape effect in a large garden. Seeds are produced abundantly and bats are very fond of carrying the fruits away before eating the outer covering. They drop the seeds and often the species can be regarded almost as a weed because so many seedlings appear in the garden. Small heaps of seeds are often found underneath the favourite roosting places of bats and most of these will germinate if not cleared away. Seedlings grow rapidly and need little attention.

Thuja (Arborvitae)

One species, *T. orientalis*, is often grown as an ornamental. It is suitable for small gardens as it does not become very tall and is not wide-spreading. The twigs and leaves resemble those of Cypress but are arranged in flat, fan-shaped groups which are held vertically. The crown is conical and dense and the tree is suitable for single planting or as an avenue for a short drive; it also makes a useful screen. Thuja can be grown in large pots or in troughs, but eventually will become too large and then must be planted out into the ground.

However, it can be kept in a large pot for many years before it becomes too large.

Bamboo

Although these plants are not trees, they are included in this section because they occupy about the same area and need the same cultivation arrangements as normal trees.

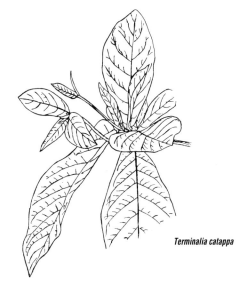

Terminalia catappa

Several species of bamboo are used as ornamentals and some of these are suitable for small gardens. Most, however, are large plants and can be invasive unless controlled very strictly. The smaller kinds make neat, dense, well-shaped plants with light, attractive foliage and are excellent as a screen or for single planting in a confined space. They are upright in growth and easily kept to a definite size by a little regular pruning. Any height from 2 to 4 m can be maintained very easily.

Larger bamboos need much more space and are suitable for large gardens only. They can reach 10–12 m in height and 6–7 m in diameter. The tall stems live for a long time and drop leaves continuously so these should be re-

Tamarindus indicus

moved frequently, otherwise they form a thick mat around the base of the bamboo and no other plants can grow near by. Bamboo stems are very hard and woody and produce a large number of branches so that they are difficult to cut down and remove from the middle of a large clump.

If all old stems are removed from a rootstock then a crop of small leafy shoots will appear and these can be kept to about 1–3 m in height, but large shoots will soon appear again and if these are not wanted they should be removed as soon as they are seen because they are soft enough to be cut easily at that stage. Disposal of old bamboo stems is often a problem as they do not rot. If they are dried they can be burnt, but great care is needed because they burn very fiercely with many loud explosions as parts of the stem break open in the heat. It is unwise to burn large quantities of bamboo in a residential area and it is best to arrange for the removal of the stems by the municipal authorities.

The yellow-stemmed bamboo makes fairly open clumps but the green-stemmed form is often very dense and the close-packed stems make an ideal breeding ground for rats. If a large bamboo is required, it is best kept to an unused corner of a large garden. Removal of a large clump of bamboo can be very difficult as the stems can be removed by chopping or sawing, but the rootstock is so hard that it may take several years before it begins to rot and soften sufficiently for it to be taken up. During this time, any shoots which appear must be cut away immediately and the rootstock can be screened by growing a trailing plant over it.

In a small garden, bamboos should be avoided and even in a large garden they can become a nuisance and after a few years they can be rather untidy.

Planting and Siting of Palms

Palms may be divided, for convenience of the present discussion, into the two groups of single-stemmed and tufted. The single-stemmed palms have only one trunk, bearing a crown of leaves at the top, and do not produce suckers from the base. Tufted palms continually produce suckers and so eventually groups of slender trunks develop, each stem having its own crown of leaves. The two kinds of palm are so different in aspect that they serve different purposes in garden design.

Single-stemmed palms are grown from seed, and a seedling will benefit by being planted out as soon as it is big enough to hold its own; it should not be kept too long in a pot, or it will be checked in growth, and start to form a trunk prematurely. Such young plants need a

good, deep soil and will benefit by occasional cultivation and manuring during their earlier years to establish a crown of good size before the trunk begins to develop. There is often a great difference between a well grown and a poor palm of the same species. Some kinds of palms need shade for their best development; these are not suitable for small gardens but in larger ones they can be grown effectively under some larger trees. For smaller gardens, the best palms are those which will stand full exposure to the sun from the beginning, but some of them benefit by a ground cover to keep their roots cool. Such palms could be grown in between shrubs or small trees so that their roots are shaded and the crown will eventually appear above the surrounding plants.

Tufted palms (such as Chrysalidocarpus) are often propagated by dividing the mass of suckers of an old plant; this method gives good-sized plants more quickly than planting from seed. It is advisable to grow a tufted palm to a good size in a pot before putting it out into the open ground. Good soil and plenty of root room are just as essential as with single-stemmed palms.

A point to remember when planting the larger kinds of palms is that their roots spread to a considerable distance, and may seriously compete with the bedded plants if they are within reach. If any plants are bedded near such a palm, they need frequent cultivation and manuring and sometimes it may be necessary to cut some of the palm roots. Sometimes palms benefit considerably from having beds of annuals, which are shallow-rooted, replanted and manured fairly frequently round their base.

Quite large palms (especially tufted palms) may be transplanted if handled with care, and this is a point worth remembering when replanning an old garden. After being moved, the plants must be watered every day during dry weather until they begin to produce new leaves and this indicates that they have produced new roots and are fairly well established.

Palms have such a distinctive appearance that they make interesting formal objects in the garden, and as such may be planted singly, in pairs, or in rows or avenues for special effect. If a row is planted, all should be of the same kind; or a single-stemmed kind may alternate with a tufted kind, or two kinds of tufted palms of different heights can be combined. Mixed species of palms may be planted in groups, where they benefit by being fairly close together; in such a group the varying habits of different kinds may be used to give form and character to the group. If the group is large, the taller palms should be in the central position but the siting of the group and its position in relation to any buildings will govern the choice of palms to be included, and also the positioning of the palms within the group.

When planting palms, it is important to have some idea of their final size and shape and it is wise also to remember how a group of palms will appear from different angles of view. This is necessary in large gardens and parks only, as there will be no room for such effects in small gardens.

Kinds of Palms

Areca catechu (Betel Palm)

A useful, quick-growing single-stemmed palm which is relatively small and has a well shaped crown of dark green leaves. The straight, slender trunk is smooth and marked with regularly arranged, ring-shaped scars left by the leaves when they fall. The palm is ideal for smaller gardens where it can be grown singly or in a small group of three to five plants. In larger gardens, it can be used for avenue planting as its appearance will never become overwhelming. Propagation is by means of seeds which germinate very easily and this is probably done most conveniently in pots. The plants are then put out into their final position when they have three or four leaves.

Arenga pinnata (Sugar Palm)

This will eventually become very large and is quite unsuitable for a small garden but single specimens can be used with effect in larger gardens, especially if grown among a group of small-leaved trees. In parks this palm can be used for avenue planting or for group planting where its large size will be most effective. The plants grow for many years before they begin to produce flowers and these are carried in very large, hanging inflorescences which give the plant a somewhat formal aspect.

Caryota mitis (Fish-tail Palm)

These palms have large leaves which are divided two or three times into a number of wedge-shaped leaflets from which the common name is derived as they are thought to resemble fish-tails. The species is often grown in gardens and can be grown as a pot plant for some time but must eventually be planted out because of its size. The palm produces a number of offsets and often only one of these will grow into a tall stem, but when well managed, three or more of such stems may grow at the same time. Each stem will grow to about 4–5 m in height and will then begin to produce flowers, commencing near the top and gradually moving downwards. When flowering has finished, and this may take two years or longer, the whole stem dies away and one of

the offsets will grow up to replace it.

As a pot plant, regular fertilizer application is necessary, otherwise the leaves will become slightly yellowish. When planted out, it should receive manuring about three or four times each year to maintain good, strong growth. It looks very good when planted singly or in a mixed border with shorter shrubs surrounding it, but can also be used for a short, informal avenue. If planted in groups, then a dense growth of shrubs or other short plants should, quite definitely, be grown around the bases of the palms in order to give the whole arrangement cohesion. Propagation is easy from rooted offsets.

Chrysalidocarpus lutescens

There is no popular name for this Madagascar palm, yet it is the commonest tufted pot palm. It makes fine, thick, bushy clumps because of the development of large numbers of offsets, and has a most graceful habit of growth as the leaves curve outwards in a very elegant manner. When planted singly, they develop an attractive shape with a dense cluster of offsets about 1–1½ m high, from which rise several curving bare stems, each carrying a neat crown of recurving leaves. Such a plant is useful in small gardens, or several plants can be used for a formal effect in larger gardens. Propagation is by removal of groups of rooted offsets which can be planted in pots. The leaves of this palm are sometimes attacked by caterpillars and will then appear a little ragged, but an occasional spraying with an insecticide will control the insects and care should be taken to spray underneath the leaves where the caterpillars are usually found.

Cocos nucifera (Coconut, Kelapa)

When space is available, this plant makes an admirable ornamental plant and the dwarf form can be used in small gardens. The tall forms are suitable for large gardens only and should be sited away from buildings to avoid damage from falling fruit. The dwarf kinds have green, yellow or orange fruits and the latter are especially attractive, besides providing material for cooking.

All kinds are easy to grow from seeds but young plants need considerable space while the stem is short as the leaves are wide-spreading. When the stem has grown to about 1½ m in height, the lowermost leaves can be cut away and there will be more room to put other plants around the base of the palm. These palms will begin to produce fruit after about four years and they should be given a little fertilizer every three months to ensure a good, continuous supply of fruits. Lack of fertilizer can result in very few or no fruits being formed and the leaves may also be yellowish

Cyrtostachys renda

Livistona chinensis

Oncosperma tigillaria

Ptychosperma macarthuri

Roystonea regia

Rhapis excelsa

Veitchia merrillii

green instead of a good, dark green. The effect of fertilizer application will not be seen for about four or five months because the growth of these palms is rather slow.

Corypha umbraculifera (Talipot)

These are the largest of the fan palms which are so called because of the shape of the leaf, in contrast to the feather palms which have long, pinnate leaves resembling a feather in shape. Corypha is a single-stemmed palm which grows for about forty years before flowering and fruiting and after this has happened, the whole plant dies. The plants are too big for most gardens but where space is available they are magnificent, especially when young, and are of great architectural value in a landscape. They look best when planted as single specimens or as an avenue, but in small groups they are not so attractive as they need to be planted widely apart because of their great size, so that when they have grown to some height they do not give the appearance of a coherent group. The crown of young plants can be 3–4 m in diameter before the trunk begins to elongate and this must be taken into consideration when planting.

Cyrtostachys renda
(Sealing Wax Palm, Pinang Raja)

This Malaysian tufted palm is one of the finest local garden plants. It prefers a damp or clay soil, and when well treated will grow almost rapidly. Very old plants sometimes become poor and thin and these can often be reconditioned by digging thoroughly all round them, removing the earth from underneath so that they sink into the ground a little, and then re-filling the hole with fresh soil. A good clump of Sealing Wax Palms makes a fine focal point for a planting scheme or an end to a vista; rows or avenues are equally effective, provided an even growth of all the plants is maintained as far as possible.

The attractive bright red colour of the leaf sheaths of this palm is its most striking feature but this colour does not show on young plants until the trunk has begun to lengthen. Many offsets are produced and although not all of these will develop a tall trunk, they do give the plant a good bushy appearance while it is young and, as the leaves are held in a very upright manner, the plant takes up very little space and can be used in a small garden. From one to five tall stems may develop on a single plant. Well rooted offsets can be detached and used for propagation. They should be planted in pots and initial growth will be very slow, but once established they make good decorative pot plants for some time, and when they finally become too large for the pot, they can be planted out. Seeds, when available, can be used for propagation, but germination and seedling growth are very slow.

Elaeis guineensis
(African Oil Palm, Kelapa Sawit)

This is too large for small gardens but it does produce a handsome crown of foliage and is very suitable for planting in larger gardens and parks. The trunk is covered with the persistent old leaf bases which form an ideal site for the growth of epiphytic ferns, orchids and other small plants. This growth of epiphytic plants can be very decorative in a garden, however undesirable it is in an estate. A little fertilizer should be applied around the palm two or three times a year, and if it develops a good crown, then a number of plants such as Balsam and Begonia can be grown in amongst the leaf bases and will cause no harm to the palm itself. Ferns will appear without any help from the gardener. This palm can be planted singly or as an avenue, or it may be used in a group of mixed species to give contrast in form and foliage.

Ravenala madagascariensis

Licuala spinosa

Veitchia merrillii (Manila Palm)

This commonly grown single-stemmed palm is a good ornamental plant and may be used in quite small gardens as it takes up very little space after the stem has grown to about 2 m in height. It may be planted singly but may also be used in a mixed group of palms, or in a mixed border; it can be effective also when used for avenue planting. The stems are greyish and the dark green leaves curve outwards from the stem. Large branched inflorescences are formed just below the leaves and make an attractive ruff around the stem. Seeds are produced abundantly but, as in most palms, germination is very slow.

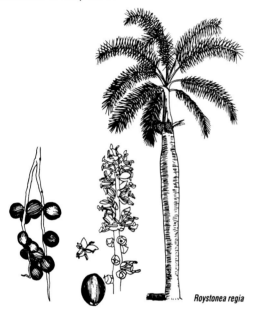

Roystonea regia

9 LAWNS

Grass lawns are the groundwork of most gardens. Against their uniform greenness we set our flowering shrubs or trees, our flower beds and palms. The essence of a good lawn is that it should be level and trim, of a uniform fine texture, so that no unevenness distracts the eye. Such a lawn helps to make a very ordinary garden look beautiful, but the finest flower beds and shrubs are robbed of their decorative value if the grass is not cared for. And yet we often find that the lawns in a garden are given no attention except the regular cutting and sweeping, with the result that the grass is poor and patchy. Grass needs well aerated soil, and manure, to keep it healthy and vigorous, just as much as any other kind of plant. With other plants, we can cultivate the soil round about them and dig in manure; with grass we cannot do this. Therefore, in some respects grass is more difficult to maintain than other plants, and its treatment requires a special technique.

The first essential for good lawns is satisfactory drainage, so that the rain water flows through the soil quickly enough and leaves it well aerated. As noted above, we cannot handle the soil underneath the grass roots; therefore it is most important that in the original planting of the lawn, arrangements should be made to secure adequate permanent drainage. The other essential is manuring. To serve its purpose properly, a lawn must be kept cut close and trim. That means we are continually removing, in the cut grass, the various substances which the roots extract from the soil. If this loss is not made good by manuring, it is obvious that the grass cannot continue to grow vigorously.

Drainage

In the case of sandy or other very light soils, the question of artificial drainage does not arise, as they never hold too much water. They may indeed hold too little for some grasses, but if the kind of grass is properly selected, excellent lawns may be made on sandy ground. Such grasses will not need watering in most parts of Malaysia, as we have sufficient rain throughout the year. These remarks apply to ordinary lawns, not to fine golf or bowling greens, which need special consideration.

But many local soils are not light, and some are decidedly heavy. Most grasses will not grow satisfactorily in such soils unless the top layer is removed and a better soil substituted, and also a permanent drainage system of some sort is provided. When houses are built in Malaysia, the top of a hill is often levelled, and the area of ground which was formerly some distance below the surface may have to be planted with grass. Such ground is usually very hard, and may sometimes be almost impervious to water. By breaking up the surface with a cangkul to the depth of a few centimetres and adding another few centimetres of good soil, it is possible to establish a reasonably good growth of grass (for methods of planting, see below), but after a time the surface becomes compacted once more, and the grass gradually loses vigour, becomes patchy, and is invaded by small sedges which flourish only in wet or badly aerated ground. Then the only remedy is to dig up the lawn and replant. The length of time taken before this condition is reached depends on how thoroughly the preparation of the ground was done. It may be a few months or it may be a few years; or if the preparation has been very thorough, and the grass is well manured at regular intervals, the lawn may be kept indefinitely in a sufficiently satisfactory condition. However, if the expense is not too great, it is far better to make a drainage system before planting is begun. Then the grass roots will have a soil which will remain in good physical condition, and continued vigorous growth will be possible. But such growth will only occur if the grass is well tended and regularly manured. The expense of laying a drainage system will be entirely wasted if the grass is not properly and regularly fed.

The most satisfactory underground drainage scheme consists of a herringbone system of rubble drains, in which a main drain runs with a gentle fall down the middle of the area, fed on either side by lateral drains of a similar nature at intervals of 2–3 m; or there may be several main drains, each with its laterals. The surface of the ground should be excavated to the depth of 16 cm, and then the drainage system marked out, its plan depending on the lie of the ground. Next, the surface should be trimmed so that every part slopes gently down to a drainage line, trenches being made along the lines and filled with rubble. Then fine rubble or cinders or sand should be laid over the whole area until it is level, and after that 15 cm of top soil in which the grass is planted.

A less elaborate scheme is to slope the ground in one direction, then put down a layer of 30 cm of rubble, and the top soil on this. The important thing is that there should be a reasonable thickness of soil into which the grass can root, and which will not dry out too quickly, and below this a drainage area which will remove surplus rain water reasonably quickly.

The top soil may be made by mixing the original surface soil with better soil from elsewhere, or with a good quantity of compost. Even a rather heavy soil will be quite satisfactory if well broken up and mixed with a good proportion of organic matter.

Planting and Establishment

Seeds or turf may be used for planting a lawn. Suitable seeds are sometimes available in Malaysia and can be used successfully, but turfing is probably the easiest and quickest method. When using seed the soil needs more preparation before sowing. The surface must be broken down as fine as possible by raking, but avoid walking over the ground too much at this stage otherwise the ground will become compacted. Grass seed is very small and light and is difficult to scatter evenly on its own, but if it is mixed with a quantity of fine, dry sand it can be handled more easily and can be distributed over the soil much more evenly. It may be necessary to sow more seeds than are usually required as birds will inevitably eat a great number.

The sand and seed mixture should be broadcast evenly over the soil surface and, if possible, the ground can be rolled lightly with a garden roller, or if this is not available then a short plank can be used to press down the soil. This ensures that the seeds will be in close contact with the soil and are better able to absorb moisture for germination. If birds are likely to be troublesome then they can be discouraged by stretching black thread, garden twine or net-

ting over the area until the seeds have germinated. One of the difficulties of establishing a lawn from seed is that if very heavy rainstorms occur after germination the tiny seedlings can be broken or so badly damaged that they will not recover. In Malaysia it is probably much easier to establish a lawn by turfing.

Turfing

Turfing means cutting up the surface of established grass into small rectangular portions called turfs and then laying them to form a continuous cover on the ground which we wish to make into a lawn. This is of course a quick method, but it is expensive, and often suitable turf is not easily available especially with the great increase in demand for turf at the present time for planting around the large numbers of new buildings which are being erected. Turf consisting of coarse grasses or containing many weeds is not worth the expense of cutting and transporting. Except for special cases in which a quick cover is essential, complete turfing of this kind is not to be recommended. One special case in which it is the only effective method is in covering rather steep banks with grass. Loose soil containing young plants is soon washed away from such banks; cut turfs protect the earth from rain wash, and if laid carefully soon become established. It may be well worth removing all the turf from a neighbouring lawn to make a good cover for such a bank, replanting the lawn with new grass. Turf should be cut to uniform size and thickness so that it can be laid neatly. It should be laid as soon as possible after being cut.

Spot-turfing

This method consists in placing small pieces of turf at regular intervals all over the ground to be grassed. The surface soil must of course be well prepared first, and the pieces of turf sunk into it so that they are flush with the surface. The turfs must contain grasses of creeping habit, which will quickly produce runners that cover the intervening bare ground. Thus again, the turf must be carefully selected or the result will be unsatisfactory. A common procedure in spot-turfing is to use turfs about 10 cm square and space them at intervals of 30–60 cm. If turf containing suitable grasses is obtained, and the surface soil is well prepared and manured, spot-turfing can be quite satisfactory; but it is not so easy by this method to obtain a final even surface for the lawn, and the additional time and trouble of the dibbling-in method is usually worthwhile.

Dibbling-in

This is the method often employed and which gives the best results in Malaysia. It consists of taking individual small pieces of grass plants, and putting them into the prepared soil at intervals of about 10 cm. Success depends partly on the proper preparation of the soil, and partly on a proper selection of grasses for planting. The method has the advantage that if the planting material is selected with care, a uniform growth of one single species of grass can be obtained. This gives a much better looking lawn than a mixture of grasses, especially if one of the fine kinds is selected. But to establish such a uniform pure growth of one species, much weeding may be necessary before the ground is completely covered, and afterwards in order to maintain the condition.

The soil for planting the grass must be of good texture, contain a sufficiency of organic matter, and preferably have rock phosphate mixed with it at the rate of about 60 g per square metre. It must also be carefully levelled. The pieces of grass to be planted may be collected from the edges of neighbouring lawns or other grass areas, or from a special grass nursery if such is available. In most parts of Malaysia, waste ground bearing suitable grasses may be found.

The pieces of grass should have stems 10 cm long, and should be buried for half their length just under the surface of the soil. If dry weather follows the planting the grass should be watered daily until the new growth is well established, which should be quite soon. When new growth has well started, it can be speeded up considerably by watering with liquid manure (see Chapter 3). Ammonium sulphate is probably the most effective and convenient fertilizer, and is quite satisfactory to use alone if rock phosphate has been mixed with soil before planting; but if this is not available any other manure containing readily available nitrogen, such as urea, will be effective. Treatment with dilute liquid manure may be continued monthly for several months. Small doses given at frequent intervals in this way are far more effective than larger doses at longer intervals.

After about two months, the young grass should have produced a continuous cover over the whole area. With it are sure to be many weeds, or coarse grasses; these must be removed. The ground should then be lightly rolled, to make the surface even, and as soon as any of the young shoots rise 10 cm above the surface the grass should be scythed carefully. If this is not done, a loose mass of young shoots will soon develop. Scything should be done two or three times, say at fortnightly intervals, followed by weeding and rolling, but the rolling should not be too heavy. When the cover of new grass is fairly even all over, it should be cut with a hand mower after scything, and thereafter mowed weekly or as often as seems necessary. Some kinds of motor mower could be used instead of a hand mower but they should not be heavy otherwise they will compact the soil too much before the grass is properly established.

Weeding should also be continued if necessary. Many weeds will soon be choked out by the grass and killed by regular mowing, but weeds which have a creeping habit may spread if not removed. The coarse grasses will also spread if they are not removed, but if the area is well drained and fully exposed to the sun, and also regularly mown close, the finer grasses will usually be the more vigorous. But as much weeding as possible in the early stages is essential for the establishment of a good turf. If intensive treatment with fertilizers and regular weeding are continued, an almost pure turf can be obtained, but as time goes on a mixture of grasses usually develops.

Manuring

The further maintenance of an ordinary garden lawn consists of regular cutting, as close as may be desired, and of regular application of fertilizer or manure. The closer and more frequent the cutting, the greater the need of regular applications of fertilizer. Thus a tennis court or golf green needs more frequent manuring than an ordinary garden lawn. In large stretches of grass which do not have to be maintained in very fine condition, it is a good thing to use a mower without a grass box, and to let the cuttings rot where they lie, sweeping them if necessary to make them lie evenly. Unless the growth is very rank, such cuttings will not show after a day or so. They undoubtedly return part of their substance to the soil, and so help to take the place of manuring. Grass treated in this way may be kept in quite good condition with the application of rock phosphate, thoroughly mixed with well rotted compost or earth, once in two years at the rate of 240 kg of phosphate to the acre, without using any of the more expensive nitrogenous fertilizers.

Grass that is cut close, with all the cuttings removed, undoubtedly needs a nitrogenous fertilizer, preferably in small quantities at intervals of not less than six months. Tennis courts should have fertilizer at least every three months, and golf greens probably more often. Each application need only be small in quantity. The best procedure is probably to apply rock phosphate or some other phosphatic manure once a year, and for the rest to use ammonium sulphate in dilute solution (30 g in four litres of water). Potash is not seriously deficient in most local soils and may be applied at long intervals, or as a minor constituent of a mixed fertilizer; it should, however, always be used on sandy or poor quartzite soils.

Watering

In most parts of Malaysia ordinary garden lawns do not need watering. There is enough rain to keep them green throughout the year, except in spells of unusually severe dry weather, when they may become brown for a short time. As soon as rain comes, they quickly recover. But lawns that have had a special drainage layer prepared and are kept cut very fine, may become too dry for vigorous growth after only a few days without rain. In such cases, as with all golf greens and fine tennis courts, watering is necessary from time to time, and a pipe laid on to the area concerned is desirable. The best method of watering is to have a hose and an automatic sprinkler that distributes a spray over a considerable area. Watering should be done in the evening, and should be sufficient to give the soil a good soaking.

Reconditioning

This should preferably be undertaken in the wet season. As noted above, if the growth of grass is very bad owing to heavy subsoil and inadequate drainage, the only practical method of improvement may be replanting, taking care at least to have a reasonably thick layer of good soil on top of the heavy subsoil. In other cases where grass has become poor owing to neglect of manuring, bare patches must be replanted, and the whole top-dressed with good soil mixed with manure, preferably a complete fertilizer mixture at the rate of 250 kg per acre. But if the surface soil has become hard, it should be broken up with a cangkul fork, used carefully so as not to damage the grass roots unnecessarily. Then after the soil and fertilizer have been spread, the ground may be lightly rolled.

Sometimes old grass consists of a mat of interlacing runners, many of them dead. This is particularly bad on a tennis court. In such cases, the grass should be thoroughly raked over with a strong rake, and as much as possible of the mat of old runners removed; after this the surface is forked if necessary and the top dressing of soil and fertilizer applied.

Kinds of Grass

The finest lawn grasses for use in Malaysia are Serangoon grass and the closely related Australian Blue Couch, Bermuda grass, and a stiff grass that grows in sandy ground near the sea, sometimes called Siglap grass. Of coarse grasses, the best is probably Carpet grass which is vigorous in growth and not so coarse as the common Buffalo grass. There are many other local grasses which are often found in mixed turf, among them all too often the Love grass, which has stiff flower stalks that no ordinary mowing machine will cut, and barbed fruits that stick to one's clothing and so are distributed.

Serangoon grass (*Digitaria didactyla*)
Serangoon grass has narrow blue-green leaves and a creeping growth of slender runners that do not readily form an undesirable stiff mat. It needs well drained soil to grow well, and will gradually die in ground that is too wet, giving place to other grasses. It is the best grass for greens and tennis courts over most of the country, but demands good preparation of the site and constant care for maintenance in first class condition. It thrives at fairly high altitudes but in the lowlands its growth is relatively weak and consequently it needs continuous care to prevent invasion by other stronger grasses and weeds.

Propagation is from cuttings and it responds very well to frequent and regular applications of nitrogenous fertilizers. On paths or areas which receive constant use, the grass can become thin with groups of leaves at the ends of the stems only, so that much of the soil surface is exposed.

Bermuda Grass (*Cynodon dactylon*)
This is a long-lived plant with a spreading habit of growth and it will grow in a wide range of soils and under different climatic conditions. It thrives best in subtropical conditions and consequently does not always grow very strongly in the central and southern parts of Malaysia; however it can be used successfully for lawns in the northern parts of the country. Improved forms have been developed in other parts of the tropics and some of these should be tried in this country. Only one form can be grown from seed and the others are propagated by cuttings. It is inferior to Serangoon grass for lawns.

Siglap Grass (*Zoysia matrella*)

This grass has relatively stout thick runners and stiff leaves which have a sharp point. The latter are grey-green and at first glance the plants resemble Serangoon grass but can be identified quite easily by the flowering head which is a single short spike in Siglap grass but a branched structure in Serangoon grass. Siglap grass is found wild on sandy sea coasts of Malaysia and thrives therefore on sandy soils and withstands dry conditions very well. It is also the best grass for lawns around houses on the coast as it will resist the salt spray from the sea. It makes a pleasant-looking fine turf but is slow to establish and its stiff nature and interlacing springy runners are not good for tennis courts or golf greens.

The grass can be used sometimes for tennis courts, in a special way. Pieces of the grass are scattered over the prepared site for the court, and then 20 cm or more of soil to cover them completely. As soon as the grass comes through the surface, it is cut, and kept very short, the ground being also well rolled. In this way a rather sparse grass cover may be maintained which holds the soil together well without making too soft a surface for play. However, the maintenance of such a court requires some care. The planting soil must be sandy, and a top dressing of sand, to make good surface wash, may be needed from time to time. Lavish fertilizer treatment is not needed, but a sufficiency of phosphate and potash must be applied, with a little nitrogenous fertilizer often enough to keep the grass in good condition.

Siglap grass makes a rather stiff, springy, upright turf which can be very dense and it can also be used for erosion control on banks. Propagation is by means of cuttings. Although it will tolerate a wide range of soil types, it does best on well drained, fine-textured soils and will not tolerate poor drainage or waterlogging. Because of its dense, tight growth it can be used in some areas to prevent or reduce the invasion of other grasses and weeds. This grass is relatively free of major disease problems compared with other turf grasses, and is tolerant of most turf grass herbicides.

Two other species of Zoysia are available now and much smaller in size. These are *Zoysia japonica* (Japanese lawngrass, or Korean lawngrass) which is coarser in texture and produces less shoots than the others, and *Zoysia tenuifolia* (Mascarene grass or Korean Velvet grass) which is the finest in texture, very dense in growth but with a rather shallow root system. It is slow in growth and is propagated from cuttings which are very small and need to be planted fairly close together. This grass is excellent for small ornamental lawns because it is very short and produces a very dense turf of dark green foliage which is decorative and neat at all times. Some care with maintenance is necessary and the grass should be trimmed fairly frequently to prevent it from becoming too tall. If this is not done then cutting will remove all of the leaf-carrying tips of the stems, leaving the old bare stems at the base of the plants. These may produce a few new shoots only so that the appearance of the lawn can be spoiled entirely. Many months may pass before the lawn recovers from such cutting and if the lower parts of the stem are too old, they may not produce new shoots. A good lawn of this grass is soft and springy to walk over and it is ideal for small areas in between paved paths or for the diminutive area in front of some of the present-day terrace houses.

Occasionally the grass is subject to a fungus attack which will cause small areas to become brown. This dead portion should be removed and burnt and fresh soil should be placed in the gap. Cuttings can be planted or the surrounding plants allowed to cover the area naturally with their own new rhizomes. Weeding will be necessary until the grass has covered the space. Provided the soil is well drained and the grass is kept fairly short, there is less chance of the fungus appearing and the turf is not usually troubled by other pests or diseases.

The species of Zoysia have been hybridized and several new forms have been produced, of which one of the more successful has been named 'Emerald'.

Carpet Grass (*Axonopus*)

This is a fairly coarse grass, usually thriving in moist soils or soils which are not quite as light as those most suited to the finer grasses. The commonest species is *A. compressus* which is found throughout the country in all open spaces and is the grass used most generally for lawns and playing fields, as well as for providing a quick cover on bare ground around new buildings and along roadsides. It makes a lawn which is rather coarse in texture though with regular mowing it becomes very dense and successfully keeps out other grasses and weeds. Sometimes in a turf composed mainly of this grass, a pathway will become completely bare because of overuse, but this can be remedied quite easily, especially when there is regular rainfall so that the soil never becomes completely dry. If the path can be closed for about two months at this time the new runners develop quickly from the plants on either side and will soon cover the bare soil. Regrowth would be much more rapid if the bare soil were loosened with a fork so that the new runners could root more easily.

When planted on roadsides or on road dividers, this grass is easy to manage as it is reasonably hard-wearing and can be maintained in good condition with little attention. It is tolerant of traffic fumes and can be used successfully for planting in the centre of towns and cities, where it will resist a considerable amount of soil compaction by constant pedestrian use before its growth is affected.

Carpet grass will grow well in full sun but can also withstand a little shade and under such conditions it becomes a little taller so that management must be more careful. Normally it is propagated by cuttings which should be planted at 20 cm intervals as the growth of the runners is very strong. However, seed is available and this can give good results although lawn formation will take a little longer. Seed has been used for planting steep banks and has been mixed with plastic or resinous materials or with a slurry made of cattle dung. The mixture is sprayed or scattered evenly over the bank so that the seeds remain stuck to the soil and will establish themselves fairly quickly. On steep banks this method is worth trying as it may be difficult or impossible to get turfs to remain on the soil until well established.

There is another species of Axonopus which is *A. affinis* and this has much narrower leaves than the previous species. It appears to be more common in the highlands but grows quite well in the lowlands although it is not as robust as *A. compressus*. Otherwise, it needs the same treatment as the previous species. Neither of these grasses should be cut too closely or bare patches will appear quickly on the lawn, but regular cutting is necessary as the leaves will be closer to the soil and the appearance of the lawn will be improved. A little fertilizer at regular intervals will keep the growth strong and the leaf colour a good dark green. Cutting should be less frequent during spells of dry weather.

St. Augustine Grass
(*Stenotaphrum secundatum*)

This imported grass is sometimes available and produces a coarse-textured lawn. It has broad leaves although not as large as those of Axonopus. The grass develops long, fairly thick runners and should not be cut too close, otherwise bare places will develop very quickly. It makes a good general purpose lawn but needs regular attention or other grasses will soon appear in it and are difficult to remove once well established. There is a form with variegated leaves which can be grown as an ornamental in a garden bed. Propagation is by means of cuttings and the grass will tolerate some shade so that it can be used in courtyards or between tall buildings where only a short period of sunlight is received each day.

Centipede Grass (*Eremochloa ophiuroides*)

This plant is a native of south China and is sometimes called Chinese lawngrass. It is a slow growing grass producing short, thick, leafy runners and has a fairly restricted root system. Although the leaves are rather narrow the turf produced is a little coarse but it makes a good lawn in places which do not have a great deal of pedestrian traffic. It is not fussy about maintenance but weeding must be done regularly while it is becoming established. It cannot be used for playing fields because of its slow growth and poor tolerance of wear.

Love Grass (*Chrysopogon aciculatus*)

On poor soil where it may be difficult to grow better grasses, a turf of Love grass can be established. It is a long, creeping grass with broad leaves and covers the ground well. However, it does have the disadvantage of producing a large number of tough flowering stems which are not easy to cut with some mowing machines. The fruits have long awns which adhere to clothing or to the coats of animals and are dispersed in this way. They can penetrate clothes and are often difficult to remove as well as being very irritant when they scratch the skin. Frequent mowing is necessary in order to prevent the development of flowering heads and to encourage the production of more leaves. It is a hardy and drought resistant grass and would only be used on areas too poor or dry for other, better varieties of grass.

Buffalo Grass (*Paspalum conjugatum*)

This grass also would not be used normally for making a lawn, but it does have some use under certain circumstances. It is a broad-leaved grass with long, creeping runners, and grows throughout the country. Frequent cutting is necessary because it is very strong-growing and tends to smother other grasses in the vicinity. It has some use in shady areas where it can be mixed with Axonopus as it will tolerate some shade, but fertilizer application should be minimal, otherwise it produces a great deal of coarse growth and can become invasive.

Grass under Shade

Under the shade of trees the finer grasses will not grow strongly and it is necessary to use the coarser ones such as Paspalum and Axonopus, as mentioned above. Under deep shade no grass will grow and then some other ground cover must be used to prevent the surface soil from being washed away.

not tolerate strong soap-oil emulsion mixtures such as are used against scale insects on most other kinds of plants. Many ferns are very sensitive to solutions of the modern insecticides and are damaged even by very dilute solutions. It is important, therefore, to read the directions for use very carefully because most of these chemicals are meant for use on flowering plants. The best treatment for ferns is to keep the plants clean by destroying infested parts, and for this to be effective constant watch is necessary, to detect the first signs of attack. The larger Maidenhair ferns are sometimes attacked badly by the caterpillars known as bagworms, and the best method of control is hand-picking as these pests are easily seen and removed. They ruin the appearance of the plant because they eat large holes in the leaflets. If the attack is very bad, all the leaves should be cut away and destroyed. The new leaves should be watched carefully as they appear and any bagworms should be removed immediately. If an attack by these insects is dealt with thoroughly, they will usually not appear again.

KINDS OF MAIDENHAIR FERNS

There are two groups of typical Maidenhair ferns grown in Malaysia, and also various much larger kinds belonging to the genus Adiantum which are, perhaps, not true Maidenhairs, though they are easily recognizable as similar in habit, with black, wiry leafstalks and leaflets of similar shape.

Adiantum cuneatum

Adiantum tenerum

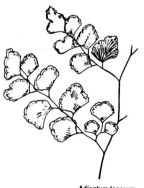

Adiantum tenerum

Glory of Moordrecht

The two groups of typical Maidenhair ferns are varieties of *Adiantum tenerum* and *Adiantum cuneatum*. The former have rather large leaflets which have a little joint at the base (easily seen with a hand lens) so that they fall separately when the leaf is old. The varieties of *A. cuneatum* have smaller leaflets that are not jointed at the base. Another distinction is in the shape of the little flaps that cover the spores at the edges of the leaflets on the lower surface. In *A. tenerum* these flaps (called indusia) are oblong in shape but in *A. cuneatum* they are circular and are placed around small indentations in the edges of the leaflets.

Typical *A. tenerum* is probably the commonest Maidenhair grown in Malaysia and often appears freely from self-sown spores among rocks and brickwork in the neighbourhood of a fern or shade house. The common small variety of *A. cuneatum* is just as easy to grow, and responds remarkably to a little manuring, producing much more bushy plants than *A. tenerum*, but it does not reproduce itself from spores in the same way.

Both of these species are commonly grown as pot plants in temperate countries.

Adiantum tenerum

This has been cultivated for many years and has occasionally given rise to finer varieties which have grown from spores. There is one group of such varieties which have very broad, much-branched fronds. The finest of all is that named var. Farleyense and it appeared as a chance sporeling at Farley Hall, Barbados about 1860. It has very large frilled overlapping leaflets but is a delicate form and is difficult to grow well in Malaysia. Usually it produces no spores but at Moordrecht in Holland, a sporeling was produced from it and proved much stronger than the parent Farleyense and almost equally fine in size and shape. This new variety was called Glory of Moordrecht (exhibited first in 1911) and has since been grown in Malaysia and Singapore where it is robust and undoubtedly the finest Maidenhair variety.

Adiantum cuneatum (A. raddianum)

This species and its varieties are suited to rather cooler conditions than the lowlands of Malaysia but with a little care some can be grown very well. For this reason these plants are not quite as common as *A. tenerum* and are less robust in growth.

THE GIANT MAIDENHAIRS

These are the large species of Adiantum mentioned above. The largest and best known is *A. peruvianum* from the Andes of Peru which may have fronds 1½ m high (including the stalks) and has leaflets 4½ cm long and 2½

Cyathea

Adiantum polyphyllum

Drynaria quercifolia

Aglaonema pseudobracteatum

Drynaria quercifolia on *Enterolobium cyclocarpum*

Aglaonema rubra

Nephrolepis duffii

Asplenium nidus

appearance. If grown in pots, small plants can be used, but it is quite easy also to use a small piece of an old plant. When full grown, the rhizome of this fern will be up to 4 cm in diameter and is densely covered with golden brown or dark brown scales.

If an old plant is used for propagation, it is best to take a piece of rhizome about 15 cm long, preferably with a growing point. It is best to use a pot of 20–30 cm diameter, about two-thirds full with a loose soil mixture. The cutting, which may be bulky, can be placed in the centre or at the side of the pot. The latter is probably best as new roots will develop quickly and will attach the rhizome to the pot, after which it will grow slowly around the side of the pot and eventually up over the rim. Branches will soon develop and spread over the surface of the soil as well as over the rim of the pot. As growth is rather slow, repotting will not be necessary for a long time.

The plants do not need watering every day and grow best in light shade, although they will tolerate short spells of direct sunshine. Two kinds of leaves are produced; there are short, broad ones, with shallow lobing and no stalk, which are pressed closely to the pot, tree trunk, or other support and are called nest leaves; and there are long, deeply lobed leaves with short stalks. The nest leaves become pale brown and remain on the rhizome permanently until they decay and are one of the attractive features of this species. Management of these plants is the same as for the Bird's Nest fern, and crumbled dried leaves can be placed in and around the bases of the leaves. If the plants are given too much water the nest leaves may not develop and only the long ones are produced, but if they are kept a little on the dry side then nest leaves will form as well as the normal kind.

Nephrolepis (Lace Fern)

N. exaltata is a commonly grown pot plant and has produced a large number of different forms of which the cultivar Bostoniensis, the Boston fern, is probably the most well known. This has long pinnate leaves which are slightly drooping and makes an attractive plant when grown in a hanging basket. Many other cultivars have been selected from this form and some have very much more finely divided leaflets, or crested leaves.

One of the more common forms with finely divided leaflets is the Lace fern which has drooping, pale green fronds and grows well in hanging pots or baskets. It often produces leaves of the normal kind and these should be removed as soon as they appear. The Lace fern needs similar treatment to the Maidenhairs and will not tolerate wet, sodden soil, so that it grows best in a mixture of well burnt

earth and dried cattle dung. It is well suited if it receives full morning sun with shade for the rest of the day, but watering must not be excessive and the plants are best kept under cover from rain. A good position for them is a house porch facing east. Each plant produces very numerous runners and the pot will quickly fill with small rooted plants which can be used for propagation.

Two other species of Nephrolepis are also grown commonly as pot plants but are, in addition, found wild throughout the country.

N. biserrata, the Sword fern, has large pinnate leaves up to 1 ½ m long, although they do not reach this size when grown in pots. This plant is very vigorous and will quickly fill a pot, but it can be planted out in the garden and will, if not checked, make a dense thicket which can be useful in a shady corner of the garden where little else will grow. It thrives in any garden soil and needs no special treatment. There is a form in which the tips of the leaflets are divided into two or more lobes, giving them a crested appearance. This form is named *cv. furcans* (Fishtail fern) and is not as robust as the normal kind but is still easy to grow, although it is not always available, and makes an attractive pot plant. It sometimes produces leaves of the normal form and these should be removed as soon as they appear. Both kinds produce numerous runners which can be used for propagation.

N. cordifolia is a smaller plant with shorter, narrower leaves, but is slower growing and makes an excellent pot plant. Small specimens can be kept in good condition for a very long time in a pot of 10 cm diameter. This species needs plenty of light, otherwise growth will stop and the leaflets will drop. If used for indoor decoration it is best kept near a window where it will receive sufficient light. Propagation is by means of runners but is more difficult than in the previous species.

There are several cultivars of this species, but the commonest in Malaysia is *cv. duffii* which has short, round leaflets closely arranged along the leafstalk. Management is the same as for the normal form.

All species are commonly used as house plants in temperate countries.

Pellaea rotundifolia

This is an imported fern, small in size, and very suitable as a house plant. It has long pinnate leaves with many flat, round, dark green leaflets and is slow in growth. Regular watering is essential and the plants need shade continuously. Plants kept indoors should be sprayed with water each week to keep the foliage clean and healthy. Propagation is by division. It is grown as a house plant in temperate countries also.

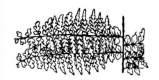

Nephrolepis

Platycerium coronarium
(Stag's Horn Fern)

A wild species often found growing on the trunks or branches of old trees. If young plants can be found they can be tied to a piece of tree branch and hung in a shady place until well rooted. The plant is not suitable for a pot but could be grown in some kind of strong basket where the pendulous fronds could be seen to the best advantage. Management is the same as for the Bird's Nest fern.

Small plants are occasionally found as house plants in temperate countries.

Polypodium scolopendria
(Phymatodes scolopendria)

One of the commonest wild ferns and yet very suitable for certain places in a garden. It will grow on the ground, or over rocks, or it will climb up tree trunks. It thrives in shade or in full sun. The large, shiny, green leaves have up to four pairs of long lobes but in very young plants the leaf blade is simple. Propagation can be done from pieces of rhizome and the plants look attractive in a trough where they can creep among other plants, or they can be planted in the ground around the base of tree trunks where few other plants would grow.

Pteris cretica

A small fern with fronds having long, narrow leaflets, which may be lobed to varying degrees. In some forms the fronds are 'crested' with many leaflets having closely arranged, short lobes at their apices. A cultivar with variegated leaves is also available.

Pteris ensiformis

This is a commonly grown pot plant of which the variegated form *cv. victoriae* is probably the best known. The fern has pinnate leaves with several long, narrow leaflets arranged along slender stalks. In the variegated form the leaflets are irregularly patterned with white. Propagation is easy by means of division and the plants will tolerate full sunlight for part of the day. These plants are best grown in pots or troughs as they are not really strong enough to compete with other plants in a border. If the pot becomes absolutely dry, the plants will recover provided they are watered soon enough afterwards, but some of the young fronds may die.

Both species are commonly grown as house plants in temperate countries.

Selaginella

These plants look rather like ferns, and are reproduced by spores; but what appears to be a single frond of Selaginella is really a branch system, with four rows of tiny leaves on each

Selaginella

Selaginella

branch, two rows spreading at right angles to the branch and two rows with smaller leaves pointing upwards. There are about thirty species of Selaginella growing wild in Malaysia and a few of them, with a few introduced ones, are often grown as pot plants. All of them need moist shady conditions, and a well drained soil with plenty of humus. They are easy to grow and some are extremely decorative. Propagation is by division of old plants or by means of pieces of stem which have developed roots, and in the latter case the cuttings should be planted in soil in a pot covered with a clear polythene bag, so that the air around them remains moist until they are well rooted.

S. wildenovii is a creeping species with long trailing stems and although it can be grown in a pot it quickly becomes far too large. However, it can be grown in a shady place around the base of a tree trunk and will make a good ground cover but it should not be allowed to dry out completely and during long dry spells should be given a good soaking with water each evening. Provided there is sufficient moisture, the leaves will always be a beautiful, iridescent blue which lights up a dark corner of the garden in a most striking manner.

Other species of Selaginella have an upright habit and shorter stems so that they make good pot plants. All, however, need continuous shade and must not be allowed to dry out. They can be grown in shaded troughs or in bottle gardens provided they can be kept sufficiently moist. Some of the wild species have young stems and leaves which are bronze or reddish brown and these are most attractive when grown among the other species which are entirely green. These plants are not suitable for indoor decoration because the air is too dry, but will do well on a shaded veranda or patio, especially if they are moistened thoroughly every evening.

Several species of Selaginella are grown in greenhouses in temperate countries and some are very suitable for growing in bottle gardens.

Sphenomeris chinensis

A small fern with deeply divided leaflets which give it a lace-like appearance. It can be grown in pots in light shade but never forms very large plants. It is a little difficult to manage in the lowlands but is easy to grow in the highlands. It is worth a little effort because of its delicate, slightly drooping fronds.

Stenochlaena palustris

This is a climbing fern found wild in swampy areas or on scrubby waste ground. It is not usually considered as a garden plant but it has elegant pinnate leaves of two kinds, fertile and sterile, and can be grown over an archway or pergola in full sun. The sterile leaves have many long, narrow leaflets about 1 ½ cm wide, and the fertile leaves have very thin, almost cylindrical leaflets which are only about 3–4 mm wide. Both kinds are bright red when young and the young fertile fronds are sometimes on sale in the market as they are used as a vegetable.

The rhizomes of this plant are long and clamber through neighbouring plants, but in a garden they can be trained over a support together with other climbers. It needs to be grown with other plants as it is not dense enough on its own. Propagation is easy from pieces of rhizome, but the initial growth is slow and some patience is needed.

Palms

Though less dainty and graceful than ferns, palms are very useful where larger plants are required. Being more robust than ferns, they will stand more exposed conditions and require less frequent attention. To maintain a potted palm in a healthy condition does, however, need some care, and plants which have been long neglected are slow to recover.

Palms are grown from seed except in the case of those with a tufted habit, which may be divided in the same way as a fern. The early seedling stages are rather slow, but in the case of most palms, useful pot plants may be grown in less than two years from the planting of seeds.

Potted palms are best in the usual burnt earth mixture, but are less exacting than some plants in their requirements as regards aeration of the soil. In any case, the palm roots will soon run all through the soil, thus helping to maintain aeration, and there is much less danger of damage from over-watering than in the case of ferns. When a plant has grown to the fullest size possible in a particular pot, it should be transferred to a larger one; if this is not done some palms will remain at about the same size (though producing new leaves) for some time, and it is often convenient to check their growth in this way. They must, however, be given a small, occasional application of manure to keep them in healthy condition, and any topsoil washed away by watering should be replaced with new soil. Manures may most conveniently be applied in the form of one of the artificial fertilizers, which are more pleasant and easy to use around the house than cattle dung.

There are very many kinds of palms but the number grown in pots is relatively small. There are two or three common tufted kinds which have a large number of shoots and make bushy plants, which are perhaps the most generally useful for decorative purposes.

Chrysalidocarpus lutescens (the Yellow-stemmed Palm), *Cyrtostachys renda* (the Sealing Wax Palm) and *Rhapis excelsa* are among the commonest of these, and are described in another chapter. Of the single-stemmed kinds of palms, the most commonly grown in pots are those with fan-shaped leaves. One which is particularly prized by many people has leaves exactly in the shape of a fan with broadly toothed edges; this is *Licuala grandis* which comes from the New Hebrides. Other kinds are species of Livistona which have very deeply toothed margins but these will quickly become too large for a pot and must be planted out. However, they make good pot plants while they are very young. There are many single-stemmed palms with feather-shaped leaves such as Pinanga and Ptychosperma, and these also make good pot plants while young.

Palms vary in their ability to withstand strong sunlight and some cannot tolerate it, quickly becoming yellow and sickly. Most, however, can stand a certain amount of sun and, indeed, benefit from it, but they are best kept sheltered from sun during the hottest part of the day. On the other hand, plants kept for too long in poor light in the house become weak, and then a sudden change to full outdoor conditions may be too much for them. The best arrangement is to change the plants in the house frequently, so that all may be kept in good condition. A sickly palm takes a long time to recover.

The Sealing-Wax Palm, which is such a characteristic Malaysian plant, does not display its decorative red leaf sheaths when young and is not suitable for small pots, but it can be grown very well in large pots, jars or tubs and is then very decorative. Another very useful palm for a large pot is Rhapis, which has numerous slender stems, each bearing small, glossy, fan-shaped, dark green leaves having several long, narrow leaflets. It is quite unlike other palms and makes a pleasant change of foliage. As a background for the display of flowering plants under a house porch, it is very effective. It rarely flowers in Malaysia but is propagated easily by division of old plants which produce a great number of suckers.

There are a few handsome and much prized Fan Palms which make good pot plants, but seeds are not obtainable in Malaysia and so the plants are not common. One of the best is a species of Pritchardia which makes a magnificent subject for large pots or jars having a bold and shapely leaf. It grows best in full sun and can be used with some effect in formal landscape gardening.

There are few pests of potted palms, the worst being beetles which eat the leaves at night, but grasshoppers and some caterpillars can be troublesome at times. Hand-picking is the easiest way of controlling them and if this is done regularly for a week or two there will be little, if any, further trouble. The larvae of some large beetles may attack the growing point of large palms and these should be sprayed with insecticide, but if the actual growing point is destroyed then the whole palm will die.

Under the heading of palms we may also mention the pretty Panama Hat plant, *Carludovica*. This is not, strictly speaking, a palm, but in leaf and habit it is palm-like and it is often used as a pot plant. The fan-shaped leaves are carried on long, slender stalks and there is no trunk, but new leaves appear continuously from the base of the plant. It produces curious club-shaped inflorescences on short stalks and is best grown in light shade. When well established, it forms a large, handsome clump of leaves so that it is suitable for single planting in shaded areas.

Aroids

There are a very large number of tropical plants of the Arum or Keladi family and a large proportion of them have decorative leaves. Some also have brightly coloured flowers, and are much cultivated especially for the cut-flower trade. The best known of these are the white Arum Lily (this of course has no relation to a true lily), which is very successful in the highlands but not in the lowlands, and the Anthuriums with their bright colours. In all aroids the flowers are very small and are grouped together on a club-like organ called the spadix, which may be completely exposed as in Anthurium or partly concealed as in the Arum Lily. In Anthuriums the flowers are easily visible on the spadix but in the Arum Lily the flowers are completely hidden inside the large leaf-like white sheath called the spathe. In some aroids the spathe is bright red, pink, purple, green or white, and may be very large as in Anthuriums, or, as in other cases, it is small and has little part in the decorative value of the plant. The flowers on the spadix eventually produce fruits which are usually red or orange berries.

Aroids vary a great deal in habit and there are climbers, rock plants, ground cover plants in shady forest, and others which have resting tubers. The edible tubers called Keladi are the fleshy stems of certain members of this family, and the leaves of some are also edible. Many aroids, however, are poisonous plants and even the edible kinds must be cooked before they are safe to eat. These plants are not troubled by pests and diseases, but some species are eaten greedily by snails.

The number of aroids available to gardeners in Malaysia has increased enormously during the last decade and many of them are very useful because they are tough plants which will tolerate a wide range of growing conditions. Consequently, many of them can be used successfully for indoor decoration in deep shade, dry air, or airconditioning. To grow them well, however, they need good treatment, and under the conditions just mentioned they will make very slow growth or none at all, although the leaves will remain on the plants for a long time, so that a reasonable appearance is maintained. Such plants need to be kept outside for some time to recover from the effect of the poor growing conditions, and if they have been kept indoors for a very long time recovery will be very slow.

It is now possible to engage commercial horticulturalists who can supply plants for the decoration of public buildings and offices, and they will maintain these plants or change them regularly. The aroids are particularly useful for this kind of work because they need changing less frequently than some other plants. The home gardener would be wise to keep more than one plant so that they can be changed around at intervals.

Most of the aroids now available are easily propagated from cuttings or by division of old plants and should be kept shaded until a new root system has developed. Many of them develop great quantities of roots and if they are grown in a trough or other such enclosed area with other plants, the latter can become starved. Regular applications of manure are essential and, if possible, it is a good idea to remove some of the aroid roots, which will not harm the plants, and will reduce their greedy absorption of nutrients from the limited amount of soil. When aroids are used as indoor plants it is not always possible to spray the foliage with water to keep it clean, but as the leaves are relatively large it is quite easy to wipe them over individually with a damp cloth, once or twice a week, in order to keep them free of dust.

Some of the aroids available to gardeners in Malaysia are mentioned below and it should be remembered that, at the present time, all of these, except for 2 or 3 species, are commonly grown as house plants in most temperate countries. The method of culture is similar.

Aglaonema commutatum and cultivars
Usually these plants grow to 30–50 cm in height and have thick stems with long, narrow, spear-shaped leaves which are variegated, either in a mixture of light green and dark green or with an irregular patterning of white. The plants will grow on practically any kind of soil and are easily propagated from cuttings. They do best in light shade, and as single

plants are not always well shaped; they look better when mixed with other plants.

Aglaonema pictum

This is a much more handsome plant with strongly coloured leaves having yellow or silver markings on a dark blue-green background. The surface of each leaf has a sheen like satin and the plants are shorter than the previous species. A few cultivars are available but are not common and this may be because the species is rather slow in growth. However, all of the cultivars are very decorative and are worth a little extra trouble in order to grow them well.

Alocasia (Elephant's Ear)

One or two species are grown and one of the most frequently seen is the very large *A. macrorrhiza* which can reach 5 m in height, with leaves up to 2 m long. The stem is very thick and stout with the flat leaves held in a close group near the tip. Each leaf blade is arranged in an almost vertical position at the end of a very long stalk and is usually light green. The plants can be grown in a border but if kept under strict control they can be used also in a small garden. They thrive in light shade with plenty of moisture at the roots but in dry conditions many leaves will drop, and the rate of growth will be very slow. Some side shoots develop and these can be used for propagation, or, if they are left on the plant, it will eventually develop into a large clump which can be striking in appearance. There is a form with variegated leaves but it is not as robust as the normal kind and produces very few side shoots.

Several other species of Alocasia are grown as ornamentals but are not commonly available and they are more difficult to manage. Some of them have strikingly coloured leaves and some have leaves of unusual shape, but in most cases each plant will carry only two or three leaves at any one time so that the appearance is somewhat meagre. They look best when placed in among a group of other pot plants. They are usually grown as pot plants but if there is a shady moist bank in the garden they can be planted there and left to their own devices. In such a place, they may at times lose all their leaves and will rest for a short while, but the gardener should not be alarmed as they will soon develop a new set of leaves.

Anthurium

These plants have handsome leaves, but some of them are grown for their flowers rather than for their foliage because of their highly coloured spathes which may be red, pink or white. Some of the species with less attractive flowers have very large and beautiful leaves,

Anthurium andreanum

such as the well known *A. crystallinum*, which has dark green, velvety leaves with pale green or almost white veins. Most Anthuriums are by nature epiphytes, growing on tree branches in the same manner as many orchids. Consequently, they need a very well drained soil and thrive best in pots more than half filled with broken bricks with a layer of fibrous leaf-mould on top, which must be renewed occasionally. To this leaf-mould may be added cattle dung or groundnut cake, or artificial fertilizer may be applied. All Anthuriums prefer a little shade, especially those with large, decorative leaves like *A. crystallinum*.

Propagation is from cuttings of the large stems, or side shoots can be detached and used. An old plant may become unsightly with a long, straggling stem, but it is often possible to rejuvenate such plants by cutting them back hard to within 20–30 cm above the soil level. The upper part of the stem can be cut into pieces which may be used as cuttings, and the lower part still in its pot can be kept in a shady place out of doors where it will develop one or more new shoots. This may take a long time but, provided the pot is watered occasionally, growth will start again and when the new leaves are large enough the plant can be used for decoration again.

The Anthuriums with bright red or pink spathes are varieties of *A. andreanum* which are often used as cut flowers. This species grows and flowers quite well in the lowlands of Malaysia. They need light shade and treatment as previously described. Many fine varieties with spathes of vivid scarlet, orange, crimson and pink have been raised in Bangkok and if seeds of these plants are grown, more new varieties could be produced.

One or two other species of Anthurium are available and are grown for their leaves as the flowers are very small and relatively inconspicuous. These species have leaves up to 30–40 cm long and broad with the margins lobed in different ways. They also have a very short stem so that they can be grown easily in pots, but these become filled with roots very quickly and regular application of fertilizer is necessary throughout the year. The roots will also grow for long distances outside the pot and must be trimmed away, especially if the plants are kept inside a house.

These Anthuriums produce inflorescences with very narrow green spathes and purple spadices, and when the yellow pollen shows on the surface of these it can be rubbed over the whole inflorescence with one finger so that, later, many fruits will develop. These are yellow or orange when ripe and the seeds germinate very easily, providing a convenient means of propagation. When no seeds are available, propagation can be done by means of cuttings of old stems, or if side shoots are developed and have one or two roots of their own, they can be detached and planted up in pots. If the main stem is used it should be cut into pieces, each of which should have some roots, but growth will be slow and it will be some time before a new shoot develops. The terminal portion of the stem which bears a few leaves will root and grow very quickly. The lowermost part of the stem can be left in the pot and treated as mentioned earlier. New shoots will not appear for one or two months and the plants will seem lifeless, but any temptations to throw it away should be resisted until there are clear signs of new shoots. Some of these plants are not freely available and so every opportunity should be taken to increase one's stock.

The foliage Anthuriums make good house plants but also look well when planted in a trough on a shaded veranda. The two commonest species available are *A. macrolobum*, with large, almost round, very deeply lobed leaves, and *A. crystallinum*, mentioned previously. Other species can sometimes be found in plant nurseries but some time is needed to search for them.

Caladium

These are probably the best known and most cultivated of the ornamental-leaved aroids. They depend for their beauty on the varied colours of the leaves which usually are more or less variegated with red. There are also some kinds which have practically white leaves, delicately veined with green. Wild Caladiums are native of South America whence they were taken to Europe, and under cultivation a very large number of cultivars were produced. A few of these have become established and grow wild in many parts of Malaysia, but they are not the most attractive varieties.

Caladiums have tuberous stems and need resting from time to time so they must be treated like other bulbous or tuberous plants. When in full growth they should be given frequent applications of fertilizer and when they have completed their growth the plants should be gradually dried off and rested. Many Caladiums will stand full sun but they are better under light shade. Some of the good varieties can be grown on shaded banks in the garden and will die down naturally during a dry spell. When the next rain moistens the soil, they will sprout again and if they are well suited they will increase naturally. Caladiums will not tolerate wet soil, and should not be overpotted or overwatered. A good burnt earth mixture or similar well aerated soil is essential and it is best to repot two to three times, increasing the size of the pot gradually, as the plants grow larger.

Caladium humboldtii

Dieffenbachia picta cv. Rudolph Roehrs

Dieffenbachia picta

Dieffenbachia splendens

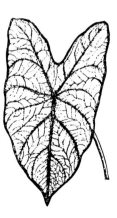

Caladium

Epipremnum giganteum

Many hybrids are available and these are usually named *C. x hortulanum*, most of which have large, broad, arrow-shaped leaves of various colours. Another series of hybrids is called *C. picturatum* and these hybrids have smaller, narrower leaves attached in a different way to the leaf-stalk but also showing the good range of bright colours. This group is not so commonly available in Malaysia, which is unfortunate; these smaller plants are better suited for indoor culture in small houses.

Caladium humboldtii is a very charming small species, quite distinct in appearance from any of the previous hybrids. It grows to about 20 cm in height and can be kept in very small pots quite easily. The leaves are attractively variegated in green and white and the leaf-blades are about 4–10 cm long and 3–5 cm broad so that they appear like miniature forms of the larger hybrids. Management is exactly the same as for the large varieties and these little plants are ideal for miniature gardens of any kind, or they can be grown on their own in a pot and when well established will make very shapely and decorative plants.

Colocasia

Although these plants are mentioned in the vegetable section, they can be used also in other parts of the garden. If there is a wet area or if there is a stream running through the garden, then some of the varieties of Colocasia can be grown and look most attractive, especially those with dark blue-green leaves. They need little attention and will increase on their own so that propagation presents no problem. The plants can be grown in gardens of any size, provided the soil is moist enough.

Dieffenbachia (Dumb Canes)

Members of this genus are among the most popular and commonly grown pot plants, often surviving the most horrifying growing conditions. Several species and hybrids are available and practically all of them have variegated leaves. Dark green, light green, white, cream and yellow are the colours found and are arranged in a wide variety of patternings. Varieties with a great deal of white or yellow in the leaves need plenty of light so that the colour will develop properly and most of the forms have thick stems and large oval or oblong leaves.

The plants need plenty of water but must not become waterlogged and if they are kept too dry the older leaves will drop, resulting in a long bare stem with a few leaves at the tip. Such bare-stemmed plants can be rejuvenated by cutting them down to about 10 cm above the soil level, and if they are watered regularly afterwards one or two new shoots will develop within a few weeks. The upper part of the stem can be cut into pieces about 15 cm long which can be used as cuttings but it is important to plant them the right way up. It is very easy to reverse these leafless stems and if planted upside down they will not, of course, grow. Cuttings of this kind take several weeks to produce roots and new leaves, but afterwards growth is rapid.

All varieties need pots of at least 20 cm diameter and in larger pots two or more cuttings can be planted as the effect will be much better after they have grown a little. If the plants are kept out of doors in pots, or if they are planted directly in the ground, they may need some support when they have become a little taller because well manured plants hold practically all of their leaves down to ground level and this makes them top-heavy, especially during rainstorms with the added weight of the water on the leaves. Strong winds will also blow them over and the leaves will very soon become discoloured if they are not raised up from the ground fairly quickly.

The commonest species is *D. maculata* which has produced very many well known cultivars, of which the most striking is that named 'Rudolph Roehrs', and in this form the young leaves are almost entirely white or cream with a very narrow green margin. Other cultivars have leaves with spotting or mottling, to varying extents, in white, yellow, cream or pale green. One very distinct form is *D. x bausei* in which the leaves are yellowish green with small irregularly shaped spots of dark green and white scattered over the whole leaf; this colour combination makes it one of the most attractive forms.

All varieties are easily grown and for those with little space available, a collection of different forms can be interesting and will provide variety. Plant nurseries should be visited as often as possible to build up the collection and very often the less popular forms will be found

Epipremnum aureum

in secluded corners of these places where they are likely to have become sadly neglected. Some of the commoner forms can now be found wild in shady places in many parts of the country.

Epipremnum aureum (Scindapsus aureus, Money Plant, Golden Pothos, Devil's Ivy)

Almost everyone has at some time or other grown a piece of this plant in a pot of water at home or in an office. It is a climbing plant with leaves irregularly patterned in yellow or white, and pieces of stem will, surprisingly, survive in water only and can actually make some growth. If grown in a trough it will trail over the sides and will also creep over the soil around the stems of other plants, but it is very good-natured and never becomes too robust under these conditions. It is a long-suffering plant and is often subjected to conditions which would kill off other plants very quickly, but it survives and produces a few small leaves which seems to satisfy the gardening instinct latent in many people.

Propagation is very easy from stem cuttings and if these are grown in a pot it is best to provide a short framework of some kind to support the long stems. When grown in this way the leaves will remain relatively small, from 5 to 10 cm long, but if a cutting is planted at the base of a tree trunk in the garden it will climb up the trunk by means of its roots which become firmly attached in the crevices of the bark, and successive leaves will be larger as the plant climbs higher. Full-sized leaves can be 30–60 cm long and often have irregularly lobed margins.

With plenty of light, the leaf colours are very bright, and because of the large size of the leaves they may seem a little too gaudy in small gardens. This plant can be grown on walls also but if the concrete or bricks become too hot in the sun, the roots are unable to attach themselves and the plant will merely grow along the base of the wall instead of climbing it. If the wall is shaded during the middle of the day there is a greater chance of success.

There is another form of this plant which is very much slower growing and has leaves finely patterned in white and green. It needs the same treatment as the previous kind but does best in light shade and is a little more sensitive to over-watering. The cultivar is named 'Marble Queen'.

Epipremnum falcifolia (Epipremnum giganteum)

This is a fine plant and is best grown on a tree trunk as it becomes very large. It has very long, rather narrow leaves about 80 cm long and 15 cm broad. Growth is slow but the leaves are retained almost down to ground level for a very long time and the plant is a most handsome addition to a shady part of the garden. Propagation is by means of cuttings which are a little slow to root.

Epipremnum pinnatum (Raphidophora pinnata)

This is an attractive plant which is found wild in Malaysia and has dark green, very deeply-lobed leaves up to 60 cm long. As it is a climbing plant, it is best grown on a tree trunk or on some kind of support, but needs shade throughout the day. Propagation is easy from stem cuttings.

Homalomena

One or two species are grown as ornamentals although they are, generally speaking, undistinguished in appearance. They are short plants, very suitable for growing in pots, and one of the best is H. wallisii and its varieties which have large, oval, dark green leaves, 15 cm or more in length, with pale green or golden markings. This is a fine foliage plant which is easy to grow and elegant, but unfortunately is not freely available. It should be sprayed regularly with water to keep the leaves in good condition, and is easily propagated by division. One of the wild species which is commonly grown in gardens is H. rubra and it is mainly useful for filling in gaps in shady places because it is rather plain in appearance.

Monstera deliciosa (Swiss Cheese Plant)

A magnificent plant but unsuitable for growing in smaller pots because of its great size. It can be kept in large jars or in troughs and when it develops full-sized leaves, it is a most striking addition to the decoration of a house or garden. This plant can also be grown at the base of a tree trunk where it will form a large mound of huge leaves and may, in addition, climb up the trunk. With care, it can be trained over a pergola but this is not usually the most effective method because the older leaves may die away, especially if the plants are exposed to hot sunshine for a large part of each day, and the stems will become bare.

Well grown leaves are very large and can be 1 m in length and about 50 cm or more in width. They are deep green with deeply lobed margins and there are round or oval holes irregularly arranged on either side of the midrib. The leaves are long-lived and a new one develops about once each month.

The plants grow very easily from cuttings but development is slow at first until the roots have made sufficient growth. If old plants are cut off near ground level, one or more new shoots will develop within a few weeks, especially if the plants are kept well watered. This

Homalomena wallisii 'Maoro'

Kalanchoe pinnata

Monstera deliciosa

Monstera deliciosa

Philodendron erubescens

Philodendron squamiferum

Philodendron gloriosum

Philodendron

Philodendron

Philodendron bipinnatifidum

Epipremnum aureum cv. 'Marble Queen'

Spathiphyllum commutatum

Xanthosoma lindenii

species produces great quantities of roots which will penetrate any cracks and crevices in concrete paths or stone paths. It is best to cut off many of these roots and to lay others on the soil surface so that they can grow into it. In a trough the quantity of roots may result in the starvation of other plants unless regular, frequent applications of fertilizer are given.

When grown in the garden, flowers and fruits are sometimes produced and the fruits are edible. In pots or troughs it is wise to put a short, stout pole in the soil to which the plant can be tied as it grows, but wherever it is planted the leaves will always be larger if the plant has a support of some kind so that it can climb a little. Outside in the garden, a good, thick piece of old tree trunk rising about 60 cm above the soil level is satisfactory and if the plant is induced to produce two or three shoots it will form a good mound of foliage which will hide the support completely.

Monstera is usually free from pest attacks but occasionally the leaves may be disfigured by stick insects which are difficult to see, although they can be up to 10 cm long. They hide during the day and it is best to remove them by hand in the evening when they appear and begin feeding; if this is done for one or two weeks, they can be cleared completely.

Monstera epipremnoides (M. leichtlinii)

Another climbing plant which can produce leaves up to one metre in length, but when it is grown in a pot the leaves are usually less than half this size. The whole plant is light green and each leaf has very large perforations which are of varying size and are arranged in two or three rows on either side of the midrib. This species can be grown in a trough where it can be allowed to creep over the soil surface amongst the other plants, but if full-sized leaves are needed then the plant must have some support on which to climb, otherwise only small leaves will be produced. Propagation is easy by means of cuttings.

Philodendron

This is one of the most popular groups of plants as they are easy to grow and will tolerate a range of growing conditions including great variations of shade and a wide range of temperatures. They will grow for some time inside a house, with very little attention, and can survive for a considerable period in air-conditioned rooms. The climbing members have very long stems and well spaced leaves, but there are species with very much shorter stems and closely arranged leaves, though even these will climb slowly if grown on a tree trunk.

The leaves show a wide range of shape and size and, as in many climbing aroids, those on young plants or unsupported stems are small and of different shape from those developed when the stem has been given some support and has begun to climb. As soon as the stem has become firmly attached to a support by its roots, then the subsequent leaves will be larger, and in a number of cases they will be totally different in shape. Although these plants will grow very well without any support, if the true leaves are needed, they must be allowed to climb. The leaves are simple or lobed in various ways and young leaves in some forms are bright red or bronze in colour. Although there are very many species and cultivars, relatively few of them have variegated leaves but this poses no problem as there are many other plants which do show this character. Some of the more easily available forms are described below.

Philodendron bipinnatifidum

This is one of the short-stemmed species and has very large, deeply lobed leaves; it needs considerable space and is therefore best grown outside in a very large pot or trough. A good plant can be 2 m in height and diameter when grown in this way, and if planted directly in the ground it can become much larger. This is a striking but slow growing plant only suitable for growing under big trees or in shady places around large buildings and in large gardens. Very large old plants grown under light shade can be 3 or 4 cm broad and high, with very thick, twisted, woody stems.

Philodendron domesticum (Philodendron hastatum, Spade-leaf Philodendron)

In this species the leaves are long and dark green with heart-shaped leaf bases and the plants can be kept for a long time in a pot. Support of some kind is needed and when the plants become overgrown, the stems may be cut into pieces which make good cuttings and root easily and quickly. This species can be grown out of doors also, in a trough or on a tree trunk as it is very adaptable and is one of the most easy to manage.

Philodendron erubescens (Red-leaf Philodendron)

This attractive species is rather slow growing and can be kept in a large pot for a long time. If given regular applications of fertilizer, it makes a very shapely plant and can be grown successfully without any support. The stems do not make any long growth and if a potted plant has two or three stems, these will provide sufficient lateral support for each other so that no stake will be needed. The leaf stems are dark purple and the leaf blades are dark green on the upper surface and red or copper-coloured on the undersurface. Young leaves

are copper-coloured and retain this colour for about two weeks until they are fully expanded, after which they gradually become dark green.

These plants may be grown in pots, troughs or on tree trunks in shade, although they will tolerate full sunlight for part of the day, provided they are well watered. They make excellent decoration for rooms of any size and the appearance is easily maintained because the leaves are large enough to be washed individually in order to remove dust.

Philodendron scandens var. oxycardium (Heart-leaf Philodendron)

A long-stemmed climbing plant with heart-shaped leaves which are bronze in colour when young. It can be grown on a tree trunk or in a trough where it will need some support; it will succeed also in a fairly small pot provided it is given a thin stake or a bamboo framework over which it can climb. In a trough it may be allowed to creep between the stems of other plants. There are several forms of this species and all can be grown in a similar manner.

Philodendron selloum

A large, short-stemmed species similar in size and shape to *P. bipinnatifidum*. The very large leaves are deeply lobed and the lobes are narrow with wavy margins. It makes a magnificent specimen if grown in a large Chinese jar in light shade, but it must be given fertilizer regularly otherwise the new leaves will be small. Watering should be carefully controlled and the pot must never become waterlogged; it is better to allow the soil to dry out almost completely after each watering. As the plant can become very large, it is unsuitable for small rooms and is best on a patio or veranda, or it can be grown in a trough.

The stems on old plants are very large and hard, and the older portions will be leafless so that they may look unsightly, but this species is not as easy to rejuvenate as some other aroids because of its slower growth. The leafy tip of the stem bearing several roots can be cut off and planted in a pot where it will establish itself quite quickly. Cuttings without roots will take much longer and are not always successful. Overwatering of such young plants must be avoided at all costs otherwise both the roots and stems will rot.

Sometimes the old, leafless part of the stem may produce one or more buds after the leafy tip has been removed and when these have made sufficient growth with some roots, they can be detached and potted up on their own. Afterwards, when they have begun to make new growth, they should be put into their final and permanent position, as they do not always take kindly to being moved: the roots sometimes seem to be especially sensitive to damage so that the plant will receive a severe check in growth until it can produce new ones. Damaged roots appear to be very prone to rotting but a very well drained potting mixture can help to prevent this.

Philodendron squamiferum

This slow growing species can be kept in a pot and is useful for decoration in small rooms. The leaf blades have three to five large lobes and long stalks which are densely covered with short, curved, soft bristles. The plant needs a short support on which to climb but sometimes produces a long stem, carrying widely spaced leaves, which creeps over the surface of the soil. This can be cut off and used for propagation as it roots very easily. As the leaves always have a good, fresh green colour the plant is an excellent subject for indoor decoration. There are a number of hybrids with this plant and some of them have more attractively lobed leaves than the parent so that they make excellent pot plants.

Many other species of Philodendron are grown as ornamentals in different parts of the tropics and there are, roughly, two main groups of these. In one group, the plants have very short stems and the leaves resemble those of Anthuriums. They are very attractive when mixed with other pot plants but on their own are less useful because each plant carries from three to five leaves only and therefore looks a little thin. The leaves are, however, in many cases very handsome as they are dark green with a velvety appearance and have light green or white veins. Despite the paucity of leaves, a single well grown plant can be used on its own with great decorative effect indoors as it takes up little space and, thanks to its very open appearance, never looks overpowering.

The other group of Philodendrons have leaves which are in appearance and arrangement very similar to those of the Bird's Nest fern, but they are scarce in Malaysia. This is unfortunate as they make excellent pot plants for small spaces and can be used also in troughs either indoors or outside in the garden.

Many of the species of Philodendron grown as ornamentals are not commonly available and often a species is more easily obtained in one part of the tropics than it is in another. A great number of the species are grown as house plants in temperate countries where they have become very popular.

Scindapsus pictus (Silver Vine)

This attractive plant has dark green, oval leaves with grey-green markings on the upper surface. The climbing stems are slow growing with the broad leaves closely arranged and

pressed firmly to the support which is almost completely hidden. Because of this method of growth, the plants are best placed at the base of a tree trunk, or a shady wall, or on some similar flat surface. If grown in a pot then a suitable support would be a piece of flat timber covered with fern root and moss.

Spathiphyllum

Spathiphyllum

The plants of this group are usually grown in pots and have long, dark green, spear-shaped leaves rising from ground level. The flowers are similar in appearance to those of Anthurium but have white spathes and produce a very strong, sweet fragrance. Light shade and well drained soil are essential and the plants can be grown also in troughs or outside in the garden, provided the soil conditions are suitable. If kept indoors the leaves need spraying with water once each week to keep them free from dust. In temperate countries, these plants are often used for indoor decoration in large rooms or halls. They are too large for small houses.

Syngonium podophyllum
(African Evergreen, Arrowhead Vine)

These are plants of strong, rapid growth and will quickly climb to the top of a tree trunk and along the branches. The leaves on an adult plant are palmate, very deeply lobed, with five to nine lobes, but on young plants the leaves may have one to three lobes only and frequently they are variegated with extensive white mottling. The leaf variegation gradually disappears as the plants become older so that on adult plants all new leaves are entirely green. This plant can cover a tree trunk completely and as there are many flower heads produced in the axils of most leaves, the appearance can become rather untidy. The number of stems growing on a tree trunk should therefore be restricted to two and all others should be removed as they appear. There are a number of cultivars differing in the amount of leaf lobing and in the amount of variegation.

Although this plant is so strong growing, young specimens with variegated leaves make excellent pot plants which are suitable for small rooms and can be kept for many months before replacement is needed. Propagation is very easy from cuttings but the plants will soon begin to produce long climbing stems. If these are cut, a bushy habit can be encouraged so that the plants can be kept to a manageable size for some time, but eventually they must be planted outside or new plants must be rooted for growing in pots.

Small plants are used commonly as indoor decoration for small rooms in temperate countries.

Xanthosoma (Yautia)

Although these plants have been mentioned in the section on vegetables, they do also make very good ornamentals. All are large herbs with short, thick stems and arrow-shaped or triangular leaves on long stalks.

X. violaceum (Blue Taro) has very dark green, sagittate leaves with purple veins and long purple stalks which have a greyish bloom on them resembling that on black grapes. Small side tubers are produced which are excellent when cooked and eaten with butter and salt. Propagation can be done from the side tubers or by dividing old plants. The colour of the leaves and stems develop best in full sunlight.

X. lindenii (Indian Kale) is a useful pot plant with long oblong or ovate leaves having large lobes at the base. The leaf blade is dark green with white veins which are bordered also with white areas of varying depth. A few cultivars are available differing mainly in the amount of white colouring in the leaf. This is an excellent and striking pot plant which grows best in light shade. Side shoots develop from ground level and propagation is easy by separating these and planting them up. Small plants make good decoration in the house and larger specimens look very well in a mixed group of pot plants, especially when decorating large halls, verandas or public buildings. When small, the plants will have up to five shoots, each with one to three leaves, but older plants may have ten or more shoots and can have a very neat and rather rounded appearance. If the plants are given regular applications of fertilizer they will produce good coloured leaves almost indefinitely, but must eventually be divided and repotted. Without fertilizer new leaves will be small and growth will be very slow.

Zantedeschia (Calla Lily, Arum Lily)

One commonly grown species is *Z. aethiopica* which is a robust plant with thick stems carrying large, broad, fleshy, dark green leaves. The flowers have a large, white funnel-shaped spathe and are very stiff in appearance. The plant will not grow well in the lowlands but does well and flowers also above 700 m, although it tends to produce a great deal of leaf and comparatively few blooms.

Another species which is available is *Z. elliotiana* and this has yellow spathes and white-spotted leaves.

Both species are best grown in plenty of light, but not in direct sunlight. Propagation is by means of division.

Bromeliads (Pineapple Family)

Many species from this family make very good pot plants because they do not grow exceptionally large and a number of them have highly coloured leaves or brightly coloured inflorescences which are interesting in shape. Although several of the genera are under cultivation in many parts of the world, only a few of these are generally available in Malaysia. Few plant nurseries keep any stock of these species, although an odd plant may sometimes be found in a neglected corner, but at flower shows, two or three kinds are often put on display by home gardeners. A number of these bromeliads are now commonly grown as house plants in temperate countries.

Practically all of the plants are native to tropical America and most of them are epiphytes. The stiff leaves generally develop in a rosette and have broad, sheathing bases together forming a cup in which water is held for long periods. This might present a small problem if mosquito larvae develop in the water but there are chemicals available now which can be dissolved in the water and will kill the mosquito larvae without harming the plant. Most of the plants grow best in good light but not in full sunlight, and the potting mixture should be very light and well drained because the plants will not tolerate waterlogging. The following species are those most frequently seen in private gardens.

Aechmea

Two species are grown commonly as pot plants. *A. fasciata*, the Urn Plant, grows to 30–50 cm high and has a rosette of long, dark green leaves which are covered with a fine white powder. The inflorescence rises from the centre of the plant and has a pink stem bearing closely arranged pink bracts and blue flowers. After flowering, side shoots develop and these can be used as cuttings. If the plant is kept indoors for some time the leaves should be sprayed frequently with clean water. There are cultivars which have variegated leaves.

Aechmea fulgens (Coral Berry) has shorter leaves up to 40 cm long which are entirely green but there is one cultivar, *cv. discolor*, in which the leaves are dark red on the undersurface. In both kinds the pale blue flowers are borne in an open inflorescence which has deep pink stems and bracts. Cultivation is the same as for the previous species.

Ananas (Pineapple)

Although normally grown for its fruit, there is one cultivar, *A. comosus cv. variegata*, which is grown as an ornamental and is very decorative. The curved leaves are striped with white or pale yellow and have short red spines along the margin and the youngest leaves are heavily tinted with red. The inflorescence develops in the same way, and has the same

Calathea lancifolia

Calathea makoyana

Calathea makoyana

Calathea ornata cv. rosea-lineata

Calathea picturata cv. argentea

Calathea picturata cv. vandenheckei

Calathea wiotii

Calathea zebrina

structure as in the edible Pineapple but the bracts are heavily tinged with pink or red and the flowers are blue. After flowering, suckers develop near the base of the plant and can be detached and used for propagation. This is one of the few genera in the group which needs full sunlight for good growth and to develop the strongest colour.

Cryptanthus

These small plants are suitable for culture in pots or in small troughs and can grow well in full sun or light shade. In Malaysia the commonest species is *Cryptanthus zonatus* (Zebra Plant) which has thin, tough leaves up to 25 cm long and 4 cm broad, with wavy margins. The normal form has green leaves with irregularly shaped, transverse bands of white, pale green or brown on the upper surface, while the undersurface is covered with a powdery or waxy white layer.

There are two or three cultivars of this species and one of these is also frequently grown in Malaysia. It is the *cv. zebrinus* in which the leaves are dark reddish or purplish brown with silver markings. Both this form and the normal one are easy to grow and produce very short inflorescences of small white flowers. The leaves tend to lie close to the soil surface so that the plants are only about 5–10 cm high. The plants are very sensitive to overwatering but if a very open potting mixture is used, there should be no trouble. Suckers are produced and can be used for propagation. These plants are ideal for the gardener with a very limited amount of space and do not need daily watering, this only being necessary once or twice a week. The plants can, if required, be grown on a tree branch in the garden and initially they must be tied on, but when new roots develop they will quickly spread in the crevices of the bark and hold the plant firmly.

A few other species of Cryptanthus are grown as ornamentals and some of them have beautiful variegated leaves but these do not appear to have been brought into Malaysia although it is possible that there are scattered specimens in a few private gardens.

Neoregelia

These are epiphytic plants with a rosette of leaves forming a deep cup at the centre. The most commonly grown species is *N. spectabilis*, the Fingernail Plant, which has leaves up to 50 cm long with bright red tips and the undersurface striped with greyish green. Flowers are produced in a short dense inflorescence from the centre of the plant.

Another species which is sometimes available in Malaysia is *N. carolinae* (Blushing Bromeliad) which is similar in appearance to the previous species but the outermost leaves of the rosette have bright red bases, and the innermost leaves, which are very much shorter, are almost entirely bright red so that the plant is very conspicuous. There are some forms available which have variegated leaves. All of these plants do very well in pots and make admirable decoration because the leaf rosettes are somewhat flattened in shape and, as they are usually viewed from above, the bright colour is seen to the greatest advantage.

Pitcairnia angustifolia

This is a tall plant which is best grown out of doors in a trough or a border where it can reach 2 m in height. It has narrow, dark green leaves about one metre long, with spiny margins, and the red flowers are borne in long, open inflorescences with slightly drooping branches. Propagation is by division and the plants will grow well in full sunlight or in light shade. Pitcairnia is probably the most frequently grown member of this group in Malaysian gardens.

Marantaceae Arrowroot Family

All members of this family are herbs, many having tubers of different sizes on their roots. The leaves of some are strikingly coloured, making them decorative foliage pot plants. There is a characteristic swelling at the junction of the leaf stalk and leaf blade.

Practically all those mentioned are common house plants in temperate countries and need high humidity. Pots can be placed on a bed of wet peat or wet sand in a tray or ornamental container, and the air around the leaves will become suitably moist.

Calathea

Several species of this genus are grown and all have strongly patterned foliage. They grow best in light shade with high humidity and may be kept in pots or troughs. The plants are rarely troubled by pests or diseases but snails can be troublesome and will eat part of the young rolled leaves as they appear at the tip of a shoot. As a result, when these leaves unroll and mature they are disfigured badly with one or more rows of jagged holes and their appearance is totally ruined. As the leaves remain on these plants for a long time it is important to take preventive measures as soon as any of the young rolled leaves show the smallest sign of damage. Hand-picking in the evening is probably the easiest method. Mature leaves are not harmed by snails.

Propagation is by division of old plants but recovery and the appearance of new shoots is very slow in some species. The plants can be grown indoors very easily, especially if the

Calathea

leaves are sprayed with water about three times each week. However, if grown out of doors, the colours of the leaves are usually much stronger and in either situation the plants respond well to the application of fertilizer, producing new leaves very shortly afterwards. In most of the species which are grown as pot plants, the colouring of the leaves consists basically of broad and narrow bands of dark green, white or pink arranged in a fishbone pattern, with all of the bands rising from the main vein of the leaf and often continuing out to the margin.

Calathea lancifolia (C. insignis)

The long-stalked, wavy-margined leaves of this plant are deep green with broad, much darker green markings on the upper surface and the whole of the undersurface is a deep wine-purple. When well grown, these plants may be one metre in height but usually in pots they are about half this height only. At night the leaf blades become vertical so that the purple undersurfaces become very conspicuous during the late evening as the light is fading. This species is very slow to establish after division and if possible, when this is done, some roots with tubers should be kept on each portion. Because of this very slow growth, small plants can be used in miniature gardens for a long time before they will need repotting.

Calathea lindeniana

A tall species up to one metre in height and very commonly grown as a pot plant. The leaf blades are broad and oval with an olive green zone on either side of the midrib and a narrow irregular band near the margin. The undersurface of the leaves is purple. This plant may be grown in shaded troughs, or may be planted in shaded areas underneath large trees where few other plants would grow satisfactorily.

Calathea makoyana (Peacock Plant)

This is an excellent and extremely decorative pot plant with large, broad, oval leaves held on long stalks, so that a good plant can be 70 cm high. The basic colour of the leaf blade is pale green with a very narrow dark green border around the margin. The very fine side veins are dark green and on either side of the midrib are broad oval or oblong bands which are also dark green. The undersurface of the leaves is a mixture of green and purple with the latter appearing underneath the dark green bands. Very young leaves, when they are newly unrolled, are a pale yellowish green with pale purplish bronze markings, and this colour changes very gradually over a period of about two weeks until the leaf is fully mature.

Propagation is by division and the young plants become established much quicker than those of the previous species. Very small plants can be grown in miniature gardens until they become too large, or they may be grown in troughs, but they make the best show when grown in pots because the restricted space results in many leafy shoots being produced close together. In a trough the shoots become more widely spaced so that the effect is much less striking. Large pots of 30–50 cm diameter are suitable, and if the plants are given fertilizer regularly they will soon develop a dense clump of shoots and leaves and are among the most striking foliage plants which can be grown. The leaves of this plant also become vertical at night and the leaf blades fold up, hence the common name of Prayer Plant.

Calathea ornata

A commonly grown pot plant which can reach 70–100 cm in height. It has long, broad, oval leaves with long stalks, and blades marked with fine, parallel, white or pale pink stripes which become green as the leaf ages. The undersurface of the leaf blade is purple. These plants are easy to grow and can be propagated by division. Two or three cultivars are available and, of these, the most common is cv. *roseo-lineata* which has narrow leaves with pink stripes changing to white as the leaf matures.

Calathea picturata

This species has broad, oval leaves with pointed apices and the blade is asymmetrical, one side being broader than the other. Normally the plants are about 40–50 cm high and the leaves are dark green, with irregular white markings on either side of the midrib and a waxy white band near the margin. In addition, two forms are commonly grown. *C. picturata cv. vandenheckei*, which is a much shorter plant, has smaller leaves with olive green or silvery green markings of similar shape and position to those of the normal form. The plants are about 15–30 cm high and are said to be a juvenile form of the species. However, the most striking form is *C. picturata cv. argentea* which grows to 40 cm or more in height with leaves of pale green or silvery green having a broad, dark green margin. This is a striking plant with a very cool appearance. All cultivars are easy to grow and small regular applications of fertilizer keep them leafy and in good condition.

Calathea wiotii

A small, rhizomatous plant with short, lanceolate mid-green leaves which have a row of conspicuous dark green blotches on either side of the midrib. These plants grow well in pots and are excellent house plants as they need shade constantly, but the soil must never be allowed to dry out. They can be grown also in a shady trough or, when the soil is moist enough, they may be grown in the shade of shrubs in a border where they can form a good ground cover.

Calathea zebrina (Zebra Plant)

This, also, is a very popular pot plant having striking, bright, emerald green leaves with a row of dark green velvety markings on either side of the midrib. The undersurface is pale purple. These plants grow from 30 to 60 cm high and the leaves have long, closely overlapping sheaths which form a short stem structure. They need spraying with water every day in order to keep the leaves in good condition and especially because the plant does not like dry air; when the humidity is low the leaves will curl up, spoiling the appearance of the plant. The species can be grown in a pot or in a shaded trough and looks extremely handsome with a mixture of other plants around it. When grown in a mixed group there is less trouble from dry air as the plants give each other mutual protection from any excessive drying out.

Maranta

Several species are used as pot plants and the leaves of some of these are as strikingly coloured as some of the Calathea species. There is one species, *M. arundinacea,* which is grown for its tubers because they are the source of arrowroot. Propagation of all kinds is easiest by division.

Maranta arundinacea cv. variegata

This species makes dense clumps of short stems, each one carrying two or three long-stalked leaves which are variegated with cream or white. The colour is arranged in irregular patterns which are different on every leaf. The plants will grow to 60 cm or more in height and are best in pots or shaded troughs. Although they can tolerate full sunlight for a very short period, the white portions of the leaves are easily scorched and will turn brown, spoiling the appearance of the plant.

Maranta leuconeura var. leuconeura
(var. Massangeana, Prayer Plant)

This is one of the more striking species as the prostrate stems carry oval, dark bluish green leaves which have white veins and a broad band of reddish brown or blackish green on either side of the midrib. There is another form in which the side veins are red. These plants can be grown in pots, bottle gardens or miniature gardens. The potting mixture must be well drained and watering must be carefully controlled, but the plants should not be allowed to dry out. In high humidity, the leaves remain flat but if the air becomes hot and dry, the leaf blades will curl upwards.

Begonia heracleifolia

Maranta leuconeura cv. kerchoviana

Maranta leuconeura var. *kerchoviana* (Prayer Plant)

This is also a short creeping plant with leaves less highly coloured than in the previous form. The oval leaves are grey-green with a row of somewhat oval, smudgy blotches on either side of the midrib and these become dark green as the leaf ages. This plant can be grown in a small pot, in a bottle garden or in a miniature garden.

Maranta leuconeura var. *erythroneura*

This is slightly larger than the last species with highly coloured leaves that are dark green with red veins bordered with cream. Management is the same as for the previous species.

Other Foliage Plants

Plants from many other families are grown for their foliage but as the number from each family is small they have been grouped all together here and are listed alphabetically. Some of these are described in other chapters and are therefore mentioned only briefly, from the point of view of their suitability as pot plants.

Aloe

This plant belongs to the Lily family and several small species are grown as pot plants. They are best treated in the same way as Cactus plants and should be kept slightly dry at all times. The very short stems have many closely arranged, thick, fleshy leaves which taper from the base to the apex. In some species the leaves are dark green with irregular bands and spots of pale green or white, while in others the leaves are more succulent with sharp spines around the margin. They will grow for many years in pots with little attention, except for the application of some fertilizer from time to time.

Most species will produce short offsets which can be removed and used for propagation. The plants may be grown also in troughs or sometimes in rockeries, provided the drainage is very good so that the roots never become too wet even at times of heavy rainfall. During long dry spells, these plants will sometimes produce flowers which are carried on tall stems above the leaves. The plants are not always available in nurseries but are often found in private homes and a few are usually seen at flower shows. They make a good addition to a small Cactus garden because they give some variation in form.

A number of the species are grown as house plants in temperate countries and are easy to manage because they require fairly dry growing conditions.

Alpinia

Two species with variegated leaves have been described earlier in the section on herbaceous plants and both can be grown for some time as pot plants provided they are given regular applications of fertilizer.

They are sometimes seen as house plants in cooler countries.

Alternanthera

These small plants are used commonly for edging borders and need full sun in order that the colours may develop strongly. They can, however, be used in miniature gardens provided they receive sufficient light, and are easy to manage because they can be pruned to keep them to any required size. Any of the forms of *A. ficoidea* may be used depending on the colour combination which is most suitable and these have been described previously. Occasionally seen as a house plant in temperate countries.

Asparagus

The species and varieties described elsewhere can be grown as pot plants but the climbing *A. setaceus* (Asparagus fern) needs a light framework over which the stems can be trained. *A. densiflorus* cv. *sprengeri* is very commonly used as a pot plant and there are several cultivars, some of which have larger leaves and more robust growth. All make admirable pot plants and with regular fertilizer applications can be kept for two or three years in a pot before the soil will need changing. These plants can be allowed to dry out almost completely between waterings. *A. densiflorus* cv. *myersii* (*meyeri*) is an excellent pot plant and more suitable for small rooms because of its short stems which are densely clothed with leaves. It will grow quite well in light shade but benefits from an occasional spraying with water to freshen up the foliage.

All of the Asparagus cultivars look best when grown singly in pots and are grown in many parts of the world for this purpose.

Bambusa ventricosa (Buddha's Belly Bamboo)

In this plant each of the stem internodes between the leaf attachment points is barrel-shaped, giving the plant a very characteristic appearance and hence its common name. It can be grown in a very large pot or jar for many years before it is necessary to plant it out in the garden. The plants will grow best in full sun but will tolerate a little shade for a short time. Potted plants must be manured regularly, otherwise most of the leaves will drop and the appearance will be spoilt. When planted out in the ground it will make a very dense clump of stems but must be kept to size

Eucharis grandiflora

Cycas rumphii

Cycas siamea

Cyperus alternifolius

Callisia elegans

that a continuous succession of well shaped and coloured leaves is produced. Propagation of the creeping forms is by division or from leaf cuttings, and the upright kinds can be propagated from cuttings.

Several other species of Begonia are grown in the lowlands but are not commonly available, although they are easy to grow provided watering is strictly controlled. It is possible also to buy seeds of Begonias and these are of two main kinds. All are hybrids and in one group they are derived from *Begonia rex* so that the plants will show large, highly coloured leaves; in the other group they are derived from several small species so these plants will be small with bright green leaves showing various patterning in purple or dark brown. The last group can be grown a little more easily in the lowlands and make admirable pot plants for small spaces. Great care is necessary when germinating the extremely tiny seeds as the young seedlings are very susceptible to damping off.

Some years ago, these Begonias were commonly grown as house plants in temperate countries and there were many named varieties, but these are not easily available now. The plants lost their popularity for various reasons, such as fashion, the introduction of other kinds of foliage plants that were easier to manage and because they were sensitive to the fumes from gas fires, gas cookers and heaters.

Callisia (Inch Plant)

These are prostrate, creeping plants having closely arranged leaves which are short and broad with sheathing bases.

Callisia elegans is the most commonly seen species and has dark green leaves with longitudinal, silvery white stripes on the upper surface and a purple undersurface. It grows very easily but the soil mixture must be well drained. It is propagated from cuttings and is a useful plant for miniature gardens because it is not invasive.

Chlorophytum comosum and cultivars (Spider Plant)

The culture of these plants has been described earlier and they make excellent pot plants or they may be grown in troughs and miniature gardens. They survive under a great variety of growing conditions and are often very long-suffering. In miniature gardens they may need to be kept in check as they may spread too fast and will smother the neighbouring plants. All forms are commonly grown as house plants in temperate countries.

Cissus discolor (Trailing or Climbing Begonia)

Despite the common name, this plant is not a true Begonia and in fact belongs to the Vine family. It is a climbing plant with slender stems and oval heart-shaped leaves which are dark, velvety green with silver or pink areas between the side veins, and deep purple or red undersurfaces. When grown in a pot, the plant needs a light framework of some kind on which to climb, but if grown in a shady trough it can be allowed to trail between other plants. High humidity is important for this plant and the leaves should be sprayed with water daily if it is kept inside a house. This is a beautiful plant but sometimes can be a little difficult to grow. Regular manuring is necessary and the plants must not be allowed to become dry or the leaves will lose their colour and may drop.

Codiaeum variegatum (Croton)

Although best grown as a shrub in the garden, these plants can be used as pot plants but must receive full sunlight and should be manured regularly. Unless these conditions are met, the plants will lose their leaves and will not develop good colour. Often grown as house plants in temperate countries but are a little difficult because they need constant strong sunlight.

Coleus amboinicus (Indian borage)

An aromatic plant with thick, fleshy, light green leaves which have a strong scent when they are crushed. It can be grown in pots or troughs and needs full sunlight. The plant is easily propagated from cuttings which should be kept slightly dry until they are rooted. Too much watering will cause rotting before the roots have developed. The stems should be pinched out to encourage branching so that a more bushy plant is obtained. The light coloured foliage provides a pleasing contrast of colour when the plants are grown among others with darker foliage. The leaves can be used as flavouring in soups and when cooking meat.

Coleus x hybridus

Commonly grown as a pot plant and can also be grown in beds where it needs full sun throughout the day. It may be used also in troughs but the colours must be given some consideration, otherwise the resulting effect might be rather gaudy. There are upright and prostrate forms, all of which make excellent pot plants. These plants grow well in the highlands and are commonly used as house plants in temperate countries.

Cordyline

These plants are often grown as shrubs or in mixed borders because of their colourful foliage, but they make good pot plants also, and some of the smaller forms can be kept in a pot for two years or more until eventually they become too large and need replacing with young plants. It is important that these plants are regularly manured when they are grown in pots, otherwise the lower leaves will drop and they will not be as attractive.

Many kinds of Cordyline take up relatively little space as pot plants because frequently they are unbranched, although sometimes they produce one or two branches only. If they are kept indoors the leaves must be sprayed with water once each week or, if possible, the plants should be put outside at night and during rainstorms. Forms with highly coloured leaves need much more light than others to ensure the best development of the colour.

Crassula argentea (Jade Plant)

A small shrub with stout stems and thick, round or oval, dark green leaves which are shiny and have very narrow red margins. Propagation is by stem or leaf cuttings and the plants must not be overwatered. It is best grown in a pot and makes good bonsai. A little fertilizer 2 or 3 times each year will prevent leaf fall and will maintain good growth. Watering must be carefully controlled and good drainage is essential. Full sun is needed at all times.

Cycas

This is a non-flowering plant and two species are seen commonly grown either as pot plants or directly in the ground.

Cycas rumphii is the smaller one and is often used as a pot plant. It will need, eventually, a very large pot, but may then remain in this indefinitely. The plant has a short crown of stiff, dark green, pinnate leaves which have very tough leathery leaflets, and a new whorl of leaves is produced once or twice a year only. Consequently, it is only necessary to apply fertilizer about once in three months, but when new leaves are developing the plants must be watered each day until the leaves have matured and become hard. The general appearance of the plant resembles that of a miniature palm as the stem is short and thick and the leaves are arranged in a very similar way. Younger plants can be up to 30 cm high and about 60 cm in diameter, especially if grown in pots, but older plants, especially if they have been put out in the ground, can grow to 60 cm or higher and will be up to 1 m in diameter. Occasionally, suckers or small side branches will develop and these can be detached and used for propagation, but their growth is very slow.

Cycas circinalis is a much larger plant and although small specimens make handsome pot plants, they will soon become too big and will be top-heavy. They are much better planted out in the ground and can be grown in full sun or light shade. This species also resembles a small palm and has a thick trunk carrying a crown of long pinnate leaves with many leaflets. Older plants often produce branches which can be detached and used as cuttings, or they may be allowed to remain and will make the plant appear more bushy.

Cultivation is the same as for the previous species, but when young leaves are produced a careful watch must be kept because they are very liable to attack by caterpillars. These can be removed by hand, or the leaves may be dusted with a powdered insecticide. It is most important that the pests are removed, otherwise they will destroy all of the new leaves and the plant will be severely checked in growth. If the young leaves are completely eaten by the caterpillars the plant will produce a smaller number of new leaves within about two months and if these are destroyed also, the plant will become very much weakened. If this process is repeated a third or fourth time, the plants will most likely die because, usually, when a new crop of leaves is produced the old leaves gradually become yellow and drop from the plant. If the young leaves are destroyed in this way before they mature, the plant is unable to make sufficient food for itself. However, this is the only trouble which is likely to affect these plants and attention is needed only two or three times a year when the new leaves are developing.

Both species are slow growing and both can be used for formal planting in a garden, but C. rumphii, when grown in pots, is excellent on verandas, patios or terraces, and around the outside of a house, but it is not really suitable for indoor decoration because of its shape, and the very dark green colour of the leaves which could be too gloomy in appearance for shaded areas.

Cyperus

One or two species of this genus are often grown as pot plants but can become very vigorous and too large for the pot within a very short time if they are given regular applications of fertilizer.

Small plants of Cyperus alternifolius (Umbrella Plant) make good pot plants and will tolerate some shade so that they can be used effectively as indoor decoration. If fertilizer is applied at two- or three-month intervals only, the growth can be kept in check, but the pot will eventually become full of rhizomes and the plants will need to be divided and repotted. This plant can also be grown in troughs or in a mixed border in full sun or light shade.

Cyperus alternifolius cv. gracilis (Dwarf Umbrella Plant) is a much smaller species which is more suitable for growing in pots but is not quite so attractive in appearance as the previous species. It needs no special soil mixture and will stand waterlogging for short periods. It can be used as indoor decoration because of its small size and will grow in full sun or in shade.

Both species are grown often as house plants in temperate countries.

Dracaena

Any of the species and cultivars mentioned in other chapters can be used effectively as foliage pot plants and some of them may be planted outside in small beds, borders or in troughs. When their growth in pots becomes unsatisfactory, they can be planted outside.

Encephalartos

This plant is closely related to Cycas and has a somewhat similar habit with a short, thick stem carrying an open crown of pinnate leaves. It can be grown in similar situations as Cycas and needs the same cultural treatment. It is not freely available but can be found occasionally in some of the plant nurseries.

Eucharis grandiflora (Amazon Lily)

A bulbous plant with long, broad leaves rising from ground level, and tall flowering stems which carry three to six large, white, fragrant flowers. These plants are best grown in pots or troughs where the watering can be controlled easily. If they are given a little fertilizer every month, they will produce flowers two or three times a year.

Euphorbia neriifolia

This is a succulent plant with thick, green stems bearing light green, rather narrow, oval leaves. The normal form can be grown in a pot but will soon become too large and must be planted out in the ground. However, there is a commonly grown variety in which the stem is somewhat flattened and undulating, giving rise to what is called a *cristate* form; this is much slower in growth so that it makes a satisfactory pot plant. The plants need a well drained soil mixture, full sunlight and must not be overwatered, otherwise the base of the stem will rot.

Other species of Euphorbia have been described in other chapters and are suitable as pot plants while they are small, but most of them will become too large eventually and must then be renewed or planted out.

Ficus

Some species of Figs have been described already and of these *F. benjamina* and *F. elastica* are commonly grown as pot plants. By careful pruning, they can be kept to a suitable size for several years but will finally become too large

and are better replaced by young plants grown from cuttings.

Ficus deltoidea (Mistletoe Fig) is a small species which makes an excellent pot plant forming an open well branched crown with small, dark green leaves which are broadest near the apex. The plants grow best in full sun but will make satisfactory growth in light shade. The species is used frequently as a house plant in temperate countries. The soil mixture must be very well drained but must not be allowed to dry out completely.

Ficus lyrata (Fiddle-leafed Fig) is a slow growing plant which is available occasionally and has interesting dark green leaves resembling a violin in shape because of the irregularly lobed margin. The plant can be kept for several years in a large pot and can be propagated from cuttings. It is frequently used as a house plant in temperate countries.

Ficus pumila (Creeping Fig) can be used as a pot plant but it is not the most satisfactory because of its creeping habit; it could, however, be used in a hanging basket so that the stems could trail down over the sides. When used as a pot plant in Malaysia, it will soon cover the pot and stems will spread into neighbouring pots and through other plants, but if the pot is placed at the base of a wall, the trailing stems will quickly become attached to it and begin climbing. As they grow over the wall, the young stems and the small leaves form interesting patterns over the surface. Plants rooted directly in the ground make an excellent wall covering but must be kept pruned so that no vertical shoots develop, because these become exceptionally vigorous, resulting in the creeping stems losing most of their leaves, and become unattractive. When this plant is grown in a pot and conditions are suitable, it will spread very rapidly, choking other pot plants and climbing up tree trunks; in these circumstances it must be controlled very strictly.

There is a cultivar with variegated leaves that is less attractive as the white pattern makes the plant look unhealthy.

Fittonia verschaffeltii (Net Leaf)

This small prostrate plant needs shade and is very suitable for bottle and miniature gardens. The leaves are dark green with red veins, but there are several cultivars in which the leaves are lighter green with white veins. The plants must not be overwatered and the soil mixture should be very well drained. Propagation is very easy from cuttings. Often available as a house plant in temperate countries.

Graptophyllum pictum (Caricature Plant)

A small shrub which makes a good pot plant and can be used as a very low hedge in the garden. It grows best in light shade and does well in a mixed border. Two or three forms are commonly grown and differ in their leaf colour which may be green with yellow patterning on either side of the midrib, or bronze with paler markings, or they may be purplish or bronze with conspicuous, irregularly shaped pale yellow areas on either side of the midrib. The plants are easy to grow from cuttings and regular manuring will keep them leafy and in good colour, but they must be pruned a little while young to encourage a more bushy growth.

Gynura aurantiaca (Purple Velvet Plant)

When grown as a foliage plant, this species must be pruned frequently to encourage the development of new young shoots in which the purple colour is most intense.

As a house plant in temperate countries, it must receive plenty of light to develop its colour satisfactorily.

Haworthia (Wart Plant, Star Cactus)

These succulent plants belong to the Lily family and there are four species which are commonly grown as pot plants in Malaysia. A number of other species are grown as ornamentals in other plants of the world. They can be grown singly in pots or they may be used in a miniature garden as they are not invasive. Flowers are often produced on tall inflorescences but are rather inconspicuous. Propagation can be done from offsets which are produced frequently.

Haworthia subfasciata is a short plant with very closely arranged thick leaves which are tapered evenly from the base to the apex. Each leaf is dark green with raised white ridges over the whole surface.

Haworthia margaritifera is very similar in habit to the last species but the leaves have raised white spots scattered over the whole surface.

Haworthia reinwardtii has long stems densely covered with short, thick, overlapping, fleshy leaves which are very dark green. The stems are erect when young but as they grow longer they become prostrate.

Haworthia linifolia is another short-stemmed species which has thick leaves with incurled margins.

Many species of Haworthia are grown as house plants in temperate countries.

Heliconia

These are short plants up to 1½ m high with a dense clump of stems carrying long, broad, spear-shaped leaves resembling those of a Banana plant, but with pointed tips. *H. striata* has pale green leaves with horizontal yellow stripes on either side of the midrib. Another cultivar, the name of which is in some doubt,

Graptophyllum pictum

Graptophyllum pictum

Jatropha podagrica

Ophiopogon intermedius

Homalocladium platyclados

has leaves irregularly patterned with red, yellow, bronze and green so that no two leaves are alike. Both of these plants can be grown in pots for a short time, but as the number of stems increases they will need to be divided and repotted. They are best grown in troughs or mixed borders and need full sun in order to develop the strongest colour, but they will tolerate light shade although the leaves will show more green and less yellow or red under such conditions.

Hemigraphis colorata (*H. alternata*, Red Ivy)

This is a prostrate plant with metallic grey leaves which are purple on the underside. It can be grown as a pot plant or in a trough where it can be allowed to trail over the sides. It is too large for miniature gardens but makes an effective edging for borders, or it may be used as a ground cover under shrubs as it will grow very well in light shade.

Hemigraphis repanda

Small, prostrate herbaceous plants with narrow, dark green leaves tinged with purple. Tiny white flowers are produced in short open inflorescences but are relatively inconspicuous. The plant is very suitable for miniature gardens and is easily grown from cuttings.

Hibiscus rosa-sinensis
cv. cooperi

Although this is a form of the ordinary Hibiscus, it is listed here because it has variegated leaves and is therefore grown as a foliage plant. It does produce some flowers which are single and red but smaller than in the normal form. The plant makes a small bush and is not as vigorous as the ordinary kind, but by careful pruning it will form a dense bush and is then most attractive. The leaves are smaller than in the normal form and are heavily patterned with creamy white, some of them showing no green colour at all.

Occasionally, branches develop which have normal green leaves and these are very vigorous but should be cut away otherwise they will dominate the whole bush very quickly and the branches with variegated leaves will be weakened and will slowly stop growing and die. The plant needs full sun and is best grown outside but it must be given regular applications of fertilizer to encourage strong growth because it is not as vigorous as those with green leaves.

Propagation can be done from cuttings which should be treated with hormone powder to help the development of roots. Rooting tends to be slower than in the green-leafed forms. It is difficult sometimes to get this plant to make a shapely bush, so it is best grown in a mixed group, either large or small, where the shape is unimportant and its foliage will provide colour and contrast.

This species is sometimes seen as a house plant in temperate countries as it is relatively slow growing.

Iresine herbstii (Beefsteak Plant)

This plant belongs to the Bayam family and is very striking because of the bright purple-red leaves that often have a deeply lobed apex. It can be grown in pots but needs to be pinched out to encourage branching, otherwise it becomes spindly in appearance. Two or three cuttings can be grown in one pot and will make a satisfactory show, but the plants can be put in a bed and allowed to grow up through other species so that their leaves provide bright spots of colour. In the highlands the colour is very much brighter and more intense so that for decoration single plants are sufficient when mixed with others. Groups of these plants should only be used when a very bold effect is needed because their intense colour takes all the attention away from the neighbouring plants.

Two or three cultivars of this plant are available, one of which has green and cream leaves with red veins.

The species is sometimes seen as a house plant in temperate countries.

Jatropha curcas (Physic Nut)

A small tree which can be grown for a long time as a foliage pot plant but will eventually become too large for the pot and must be planted outside. It has large leaves with three to five shallow lobes and inconspicuous flowers. The plants can be grown also in a mixed border in full sun and propagation is from cuttings or seeds.

Jatropha podagrica (Tartigo)

Although described earlier, this plant can be used also as a foliage pot plant and is very decorative with its large, dark green leaves and bright red inflorescence stems and flowers. It has a single stem which is swollen to a great size at the base and the plant should not be manured too frequently, otherwise the leaves become over-large and succulent. The plant then loses some of its character, especially as these large leaves tend to curl up around the edges and give the plant the appearance of being slightly diseased. In pots this species can be kept quite dry and, in fact, it may be planted in a rockery where the flowers provide good colour.

Kalanchoe

Some species of this genus have been described already in the section on rock gardens and of these K. pinnata (Air Plant, Life Plant) can be grown in pots but they become too tall and top-heavy; it is a little too large and coarse to be grown in a group with smaller plants. K. daigremontiana (Devil's Backbone) and K. tubiflora (Chandelier Plant) can both be used in miniature gardens but need full sunlight.

There are two other species which can be grown as pot plants and need very little space. They may be grown singly or in a small group of other sun-loving plants in miniature gardens. K. marmorata (Pen-wiper Plant) has large, closely-arranged, broad, oval, pale green leaves with small purple spots and blotches scattered over the whole surface. The leaves are thick and succulent and are held on the plant for a very long time. Several branches are produced and the plants make a most attractive addition to a small Cactus garden. K. tomentosa (Panda Plant) has long, oval, densely hairy leaves which are dull olive green with dark red tips to the teeth around the margin. It can be grown in a similar way to the previous species and in similar situations. Both species can be propagated very easily from leaf cuttings and this is done by detaching leaves and inserting their stems into moist sand. They can, if required, be dipped into rooting powder beforehand and will develop buds and roots within a few weeks at the ends of the leaf-stalks.

K. orgyalis is available very occasionally and has woody stems with large, thick, round or oval leaves which are brown when young and silver grey at maturity. Very dry conditions are needed and propagation is by stem or leaf cuttings, kept fairly dry until rooted.

All of these species, except the last described, are often seen as house plants in temperate countries.

Kochia scoparia (Fire Bush, Burning Bush)

These are densely branched annual plants which are round or conical in shape with very many small, narrow, light green leaves. In temperate countries, the foliage becomes purplish red in the autumn before the plants die down, but in Malaysia this does not happen and it remains green throughout the life of the plant. Kochia can be grown in pots or troughs but must have full sunlight. It is usually available in nursery gardens and will grow to about 25–50 cm in height. It is useful in a small space for a formal effect and will continue growing for many months before replacement is needed. It is propagated from imported seed which is available from most seed merchants.

Muehlenbeckia
(Homalocladium, Centipede Plant)

Although described earlier under dwarf shrubs, this plant is excellent as a foliage pot plant and will develop a good shape and size, especially if it is given regular applications of fertilizer. Normally it grows best in full sun but it will tolerate light shade though it will be slightly more open in appearance and the stems will remain a darker green. In a large pot it may grow to one metre in height but in troughs it can become taller than this.

Musa (Bananas)

There are some varieties of Banana which make attractive foliage plants because the young leaves are pale green with irregular markings of dark brown or purple over the whole leaf surface. These colours last several weeks but gradually disappear as the leaves mature and change to an even dark green. The young leaves on older and taller shoots do not show this coloration so that the management of the plants must be arranged in order to have one or more suckers developing around the base of an older shoot. These plants grow well in light shade but are really too large for pots, although they could be used in a large trough.

Nautilocalyx lynchii

This is a striking plant belonging to the Saintpaulia family. It grows to 60 cm high and has long, elliptic leaves with pointed tips and coarsely toothed margins. The shiny upper surface of each leaf is purplish red or very dark green and the undersurface is red or purple. Small groups of pale yellow flowers are produced in the axils of the leaves and the plant needs shade to grow well. Propagation is by means of cuttings and as soon as the plant has begun to grow strongly it should be pinched out to encourage branching. It can be grown in a pot and looks best with a trailing plant grown around the stem base so that the soil is concealed. Nautilocalyx will grow well in a trough in the shade of other plants and helps to conceal their bare stem bases which are often unavoidable in such situations. It needs plenty of moisture but must have a well drained soil mixture.

Ophiopogon intermedius (Lilyturf)

This small plant is most usually grown in a pot but it can be grown outside also as a ground cover in light shade beneath shrubs or small trees. It has curved, strap-shaped leaves 1 cm wide which have broad white margins, and occasionally small sprays of white flowers are produced. It can be used in miniature gardens with good effect as it does not spread too rapidly and it is easily propagated by division.

Oplismenus hirtellus
(variegated form, Basket Grass)

This is a short, creeping grass which is found wild in several parts of Malaysia. However, there is a cultivated form with variegated leaves which is sometimes available and it makes a most agreeable plant when grown in a pot with the stems trailing over the sides. The leaves are striped longitudinally in white, pink and green and the plant is best grown in a small pot on its own, or in a miniature garden because it is not aggressive and dislikes too much competition from other plants. The plant has a very delicate appearance and because of its very small size it is appreciated best when looked at from a very short distance. Full sunlight is necessary for the leaf colour to develop well and the soil can be kept slightly dry. Propagation is by means of cuttings which can be a little slow to root, and overwatering must be avoided as the plants are very sensitive to too much moisture around their roots. This is a gentle little plant well suited to sunny window-sills where space is very limited.

In temperate countries it can be more robust and may need careful control when grown as a house plant.

Opuntia (Prickly Pear)

Some species of this genus are described later but there are others which make good pot plants or can be grown in miniature gardens because they are much smaller. All have flattened, fleshy stems shaped like oval segments placed end to end. They need full sunlight and dry conditions so that they can be grown with other Cacti or succulents. The very smallest ones are suitable for miniature Cactus gardens but they do have tiny sharp hairs which may cause some skin irritation and so a little care is necessary when handling the plants. When re-potting or taking cuttings, it is wise to use a pair of thin gardening gloves to prevent the hairs from penetrating the skin on one's fingers.

A number of species are used as house plants in temperate countries.

Pandanus (Screw Pine)

These plants have been described in the chapter on shrubs but small specimens are often used as foliage pot plants and can be kept for about two years before they become too large for the pot. Many side shoots develop and these can be detached and potted up on their own as replacement plants while the old plants can be discarded. Plants with variegated leaves may produce some shoots with entirely green leaves and these should be removed immediately, otherwise they will develop at the expense of the variegated shoots.

All of the Pandanus species have sharp spines along the leaf margins and main veins so that they must be handled carefully and, in addition, pots should not be placed where people will brush against them as they walk by

Pandanus dubius

Pandanus pygmaeus

Pellionia daveauana

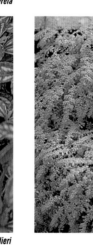

Peperomia argyreia

Peperomia obtusifolia

Peperomia obtusifolia variegata

Pilea cardieri

Pilea microphylla

Pilea nummulariifolia

Pereskia aculeata

because they can be severely scratched and clothes can be torn. When these plants are used for decoration on a veranda or other such area, great care must be exercised if there are small children about because the leaf spines can cause quite deep cuts in little hands. The pots are best placed behind others so that children cannot reach them easily.

Pellionia

Two species are commonly grown and both are creeping plants with relatively inconspicuous flowers. They may be grown singly and allowed to trail over the sides of the pot, or used as a ground cover in troughs because they do best in light shade. They will grow in full sunshine but are not happy, and growth will soon become slow and the general condition of the plants will deteriorate. Propagation is very easy as the creeping stems produce roots where they touch the soil and short pieces can be removed and potted up separately.

P. daveauana (*P. repens*, Trailing Watermelon Begonia) has oval leaves which are light green or greyish green with dark green or bronze borders. The colour varies a little, depending on the amount of light which the plant receives.

P. pulchra (Satin Pellionia, Rainbow Vine) has smaller, shorter leaves which are crinkled and light to mid-green with purple veins.

Growth of both species is rather slow so they can be used with some success in bottle gardens.

Both species are used as house plants in cooler climates and are easy to manage as they grow well in light shade.

Peperomia (Radiator Plant)

This group of plants belongs to the Pepper family and many of them are very popular as pot plants in the tropics and as house plants in temperate countries. Some of them are trailing and others are erect in habit and there are a number of cultivars with variegated leaves. In all species, tiny flowers are produced in long slender spikes which are, in some cases, conspicuous. Most of the species are small, succulent, herbaceous plants native to the tropical and subtropical regions of the world, and many of them grow epiphytically. Consequently, they appreciate a fairly humid atmosphere and little water in the potting mixture. It is often thought, quite mistakenly, that they should be watered daily, but if this is done then the roots will rot very quickly. It is better to let the soil in the pot become quite dry before watering. The plants need shade and in full sunlight the leaves will become scorched. Propagation is by stem cuttings, division, or from leaves with a portion of stem which can be inserted into sand until rooted.

P. argyreia (Watermelon Peperomia, *P. sandersii*) is a small plant that may grow to 20 cm high but is often much less when grown in pots. The leaves have dark red stems and the peltate blades are broad, oval and pointed at one end. They are bright green or bluish green with broad bands of silver or pale green radiating from the point where the blade is attached to the stem. These plants are very decorative when grown singly in small pots but they look good also when grown in a miniature garden.

P. caperata (Green-ripple Peperomia) is a very small species growing to about 15 cm only in height. It has small rounded leaves which have a quilted or corrugated appearance on the upper surface. The leaves are carried on long stalks and the white flower spikes are up to 10 cm long and are very decorative. The plant is best grown singly in a small pot as it makes a well-shaped mound of foliage and is always neat in appearance. There is a form with variegated leaves.

P. griseoargentea (*hederifolia*) (Ivy-leaf Peperomia) is very similar to the last species in shape and size but the leaves are greyish green with an undulating surface which is smoother in appearance.

In *P. magnoliifolia* the young stems are erect so that the plants can be shrubby in appearance, but as the stems grow longer they fall over and become trailing in habit. The stems and leaf-stalks are reddish, and the leaves are large, oval, thick and fleshy so that they are very heavy and are partly responsible for the falling over of the stems. The normal form has dark green, shiny leaves but there is also an extremely attractive cultivar with leaves very irregularly patterned in pale green, cream and dark green.

P. obtusifolia (Baby Rubber Plant, Pepperface) is very similar to the last species but makes a slightly larger plant and the leaves are a little smaller with dark red margins. There is a form with variegated leaves also, and either kind make good pot plants or may be grown in a trough so that the stems can trail over the sides.

P. scandens (*P. serpens*) is another trailing species much faster growing than the last two and having heart-shaped leaves so that it is easily recognised. The usual form has dark green leaves but there is a cultivar in which the leaves are irregularly margined in creamy white. It looks good grown in hanging baskets or in a trough trailing over the sides.

All species are grown as house plants in temperate countries and are best kept slightly dry. Overwatering will quickly cause rotting.

Pereskia aculeata

Although this has been described elsewhere, it

can be used effectively as a foliage pot plant also, and very small specimens can be used in a miniature garden as they are slow growing and will not need replacement for at least twelve or eighteen months. The young coloured leaves are most attractive and remain so for two or three months before becoming green.

Pilea

Several species of this genus are grown for their foliage and all are easy to manage. They can be used in shade rockeries, miniature gardens and bottle gardens, or grown singly in small pots, and some can be kept in hanging baskets. However, all of them need shade and must be watered regularly.

Pilea cadieri (Aluminium Plant) is a short herbaceous plant which can grow to 30 cm high and has oval leaves which are dark green with irregular bands of white alongside the midrib and main veins. Older plants may lose the lower leaves but if they are pruned and given a little fertilizer new leafy shoots will soon develop and the appearance of the plant will be restored. There is a dwarf form of this species which is very suitable for miniature gardens but can be used also in a small shade rockery.

Propagation of both kinds of *P. cadieri* is by means of cuttings which root very easily.

Pilea involucrata (Friendship Plant) is a small plant which has prostrate and semi-erect stems and can be used as a trailing plant if required. It has oval, deep green leaves which are quilted in appearance and the young leaves are reddish brown or bronze until they mature.

P. involucrata is propagated easily from cuttings.

Pilea microphylla is a very small species which often appears spontaneously in moist shaded areas in most gardens and is very suitable for miniature rock gardens or shade rockeries. Small plants may be less than 10 cm high but with a small amount of fertilizer a plant may grow to 20 cm high and 30 cm wide. The branches are almost horizontal so that a well grown plant is somewhat dome-shaped. Both flowers and leaves are very tiny, but as the latter are always a bright, fresh green colour the plants are useful for brightening shaded areas where little sunlight penetrates. Although the plant can grow in full sunlight, it does very much better in shade and is a better size and colour. When established, it will seed itself freely and a plentiful supply of young seedlings will be found everywhere. Cuttings can be used also for propagation.

Pilea nummularifolia (Creeping Charlie) is a perennial, creeping species with small, round, fresh green leaves and is very useful in hanging baskets or in a shady rockery where it can creep among other plants. It is not invasive and is easily controlled. As the creeping stems root where they touch the soil, short pieces can be detached and used for propagation.

All species are often grown as house plants in temperate countries.

Piper porphyrophyllum

A slender, climbing plant which is native to Malaysia but is often grown as an ornamental foliage plant. It has red stems and leaf-stalks and the leaves are oval, broad and dark olive green with pink spots scattered over the upper surfaces. Shade is essential and the plants can be allowed to creep over the soil surface or they may be grown in a pot over a light bamboo framework for support. When allowed to trail over the soil, the stems will produce roots frequently and these portions can be used for propagation.

Piper sarmentosa

A creeping plant belonging to the Pepper family and having some medicinal uses. It makes a good garden plant as it thrives in shady places and has attractive dark green, shiny leaves which are slightly crinkled on the upper surface. The flowers are inconspicuous and are produced in short white spikes. It spreads by means of creeping stems which can be used also for propagation. This plant makes an excellent ground cover in shaded areas such as underneath trees or near the base of a wall where other plants would be unable to grow successfully. It can be allowed to creep around the stems of shrubs in a mixed border as it is easily controlled and is useful for filling small gaps between the shrubs.

Polyscias

Although described elsewhere, this group of plants is mentioned again as they are often used as foliage pot plants and some of them are especially suitable for bonsai work. All make good, long-lasting pot plants, provided they are manured regularly in order to keep them leafy.

Portulacaria afra (Elephant Bush)

In the last few years, this plant has appeared in Malaysia and grows quite well provided it is managed properly. It makes a small tree with a rather fleshy stem and widely spaced branches which grow almost horizontally. The round, glossy green leaves are small and set wide apart so that the plant always has a light, thin appearance. Flowers are sometimes produced and these are small with pink petals. The soil mixture must be very well drained and the plants are best treated in the same way as succulents. They can be propagated from cuttings which should be kept fairly dry until they have rooted. This plant can be grown singly in a small pot and looks good if the soil is covered with fine gravel. It may be used as a bonsai plant or grown in a miniature garden of small succulent plants. A small application of fertilizer about once each month will keep the plant in good condition.

Pseuderanthemum

Two species are described elsewhere and of these *P. reticulatum* is the better one for use as a foliage pot plant. *P. atropurpureum* does not branch well enough to make a good shapely single pot plant, though it can be used with effect in a mixed group of such plants.

Rhoeo spathacea (Oyster Plant, Boat Lily)

This is an easily grown plant with a short, thick stem carrying closely arranged, long, broad, strap-shaped leaves which are very dark green on the upper surface and purple on the lower surface. Short inflorescences are produced between the leaf bases and each has a small group of white flowers which are partly enclosed between two very large, boat-shaped bracts. Fruits and seeds develop freely and seedlings are often found around old plants. These can be lifted and potted up for use as replacements at any time. The plants can be grown singly in pots or used with great effect in a bed, and very small plants can be used for some time in miniature gardens. When used for bedding they can be planted as a ground cover underneath shrubs or small trees as they grow best with a little shade for part of the day. They are very susceptible to damage by snails so a careful watch must be kept for these pests which can totally destroy whole plants within a day or so.

Although the plants do produce a few side shoots they do not become very bushy and if a dense effect is desired in a pot then it is best to grow two or three plants together. Small groups look very good in troughs and may also be grown in shade rockeries where they will spread gradually by means of the seeds. There is one cultivar, which has variegated leaves with narrow, pale yellow, longitudinal stripes, but it is not always easily available in Malaysia. Rhoeo plants have some use in Chinese medicine. Both forms are grown as house plants in cooler climates.

Sansevieria (Mother-in-law's Tongue)

As foliage pot plants, *S. trifasciata* and its cultivars are the most suitable, especially the *cv. hahnii* which is very short. The leaves of *S. cylindrica* spread too widely so that it is difficult to manage in a pot and because the leaves are widely spread it is more curious than attractive.

S. trifasciata and its cultivars are some of the most common and long suffering house plants grown in temperate countries. They need quite dry conditions and will survive with the minimum of attention.

Small plants of *S. cylindrica* are sometimes grown in these countries and while they are young the stiff leaves are straight and almost vertical in position so that the plants occupy little space. However, this species is not as attractive in appearance as the previous one.

Schefflera (Umbrella Tree)

Several species of this genus grow wild in Malaysia and a few are sometimes available in nurseries. They are popular as house plants in temperate countries as they are slow growing and do not need repotting for at least two years. They grow best in light shade but will tolerate full sun for part of the day and it should be remembered that in the wild many of them grow as epiphytes on the trunks or branches of large trees. Consequently, when grown in pots, they should be given a porous soil mixture. They can also be grown in the ground with no trouble and some of the species make very fine garden plants.

The plants are usually sparingly branched and the leaves have very long stalks with many, palmately arranged, long leaflets and the appearance is therefore interesting and attractive. Frequently, only one stem develops but as the leaflets are large this is no disadvantage and, in fact, the plants make very good indoor decoration as they are not too heavy in appearance. They can be kept in medium-sized pots for a very long time but if transferred to a very large pot, they can grow to 1½–2 m high.

When grown outside on the ground they can be very vigorous, the stem reaching 2–3 m and having much larger leaves. Such plants may become leafless at the base and the group of leaves left near the stem tip may make it heavy so that it bends over and the appearance is spoilt. If this seems likely to happen, the stem can be pruned back to about one metre in height and will produce one to three new branches and in about two or three months the appearance of the plant will be restored. Plants in pots can be pruned in this way also and the process can be repeated until the rootstock eventually becomes too big for the pot.

In temperate countries 2 or 3 species of Schefflera are often grown in large pots for decorating public buildings. They will often reach 1½ m or more in height and are too big for small rooms.

Cuttings are difficult to root but marcotting can be done or long stems can be pinned to the ground as is done for layering. Regular application of fertilizer will help to prevent the dropping of leaves from the lower part of the

Tribulus terrestris

Costus malortieanus

Setcreasia pallida

Epipremnum pinnateum

Strobilanthus dyerianus

Talinum triangulare variegata

stem. Small plants make good room decoration and larger ones may be grown in troughs. In a large garden, small plants of Schefflera can be tied to a tree trunk or a large, low-hanging branch where the roots will eventually attach them firmly, and when new leaves have developed they make an interesting and unusual addition to the garden.

Sedum morganianum
(Burro's Tail, Donkey's Tail)

This plant is usually grown in hanging baskets as it produces long trailing stems, densely clothed with grey-green leaves which are almost cylindrical and have pointed tips. Careful watering is necessary and the plant should receive as much sunlight as possible. When the basket containing the plant is moved, some care is necessary as the leaves fall very easily from the stems even if touched very lightly only. Rough handling will result in a basket of bare stems. Propagation is from stem or leaf cuttings.

Setcreasea pallida (S. purpurea, Purple Heart)

This trailing plant has long purple leaves and may be grown in large pots, hanging baskets or troughs. Full sun is necessary for the leaves to develop their most intense colour and small pale purple flowers are produced on long stalks. Propagation is by means of cuttings which root very easily, and although the plants will tolerate a great deal of heat, the soil should

never be allowed to dry out completely. Young plants should be pinched out to encourage the growth of more shoots and a highly bushy plant will be obtained. Snails are a great nuisance and can destroy whole plants overnight, so if these plants are grown outside in a bed a constant watch is needed to detect the first signs of damage by these pests.

Sometimes seen as a house plant in cooler climates where it needs plenty of light to develop the full colour.

Strobilanthes dyerianus (Persian Shield)

A short, herbaceous plant best grown in pots in shade where the young leaves will develop a strong silvery purple flush over their whole surface. The stems are sparingly branched but pinching of young plants will encourage a more bushy habit. The long narrow leaves are purple on the undersurface and on the upper surface the margin is dark green and the central portion is silvery purple. Propagation is by means of cuttings.

Tacca (Bat Lily)

A shade-loving forest plant which grows very well in cultivation, either in pots or troughs, and may also be planted beneath trees or shrubs in the garden. The plants have short rhizomes producing a dense clump of many tall, broad, spear-shaped leaves up to 60 cm or higher. Tall flowering stems develop frequently and are about 60 cm high with a group

Tacca cristata

plant will have a large clump of stems and inflorescences, making a very bold sight.

Other slightly smaller species of Zingiber are sometimes seen and these have shorter leafy stems and inflorescences. The latter are narrow with a pointed apex and carry pale green or bright orange-pink bracts which are pressed closely together. These species do not flower quite as freely as the previous one but are still attractive, even when they have leaves only.

There are several other members of this family which make good foliage plants as the leafy stems carry elegant, narrow leaves which are purple on the undersurface and this colour shows up well because of the way in which the leaves are held on the stem. One or two species produce tall, leafy stems on which the young leaves are bright green with striking purple or dark red markings. These plants are highly ornamental, but the bright colours of the young leaves change eventually to an even dark green as the leaves mature. The young leaves retain their bright colours for two to four weeks before they begin to change and the plants are well worth growing for this display which can be quite magnificent.

Sanchezia nobilis

11 ORCHIDS

It is impossible in a single chapter to do justice to the subject of orchids, but an attempt is made here to give a summary which will serve as a guide to the use of orchid books and to the articles which have been published in the *Malayan Orchid Review* and other journals. A large number of the most useful orchids for Malaysian cultivation are mentioned below, with notes on local conditions as regards details of cultivation. It must be emphasized strongly that instructions for orchid culture published in other countries, with climates different from that of Malaysia, are unsafe to take as guidelines for cultivation in Malaysia. Our climate is so humid that methods very suitable elsewhere may be fatal to our plants if adopted here.

There are many thousands of species of orchids, found wild in almost all countries of the world, but mostly in the tropics. In the Malay Peninsula alone there are known to be about 780 species, and probably a number more remain to be discovered. The great majority of these have small or shortlived flowers, or are otherwise unsuitable for use as garden plants. A few, however, are very useful, and others have been imported from Burma, Java, the Moluccas, New Guinea, and also (by way of Europe) from tropical America.

In addition to the natural species, as they are found growing wild, there are thousands of hybrids, which have been produced artificially by breeding different but related species together. This process of hybridization has been carried out to great lengths in Europe and America, especially with tropical American orchids, but also with species from Burma. Unfortunately, some of these are quite unsuited to lowland Malaysian conditions, as they are adapted to much cooler temperatures, or in some cases need dry resting periods to induce them to flower. Some of those adapted to cool conditions can be grown in the hill stations and a few of them do very well.

In recent years, the breeding of Malaysian orchids has been carried out in Indonesia and Malaysia, with the object of producing new orchids suited to the climate of this region. This has been successful and there is at present a large range of beautiful new flowers for local gardens and each year new hybrids are produced. It is now possible to buy new hybrid

seedlings with three or four leaves, from many nurseries, and these must be grown on until they flower before their quality can be assessed. This provides a good source of supply for beginners in orchid culture and there is the possibility that a good new form will be obtained. But although the hybrid seedlings may have been obtained by crossing two good parent plants, not all of them will produce flowers which would be suitable for entering in any kind of flower show; most of them would be suitable for decoration only. This should not deter would-be growers as the element of luck can provide a little excitement.

Some seedlings will flower earlier than others; some will flower more freely and some will show both of these characters together with well-formed, well-coloured flowers which may prove to be successful as exhibition plants. Great patience is needed as orchids are usually rather slow in growth and several years may pass before the first flowers are produced. But again, a word of warning is necessary. These orchids which are best suited to Malaysia are in many cases difficult to handle, or may fail to flower in other climates, especially those in which greenhouse culture must be practised. It is therefore not worthwhile sending orchid plants from Malaysia to other countries without first making a careful enquiry as to which are suitable to send. Failure to do this will mean waste of time, money and plants.

Over the last few years there has been a great increase in the export of orchids as cut flowers to different parts of the world. This is because the flowers can be sent by air and arrive at their destination very quickly after they have been cut, and also orchid flowers last a long time in vases and are therefore economical to buy, whereas many other kinds of cut flowers last one or two days only, or at the most one week. Some hybrids are grown specifically for the export trade and planting material is therefore easily available, so that a gardener with a small area of land could grow one or more of such hybrids and the sale of flowers would even provide a small income. Flowers of other hybrids are always welcomed by the many florist shops in Malaysia. The export of flowers is not easy for beginners as there are many rules and regulations to be followed, but any gardener in Malaysia interested in this aspect of orchid growing should write to the Ministry of Agriculture for all details of procedure.

Before proceeding further, it will be well to describe an orchid flower and its various parts briefly, as it will be necessary to mention some of these parts in the descriptive notes given below.

An orchid flower has three **sepals**, one usually at the top of the flower, and the other two on either side below the middle line; the sepals are all alike, or often the two at the sides (lateral sepals) are rather different from the upper one. Then there are three **petals**, alternating with the sepals. The petal at the bottom of the flower is different from the other two, usually larger and of rather complicated shape; this is called the **lip** or **labellum**. The lip is usually more or less clearly divided into three parts or **lobes**, the two **side-lobes**, on either side near the base, and the **mid-lobe**. In the centre of the flower, facing the lip, is the **column**, which may be short or long; this has the **anther** (containing the pollen or male element) at its end, and in its front is a hollow **stigma**, which receives the pollen when fertilization of the flower takes place. At the foot of the column, behind the flower, is the ovary, containing the rudimentary seeds; this ovary develops into a fruit if the flower is pollinated. The pollen in the anther is not powdery, like most pollen, but is stuck together in little round or oblong lumps, each containing some thousands of pollen grains. These lumps of pollen are called **pollinia**. They usually have a spot of sticky substance at their base; this attaches them to visiting insects, which may thus transfer them to other flowers.

For purposes of cultivation, orchids may be conveniently divided into three groups, terrestrial, climbing, and epiphytic. **Terrestrial orchids** (or ground orchids) are those which are rooted in the ground like other plants, and have no long climbing stem, nor roots above ground. **Climbing orchids** have long climbing stems, capable of continuous growth at the end, bearing at frequent intervals aerial roots, which serve to hold them to their supports. Some of the roots may also reach the ground. **Epiphytic orchids** are those which live quite away from the ground, on trees (or sometimes on rocks); they usually produce a succession of shoots of limited growth from a basal rootstock, not a long stem of unlimited growth like the climbers. Epiphytes are therefore usually more or less compact plants, but climbers are long and straggling. The short, fleshy shoots found in most terrestrial and epiphytic orchids are called **pseudobulbs**; though often bulb-like in shape, they are solid and have not the structure of true bulbs.

Terrestrial Orchids

The Jewel Orchids

These are small terrestrial orchids which have extremely beautiful foliage and there are three genera grown for this character. They are *Anoectochilus*, *Haemaria* and *Macodes*. Of these, *Haemaria* is the easiest to grow and has leaves of dark purple or dark green with gold or red veins, or the veins may be pale green. It can be grown in broken brick and charcoal or in burnt earth but must be given shelter from rain and must be shaded from direct sunlight. It can be propagated from cuttings of the fleshy stems, but the plants are rather slow in growth, producing only three to five leaves each year. *Anoectochilus* has leaves of similar colour, but is not so easy to cultivate as it is a plant which grows naturally in moist leaf litter in the deep shade of the forest. It has been hybridized with *Haemaria*. *Macodes* has very dark green leaves with golden veins and this genus also has been hybridized with *Haemaria*. Cultivation is the same as for *Haemaria*.

Arundina

Orchids of this genus have slender, erect stems, one metre or more in height, and narrow grass-like leaves, for which reason they are sometimes called Bamboo Orchids. One species, which has many varieties differing in size of flower and in details of colouring, is found throughout Malaysia in open places, sometimes quite abundantly. It is found in both the lowlands and highlands and can be grown as garden plants in both areas. This has been variously called *A. bambusaefolia* and *A. speciosa*, but the oldest name is *A. graminifolia* (grass-leafed). A local name is Kinta Weed. *A. chinensis* is also grown in Malaysia, and differs only slightly from the local species.

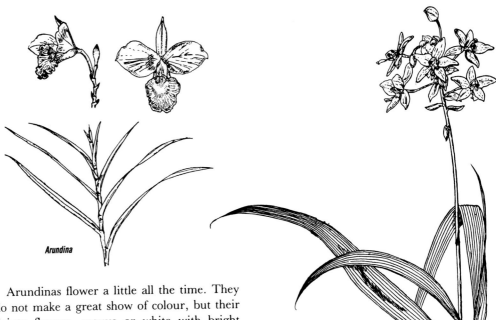

Arundina

Arundinas flower a little all the time. They do not make a great show of colour, but their dainty flowers, mauve or white with bright purple and yellow on the lip, are very attractive and useful for cutting, so that a bed in the cut-flower garden, or some inconspicuous place, is best because the flowers are produced at the tops of the stems and the plants need full sun so that it is not easy to screen the basal parts with other plants. Visitors to this country sometimes think that the flowers are a form of *Cattleya* because of a slight resemblance in shape. The plants need a well-dug bed containing plenty of compost, and a sunny position. A little organic fertilizer (such as cattle dung) every few months keeps them vigorous; and a little balanced inorganic fertilizer applied more frequently would be a good substitute. When the plants become too thick they may be lifted, divided at the base and replanted, the tops being cut back halfway to the ground. The large-flowered kinds are the most handsome, but some of the smaller-flowered kinds are more free-flowering. After flowering the old stems produce short side shoots which may be removed and rooted in sand.

Spathoglottis plicata

Spathoglottis

The purple *Spathoglottis* (*S. plicata*) used to be the commonest terrestrial orchid in Malaysian gardens. It has leaves 45 cm or more long and 5–7 cm wide which appear to have tiny pleats throughout their length; all grow from the ground. From among the leaves spring slender flower stalks 45 cm or more tall, each bearing a cluster of small purple flowers at the end. There are several varieties, with flowers in shades of mauve and purple, or white.

S. plicata is grown either in flower pots or in garden beds. In pots, good burnt earth mixture, or any other mixture giving free drainage and aeration of the soil, is essential for good growth. Liquid manure in small quantities every two or three weeks is desirable. The plants should not be overwatered; it is best to give them a good soaking and then let the earth become nearly dry before watering again. In garden beds, drainage is the most important factor to be considered. The plants will not grow successfully if their roots are in constantly wet soil. If the earth in the garden is at all heavy, therefore, it must be dug deeply, or some sort of subsoil drain provided for the bed; or alternatively the whole bed may be raised by building up the edges with rocks or bricks. If the whole bed can be made up with a burnt earth mixture, that is ideal; but failing this, a layer of brick rubble at the bottom, covered with 30 cm of good soil generously

Arundina

Spathoglottis plicata

Calanthe vestita

Phaius Tankervilliae

mixed with compost, is usually quite satisfactory. The plants must not be planted too deeply, and should be shaded for two weeks after planting. Once established, they only need watering in very dry weather. A top dressing of compost every few months, and more frequent watering with some sort of liquid manure are desirable. The chief pest is a beetle which lays its eggs at the base of the young leaves; if this appears, regular spraying with Tuba root (if this is available) for a few weeks should give sufficient control. Sevin (Carbaryl) or Tamaron (Methamidophos) are good alternatives to Tuba root.

Crossing between different varieties of *S. plicata* has resulted in the production of 'Singapore Giant', a very fine and free-flowering bedding plant which has inflorescences one metre tall.

In the mountains of Malaysia, there is another *Spathoglottis*, which has larger deep yellow flowers; it is called *S. aurea* (golden). This species cannot be cultivated easily in the lowlands, but has been hybridized with *S. plicata*, and some very attractive pale yellow varieties have been produced. The best have little mauve colour on petals and sepals, but the side-lobes of the lip are a good rich purple. The hybrids are called *Spathoglottis* Primrose. As pot plants, they need rather more careful handling than *S. plicata*, but when well handled, grow strongly and flower well. A very well aerated soil is absolutely essential and liquid manure when the plants are in active growth; watering should be as described above and not daily. The plants may have full sun or light shade in the afternoon. Other hybrids have also been raised in Singapore but are not commonly in cultivation. The best were raised by crossing the Philippine *S.* Parsonsii with *S.* Primrose and the resulting hybrid with *S. tomentosa*; the offspring, called *S.* Dwarf Legion, have flowers of many shades of pink. There are one or two other yellow-flowered species of *Spathoglottis*

found in the highlands of Malaysia and it would be well worthwhile trying to cross these with some of the hybrids just mentioned and with *S. plicata*.

A different range of fine hybrids has been produced in Bangkok; the yellow parent used has been *S. kimballiana*. These hybrids may usually be known from the purple suffusion on the backs of the sepals. They appear to have no distinctive names.

Paph. barbatum

Calanthe

There are several species of this genus in Malaysia, but the only one worth cultivating is *C. veratrifolia*, which grows in freshwater swamp forest. In nature, it grows with its wide-spreading roots among half-decayed moist leaves, under shade. It has leaves something like those of *Spathoglottis*, but softer in appearance, and produces an erect inflorescence of mainly dainty, small, white flowers. In cultivation, it grows best in pots, in a mixture containing plenty of compost, which is kept moist (not sodden), the plant always under light shade. Some of the other wild species have yellow or orange flowers and if any plants were available to gardeners it would be worth trying some crossing with the white-flowered species.

There are other Calanthes from more seasonal climates which lose their leaves and then flower in a leafless condition after resting; the best of these is *C. vestita*, which has been much hybridized in Europe. *C. vestita* is difficult to manage in Singapore, but with care may be artificially rested and kept dry until it begins new growth. Its management would be easier in the more northern part of the Malaysian peninsula. The plant has a large, pear-shaped pseudobulb.

Phaius

Two species of *Phaius* are found in Malaysia, and one of them may be grown with success in the lowlands. It needs a potting soil which is well aerated, and light shade; manure water at intervals, when the plants are growing, is desirable. The leaves are something like *Spathoglottis* but much larger, and the flower stalk is taller and stouter, with much larger flowers which are brownish with purple lip, and fragrant. Hybrids between *Phaius* and *Calanthe* have been made and crossing between the local species should be tried.

Paphiopedilum (Slipper Orchids)

There are a number of species of this genus in Burma and Malaysia which have been much hybridized in Europe and America. The hybrids, however, are nearly all suited to cool conditions, as the species are mostly native on mountains, and not so well suited to our Malaysian lowlands (though some of them do well at Cameron Highlands). None of the mountain species are really successful in the lowlands but there are a few lowland species which may be grown, with care, in pots, and flower fairly often; none are really free-flowering. The most free-flowering species is *P. glaucophyllum* from east Java. *P. niveum, P. exul* and *P. bellatulum* from peninsular Thailand, which grow on limestone rocks, also flower fairly freely but are difficult to manage. They

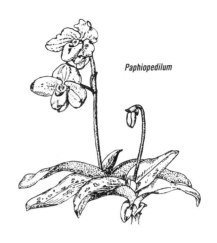

Paphiopedilum

are best kept protected from rain, under light shade. *P. praestans* from New Guinea and *P. philippinense* grow well and flower occasionally, the long and twisted petals giving them a peculiar appearance. The native Malaysian *P. barbatum* flowers rarely in Singapore, but the closely related *P. callosum* from Thailand is strong and free-flowering; *P. lowii*, an epiphytic species from the mountains, will flower occasionally in the lowlands.

Successful hybrids between *P. philippinense* and *P. callosum* have been raised in Singapore; the hybrid name is *P. Milmanii*. The plants are strong and flower well. Other hybrids of the abovenamed species should be well worth producing. In the lowlands all Paphiopedilums seem to grow best in a mixture of clean broken bricks with chopped fern root and a little leaf mould. They will respond to careful manuring when in active growth. They all need light shade.

Slipper Orchids are considered to be highly threatened with extinction. Trade in endangered orchid species such as Paphiopedilums is prohibited under the regulations of the Convention of Trade in Endangered Species (CITES) enforced by over 90 signatory countries including Malaysia.

Peristeria

The Dove Orchid from tropical America can be grown quite successfully in Malaysia, but is not common. The beautiful waxy, white, fragrant flowers are borne on tall erect spikes. The plants when well grown are vigorous and need large pots. A potting mixture of burnt earth and fern root or broken bricks and fern root is quite satisfactory, or the plants may be grown in a lightly shaded rockery in a large pocket of earth or broken bricks, with good drainage beneath. When new pseudobulbs are developing frequent applications of manure water or other fertilizer are necessary. The plants need light shade and well drained soil.

Climbing Orchids

Malaysian climbing orchids belong to a group of related genera, the chief of which are *Vanda*, *Arachnis* and *Renanthera*; all are native in tropical Asia. All have a similar climbing habit, though they differ in size and in the shape of their leaves. All need essentially the same treatment, which will be described briefly before we proceed to the individual species and hybrids.

As stated above, these climbing orchids have stems of unlimited growth, the tip continuing to grow in length, and produce new leaves indefinitely, unless damaged. They produce a certain number of lateral branches, and in time a single plant may produce a thicket. Each stem produces a number of aerial roots, which grow away from the light and attach themselves to any support (such as the branch of a tree) which they may meet. In this way, in nature, the plants scramble over small trees, some of their roots descending to the moist shady ground below, where they branch among a litter of dead leaves and collect food for the plant. The flowers are borne only at the top of the supporting shrub or tree. Thus we see that these orchids must have (a) a support of some kind, (b) sun above, to induce flowering, and (c) a moist shaded litter below, in which the descending roots can find the necessary moisture and food to maintain the plants in good health.

In practice, the different species of climbing orchids need slightly different treatment on account of their differing size; these differences will be mentioned below. In general, the treatment in establishing a bed of climbing orchids is as follows. The bed should be dug in a sunny place, and filled with broken bricks if possible, to ensure good drainage, and the necessary posts put into it. To each post are tied an appropriate number of cuttings taken from the growing ends of stems, usually 45–100 cm long. Each cutting should bear several aerial roots. The bottom of the cutting is placed at the level of the top of the layer of broken bricks in the bed. A layer of compost and grass cuttings (or mulch) about 10 cm thick is then laid over the bricks, and the plants are shaded with palm leaves or shade cloth. The shade is continued for about a month, by which time new root growth should be well established. They should be syringed every day, if there is no rain, in the evening.

An alternative method is to keep the cuttings in a shady place until they have begun to make root growth, and then transfer them to the bed. Fresh compost and grass cuttings, to which may be added a little cattle dung (when available) or other organic fertilizer, should be placed around the plants at intervals to maintain a good medium for the growth of the feeding roots.

Fresh grass cuttings should not be used on their own as they pack down too tightly and heat up so much that the plants will be damaged and no roots will develop. Grass cuttings should always be mixed with compost or, if this is not available, then dead leaves make an admirable substitute as they keep the grass clippings open so that the heat generated as they decay can disperse without harming the plants. A safe substitute are the commercial mulches that are now available, for example cocopeat made from coconut husks. If the compost mixture falls out on to the path, it can look very untidy, and this can be avoided by putting a short width of galvanized wire netting around the edge of the bed to retain it. The netting will be partly hidden by successive layers of compost and thus scarcely visible.

Another alternative method is to dig the beds 45-60 cm deep (removing all the earth), fix the posts and fill the bed half full of broken bricks. Then complete the filling with compost, the surface of which will be flush with the ground level.

When the plants have grown beyond the tops of their supports, they will usually begin to flower (some are seasonal in flowering, and others flower continuously). When the flower buds appear, spraying with Rogor or Tamaron is essential to prevent the attack of pests which will spoil the flowers. The most obvious pest is a yellow beetle, which lays its eggs on the flower stalks; the fat, slimy grubs soon do much damage to the buds and flowers. These beetles are easy to see and may be controlled by hand-picking.

A much worse pest is not so easily seen, namely a tiny flying insect called Thrips, which appears in large numbers and damages the flower buds and the opened flowers. A bad attack of Thrips distorts every flower, causing brown patches also, and many buds may fail to develop entirely. Unless flowering orchids of this kind are regularly sprayed with Rogor 40, attack by Thrips is certain. Spraying once a week is sufficient to maintain control, but if the plants are badly infested more frequent spraying is necessary until the numbers of insects are reduced. The adult Thrips are tiny, narrow, black objects and may usually be seen on careful examination of damaged flowers, but most of the damage is done by the young insects which are pale in colour, often hiding in the buds, and difficult to see. Fortunately, the less fleshy flowers of Dendrobiums and some other orchids are not badly attacked by Thrips; but in any case it is a good practice to spray all orchid plants regularly with Tuba root, as this will keep away nearly all the pests which are liable to trouble the orchid grower. Other liquid insecticides may be used but it is important to make them up to the recom-

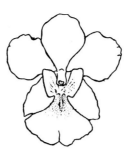

Vanda Miss Joaquim

Vanda Miss Joaquim

Dendrobium crumenatum

Vanda teres

mended concentration. If they are too weak they will have no effect, and if they are too strong they will damage the plants.

Vanda Miss Joaquim

This was, and may still be, the commonest orchid of Malaysian gardens, because it is easy to propagate and flowers freely and continuously. It is a hybrid between *Vanda teres* and *Vanda hookeriana* (see below), which appeared in the garden of Miss Joaquim in the year 1893. It has curious cylindrical or terete (not flattened) leaves, which have a little kink near the tip, like the joint of one's finger. The flowers are fairly large, in colour rosy mauve, with suffusion of orange on the side lobes of the lip, a combination of colours which is not very pleasing. They are far more attractive by artificial light than by daylight, as the yellower artificial light gives them a brighter rosy shade.

The details of cultivation have been mentioned above. Full sun is essential. Supporting stakes about one metre high above ground level are usually most satisfactory. As the plants flower continuously, regular weekly spraying with Rogor is absolutely essential. When the plants are too tall to be manageable, the topmost metre is cut off and started again as cuttings. A garden bed planted entirely with this *Vanda* can be a very fine sight while the plants are young, but when they have grown tall the lower parts with all the roots are not a very pleasing sight. If possible, they should be screened by growing some short bushes in front of the bed, provided they do not shade the orchids. *Vanda* Miss Joaquim is a good cut flower and lasts very well in water, but if bees come into the house and remove the pollinia then the flowers will fade very quickly and will become almost white within twenty-four hours or less.

Vanda teres

This is one of the parent species of Miss Joaquim and is native in Burma. There are several varieties, the most highly prized being a white one. All are seasonal in flowering, being stimulated to flower by dry weather, and rarely give a full show of blossom in Singapore. They are better in the north of Malaysia. The flowers of the best varieties are very large and handsome, but the lip is smaller than in Miss Joaquim.

Vanda hookeriana

This is a Malaysian species, being found in open swampy jungle in various parts of the country. It is much less vigorous in growth than *V. teres*, needs more careful treatment, and more moisture. It will respond to heavy manuring when well established. The flowers have a most beautiful broad lip, the side-lobes a deep purple, and the wide mid-lobe white or mauve with rich purple markings. Strong plants will flower continuously, but not as freely as *Vanda* Miss Joaquim.

Vanda tricuspidata

This is a species from the island of Alor which has a lip of unusual shape, the side lobes being very narrow and the mid-lobe ending in three slender points. Some plants have better coloured flowers than others, but none are really free-flowering in Singapore. It is treated as the other climbing Vandas.

Hybrid Terete Vandas

New hybrids have been produced within the group of climbing Vandas, and also between these and the Scorpion Orchids, and the epiphytic Vandas (see below). Within the group of climbing terete-leafed Vandas, the cross *V. Miss Joaquim x V. hookeriana* has given a range of forms, more or less resembling *V. hookeriana*, but larger and more robust. Not all of these are good. *Vanda hookeriana x V. tricuspidata (Vanda Amy)* is a very attractive hybrid, more free-flowering than *V. tricuspidata* and also richer in colouring. *V. Miss Joaquim x V. teres* has produced some large-flowered hybrids, but none of striking colour. More hybrids have been produced in this group, the object being free-flowering plants with large flowers having a broad richly-coloured lip.

There is a white-flowered form of *V. Miss Joaquim* and there is another white-flowered hybrid terete *Vanda* named *V. Diana*, both of which are as easy to grow as *V. Miss Joaquim* and need the same treatment. The flowers are excellent for cutting but are subject to a little spotting when the weather is very wet.

Arachnis flos-aeris (previously *A. moschifera*)

This is the common Scorpion Orchid, bearing large flowers of scorpion-like shape, coloured chocolate-purple and pale greenish yellow, in broad uneven bands, with a small lip. The plants are very robust, with stout climbing stems and two rows of flattened leaves. They are probably best grown on strong posts about 2 m high and about 1 m or more apart. The

Vanda hookeriana

Arachnis hookeriana

Arachnis maingayi Maggie Oei

Renantanda

Grammatophyllum speciosum

Arachnis flos-aeris

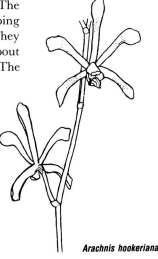

Arachnis hookeriana

Vanda dearei

Vanda merrillii

Vanda sanderana

Vanda Rothschildiana

as this can be a little smelly it should be done well away from the house. In towns this may not be possible as there may be complaints from neighbours and there may be some trouble from mosquitoes. The containers used should be covered and this will prevent or reduce the mosquito problem. Very successful results have been obtained by using a dilute watery extract of finely chopped fish. Discarded fish from the market can be used for this purpose, but care should be taken to make sure that flies do not become a nuisance, otherwise there will be complaints from neighbouring houses. Unfortunately, pieces of raw fish sometimes encourage the breeding of maggots. Commercially prepared fish emulsion is now available which is not only more hygienic but also less odorous.

Fresh cattle dung, if available, may be mixed with water, the liquid strained, and then applied. Groundnut or soybean cake may be soaked in water until rotten, and the liquid used. Urine, diluted with four or five times its bulk of water and kept for a few days, is an excellent manure for orchids. All these solutions of organic material are liable to be very strong smelling, and after they have been applied to the potting mixture, the smell will persist for some time, possibly attracting flies, which would be unacceptable to housewives who are not keen orchid growers. When possible, manuring should be continued, in small amounts every week or so, while growth continues. Many orchids rest after completing a stage of growth, and at this time no manure should be given.

Orchid Houses in Malaysia

As has been noted above, most epiphytic orchids need some shade, and all need some sort of bench for supporting the pots, or a bar on which to hang them. Shade can of course be provided by trees, and the hanging plants can be suspended from the branches, but usually it is more convenient to have some sort of house in which to keep the plants. In choosing the site for the house, it is most desirable to have it exposed to the morning sun on one side and sheltered by trees from the afternoon sun on the other. If this is done, the plants needing more light can be placed on the eastern side of the house, and those needing more shade on the western side where they will get less direct morning sun, and shade in the afternoon.

As regards a roof, there seems no reason for one of ridge shape, unless it is to be covered with glass. A flat roof covered with horizontal wooden laths is quite satisfactory. The laths should run north and south; then their shadows keep moving all day, and no plant is ever exposed to direct sun for any length of time. There should be about the same space between the laths as the width of the laths themselves. Special plastic netting of varying densities is now made and this cuts out different amounts of light. It can be used in place of laths but is best stretched firmly over a framework so that it does not sag, and the border should be firmly held under a wooden lath; otherwise it will fray and eventually the netting will fall down. It is a little expensive but lasts a very long time and has the additional advantage of preventing heavy rain from damaging the plants underneath.

Orchids requiring plenty of light and air (e.g. most Dendrobiums) are best hung beneath a narrow roof which gives shade in the middle of the day only; it may be supported by a row of short-armed T-shaped steel posts 2½ m tall. Benches for the plants may be arranged in any way found convenient. It is desirable to have them so that there is a free circulation of air around the plants. If practicable, it is useful to have part of the benches covered with glass, to keep rain off the plants which have been repotted or others that need shelter from heavy rain; this can be done by fixing sloping glazed frames in suitable positions, without the trouble and expense of making a ridged roof. It is possible also to use sheets of polythene film for protecting the plants and although this is easy to use it does deteriorate after it has been exposed to strong sunlight for many months. A plant house could be roofed entirely with sheets of polythene film, provided the supporting framework is adequate to prevent sagging of the polythene. If it does sag, water will gather and as this can be very heavy it may result in the tearing of the polythene film.

It is important to have a good potting shed if the garden is sufficiently large, so that there is plenty of room to store burnt earth, broken bricks, etc. under cover from the rain, a good roomy working bench, a place for keeping spare pots and for spraying materials. Obviously, in a small garden there would be no

Aranda Tyersall

Ascocentrum miniatum

Rhynchostylis gigantea varieties

room for a potting shed but if a small plant house can be built then most of the equipment used can be stored underneath the benches or in a waterproof cupboard. Artificial fertilizers and other chemicals should be stored in a dry place and unused pots are best kept under cover; if they are left outside in the garden they will become green very quickly and will need to be thoroughly scrubbed before they can be used again.

Epiphytic Vandas

These are exceptions to the general rule that epiphytes consist of a series of short shoots arising from a basal rootstock. Like *Vanda teres*, the epiphytic Vandas continue to grow indefinitely at the top of the stem, but much more slowly than the climbing species. The principal epiphytic Vandas grown in Malaysia are *V. tricolor* from Java (with the closely related *V. suavis*), *V. coerulea* from Burma, *V. insignis* from the Lesser Sunda islands, *V. dearei* from Borneo, *V. sumatrana* from Sumatra, *V. luzonica* and *V. sanderana* from the Philippines. These all have fairly stout, erect stems, with flattened strap-shaped leaves of varying size, and thick roots. They are grown in pots or baskets; the pots need not have perforated sides if the potting mixture is sufficiently open to give good aeration. Rather large pieces of clean bricks and charcoal, with some pieces of coconut husk also, make a satisfactory potting medium; but the coconut husk becomes rotten after a time and is best used only in perforated pots or baskets. As new aerial roots are produced by the plant, it is well to train them to grow into the pot, so that they may absorb the manure which is given in solution from time to time.

Plants of this kind produce lateral shoots, and they may be propagated by cutting off such shoots, but no shoot should be cut until it has a few well grown aerial roots. When potting such a newly cut shoot, its base may be covered with the potting mixture of broken bricks, etc., deeply enough to hold it firmly, and also the ends of any aerial roots that are long enough. The roots should be handled carefully, so as not to damage them. Although they may feel quite firm and strong, they will snap very quickly and easily if they are bent too sharply. The newly potted plant should be kept in a shady place until it has begun to make new growth, when it may be moved gradually to a more exposed position.

If an old plant of this kind does not produce side shoots, the whole top of the plant may be removed, including all the leafy part if necessary. The base will then produce side shoots, which may be removed as cuttings when they are big enough and have aerial roots of their own. The top of the plant can also be used as a cutting. This is the quickest way of propagating plants of this group. For propagating large quantities, tissue culture techniques are employed. These give uniform and unlimited reproduction of selected clones.

Vanda coerulea

This is one of the most beautiful species but really requires a seasonal climate with quite a cool season, and does well at Cameron Highlands. In the lowlands, newly imported plants will flower well once or twice but are difficult to keep in vigorous growth. There are many varieties, all having large flowers in shades of blue or blue-mauve and there are forms with pink or white flowers. These have been hybridized and some of the plants obtained flower well in the lowlands of Malaysia. Many of the varieties have an attractive tessellated pattern on the petals and sepals. The plants seem to grow best with full exposure to sun.

Vanda dearei

A large plant with long, curved, broad leaves. It has creamy yellow flowers, sometimes partly flushed with a brownish tinge, with broad petals and sepals, and they are very fragrant. Unfortunately, only a few flowers are borne on an inflorescence and the stalk is short; but on account of the unusual colour and size of the flowers the species is popular. It has been used extensively for hybridizing. The plants prefer light shade and will become very large, flowering every few months.

Vanda denisoniana

This species also needs more seasonal conditions and a slightly cooler climate so that it is not vigorous in growth in the lowlands. It has good-sized flowers which are available in several colours from white to yellow, orange or brown. The species has been used for hybridizing, and there are a number of very attractive hybrids available.

Vanda insignis

This plant has rather larger and more richly coloured flowers than *V. tricolor*, with the end of the lip broadly rounded, but it is not so easy to grow in Malaysia, preferring a more seasonal climate. It has been used very successfully for hybridizing, some notable plants

Vanda insignis

having been produced, and from these other well known hybrids such as *Vanda* Tan Chay Yan were derived. Many of the hybrids from this species have been used for crossing with other genera such as *Vanda*, *Arachnis*, *Renanthera* and *Ascocentrum*.

Vanda lamellata

A small-flowered species, native to the Philippines, which is easily grown in the lowlands of Malaysia. The long inflorescence carries many pale yellow flowers which have brownish markings. It was one of the first Vandas used for crossing with the Scorpion Orchids and several good, free-flowering hybrids were produced.

Vanda luzonica

This species has beautiful pure white flowers with rich purple markings, but does not flower so freely as the others in Singapore. It also grows best under light shade.

Vanda sanderana (Euanthe sanderana)

This is the most prized species of the group and is also the most expensive. It has rather narrow leaves, is not such a robust plant as the others already mentioned, and is not easy to grow successfully in the lowlands of Malaysia. The inflorescence is relatively short but carries up to fifteen large flowers which are round and flat, and are arranged quite close together all around the stem. They are pale lilac-mauve with brown markings and the large lateral sepals have a close network of brown veins. The species has been the parent of many outstanding hybrids.

Vanda sumatrana

The plant is very similar in habit to *V. dearei*, and has flowers of similar shape, with shining petals and sepals of a brownish colour.

Hybrids of Epiphytic Vandas

Some very fine hybrids have been produced, especially in Honolulu, between *V. coerulea*, *V. sanderana* and other species. One of the most outstanding hybrids was *Vanda* Rothschildiana which was the result of combining *V. coerulea* and *V. sanderana*. Crossing between other species has given a wide range of extremely attractive plants with flowers in yellow, orange, pink, red and blue and many of these make excellent cut flowers as only a single spray need be used for a display and will last a very long time in water.

Semi-terete Vanda Hybrids

Many hybrids have been made between the terete climbing Vandas and the epiphytic Vandas. These hybrids have long and deeply channelled leaves, U-shaped in section. They will grow quite tall and may be treated either

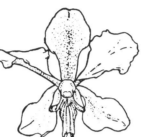

Vanda Marguerite Maron

as pot plants or grown in beds like the climbing species. They are vigorous in growth when well treated, and many of them flower quite freely. As regards cultural treatment, they are best in full sun potted in unperforated pots, with bricks and charcoal, or with rather large pieces of good burnt earth; but the burnt earth needs renewal from time to time, as it becomes too compact. The roots will enter this mixture and branch freely; liquid manure should then be given regularly. The surface of the potting material may be covered with small pieces of coconut husk, to prevent undue heating by the sun; these need renewal from time to time.

One of the best of these hybrids is the earliest, *V.* Marguerite Maron (*V. teres* x *V. suavis*). Strong plants will flower regularly; the inflorescences have good long stalks and they may have eight or more flowers open simultaneously. The hybrid *V.* Miss Joaquim has been much crossed with the epiphytic Vandas; its offspring is always variable, and not all seedlings are satisfactory. The best varieties of the cross *V.* Miss Joaquim x *V. tricolor* (*V.* Madame E.M.E. Dinger) are good and free-flowering, but some are very poor. From the cross of *V. teres* x *V. insignis*, the very fine hybrid V. Josephine van Brero was obtained and has a predominating orange shade. This plant has been used for crossing with other *Vanda* species and hybrids as well as with other related genera, and large numbers of excellent plants have been produced.

For growers who may wish to find out more details of these hybrids, there are a number of books available dealing with orchids only and enquiries can always be sent to the Botanic Gardens in Singapore. Some very good plants have been produced by crossing *V. coerulea* with *V. teres* and *V.* Miss Joaquim but many of the seedlings are disappointing in the shape of the flowers, or their colour, and some are not free-flowering.

Vanda-Arachnis Hybrids

Some good and free-flowering hybrids have been produced by crossing the epiphytic Vandas with the Scorpion Orchids. One of the best produced in Malaysia is *Aranda* Deborah, *V. lamellata* x *V. hookerana*. The *Vanda* parent (from the Philippines) has quite small yellowish flowers, but has many on an inflorescence. The hybrid has a graceful erect inflorescence of many flowers, about as large as those of the *Arachnis* parent, the petals and sepals cream with attractive small markings, the lip yellow. *Aranda* Tyersall, *V. dearei* x *A. hookerana*, has fewer flowers on an inflorescence, but is an attractive cream colour. *Aranda* Hilda Galistan, *V. tricolor* x *A. hookerana*, is very free-flowering when well grown, with long-stalked sprays. *Aranda* City of Singapore (*A. flos-aeris* x *V. dearei*)

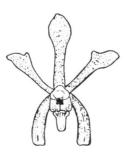

Aranda Hilda Galistan

Ascocenda

Mokara Bibi

flowered for the first time in 1951. *V. coerulea* x *Arachnis* hybrids unfortunately seem shy of flowering.

Of all the orchid hybrids produced, *Aranda* is probably the most widely grown and has been one of the mainstays of the orchid cut flower industry in Malaysia. The plants may be treated as climbing orchids and need full sun, but they are slower in growth than *Arachnis*.

Rhynchostylis

A small genus sometimes called the 'Foxtail Orchids' because of the appearance of the inflorescence which has many flowers arranged densely on all sides of the stem. They are seasonal and flower once each year but are then unforgettable because of the abundance and fragrance of the flowers. The species will not grow well in the lowlands of Malaysia but in cooler, more northern areas they are easy to grow and flower freely in the lowlands. Hybrids have been obtained by crossing with *Renanthera* and *Vanda* and these are known as *Renanstylis* and *Rhyncovanda* respectively. They grow well in the lowlands and flower freely and continuously in Singapore and Malaysia.

Ascocentrum

This is a small genus of plants which resemble miniature strap-leafed Vandas and they produce small flat flowers arranged densely around the whole stem. Some of the species and most of the hybrids are easy to grow, flower continuously, and are tolerant of a wide range of growing conditions. For gardeners who have only a small space available, these plants are ideal and provide quantities of flowers with the minimum of time and effort.

The species have been crossed with *Vanda*, giving plants called *Ascocenda*, and they have also been crossed with *Phalaenopsis*, giving *Asconopsis*. Some of these hybrids have been crossed with *Renanthera* and *Arachnis* in order to produce miniature forms of those genera.

Dendrobium crumenatum (close-up)

Commercially, multi-generic hybrids that involve the three genera, *Vanda*, *Arachnis* and *Renanthera*, and the genus of miniature Vandaceous species, *Ascocentrum*, are most important. These free-flowering, brilliantly coloured hybrids enhance most orchid collections and are among the most popular items for cut-flower production. Examples are Ascocendas, Mokaras and Kagawaras.

Phalaenopsis

The species of this genus are often known as Moth Orchids or Moon Orchids and are widely distributed in Southeast Asia, mostly in the lowlands. They are easy to grow and require continuous shade and flower almost continuously if well treated. *Phalaenopsis* is part of the *Vanda* group but has very short stems, with large, usually flat but rather fleshy, hanging leaves. The finest and best known species is *P. amabilis* (sometimes called *P. grandiflora*), with long sprays of beautiful white flowers having almost round petals. In Malaysia, the native species are *P. amabilis*, *P. cochlearis*, *P. cornu-cervi*, *P. fuscata*, *P. gigantea*, *P. mariae*, *P. sumatrana*, and *P. violacea*, which are sometimes cultivated; in all except the first mentioned, the flowers are smaller and borne only a few at a time. In the Philippines are some very handsome species, with long branched inflorescences bearing many flowers, but they are not suited to the lowland climate, though they will flourish at our hill stations. These include *P. sanderana*, *P. schillerana*, *P. stuartiana*, *P. amboinensis*, *P. lindenii*, and *P. lueddemanniana*. In West Borneo, several years ago, a very curious group of species was

Phalaenopsis hybrid

Dendrobium anosmum

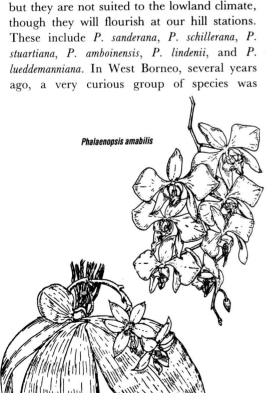
Phalaenopsis amabilis

Phalaenopsis violacea

Phalaenopsis violacea

discovered, with long cylindrical leaves, rather like those of *Vanda teres*, but longer. The best known of these is *P. denevei* (now known as *Paraphalaenopsis denevei*), which has attractive cinnamon-brown and purple flowers, several open at a time, but a short inflorescence.

If *Phalaenopsis* plants have correct treatment they will grow strongly and flower well. But they are easily spoilt by bad treatment, and are sometimes very subject to attack from a black weevil which bores to the bud of the plant and destroys it, often before the attack is observed. For this reason, it pays to spray Phalaenopsis plants, like all other orchids, regularly with Tuba root, which discourages undesirable insects.

Opinions differ as to the best treatment for *P. amabilis*, but it certainly needs some shade (preferably after noon) and must hang in an airy place. Plants are usually attached to pieces of wood, or of tree fern root, or coconut husk, to which their roots become attached. They can also be grown in pots with any of the usual open-textured potting mixtures for orchids. New plants, which have no roots, need to be kept in a place sheltered from heavy rain until they have begun to produce new roots, and excessive watering of all plants should be avoided. Some people prefer to keep all plants under shelter from the rain, and so control watering.

When plants are in active growth, they need manuring, preferably with liquid manure. Some growers cover the roots with fresh cattle dung now and then, so that it forms a crust, but this is liable to harbour insects and to become too wet in rainy weather. If kept under cover from rain, another treatment, devised by a local grower, is possible. A plant established on a piece of wood is placed in a wooden basket, so that its leaves project through the side of the basket and its roots (on the piece of wood) are inside. The basket is then filled with pieces of the root of Bird's Nest fern which have been soaked in fresh cattle dung and water and then dried. The basket must be kept under cover from rain, and watered only at intervals of a few days; excessive watering or exposure to heavy rain will cause the roots to rot. The method may also be adopted for *P. violacea* with success; but *P. violacea* always requires more shade and moisture than *P. amabilis*.

Flowers may remain on the inflorescence for up to three months and when the last one has faded, the stem may be cut just above the first flower which will result in a new flowering stem appearing from the node just below. Flowering can be prolonged in this way but the blooms on the subsequent side branches will not be quite as large as those on the original stem.

Hybrids of *Phalaenopsis*

Several thousand hybrids have been produced, both between species within this genus and between it and other genera such as *Vanda*, *Doritis*, *Renanthera* and *Ascocentrum*. It has been used in combinations of three genera in one hybrid. There is a wide variety of flower colour in all these hybrids and all colours can be found except blue. *Paraphalaenopsis* has also been used a great deal for hybridizing with *Aerides*, *Renanthera*, *Vanda* and *Arachnis*, and a number of named forms have been produced.

Aerides

Another genus of the *Vanda* group, in habit resembling the epiphytic Vandas, but less erect in growth and branching more freely. The flowers are arranged all around the stem of the lateral inflorescences and are usually waxy in appearance with a strong fragrance. Practically all of the flowers on one inflorescence will open at the same time. When well grown, the plants will flower freely from time to time; their flowering seems to be dependent on dry weather following a wet period.

Owing to their sprawling habit, *Aerides* are a little troublesome to manage. The easiest method is to tie them to an old palm trunk which has persistent leaf bases (like the oil palm), or to a tree which is not too shady and has bark with crevices into which the orchid roots may grow. In a basket, they are best kept hanging in a place where they get the morning sun. To keep the plants shapely, they must be tied to some sort of support and their spreading roots should be brought into the basket as far as possible, so that they may obtain food. The usual brick and charcoal potting mixture may be used, or in a wide basket pieces of coconut husk and Bird's Nest fern root may be included, being removed and replaced when rotten. The plants respond to regular manuring, always provided of course that they have healthy roots. When tied to a tree trunk, the stems are slightly pendulous with the tips curved upwards and the long roots tend to grow towards the tree trunk where they grow along the cracks in the bark. When a number of the roots have grown in this way the plants may appear as though supported on a fine trellis of roots.

Another method of treating *Aerides* which may be very successful if carefully managed is to tie the plants to a short stout stump of wood (say 60 cm long and 15 cm thick) and place it vertically in the ground, so that the roots of the plants are at ground level. A place that has sun at least all morning is necessary, and when well established under these conditions the plants will stand sun all day. A light cover of leaves and cut grass over the spreading roots is required and should be renewed from time to time. Clumps of plants so treated will flower very freely, and their growth will be vigorous.

The common local species is *A. odoratum*; it is variable in colouring, but the prevailing tone is mauve. The lip has a curious spur which is curved forwards at the tip, and is horn-like in shape.

A. lawrenceae is a Philippine species which is more robust than the local *A. odoratum* and has finer inflorescences. The beautiful species of *Aerides* from Burma unfortunately do not flower well in Malaysia.

Aerides has been hybridized with other genera such as *Vanda*, *Arachnis*, *Renanthera*, *Ascocentrum*, *Phalaenopsis* and *Rhynchostylis* and most of the plants are vigorous and free-flowering.

Dendrobium

This is one of the largest genera of orchids in the tropics of Asia, and there are many wild species in Malaysia. Unfortunately, most of our local species have either small or shortlived flowers. The commonest one in Malaysia is *Dendrobium crumenatum*, the Pigeon Orchid, which can be found on almost any old tree; its beautiful fragrant flowers only last a few hours. The principal Dendrobiums cultivated in Malaysia are imported either from the Moluccas and New Guinea, or from Thailand. The former group are the most useful, as their flowers are usually in long sprays, and last a considerable period. Some of the Thai species are very beautiful, but their flowers are in short sprays, not fit for cutting, and not lasting many days.

All Dendrobiums have a succession of shoots (or pseudobulbs) of limited growth; these shoots vary much in length in different species, in some being long and stiffly erect, in some long and slender, hanging down, in others quite short. Their leaves are equally various, but most have two rows of moderate-sized leaves along the shoots to their tip. The flowers are produced either all along the shoots, or only towards their tip; in some species the shoots only flower after they have lost all of their leaves (this is true of most Thai species), while others flower on the leafy stem (most New Guinea species have this character). Some of the Thai species require a rest in dry, cool weather to make them flower. Such plants are not successful in Malaysia, as we have no dry or cool seasons; some of them will grow indefinitely but hardly flower at all.

In general, Dendrobiums are treated as described under the main heading of Epiphytic Orchids; and differences of treatment or peculiarities of the individual species are noted below.

The general structure of a *Dendrobium* flower is as follows. The column is short, but has a more or less prolonged base, called a foot; the lateral sepals are attached to the sides of the foot, so that they are more or less triangular and of a different shape from the upper sepal. The lip is attached to the end of the foot. The foot with the bases of the sepals and of the lip forms a projection of greater or less size behind the flower, often shaped rather like a chin, and this is called the **mentum**. The side lobes of the lip are usually less clearly defined than in the Vandas, and the mid-lobe often has ridges or keels or other structures upon it. The anther contains four pollinia, but they have no connecting membrane as in *Vanda*; there is, however, a sticky substance which attaches them to a visiting insect (or to the hybridizer's matchstick).

Malaysian Dendrobiums

The most beautiful *Dendrobium* native in Malaysia is probably *D. farmeri*, which is found on trees by rivers in the northeastern part of Peninsular Malaysia and north into Thailand and Burma. Plants imported from Thailand do not flower well as far south as Singapore, but Malaysian plants usually flower well there once a year. The pseudobulbs are rather short, and square in section, each having only a few leaves. The flowers are in graceful hanging bunches, the petals and sepals pale mauve or white and the lip yellow; unfortunately, they only last a week. They need light shade, and are better in hanging baskets or pots than when placed on a bench.

D. superbum (also called *D. anosmum*) is distributed throughout the Malaysian region from Sumatra to the Philippines, but is not common in Malaysia, and local plants are not of the finest variety, having usually rather small flowers. The best varieties are from the Philippines. This species has long slender pendulous shoots which bear flowers throughout their length after losing their leaves. In general, they do not flower so freely in Malaysia as in more seasonal climates.

Owing to the long hanging shape of the stems, *D. superbum* requires special treatment, either in hanging pots or baskets (which must be hung high enough to allow free room for the hanging stems) or, even better, attached to the spreading branch of a tree. The latter treatment has the disadvantage that the plant cannot be moved for display purposes, but such a plant usually grows more strongly than in a basket. The flowers are large, mauve with a hairy lip of deeper colour, and fragrant. There is a fine variety with white petals and sepals, the lip alone mauve, often called var. *huttonii*. There are also smaller varieties with this colouring.

D. crumenatum is distributed throughout Southeast Asia and usually grows in exposed situations. The short plump pseudobulbs

Dendrobium nobile

Dendrobium lineale

Dendrobium phalaenopsis hybrid

Dendrobium lasianthera

Dendrobium antennatum

Coelogyne pandurata

become wrinkled as they age and at the top of each one there is a thin stem carrying a number of thick, dark green leaves. Some of these stems produce a long, thin, leafless stalk on which the white flowers are borne. The Pigeon Orchid flowers gregariously about nine days after a heavy storm which causes a sudden drop in temperature. Though the flowers are shortlived, they are beautiful and fragrant, and often produced in large numbers, so that it is worthwhile growing a few plants.

They may be grown in pots, as described for epiphytes in general, or in a hanging coconut husk, or they may be tied to tree trunks or branches and their new roots will soon hold them in place without any other support, but they must be in a position where they receive sunlight for most of the day. They grow quite well in a little shade but do not seem to flower quite as well.

Dendrobiums of Burma and Thailand

The most free-flowering of these in Malaysia are *D. dalhousianum* and *D. moschatum*, both with large and beautiful flowers and tall, erect shoots, making them suitable for treatment as pot plants. They need morning sun, and will, if hardened, stand full sun. They only flower on the old shoots which have lost their leaves. Unfortunately the flowers last no more than a

Dendrobium chrysotoxum

Dendrobium phalaenopsis

week (sometimes less) and, being in pendulous inflorescences with short stalks, they are not suitable for cutting. *D. fimbriatum* has bright yellow flowers, rather smaller than those of *D. moschatum*, but it is less free-flowering in Singapore. *D. chrysanthum* has pendulous stems, and bright yellow flowers which appear before the leaves fall; it is treated as *D. superbum*, but is not very strong in growth in Malaysia. *D. farmeri* has shortlived flowers but these are produced regularly once a year in Singapore. The pseudobulbs are four-angled and up to 30 cm long with three or four leaves only. Twenty or more of the large flowers are produced in a dense cluster on the drooping inflorescence. *D. thyrsiflorum* has a habit much like the previous species (the longer pseudobulbs have more than four angles) and a similar type of inflorescence but rarely flowers in Singapore. *D. pierardii* has a habit much like *D. superbum*, but with more slender stems. In a seasonal climate, the old bare stems are covered with flowers after resting, but in Malaysia it usually bears not more than a few flowers at a time at uncertain intervals. It does much better in the northern parts of the peninsula. The thin hanging pseudobulbs may be up to 2 m long and the flowers are mauve with a pale yellow lip. *D. chrysotoxum* has short, swollen, erect pseudobulbs and terminal inflorescences of beautiful golden flowers, of moderate size; it grows very well when properly potted and manured, requiring full morning sun, but does not flower very freely. *D. aggregatum*, one of the prettiest of the Burmese Dendrobiums, rarely flowers in Singapore, and *D. nobile* (and many others) are even more shy of flowering, probably because they need a cool season to mature their flower buds. More success might be obtained in the northern parts of the Malaysian peninsula.

Dendrobium phalaenopsis

This species is found from the Moluccas through Indonesia and down to Queensland and is often very abundant. It is easy to grow, flowers well and the flowers are always beautiful because they are of a good full shape, long lasting and held in graceful sprays. It has fairly stout pseudobulbs, erect or nearly so in growth, and flowers near the ends of both new and old growths. It needs full morning sun.

D. phalaenopsis varies a great deal in the flower colour and there are forms with rich purple sepals and petals while in others they are white. There are intermediate forms and there are some in which only the margins of the sepals and petals are coloured, the remainder of the flowers being white. There is also some variation in the size of the flowers and in the shape of the petals and sepals. Owing to its broad petals and shapely inflorescence, it has been much used for hybridizing, and is the parent of many beautiful plants. The range of colour in the flowers resulted in much variation in the hybrid offspring, and very many fine plants have been produced, especially in Europe and Hawaii. One of the most well known of these is the variety called *D.* Pompadour, which is used extensively for cut flower production in several countries. Many hybrids produced by crossing this variety with other *Dendrobium* species are also used extensively now in the cut flower trade, especially in the growing export trade.

The *Dendrobium* Section *Spatulata*, formerly *Ceratobium*

Dendrobium veratrifolium

This group of species occur mostly in New Guinea, and many of them are very beautiful; all also have long-lasting flowers in graceful sprays, which should make them excellent subjects for cultivation. Their petals are, however, narrow, and usually twisted (the sepals often still more twisted) and they lack the fullness usually demanded of a cut flower. For this reason they have been crossed with *D. phalaenopsis*, which brings a wide-petal character to combine with the narrow-petal *Spatulata* type. The result is a series of graceful hybrids which are mentioned below. In general, these hybrids are both easier to grow and more free-flowering in Malaysia than the parent species, but there are a few species which are quite easy to manage and well worth growing.

The species described below, belonging to this *Dendrobium* section, are *D. antennatum*, *D. discolor*, *D. lasianthera*, *D. lineale*, *D. schulleri*, *D. stratiotes* and *D. superbiens*.

Dendrobium antennatum

This is a small plant which flowers well in Singapore and has thin pseudobulbs with sprays of white and green blooms.

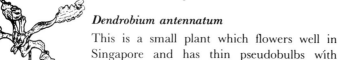

Dendrobium undulatum

Dendrobium discolor, sometimes *D. undulatum*

An unmistakable species with twisted sepals and petals which also have undulating margins. The pseudobulbs are one metre or more in length and the inflorescences, which may be 45 cm long, are produced at the ends or in the axils of the leaves. Each inflorescence can carry up to thirty flowers which are arranged attractively all around the stem for its whole length. The species shows great variation in the habit of the plant, the size, shape, and colour of the flowers, but has been used a great deal for hybridizing with enormous success. Some of the hybrids are *D.* Constance, *D.* Pauline and *D.* Champagne.

Dendrobium lasianthera

Dendrobium stratiotes

This is a very tall species with pseudobulbs up to 3 m in height bearing inflorescences up to 20 cm long, with flowers carried close together on the upper half of the stem. Natural hybrids between this species and *D. discolor* are thought to occur in New Guinea.

Dendrobium lineale, formerly *D. veratrifolium*

A large, robust species with long pseudobulbs up to 3 m long when well grown, and flowering freely once each year with a little flowering at other times. The slender, erect inflorescences carry many small, pale lilac flowers which have erect, hardly twisted petals. The free-flowering character is transmitted to all of its offspring. The plants do best in almost full sun and can be grown in pots or on tree stumps with the usual treatment for epiphytes. In the wild there is a wide range of differences in flower colour and shape and some of this may be due to natural hybridization with one or two other species. The inflorescences can be 70 cm or more long and may carry more than thirty flowers; consequently when one pseudobulb carries several such inflorescences and the whole plant has many pseudobulbs the effect is most striking.

Dendrobium schulleri

Many green-flowered Dendrobium hybrids owe their colour to crossing at some stage with this species. The plants have pseudobulbs up to a metre long and inflorescences up to 50 cm. The flowers are pale brownish green but there are forms available with pale yellow or green flowers.

Dendrobium stratiotes

Probably the most commonly grown of a group of smaller species which have stiffly erect inflorescences bearing fewer flowers of more formal shape, with stiff, erect, twisted, narrow petals, like the horns of an antelope. Other species of the group are *D. antennatum*, *D. leporinum*, and *D. taurinum*. *D. stratiotes* is a fine species with graceful long-lasting flowers. The plants are strong growing and were used in producing some of the early hybrids in Singapore, but a slight disadvantage of many of these was the short inflorescence stalk carrying only a few flowers.

One of the most well known and successful hybrids is *D.* Caesar. The plants grow better in a hanging pot or basket than on a bench, and the roots need more air than *D. veratrifolium*. It is best, in fact, for the base of the plant to be well above the potting mixture, the roots growing down like stilts and supporting the stems. As the plant spreads out of the pot, some loose bunches of fern root may be tied on outside, to hold the orchid on the new growth. The less the plant is disturbed the better. The flowers of this group of orchids are extraordinarily long-lasting.

Dendrobium superbiens

This is a natural hybrid between *D. phalaenopsis* and some member of the *Spatulata* group, probably a small variety of *D. undulatum* (*D. discolor*). It is found on Thursday Island and neighbouring territories, and is very variable. *D. goldii* should probably be regarded as one of its varieties. It has graceful, arching inflorescences of medium-sized flowers, usually of a rich purple, with petals intermediate in shape between the round ones of *D. phalaenopsis* and the narrow twisted ones of *D. undulatum*. The finest varieties of *D. superbiens* are very handsome, and the flowers are long-lasting. They are also quite free-flowering in Malaysia, flowering again and again on the old stems, but they need careful management, and repotting at least every two years, as the old roots tend to become rotten and have to be removed. Fine hybrids obtained by crossing *D. superbiens* with *D. phalaenopsis* are called *D. Louis Bleriot* and *D. Madame Pompadour*. The best of them are very rich in colouring, with larger flowers than *D. superbiens*.

Dendrobium Hybrids

Many *Dendrobium* hybrids have been raised in Europe, but nearly all are from the *D. nobile* group and other species from Burma and Thailand which are not very satisfactory in Malaysia, owing to the absence here of a cool, dry season. In recent years, however, a large number of new hybrids have been raised in Java and Singapore from the *Spatulata* group and *D. phalaenopsis*, most of which have proved well suited to our climate. As noted above, *D. phalaenopsis* gives the valuable character of broad petals, which adds a fullness to the rather delicate beauty of the *Spatulata* species. One of the first of the hybrids and still one of the best, is *D. Pauline*, *D. phalaenopsis* x *D. undulatum*. This has long, graceful inflorescences of quite large flowers, with long and slightly twisted petals, mauve in colour.

Owing to the variability of *D. phalaenopsis* in colour depth, there is much variation in its hybrids and many plants of *D. Pauline* are too pale to be first-class. All are graceful, however, and have a certain informality, due to lack of stiffness in flowers of *D. undulatum*, not found in the more stiffly formal shape of the hybrids of most of the other Spatulata species. *D. Caesar* (*D. stratiotes* x *D. phalaenopsis*), *D. Rose-Marie* (*D. leporinum* x *D. phalaenopsis*) and *D. Wilhelm Stuber* (*D. lasianthera* x *D. phalaenopsis*) all have more formal shape than *D. Pauline*, and when deeply coloured are very handsome. The best forms of *D. Bali* (*D. taurinum* x *D. phalaenopsis*) are also very fine. *D. Louisae* is the product of *D. veratrifolium* and *D. phalaenopsis*, and has

Dendrobium Helen Park

Dendrobium 'Pauline'

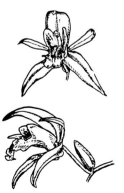

Coelogyne asperata

smaller flowers, but is very attractive, as also is *D. Helen Park* (*D. veratrifolium* x *D. bigibbum*) which sometimes has very long inflorescences.

Further generations of hybrids in this group have been produced, resulting in forms with deeper colour, large-flowered white forms and many others with broader petals. Much to be desired is a good yellow hybrid of this type. Unfortunately, the *Spatulata* species will not cross with the yellow species from Thailand and Burma, such as *D. chrysotoxum*, and the yellow of *D. undulatum* hardly shows when it is mated with a mauve species. In any case this group of hybrids has been much developed and has become very popular, as the long sprays of flowers are very graceful, long-lasting and have proved excellent for the cut-flower trade, both locally and overseas.

Coelogyne

This genus is well represented in Malaysia, and several species have quite large and handsome flowers. They are not, however, very free-flowering, the flowers do not last very long and the plants are rather bulky. Consequently they are not very popular. All require more shade than the epiphytes hitherto mentioned; light shade throughout the day is probably the best for them. They have large, swollen pseudobulbs, usually close together, each bearing two large leaves and sometimes a terminal inflorescence. They may be potted in the usual brick and charcoal mixture, and given liquid manure as other orchids. The species with more or less erect inflorescences may be grown in large perforated pots and kept on benches, but the species with long, hanging inflorescences must be hung, and for this purpose wooden baskets are perhaps preferable.

The best species are *C. asperata* (cream and brown flowers) and *C. pandurata* (pale green and black flowers, and flattened pseudobulbs), which have ascending inflorescences, and *C. dayana* (cream and brown flowers, with long, slender pseudobulbs), which has long, hanging inflorescences and occurs on the hills. *C. speciosa* and related species have only one flower open at a time but are beautiful. *C. rochusseni* is a lowland species with long, hanging inflorescences of rather small flowers. *C. kingii* has erect inflorescences of beautiful white and gold flowers but does not flower well in Singapore. On high branches of forest trees near Gemas (a town in Peninsular Malaysia) and elsewhere, it flowers very profusely at certain seasons. *C. mayeriana* is a second green-flowered species with smaller flowers than *C. pandurata*. A few hybrids have been raised but none are commonly cultivated.

Grammatophyllum

This genus is represented in the Peninsula by

Cattleya hybrid

Cymbidium ensifolium

Oncidium kramerianum

Epidendrum radicans (from Costa Rica)

Grammatophyllum speciosum (close-up)

Cattleya hybrid

one species, *G. speciosum*, which forms larger plants than any other known epiphytic orchid. It grows wild in the crowns of tall trees, but is so large that in the garden it is usually grown on the ground; no pot is big enough for it. But as it is an epiphyte, it needs aeration for its roots, and it must be grown on a raised bed of coarse broken bricks, to provide the necessary drainage. This need be no more than 30 cm high. If the plant is large, it will probably stand firmly enough in a depression in the pile of bricks, but if it is liable to fall over then it must be supported by tying it to a stout stake driven into the ground. The base of the plant should not be covered with stones to make it stable. After staking, some small rocks and pieces of fern root can be packed very lightly around the base of the plant, but not sufficient to interfere in any way with the drainage, and some garden compost can be scattered over afterwards. The plant should be screened from the sun for several months and, when growth has begun, occasional doses of liquid manure can be applied. An established plant needs little attention apart from a small application of garden compost and organic fertilizer twice a year. The plant will produce a dense mass of erect, much branched white roots around its base and compost or dead leaves can be scattered on these and allowed to rot down undisturbed. Plants grown in pots dislike being disturbed; when they become too big for the container, the whole thing should be placed in a larger container but the roots should not be covered with stones or broken brick.

In a large garden, if an old tree with suitable branches is available then this will provide the most ideal conditions for the orchid. The long leafy stems will curve downwards and can reach 3 m in length (on the ground they will be more or less erect with a slight curvature only) and the inflorescences when they appear will be erect and may be 2 m in length; each can carry up to forty large flowers which last for a very long time. Flowering occurs once each year, often after the dry spell at the beginning of the year in the north of the Malaysian peninsula, but further south flowering may be more irregular. An old plant with many inflorescences is a magnificent sight.

G. scriptum is native in the Moluccas. It has quite short, thick pseudobulbs, each with a few leaves, and a mass of upward growing branched white roots. The inflorescence is long and has many flowers, but they are dull (greenish and brown). It is quite handsome, however, when grown well and flowering. It needs quite an exposed situation.

Cymbidium

In this genus are species and hybrids which are among the most popular spray orchids in temperate countries. The original plants were obtained from the mountains of Burma and the foothills of the Himalayas and consequently will not do well in the lowlands of Malaysia. The plants will grow here but will not flower because they need a low night temperature when the flowers are developing and opening. Some of them grow and flower very well at Cameron Highlands. There are lowland species of *Cymbidium* but these are not very satisfactory as garden plants, as some of them have pendulous inflorescences and others have small flowers which are not well coloured. This should not deter gardeners from trying to hybridize them as some interesting results might be obtained.

Cymbidium finlaysonianum is one of the commoner species found wild throughout the lowlands and grows as an epiphyte in exposed places. It often makes very large clumps and in a garden should be given a similar kind of position on a tree branch. It needs little attention and will flower quite well but not continuously, and the long, hanging inflorescences can be very striking, especially if they can be viewed at close quarters so that the colouring of the individual flowers can be appreciated. The inflorescences can grow to 90 cm or more in length. The plants can be grown in pots but these should be set on a high bench or hung from a suitable support so that the inflorescences can hang freely. *C. pubescens* is another species which could be grown in a similar way as it has hanging inflorescences also, but the flowers are a little smaller than in the previous species.

Cymbidium finlaysonianum

C. ensifolium is a small terrestrial species with narrow leaves and erect inflorescences carrying up to seven pale green fragrant flowers which sometimes have red markings. In the lowlands it can be grown quite easily in pots with the lower half filled with charcoal and the top with good coarse, burnt earth. The plants need light shade and can also be grown successfully in the highlands. When grown in pots they can be brought indoors as the plants begin to bloom.

Cattleya

The treatment for Cattleyas (both species and hybrids) is very much as described for Dendrobiums. They are most conveniently handled in pots, and the usual local potting material is broken bricks and charcoal. As noted above, the bricks must be newly broken and clean. Old blackened pieces of brick are covered with algae and probably bacteria, which appear to have a bad effect on the orchid roots. The other points to remember when repotting are to fix the orchid plant on top of the bricks, so that everything but the actual roots is exposed to the air, and to fix it firmly, so that no move-

ment is possible, by tying it to a stick firmly embedded in the potting mixture.

Each new shoot starts as a bud at the base of the last-formed pseudobulb, and grows obliquely upwards. As soon as it has started well into growth, new roots appear at its base; this is the time when care must be given to water sufficiently, and when dilute manure water will have the maximum effect. If one wishes to divide a plant, for purposes of propagation, the right time to cut off the leading part is when a new bud has begun to make new growth. Great care must naturally be taken to avoid injuring the growing bud. Two or three pseudobulbs should be removed; if more are taken the old part of the plant will be slow to resume growth. It is best to wait until a plant has at least two branches (or 'leads') before attempting to propagate it.

If Cattleyas are kept in an open house, exposed to rain, they must have a potting material which allows very good aeration for their roots; this is provided by the usual brick and charcoal mixture. Plants grown in greenhouses in Europe and other temperate regions are potted in a very close mixture of Osmunda fern root and sphagnum moss. Plants potted in this way and imported to Malaysia must have all the material carefully removed from their roots, or these will rot and the plant may die. It is, however, possible in Malaysia to use a close filling of Osmunda fern roots for the top of the pot in place of small broken bricks and charcoal; the fern roots must be well packed. There does not appear to be a common Malaysian fern with roots which are a suitable substitute for Osmunda; most are too harsh or too soft and spongy. If Osmunda root or a similar material is used in Malaysia, the plants are best kept under cover from heavy rain, and the watering carefully controlled according to the weather and the condition of the plants.

Light shade all day, or morning sun until ten o'clock and then shade, is best for Cattleyas. Too much shade checks flowering. Cattleyas are slow growing and each pseudobulb flowers once only so that they are not so free-

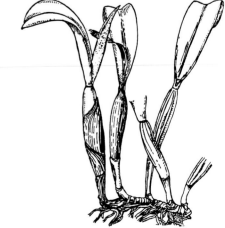

Cattleya plant, showing habit of branching

flowering as some of the other orchids grown in Malaysia.

Cattleya has been hybridized a great deal with closely related genera, especially Laelia which has given rise to plants named *Laelio-cattleya*, but very often all of these hybrids are loosely called *Cattleya*. Their flowers are usually large and often flamboyant as they are available in all shades of purple or purple and red and orange or white.

As regards choice of hybrids, advice is difficult, and a large number have not been tried. If one is buying locally, a good strong plant, well established under Malaysian conditions and showing signs of having flowered, is a safe choice, and all Cattleyas are handsome. If importing from a cooler climate, it is best to choose hybrids suited to the warmest temperatures; but some that are regarded as intermediate are quite satisfactory in the lowlands and can be grown successfully also in the highlands. The following Cattleyas are known to be free-flowering and easy to manage: *C. bowringiana* and its hybrid *C. mantinii; C. hardyana; C. intermedia* and *C. ashtoni.* Many hybrids within the genus *Cattleya* are strong-growing and fairly free-flowering in the lowlands, but hybrids with the genus *Laelia* are usually less vigorous, probably because the *Laelia* species are mountain plants. However, they grow fairly well, but flower less than the *Cattleya* hybrids in the lowlands; practically all of the *Cattleya* hybrids will grow and flower much better in the highlands.

Cattleyas need fairly bright light and if they have too much shade will not flower well. Full sun in the early morning followed by broken shade would be excellent, although some hybrids will tolerate almost full exposure. As with most other orchids, Cattleyas are best with a little liquid manure while they are in active growth. Plants which have been potted recently, or which are in a resting phase should on no account be given any manuring. The liquid from rotting organic materials such as groundnut cake, fish, prawn dust or fresh cattle dung, or dilute urine can be used. These may prove to have a smell which is too objectionable and then a solution of a mixed organic fertilizer (there are several on the market) is very satisfactory. There are few kinds of plants that repay a little care so handsomely as Cattleyas, and for a man who wants to have a few orchids only, Cattleyas are a good choice.

Epidendrum

This is the largest genus of tropical American orchids, comprising several hundred species. Some are cultivated, but the best of these are not suited to the lowlands of Malaysia. *E. radicans* and a few of its hybrids are reasonably strong in our lowland climate but are much

Brassocattleya flower

Hybrid of Epidendrum radicans

better at the hill stations. *E. radicans*, as the name implies, is a climbing species with aerial roots, but does not attain the size of our Malaysian climbing Scorpion Orchids. It has leafy stems 60 cm long or so, each ending in a tall, slender inflorescence, bearing a group of scarlet flowers at the top. The flowers are not large, but they are attractive in shape, and their colour is unusual among orchids. They make good cut flowers and should be grown more at our hill stations. *E. radicans* is easily propagated from cuttings. There is a related species or hybrid with rich purple-crimson flowers, and others with yellow, yellow-orange or mauve flowers. Probably more hybrids of this group could be raised locally and in this way something better suited to the lowland climate might be found.

Some Epidendrums have pseudobulbs, and rather the habit of Cattleyas. One of these, *E. stamfordianum*, flowers quite well in Colombo, but has not so far proved very successful in Singapore. The curious *E. cochleatum* (now known as *Encyclia cochleata*), with small greenish yellow flowers, is quite successful in the lowlands of Malaysia. Hybrids between *Epidendrum* and *Cattleya* have been raised and some of these are now available in Malaysia.

Oncidium

A large genus of orchids with an extensive distribution from Central to South America and consequently adapted to a wide range of habitats. They prefer fairly dry growing conditions and the roots must not, on any account, be allowed to become too wet or waterlogged.

Several species are grown in Malaysia and some of these have yellow flowers which are a welcome change from the prevailing mauve shades in other orchids. The mid-lobe of the lip of most Oncidiums is very elaborate, with a complex warty structure near the base, which gives the flower a characteristic appearance. Some species have short, thick pseudobulbs, and others have none, but instead produce a series of short shoots, each bearing one leaf. Few of the species have large flowers, but many of them have very attractive colouring combined with an unusual and graceful form, and consequently they are popular as cultivated plants.

A number of hybrids have been raised and some of these are extremely successful as cultivated plants in the tropical lowlands. One of the best known is *Oncidium* Golden Shower which is a hybrid between *O. flexuosum* and *O. sphacelatum* raised in Singapore and now cultivated in great quantity throughout Southeast Asia for the cut-flower trade. Both of the parent species are also grown as garden plants but are not as attractive or as free-flowering as the hybrid. *O. sphacelatum* is the commonest species in local cultivation, having long, narrow, flattened pseudobulbs with rather grass-like leaves and an inflorescence, up to one metre in length, bearing numerous rather pale yellow flowers. *O. flexuosum* is a related, but smaller species, with a shorter but more widely branched inflorescence of bright yellow flowers; it is very dainty and excellent for decorative purposes, but its cultivation requires care. It is best kept away from heavy rain. The hybrid between the two species is more robust than *O. flexuosum* and quite as free-flowering, and has the rich colour of that species. Other Oncidiums are *O. splendidum, O. varicosum* and *O. cebollata*. A very fine species with large yellow flowers of most remarkable shape is *O. kramerianum*; this is a little difficult to manage, but when flowering it produces a succession of many flowers, one at a time, on the same inflorescence.

Oncidium lanceanum

This species does not have pseudobulbs but has large, slightly mottled leaves and stout, erect inflorescences bearing several fragrant flowers rather larger than most Oncidiums, of rich purple, chocolate and greenish yellow. Its culture requires some care, as its roots will not tolerate wet conditions, but a strong plant will flower well, and is very handsome. A hybrid between this species and *O. luridum*, known as *O. haematochilum*, is easier to grow and more free-flowering, with taller inflorescence, but has flowers of weaker colour, including various shades of pale yellow, cinnamon brown and mauve. The hybrid occurs naturally in the West Indies and has been made artificially in Singapore.

Oncidium Golden Shower

12 OTHER KINDS OF GARDENS

In this section are included other kinds of gardens which may be regarded as more specialized types, and these can be roughly grouped into small and miniature kinds.

Small Gardens

Rock gardens and water gardens are included as part of this group although the size of either kind will vary depending on the amount of space available. They can form part of a very large garden or they may be the only kind used in a very small area. Troughs can be included here also as they can be built in a garden of any size and may be made of a variety of materials. The size can be arranged to suit the space available, and in a large area they may be purely decorative, forming part of the general garden design, but in smaller places where space is restricted, they may be the only means of growing plants.

Sometimes roof gardens can be created and although a wide range of plants may be grown the choice of species will depend on a number of climatic factors. The amount of wind is important as this can dry out plants very quickly, or uproot them, but if some kind of screen can be arranged to protect the plants they will usually grow very well as they have full sunlight every day and benefit from any rainfall. Usually, sunlight is uninterrupted in a roof garden and there is a great deal of reflected heat and light; plants selected must therefore be able to withstand these conditions.

Adequate and efficient drainage must be provided otherwise the plants may suffer from waterlogging during heavy storms. It is most important to ensure that the roof is sealed properly so that there can be no leakage of water into the rooms beneath. Surplus water should be drained away through gutters and drainpipes, and should not be allowed to run down the outside walls of the building as this would, very quickly, cause discoloration and damage to the plaster or cement and the appearance of the building would be ruined.

If it is possible to cover as much of the roof surface as possible with plants, this will reduce the amount of reflected heat and light considerably so that all species will grow very much better. With adequate facilities it is sometimes possible to make a small lawn on the roof but this needs careful thought and preparation and a fair amount of attention until the grass has covered the soil. It must be remembered that in order to make a garden of this kind, on the top of a building, all soil, rocks, plants and any other materials needed must be raised to the roof, which may cause some problems. A storage place for pesticides, fertilizers and tools will be needed, and a convenient water supply point is essential.

Miniature Gardens

At the present time when many people live in flats, apartments or small houses which have very little or no outdoor space for growing plants, it is still possible, with a little ingenuity, to create a tiny garden which can form part of the interior decoration. Most usually, plants which are kept indoors are grown singly in pots, but this is not always necessary, and instead, a group of small plants can be grown, the maintenance being exactly the same as for single plants. This will create a totally different effect and the appearance will be of a small bed of plants growing in the house. Such groups of plants are sometimes on sale in shops but it is much more satisfactory to grow one's own. In temperate countries such little groups of plants are available throughout the year and many of them are mixtures of house plants (most of which are tropical in origin) grown in ornamental containers and selected to give a floral or foliage display. These miniature gardens need little attention and last a long time before any major change is necessary. In the tropics, where plant growth is so easy and rapid, it is not difficult to create similar small gardens and the main problem is to control the growth of the plants so that they do not become too large within a very short time. If any one plant grows too strongly it will smother all the other plants quickly. Strict control is necessary.

Several different kinds of these miniature gardens can be created, all needing a small space only, and the choice of plants would be governed by the position in which the garden is to be kept for most of the time. For instance, it may be kept inside a room continuously, or on a veranda or balcony, which may or may not be covered. In a room it will be shaded for part or all of the day and the air will be dry and dusty; on a veranda or balcony it will also be shaded, but will have good air circulation and may even receive a little rainfall. Consequently, the choice of plants must be given careful thought. Airconditioned rooms have much drier air and slightly lower temperature and although many plants will survive for some time in these conditions their growth will be slow and they will eventually deteriorate. The choice of plants for such rooms is limited because thin-leaved kinds will die very quickly in the dry air. Alternatively, bottle gardens can be used as the enclosed plants are not affected by the dry air. If miniature gardens are to be kept in airconditioned rooms, it is better to have three or four of them so that they can be changed at about weekly intervals. The extra miniature gardens should be kept in another room which is not airconditioned or, if possible, outside the building, until they are needed again in the airconditioned room.

Although miniature gardens are ideal for small spaces, it should be remembered by those who live in high-rise buildings that there may be a problem in transporting materials to and from the apartment. New soil, old soil, pots, fertilizer and plants must all be carried up and down by hand in such places. When there is no space for propagation, the tiny garden must be planted directly with young plants and should be kept in the allotted position while they grow. Some patience is necessary as many weeks may pass before the growth of the little plants is sufficient to create the appearance of a small garden.

Lack of space may be a problem when it comes to the storage of soil and fertilizer; it may be necessary to buy ready-mixed potting soil which is available commercially. These soil mixtures are packed in polythene bags of various sizes and can be used immediately, so that they are very convenient for people living in flats. Fertilizer is also needed and various kinds are available in solid or liquid form. These can be bought in small quantities and will last for a long time if only one or two groups of plants are grown. Slow release fertilizer is available and a small packet of this, although expensive to buy, will last for a considerable length of time and is very worthwhile as it needs to be applied at infrequent intervals only. If storage space is available, it is a good idea to keep a small bag each of burnt earth or garden soil, peat and sand, so that one can make up one's own potting mixture to suit different kinds of plant. In a flat, potting may have to be done on the floor or on a table and it is useful to have a large sheet of thick polythene to lay down. All work can be done on this and there will be no mess inside the flat afterwards. Planting and preparation of small plants for miniature gardens is more easily done on a bench or table.

Rock Gardens

These are for the cultivation of those plants that need specially exposed positions or good drainage and they are usually plants native to drier climates than that in Malaysia. Special construction work is needed in order to accommodate these plants and as a rock garden is essentially informal, its position must be considered carefully. It may be in full sun or it may be in shade and the kinds of plants for either situation will be quite different. A sun rockery is for those plants which require full sun and good drainage and such plants are usually from drier climates. It is essential, therefore, that such a rockery should receive full sun for the whole day as far as possible and it should be away from large trees. The trees would cast shade at some time of day, their leaves would drop and spoil the rockery and the roots would penetrate into the soil and starve the rockery plants. Rainwater falling from the tree crown would also damage the rockery. An east or southerly aspect is best.

Because rock gardens are informal in appearance, they should be kept away from all formal arrangements and in a small garden this may not be possible always. Obviously artificial structures can generally be avoided by planting informal hedges or a group of bushes arranged in a staggered manner to act as a screen. With a new house, there is sometimes an untidy corner which one may find difficulty in using; it may have been a dump for builder's rubble and this would make a good base for a sun rockery.

The form or outline must be considered now before any work is started, and this is largely governed by the type of ground at our disposal. The prospective site may be of diverse nature, a steep bank, a natural depression or a piece of level ground; and all can be dealt with alike. When choosing stone one must bear in mind always the piece of ground which is to be used. For instance, a steep bank would require larger rocks and of a more precipitous nature than an undulating piece of ground.

The first consideration is drainage. The site must be well excavated and a rather close series of rubble drains made as a basis; they should all lead into one main drain and arrangements must be made for this to carry off water to some convenient point. On the top of the foundation with its drains, a considerable quantity of rubble should be piled; broken bricks and other builder's discarded material are suitable. This layer should be quite thin at the edges of the area where the rocks will only rise a little above the surrounding ground, and high in the middle; it should be built up in accordance with the intended contour of the finished garden and will serve as the base on which the rocks and earth will be arranged. The contour of the finished garden should harmonize with that of the surrounding ground, so as to look as natural as possible.

In most parts of Malaysia there is little choice of rock, and bedded sedimentary, of the kind that makes the most natural looking rock garden, is hardly obtainable anywhere. Granite is less easy to use but it is often the only obtainable rock and in limestone areas native limestone would be a good choice, but in a single rock garden different types of rock should not be used together.

The soil on which the rocks have to be placed may be carted on as required. It is seldom in Malaysia that the virgin soil of any area is really suitable for our rock garden, so a good friable and porous mixture has to be made. This should consist of half rough chippings and sand and half cattle dung and leaf soil. Together with this, there should be a fair sprinkling of rock phosphate. If the natural soil is sandy, no drainage or special soil preparation is necessary beyond the addition of a little humus and cattle dung when planting. Rough chippings are very useful when placed around the essentially succulent plants after they have been planted as they prevent the soft stems and leaves from coming into contact with the soil which might cause rotting. At this stage also it is essential that all weeds, particularly those which have creeping roots, should be eradicated. Such pests as Lallang and Nutgrass, when once the rocks have been put in place, are almost impossible to clear.

The actual building requires serious thought and no little artistic ability, and here we find the most obvious blunders. It will be noticed in natural formations how rocks invariably lie to the hillside or bank, arresting downward progress of the soil and seed. They also act as retainers of moisture, and by their tendency to incline towards the hillside, conduct moisture to the roots of the plants. They prevent damage to the roots from the heat of the sun and roots then always remain cool and moist. In the constructive work on a larger type of rock garden, the question of stability is of vital importance. In such cases where much soil has been piled up, great care must be taken to ensure a firm foundation. If this is not properly done the rocks are liable to sink, thus destroying the whole effect and making unnecessary work.

In the matter of outline, informality is essential; bays, recesses and promontories are necessary in order to accommodate the greatest variety of plants by reason of the diverse aspects they present. Such constructions are important in either a large or a small rock garden. Where a path is desired, it should take the form of a meandering stream and should never be formally curved or straight. Too much of the path should not be seen from any one point. All rocks should be kept as much as possible from forming straight lines; the more informal the arrangement the better. It is particularly important to see that each rock is placed firmly and the surrounding soil beaten down to prevent airspaces which make an excellent hideout for vermin and in which the roots of plants may rot. All rocks should be placed on their broadest surface and not, as is often done, on their ends which gives the appearance of a cemetery instead of a rock garden.·

When starting to place rocks in position it is best to begin from the back or from the highest point. If the foreground is built first then the moving of large and very heavy stones to positions above and behind it may cause displacement of rocks which are already in position and any alternative way of putting the rocks into place could be very laboursome. These remarks, naturally, only apply to the construction of large rock gardens.

With the first rock placed, shall we say in the background, the next must be selected and arranged near it to give the appearance of natural sequence. All rocks should be positioned so that they present a harmonious appearance in relation to each other and to the overall form of the rock garden. Although the garden is built primarily for plants there should be a balanced effect between these and the arrangement of rocks.

Another important point to remember during construction is to leave ample depth of soil for herbaceous plants and dwarf shrubs. Deep crevices between the rocks are necessary to enable the roots of the plants to penetrate far enough to obtain the cooler moisture and nourishment. Where space is available, a rock garden may consist of a series of outcrops arranged as informally as possible with pathways meandering between them, giving access to all or practically all of the garden. By this method, quite a large area of ground can be covered with the minimum amount of rock and the result can be just as pleasing as if the rocks were arranged in one large outcrop comprising the whole garden.

Some of the plants suitable for rock gardens are described below but a few general principles must be considered first. One of the objects of a rock garden is to be able to see the plants interspersed among rocks in a decorative way, but if the plants are allowed to grow so strongly that they hide the rocks completely then one does not have a rock garden. In the tropics where plants grow so easily and quickly their growth in a rock garden must be strictly controlled to achieve the right effect and careful pruning is necessary to preserve the informal appearance. Some of the plants which can be used are quite large, almost like small trees, and it is obvious that these will dominate the scheme when they are well grown so that they can be used in a large rock garden only. The sites for such plants should be chosen first as these will form the focal points around which other plants will be grouped. Shorter plants can be positioned around the large ones and finally creeping plants or very short plants can be added to complete the effect. There is always room for small plants and these can be changed from time to time as desired, but the first essential is to decide on the large plants and their siting, and not to have too many of them or too large kinds which would dominate the area unduly. The number and selection will naturally depend on the size and position of the rock garden and also on the taste of the designer.

In a small rock garden large plants would be entirely out of place and therefore plants must be chosen more carefully. It is most important that some of the rocks remain visible at all times in such a small garden because if they become completely covered by the plants the whole effect will be lost and the area will look like a peculiarly shaped raised garden bed. In a small or medium-sized garden it may be possible to combine a small rockery with a pool because the rockery could be used to cover the piping necessary to provide a small cascade of water. This kind of arrangement would give the gardener an opportunity of growing two kinds of plants, requiring totally different growing conditions in a relatively small area. The plants in the pool and those on the rockery require full sun for as long as possible and this single common requirement makes such an arrangement feasible.

Adenium coetaneum

Agave angustifolia

Large plants will not require much attention, but should be given a little manure every few months. Probably dried cattle dung is the best thing for them, or small quantities of the more concentrated manures such as groundnut cake. Artificial fertilizers can be used also, but heavy manuring with any kind of fertilizer should be avoided. As regards smaller plants, treatment will vary with individual kinds; quick growing species will need more manure and may well be given small doses in liquid form, while the slower growing species will need less frequent manuring. Excessive manuring will lead to abundant plant growth and this will spoil the appearance of the rockery. Watering should be limited to that needed for the early stages of establishment of any herbaceous plants which are used.

One of the objects of a rock garden is to grow plants that need less than the normal amount of water and which are not harmed by dry soil. In fact, at most seasons of the year in Malaysia they will have too much water from rain, which is the reason why we build the rock garden with such an efficient drainage scheme.

Rock gardens provide an excellent hiding place for slugs and snails which can do a great deal of damage to succulent plants, especially when they are young and have a high proportion of soft tissues. It is well to use a pesticide to control both slugs and snails as soon as any damage is noticed and this should be done from the time of establishment of the rockery.

Plants for Rock Gardens

Very small herbaceous plants can be used and, of course, most cacti and succulents can be grown. Some trailing plants can be used but their growth should be controlled to prevent them from smothering smaller plants and from covering too much of the ground. It is best to grow perennials although some annuals can be used, especially if they seed themselves so that self-sown plants will appear at odd places in the rockery and will provide extra spots of colour. It is not necessary for these annuals to grow to their full normal size; they will flower usually when they are quite small so that they are more suitable for a rockery at that stage.

Cacti and Succulents

These plants require full sunlight and fairly dry conditions and then are more likely to flower. In the humid tropics the main problem is the excessive rain during some periods of the year, combined with lack of sunshine for several days which results in the soil and the plants remaining very wet so that the roots would begin to rot. A few hours of sunshine each day is sufficient to dry out the rockery

and prevent rotting of the plant roots. Most cacti require very dry conditions, but some succulents need a more humid atmosphere and grow well in the Malaysian climate. Several of the larger members of the Cactus family grow very well in Malaysia, given the good drainage and exposure provided in a rock garden constructed as described; but few of them will flower. The most free-flowering kinds are some of the Prickly Pears (genus Opuntia) and two of the large columnar cacti (genus Cereus), which flower at night. Some of the smaller members of the family, such as Mammillaria, Rebutia, Cephalocereus, Notocactus and a number of other genera, could be grown but some of them are densely hairy and such species need protection from too much rain. There are also a number of small species of Opuntia which could be used on a rockery. A scandent small woody plant called Pereskia is also useful and any long stems, when they develop, can be cut back. The young leaves of this plant are pale pink and cream in colour and remain so for a long time before becoming green so that the plant is attractive for quite a long period of time.

Imported packets of seeds are available and these grow quite easily, but it is very important not to overwater and the seedlings are best kept under glass until they are well established and large enough to handle easily for transplanting. A number of species which are normally grown in pots should be tried out on the rockery as they should do well because of the good drainage and the cool root room. When transplanting from a pot it is well to moisten the soil in it thoroughly before removing the plant, otherwise the very dry soil will fall away from the roots which can then be damaged very easily and the plants will receive a severe check in growth. Such plants may take a long time to recover before beginning new growth. Many cacti are very spiny and it is wise to wear some thick gardening gloves when handling them, to prevent bad scratching of the hands and arms.

The larger cacti can grow to 2 m or more in height and are suitable for large rockeries only, so that a careful choice of species must be made to suit the size of the garden. Some of the Opuntias and Cereus species come into this group and there are also cactus-like members of the Rubber family (Euphorbia) which can be used.

Many succulent plants are easier to manage than true cacti, but all require dry growing conditions if they are to establish well. Among these are Kalanchoe, Crassula, Cotyledon, Stapelia, Euphorbia, Aloe and Agave. Some of them are prostrate in habit, others rather bushy and the remainder fairly erect so that planting can be arranged to give different

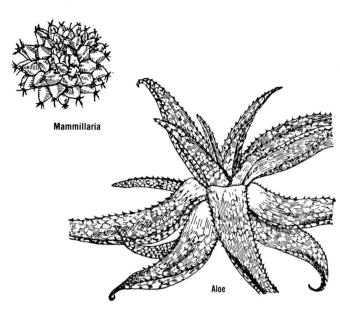

Mammillaria

Aloe

effects. Brief notes on suitable plants are given below.

Adenium

This genus is native to Arabia and the drier parts of East Africa. One species has proved very successful in Malaysia and can be grown in pots with good drainage or it can be planted in a rock garden in full sun. The species is *A. coetaneum* which is a bushy shrub up to one metre is height with thick fleshy branches and vivid crimson flowers, rather like the purple Allamanda in shape. It flowers continuously and liberal manuring increases flowering. It can be planted in a garden bed if the soil is sandy, but it will not tolerate wet clay soil and the roots will soon rot in such a position.

This plant makes an excellent subject also for growing in large earthenware jars, and a row of such plants in full sun on a veranda remains decorative for a very long time, needing very little attention. Propagation is by means of cuttings and as the twigs are rather large they are best planted singly in small pots. The potting mixture must be open and well drained and should be kept fairly dry until the cuttings are rooted. The pots with the cuttings can be kept in full sun but should be protected when there is heavy rain as the soil would become too wet. As soon as the cuttings are well rooted, the plants can be given small quantities of liquid manure and will soon be ready for potting on. Sometimes old plants will produce fruits and when these are ripe the seeds can be collected and planted. They should be sown in a sandy potting mixture and kept fairly dry until after germination. Seeds are best sown as soon as they are harvested and germination will then be excellent. Well grown seedlings should begin flowering about two years from sowing.

Agave

This genus is native in Mexico and neighbouring countries. The best known species is the Sisal Hemp which is grown for its fibre. Agaves have rosettes of long stiff leaves (a metre or more in length) with pointed ends and often with thorny margins. They grow for several years then producing a very tall inflorescence up to 3 m or more in height, and after the fruits have ripened the whole plant dies. Hundreds of seeds are produced and the plant is easily propagated from these. In some forms no seeds develop but very small bulbils arise on the branches of the inflorescence and these look like small seedlings. They can be planted in the usual way and will soon grow to a good size. Two or three species are commonly grown and some of them have bluish leaves while others have variegated leaves. Large plants are striking and need plenty of space so that they are only suitable for a large rockery. They can be grown also as single plants elsewhere in the garden but are rather stiff in appearance and must be sited carefully. Young plants can be used in a small rockery but may be difficult to remove when they become large, especially as a great number of underground suckers are usually produced.

Agave americana has grey-green leaves but there is a form with variegated leaves having longitudinal yellow stripes. In some of the forms the leaves are not held stiffly at a sharp angle but are curled backwards, giving the plants a very distinctive appearance. *Agave angustifolia* is commonly grown as a garden plant and as a pot plant and will attain a total diameter of about one metre. The most usual form seen has longitudinal white stripes on the leaves and because the plants are not as large as the previous species they are more suitable for a smaller rockery. These plants are often seen with inverted empty egg-shells placed on the sharply pointed tips of the leaves. *Agave sisalana* is a large plant which may become 2–3 m in diameter and is therefore suitable for large rockeries only. It can be planted also in the garden as a single specimen but should not be placed where children play frequently as the tips of the leaves have very hard, sharp points and can cause quite deep wounds.

One or two other species of Agave are sometimes available and are usually seen as pot plants, but they would be quite happy grown in a rockery. As they are much smaller plants than the previous species, they would be very suitable for small gardens.

Cactaceae (Cactus Family)

Many members of this family can be used on a sun rockery and it is important to ensure that they receive as much heat and light as possible from the sun, and that the soil is very well drained so that there is no waterlogging even after several days of continuous rain. Some of the species are too small for growing in a large rockery and are best in pots or in miniature gardens, or they would be suitable for small outdoor rockeries more appropriate to their size.

Two species of Pereskia can be used in a large rockery. These are *Pereskia bleo* and *P. aculeata*, both of which have very spiny stems but are quite different in habit. *P. bleo* has tall, erect, thick stems which bear clusters of large pink flowers at frequent intervals. The young stems carry large, dark green leaves which remain on the plant for a short time only before they drop. *P. aculeata* is a short plant with slender stems, some of which become very long and scramble through neighbouring plants. The ovate leaves are cream and pink when they are young and retain this colour for a long time, so that the plants are highly attractive until the leaf colour changes through bronze to dark green. The plants can be kept short by pruning, or the long, scrambling stems can be allowed to trail over some of the rocks. However, these trailing stems are not as leafy as the shorter ones, often carrying a group of leaves near the tip only; it is therefore better to keep the plants short as they will then be more leafy and will provide a useful patch of colour on the rockery. This species is quite adaptable and can be grown successfully also in a trough. Growth is rather slow and a small plant can be kept easily in a miniature garden for a very long time before it will need to be replaced.

Two or three species of Cereus are available and grow well on a rockery but as they produce a group of thick, upright stems their position on the rockery, in view of the final shape of these plants, must be given some thought.

Several species of Opuntia (Prickly Pear) can be obtained and the larger ones are easy to grow on a sun rockery, but the smaller ones are suitable only for pots or a very small rockery or a miniature garden of succulents. The larger Opuntias grow well in an ordinary garden bed or in a trough and are sometimes used in this way around public buildings, but unfortunately, in such situations, some members of the public have an irresistible urge to write their names on the flat stems which are then badly disfigured.

Other kinds of cactus, which are much smaller, are mentioned in the section on miniature gardens.

Crassulaceae (Stonecrop Family)

Several members of this family are suitable for a large sun rockery and there are also many other species which are useful for miniature gardens. Two of the most useful genera in a rockery are Kalanchoe and Bryophyllum (which is now included in Kalanchoe). In both kinds, small plantlets are produced around the margins of the leaves and these provide an easy and convenient means of propagation. *Kalanchoe pinnatum* will grow to about one metre in height and has large leaves with from one to five oval leaflets. A long inflorescence of greenish tubular flowers is produced at the end of each stem when growing conditions are favourable. A group of these plants has a softer appearance than the cacti, which can look rather uncompromising. Bryophyllum plants tend to remain unbranched or sparingly branched so that it is best to grow several in a small group if a bold effect is needed. Leaflets which fall to the ground will usually develop several small plants around the margin and if these are allowed to grow, the group of plants will soon become very dense, a problem easily controlled by judicious thinning.

Two small species of Kalanchoe which are seen frequently are *K. tubiflora* with long, narrow, cylindrical leaves and *K. daigremontiana* with long, narrow, ovate, flat leaves. In both species, the stems are unbranched and the

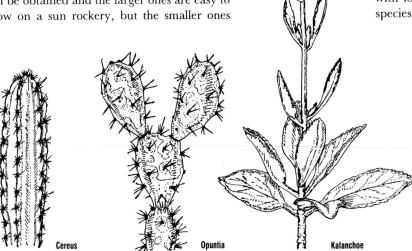

Cereus   Opuntia   Kalanchoe

Euphorbia

leaves develop many small plantlets around their margins, giving the plants a very distinctive appearance. Both species spread very easily by means of the plantlets from the leaves and can sometimes become weeds. In a large rockery they are useful for filling small crevices and can be left to their own devices, provided their spread is controlled. These plants are suitable also for small rockeries and miniature gardens and, when once established, a constant supply of young plants for replacement will be available always, sometimes in the most unexpected places elsewhere in the garden. With restricted root space and very little water, these plants will remain small for a very long time, but if they are given ample water they will quickly become tall and are less suitable for miniature gardens. In good soil they show very rapid growth and become very tall but must receive full sun otherwise the stems become weak and fall over.

One other species, *K. blossfeldiana*, is often sold in nurseries as a pot plant and is a short, much branched plant with dark green leaves. Many flowers are produced in a short inflorescence held just above the leaves and the whole plant will grow to about 20–30 cm in height. The most commonly available form has red flowers but other kinds with pink or yellow flowers can also be obtained. These plants can be grown on any kind of rockery or as single pot plants, but are not really suitable for miniature gardens. They are 'short day' plants and sometimes a little shy in flowering. Unless well grown, they do not make very shapely plants.

Euphorbiaceae (Rubber Family)

There are several succulent members of this family which are suitable for growing in a large sun rockery. All of them will eventually make very large plants, unsuitable for small areas as most of them are thorny, but they can be used as pot plants for some time. Most of the suitable species belong to the genus Euphorbia (which includes the Poinsettia). Several have thick, succulent but hard stems with three or more angles on which the thorns are situated. Leaves are present on the young stems but drop away very quickly, and flowers are produced at intervals throughout the year. Some species have abnormal forms in which several branches are joined into a massive, flattened, undulating structure and these forms are slow growing. They are usually described as cristate and are well suited to a sun rockery, but they must be positioned with care because of their unusual shape and form.

The most commonly grown species are *E. lactea*, *E. neriifolia*, *E. polyacantha*, and *E. antiquorum*, all of which have cristate forms, and all can grow to the size of a small tree with a round or oval crown of densely arranged, erect branches. Although they would need many years to reach this size, it would be unwise to plant more than two or three of these plants in a large rockery; in a small rockery their growth would need to be controlled by pruning. These species will grow well in any other sunny part of the garden but look best when planted singly as their stiff, upright habit does not combine very well with the softer outlines of normal leafy plants. Any of these plants can be propagated very easily by means of cuttings 15–60 cm long. The stems contain a great deal of white latex and the flow of this, after cutting, can be slowed down by dipping the ends into dry sand or dry soil. The cuttings can be kept for several days, if necessary, before planting and this will allow the cut surfaces to dry a little so that there will be less danger of rotting after planting. The cuttings may be planted in pure sand or in a mixture of sand and ordinary garden soil, but they must be kept fairly dry until roots have developed. Overwatering at this stage will rapidly cause rotting. Rooting is slow and the cuttings are best kept in full sun until they are ready for planting out.

Euphorbia cotinifolia

Although this plant is not cactus-like in appearance, it can be used in large rockeries provided it is pruned to keep it to a suitable size. The plant has normal leafy twigs and leaves and will grow into a large bush or a

Euphorbia millii

small tree. It is striking in appearance with dark red stems, leaf-stalks and leaves and the latter are usually carried in whorls of three along the stems. This plant needs regular and frequent application of fertilizer which will result in fast growth with large leaves, and it must receive full sun for as long as possible in order to develop the most brilliant colour. If it is not pruned regularly or given fertilizer, the branches tend to become long and slightly drooping, with small poorly coloured leaves, and the basal portions will be leafless so that the plant will look straggly. Fortunately, the plant responds very quickly to improved treatment and hard pruning, combined with application of fertilizer, will result in the production of strong, well-coloured shoots within two or three weeks.

The plant can also be grown in troughs or pots but is not really suitable for small rockeries. Only small plants make a good show in pots and as soon as they become larger and the roots have filled the pot, no amount of pruning and application of fertilizer will give good new growth. This species is useful in a shrub border as it provides a good splash of colour, but if shaded by other plants the leaves will become dark green. The best effect is obtained when the shrub is planted so that it can be viewed with the sun shining through the leaves: the red coloration will then be most brilliant.

Euphorbia millii var. splendens (Crown of Thorns)

This is a small much branched shrub with thick, grey, angular stems which carry many strong thorns. Young stems retain the fresh green leaves for a long time if the plants are watered regularly, but if the soil is allowed to become dry then the leaves will drop very quickly although flowering will continue. The leaves are retained for a much longer time in very light shade, but flowering will not be quite as abundant. Small groups of bright red flowers are produced almost continuously and the plant is suitable for a rockery of any size. Some pruning is necessary to encourage the development of a shapely bush. The species is often grown in pots but the long spines make handling difficult when repotting is necessary.

Euphorbia tirucalli (Bone Bush)

This plant is slightly unusual in appearance as it has thick, round, green branches which are about the size and shape of an average pencil (older branches will of course be larger), and these bear a few scattered small leaves when they are young. Branching is profuse and the leaves drop as soon as each branch is mature. The plant will grow to 2 m in height, and is best used in a large rockery or as a single speci-

men elsewhere in the garden. It is interesting if not very comely. It can also be used at the back of a border where it provides a useful variation in form. All parts of the plant contain a great deal of white latex which is said to be good for skin troubles. The species is easily propagated from cuttings which should be kept fairly dry until they are well rooted. When well established these plants will tolerate much more water in the soil than is usually expected of succulent plants.

Jatropha podagrica

This plant has a swollen, fleshy stem carrying large lobed leaves and an erect inflorescence bearing numerous small coral-red flowers on red branches. The colour of the inflorescences is very striking and the plant is suitable for rockeries of any size. It should not be given too much fertilizer, otherwise it develops very large, dark green leaves which are liable to crinkle in dry weather. Many seeds are produced and provide an easy means of propagation as they germinate readily.

Mesembryanthemum (Icicle Plant, Ice Plant)

This large genus of beautiful and interesting succulents is very difficult to manage in Malaysia, and few species will flower. The species which give such brilliant displays of colour in cooler climates should be tried at the hill stations, but it is probable that the climate there is too wet and uniform to suit them; they can be kept alive under glass in the lowlands.

Pedilanthus tithymaloides (Slipper Flower)

There are two or three forms of this succulent species and all may be used in rockeries of any size. They have thick, erect stems with two rows of narrow, pointed leaves arranged fairly closely and regularly along the whole length of the stem. One form is entirely dark green with very closely arranged leaves and only grows to 20–40 cm in height. This is very suitable for small rockeries, troughs or miniature gardens. The other forms are much taller and can reach 1 ½ m in height unless pruned. The stems and leaves may be entirely green or they may be variegated in green and white or green, white and pink or purple.

When conditions are right, small groups of flowers are produced at the tips of the stems and each group is enclosed in pink or red bracts. All varieties should be pruned early to encourage branching from near the base so that the plants will become bushy. Without pruning these plants are liable to become long and straggling but this habit might be suitable in some places on a large rockery. All of the variegated forms need full sun in order to develop their best colour, but the short, dark green form will tolerate a little shade. Propaga-

Mesembryanthemum

tion of all forms can be done by taking cuttings which should be kept fairly dry until they have rooted.

Portulaca

This succulent plant grows best in slightly dry conditions and can therefore be used in rockeries, pots or troughs where drainage is good and watering can be controlled. The plants are, however, very subject to attack by snails which can destroy whole plants overnight. Two forms are available of which one is grown from seeds and produces single and semi-double flowers of yellow, pink, orange, red and magenta. This form never seems to be really robust and does not cover the soil very well, although numbers of flowers are produced for a short time. It looks better when grown in crevices in a rockery or when several plants are grown together in a single pot. It is usually grown from imported seed and the flowers are rather small.

The second form appears to be much better adapted to the lowland climate and makes a much more satisfactory garden plant. Provided there are no snails present, it can be used most effectively as an edging to a sunny border, on a rockery or in a sunny trough. It is easily propagated from cuttings and if these are planted fairly close together they will soon make thick growth and cover the ground completely. The double, brilliant magenta flowers are produced abundantly and though they last one day only, a new crop will open each day for many weeks, especially during hot, dry weather. The foliage may be half concealed by the flowers and their colour is so intense that it is almost painful to look at them. These plants only flower in full sun and during wet periods they make a great deal of leafy growth and produce few flowers.

Sansevieria

Two or three species and their varieties are commonly grown as pot plants, but all are suitable for use in a sun rockery. The smaller kinds can be used quite successfully in small rockeries as they are not invasive. Descriptions of the different kinds are given in the chapter on pot plants. The two biggest species are suitable for large rockeries but must be positioned carefully because of their very stiff and uncompromising habit. *S. trifasciata* makes large, dense clumps of thick, vertical leaves and will spread quite quickly. *S. cylindrica* is an open plant with long, curved, cylindrical leaves up to 1½ m long which look well when arching over a rock surface. These plants can be grown in troughs satisfactorily and they can also be grown in pots for a short time but very quickly become too large and are liable to burst the pot.

Sansevieria

Stapelia

Stapelia (Starfish Flower)

This is a well known genus of African succulents, many of which have remarkable flowers, but they are not very successful in open rockeries, though some of them, including the related genus, Huernia, will grow and flower quite well under glass. They can be used with great success in miniature gardens.

Yucca

Plants of this genus are native to the drier parts of North America. One species is hardy in England and there is a Mexican species which grows well in Malaysia, flowering very beautifully but not frequently. Young plants look rather like an Agave with stiffer, narrower, very sharply pointed leaves; old plants develop a branching stem. The inflorescences are tall and erect with numerous branches, each bearing rather large white flowers which open at night. The plants are easily propagated from suckers or from seeds.

SMALL SHRUBS

Creeping Juniper

Two kinds of Creeping Juniper grow well and make good subjects for a large garden; they are slow growing and if they become too large they should be pruned with some care in order to preserve the general shape. Light pruning is best done before the plants become too large as the younger branches recover better than older ones and shaping is easier. Junipers are propagated from small cuttings or from marcots.

Cuphea

One species of Cuphea has become fairly common as a garden plant during the last few years and this makes a short, low bush which tends to be flat-topped. *C. hyssopifolia* is best planted where it can be viewed from above as the plants tend to be funnel-shaped and are not so attractive when looked at from the side. The flowers are very small and several colour forms are available, ranging from white through pale pink to red and pale purple. The leaves are tiny also and are dark green. The plants can be grown on a rockery of any size and are propagated by means of cuttings.

Ixora

The dwarf Ixora known as 'Sunkist' is very suitable for rock gardens, flowering continuously and brilliantly. There are forms with red flowers and others with pink flowers, but all grow equally well and make short, dense plants up to 60 cm high. They are slow growing and when established flowers are produced over the whole bush almost throughout the year. Spraying is necessary to protect the leaves against beetle attack and the flowers against caterpillar damage.

Lantana

The creeping *Lantana sellowiana* can be used on rockeries of any size and will flower continuously. It is not likely to smother neighbouring plants but if it becomes straggly a little pruning may be done to encourage the growth of some new shoots which will improve the shape.

Phyllanthus

Only one species of Phyllanthus is suitable for rock gardens and even this is not suitable for small areas because if it is allowed to grow unchecked it will form a low mound about 1 m high and 2 m in diameter. *P. myrtifolius* is an attractive plant with very thin stems and small, narrow, closely arranged leaves. When established, it is strong growing and the branches will eventually root where they touch the ground. It can be propagated from woody cuttings but disappointing results are often obtained. All branches arch outwards, becoming horizontal and then slightly drooping, so that the final shape of a single plant will be hemispherical and in a rockery its spread must be limited by pruning. It recovers well from fairly hard pruning and the branches are soon covered with new, fresh, green leaves. This Phyllanthus grows best in full sun but can tolerate a little shade only and is excellent when planted at the edge of a rockery or a bed of shrubs as it softens the outline of each, giving a more natural appearance.

SMALL FLOWERING PLANTS

The common perennial Coreopsis and the Black-eyed Susan (Rudbeckia) are useful and permanent plants. Hymenatherum and *Zinnia linearis* are shortlived, but very attractive, and easy to raise from seeds. Two small species of Cuphea are also useful: *C. ignea* with small tubular orange flowers, and *C. miniata* with purple, red, pink or white flowers. Both are easily grown from seeds and will perpetuate themselves with self-sown plants. The large-flowered hybrid Portulacas may also be used, but tend to be weak in growth and several plants need to be grown close together to make a reasonable showing. There is, however, a double-flowered form with petals of an intense magenta colour and this grows easily and strongly. The flowers are open in the morning only but make a very striking sight. All Portulacas open their flowers when the sun comes upon them only and they should therefore not be shaded at all. They are very prone to snail attack and on a rockery, where there are many

hiding places for snails, careful control of these pests is needed, otherwise the plants will be eaten down to the ground and will not recover. The double-flowered form produces flowers for several months but then needs to be replanted. Propagation is easy from cuttings.

BULBS

Any small bulbs may be used and some of the Zephyranthes species are especially suitable. These have flowers of various sizes and may be white, pink or yellow. As the plants are small the bulbs can be planted in narrow crevices between the rocks and will thrive and increase very easily. Haemanthus look well with their large, round heads of spidery red flowers, but they need artificial resting as for Hippeastrum, in order to induce them to flower. Some Hippeastrums may also be used and the small pink kind will flower after a moderately dry spell without artificial resting. The larger Hippeastrums produce a great deal of leaf and are less satisfactory as permanent occupants of the rock garden because the leaves are not particularly decorative.

Shade Rockeries

The natural habitat of Maidenhair and many other ferns, and of some other attractive plants such as Begonias, is rock crevices, and a shade rockery properly constructed will allow such plants to grow under natural conditions. The rockery should receive light shade only and must be kept moist by spraying during any rainless periods. It is often difficult in a small garden to find space for such a rockery; but a steep earth bank, if available, built up with a facing of large stones or rocks, is all that is needed and is, in fact, more suitable than an artificial built-up structure. The horizontal crevices between the rocks provide an ideal position for the stems and rootstocks of the plants which are not then exposed to the drip and wash of rain. The type of rock garden used for sun-loving plants is not, therefore, suitable for this kind of situation, though it might be used for Begonias and some other plants on sloping ground at the top of the wall.

The essential thing is that there must be rocks with horizontal crevices between them, the upper rock flush with the one below, or even slightly overhanging, which helps to prevent rain-wash. A wall of any kind, if in a slightly shady place and kept moist, will soon develop a crop of ferns, without any special planting. If artificial planting is to be done, room should be left between the rocks for this to be carried out, but the cracks must in no case be too wide, and it is best to start with rather small plants, pushed carefully into the crevices so that their rootstocks are just enclosed.

Behind the wall should be a reasonable thickness of good earth, into which compost and phosphate have been mixed. Sufficient nutrient will drain out of this into the cracks between the rocks to reach the roots of the ferns. There may be some danger of the pressure of this earth being too much for the strength of the wall. The base of the wall should therefore be thick, and the rocks built up carefully so as to be stable. Some cement may be used at the back if desired, but not too much or it will stop free drainage and aeration.

The kinds of plants which will establish themselves in such a wall will vary according to the degree of exposure or shading, the frequency of watering and the presence of suitable plants near enough to provide spores or seeds for propagation. The most attractive ferns will not develop unless conditions are distinctly moist. A low water tank near by will help to keep the air moist, and will facilitate spraying; but care must be taken to prevent mosquitoes from breeding in the water and the easiest method of control is to keep a few guppies in the tank. All Maidenhair ferns are suitable, and grow in their natural way with the fronds hanging down gracefully. Many of the foliage Begonias are also suitable, and some of the native limestone plants, including the pretty little Slipper Orchid (*Paphiopedilum niveum*), and some of the aroids.

The smaller Selaginellas help to add a continuous cover, if that is desired, but may become too abundant, and will smother other plants. Saintpaulia and Episcia are two attractive flowering plants which are suitable. If small plants of *Pilea microphylla* can be established they will quickly seed themselves and young plants will appear everywhere within a very short time. Such self-sown plants will often establish themselves in crevices or positions where it would be impossible to plant them by hand, and will grow very well.

When a wall is sufficiently moist, mosses will begin to grow on the rocks and these can be very attractive because of their bright green colour. They often form small hummocks which help to hold moisture and when they are well established the wall will need less frequent spraying with water. Clumps of moss will help to prevent soil from being washed away and will provide convenient places for seeds of other plants to germinate.

If an ordinary rockery construction, with exposed pockets of well drained soil, can be combined with this wall garden, some of the larger, erect growing Begonias which need some shade can be grown as well as a considerable selection of aroids, including the finer Anthuriums and Caladiums. Gloxinias (Sinningia), dwarf Ixoras, *Clerodendron nutans* with its nodding inflorescence of pure white flowers, and some of the local forest ferns could be grown also. At the hill stations more effort should be made to grow some of the charming small flowering plants which are found in the forest as most of these will not grow in the lowlands or are very difficult to manage. The native mountain flora has been very little investigated for garden purposes, partly because most of the more decorative ones need shade and also slightly lower temperatures than can be obtained in the lowlands.

A shade rockery implies trees or buildings of some sort to provide the shade. Buildings should cast shade throughout the day, as in internal courtyards or between very tall buildings. Trees may be of any kind preferred, so long as they give a suitable shade that is not too dense. One difficulty is that the tree roots spread rapidly and will quickly invade the soil of the rockery and, by removing the plant nutrients, cause poor growth of the rock plants. When this happens the tree roots must be cut from time to time. Fallen leaves from trees should not be allowed to gather in any quantity otherwise they will smother the rock plants and may make conditions too wet for the growth of some of the plants. Some dead leaves could be allowed to remain as they will rot down and provide a little additional plant food.

Water Gardens

When water plants are desired, it is necessary to grow these in tanks in most gardens, though on clay soils it may be possible to make a small pond of puddled clay. Tanks may be raised or sunk below soil level and may be made of concrete or bricks with a lining of mosaic tiles or plastic sheeting if desired. It is possible also to buy ready moulded pool liners made out of fibreglass or tough plastic material and these are available in various shapes and depths which can be set directly in the ground. Whichever kind is chosen, some thought must be given to a supply of water and also to a drainage pipe and an overflow pipe. Some provision may be needed for a supply of electricity to run a pump or for illumination of the pool.

When concrete or brick tanks are being constructed a drainage pipe should be included if possible so that the pool may be emptied for cleaning and maintenance from time to time. It is an advantage to have a water supply pipe taken to the pool, otherwise filling must be done by means of a hose pipe attached to a tap outside the house or one of the taps inside the house, provided this is not too far away. If it is not practical to arrange for a drainage pipe to be built in then the pool must be emptied by means of a small pump and there are a number of different kinds available which will work a fountain or can be used to remove the water. Pools lined with special sheeting or those with moulded pool liners cannot have a drainage pipe attached and must be emptied, when necessary, by means of a pump.

A pool of any kind is best placed in full sun because most water plants require as much sunlight as possible. Raised tanks are more expensive to make and are more difficult to fit into a garden design. A concrete tank is essentially of formal shape and should be part of a definite scheme of paving, paths or planting. So used, it can play its own part in a design, by virtue of its shape, apart from the beauty of the plants it may contain.

The size of the pool will naturally depend on the space available. In a large garden the minimum size to be effective is about 2 m by 1 m. The shape can be varied to suit the scheme as a whole, which will again depend on the shape and situation of the area to be dealt with. Pools are best kept as a simple shape, either square, rectangular or round, and should be at least 30 cm deep. If they are shallower than this then the water will become very hot on clear sunny days and if the pool is lined with concrete or mosaic tiles these materials also will absorb a great deal of heat and will aggravate the condition. Plants and fish would be killed very quickly under these conditions.

Pools may be surrounded by a paved area or by grass and in both cases a simple scheme of formal planting with small beds or paths or a combination of both may be used. The arrangement may be supplemented by suitably placed formal shrubs or conifers grown in large jars but the pool should be the focal point of the whole scheme. If the rim of the pool is sufficiently broad then some suitable potted plants can be placed on it but the number should be limited otherwise they will obscure the view of the pool with its plants and fish. A fountain and one or more stone ornaments may be added and may stand directly in the water or at the margin of the pool as part of the general design. An informal planting arrangement is easier to arrange and would need less maintenance, but shrubs and other larger plants should be placed so that they do not overhang the water when they have grown to their full size. Pools of any size should not be shaded by trees otherwise the water plants will not grow well and when leaves fall into the water they may cause a great deal of trouble because they will decay, making the water foul; the fish will die and water plants may be smothered.

When a large pool is to be constructed, the necessary piping should be laid before any concrete work is done. The position of the water supply pipe, the drainage pipe and the overflow pipe should be related to any drainage scheme for the remainder of the garden. In the Malaysian climate, with its excessively heavy rains coming at all times of the year, a proper drainage scheme to carry off the storm water efficiently is well worth the extra time and expense it involves, even if this means reducing the size of the formal water garden.

A newly made concrete pool has a certain amount of soluble lime in its structure which will make the water alkaline until it has been washed away completely, and consequently a new pool cannot be used for planting until several changes of water have passed through it; this may take a week or more to accomplish. Sealing compounds are available which can be painted on to the surface of the concrete and these neutralize the lime as well as simultaneously reacting with it to produce a form of internal glazing. If this is done the pool can be filled with water and stocked with plants immediately. These compounds are best used for new concrete pools because when used on old concrete there is no free lime with which they can react to produce the glazing effect. Other kinds of sealing mixtures can be used and these form a protective skin over the concrete. They can be used on new or old concrete but in the case of new concrete a special primer must be applied first to neutralize any lime present. The sealing materials are plastic compounds and must be applied while the concrete is clean and dry. Only sealing compounds recommended for garden pools should be used as other kinds are poisonous to both plants and fish.

When marsh plants are required as well as submerged plants, some provision must be made to accommodate them and the pool should be constructed with a deep centre portion and a shallow ledge around part or all of the margin. Pots of marsh plants can be placed on this ledge as they need shallow water only in order to grow successfully. If very strong growing plants are desired then the ledge can be divided into several separate sections so that the growth of individual plants can be controlled to prevent them crowding out other species.

In a large pool separate containers can be built of bricks and for this purpose no cement is needed. The bricks are merely placed loosely on top of each other, leaving small spaces between adjacent ones and they can be arranged to make a container of any size that is desired. The upper edge of the container should be well below the water surface and in a pool of average size this means that the container sides should be less than 30 cm high. Any good garden soil mixed with some rock phosphate can be used to fill the container and planting is best done immediately before the pool is filled with water. This will mean that the water will remain fairly clear. If planting is done after the pool is filled then the digging necessary in the soil in order to position the plants will create a fine suspension of soil particles in the water, and although this will eventually settle it will also leave a fine deposit on the plants which will make them unsightly and hinder their growth. A layer of clean, washed gravel can be placed over the surface of the soil after planting and this will prevent it from falling about. It will also prevent fish from rooting in it and loosening the roots of the plants so that they float to the surface. When the plants are well established, they should be given a little manure about once a month, and some pieces of groundnut cake pushed beneath the soil surface are quite effective for this purpose. Alternatively, small paper parcels of manure and compost may be put around the plant.

In a small pool, earth may be spread over the bottom and then covered with a layer of gravel, but when the pool needs cleaning this will cause some problems because it will be difficult to drain off the water without clogging the pipes. In such a situation it would be better to grow the plants in suitable containers which can be removed fairly easily when cleaning; and at the same time it is much easier to give the plants any attention which is necessary. Ordinary flower pots should not be used as the soil in them quickly becomes sour and the plants die or their growth becomes very slow. For small plants, earthenware orchid pots are useful as there are large holes in the sides allowing water to penetrate easily and the roots of the plants can grow out into the water without hindrance. These pots should be lined with a piece of small-mesh wire netting to prevent the soil from falling out into the water. Plastic containers of various shapes and sizes with perforated sides can be used for holding soil and growing plants. Unfortunately, these are often made in rather lurid colours and would not look very ornamental in a pool, but when the plants have grown a little the containers will be hidden and if they are still too conspicuous they can be concealed with an arrangement of clean rocks or large stones.

Pools lined with mosaic tiles are easily scrubbed when cleaning is necessary, but concrete linings are more difficult to deal with unless the surface is reasonably smooth; a good hard broom is needed in order to clean it effectively.

It is possible nowadays to make a garden pool by using special waterproof plastic sheeting and although several kinds are available careful selection is necessary as some of them may be unsuitable for use in hot countries because they deteriorate rapidly in the strong sunlight and heat, and would need replacing every few years. Other kinds are far less affected by these conditions and consequently are much more permanent, lasting for many years before replacement is necessary. This sheeting can also be used for lining concrete tanks and avoids the necessity for sealing the inner surface or for making several changes of water before the pool can be stocked. It is not usual to put earth over the bottom of a pool lined with plastic sheeting and the plants are usually grown in very open containers so that they can be removed easily for attention. Although the plastic sheeting is fairly tough it can be punctured quite easily and as far as possible one should avoid walking through a pool lined with this material. Plant containers in the middle of such a pool should be removed by placing a broad plank across the pool and working from this. Garden tools should not be used for lifting plant containers as only a small slip could mean a puncture in the pool lining.

A pond may be constructed using the plastic sheeting only and this is relatively simple to do as well as being less expensive than making a concrete tank. It is only necessary to dig out the soil to the required depth, shape and size of the pool that is needed and the walls should then be smoothed to make sure that there are no sharp stones or pieces of broken roots which might puncture the plastic sheeting. In order to help prevent this from happening, it is beneficial – although not absolutely necessary – to put a thin layer of sand over the whole of the inner surface and this will smooth over any irregularities in the soil which might cause damage to the plastic sheeting. It should be remembered that the weight of water in a pool after it has been filled is considerable and the pressure of this on the lining could easily cause a puncture by any sharp irregularities on the surface of the excavation underneath. A layer of sand would act as a sort of cushion and would help to prevent any such unfortunate accident.

When the hole has been excavated, the plastic sheeting is placed over it and the edges are held down firmly with large stones or concrete slabs. Water is directed slowly from a hosepipe on to the sheeting which will gradually sink into the hole, shaping itself automatically. The rim of the pool should be slightly raised above the surrounding ground so that water can drain away easily during heavy storms. When the pool is full of water, flat stones or concrete slabs are arranged close together around the margin to hold the lining sheet firmly and also

because of the lack of light. Some water plants must be rooted in soil, although the development of roots in some of these species is weak, and other plants are free-floating. Most of the plants grow very rapidly and must be controlled very firmly otherwise they would quickly fill the pool. This is especially true of floating plants and some species which grow totally submerged. Plants which root in soil at the bottom of the pool and hold their leaves above the water surface are not usually quite so invasive. Some of these need deep water and others shallow water in order to grow at their best; this must be considered when making a choice for the garden pool. All water plants are best renewed and replanted about once each year and if they are grown in containers then this is an easy task which can be done gradually so that the pool is never without plants at any time. Also, there is no necessity for removing the fish as the water should need no changing and in a well balanced pool it will remain clear and odourless indefinitely. When rainstorms are frequent the pool will be kept full with no effort and the rain will freshen and aerate the water.

Water plants are sometimes attacked by pests and these can be a little difficult to control because most of the chemicals normally used to destroy them are poisonous to fish so that they cannot be sprayed on to the plants in the usual way. Fish are highly sensitive to very small quantities of these chemicals and will die very quickly. Beetles and caterpillars can be hand-picked when they are seen and if a plant is badly damaged it is best to cut it back so that clean new growth will be produced. Unless they are overcrowded water plants are not usually affected by fungus diseases in a well balanced pool.

Some notes on suitable plants and their management are given below.

Aponogeton

One or two species and hybrids of this genus are sometimes available and make fine plants in an outdoor pool. They have long, narrow, dark green leaves, often with undulating margins and frequently, long spikes of small flowers are produced which project for 10–15 cm above the water surface. The plants grow completely submerged and need full sunlight in order to make good growth. They dislike competition from other submerged plants such as Cabomba. These tend to grow over the Aponogeton leaves and reduce the amount of sunlight, causing poor growth and eventually the death of the plant.

The plants will grow in water 30–50 cm deep and if placed away from other underwater species they will make magnificent specimens which will flower well and produce many tiny fruits. The fruits are a convenient means of propagation. Young plants can be grown in an aquarium garden for a short time but will eventually become too large and must then be moved into an outdoor pool.

Azolla pinnata (Fairy Moss)

This is a very small free-floating water fern which is dark green and becomes red in full sun. It will quickly cover the surface of the water but is easily controlled and gives some shade for fish as well as keeps the water cool. Other species are grown in pools in temperate countries. They will not thrive in shade.

Blyxa

These are grass-like plants making small clumps on the bottom of pools or clear slow-moving streams. They grow quite well in an aquarium and the leaves are usually pale green or greyish green. These plants do well in shallow outdoor pools where the light is fairly strong, but they are less successful in deeper pools. They are attractive plants for growing in an aquarium under artificial illumination. Propagation is by means of division.

Cabomba caroliniana

This is an excellent and very decorative plant commonly used in indoor aquaria but grows very well in outdoor pools in full sunlight. It has fan-shaped leaves divided into very narrow segments which give it a very elegant appearance, and the young leaves are often tinted with red or bronze. Few roots are produced but the stems can be pushed into some soil, or a bunch of stems can be tied to a small stone to weight them down so that they rest on the bottom of the pool.

Growth is very rapid and the tips of the stems will soon reach the surface of the water where they will sometimes produce a few small white flowers. The stems and leaves will quickly cover the surface of the pool and need cutting back fairly frequently, but the plants always have a fresh, bright green appearance which is most attractive.

Propagation is easy by means of cuttings which are obtained by cutting off the young ends of the stems. These can be tied in bunches to a small stone, put at the bottom of the pool, and within two weeks or less, depending on the depth of the pool, they will have grown to the surface. The older plants can be removed at this time. Growth is slower in an indoor aquarium.

Ceratopteris thalictroides

This is a fern which can be grown as a free-floating plant or in a container of soil. When grown as a free-floating plant, the leaves become arranged in a rosette but never become very large, and often produce bulbils on the margins. In this form the plants are very useful for shading part of the water surface and at the same time provide a good hiding place for the fish.

When rooted in soil the plants are totally different in habit with leaves held almost vertically above the water surface. The leaves are very deeply divided, up to 30 cm or more in length, and when they fall over on to the water surface they develop bulbils around the margins that provide a very convenient method of propagation. Young plants can be put into a container of soil which can be submerged in a part of the pool not more than 20 cm deep and they will soon produce leaves above the water surface. Free-floating plants can be used effectively in an indoor aquarium, but those rooted in soil may become too tall in such a place and are more suited then for a display of aquatic plants as a decorative item.

Chara (Stonewort)

These are green, leafless plants found wild, growing at the bottom of ponds. The stems bear whorls of straight branches and although the plants can be kept growing for some time they are difficult to maintain for very long periods. They will grow in quite deep water in an outdoor pool but as they prefer hard water, and fish thrive better in softer water, it is often difficult to provide such growing conditions when fish are kept also. These plants can be used in an indoor aquarium and are very decorative, but the branches tend to become covered with any particles floating in the water and can then look untidy.

Cryptocoryne

Several species of this genus are available and although all can be grown in an outdoor pool, some of them are better in an aquarium garden where their attractive appearance is more effective. All may be grown completely submerged but some of the species are able to grow also with their leaves above the water surface and so can be used in a shallow part of the pool. The leaves vary in shape from broadly oval to long and narrow and, while some are attractively coloured and often have wavy margins, others are undistinguished in appearance. Consequently these plants can provide useful furnishing in a garden pool, especially as they are better left undisturbed for a long time. Those with attractive leaves can be used also with great effect in an aquarium garden where their colour and shape can be seen more easily.

Cyperus

Several native species of this sedge genus are very decorative when in flower and would make an excellent addition to the planting scheme of an outdoor pool. Most of them develop a dense tuft of stems, many of which will carry large, much branched flowering heads. All should be grown in containers of soil which can be set in a shallow part of the pool. They are useful in providing a little height to the plant arrangement in and around the pool and are not invasive. There is one species, though unfortunately not easily obtainable, which grows completely submerged and has long, slender, rather thread-like stems.

An introduced and very large species is *C. papyrus* which can be grown also in the highlands. This can grow to 2 m in height and has very large, thick rhizomes so that it is suitable for large pools only. However, it can be grown as an ornamental in other parts of the garden, especially in places where the soil remains very wet most of the time. In a pool the plants are best grown in a brick-built container as they are too large for pots. When well grown they make a striking and majestic sight in the pool and are excellent as part of a large landscape design.

Echinodorus

Many species of this genus are used in aquaria but those most commonly available in Malaysia will eventually make very large plants and can be grown quite easily in an outdoor pool. They are often referred to as Amazon Sword plants because they have long, broad, pointed leaves and these are always totally submerged. There is, however, an attractive species with long-stalked oval leaves held well above the water and this also produces long, flowering stems carrying large white flowers which are extremely decorative. All species need full sun and the submerged species will thrive in water up to 50–60 cm deep, but the species with aerial leaves grows best in shallower water 20–30 cm deep. The flowering stems of this species will eventually fall over on to the water surface and young plants will develop on it

Rhynchospora aurea

which can be used for propagation. The submerged species become tufted and propagation is by means of division, but in some other cases the plants produce long runners bearing small plantlets and these can be used for propagation.

The commonest submerged species is *E. brevipedicellatus* which will eventually form large clumps providing good shelter for fish. Although it will survive for a long time in subdued light in indoor pools, it will not become very vigorous under such conditions. The species producing flowering stems above the water is *E. cordifolius*.

Eichornia crassipes (Water Hyacinth)

This floating plant with inflated leaf-stalks and long inflorescences of mauve flowers is most attractive but is very invasive and must be strictly controlled otherwise it will quickly cover the whole surface of the pool. In Malaysia it is often grown in quantity on ponds for use as pig food, but in some parts of the country and also in other parts of the tropics it is a noxious weed because it chokes water channels by its very rapid spread. It appears to grow much better in shallower water where its roots can touch some soil and it is suitable for large pools only. Many short offsets are produced and these can be used for propagation. Young plants can be kept in a small pool for a short time but they will soon become too large and must be removed. The plants need full sun at all times.

Hydrilla verticillata

One of the commonest water plants used in ornamental aquaria and found wild in many streams and ditches throughout the country. It grows strongly in full sunshine and is useful as it is a good oxygenating plant, but it grows very rapidly and must be cut back regularly to prevent it from smothering other plants. Groups of short cuttings can be inserted in small pots of sand which can then be placed at the bottom of the pool. They will grow very quickly and will soon reach the surface of the water where they will form a dense layer just underneath the surface. A small area of this dense cover is useful as it provides some shade in the water, with no leaves visible above the surface, and it helps to keep the water clear.

The growth of Hydrilla is easily controlled by pruning and the plants will rapidly produce new shoots. Some roots are developed and these help to hold the plants in the sand. The plants have short, narrow leaves which are closely arranged in whorls along the stem and when well nourished and in full sun they are a most attractive shade of bright, dark green. In poor light the stems become long, thin and straggly and are then unattractive. In a big

outdoor pool containing carp, this plant may be eaten by the larger fish.

Hydrocleys nymphoides (Water Poppy)

This plant has short, rounded leaves above water level and carries, on short stalks, clear, pale yellow, poppy-like flowers with dark centres. Although each flower lasts for one day only the plants produce many flowers continuously if they are in a sunny position. The plants need to root in mud near the surface and respond to regular manuring.

Hygrophila difformis
(Synnema triflorum, Water Wistaria)

In a large outdoor pool these plants are robust and strong growing and will eventually produce flowering stems above the water surface. The underwater leaves are usually deeply lobed but near the water surface they are often much less lobed; on the flowering stem above the water the leaves are usually entire. The stems root strongly and propagation is very easy by means of cuttings. Detached leaves if left floating in the water will produce young plantlets from the cut surface of the petiole. This species is suitable for pools of any size as it is easily controlled, but only small plants can be used in an aquarium garden.

Lemna (Duckweed)

These are small floating plants which need full sunlight and will spread extremely rapidly so that the whole surface of the pool can be covered within a week. It does, however, provide shade and the water underneath will remain clear. The plants need no special attention but if goldfish are kept in the pool they will eat the duckweed greedily as their diet is partly vegetarian, and the plants will survive only in small places between the stems of other water plants where the fish are unable to reach them.

Hydrocleys nymphoides

Ludwigia repens

Ludwigia natans

Limnocharis flava

These attractive plants are most suitable for outdoor pools and need full sun for their best development. They can be grown in containers of soil placed in water up to 30 cm or more in depth. While young, the plants are completely submerged but as they become larger the leaves are produced above the water surface and are a fresh pale green. Groups of large, yellow flowers are also produced at the ends of long stems held well above the water. Quantities of seeds are produced and once established propagation is easy as there will always be numbers of seedlings available to replace old plants. The plants never become invasive and small ones can be kept in an aquarium garden for some time before they become too large. The leaves are sometimes eaten as a vegetable.

Limnophila indica

Two or three species of this genus are native to Malaysia and all have finely divided underwater leaves and small entire leaves above the water. They can be rooted in pots of sand and grow easily and rapidly, but need plenty of light. They are very decorative and do not spread as quickly as some of the other water plants. Propagation is easy from cuttings and the plants are very attractive in indoor aquarium gardens.

Ludwigia natans

These are attractive plants needing full sunlight and can be planted in containers or they will grow quite well floating on the surface of the water. The leaves are dark, glossy green with red or purple coloration on the undersurface, and small, rather inconspicuous flowers are produced in their axils. Although they grow fairly quickly, they are easily controlled by pruning and the pieces which are cut away can be used for propagation if necessary. The plants may be rooted in a container at one side

of the pool and can be allowed to trail out over the water surface for a short distance. Ludwigia can be grown in pools of any size and small plants are suitable for an aquarium garden provided they receive sufficient light.

There is also a wild species which would be useful in outdoor pools and this is *L. repens*, which has stems trailing over the surface of the water. When submerged for any length of time they develop a large amount of spongy white tissue to help them float. White flowers about 3 cm in diameter are produced almost continuously. Plants collected from ponds in the countryside should be isolated for several weeks before they are put into the garden pool to ensure that no diseases or pests are introduced.

Marsilea crenata

This is a small fern species which is best grown in rather shallow water and can be used near the sides of larger pools where it may be allowed to grow in and around the stems of taller plants. It is not invasive and has long, slender, creeping rhizomes which carry well spaced leaves almost circular in general outline but divided into four leaflets. The plants can be grown totally submerged, but it is better to allow the leaves to appear above the water surface where their shape and light green colour will provide a great deal of interest among the stems of the other plants. Propagation is by means of division and the plants grow best in full sunlight.

Monochoria

Three species of this genus are found growing wild in Malaysia, two of them (*M. hastata* and *M. vaginalis*) being common in ditches and ricefields over most of the country and the third being found in the north only. All have pretty blue flowers which last for a few hours (from early morning to about three o'clock in the afternoon). The two common species are

Monochoria elata

worth a place in an outdoor pool, especially if several plants are grown together in a single container so that the colour of the flowers is seen to better effect. In a very small pool single plants can be very effective because of their small size, their flower colour, and because they do not spread rapidly. The northern species *M. elata* has much larger flowers and a graceful habit. It rises one metre or more out of the water with erect leaf-stalks carrying narrow blades which are curved downwards at the top. Out of some of the leaf sheaths heads of blue, star-shaped flowers will appear and each head produces a succession of flowers every day for several days. The plants grow easily from seeds.

Myriophyllum (Water Milfoil)

These are attractive plants which are best used in an aquarium garden where they can be seen more easily and to better advantage than in a pool where their dark green, finely-divided leaves are not so clearly visible. Good light is essential and the plants will then grow very rapidly and need to be cut back very frequently. Groups of stems can be tied to a little stone or may be inserted into a small pot of coarse sand which can be placed at the bottom of the pool or aquarium. After the stems have reached the surface of the water they will grow above it and then small flowers may be produced but this should not be encouraged as the underwater leaves will drop from the stems when it happens. Propagation is very easy by means of cuttings.

Nelumbo nucifera (Indian Lotus)

These are large, vigorous plants with long, creeping rootstocks, tall leaves raised for some distance above the water and large flowers, also on long stalks above the water. Because of their size and vigour, these plants are unsuitable for small pools and even in large pools they are best grown in a large container or a specially built up section of the pool so that their spread can be controlled. If they are unrestricted they will soon take over the whole pool.

In order to grow well, they need an area of one square metre or more for rooting and do best when the soil level is fairly near the surface of the water. The leaf and flower stalks can reach 1–2 m in length. The position of the plants must therefore be given careful thought otherwise they will look out of place and will dwarf the neighbouring plants and the proportions of the whole planting scheme will be spoilt. Lotus can be grown in a central container with no other plants, or they can be placed at one end of the pool, if it is desired to keep the centre planting low; alternatively, if they are grown in a pool of their own this may be situated at the end of a path or terrace. When well grown, they are very handsome and will bloom quite freely throughout the year.

Propagation is most easy from seeds just covered with soil in broad shallow pans which are placed in water in a lightly shaded place and with the soil surface about 5 cm below the water. Fresh seeds will soon germinate and the young plants grow very quickly. The first leaves are floating but later ones are held above the water surface as in fully grown plants. In a tank or pool 45 cm deep, soil should be laid to within 8 cm of the surface, plenty of organic matter (compost) being incorporated, together with a little rock phosphate. As the plants grow they respond rapidly to treatment with nitrogenous manure, which should be applied about once every two months, but as a result of this frequent manuring the soil may become foul and will need to be renewed about once each year.

The common Lotus has pink flowers, but there is also a white variety which is very beautiful. Other varieties exist in China and Japan but do not seem to have been tried in Malaysia. In North America is the yellow Lotus (*N. lutea*) which should grow at the hill stations in Malaysia; the two kinds have been hybridized in Honolulu. Some hybrids are very fine and should be tried in this climate.

Neptunia oleracea

This leguminous plant can be found in many parts of the country in ditches and ponds and makes an interesting addition to the garden pool. It grows best if some of the roots can reach soil in a shallow part of the pool. Long stems are produced, which float on the surface of the water, and these are very attractive as they carry light green bipinnate leaves (resembling those of *Mimosa pudica*, the Sensitive Plant). Fluffy heads of bright yellow flowers are produced almost continuously. The floating stems often become enlarged with white spongy tissue which makes them buoyant but does not make them unsightly. Propagation is by means of cuttings which are best rooted in a pot placed in shallow water in full sun, and when growth has started it may be put into the pool so that the stems can grow over the surface of the water.

Nymphaea (Waterlilies)

There are three different groups of Waterlilies belonging to this genus which are grown in Malaysia. They are the hybrids of *N. lotus* (Egyptian Lotus), *N. capensis* (Cape Blue Waterlily) and its relatives, and *N. mexicana* (Yellow Waterlily). All have short rootstocks bearing groups of floating leaves and the flowers are held just above the water surface.

Nymphaea lotus hybrids have large flowers which are white, various shades of pink and crimson. When well grown, all are large plants, and need plenty of room; a circle of 1½ m is enough, but some plants may need even more space. The flowers open at night and close at about ten o'clock in the morning, as soon as the sun is hot. Each flower will last for about three days and the plants produce many seeds which are easy to germinate.

Nymphaea capensis has beautiful fragrant blue flowers which open between ten and eleven o'clock in the morning and remain open until late afternoon. The cultivar *N. zanzibarensis*, with flowers in various shades of mauve, and also fragrant, blooms at the same time during the day. These plants are especially suitable for water gardens. Most of them do not grow as large as the *N. lotus* hybrids, but it is a general rule with Waterlilies that the better a plant is fed, the larger it will grow and the larger will be its flowers. A good plant can produce flowers twice as large as one of the same kind which has been neglected.

The third group is made up of much smaller plants. They are usually called *N. pygmaea*, but it seems likely that they are hybrids of *N. mexicana*, many of which were raised in France and America in the latter part of the nineteenth century. More of these hybrids should be tried in Malaysia as some of them should be very successful. There are two hybrids which grow very well; one has pale yellow flowers about 8 cm across, with deep yellow stamens in the centre and leaves up to 8 cm by 13 cm which are mottled with purple. The other is larger with flowers 10 cm or more across, the outer petals a very pale creamy yellow, slightly flushed with crimson which becomes more intense as the flower gets older, the centre being filled with deep orange-yellow stamens. Both these flowers open at about eleven o'clock in the morning and remain open for the rest of the day. Because of their small size, their dainty colouring and their day-flowering habit, they are very suitable for the small water garden.

Seeds of Waterlilies can be planted and germinated as described for Nelumbium. They will soon germinate and when the seedlings are large enough to handle they should be transplanted into separate pots with the depth of water above them being increased gradually as the plants grow larger. When the leaves are about 8 cm in diameter the plants are large enough to move into their permanent position in the pool.

Nymphoides indica (Water Snowflake)

This plant is native to Southeast Asia and has white flowers and round floating leaves. They are best grown in containers in pools of any size and they spread by means of runners. Flowers develop from the upper end of the leaf-stalk and are produced for several months. Propagation can be done easily by placing a leaf on moist soil where it will quickly produce roots, and afterwards the young plants can be put into containers of soil which may then be placed in the pool. These plants need full sun and sometimes can be a little temperamental as they will not persist for very long. They are also subject to insect attack so that the leaves can become unsightly and ragged in appearance. When these plants grow well they are attractive, but if they begin to deteriorate, or if their growth is weak, they are not worth a great deal of attention as there are other water plants, equally attractive, which can be grown with less trouble.

Oryza sativa (Rice)

Although this may seem a strange choice as an ornamental plant, it should not be ignored. Young, well grown rice plants are very attractive as they have a good, fresh green colour and develop into small well-shaped clumps. They are easily grown in pots which can be placed in a shallow part of the pool in full sunlight. The plants are suitable for pools of any size and can be positioned to fit in with the general garden design. They will eventually produce flowering stems but when the grain develops the whole plant will become yellow and should be replaced by young plants. Rice plants are useful because they give some height to the general planting scheme of a pool.

Pistia stratiotes (Water Lettuce)

This small free-floating water plant resembles a little Lettuce because of its light green, crisp leaves. It belongs to the Keladi family but its flowers are very tiny and not easily visible. Full sun is needed and, provided there are sufficient nutrients in the water, it will thrive and increase. Although it is slightly difficult to grow well, it is worth a little trouble because it is very decorative and success is very rewarding. It propagates itself rapidly by means of short offsets and will tolerate much cooler temperatures than those of the lowland tropics because it can be outside, for the summer only, in some temperate countries.

Sagittaria (Arrowhead)

Usually these plants are found in the temperate regions of Europe and Asia but they grow very well in the lowlands of Malaysia and will produce edible tubers. These can be found in the market at all times and if planted in some moist soil they will sprout very quickly and can then be transferred to shallow water. When grown in deep water, the first leaves will be strap-shaped but the leaves which appear

Nymphaea

Nymphaea

Portulaca grandiflora (mixed hybrids)

later above the water surface will have the arrow shape responsible for the common name of the plant.

In the northern parts of the country the plants will flower and produce tall inflorescences carrying a number of white flowers. A much finer species is *S. montevidensis* from South America. This flowers freely and tall inflorescences are produced with large flowers having white petals with a dark blotch at the base of each. The flowers last for one day only but new ones open each morning. The leaf blade, although arrow-shaped, is very narrow. The plant needs the same treatment as for Indian Lotus and if not well manured growth will be poor and the flowers will be small.

Salvinia cucullata

In some parts of the tropics this floating water fern can be very troublesome because it grows very rapidly and chokes waterways and ditches. Full sunlight is needed for best growth when large, closely arranged leaves will be produced, but strict control is necessary otherwise the plants will quickly cover the whole surface of the pool. This thick growth will keep the water cool but will also prevent sunlight from reaching underwater plants so that they will not grow well and may even die. Salvinia will also grow under subdued light in indoor pools and can survive for a long time under such conditions, but it will produce smaller leaves more widely spaced along the stems, giving the plants a most delicate appearance. Growth will be much slower under these conditions and the plants will take much longer to spread over the water surface. In full sun the leaves are usually yellowish green with upturned sides, but in subdued light they are light green and usually rest flat on the water surface. No special cultural treatment is necessary and the plants will survive in most situations, provided there is sufficient water.

Trapa bicornis

The large, black, two-horned fruits of this

Sagittaria montevidensis

298

plant are available in the market at certain times of the year and if they are fresh it is possible to grow plants from them, provided they receive plenty of light. Germination may take several weeks and the fruits should be completely submerged in water. The first leaves which are produced are very deeply lobed, but as the stem approaches the water surface the later leaves are more triangular with enlarged stalks and they become arranged in a close rosette at the surface, where they look most attractive. Germination is best done in an aquarium garden but as the plants are really too large for such a small container they must be planted out in a pool as soon as they are large enough to be handled without damage. Most of the fruits available in the market will have been cooked and are therefore useless for germination but uncooked ones are sometimes obtainable and it is worthwhile asking for these as the plants are very attractive and not invasive.

Typha angustifolia (Reed Mace, often wrongly called Bulrush)

This tall plant is very useful in garden pools because it adds height to the planting scheme and does not spread a great deal. It produces a number of stems carrying long, narrow leaves and finally the familiar dense heads of flowers and fruits which are much used by flower arrangers. The plant is best suited to large pools but can be grown for short periods in smaller ones although it will not grow as large and will need replanting more frequently. It is an excellent choice for a formal pool especially if used with Waterlilies only, and the scheme could include a simple fountain. Propagation is by means of division.

Utricularia (Bladderwort)

One species of this genus is suitable for use as an ornamental plant and that is *U. flexuosa*, which is free-floating, usually without roots and having whorls of finely divided leaves. Single plants will therefore appear very delicate but if the plants are crowded this appearance will be lost. They grow just beneath the surface of the water and need full sun, but will spread rapidly and so must be controlled frequently. The young leaves are often bronze in colour and when growing conditions are right many bright yellow flowers will be produced. These are carried on stems about 8 cm high held above the water surface. Propagation is by means of cuttings which are merely allowed to float in the water.

Vallisneria spiralis (Eel Grass)

Although this plant is normally associated with indoor aquaria it can now be found growing wild in many undisturbed ponds throughout the country and may be used very effectively in outdoor pools of any size. The leaves are long, narrow and strap-shaped and although flowers are not produced very frequently the plants spread easily by means of freely-produced runners. However, the plants are not invasive and will develop into dense clumps from which the runners will spread over the bottom of the pool. They are easily removed when necessary and cause no damage to any pool liners. Some of the runners can be allowed to grow around any other containers at the bottom of the pool and will help to conceal them without hindering the growth of other plants.

In full sunlight and shallow water, the leaves will be dark green and short, but in deeper water and with less light they will be longer and paler in colour. This species can be grown in indoor pools where there is poor light but the plants will not be as robust as those which receive strong light. In concrete pools or those with mosaic tile lining, they make a useful green cover over the bottom of the pool, helping to keep the water cool as well as providing ample hiding space for fish. Propagation is by means of division and the young plants are best started off in small pots and then moved to larger ones before being placed finally in the garden pool.

Victoria amazonica (*V. regia*, Amazon Waterlily)

This is the giant Waterlily of the Amazon region and is much too large for small gardens. It needs a very large pool with a diameter of at least 4 m and can be very handsome. Seeds are difficult to obtain and are slow to germinate but if the plants are treated correctly they will be very vigorous. They need plenty of room for their roots and very generous manuring. A well grown plant should persist for many years.

It is important, when stocking a pool with plants, to keep a good balance between submerged and floating plants. Both types can be very strong growing and must be rigorously controlled if the pond is to look well at all times. Many of the free-floating plants such as Utricularia and Salvinia would quickly cover the water surface with a thick mat of stems and leaves, and although the water would remain cool and clear and the fish would be healthy, the appearance of the pool would be spoilt and it would look neglected. The plants should be thinned, either every week or every two weeks, depending on their rate of growth. A part of the water surface should be kept free of plants at all times so that the fish can be seen and some sunlight can reach the submerged plants. In addition, when free the surface water becomes greatly disturbed by falling raindrops during heavy storms; the fish appear to enjoy this action as they swim near the surface and are very active because the water is better aerated at this time.

Plants such as Waterlilies which are rooted in containers and have floating leaves may also become overgrown and the leaves then become pushed upwards out of the water so that the pool will look untidy and any formal aspect will be lost completely. Older leaves should be removed carefully, leaving a sufficient number nicely spaced out on the water surface. The pool will then retain a formal appearance.

Trough Gardens

Troughs can be built of concrete or bricks and vary considerably in size and height. Often in small modern houses or flats, a trough is part of the original design and may be situated alongside a wall or as the outer border of a veranda or balcony. They are used frequently around large public buildings, both inside and outside. Larger troughs usually have drainage holes provided at the base, often with small pipes extending to the nearest storm drain or to the edge of a balcony. Small troughs, especially those inside a building, must have metal containers made to fit inside them so that excess water cannot drain out and run over the floor. Any troughs which are to be filled with soil should have a layer of gravel or small stones placed at the bottom to a depth of 5–8 cm. This can be covered with a layer of coarse leaf mould or partly rotted grass trimmings and the remaining space can be filled with soil to within 6 cm of the rim of the trough. It should be allowed to settle for several days before any planting is done.

The choice of plants will depend on the position of the trough and the amount of light which it receives. In full sunlight a wide variety of plants, except trees, can be grown, but in very shaded situations the choice of plants will be more restricted. If the trough is the only place available for growing plants then the owner may wish to grow a few vegetables or spices and this can be done easily provided regular manuring is carried out. However, if the trough is of sufficient size, a mixture of ornamentals and vegetables can be grown. Ordinary garden soil can be used to fill the trough and if it is possible to mix it with some compost or old cattle dung beforehand, this will be of great benefit.

Shrubs and large herbaceous plants can be grown easily and well in big troughs and can be especially decorative around large public buildings. In small houses and flats some taller plants in a trough would provide shade to part of the room and would also give a little privacy to the occupants. One of the advantages of growing plants in a trough is that watering can be less frequent and the plants need less attention than when they are grown in pots. The arrangement of the various plants in a trough will depend on its situation and any specific purpose which the owner has in mind. A trough may be regarded as a small garden and can be planned accordingly as there is a wide variety of plants of different shapes, sizes and colours from which to choose in order to create many different kinds of small landscapes. Tall and short plants can be combined with trailing plants that are allowed to grow over the sides of the trough. In flats which have a trough as part of the balcony it should be remembered that plants will tend to grow outwards towards the light and they cannot be turned around as is done with pot plants. A little careful pruning can be helpful or sun-loving plants can be grown along the outer edge of the trough and shade-loving plants on the inner side. A trough in full sun throughout the day could be planted with a mixture of cacti and short succulents; if the trough were shaded continuously then a mixture of ferns and other foliage plants could be grown. When there are many plants in the trough regular fertilizer application is necessary in order to maintain good growth, but the plants will always thrive much better than those which are grown in pots because they have more space for their roots to spread.

The choice of plants depends on the situation of the trough and the personal taste of the house owner. In a very sunny situation the whole trough could be planted with mixed varieties of Coleus or two or three of these varieties could be planted to form a definite colour pattern. This would be very attractive, especially as the plants grow for a long time with little attention and when replanting becomes necessary a totally different colour pattern can be arranged. In shady places a mixture of ferns is very satisfactory and Selaginellas and mosses can be used with them. Flowering plants are not quite as useful, especially in troughs which are arranged so that one side faces outwards with strong light and the other side faces inwards towards a room and therefore will be much more shady. The stems of the plants will grow towards the light and the leaves also will turn towards it so that the plants will not be seen to the best advantage. Flowers also will tend to be produced on the outer side of the plants in the stronger light and cannot, therefore, be seen from inside the room. This is especially true of trailing plants which are grown for their flowers. Gardeners living in flats should take this into consideration when planting because they may be unable to walk outside in order to see the flowers on their plants.

Any of the foliage plants described elsewhere in this book can be grown in troughs, but some of the larger kinds of aroids such as Monstera and Philodendron develop great quantities of roots and are liable to starve any other plants in the trough unless fertilizer is applied regularly and frequently. Flowering plants are suitable only when there is plenty of light but in outdoor troughs around large buildings they can be used without hesitation and it is surprising how well some of the small and medium-sized shrubs will grow under such conditions. With regular attention to keep them healthy and in good shape, they can be left in the trough for a number of years before they need to be replaced with younger plants.

Indoor troughs with a metal container inside can be filled with pot plants and this arrangement makes management very easy as the pots can be changed when the plants have become too old or have lost their leaves and shape. If a few pots of trailing plants are included their stems can be encouraged to grow in and around the other plants so that the pots will be concealed and some of the stems can also hang over the sides of the trough. Such troughs are very often placed in continuous shade and the choice of plants will be slightly limited; it would probably be better to use foliage plants only in such situations. If flowering plants are used then they should be changed around frequently because if they are kept in the shade too long they will lose both their flowers and their leaves. Watering must be done carefully, otherwise excess water will gather at the bottom of the container and mosquito larvae will soon appear, although there are now some insecticides which can be put into the water to control these pests. Surplus water could also make the soil in the pots waterlogged and the plants will die quickly if this happens. A thin layer of gravel at the bottom of the container will help to avoid this problem. In metal containers filled with soil for direct planting, watering must be very strictly controlled because excess water cannot drain away and will not evaporate quickly; if the soil is permanently wet, plant roots will rot. It is much easier to use pot plants in these metal containers.

Miniature Gardens

In this section are included bottle gardens, aquarium gardens, bonsai culture and true miniature gardens which are groups of small plants grown together in a single container. The first two kinds can be kept inside a room as part of the decoration but the last two kinds will thrive very much better if they can be kept in some place such as an open veranda or balcony where there is plenty of air circulation and also a slight change of temperature at night. If such small gardens are kept permanently inside a house they will eventually become very dusty and, because the air is much drier indoors and there is much less difference in temperature at night, the plants will not make such good growth and the garden will lose a great deal of its attractive appearance. The plants will benefit from spraying with a very fine mist of water from a hand spray at regular intervals and they will make better growth as well as be much improved in appearance.

Bottle Gardens

These are small collections of plants grown together in some kind of glass container such as large jars, old carboys or acid bottles and even old aquaria can be used. Whichever type is used, it must be thoroughly cleaned and washed beforehand. If large bottles are used it is an advantage if the neck is not less than about 5 cm in diameter, otherwise it is too difficult to put in soil and plants. Smaller bottles can be used but setting up the garden is then a much more painstaking job.

A layer of coarse gravel should be put in first and then a layer of coarsely ground charcoal. This is covered afterwards to a depth of 10–15 cm with the planting mixture made up of sterilized garden soil, sand, a little bone meal and a very small quantity of a balanced artificial fertilizer. If one of the commercially made potting mixtures is used then this will not need sterilizing and one of the slow release fertilizers can also be used instead of the ordinary balanced mixture. The planting medium should be well mixed before it is put into the bottle and if possible avoid getting any of it on the sides of the bottle as it is difficult to clean it away completely afterwards and may look unsightly.

A few simple tools are needed and these must have long handles so that the soil can be reached through the neck of the bottle. They can be made quite easily by the gardener and may be entirely of wood, or discarded spoons and forks from the kitchen may be pressed into service. When made of wood, long narrow pieces are needed and one end should be carved into the shape of a two-pronged fork and the other end flattened like a spatula. Old forks or spoons can be tied firmly to long wooden handles and may need to be flattened or bent to suit their purpose. A fairly stiff piece of wire bent into a small hook at one end is useful for lowering the plants into position in the bottle. After the soil has been made ready the plants can be lowered carefully through the neck of the bottle; the roots must be pressed gently into it and covered over, using the long-handled spatula or fork. Some patience is needed for the planting operation until one has become accustomed to manipulating the planting tools through the neck of the bottle. It might be of advantage to put in a little practice beforehand, using the long-handled tools in a container with a very wide mouth.

After planting, only a small quantity of water should be added and this can be done by inserting a short length of plastic tubing until it reaches the soil level. Water can be poured very slowly through it and will settle in the layer of gravel in the bottom from where it will gradually soak up into the soil. On no account should a large quantity of water be added because it does not evaporate very quickly inside the bottle and the soil will become waterlogged so that the plants will die. In a bottle garden condensation can be a great problem so too much water must not be added initially otherwise the atmosphere inside the bottle will become too humid and its sides will be covered with droplets of water and the plants will not be visible. Water should not be added regularly or the soil will be saturated continuously; it is best to add it at infrequent intervals only, these intervals to be estimated by the appearance of the plants. Bottle gardens should be kept out of direct sunlight which will cause a great deal of condensation; also, if the sides of the bottle are strongly curved, they will act in the same way as a lens and the plants may be scorched.

When space is very limited, bottle gardens provide a good way of enjoying a little practical gardening and is challenging because it can be difficult unless managed carefully. It needs a great deal of thought if it is to be done successfully and this makes it more interesting besides providing an attractive addition to the decoration of the room. The position of a bottle garden in a room will affect the choice of plants somewhat because of the amount of light which it will receive, but it is quite possible to have it in a very dark corner where it can be illuminated in the same manner as an aquarium.

Only small plants can be used when making a bottle garden and initially they must be small enough to pass through the neck of the bottle without being damaged. After planting they will soon produce new leaves and shoots and will quickly form a tiny landscape in the bottle. Growth may be fairly rapid at first but will slow down later. The garden may require little or no attention, apart from watering, for about one year before pruning or rearranging is necessary.

Old aquaria can also be used in a similar way and are easier to manage because planting and arrangement of soil, stones and plants can be done by hand without the aid of any special tools. An aquarium used in this way is usually called a terrarium and should be fitted with a glass lid with or without illumination, depending on its position in a room. The preparation of the planting medium should be done in exactly the same way as described for bottle gardens and because the work can be done by hand it is possible to introduce stones or rocks of interesting shapes to create a miniature landscape. Watering must be controlled carefully but condensation should be less of a problem as the glass lid can be raised if it should occur, and can be replaced as soon as the glass walls are dry. A terrarium of this kind can be used as part of the room decoration in the same manner as a bottle garden and is sometimes easier to display as it can be illuminated like an aquarium by using a built-in overhead light, concealed if required behind a screen cut to the correct size and shape. One precaution is to ensure that the light bulb does not give out too much heat which might scorch the plants or make conditions too dry for them to grow well.

Plants suitable for these little gardens are small ferns and foliage plants, mosses and some Selaginellas. Flowering plants are not the most suitable because they often need different conditions in order to produce flower buds, although they develop plenty of leaves. It is unwise to use fast growing plants such as Zebrina, as they will fill a bottle very quickly, smothering all other plants and eventually growing out through the neck of the bottle. It must always be remembered that conditions inside any container will be very humid and the plants chosen ought to be those able to tolerate these conditions continuously. Descriptions of plants which would be suitable are given elsewhere in the book and a selection can be made from these.

Aquarium Gardens

These are useful in small houses and flats where very little space is available, and the emphasis is on the plants and not on fish. Preparation of such a little garden can be done in the usual kind of aquarium and in exactly the same way as for a collection of fish, including the illumination and positioning in a room. However, it is necessary to introduce one or two small fish such as guppies to prevent any mosquito larvae from appearing although there is a soluble insecticide available which can be used and is said to be harmless to plants. A large number of different water plants can be ob-

tained and a suitable selection can form a most attractive underwater landscape. These plants, however, tend to grow faster than terrestrial ones so that their growth will need strict control if the appearance is to be preserved. An aquarium garden can be placed in any part of the room and if it is illuminated there is no difficulty in the choice of plants which can be used.

For plants to grow satisfactorily, there should be a minimum of 60 litres of water, and 100 litres would make it easier to establish and maintain a good balance. The planting medium should have no organic matter which would decay and cause the water to become foul. A layer of gravel should be placed over the bottom of the aquarium and some charcoal broken into small pieces can be scattered over this. Finally, a layer of coarse sand is placed over the surface to a depth of 4–5 cm, or a little more if the aquarium is tall enough. The sand can be arranged to different heights and it is better for it to slope from the back of the tank to the front; rocks or stones may be placed on the sand and, if required, a layer of small gravel chippings can be spread over its surface.

The aquarium may be filled with water before or after the plants are put in and this is a matter of personal preference. It must be poured in carefully to avoid shifting the sand, otherwise small particles will float for some time in the water and will eventually settle on the leaves of the plants, making them unsightly. An easy way of avoiding this trouble is to place a piece of paper, cardboard or polythene on the surface of the soil and to let the water fall on this slowly until there is a depth of about 2–3 cm, after which it can run in faster with little disturbance. Tap or rain water may be used and at first it may be a little cloudy, but this should clear within one week and if the aquarium is well balanced the water should remain clear and odourless indefinitely.

If the aquarium is kept in a dark part of the room, then illumination will be necessary otherwise the plants will not grow well; about twelve hours of light will be sufficient for satisfactory growth. Fluorescent lighting is suitable and can be arranged above the tank in the same manner as for fish tanks.

Aquarium fertilizers are available but ordinary garden artificial fertilizers can be used, provided they are diluted sufficiently. These should not be used in outdoor pools as they can be poisonous to fish. Some of the balanced fertilizers which are available in liquid form are suitable, but again, must be used in more dilute form than for plants grown in pots.

An aquarium garden should not be placed in direct sunlight as the water will become green and the inner surface of the glass will be covered with green algae which can be very difficult to remove. The green water may clear itself if the aquarium can be shaded or moved away from the strong light but it is better to keep the aquarium garden in a shaded position, giving it a little artificial light occasionally to keep the plants healthy. If the plants are to be grown entirely under artificial light then the aquarium garden will probably be kept permanently in one place at the side of the room. It can then be constructed with one side only made of glass and this is perfectly satisfactory because the plants can be arranged to form a very decorative miniature landscape.

Plants suitable for growing in these small water gardens can be obtained from most aquarium shops, but regular visits are necessary because new plants appear at intervals and are quickly sold. A good collection can soon be obtained in this way and the plants should be grouped in an attractive manner, generally with the shorter ones near the front and the taller ones at the back of the tank. Much denser planting can be arranged than is usual in an aquarium which is set up to display ornamental fish. Practically all of the plants which are suitable will be grown for their foliage only in these small gardens. It is best, therefore, to collect a number of species showing different leaf shapes and colours which will create variety in the planting and make the garden more interesting in appearance. In a collection such as this it is wise to include only plants which normally grow completely submerged in water because the garden will be viewed from the side and the top will be covered with a lid to which a light bulb will be attached. For the same reason, it is pointless to grow floating plants as only their roots would be visible if the garden were seen through the side of the tank. Plants suitable for this kind of garden are Hydrilla, Ludwigia, Cabomba, some species of Echinodorus, Synnema, Vallisneria, Limnophila, Myriophyllum, Cryptocoryne and small specimens of some of the other plants described earlier, although these will need to be replaced as soon as they become too large for the garden.

A different kind of small water garden can be created by using bog plants only, or a mixture of bog plants and floating plants, and such collections cannot be grown in an aquarium because they need much more light for the plants to thrive. Also, as the bog plants usually grow to some height above the water surface it

Miniature garden in a dish

would be difficult, if not impossible, to arrange for suitable artificial lighting. This kind of garden is best grown in shallow containers 5–10 cm deep and there are many ornamental earthenware kinds available which are very attractive, but they must be glazed on the inside. Containers of any material may be used provided they are waterproof and strong enough to hold the weight of the soil, and it is best to conceal this completely under a layer of very coarse sand or gravel chips which will help to prevent the water from becoming muddy. If the water level is not above the gravel chips, then only bog plants can be grown, but if it is well above the gravel, floating plants can be grown also, and these do give the little garden a very natural appearance.

All these plants need ample light in order to grow well. About once every two months a very small quantity of a balanced artificial fertilizer should be applied and one of the proprietary liquid kinds would be most convenient as it can be mixed with a little water and gently stirred into the pond water. The concentration used should be much less than for pot plants. Great care must be taken to · prevent the appearance of mosquito larvae and when there is free standing water one or two guppies can be introduced to provide an easy means of control.

This kind of small garden can be kept in full sunlight on a window sill inside a house and if bog plants only are grown then the gravel will help to keep the water cool; when floating plants are included these also will help to keep the water cool and prevent it from becoming green. If there is sufficient sunlight the plants will flower and are very attractive, but even without flowers they will be decorative because the leaves are usually a good, fresh, bright green. If the little garden can be kept on a veranda or patio, in addition to receiving sufficient sunlight it will also benefit from lower temperatures at night, and from some rain which will freshen up the plants and replenish the water in the container. A great deal of water will be lost by evaporation and through the leaves of the plants, so that it is important to check on the water level every few days and to make up any loss with tap water, this being no more troublesome than the care of ordinary pot plants. Replacement of water is especially important when floating plants are grown, otherwise they will deteriorate very quickly.

Suitable plants for such a water garden are Sagittaria, Echinodorus, Monochoria, Scirpus, Cyperus, Ludwigia, Ipomoea (Kangkung), Limnocharis, Ceratopteris, Lemna and Azolla. Other plants can be tried, but it is important to remember that most of such plants will need full sunlight for as long as possible in order to grow well. They will remain decorative for a long time if they are in ample sunlight for part of the day only, but under such conditions some may become too tall and it is impossible to use stakes of any kind for support because the soil in the container is not deep enough.

Miniature Gardens in Pots

These are convenient for very small spaces and if suitable plants are chosen they can be kept in many places in a house or flat, even if the amount of light is limited. Ordinary earthenware or plastic pots can be used and it is better that they should be not less than 12 cm in diameter as several plants will be grown in a single pot. These pots may be placed inside ornamental glazed containers if desired, to improve their appearance. Fancy containers of other shapes and sizes can be used also, but they must have drainage holes in the base and will need to stand on glazed saucers of some kind to hold any water which runs through the soil.

If such small gardens can be kept on an open veranda or balcony, where there is plenty of air and a slight change of temperature at night, the plants will be much healthier than if they are kept inside a room the whole time. Plants kept entirely indoors will become dusty and will not make good growth, but they can be sprayed with a fine mist of water from a hand-spray, or, if the leaves are large enough, they can be wiped over with a damp cloth. The container should be placed outside on a window sill overnight as often as possible and the plants will thrive much better. When the foliage is sprayed with water it is best done on a hot, dry day so that the leaves will dry quickly, but if the plants have been kept indoors continuously they should not be put out into direct sunlight to dry off as the leaves will be scorched badly. If spraying is done during dull or wet weather, the leaves must dry fairly quickly or they may begin to rot, and it is better to wait for a good dry day before spraying.

Many different kinds of plants can be used for a miniature garden and it must be remembered that most plants in the tropics grow very quickly and thus need to be pruned in order to keep them to a size suitable for the little garden. Some plants grow faster than others and these must be kept rigidly under control, or they will take over the entire space. When stems become too long they often lose the leaves on the lower parts and will then look a little bare and straggly, but if they are cut back new, young shoots will develop and the appearance of the tiny garden will be restored. When several plants are grown together in a single container in this way, it is important to give regular applications of fertilizer and the balanced artificial kinds are the most convenient for this purpose. Some fertilizer should always be given after the plants have been pruned as this will encourage the growth of strong new shoots.

Suitable plants for these tiny gardens are cacti and succulents, small flowering plants and small foliage plants, but in many cases it is necessary to use small specimens of any of those species and to replace them when they become too large. Although such small gardens can be kept for a long time without change, it is wise to remake one completely as soon as the plants show signs of becoming weak.

Cacti and Succulents

These plants need full sunlight, and fairly dry growing conditions, and if the daytime temperatures are high the plants are more likely to produce flowers. Small plants are available from many of the plant nurseries, but packets of imported seeds are also available and are easy to germinate. The seedlings are slow in growth and must not be overwatered. It is wise to plant the seeds in 12–15 cm pots so that they can make good root growth by the time they are large enough to be transplanted. In shallow pots the roots will be distorted and will make poor growth and the plants will be weak.

When this kind of plant is grown, the containers should have a layer of coarse gravel over the bottom and the soil mixture should have plenty of sand mixed in it so that drainage will be very good. If small plants are bought in pots then the soil should be thoroughly soaked before they are transplanted into the miniature garden. If this is not done the dry soil will fall away from around the roots and it is difficult to get the new soil between the roots without damaging them. Many cacti are very spiny and difficult to handle when repotting, so that it is wise to use gloves if possible, to hold them while soil is

pushed around the roots. A small kitchen fork or a small piece of wood are useful implements for moving the soil and pushing it between the roots.

With plants of this kind it is wise to choose those showing different shapes and sizes so that there will be some variation in the little garden. Many of the commonly grown cacti are bun-shaped and a collection of these in one small garden would be rather dull. If possible, a mixture of bun-shaped cacti, taller thick-stemmed kinds and succulents with fleshy leaves should be grown and would make an interesting small garden. Cacti such as species of Mammillaria, Rebutia, Opuntia and Cereus are suitable and succulents such as Kalanchoe, Cotyledon, Echeveria, Crassula, Stapelia, Euphorbia, Haworthia and Aloe can be used effectively with them. Most of these are described elsewhere in this book. Other species are available but are not suitable for a miniature garden as they are too large. The number of species planted must be limited by the size of the container used and it is better to have two or three well grown plants only, than to have many species crowded together and consequently showing poor growth.

Small Flowering Herbaceous Plants

Many such plants can be grown but unfortunately they usually become too large for the container in a very short time and it is always possible to keep them to a manageable size by continuous pruning. One or other of these plants will often grow so fast that it will eventually smother the remaining species and the result will be a container with one species only, not a small garden. Most flowering plants will need full sunlight or sunlight for a great part of the day in order to flower well, but some plants such as Saintpaulia or some Begonias will thrive and flower well in subdued light. Other small plants, such as *Zinnia linearis*, Impatiens (Busy Lizzie) and some small annuals would be suitable but, in general, small flowering herbaceous plants are not the ideal subjects for a miniature garden.

Foliage Plants

In miniature gardens it is often possible to grow small specimens of foliage plants which, with different management, would be much too large for this kind of work. Many of the suitable plants are shade-loving and their growth is not as rapid as that of some flowering plants so that small specimens can be kept in a container for a long time before they need to be replanted. The rate of growth can be controlled somewhat by applying fertilizer at infrequent intervals; this will keep the plants healthy without the production of too much foliage. Unless the miniature garden is to be kept in full sun, many plants with coloured leaves cannot be grown. However, there are many plants with leaves of different shapes and sizes which can be combined into an interesting collection and there will also be some variation in the green colour of their leaves. A miniature garden of foliage plants which is kept indoors continuously must be sprayed with water about once every week in order to wash dust from the leaves and to freshen up the plants. Leaves which are large enough can be wiped over individually with a damp cloth. It is important that the growth of all the plants is kept under control to prevent some from smothering others or from becoming too large for the container.

Suitable plants for this kind of garden are small specimens of some of the ferns described elsewhere, some Begonias and seedlings of some trees. Trailing plants must be controlled strictly and the larger aroids should not be used in groups of small plants because they produce large numbers of roots which fill the container quickly so that other plants become starved. Seedlings of trees or shrubs are often suitable as many are slow in growth while they are small, and if kept in a small container (which restricts their root growth) they will not need to be replaced for two or three years. However, if these seedlings begin to grow very fast they may become too high for the container and their roots will increase so much that the other plants will be unable to grow. Many of these seedlings will tolerate some shade and can be kept inside a house for a long time without harm.

Small plants of ferns such as *Nephrolepis biserrata*, *Pteris ensiformis*, *Davallia denticulata*, Adiantum varieties and *Asplenium nidus* are suitable and could be kept for at least one year before replacement would be necessary. Other foliage plants such as Begonia, Maranta or Calathea can be used also and can be grown effectively with some of the ferns to give the group some variation in colour and form.

Do not be tempted to use large plants in order to fill the container for an immediate effect because such plants will have larger root systems and it will be difficult to include sufficient soil mixture for them to recover and grow well. It is much better to use very small plants in plenty of good soil mixture and these will quickly grow together in a very natural way which will give a more satisfactory appearance. With this method the miniature garden will look a little bare initially because of the earth showing between the plants, but this can be covered with clean gravel if necessary, and the plants will soon grow over it. Some experimenting with different combinations of plants is worthwhile in order to find out which ones grow best or produce the best effect in the places

that must be used, because growing conditions may not be ideal and good management is therefore important to keep the plants in reasonable health.

Very simple miniature gardens can be created without using soil and for this purpose, shallow, glazed, ornamental containers can be used. They should be filled with clean washed gravel or small stones and two or more pieces of Dracaena stem can be arranged to stand in the bowl with water to a depth of about 1½-2 cm at all times. The thick stem cuttings will produce one or more leafy shoots which are slow growing and the arrangement can be kept for many months before it needs any attention. A little care is necessary to ensure that no mosquito larvae appear but if the water surface is well below the gravel there is little likelihood of this happening; a soluble insecticide can be dissolved in the water for added protection and will not harm the plants. This little garden can be kept in shade or sunlight and as soon as the leaves are sufficiently large they will benefit from a weekly spray with water. Other plants which can be grown in this way are Arrowhead (Sagittaria) and some species of Echinodorus. A little liquid fertilizer should be added to the water when growth has commenced.

Another kind of miniature garden which can be made is a tiny rock garden. For this purpose a small rock of irregular but interesting shape can be used and this should be soaked in water for one or more days before being placed in a shallow ornamental container. Smaller rocks or large stones can be arranged around the base and the arrangement is then ready for planting. Various kinds of moss can be attached to the rock and one or two small fern or Selaginella plants can be placed in any small crevices or hollows in the rock. Initially the plants should be tied to the rock with thread until they become firmly attached. They must be sprayed with water every day. With this kind of garden, the plants must be kept moist continuously in order to remain in good condition but if there is any standing water in the container the usual precautions must be taken against the appearance of mosquito larvae. Several different kinds of moss can be used and can be very attractive, but this kind of small garden takes a longer time to establish than one in which the plants are rooted in soil. Other kinds of plants which can be used successfully are those such as *Pilea microphylla* which appear naturally on moist walls and similar situations. It is also possible to use small seedlings of some big trees, such as *Ficus benjamina* (Waringin), which must be tied to the rock until their roots have taken firm hold. When established they need not be kept as moist as some of the other kinds of plants which can be used.

Bonsai

Although only a brief account of bonsai culture is given here, it is a section of gardening which should be considered by those living in houses with very little outdoor space or in flats with a small balcony.

For beginners it is best to use plants which are fairly tough and undemanding with regard to growing conditions, and when success has been achieved with these, other more difficult or more delicate plants can be tried out. Seedlings of wild plants can be obtained from all sorts of situations such as wall crevices, roadsides and banks where the plants are often stunted in growth, and from old oil palm trunks or from rocky areas either on the coast or inland. Bonsai culture is usually associated with Japan but it is now very popular in many parts of the world, especially in countries with a more temperate climate, where it is possible to buy tree seeds specially for bonsai culture. Unfortunately, these seeds are not suitable for growth in the tropics but there is no reason why tropical plants could not be used as there are many species of both wild and cultivated tropical trees which would be suitable for this purpose. The main difference in the tropics is the continuous growing season and the vigorous growth of many of the plants.

Bonsai trees are managed in a way which limits their growth so that the plants remain small at all times, and they can range from 10 cm to 90 cm in height. The growing of bonsai is exacting and needs a great deal of patience but this should not deter anyone from attempting it because it is a fascinating hobby and when successful provides a most satisfying form of decoration for small outdoor areas. Although bonsai should be kept outside most of the time, it is worthwhile experimenting with different plants in order to find some which could be grown satisfactorily in this way indoors. Provided they receive sufficient light,

some of these small trees can survive for a long time under rather poor conditions, and some can even be kept in airconditioned rooms for a long period before they begin to deteriorate. However, all such plants kept indoors will eventually make poor growth and drop their leaves. And even if they are placed outdoors at this time they will be very slow to recover. They should be left outside until a complete change of foliage has developed.

The trees are usually grown in small, often shallow containers which restrict the root growth considerably, and by careful pruning of the above-ground parts of the tree, it can be kept to a size appropriate to the root system. These little trees can be encouraged to develop the shape of a normally grown specimen and with good management they will flower and fruit as well. Careful pruning or pinching is needed to encourage suitable branching, and the trunk or branches can be trained in various ways to form interesting shapes. In order to achieve this effect, the branches are wired in position while they are still flexible and the wire is kept in position until the stems have become sufficiently hard to retain the desired position.

Because bonsai are grown in relatively shallow containers they will need a complete change of soil at intervals as the root system becomes very dense and the soil will be exhausted. Repotting may be done every year or every third or fourth year, depending on the condition of the plant, but whenever it is done some root pruning is necessary at the same time. Large roots should be cut back to encourage the development of a mass of small roots around the base of the trunk. Pruning of the stems and branches should be done when the plant is established, with the object of encouraging the development of a well shaped crown. Regular watering and application of fertilizer is necessary, but both must be carefully controlled in the tropics so that, while growth is maintained, it is not too rapid.

A number of tropical plants are suitable for bonsai culture and may be grown from seeds or cuttings. Another way of obtaining suitable plants would be to look for small seedlings of wild or cultivated plants which are stunted because of poor growing conditions. If these are lifted carefully and planted in small pots so that their roots are restricted in growth, they will make an admirable beginning for bonsai culture. The little plants should be kept in the small pots for as long as possible before they are planted finally in the ornamental containers. Bonsai plants may be grown singly or in groups depending on the effect desired, and the size of the container used will depend on the amount of space available.

Seedlings and young rooted cuttings are

easily handled and need no support, but when repotting an older bonsai plant with a good root system, it must be wired to the container before soil is put in because it would be top-heavy and the new, fairly loose soil would not hold it sufficiently firmly. This is especially true when very shallow containers are used. Most containers will have at least two drainage holes in the base and when older plants are repotted, plastic covered wire can be passed around some of the larger roots and out through the drainage holes, where it can be tied to hold the plant firmly in place. The container may then be filled with soil, gently pushing it between the roots with a small stick, to ensure that no spaces are left. Afterwards, the soil can be levelled off and, if required, it can be covered with moss which will give a more natural appearance and will help to prevent the soil from drying out too quickly.

Watering must be done very carefully so that soil is not washed out of the container and the plant must be kept in very light shade until it is established. It should not be put out into direct sunlight at this time because the shallow soil would dry out very quickly and the roots would be killed. During long periods of heavy rain the plants may need some protection to prevent waterlogging, loss of nutrients and loss of soil. Provided there is sufficient light, a position on a covered balcony or a patio would be excellent and the plants should thrive. Bonsai plants which have been kept outside continuously can be brought into the house for one or two days, but if possible, they should be put outside at night during this period.

Because the root system is restricted, it is important in the tropics to make sure that when the plants are being repotted the roots are not allowed to dry out completely. When the soil has been removed from around them they should be covered with a wet cloth while the other preparations are being made. New soil mixture should be fairly dry so that it can

be pushed between the roots more easily and the first watering should be done very gently so that the soil is disturbed as little as possible. After a week or so the soil will have settled and become more firm so that less care will be needed when watering. Small plants can be potted into the container in the usual way and no wiring will be necessary because they will be held firmly in the soil.

Many of the well known shrubs should be tried for bonsai culture but they should not be expected to produce such quantities of flowers as they would when planted out in the garden. Shrubs such as Murraya, Barleria, Bauhinia, Tecoma, Brunfelsia and Galphimia should be tried out, and even if they produced a few flower clusters only, this would be entirely satisfactory and would be more suited to the small size of the plants. Some of the foliage shrubs can also be used, especially Malpighia, Ehretia, Phyllanthus, Polyscias, *Acalypha siamea* and dwarf Pandanus. Trees which would be suitable, especially if grown from seed, are Muntingia, Ficus, Eugenia, Thevetia, Pinus, Cupressus, Podocarpus, Citrus, Pithecellobium, Gardenia, Zizyphus, Fortunella, Salix, Tamarindus, Wrightia, Melia, Mimusops, Michaelia and Lagerstroemia. Some of these can be found as seedlings growing wild, and the smaller specimens can be potted up more successfully than the larger ones because they adapt better to the restricted growing conditions which are necessary.

Bonsai plants are viewed at close quarters so that the details of flowers and foliage are better appreciated than on large plants of normal size grown outside in the garden.

Highland Gardening

In Malaysia there are a few places only where gardening can be done at higher elevations, but in other parts of the tropics much greater

Bonsai growing necessitates care and patience, but it is a very rewarding hobby

areas are available. The main differences from lowland conditions are with regard to temperature, humidity and the amount of ultra-violet light. With increasing elevation, conditions become cooler and more moist and, in general, the temperature will fall about 1° Centigrade for each 100 m in altitude, but this varies in different places according to the season, the time of day, the water content of the air, the amount of rainfall and other factors.

As the temperature falls with increasing elevation, the air becomes more saturated with moisture and the cloud line is reached at about 1200 m. The increase in ultra-violet light results in slower growth and more intense coloration of plant organs. Cloud is more frequent at higher elevations and the plants remove a great deal of moisture from the air as it moves through the foliage. Above the cloud line plants can suffer from lack of water at certain seasons and this is reflected in the kinds of plants which grow in such situations. The soils also show some change and, in general, contain more humus and less minerals. Earthworms and termites are not found above 1200 m and there is a great deal more surface peat and leaf litter. The amount of peat often increases considerably at the cloud line because the abundant moisture and low temperature inhibit the decaying process. Some of the plants have leathery leaves which are resistant to decay and remain as leaf litter for a long time. At the cloud level conditions are continuously very moist and the trunks and branches of trees become concealed with a thick, dense cover of mosses, liverwort and filmy ferns. In other parts of the tropics, different species of epiphytic ferns, orchids and bromeliads also occur abundantly in this situation. Above this region where the air becomes drier, these plants are far less abundant and frequently the trees are very much shorter.

When gardening in the highlands it is im-

portant, therefore, to take into account these climatic conditions as they will affect the choice of plants and the methods of cultivation. Highland areas often include steep-sided valleys separated by narrow ridges so that gardens will need some careful planning. Terracing may be necessary on very steep slopes and flower beds may need to be raised to ensure good drainage when some kinds of plants are grown, especially during a wet season. However, the basic routines of gardening, such as preparation of the ground by digging, manuring, mulching and composting, pruning and maintenance of plants, propagation of plants, as well as spraying against pests and diseases, will be the same as in the lowlands.

Propagating pans may need some protection from too much rain and polythene sheeting or glass panes may be used for this purpose. In unused flower beds, the soil may become compacted and hard as a result of the heavy rainfall, so that it is best to try and keep it covered to prevent this from happening. A thick planting of annuals or similar quick-growing plants would be suitable and after flowering they could be dug into the ground as a form of green manure.

In highland gardens situated on steep slopes, mulching will be of great help in protecting the soil from heavy rain wash and some terracing will also help in this respect. The arrangement of such gardens needs careful consideration if they are to be managed fairly easily. Too many small terraces may look unattractive and will also make movement through the garden very awkward. Paths and steps should be arranged to fit in with the contours of the ground and will provide easy access to plants on either side. On steep slopes it would be wise to plant trees and shrubs which need little attention as it is extremely tiring and difficult to work in such areas.

Planning a garden in the highlands needs the same considerations as in the lowlands but the choice of plants, especially tree species, will be quite different. There is a complete change of wild species of plants above 1000 m so that the tree species which can be grown will be quite different from those in the lowlands. Many of the wild tree species in the highlands make good garden plants as they are shapely, with good foliage, and some of them are deciduous or have highly coloured young foliage which makes them exceedingly attractive for several weeks each year. Some of the wild shrubs and herbaceous plants in the highlands also make good ornamentals as many of them flower abundantly or have interesting foliage. However, these plants will not grow in the lowlands and will only make very spindly growth there. On the other hand, many of the lowland shrubs and herbaceous plants can be

Tea grows quite well in the highlands

Photo: H S Yong

grown successfully in places up to 1000–1500 m in altitude and frequently the flowers are better coloured and last longer than in the lowlands.

At these elevations, many of the lowland plants with coloured foliage also grow very successfully and the leaf colour is more intense, so that striking displays can be obtained in the garden. Red, blue and purple colours appear much brighter at higher elevations but other colours seem to be little affected. Purple-flowered Bougainvilleas are much more intensely coloured if planted in a well drained position in the highlands. Hibiscus and Ipomoea flowers remain open the whole day whereas in the lowlands they close at noon or earlier.

In the highlands, with the lower tempe-rature and the almost constant high humidity, stone surfaces such as walls or sides of troughs can become covered very quickly with mosses and lichens, especially if they are slightly shaded. Steep banks which are lightly shaded will also become covered with ferns, small flo-wering plants and mosses so a different style of gardening could be arranged. On such steep slopes it may not be possible to plant trees or shrubs but the smaller herbaceous species will make an admirable and most attractive cover which will also protect the soil from rain

wash. Many epiphytic plants grow well in the highlands because they are able to obtain all the water they need during the long cloudy periods when moisture condenses on the leaves and stems. It is possible therefore to arrange a garden with trees forming the main planting and small orchids, ferns and mosses grown as epiphytes on the trunks and main branches. Initially, these small plants can be tied in place and will quickly produce new roots which will attach them firmly to the bark. A very natural effect can be developed, especially if one or more different tree shapes are included in the planting scheme. In a large garden a group of tree ferns make a striking and beautiful feature but they need a considerable amount of space while they are young because the fronds are very long and broad.

In the shade of these larger plants, small shrubs, ferns and flowering herbaceous plants can be grown and may be planted in a formal or an informal manner. There are a number of attractive species of ferns which can be grown easily and several members of the Sendudok family grow and flower well in the shade of other plants. A number of Gingers can be grown, as well as forms of Impatiens and Begonia. Some of the ornamental plants from temperate countries can often be grown in the highlands, especially annuals, and these grow luxuriantly; also many of the plants regarded as half hardy or tender in temperate countries will grow very successfully in the tropical highlands.

Gardeners in the highlands need to try out more species of plants to find out how they behave and how well they grow and flower. Both wild and cultivated species should be tried in order to discover the most suitable management which will give the best display in the garden.

13 VEGETABLES

A considerable variety of vegetables may be grown successfully in the lowlands of Malaysia. It is necessary to import seeds of some of them, but many will mature seeds locally if plants are saved for the purpose. If there is a ready supply of seeds from local growers or dealers, it may pay the small gardener to purchase, as time and ground are saved; but if there is any difficulty about supply, a few plants must be kept for seeds. Notes on this subject are given below under each kind of vegetable.

Good cultivation is of the utmost importance in vegetable gardening. Without proper cultivation and the addition of plenty of compost to the soil, results will be poor; but if these matters are properly attended to, and manuring practised as described in Chapter 3 of this book, rapid and excellent results are possible.

The next important matter is the control of pests. These are dealt with in a special chapter of this book, but a few words on the special problems of pests on vegetables are appropriate here. The first thing the novice will discover is that seedlings are very vulnerable to attack by insects. A seedling has little power of resistance, and is easily killed by repeated attacks, especially of night-feeding beetles. If spraying of all plants is regularly carried out, as recommended here, the local pest population will be reduced to small proportions, but negligence will soon lead to the increase of pests with disastrous results. Careful inspection of plants each morning is most desirable, and also in the evening, when many pests may be found which are not seen during the day.

Tuba root (Derris) is still one of the best general local insecticides and if used freely will control most vegetable pests in a small garden. Tobacco infusion, in a soapy solution, is also effective. There are available now modern insecticides which are effective against a large number of diseases and pests but many of these must be used with great care as the vegetables cannot be eaten immediately after spraying and a varying amount of time must be allowed to elapse (depending on the chemical used) before harvest and use.

The choice of site for a vegetable garden is important, though in a small compound there may not be any alternatives from which to select. The site must be reasonably open to sun and air, and away from large trees and high buildings, or most plants will not flourish. If the site is sloping, it should be terraced to prevent erosion, the beds following the contour of the land. A ready supply of water is important, as seedlings and most green vegetables need water in dry weather. A site for composting adjacent to the vegetable plot is also useful, as much time and labour in the transport of compost may thereby be saved.

Rotation of crops is essential, chiefly as a measure of control of pests and diseases inhabiting the soil, and also because different crops have different nutrient requirements, continuous cropping with one kind of plant tending to exhaust the soil. It is usual to practise a rotation of four different crops, one of them being beans, as these have nitrogen-fixing bacteria in their roots. The possible rotation may be limited by the nature of the soil, as some crops do not succeed in light sandy soil, and others will not grow well in black valley soils which have water near the surface. A medium loam, well drained, is best for most purposes, but either light or heavy soils will improve greatly with continued cultivation and a generous supply of compost.

Heavy rain, which is of frequent occurrence in Malaysia, may do serious damage to small seedlings, especially of some of the leaf vegetables, such as Bayam. In such cases it is best to grow the plants first in pans or boxes, under cover from the rain, and transplant when they are large enough to handle. After planting they should be protected from both sun and rain by cut palm leaves. Sometimes continuous rainy weather will make establishment of such small seedlings very difficult, and in parts of the country which have a regular wet season this should be avoided as a time for planting except for crops with large seeds, young plants of which can hold their own, or those grown from cuttings.

The storage of seeds is important, as many kinds (especially the smaller seeds) do not keep well in the climate of Malaysia unless they are dry. Freshly gathered seeds should be spread out to dry on fine days, and then packed in tightly stoppered bottles, or tins with very close fitting lids. Seeds should in any case not be kept longer than is necessary, as nearly all of them deteriorate in storage. Germination of old seeds is often slow and irregular, and the percentage of bad seeds increases with the length of storage.

The following notes refer to lowland conditions in Malaysia. On the hills, a large number of vegetables from temperate countries can be grown successfully, including Potatoes, Cabbages, Cauliflowers, true Spinach, Carrots and Leeks. Of the green vegetables it is usually those which have a short and rapid life-cycle which are the most successful.

Starchy Tubers

Sweet Potato (Ubi Keledek, *Ipomoea batatus*)

These produce quicker though no heavier yields than any other root crop, and have better food value than Tapioca. The varieties with yellow or orange flesh have the highest vitamin content and are usually the sweetest; some people prefer the less sweet varieties which have a firmer paler flesh or are white. The orange-fleshed forms have the best flavour and cook well with the minimum of fibre. More selection for good varieties should be undertaken in Malaysia.

A bed for Sweet Potatoes should be in the form of a ridge 45-60 cm high; the cuttings are planted along the top of the ridge. A light soil is best, and compost and phosphate may be mixed with it, but not any nitrogenous manure, excess of which in the early stages of growth appears to prevent the formation of tubers. If an ordinary flat bed is used, most varieties do not crop well, but there is one variety which yields well even in a rather wet, heavy soil not made into ridges. This has deeply lobed leaves, purplish when young, and rather long, white tubers.

Propagation is from cuttings of old plants. There are several methods, the most usual being to take stem-tip cuttings about 30 cm long, inserting the lower half of the cuttings obliquely into the ground and planting them 40 cm apart. Another method is to take lengths of 30-45 cm from the older parts of the stems, and bury them horizontally, with only the leaf blades projecting. Stem-tip cuttings start growth more quickly, but in some circumstances the other method may yield a more uniform crop of larger tubers. The matter has not been fully investigated under local conditions. My experience is that Sweet Potatoes are a temperamental crop with which it is difficult to carry out controlled experiments

When new growth begins, the stems trail along the ground, and if undisturbed soon form roots. To prevent this, they should be moved from one side of the ridge to the other every week. If roots are allowed to form all along the trailing stems, the main root tubers will suffer.

After the plants have been in active growth for at least a month, liquid manure may be given, but not before. The tubers of the quickest maturing kind should be full grown in about three months, but they will take longer if ridging is not practised. Varieties maturing in four to six months are also sometimes grown. One variety is grown for the young leafy shoots which are used as a green vegetable but it produces very few tubers.

A borer often attacks the tubers if they are left too long in the ground, and will certainly attack subsequent crops unless rotation is practised.

Tapioca (Ubi Kayu, *Manihot esculenta*)

This is the easiest starchy root crop to grow, but is inferior in food value to Sweet Potato, and takes longer to mature; under good conditions it gives heavy yields, but in poor soil the tubers may be small and woody. There are a number of good varieties commonly grown locally as vegetables. The varieties grown to produce prepared Tapioca mature slowly and some may contain an appreciable amount of prussic acid; they are therefore unsuitable for our present purposes.

Propagation is by cuttings of the stem (not of the tubers). Cuttings should be of mature stems, 12–15 cm long, planted at thirty degrees to the horizontal with three-quarters of the cutting below the surface of the soil. They are best planted on ridges 1 m apart, at intervals of 60–100 cm in the ridges. Monthly manuring is desirable. The crop is mature at four to ten months, according to the variety. The tubers are more palatable if not too old, otherwise they can be very fibrous and woody in texture.

The best variety grown as a vegetable matures in four or five months. It has very pale green leaf-stalks (sometimes tinged with red near the base) and rather broad leaflets. This variety has a very low prussic acid content, and its leaves when cooked make a good green vegetable. The leaves of some other varieties

Tapioca

Tapioca tubers

are not good to eat. Cooking destroys the prussic acid in all parts of the plant so that it is then perfectly safe to eat.

All Tapioca varieties take a large amount of nutrients out of the soil so that regular manuring is essential otherwise the soil will become impoverished and growth of any subsequent crops will be slow.

Keladi or Taro
(*Colocasia esculenta* and cultivars)

These are sometimes miscalled Yams. Yams are climbing plants with small leaves; Keladis have short, erect rootstocks and large, triangular leaves on fleshy stalks 60 cm or more long. The stalk is attached near the base of the blade, but not on its edge.

Propagation is from small side tubers, or from cuttings of the main tuber. The plants should be 30–60 cm apart. They will grow in wetter ground than most other vegetables. As they grow, earth should be piled up around them. Manuring at intervals of a month is desirable.

The crop is mature at seven to ten months according to variety. Many varieties are grown; that grown by Chinese for the markets (Keladi China) is probably the best for general use.

All Keladis are more or less acrid if eaten when raw because the tissues contain numbers of very tiny sharp crystals which are irritating to the lining of the mouth. Some varieties have more crystals than others and those with very few can be eaten raw with no ill effects, but all of the others must be cooked in order to destroy the crystals.

The leaf-stalks and the leaf blades are also cooked and eaten. They contain a good deal of mucilage and although they have good food value, many people dislike them on account of their rather slimy texture.

Keladis are useful as a crop for rather wet ground that will not bear other vegetables.

Yautia (Keladi Betawi)

These plants are related to Keladis, but originate from tropical America. They have large leaves shaped like an arrowhead with the blade cut back to the insertion of the stalk. The rootstock produces numerous small side tubers, each as big as a moderate-sized potato, and these are the parts which are eaten. They are of better texture than Keladi.

Two varieties are grown, one with purple leaf-stalks (*Xanthosoma violaceum*) and one with pale green leaf-stalks (*Xanthosoma sagittifolium*). Propagation is as for Keladis.

Yam (Ubi Nasi, Ubi Torak)

Yams are climbing plants, and need strong supports 2–3 m or more high for their stems.

Keladi China

Yam Bean

Propagation is from portions of an old tuber (not from stem cuttings), planted 60 cm apart, and maturation takes eight to ten months. When the tubers are fully developed, the leafy stems begin to wither; this is the sign for lifting the crop.

Yams will keep longer than most tubers. After they have been in store for a while, they will sprout near the top end. These sprouting top ends should be cut off and planted, the rest of the tuber being eaten. The lower parts of the tuber sprout later than the top, so that it is not good to cut one tuber into several pieces and plant all together.

The Greater Yam (Ubi Nasi, *Dioscorea alata*) has thornless stems and very large tubers. There are many varieties, with tubers of different shapes and sizes, differing also in colour of flesh (the flesh of some is bright purple). The Lesser Yam (Ubi Torak, *Dioscorea esculenta*) has thorny stems and smaller but more numerous tubers which are considered by some people to be of superior flavour. Yams are more like potatoes in texture and flavour than any other local tubers.

There is another kind of Yam which bears potato-like tubers on its climbing stems; it is sometimes called Ubi Atas (*Dioscorea bulbifera*). These tubers are quite good, but more soapy in texture than the tubers of the Greater Yam. They can be kept aside for months without taking any harm, but eventually they will begin to grow and must then be planted out.

Yam Bean
(Bengkuang, *Pachyrhizus tuberosus*)

This is a climbing bean which produces a tuberous root rather like a large turnip in shape and texture. This root is edible but the pods and beans are poisonous. Its botanical name is Pachyrhizus. Plants are grown from seeds, planted 40 cm apart; the climbing stems need support like other bean stems. If the flowers are removed the climbing stems continue to grow for as long as ten months, and the root tubers also; if the flowers are not removed the stems die sooner and the tuber is smaller. Occasional manuring during growth is necessary. The root is firmer than a turnip when cooked and is pleasant to eat, though having a very mild flavour. It can also be eaten raw and makes an excellent addition to a vegetable salad. The root is not related in any way to the true turnip which is not available in Malaysia, but in most markets and in many published recipes for local cooking, when the word turnip is mentioned, it refers to the root of Yam Bean.

When grown on raised beds without any support for climbing, the plants can be highly ornamental and for this purpose the plants are allowed to flower and any long stems are bent

Greater Yam

Greater Yam

Lesser Yam

back on to the bed. The flowers are produced in quantity and are deep blue, a colour which is scarce among tropical garden flowers. The display lasts for some time but when fruits develop, flowers will no longer be produced. The plant therefore deserves some attention as an ornamental but its management would need to be adjusted to suit the type of garden planting for which it would be required.

Jerusalem Artichoke (*Helianthus tuberosus*)

These are easy to grow, but do not crop heavily. A light soil is best, as wet conditions encourage the growth of a fungus rot which can destroy a crop completely. Small pieces of old tuber are planted about 30 cm apart and the crop is mature in about four months. Tubers for planting can sometimes be obtained in the local markets but it is not a common vegetable.

Beans

French Bean
(Kacang Buncis, *Phaseolus vulgaris*)

These are more difficult to grow than the other kinds of beans, as they are more subject to attack by a stem borer in the seedling stage. Frequent spraying with Tuba root is the best preventive treatment, but by no means a certain one.

Both climbing and dwarf bushy varieties can be grown. Seeds of the former should be planted in two rows in a bed, 20 cm apart in the row; the latter need to be more widely spaced. Climbing kinds need supports 1½–2 m high. Chinese market gardeners grow a climbing variety that crops well and seeds of this are always obtainable from dealers. Several imported varieties are also satisfactory, both dwarf and climbing.

The plants should be manured once a fortnight. Cropping begins at two months and continues for about six weeks.

Long Bean (Kacang Panjang, Kacang Perut Ayam, *Vigna unguiculata* and cultivars)

These have long, cylindrical pods 30 cm or more in length. They crop better than French Beans but are inferior in flavour. Seeds are available always from seed dealers or growers, or you can save your own seed.

A number of varieties are available which differ in size and length of pod, colour of pod, colour of seeds and habit of plant. Some forms are climbing while others are more bushy in form but also produce some long stems. In the market the usual form on sale is the fruit, about 30–50 cm long, and these may be very thin and dark green, or much thicker and pale yellowish green, or they may be purple. The latter variety is not very popular as the colour is not good after cooking and one always seems to expect that beans should be green. The very long variety known as Kacang Perut Ayam has pods up to one metre in length and is superior, although it is not usually grown for the market.

Planting should be done as for French Beans, but allowing 30 cm apart in the rows. Cropping begins at two months from planting and continues for six weeks.

Four-angled Bean (Kacang Botor, *Psophocarpus tetragonolobus*)

The pods of this plant are four-angled and have a broad, crinkled wing along the whole length of each angle. They are bright green and make an excellent vegetable, especially as they retain a good colour after cooking. Young pods can be eaten raw in salads and have a very good flavour. Seeds can be obtained at most times from Chinese seed dealers.

Plant 50 cm apart and use strong supports as the plants grow for at least one year. Cropping begins at three to four months and continues for many months. Manuring once a fortnight in the early stages is desirable.

Sword or Jack Bean (Kacang Parang)

These are very similar in appearance and the pods of both are good to eat as a green vegetable, but only when very young. Older pods are very hard and old seeds are poisonous.

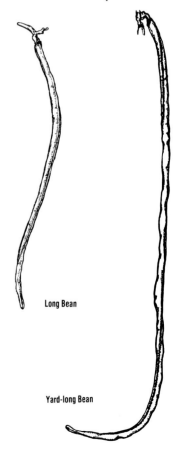

Long Bean

Yard-long Bean

dens the best remedy is to burn all fallen or infested fruit; all wilted branches should be cut off and burnt. Young fruits should be covered with paper bags about two days after the fruit has set. The leaves are often eaten by night-flying beetles but these can be controlled by spraying with an insecticide. The fruit fly is an especially troublesome pest and can be so bad that it is not worthwhile growing this vegetable.

Tomatoes (*Lycopersicon esculentum*)

These are highly susceptible to a bacterial wilt disease prevalent in most old garden soils, and can be grown safely only in sterilized soil, and are best in large pots, kerosene tins or boxes. When well treated, most imported seeds of good varieties can be grown with reasonable success.

Seeds should be planted in boxes or pans and the seedlings transplanted when 10 cm high. The plants should have a little liquid manure once a week. They need staking and side shoots should be nipped off. If the bushy kind of Tomato plants are grown, there is no need to pinch out the side shoots. If grown in a sandy soil care should be taken to water sufficiently, as the drying of the roots may cause falling of flowers and so failure of fruit. Cropping begins at two months and continues for about two months. One or two fruits should always be kept for seed.

Another method of growing Tomatoes is in open-ended rings. Cylinders of metal such as galvanized iron, are made which are open at the top and at the bottom. These are placed upright on a bed of gravel or very coarse sand which is kept in place by means of a very low concrete or brick wall to retain water. Any other material may be used for this purpose provided water can be retained. A thick sheet of some polythene film or any other strong plastic material could be used and the edges could be fixed to an upright wooden framework. Such a container for gravel or sand can be 20–30 cm in height and the length and width can be of any size convenient for the space available.

The rings are placed on the gravel and filled with the soil mixture for planting. Seedlings can be transplanted into the rings and when established they can be given liquid manure which should be poured into the top of each ring. Watering should not be done in the same way, and all water should be poured into the gravel at the base. The Tomatoes will produce a large number of feeding roots inside the ring and longer roots into the gravel from where they will absorb all the necessary water. If this system is used it would be a good idea, if the plants are to be grown outdoors, to protect them from heavy rain which might make the gravel base waterlogged, or to provide a controllable outlet so that excess water could be drained off at any time.

The small Cherry Tomato is much more resistant to the root disease than the large fruited kinds, and may be grown successfully in open beds. The fruits have an excellent flavour.

Gourds

Cucumber (Timun, *Cucumis sativus*)

The only satisfactory kind is that grown by local Chinese market gardeners; seeds are obtainable from dealers at any time of the year. Seeds are sown two to a hole, in two rows in each bed, 45 cm apart in the rows. A framework or trellis is needed. Manure once a week with liquid manure as rapid growth is essential. Cropping begins at six weeks from planting and continues for several weeks.

Seedlings are much subject to beetle attack, both by day and night, and should be hand-picked if necessary as well as sprayed with Tuba root or some other insecticide. It may be necessary to cover the fruits with paper bags to prevent attack by insects or birds, but in some parts of the country this is not troublesome.

Young green fruits 15–25 cm long are picked and eaten raw or as a cooked vegetable, but if allowed to mature the fruits will reach about 30 cm in length and will have a thick, hard, orange-brown rind. Usually then they are used for making soup.

Bottle Gourd
(Labu Air, *Lagenaria siceraria*)

The young fruits of this gourd are eaten as a cooked vegetable but are a little tasteless, and the young shoots are also used as a green vegetable.

There are several varieties; that commonly grown for the market has long fruits gradually narrowed to the stalk end, very pale green. The plants are large and vigorous, needing plenty of room and strong supports; a horizontal framework of bamboo or other material about 2 m above the ground makes a good support.

Angled Loofah (Ketola Sanding,
K. Sagi, *Luffa angulata*)

The fruits of this vegetable are like long Cucumbers with strong ridges from one end to the other. They are eaten cooked and have a strong musky flavour which does not appeal to everyone. Seeds are available always from Chinese dealers and growers and the plants are treated exactly as for Cucumbers.

Control of pests at the seedling stage is very important, and older plants are sometimes also

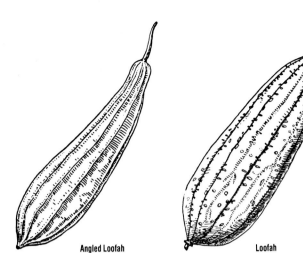

Angled Loofah

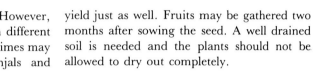

Loofah

Bitter Cucumber

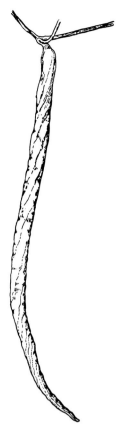

Snake Gourd

much subject to attack by beetles. However, the severity of the problem varies in different parts of the country, and fruits sometimes may need to be bagged as with Brinjals and Cucumbers.

The plants are fast growing and need some kind of support on which to climb. Fruits can be picked about two months after planting but only young fruits can be used as a vegetable as they become very fibrous when older. The plants are too big to be grown in pots, but a few could be grown in troughs or in a raised bed in a small garden.

Smooth Loofah (*Luffa cylindrica*)

This plant is just as easy to grow as the previous species and has similar requirements. The fruits are cylindrical with a smooth surface and can be eaten raw when very young, or they may be cooked and eaten as a vegetable. Ripe fruits are too fibrous to eat but the network of fibres in the fruit wall can be separated and may be used in a variety of ways. Heavy rainfall at flowering will result in lower yield.

Bitter Gourd or Bitter Cucumber (*Momordica charantia*)

The fruits of this plant are very bitter in flavour and two forms are available in Malaysia, although other varieties have been developed in different parts of the tropics. Of the two local forms, one has small fruits up to 10 cm long with a very wrinkled and warted surface, and the other is up to 40 cm long with a smooth, pale green surface and longitudinal ridges and tubercles.

Both kinds become orange when ripe and will split open, revealing the pale cream or yellow seeds which are completely enclosed in bright red, fleshy arils. Both can be grown on supports but the short fruited form may be allowed to trail over the ground also and will

yield just as well. Fruits may be gathered two months after sowing the seed. A well drained soil is needed and the plants should not be allowed to dry out completely.

Snake Gourd (Ketola Ular, *Trichosanthes anguina*)

Seeds should be planted one metre apart and the plants need a trellis which will allow ample space for the long, hanging fruits. The fruits may become curved while growing but if straight fruits are needed then a small stone should be tied to the tip of the young fruit and its weight will keep the fruit straight until it reaches full size.

The fruits are coloured strikingly in dark green and white, often with the white markings predominating. When cut open, the inner tissues are also dark green and retain this colour after cooking. Ripe fruits may be 1–2 m in length but are picked when they are 30–60 cm long if they are to be used as a vegetable. They are orange or dark red when ripe and have a strong smell when broken open, but this disappears after cooking.

The plants are quick growing and need a well drained soil with one or two applications of fertilizer until fruiting begins. Fruits may be picked about three months after seed sowing and for a further three months. Sometimes fruit flies are troublesome and the fruits must be covered with newspaper while they are developing. Seeds are always available from local growers.

Wax Gourd (*Benincasa hispida*, Kundor)

The fruits of this plant are always available in the market and two forms are seen. In one kind the fruits are dark green and in the other this colour is completely hidden by a thick covering of white wax so that the fruits appear greyish white. The fruits may be round or elongated and when ripe can be very large and

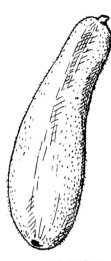

Hairy Wax Gourd

heavy. They range from 1 m to 1½ m in length and weigh 12-50 kg.

In both kinds, the young fruits are dark green with a coating of soft, long, silky, white hairs and in the market they are often called marrows although this name refers to the fruit of another member of the Cucumber family. The plants may be grown on strong supports or allowed to trail over the ground. If grown on a framework, the large fruits may need additional support in the form of a piece of old fishing net, otherwise their weight may cause the stem to break. If, however, they are grown on the ground, then some rice straw or similar material should be placed under the growing fruit to keep it away from the soil so that there is less chance of it rotting before it is ready for use.

The ripe fruits can be eaten raw or cooked, or they can be sliced and candied with sugar. Seeds should be sown about one metre apart and young fruits may be picked in about three months, but the full sized fruits need six months for their development. Regular fertilizer application is necessary to produce good fruits. The form with wax-covered fruits is best grown in areas which have a definite dry season.

Pumpkin (*Cucurbita spps*)

These plants can be grown quite easily but need a great deal of space and heavy manuring for best results. The fruits seen in the markets are usually 20-40 cm in diameter and have orange flesh. Seeds are not always available but may possibly be obtained from stall-holders who sell the fruit in the market.

Watermelon (*Citrullus lanatus*)

These are grown extensively in some parts of Malaysia where there is light, well-drained soil and a slightly dry season. The fruits may be entirely dark green or dark green mottled with lighter green and the flesh is usually pink or white. The plants are allowed to trail on the ground and when the fruits are growing they can be raised on rice straw or similar dry material to prevent rotting and attacks from insects. The plants spread for some distance and are really suitable for large gardens only.

Chayote (*Sechium edule*)

The fruits of this plant are unusual in the Gourd family because they contain a single large seed only. The plants are easily grown and need some support, but in the lowlands, although many flowers are produced, fruiting is not common. However, in the highlands, from 900 m to 2000 m altitude, they are more vigorous and fruit very well.

Propagation is easy and if a fruit is left on a shelf, germination will soon begin and it can

be planted out in the garden. Well drained soil is necessary and regular application of liquid manure or artificial fertilizer is recommended. The pear-shaped fruits are an excellent cooked vegetable and have a very delicate flavour. The first fruit can be picked about four months after planting and as the plants are perennial they will continue to crop for a long time.

Root Vegetables

Radish (*Raphanus sativus*)

Radishes to be eaten raw with salad are easy to grow. Imported seeds from any good dealer are satisfactory. Plants do not produce seed in the lowlands of Malaysia. The ground should first be well manured. The seeds should be sown in rows 15 cm apart and the seedlings thinned as soon as they are big enough to handle. They must be watered in dry weather and the first Radishes should be ready in three to four weeks.

Radishes should be grown as quickly as possible so that the swollen roots will be crisp; if growth is slow then the roots will be tough or woolly in texture. The leaves can also be used in salads. Radishes can be grown in large pots, in troughs, or directly in the ground.

Chinese Radish (Lobak, *Raphanus sativus var. longipinnatus*)

These are much larger than the ordinary Radishes, are white and as vegetables can take the place of Turnips, or may be eaten raw.

Imported seed is normally available from Chinese dealers and the plants will sometimes flower and fruit in Malaysia but the seed crop is less certain than in a more favourable climate. Seeds should be planted in rows 20 cm apart and the seedlings thinned out when they have grown to a height of 5-7 cm, leaving 15 cm between the remaining plants. Liquid manure should be applied every ten days, and the crop is ready about two months after planting.

Carrot (*Daucus carota*)

Carrots will not grow to their full size in the lowlands of Malaysia but small roots can be produced and make excellent vegetables. Seeds of many varieties from Europe, Australia and America are satisfactory; the 'earlier' or quicker maturing kinds should be chosen as such plants do better under tropical conditions than temperate plants which need a long growing season. If plants are kept long enough they may flower and fruit but the seed crop is rather uncertain.

The soil in the bed must be in a good friable condition and not recently manured. Seeds are sown in rows 20 cm apart, and the seedlings thinned out to 50–70 cm apart. They cannot be safely transplanted. When the plants are well grown they must have earth pulled up around them. It is best to use liquid manure. The crop takes three months or more to reach its full size, but young plants may be lifted earlier. This is not a profitable crop as regards yield but is useful to provide a variety of food

Onion (Bawang, *Allium sp.*)

Most varieties of true Onions will not mature in Malaysia though some plants can be grown satisfactorily from seed and eaten as young plants (Spring Onions) in salads or used as garnishing for other dishes. But for this purpose it is easier to grow Shallots or a small kind of white Onion, both of which produce tufts of small new bulbs from one old bulb planted out.

The beds are well manured with cattle dung or good compost before planting, and the bulbs are planted singly at intervals of 15 cm in rows not less than 15 cm apart. The crop is ready in about six weeks. Shallots will not form new bulbs in wet weather and it is necessary to buy imported bulbs for propagation. The small white Onion can be propagated easily from the young shoots at any time without drying off and so is much more convenient.

Leaf Vegetables

Lettuce (*Lactuca sativa*)

Many kinds of Lettuces will grow in the lowlands of Malaysia, but none have their full flavour, and they do not produce good hearts. For proper development, soil of good texture, plenty of water, and frequent manuring are essential.

The best type of Lettuce is probably the small Cabbage Lettuce of which seeds must be imported from a cooler climate. Varieties which mature quickly should be chosen for growing in the lowlands. Chinese dealers stock seeds of a large Chinese Lettuce which produces good crops. Some Lettuces will flower and produce good seeds in Malaysia, and it is worth keeping a few plants for seed if supplies are uncertain.

Seeds should be sown in pans or boxes, in a sheltered place and protected from ants, the seedlings planted out in beds at 20 cm spacing when they are 5 cm high. Shading with attaps about one metre from the ground is desirable for a week or more at this stage. Liquid manure should be given once a week after the plants have recovered from transplanting. The Lettuces should be ready to eat in thirty to thirty-five days from transplanting. The best and most crisp Lettuces are produced when

rapid growth is maintained until the plants are ready for cutting.

Cabbage (*Brassica oleracea* and varieties)

In the lowlands of Malaysia several kinds of true Cabbage can be grown successfully from imported seed and although they do not produce large hearts, they are of good flavour. However, in the last few years several varieties of Cabbages and Cauliflowers suitable for growing in the lowland tropics have been produced in the Philippines, and these give plants with good-sized hearts or heads of flowers. Seeds are available but are sometimes in short supply.

Seeds and seedlings should be treated as described for Lettuces, but spaced at 30 cm intervals. They should not be overwatered or intensively manured. Slow growth is desirable for the production of hearts, which takes about three months from sowing. Cabbages may also be grown from cuttings made from the side shoots which appear on old plants after the heads have been removed. Plants grown from seeds imported from temperate countries do much better in the highlands. They are very susceptible to attack by caterpillars and regular spraying is necessary otherwise the plants can be destroyed completely.

Chinese Cabbage and Mustard (Sawi)

Several kinds of these are grown abundantly by Chinese market gardeners and they provide very useful green foodstuffs. Seeds are imported from China but are always available from dealers.

The most useful kind is the white-stalked Pak Choy or Pek Chye (*Brassica rapa chinensis* group). Choy Sam or Choy Sim (*Brassica parachinensis*), the Spinach Mustard, has green stalks and flowers freely in Malaysia as well as produces good seeds. Kai Choy or Toa Chye (*Brassica juncea*) is a pungent Mustard of large size and many varieties are bitter in flavour. Kai Lan (*Brassica oleracea alboglabra* group) is a Kale with blue-green leaves, tasting much like a true Cabbage.

The plants are handled much in the same way as described for Lettuces, and are mature at about twenty-five days from transplanting. Many varieties are available and these are named by Chinese gardeners according to the colour of the flowers, the leaf shape and the number of days needed to reach harvesting stage. Frequent manuring is essential for good results. Kai Lan takes longer to mature than the others.

Seedlings of these plants may be eaten raw in the same way as Mustard and Cress. They are ready to eat five or six days from planting.

(Pek Chye or *Brassica rapa, pekinensis* group, is sometimes called Celery Cabbage and has a

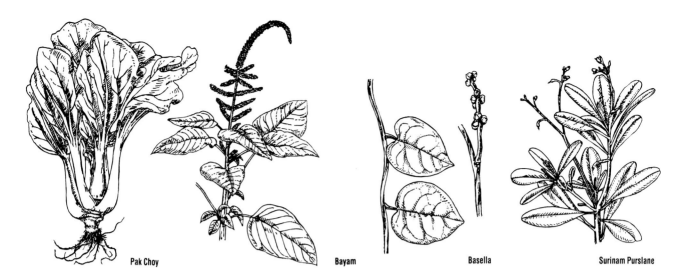

Pak Choy   Bayam   Basella   Surinam Purslane

long, dense head of crinkled leaves with very broad white stalks.)

Indian Spinach
(Bayam, *Amaranthus hybridus*)

Several kinds of Bayam are available, the commonest being a rather short plant with large green leaves. This makes a good substitute for Spinach. Locally produced seeds are quite satisfactory and may be obtained from growers. A few plants should be kept for seed which is produced abundantly.

The plants need handling in much the same way as Lettuces, and are mature in about a month. Regular manuring is essential. The seedlings are very small and need very careful handling, especially in rainy weather. When once well started in growth, the plants are quite vigorous.

The tall red- and green-leafed Bayams have thick stems which are excellent and very tender when young (eaten like Asparagus), though the leaves are not as good as those of the green-leafed Bayam. Some of the small-leafed kinds have a better flavour than the large-leafed kinds but give a smaller yield and so are not generally grown for the market. Large Bayams may be cut back, the tops eaten, and the stock allowed to produce a second crop of shoots. The botanical name for Bayam is Amaranthus.

Climbing Spinach (*Basella alba*)

This is a climbing plant available in two forms, one of which has purple stems and leaf-stalks and the other having pale green stems and leaf-stalks. It is easily grown from seeds or cuttings and is perennial. The plants have succulent stems and thick, fleshy leaves which are cooked in the same way as Spinach but contain a great deal of mucilage which is disliked by some people.

Seeds are planted either in beds or boxes. In the latter case they should be transplanted when they are 5–6 cm high and spaced 30 cm apart in two rows in each bed. Supports are needed for the long stems and leaves may be plucked after about one month from planting. Harvesting can continue for as long as the plants remain in good condition.

Water Convolvulus
(Kangkung, *Ipomoea aquatica*)

This is an excellent green vegetable and is very easy to grow. There are two kinds, one grown in water and one in ordinary vegetable beds. The latter is usually considered superior. Seeds of this are available always from Chinese seed merchants.

The beds must be well manured before planting. Seeds may be broadcast or sown in rows, and are thinned out as required. The plants soon make a trailing mat all over the bed. The first crop of young shoots is taken about three weeks from planting, and other crops later until the plants become weak. Plenty of watering is required in dry weather. The plants will flower and produce seeds in the lowlands. They may also be grown from cuttings.

Watercress (*Nasturtium officinale*)

This salad vegetable is easily grown from seeds or cuttings and is easily maintained. Seeds are not always available but if a bunch of stems are bought in the market, they can be used as cuttings and will root quite well. The plants require a sheltered place and plenty of water. Application of liquid manure (groundnut cake or artificials) once a month promotes vigorous growth.

Surinam Purslane (*Talinum triangulare*)

This green crop is of relatively recent introduction to Malaysia and makes a pleasant vegetable as well as being easy to cultivate. Plants are most easily grown from cuttings about 15 cm long; these root quickly, but should be shaded for a week after planting. They are best spaced about 30 cm apart. When the plants are about 50 cm high, the leafy shoots are cut off and both stems and leaves used as a vegetable.

The plants will soon produce new shoots which can be used in the same way. If shoots are cut very often the plants will need renewing about every six months; this can be managed by taking fresh cuttings.

Gardeners wishing to grow this vegetable can buy a bunch of leafy stems from the market, where they are often available now, and these can be used as cuttings to produce the first crop. If the shoots are not harvested the plants will flower freely and produce large numbers of tiny pink flowers with very slender stalks in quite large and much branched inflorescences. Almost every flower will produce seeds and these can be used for propagation, but the seedlings are a little slow in growth and need to grow for a long time before harvesting can be started. Propagation from cuttings is quicker and cutting can be done much earlier.

The plants will grow well in full sun but will tolerate a little light shade for part of the day. They can be grown on their own or used in a mixed border of ornamental plants, or they may be grown in pots and troughs, provided the soil is well drained. There is a form with variegated leaves which is used as an ornamental but there is no reason why it should not be used as a vegetable also. It needs exactly the same treatment as the normal form.

Roselle (*Hibiscus sabdariffa*)

This is not a common vegetable but is worth a place in a small garden. The plant is a shrub which will grow to about 2 m in height but can be kept to any convenient size by pruning. Young shoots are sometimes available in the market and these provide the easiest method of getting propagating material. The shoots are used as cuttings and are treated in the same way as the Hibiscus which is grown as a hedge plant.

The plants have red stems and leaf-stalks and the leaves are deeply lobed. Branching should be encouraged by pruning and when the plants are about 1 m high, harvesting can begin. Only the youngest shoots are used and of course, as these are removed, new shoots will develop. The young leaves and stems can be eaten raw or cooked as a vegetable, or used to make an excellent sour soup. If the stems are allowed to continue growing they will eventually produce flowers and fruit and the latter can be used for making jam. As a vegetable, the flavour is very similar to that of Rhubarb.

Daun Kesom (*Polygonum*)

This is an easily grown plant and the leaves are an excellent addition to salads and rice dishes. Bunches of stems are nearly always available in the market and can be used as cuttings to produce the first crop. Growing conditions and treatment are the same as for Watercress and if cutting is not too frequent the plants will continue growing for a long time. Should they become weak, replacement is easy by planting more cuttings. The plants appreciate a moist soil and can be planted beside a pond or small stream if these are available.

Spices and Flavourings

Many gardeners would like to grow their own spices and as these are usually used in small quantities there is generally no need for many plants. One or two plants may be sufficient and these can be grown in pots or troughs in the minimum of space. Alternatively, a collection of spice plants could be grown together in one garden bed as long as suitable growing conditions can be provided for each. With good soil and regular applications of fertilizer, the plants should last for a long time and the gardener will have the satisfaction of being able to gather fresh material whenever it is needed.

Chilli (*Capsicum annuum*)

The fruit of this plant is probably the most commonly used flavouring for food in the tropics. In Malaysia the price of Chillies varies considerably throughout the year and it would be of some advantage, therefore, to grow a few plants so that a supply of fresh material is available at all times.

There are a large number of forms which differ in the position, shape and size of the fruits; these may be pendent or erect, and round, oval or cylindrical in shape. They also differ a great deal in pungency though it is possible that weather conditions may have some effect on this and when it is very wet there appears to be, sometimes, very little pungency. Some varieties, such as the Sweet Pepper or Paprika, lack pungency naturally and are grown for the plain flavour of the fruits. In all forms, the fruits are bright red when ripe and are used either fresh or dried. Cayenne pepper is the powder obtained by grinding dried Chilli fruits.

The plants can be grown from seeds in pots, troughs or in a garden bed. If seedlings are transplanted, branching will be encouraged. If this does not occur, the main shoot should be pinched out to ensure the development of several branches. The soil must be well drained as waterlogging will stop growth and cause leaf fall. The first fruits should be ripe in about two or three months after transplanting.

When space is very limited, Chillies can be

grown in pots but the drainage must be good and the plants will need regular application of fertilizer. They will then fruit for many weeks and if planting is done in succession, a continuous supply of fruits can be obtained. When grown in pots it is wise to use burnt earth or sterilized soil in order to prevent infection by viral diseases which cause leaf curl and distortion. Chillies are very prone to these diseases so infected plants should be burnt and new ones raised in fresh burnt earth. The viruses are transmitted by Thrips so spraying to control these pests may help to prevent infection.

Too much rain may cause rotting of the fruits before they are ripe and often great damage is done to young fruits by insects. Fruit may be picked for about three months or longer, especially from plants grown in a raised bed, and if a few fruits are saved they will provide an adequate supply of seed for a new crop.

Chilli Padi (*Capsicum frutescens*)

This is a perennial plant with small conical fruits which are erect and borne in small clusters on the branches. They are exceedingly pungent and should be used with caution by those who are not used to chilli pungency. Cultivation is the same as for *C. annuum* but these plants will continue to produce fruit for two years or more. One or two plants would supply the entire needs for a family and can be grown in an odd, unused corner of the garden.

Sweet Pepper or Paprika (*C. annuum var. grossum*)

This plant will grow in the lowlands but is more vigorous in the highlands and more fruits are produced there. Few branches are developed and consequently only a few fruits can be gathered from a single plant. In the lowlands these plants are best grown in large pots or troughs where the watering can be controlled.

Coriander (*Coriandrum sativum*, Ketumbar)

The small round fruits of this plant are one of the most commonly used spices in the tropics and the young seedlings are used also as flavouring in many dishes, both cooked and raw. The fruits are always available in the market because they are ground to form the main ingredient of curry powder. These fruits can be used for growing but germination may be slow. They can be grown quite well in raised beds that give good drainage and need a little protection from rain, especially when the fruits begin to ripen. At this stage, when most of the fruits are ready for harvest, the plants can be allowed to dry out completely. If seedlings are

Ocimum canum

needed for fresh consumption they should be grown until they have about five or six leaves and are about 10–15 cm high. It would not be possible to produce enough fruits for grinding for one family, but seedlings could be produced in sufficient quantity quite easily for family use. When grown for seed, gardeners should note that the kind of leaves produced on the flowering stem is quite different in appearance from those found in the seedlings.

Celery (*Apium graveolens*)

When Coriander seedlings are not available, it is possible to use Celery seedlings as a substitute as both plants belong to the same family, though the flavour will be slightly different. Imported Celery seeds are usually available and will germinate easily; the seedlings are used in exactly the same way as Coriander seedlings. In the lowlands, Celery will not grow to any great size, but this is of no consequence if only seedlings are required.

Basil (*Ocimum canum*, Biji Selasih)

This is a small, bushy plant needing little attention or space. It is grown for the leaves which are used for flavouring. Large numbers of flowers are also produced and these give a good supply of seed which can be used for propagation if necessary.

Another species of Basil (*Ocimum basilicum*) is an easily grown herb which can be used as an ornamental as well as for the normal culinary uses. The leaves are the parts used in cooking and one variety has purple stems and leaves although the flavour is exactly the same as the normal form.

Packeted seeds are usually available and the

Ipomoea aquatica

Nicolaia speciosa

Ocimum (Purple-leaf Basil)

plants can be grown in pots, troughs, or in a bed, provided the soil is well drained. Plants grow best under slightly dry conditions and although they are annuals, can be kept growing quite well for more than a year. If they are allowed to flower, seed will be produced and can be used to raise new stock. Full sun and a little application of fertilizer are required and light pruning will encourage the growth of young leafy shoots. If the leaves are moved a very pleasant aromatic scent is produced and this could be an added attraction if the plants were grown in pots or troughs near the house or in a flat.

Mint (*Mentha spicata*)

This herb is grown in many parts of the world and is always available in local markets. If a small bunch of leafy stems is bought in the market they can be rooted in water or planted directly in a pot as cuttings. As soon as they have sufficient roots they should be planted out in a lightly shaded position in well dug soil which has had some good compost mixed with it. Plants may be grown in large pots and will need replanting each year, but if they are planted in a bed replanting need not be done for a longer period, and only when the plants are showing signs of less vigorous growth.

Mint produces long underground stems which may need to be controlled. This can be done by sinking thin wooden planks or galvanized iron sheet, about 15 cm wide, into the ground vertically around the plants. This should contain the underground stems effectively.

Parsley (*Petroselinum crispum*)

A plant which is not always available in markets but which is easy to grow from seed. It is best grown in pots or boxes so that watering can be controlled easily and drainage is good. Packets of seeds are available from many dealers and are slow to germinate, but once the plants are established they can be kept growing well for many months.

If flower stalks begin to appear, they should be removed to encourage the production of more leaves. When leaves are needed, they should be cut off with scissors or a sharp knife and not pulled away from the plant. Pulling may cause damage to the stem so that disease organisms enter and the plants die very quickly. The plants are best grown in a little light shade or at the side of a house where they receive a little sunshine for part of the day only.

Coleus (*Coleus amboinicus*)

This is a perennial plant with thick, stiff, fleshy leaves which are very aromatic when rubbed between the fingers. It is easily grown from cuttings but needs a fairly dry, sunny position and does well in pots or troughs, provided it receives a little artificial fertilizer regularly. The leaves are light green and attractive and a bushy plant is very decorative; it could quite well be used in a bed of ornamental plants. The leaves can be used as a substitute for Sage.

Chives (*Allium schoenoprasum*)

Although this plant is widely grown in many parts of the world, it is not commonly seen in the lowland tropics, but it can be grown quite easily in pots or troughs which should have a little light shade for part of each day. It will eventually form a small dense clump of dark green leaves and at about 10 cm below the surface of the soil there will be very small bulbs. Only the tips of the leaves are used and, provided the plants are not overwatered, they can be kept growing indefinitely. When the clumps of leaves become too dense, they can be split up and replanted. These plants make much stronger growth in the highlands.

Chinese Chives (*Allium tuberosum*, Kuchai)

Leaves and flower buds of this plant are always on sale in the market and one or two clumps in the garden would supply the requirements of a family indefinitely.

For propagating, a small group of complete shoots is necessary and this may be obtained from growers as the material seen in the market will not have the basal part of the shoot and cannot therefore be used for propagation. Well dug soil with some compost mixed into it is suitable and the plants will soon develop into a large clump. When well established, flower heads will also be produced. Little care is needed except for a little application of fertilizer at long intervals and watering during dry spells.

Garlic (*Allium sativum*)

Small plants are easy to grow from bulbs in a well drained bed or even in a trough. After several of the flat leaves have been produced, a small bulb will begin to form at the base of the plant. The whole plant can be used as a vegetable at this stage and if the bulb becomes sufficiently large, it could be encouraged to ripen by cutting down the water supply; when the leaves begin to turn yellow, the plants can be lifted and dried off. The bulbs can then be used in the usual way. It is unlikely that large bulbs would be produced in the lowlands but better success might be obtained in the highlands.

Three members of the Ginger family can also be grown in a small garden and to a small extent in large pots. These are Turmeric, Ginger and Languas.

Languas (*Languas galanga*)

The fresh rhizomes of this plant are always available in the market as it is used such a great deal for flavouring in local food. It is, however, very easy to grow and when well developed forms a large clump of leafy stems up to 1–1½ m in height. Rather small white or cream flowers are produced at the tops of many of the stems and these have some decorative value so that the plant could be included in a mixed border of ornamentals, if space is very limited.

The plants will grow equally well in light shade or full sun, but in the latter case the leaves may become a little yellowish. Young plants are best left undisturbed until at least ten stems have been produced so that the underground rhizomes will have made sufficient growth before harvesting can begin. As the rhizomes become older, they are very hard and if the ground is dry, it can be difficult to remove pieces for use.

Ginger (*Zingiber officinalis*, Halia)

Fresh rhizomes of this plant are always available in the market and provide a convenient and easy method of propagation. Ginger is best grown on a raised bed which has been well dug and has had a quantity of well rotted compost mixed with the soil. Small pieces of the rhizome are planted about 30–50 cm apart and each will produce a small group of leafy stems which are about 30–40 cm high. New rhizomes will be produced underground and these will be ready for harvest in about eight or nine months. The plants need watering in dry weather and are usually grown in full sun, but they will tolerate a little shade for part of each day. Good drainage is essential.

Turmeric (*Curcuma domestica*, Kunyit)

This plant is also grown from pieces of rhizome which can be bought initially from the market. These rhizomes are small and when cut open are bright orange. They are used for the flavour and colour and when powdered are used also as a substitute for the more expensive saffron.

The growing requirements are the same as for Ginger. The plants flower frequently and the inflorescences are eaten raw in salads or they can be used for flavouring; the leaves are also used for flavouring. As the rhizomes are comparatively small, it is possible to grow one or two plants of Turmeric in a large pot where drainage should be good. A little fertilizer applied at regular intervals keeps the plants in good condition when grown in this way.

Lemon Grass (*Cymbopogon citratus*, Serai)

The young shoots of this plant are used in many dishes and the plants are easy to grow as they need little attention. One or two plants can be grown quite easily in odd, unused places in the garden, or in a mixed herb bed. The shoots bought in the market will be satisfactory as planting material, provided the basal portion is undamaged, because it will then be able to produce roots very quickly. Small plants can be grown in pots but will not become as large as those grown in the ground.

The soil should be well dug and the plants should not be allowed to dry out before they are established. New shoots will appear quickly and eventually a dense clump of stems will be formed. Cutting should not be too frequent until the clump has reached a good size. When cutting pieces for the kitchen, some soil will have to be removed from the base of the plant as the basal part of the stems is just below the soil surface. As soon as the stems are removed, the soil should be replaced and the plant will respond by producing more shoots within a very short time.

Drumsticks (*Moringa oleifera*)

This small tree has much-divided pale green leaves and white flowers which resemble Bean flowers. Long, cylindrical pods are produced which are used for cooking while they are still young and green as they are very hard and fibrous when they become older. Propagation is by means of seeds or cuttings and the latter may be up to 1½ m long.

The tree gives light shade and if not pruned it will become straggly and will also grow too high for easy harvesting of the fruits. Fruits are produced three or four times each year and the plants are partly deciduous. After a dry spell the tree may lose all its leaves, but when rain is more frequent, the older leaves will fall, leaving some of the younger ones near the tips of the twigs. New leaves develop very quickly and flowers appear at the same time. The young leaves can be used as a vegetable and the roots as a substitute for Horseradish in European cooking, although the flavour is not as good.

The tree can be kept to about 2–3 m in height by pruning and this will make it bushy in appearance. It will grow in most kinds of soil and little, if any, preparation is needed, so that only a small space is necessary. If flowering shrubs were used to conceal the trunk it could be part of an ornamental display. The fruits are dark brown or black when ripe and as they are produced in large clusters, the tree can look unsightly. Old, unused fruits should, therefore, be removed when pruning is done.

Kantan
(*Nicolaia speciosa*, formerly Phaeomeria)

These are large plants belonging to the Ginger family and can be used as part of an ornamental scheme. They grow best in light shade but will tolerate full sun for part of the day. The leafy stems grow to 2–3 m in height, so that these plants are not suitable for the smallest gardens.

Flowering heads are produced on separate stalks from ground level and when young are eaten raw in salads, but if allowed to mature they make excellent floral decoration. Propagation is by means of pieces of rhizome bearing two or three leafy shoots. The shoots should be cut short before planting and the soil should be well dug and mixed with compost beforehand.

14 FRUITS AND FRUIT TREES

Many local fruit trees are large, and there is hardly room for them in a small garden, but a few fruit trees could be used for screening or shade instead of ornamental trees. Thus, while it is recognised that fruit growing in most gardens is necessarily limited, probably all gardeners want to know something about fruit trees, if only for the reason that they may have inherited an old garden with such trees in it.

Fruits tree vary in habit and the kinds a gardener may plant will depend on the site available. Durian trees are unsuitable for any but quite large gardens. Mangosteens are small but very spreading trees, giving dense shade; they are also slow in growth and not suitable where quick screening is desired. Guavas are light and open, giving little screening. Avocado Pears must have a really good soil that is not inclined to remain wet after rain. Considerations of this kind are mentioned below under each kind of tree. In general, all fruit trees need a fairly open place, and they naturally need good soil to produce good growth. Like all trees, their roots spread some distance from the trunk, often far beyond the spread of the crown, and they may be troublesome to nearby flower beds.

The next point to remember is that only good varieties of fruit trees should be planted. In the chapter on propagation it is explained that by the use of cuttings, marcots or budding we can propagate plants vegetatively, so that the resulting plants are all identical with the parent plant; they are in fact part of it. But seeds are produced by the union of two cells, often from different plants, and the resulting seedlings are frequently not alike. Therefore, seedlings from a good fruit tree are not all as good as their parent. There are only too many inferior varieties of such fruits as Rambutan, which may become crossed with poor varieties growing in their neighbourhood, and the danger of raising inferior seedlings is a real one; it is the more dangerous that we do not discover our mistake until, after several years, the seedling tree begins to fruit. Therefore, the only safe method is to plant budded or marcotted trees derived from known good varieties.

Budding material can be obtained from trees known to the gardener and used on stocks raised by himself, or branches of these trees can be marcotted. If plants must be bought, they should be obtained from a nursery garden which specializes in fruit tree production and is known to be reliable. There are a few cases, such as Mangosteen, in which budding and marcotting are both extremely difficult, and then we have no alternative but to use seeds. Fortunately, in the case of Mangosteens, there seems to be little variation between seedlings.

Fruits grown in Malaysia vary much in quality. Some are hardly more than local wild trees which have received little or no selection. Among these is admittedly the Mangosteen, one of the most delicious Malaysian fruits, but others cannot be classed as of high quality. These grade off into local wild trees with fruits that are edible but certainly not worth cultivating for their fruit. Thus, it is not easy to know just where to draw the line when selecting trees for inclusion here. Personal judgement is bound to affect the selection, and some readers may feel that scant justice has been done to some of the fruits. All of the more important local fruits are included, though some are only mentioned briefly.

Some fruit trees are seasonal in flowering and so in fruiting, while others bear continuously. The latter are naturally the more useful in a garden, but the seasonal fruits include the more characteristic local kinds, such as Durians and Mangosteens. These are dependent on dry weather which stimulates them to flower. In those parts of Malaysia which have a regular dry season, even if it is not a long one, fruiting is regular; but, especially in the south, dry weather is very uncertain and fruiting is consequently irregular. In Singapore, there tend to be two main fruit seasons, about the middle and the end of the year, and sometimes one, sometimes the other, is the more prolific; and sometimes there is an interval of eighteen months or even two years between one good Durian or Mangosteen crop and the next. Rambutans appear to respond to a less pronounced drought, and so their fruiting is more frequent, some varieties giving two crops in a year. Further north in Malaysia where there is a more marked change in season, the fruit trees are more regular in their cropping and usually the mid-year crop is the largest. Some kinds of fruit trees may give reasonable crops each year, but others may give an outstanding crop at intervals of about five years with smaller crops in the intervening years. Some kinds of fruit trees give a good crop every two years with very little yield at other times and some Mango varieties show this behaviour. Weather conditions at critical times of the year can vary a great deal in different parts of the country, and may affect flower and fruit production considerably.

Other fruit-bearing plants are not trees but it is convenient to include them here. They are Pineapple, Passion fruit, and Banana. Papaya and some bushy plants such as Lime are also hardly trees. The following pages include brief descriptions of all fruit-bearing plants. Further information about all of them will be found in Burkill's *Dictionary of the Economic Products of the Malay Peninsula*, and in Corner's *Wayside Trees of Malaya*.

Annona Family

The name Annona is of South American origin, and a variation of the name is still used for two of the three fruit trees commonly grown in Malaysia. The three are Soursop (*Annona muricata*, Durian Belanda), Sweet Sop (*Annona squamosa*, Nona Sri Kaya) and Custard Apple or Bullock's Heart (*Annona reticulata*, Nona Kapri). The first two are common throughout Malaysia, the third chiefly on the east coast of the peninsula. In all three, the fruit is fairly large, containing a soft pulp with many black seeds embedded in it. All are small trees with open branching, and grow best in a sunny place with good, well-drained soil. They flower and fruit throughout the year.

Probably the easiest to grow and the most prolific in fruiting is the Soursop, which often has very large fruits. These are dark green, roughly oval fruits, though they can be irregular in shape, with soft spines over the surface and may weigh ½–2 kg. In poor varieties, the pulp may contain a large amount of fibrous tissue, but good varieties lack this and are excellent served fresh and chilled. The pulp can also be used for flavouring ices and drinks, and loses little flavour after cooking.

The Sweet Sop is a much smaller tree, often hardly more than a bush, with smaller fruits, containing a very sweet, fragrant pulp. If not well grown, the fruits are small with little flesh and many seeds so that they are not really worth any attention. The Custard Apple is deciduous, for which reason it is only suited to

the more seasonal parts of the country. This tree also, if not well grown, gives poor fruits with little flesh.

Both the Soursop and the Sweet Sop (also called the Sugar Apple) are very liable to attack by mealy bugs, brought by ants. Constant watching for this attack, and spraying with kerosene emulsion or a suitable insecticide, are necessary to obtain good fruits. As noted above, a good, deep soil and regular manuring are also needed to keep the trees healthy. The trees are not ornamental and can be rather irregular in shape, so that they should be placed in some part of the garden where they are less visible.

The trees can be grown from seeds quite easily, but are best propagated vegetatively, by marcotting, to maintain good varieties.

Avocado Pear (*Persea americana*)

This is a tropical American fruit of the Laurel family, which is not in common cultivation in Malaysia. It has large fruits, almost round to pear-shaped, purple or green when ripe, with a single large seed surrounded by firm flesh which contains much fat and has a high food value. It is not a sweet fruit and may be eaten fresh with various seasonings, in salads, or in cold soups and sauces. If cooked it loses some of its flavour, so care is needed.

In America, a large number of varieties of Avocado have been produced. Those suited to Southern California are not successful in Malaysia. A few West Indian varieties have been tried, but there is need for more trials and breeding work should be done to try and produce varieties well suited to our uniform climate. A few imported varieties have been proved to fruit well in Malaysia and these have been propagated by budding on to seedling stocks, but unfortunately they are not commonly available. Seeds are easy to germinate, and the plants attain fruiting size in about six years; but all are hybrids, and it is not certain therefore that seedlings from a freely fruiting tree will be as successful as their parent. It is far better to do your own budding or try and buy budded trees.

Avocado trees when well grown will reach 10 m or more in height, and are of a good bushy shape. The foliage of most kinds is a rather yellowish green. The trees are not particularly handsome, but have quite a pleasant

Persea americana

Persea americana (Avocado)

Persea americana (Avocado)

Breadfruit (*Artocarpus altilis*)

Averrhoa bilimbi

Averrhoa bilimbi

Artocarpus altilis (Breadfruit)

Artocarpus altilis (Breadfruit)

Averrhoa carambola (Starfruit)

aspect when well grown. They will not stand wet ground or ground that holds water for long after rain. Good, deep, well drained soil and an open situation are necessary. It pays to cultivate and manure the trees regularly. They do not appear to have any serious pests. The best kinds fruit quite heavily about once a year in the lowlands.

Banana (Musa)

Bananas are an important local food crop, and easy to grow. They have certain drawbacks in the home garden, and probably are best produced in small· orchards; but if there is room, the householder may wish to plant one or two clumps. Each clump produces a large bunch of fruits at intervals of a few months; but the fruits do not keep long, and in a small household, a whole bunch can hardly be consumed while it remains in good condition.

There are many varieties of Banana in Malaysia. Most of them are good for eating raw, but a few are not sweet and only useful for cooking. The best of the former are the common Banana (Pisang Embun, identical with the Gros Michel which is grown for export in the West Indies), the small golden Banana (Pisang Mas), the red Banana (Pisang Raja Udang) and a yellow Banana known as Pisang Rajah. There are other kinds which are slightly acid when ripe and break away at the stalk very easily, a common one being Pisang Rastali. These are very pleasant to eat but must be fully ripe, when the breaking of the stalks makes them troublesome to handle.

Bananas are propagated from the suckers which grow around the base of old plants. The ground should be well dug and mixed with compost, and the suckers planted about 2½ m apart. When they are well started in growth they should be manured, and when they have attained a good size, a heap of garden refuse, mixed with manure, may be put around each plant. As the plants grow, they in turn produce suckers at the base. Too many suckers will not grow successfully together and it is best to select the strongest one every four months or so, removing the others, which may if desired be used for propagation. This means that the plant will have three stems at any one time: one which will be about to produce a flowering stem and then fruit; one which is half grown and one which is just starting into growth from the sucker stage.

The oldest stem will carry a crown of four to eight very large leaves which will be torn into strips in windy areas, although this does not decrease their efficiency. The stem of the Banana plant is actually made up of a number of leaf-stalks and leaf sheaths which enclose each other. This is very clearly seen when a Banana stem is cut down. At about a year

Chiku

Jackfruit

Artocarpus heterophyllus

after planting, the original sucker will produce a flowering stem and subsequently a bunch of fruit. The flowering stem pushes its way up through the leaf bases and then appears at the apex of the plant between the leaf blades. At first, it is erect, but very quickly it will bend over to one side. The first flowers are all female ones and are the ones which will form fruit. They are in groups, each protected by a large, boat-shaped structure called a bract. Several groups of female flowers are produced and then there is a sudden change and all subsequent flowers are male. The terminal bud with its male flowers protected by the bract is often sold in the market as it can be used as a vegetable. The fruits develop in groups on the stem and each group is called a hand; individual Bananas in a hand are called fingers.

After fruiting, the stem is no longer productive and is cut down to the ground. The leaves may be used as plates and the stem portion can be used as pig food. Part of the stem is also used by batik printers on the tables used for printing the fabrics. When the old stem has been removed, the base of the plant is mounded up again with garden refuse and manure, and the next sucker will soon reach the fruiting stage. If a proper succession of suckers is maintained, they will fruit in turn at intervals of a few months, and the clump will remain productive for about five years. After this, it is better to uproot it and start with a new sucker. The bases of the plants should be kept free of grass and weeds and the dressing of compost will help to do this.

Belimbing (*Averrhoa bilimbi*) and Carambola (*Averrhoa carambola*)

These common fruit trees are both members of the Wood-Sorrel family (Oxalidaceae) and are quite distinct from each other in appearance.

Belimbing or Belimbing Asam is a small tree which usually has an open crown but in very old plants it can become quite dense. The pinnate leaves are light green or yellowish green and often crowded near the ends of the branches, giving the tree a very characteristic appearance. The flowers develop in short inflorescences on the older, bare parts of the branches and also on the tree trunk. Fruits resemble small cucumbers and are 5–10 cm long. They are smooth-skinned and yellowish green when ripe, with very juicy, but extremely sour, pulp. These fruits make an excellent substitute for gherkins when pickled and are very good in chutneys and curries. The juice can be used to remove stains from cloth. There appear to be no well marked varieties in Malaysia and for good growth the tree prefers an open, sunny place which is well drained. It is propagated by marcotting and fruits are produced throughout the year.

Carambola or Belimbing Manis is a small tree up to 7 m high, with an oval crown of dark green pinnate leaves which are much shorter than in the last species. The small, purplish-pink flowers are borne in branched inflorescences on the twigs between the leaves. There are a number of varieties, some having sour fruit and others having sweet fruit. The size of the fruit also shows great variation, ranging from 10 cm to 20 cm in length. It is distinctive in appearance as it has a smooth skin with a waxy appearance and five broad, deep grooves running longitudinally the whole length of the fruit, so that, when cut in half, it has the appearance of a star and is sometimes called Starfruit.

Good varieties are propagated by marcotting and the fruits need to be covered with paper, very often until they ripen, to protect them from the attack of fruit flies which can be extremely troublesome. The fruits are eaten raw or cooked in a variety of ways; they can also be used for flavouring soft drinks and salads. The juice of this species can also be used for cleaning metal surfaces and for removing stains from cloth. The tree is suitable for a small garden and is attractive as well as useful. It would make a good subject for bonsai culture. The plant needs full sun and good, well drained soil.

Brazil Nut (*Bertholettia excelsa*)

A full-grown Brazil Nut tree may be 25–30 m high, with a broad, oval crown and slightly drooping branches. It has large, drooping, dark green, shiny leaves which become red before they fall. The trees are far too large for a small garden but could be grown in a larger one, and a group of them used in the landscaping of a park are magnificent.

Yellow flowers are produced in large inflorescences over the top of the tree crown and as they need to be cross-pollinated before fruits develop, the trees should be planted in groups. Single trees will not, as a rule, produce any fruit. Plants can be grown from seed but germination may be very slow. They will begin to bear fruit when they are about eight years old and the fruits take about one year to reach maturity. Fruits have a very thick, woody covering and are very heavy, so trees should not be planted near public pathways as falling fruit could cause serious injury.

Breadfruit and its Allies (genus Artocarpus)

The fruits of these trees are, in actual fact, whole inflorescences. They are therefore made up of many small fruits fused together to give one large structure. In Malaysia, there are some twenty species, several of which have edible fruits, but the principle cultivated trees are the Breadfruit, the Jackfruit and the Chempedak.

Breadfruit (Sukun, *Artocarpus altilis*)

This is a medium-sized tree up to 10–15 m in height. It has very dark green, shiny leaves which are deeply lobed and look most decorative. The veins are light green and stand out in sharp contrast to the dark leaf blade. It has long club-shaped male inflorescences and large round fruit.

There are several varieties known and the one most usually grown here is seedless with smooth fruits. The flesh is white, and when baked or boiled has somewhat the texture of potato. This variety must be propagated vegetatively from root suckers or root cuttings because no seeds are available.

The seeds of seed-bearing varieties can be cooked and eaten. As a garden tree, it is interesting and handsome when well grown and leafy; in Malaysia it is partly deciduous and although some leaves drop, a few are retained and the crown can look somewhat thin at this time. It fruits about twice a year. Because of the open branching, it cannot be used for screening, but makes an interesting plant when grown singly or to provide an interesting contrast of foliage in a group of trees. It does not like wet clay soil, but in a medium soil grows well with little attention.

Jackfruit
(Nangka, *Artocarpus heterophyllus*)

An evergreen medium-sized tree growing to 20 m high, with much smaller, dark green, shiny leaves which are slightly lobed in seedlings; in older plants, all the leaves are entire with smooth margins. Young trees are shapely and quick-growing but can become a little untidy in appearance when they are older. The fruits are developed on the trunk and main branches and are sometimes very large; they may indeed be one of the largest fruits in the world. They are produced almost throughout the year and need to be covered with paper or other suitable material while developing, to prevent damage from insect or animal pests. The fruits are covered with small prickles and contain very large seeds embedded in firm, fleshy pulp. There are a number of varieties which differ in the firmness of the pulp, its juiciness, thickness and flavour. Good varieties have crisp, sweet pulp which is refreshing to eat, especially when chilled.

Chempedak (*Artocarpus champeden*)

The Chempedak is also an evergreen tree up to 20 m high, with small, dark green, shiny leaves and stiff brown hairs on the twigs, leaf and flower stalks. It is not really suitable for small gardens, but its size can be controlled by a little careful pruning. The fruits develop on the trunk and main branches, often in considerable quantity. The fruits are smaller than those of Jackfruit and may be up to 40 cm long. They are yellow or pale brown when ripe, somewhat cylindrical in shape, and the rind is covered with very many small, cone-shaped mounds, each having a dark tip. These fruits have a very strong smell when ripe and the central core can be removed easily. The pulp is remarkably sweet in some varieties but there are poor forms and these are not worth having in the garden. The seeds can be cooked and eaten and the fruit can be used in the same way as Jackfruit.

Propagation is best done vegetatively when a good variety is available but seeds can be used and germinate easily. The trees are a little slow in growth, require little attention, and are seasonal in fruiting.

Chiku (*Manilkara zapota*, formerly *Achras zapota*)

This is one of the best fruits for garden planting in the tropics as it fruits almost continuously throughout the year and is suitable for small gardens. It is a slow-growing evergreen tree which can eventually reach 10 m or more if unpruned. The crown is dense and the tree provides good shade, so it should not be planted too near the house.

The fruits are 5–8 cm long, oval in shape with pinkish or whitish brown flesh, in which three to six seeds are embedded, and have a thin brown skin. There are a number of varieties and the better ones are best propagated by marcotting. Seeds germinate easily but the seedlings are slow in growth and take a long time to begin fruiting. Marcotted plants will begin fruiting in two or three years. The trees need full sun, good soil and manuring every six months. While they are young, the surrounding ground may be used for vegetables or some other small plants, the cultivation and manuring of which will benefit the Chiku tree.

Citrus Family

The finest of the Citrus fruits are suited to a drier and more seasonal climate than that of the wet tropics, but a number of kinds can be grown successfully in the lowlands, and more at the hill stations. Some experimental work has been done in Malaysia, especially in the hills, but more is needed in the matter of introducing new varieties, propagation and breeding. All Citrus trees need manuring, especially with phosphate, but too much nitrogen should be avoided as it is bad for them.

All Citrus species are evergreen and many of them are thorny. They are small shrubs although some of them can grow into small trees. All of them, when damaged, give off a

Musk lime (*Citrus madurensis*)

Sweet orange (*Citrus sinensis*)

and watering are important when grown in pots, but overwatering must be avoided. The leaves can be 2–6 cm long and the fruits are about 2–4 cm in diameter, always soft, and become pale yellowish orange when ripe. They have a thin skin, and contain a number of large seeds, but are very juicy and have a distinct flavour and scent. The fruits have a number of uses in the kitchen and also make the most pleasant drinks with a characteristic flavour.

When grown in pots, the plants must not be allowed to dry out completely, otherwise the leaves will drop, so regular watering is necessary and a good, well drained potting compost should be used. A mulch of compost can be placed on the surface of the soil in the pot, but it should be kept 2–3 cm away from the stem of the plant. This will ensure that the stem remains dry at the base and will be less liable to attack by disease organisms than if it were continuously moist. The mulch of compost keeps the soil surface cool and prevents too much loss of water while at the same time it gradually decays, providing some nutrients for the plant.

Full sun is needed and regular application of a balanced artificial fertilizer will help to keep the plant leafy and assist in the production of good-sized fruits. In pots, the plants will shape themselves and the only pruning needed will be to remove any dead twigs. To prevent water from gathering underneath the pot and in its lower part, it can be placed on a small quantity of gravel or on two bricks and the water can drain away easily. The pots are best kept away from the wall of the house as they can become too hot in the middle of the day.

Common Lime (Limau Asam, Limau Nipis, *Citrus aurantifolia*)

All of the Limes are more suited to tropical conditions than any other Citrus fruit, and so are among the easiest to grow. They will grow into large bushes or small trees and need full sun, good soil and regular manuring. There are a number of different forms of the common Lime, the best having thin skins and very juicy flesh, while the poorer forms have thick skins and rather dry pulp. The better forms can be propagated by marcotting and this is essential in order to secure free-fruiting varieties.

The leaves on this plant can be up to 8 cm long and have a narrow wing on each side of the stalks. The fruits are round, with smooth or slightly rough skin and are usually green when bought in the market. If kept for some time, they will ripen and become yellow or pale orange. The number of seeds in each fruit and the amount and flavour of the pulp is variable. Although seeds germinate easily, it is not wise to use them for propagation as the plants do not come true from seed.

strong aromatic smell. The flowers are usually white and have a very sweet smell and the fruits of the different kinds vary considerably in size, thickness of skin and amount and flavour of juice. Several kinds can be grown in pots and when space is limited, the plants can be ornamental and useful at the same time.

Most Citrus trees of all kinds are liable to attack by scale insects, often carried by ants, especially on the young stems. A careful watch should be kept for these and a kerosene emulsion spray or other insecticide applied. Otherwise the chief pests are fruit flies, which lay their eggs in the young fruits. The most effective remedy is to burn all infected fruits and, if necessary, to bag each young fruit as it forms. This is especially necessary with Pomelos. Spraying with insecticide can be done but would need to be repeated after heavy rain.

Musk Lime (Limau Kesturi, *Citrus madurensis*)

This is a small shrub which can grow to 4 m in height when planted in the ground, but it can be grown successfully also in large pots and if well treated will flower and fruit at intervals throughout the year. Regular manuring

Pomelo (*Citrus maxima*)

Grapefruit (*Citrus* x *paradisi*)

Lemon (*Citrus limon*)

Green dwarf coconut

Fruits of green dwarf, yellow dwarf and
brown dwarf coconuts

The Italian Lime, with fruits shaped like a lemon, grows well and fruits continuously in the lowlands, and is well worth more frequent cultivation. It is a small bushy tree to 3 m high and there is a short thorn at the base of each leaf-stalk. The leaf-stalks have a narrow wing on each side. The fruits are usually about 10–13 cm long and oval with an uneven surface to the skin. They are green at first but become yellow as they ripen. There are a number of varieties and good ones should be propagated by marcotting. Cultivation is the same as for Limau Asam.

Orange (Limau Manis)

There are many kinds of oranges, thick and thin skinned, loose-skinned or otherwise, large and small. In the lowlands of Malaysia, three fruits normally classed as oranges may be grown. One is the Chinese sweet green orange (*Citrus sinensis*), which fruits fairly freely but needs considerable care in the matter of well drained soil, cultivation and manuring. The fruits are green turning yellowish when ripe, and have a thin, firmly adherent peel. The flesh is pale and very sweet. A loose-skinned orange is also grown, especially in Java; the fruits are yellowish green when ripe. They are rather watery, but have a pleasant taste and make a good drink. The third kind has a thin skin which is not loose, though quite easily peeled. It is also partly green when ripe, and has quite a pleasant flavour. All these oranges are better suited to a drier climate, so great care is necessary in handling them in the wet tropics. More breeding work is needed in order to obtain new forms which are better suited to the climate. As with all other Citrus fruits, marcots from good trees or grafted plants should always be planted, not seedlings.

The plants grow into small trees about 5 m high and in good specimens the crown is rounded but very often it becomes a little untidy in appearance, so the plant is best grown where it does not form part of the general garden scheme. The leaves do not have wings on the stalks and the fruits which are most frequently available have shiny skins which are green or green and yellow. Other forms with rougher skins are of more limited distribution and often more frequent in certain parts of the country only.

Pomelo (Limau Betawi, *Citrus maxima*)

This is the largest of Citrus fruits, and also makes the largest tree. A well grown Pomelo is 10 m or more high, very bushy, with a handsome, glossy, dark green foliage, and makes a good screening tree. It needs less attention as regards cultivation than the smaller Citrus trees but will repay care in this matter, fruiting continuously and freely.

The trees have some long thorns on the twigs and branches and the white flowers are strongly scented. The fruits are very large, ranging from 13 cm to 25 cm in diameter, and are pale green or pale yellow. The skin is smooth but varies considerably in thickness in different varieties and can be 1–3 cm thick. The flesh is semi-transparent, whitish, pink or very deep pink and the amount of juice is also variable. Many different varieties are available and there are also seedless forms which often have pink flesh. Poor forms are not worth growing as the skin is thick and the flesh quite dry with poor flavour. Good forms should be propagated by marcotting or budding.

Pomelo plants grow and fruit better where the climate is more seasonal. Fruit flies can be troublesome and young fruits may need to be covered with paper bags to protect them, although this may be difficult because of the thorns on the twigs.

Grapefruit (*Citrus x paradisi*)

Most of the Grapefruit offered for sale are imported but there are a few varieties grown in the country which are equal to, or better than, many of the imported fruit. Unfortunately, the plants grow best in the more northern parts of the country and production is limited. They can also be grown very successfully in the highlands. The best varieties have a thin skin and very juicy flesh. Thick-skinned forms always seem to have much drier flesh.

Lemon (*Citrus limon*)

One or two varieties of Lemon are grown in Malaysia but it does best where the climate is more seasonal. The large oval fruits have a raised apex and tend to remain green when ripe instead of becoming yellow. However, they are uncommon as they are not used a great deal in local cooking, in which Limes are used instead.

Coconut (Kelapa, *Cocos nucifera*)

One of the most common trees of the tropics and often grown in the smallest gardens (although it is really too big in such locations) because the fruits are used such a great deal in Southeast Asian cooking. There are tall and short forms and the latter may have green, yellow or orange fruit. Many varieties exist and all parts of the fruit are used for various purposes.

The palms are easily grown from seed and sometimes the fruits will begin to sprout before they drop from the tree. Fruits can be stored in a lightly shaded place until the first leaf and root appear through the husk. They can then be planted in a shallow hole in the soil without covering the new young shoot. In dry weather the young plant should be watered but when it is well established, with three or four leaves, watering can be discontinued. Regular manuring is necessary while the plant is young and after it has reached flowering stage, fertilizer should be applied about four times each year. In this way, flowers and fruits will be produced continuously throughout the year. But if the soil becomes poor, the number of fruits produced will be considerably reduced or may cease for several months.

The tall forms are only suitable for larger gardens and when they become too tall, harvesting is difficult unless one is very agile or has friends who can climb the trees. The dwarf forms are more suitable for small gardens and those with orange fruits are also very decorative. The fruits are smaller than the tall forms but usually two trees will keep a household well supplied with fruit for the kitchen. Young palms can take up a great deal of space until the stem has grown tall enough to raise the crown of leaves well above the ground.

Duku Family

The Duku (*Lansium domesticum*) and its close relative, the Langsat (*Lansium domesticum*), are among the best of the local fruits, though they are not very large. The Duku has a round fruit with rather thick skin; the Langsat fruit is smaller, oblong, with thinner skin. The Duku is the larger and more vigorous tree, attaining 17 m in height. Leaves of both kinds are compound with five to seven leaflets and the flowers are borne on drooping inflorescences on the older parts of the branches. In Langsat fruits, the skin contains a milky juice. Many of the fruits produce no seed but as there are a number of varieties it is better to plant marcotted or budded plants. The latter will fruit more quickly than seedlings which may take fifteen years before they come into bearing. Fruiting is seasonal, usually twice a year; but too much dry weather may result in one fruiting season only.

The Duku is a tree of good appearance and is excellent for shade; the Langsat is less satisfactory as the crown is much thinner. The trees are slow-growing and not suitable for small gardens.

The Sentul is another fruit of this family, but inferior in texture and flavour. There are two kinds, both being large, handsome trees up to 50 m high, and have been called the Red Sentul and the Yellow Sentul, but there are many varieties of each. The leaves are compound with three leaflets. In the Red Sentul they are velvety, but in the Yellow Sentul they are smooth. The fruits are almost round with a downy surface and faint longitudinal wrinkling, but in the Yellow Sentul the rind is thin and there is a thick layer of juicy flesh around the seeds. In the Red Sentul the rind is thick and there is very little flesh around the seeds. The trees are quick-growing but, because of their size, they are not suitable for small gardens. They make fine large avenue trees, being shapely and having a foliage of pleasant texture. It is likely that better forms could be obtained if some breeding work were done with these trees.

Durian (*Durio zibethinus*)

The Durian is the most renowned of all native Malaysian fruits and is commonly planted throughout the country, although it is not suitable for small gardens. Trees can be grown easily from seed and will begin fruiting in five to seven years, but it is possible to propagate by budding and for all good forms, this method should be used. Seedlings are not likely to produce fruits as good as those from the parent plant.

The trees are conical when young and if well grown have a dense crown, but as they become older the crown grows more open and irregular so that the general appearance is not so attractive. In a large garden, they can be grown successfully with a group of other trees and appear to prefer their roots to be shaded while the plants are young. Good, deeply cultivated soil is best for them and a little fertilizer application three or four times a year encourages good growth, especially before the plants begin to flower and fruit. The leaves are dull green but have a thin covering of scales, especially on the undersurfaces, and this gives them a shiny bronze colour which is very at-

Durian (*Durio zibethinus*)

tractive as the leaves appear to change colour when the wind blows through the tree.

The large white flowers appear in clusters along the older parts of the branches and have a very strong smell. The olive green or yellowish fruits range from 20 cm to 35 cm in length and have a thick tough rind which is covered with short, sharply pointed spines that make the fruit difficult to handle. When ripe, fruits drop from the tree and are not harmed because of the tough coat. They can split into five parts and in each there will be one or more seeds covered with a thick, soft cream-coloured pulp. The pulp is the part which is eaten, but the fruit has a strong smell and this deters many from sampling it. However, it is one of the best fruits in the country although there is a great deal of variation in the thickness, consistency and flavour of the pulp surrounding the seeds. Poor varieties have thin, rather dry and hard pulp, but in good varieties it is thick, well-flavoured and the consistency is like very thick cream or custard. The colour also shows some variation and will range from almost white to deep cream or yellow, and there are a few varieties in which the pulp is orange.

The trees are usually up to 40 m high but there is sometimes available a short form from Thailand and this has been propagated by budding. This form is suitable for small gardens but the fruit quality may not be as good as some of the tall-growing forms. Trees may fruit twice a year with the heavier crop produced between June and August. The fruits take three months to develop.

Figs (Ficus)

There are a large number of wild Figs in Malaysia, and some of them have edible fruit, but few are worth eating and none (unless it be *Ficus roxburghii*) worth cultivating for their fruits. The edible Mediterranean Fig is not well adapted to Malaysia, but some varieties will grow quite well, with care, and will bear fruit. They need a deeply cultivated soil and much care in the prevention of attacks by pests. Probably they could be grafted on to one of the local wild Figs to be more successful.

The Indian species *Ficus roxburghii* grows strongly from marcots and fruits well in the lowlands. The fruits are produced on short branches near the base of the trunk and are edible but lacking in flavour. The trees have a broad, rounded crown up to 4 m or more in height and 3–6 m in diameter. The leaves are very large and dark green when fully grown but pinkish or bronze when young and expanding. The plants make a striking feature in a garden and can be kept to a small size by pruning. They can also be used in partly shaded courtyards or as single plants in full sun.

Guava (*Psidium guajava*)

Red Guava

Kwini fruit (*Mangifera odorata*)

Mango (*Mangifera indica*)

Syzygium aquea (Jambu Air)

Syzygium aquea (Jambu Air)

Jambu Bol (*Syzygium malaccense*)

Jambu Air (Water Apple, *Syzygium aqueum*)

Mangifera indica

Kwini tree (*Mangifera odorata*)

Mangifera indica

Guavas (*Psidium guajava*)

Guavas originated in tropical America, but are now so well established in Asia as to appear native. The trees are small, with open branching, and their peeling bark is characteristic. They fruit almost continuously. The common semi-wild village Guava is a very inferior fruit, small and of poor flavour, and it is not easy in Malaysia to secure good varieties. Some of the better kinds do not fruit so well as the poor kinds, but it is worth planting good varieties when they can be obtained.

The trees need a sunny place and repay good cultivation and manuring. They can be propagated by marcotting or budding and seedlings will begin fruiting at about two years old. Because of their open branching, the trees are not particularly ornamental and are of no use for screening so that their best position would be in some less frequented part of the garden. Good varieties have large fruits and are well flavoured, but most of them contain very many small seeds, although there are a few seedless varieties available. The latter must always be propagated vegetatively. The fruits are sometimes attacked by fruit flies and if this happens they must be bagged or sprayed frequently until ripe.

Jambu

The tropical fruits known as Jambu in Malaysia belong to the genus Eugenia (Syzygium), of which some 140 species, all trees, occur in Peninsular Malaysia. Some of the others, besides those known as Jambu, have edible fruits and are known as Kelat, but they are small and not worth cultivation. However, some of them would be of use as ornamentals, especially for smaller gardens as they are small trees with crowns of good shape and attractive foliage. The common Jambu kinds are Jambu Chili, J. Mawar, J. Air (J. Merah and J. Hijau) and J. Bol. To them we may add a South American relative, though it has a fruit of different texture and would not be called a Jambu; it is the Cayenne Cherry or Chermai Belanda.

Jambu Chili (J. Air, Water Apple, *Syzygium aqueum*)

This is a small, bushy tree, 5–8 m tall, with opposite leaves which have very short stalks so that the base of the leaf blade appears to clasp the stem. The flowers develop in bunches on new wood and are followed by attractive top-shaped fruits which have a narrow base and a broad apex. The skin is smooth and glistening and may be white or bright pink. Each fruit is about 2–4 cm long and broad. The pink fruits are most attractive and make good table decoration in a bowl, provided they are not eaten too quickly. They are an excellent thirst quencher when eaten raw, but can also be lightly boiled with very little water and a trace of sugar and then have the delightful fragrance of rose water.

Some forms are better than others for this character and the fruits also vary a great deal in quality. Good varieties can be propagated by marcotting and most of the fruits are seedless. The trees grow best in a reasonably open place and can be planted at the edge of a screen of trees. They are fast-growing and will fruit within two or three years after planting. The tree crown is dense and in smaller gardens can be grown singly as it is both ornamental and useful. A tree in full bearing is a beautiful sight.

Jambu Mawar (Rose Apple, *Syzygium jambos*)

This is a small, bushy tree up to 7 m high, with long, narrow leaves, and bears large, white, fragrant flowers followed by dull, pale-coloured fruits which have a distinctive scented flavour. Good and poor varieties exist and it is best to propagate by marcot from a good variety if possible. Fruiting occurs several times in the year and the plants prefer an open place with deep soil.

Jambu Air (J. Air Rhio, J. Merah, J. Hijau, Java Apple, *Syzygium samarangense*, formerly *E. javanicum*)

This tree will grow to 14 m high and has white flowers followed by fairly large fruits which may be round, oval, or slightly pear-shaped. These are mostly green or whitish but there are some forms in which the fruits are pink or red. There are many varieties; the better ones do not seem to be available in Malaysia, and little selection has been done here.

Jambu Bol (J. Melaka, J. Merah, Malay Apple, *Syzygium malaccense*)

This fairly large tree will grow to 12–20 m in height and has large, oval, distinctive leaves which give it a characteristic appearance. Two or three times a year, it produces large, bright crimson flowers which are very decorative although the tree crown itself is not always of good shape. Fruits are oblong or pear-shaped and may be white with pink markings, or wholly pinkish or purplish. The flesh has a faint scent but tends to be flavourless and in some varieties is a little dry. No systematic selection has been done for better varieties.

Cayenne Cherry (Chermai Belanda, Surinam Cherry, *Eugenia uniflora*, previously *E. michelii*)

This is a little bushy tree which will grow to 5 m high and has attractive dark green foliage.

It needs full sun and good soil and can then be grown as a hedge or singly. Young leaves are bright red and very cheerful in appearance.

The small white flowers are produced almost throughout the year and are followed by small, round, deeply grooved fruits which appear like small lanterns hanging on the branches. The fruits can be eaten raw, but are very sour. They can also be cooked or made into jam or other preserves. Each contains a large seed which is often greenish and can be used for propagation as there seems to be only one variety in the country and it comes true from seed. Germination may be slow and takes several months although some seeds will germinate earlier than this. Plants grown from seed will fruit in two or three years. Flowering will be considerably reduced if the plants are shaded. When the plants are grown as a hedge they must be planted closer together than if they were needed for fruit production.

Mango Family (Anacardiaceae)

Most varieties of the true Mango (*Mangifera indica*) are unsuccessful in the south of Malaysia, as they need a dry season to induce them to flower and dry weather also at the time of setting of the fruit. The best Indian Mangoes are not very successful even in the north of the Peninsula, but a number of varieties of quite good quality are established and well worth cultivation. Fruiting of some of these is uncertain in Singapore.

As with other fruits, desirable varieties should be vegetatively propagated and this is commonly done by inarch grafting or by budding. Young trees planted in good soil grow rapidly, and grafted trees should flower within two or three years after planting. They need full sun and are sometimes troubled by caterpillar attacks on the young leaves and flowers. Spraying with insecticide will help control this problem.

Budded trees of good varieties are often available grown in very large pots and these need careful management to keep them in good condition. The soil must not become waterlogged and the plants should be given regular applications of fertilizer. A mulch of old compost can be placed on top of the soil in the pot but should not be in contact with the trunk of the plant. When these plants stop growing well, try and plant them out in the ground as repotting would be very difficult because of the size of the plant and the weight of the pot when full of soil. In a large garden, grafted or budded trees should be planted about 7 m apart.

The local relatives of the Mango are not its equal; they are the Bachang, Binjai and Kwini. Belonging to the same family, but less nearly related, are the Kundangan, Rumenia, the Cashew Nut and the Hog Plum (Kedondong). These trees are common in villages and often found in old gardens.

Bachang (*Mangifera foetida*), Binjai (*M. caesia*) and Kwini (*M. odorata*)

These trees fruit seasonally, and bear freely all over the country. They are quite large trees, and there are good and bad varieties of all of them. With selection and breeding, they could be improved, but this would take many years to accomplish. At present only the best varieties are worth planting as garden trees, except for screening or ornamental purposes. Well grown trees of Bachang and Binjai are very shapely and have dense crowns which are round or oblong in shape. In a good season, the whole crown of the tree will be covered with flowers and is a really magnificent sight as the foliage is almost completely hidden from view.

Kwini trees are more open in branching and not quite as ornamental in appearance. The best varieties of Kwini are sweet, and also better than the other Mango relatives for such purposes as making chutney. Probably budding would be possible for all these trees as a method of propagating good varieties, but little experimental work on this has been carried out.

Many members of the Mango family have sap in the stems or fruits which can be very irritating to the human skin, and the most well known of these are the group called Rengas trees. The sap from these will cause severe blistering of the skin and needs prompt treatment by a doctor. The sap of the fruit trees is less powerful but can still cause mild skin irritations on some people. A few are unfortunate enough to develop skin irritations after eating the fruits. When such troubles occur, Mango fruits should be one of the first foods to come under suspicion.

Rumenia (*Bouea microphylla*) and Kundangan (*Bouea macrophylla*)

Both these trees have smaller fruits than the ones just mentioned. They are slow-growing, handsome trees with dense oval or oblong crowns of dark green, shiny leaves, and are very ornamental. The fruits are very sour but there is some variation in the flavour though no selection has been done. Rumenia is deciduous and Kundangan is evergreen, but both could be grown solely for ornament and may then be planted singly, in groups or in avenues.

Cashew Nut (Gajus, *Anacardium occidentale*)

An open-crowned, spreading tree, to 14 m high, flowering in dry weather and having one

Anacardium occidentale

Passion fruit (*Passiflora laurifolia*)

Baccaurea motleyana

Flacourtia inermis

Flacourtia inermis

Mangosteen (*Garcinia mangostana*)

Persimmon (*Diospyros kaki*)

principal fruiting season in the year and several subsidiary ones. The sap of all parts of the tree is irritating to the skin so it should be handled with care. The leaves are large, dark green and rounded and the fruits are produced at the ends of the leafy twigs.

Each fruit has two parts: the nut, which is hard, and is held at the end of the other part, the swollen stalk which becomes soft and juicy when the fruit is ripe. The pulpy stalk may be eaten but care must be exercised because of the sap. The nut must be heated to destroy the poisonous sap and is then perfectly safe. The edible portion is the seed which is enclosed in a thin, hard shell. Raw fruits should be handled with great care as the sap is extremely irritating to the skin and should be kept away from the face, especially the eyes.

In places with a more seasonal climate, and especially in sandy, coastal areas, these trees grow very well, but are not really worthwhile growing by the ordinary gardener. They thrive in poor sandy soil but do much better if they are regularly manured. There are not many local varieties, and propagation from seed is satisfactory, but if a good variety is found it should be budded on to seedling stock.

Hog Plum (Kedondong, *Spondias pinnata*)

Two species of these plants are grown here and the fruits are mainly used for pickles or as flavouring as they are very sour. There are forms with sweeter fruits and more selection is needed. The trees are rather untidy in appearance and have pinnate leaves and a very open crown. They grow rapidly from seed and will begin fruiting about four years after planting.

Mangosteen Family (Clusiaceae, formerly Guttiferae)

The Mangosteen (*Garcinia mangostana*) is one of the most generally esteemed of all tropical fruit. It is seasonal in fruiting, and crops are uncertain in the south of Malaysia where dry weather is irregular in occurrence. Besides the Mangosteen itself, there are several related species which have edible fruits and are common village trees. Of these, the Asam Gelugor is used as a substitute for tamarind in curries, especially fish curries, and the sour fruits of the Mundu are good when candied or made into jam. The Kandis and Kechupu have fruits which may be eaten raw.

The Mangosteen is a slow-growing evergreen tree which can reach 14 m in height and gives deep shade as the crown is very dense. It is a handsome tree and very ornamental, but patience is needed as its growth is slow and it will not begin to fruit for about fifteen years. The fruits are round and when ripe are dark purplish red with a thick rind enclosing five to

Papaya (*Carica papaya*)

eight white fleshy segments, some of which will contain a single seed. The seeds germinate easily, but the seedlings are very slow in growth and because of this the trees are less commonly planted than other quicker-growing fruit trees.

Mangosteen trees grow best in light shade but if this is not available they will tolerate full sun. They fruit twice each year but weather conditions may affect fruiting so that some trees may produce one crop only. The rind of the fruit contains a juice which will stain clothing heavily and these stains are almost impossible to remove. Mangosteen fruits at the same time as Durian and it is said that a meal of Durian should be completed by eating several Mangosteens.

Asam Gelugor (*Garcinia atroviridis*)

This is a small, narrow tree which may grow to 20 m high and could be grown in a small garden as it has dark green, shiny foliage which is very ornamental. The flowers have red petals and the fruits are about 7–10 cm in diameter, round and bright green while young. The surface is deeply grooved from top to bottom and the fruits become orange-yellow when ripe. The sliced dried fruits are always available in shops and markets. These are soaked in water, and prawns or fish are steeped in the solution before they are cooked.

Papaya (*Carica papaya*)

Papayas are one of the best fruit for garden planting as they are not too large and bear fruit freely and continuously. They are usually grown from seeds but grafting and budding are practised in some countries, though not usually in Malaysia.

Normally the plant has a single stem but very old specimens may develop a few branches. If the growing point of the young plant is damaged, one or more branches will develop and one of these will become the main stem of the plant.

In Malaysia, the fruits vary a great deal in size, flavour and quality as they are grown from seed; consequently, if one wishes to grow Papaya, it is best to use seed from a good, well-flavoured fruit. There is one variety sometimes available which has rather small, round fruits of excellent flavour and this comes fairly true from seed.

Papaya plants are of three kinds. Some have male flowers only; some have female flowers only; and others have bisexual flowers. Only the last two forms produce edible fruit freely and these will show considerable variation in size, shape and colour of flesh. The male-flowered trees are useful for planting at the back of a mixed border as the flowers have a very strong, sweet fragrance and are produced in long, arching inflorescences up to a metre in length. All types of fruit will be orange or yellow when ripe but the flesh will vary from pale yellow to red.

Seeds may be planted in pots or seed beds and the young plants transplanted when they are large enough. In some areas, birds such as sparrows may destroy seedlings before they develop the first pair of leaves and some protection is needed until the plants are a little older. The ground for the final planting should be well dug and manured and when several plants are grown they should be spaced about 2 m apart. Generous manuring twice a year afterwards is necessary for good results.

Plants may be grown from sea level up to about 1000 m in the highlands. Fruits will be produced within about six months on some trees and in about ten months on others, but production will continue for three or four years provided the plants are well manured regularly. If artificial fertilizers are used, a high content of potash is necessary. Old plants should be discarded and replaced with new seedlings.

Because the Papaya has separate male and female plants, it is necessary to keep some male or bisexual plants to provide pollen for fertilizing the female flowers but as the plants are so frequently cultivated there is usually no difficulty about this, even if a single tree only is grown in a garden. It is unfortunate that the male or female flowered plants cannot be distinguished at the seedling stage and one must wait for the flowers to appear before discarding any plants.

Papaya leaves can be used for tenderizing meat and the plants have a number of industrial uses.

Passion Fruit

Passion fruits are borne on large climbing plants that need considerable supports, and a vertical screen of wire netting is probably the best. Three kinds are grown locally. In the lowlands, we have the yellow Passion fruit or Buah Susu and the Granadilla (Marquesa or Timun Belanda); on the mountains there is the purple Passion fruit. All originated in tropical America.

The Buah Susu (*Passiflora laurifolia*) has simple glossy leaves, and is very rampant. It flowers almost continuously, but in order that fruits may develop, it is necessary for two separate seedling plants to be grown together so that the flowers can be cross-pollinated. Pollination is usually effected by insects, but it is likely that the fruit crops could always be improved by artificial pollination. The flowers are fragrant and the pulp inside the fruit also has a sweet smell. Fruits are oval and yellow or pale orange when ripe. Plants can be grown from seeds or cuttings and will begin fruiting about one year after planting.

The Granadilla (*Passiflora quadrangularis*) has a larger, light green foliage and more than one plant is needed so that cross-pollination can occur. The fruits are much larger than those of the Buah Susu; they may be eaten when full grown but still green, as a cooked vegetable, or when fully ripe for their very fragrant juice. The plants are easily grown from seeds or cuttings and will fruit throughout the year. But they are large climbers and take up a considerable amount of room so are not really suitable for a small garden unless grown on a trellis as a screen between two houses, or for light shade over a patio. Granadillas are little grown in Malaysia and there are better varieties than the one already found here.

The purple Passion fruit (*Passiflora edulis*) has lobed leaves and will grow well in the lowlands but hardly fruits at all. However, in the highlands it grows and fruits well all through the year and should be cultivated there much more as the fruits are excellent for dessert, fruit salads or drinks. As the plants are climbers, they need to be grown over some kind of support, but they are easily propagated from seeds or cuttings.

Persimmon (*Diospyros kaki*)

The Asiatic Persimmon, known to the Chinese and Japanese as Kaki, will not grow in the plains of Malaysia. And while it does well in the highlands, its fruiting habits there are not known. It produces fruit on the mountains of Java, which have a more seasonal climate, and trees are grown and fruit well in some parts of the Mediterranean region.

There is, however, a tropical relative of the Persimmon which is common in the lowlands of Malaysia; this is the Mabolo or Buah Mentega (*Diospyros discolor*), native of the Philippine Islands. It is a slow-growing, bushy tree which can reach 20 m in height but rarely does so in Malaysia. It is evergreen, with slightly drooping branches and can become a little straggly unless some light pruning is done. Male and female flowers are on different trees so more than one plant should be grown if fruits are needed. The fruits are borne almost throughout the year; they are round, hairy and pink (the colour of the skin is purple-red, but this is partly obscured by the dense covering of pale hairs), with creamy, sweet flesh. The smell of the fruits is less attractive than the taste. Trees may be grown from seed, but take a number of years before they produce fruit. The foliage is pleasant and new leaves are pink and cream so that the trees have some ornamental value, and if the crown is not allowed to become straggly they make good avenue trees. The timber is an ebony of good quality.

Pineapple (*Ananas comosus*)

Several kinds of Pineapple are grown in the tropics, the best for dessert purposes being the large kind known as the Sarawak Pineapple and a small kind with little juice but of good flavour called the Mauritius Pineapple. The common canning Pineapple has a poor flavour when eaten raw.

Pineapple plants are grown from suckers which appear at the base of old plants. They need a sunny place and soil containing a good quantity of compost. Plants will fruit about eighteen months from planting but good varieties rarely produce seeds so that propagation must be from suckers or slips. For good results they need regular manuring, and the maintenance of a mulch of dead leaves around the plants. The roots are always near the surface and the mulch prevents them from being dried in hot sun. Plants need to be spaced about one metre, or a little less, apart.

Rambai and Tampoi (Tempui)

The Rambai (*Baccaurea motleyana*) is a common village tree, and the Tampoi is a related species found wild in the forest. The best varieties of both have quite palatable fruits, but no systematic selection has been undertaken.

The Rambai is a very handsome tree, often only about 10 m high, but older specimens can reach twice that height and are then majestic. They are evergreen with a dense crown of large, dark green leaves and the flowering is seasonal. Flowers are produced on long, hanging inflorescences on the twigs and main branches, with a few on the trunk of the tree. Male and female flowers are on separate trees and there is no way of distinguishing the two kinds at the seedling stage. The male flowers have a strong, sweet fragrance and all of the flowers in one area will open at the same time.

The trees are too large for small gardens but where space is available, they are excellent grown singly or as an avenue as older trees are

very wide-spreading and have a broad, rounded crown which always has a tidy appearance. An avenue of male trees would be remarkable when in flower because of the fine fragrance which can be appreciated even from inside passing vehicles. Male flowers are produced more abundantly than female flowers but the female inflorescences are much longer than the male ones. Regular manuring is required while the trees are young, but later, when they begin to flower, manuring about twice a year would be sufficient.

The Tampoi (*Baccaurea griffithii*) is very similar to the Rambai but is shorter and has smaller leaves. It is less common and needs the same treatment as Rambai and could also be used as an ornamental.

Rambutan Family (Sapindaceae)

This is another group of endemic Malaysian fruits, and comprises the Rambutan, Pulasan and Mata Kuching. The Chinese Lychee (*Litchi chinensis*) is closely related to the Mata Kuching; it grows well in the lowlands of Malaysia, though slowly, and makes a handsome shade tree but does not fruit here.

Rambutan (*Nephelium lappaceum*) and Pulasan (*N. mutabile*)

These are medium-sized trees, up to 20 m high, which are bushy in growth and flower seasonally; there is usually one principal fruit season in the year, depending on the time of the dry season which stimulates flowering, and sometimes a subsidiary season also. There are many races of Rambutan and Pulasan, and propagation by budding or marcotting is necessary to secure good varieties. Budded trees will fruit sooner than seedlings and may produce a few fruit in one or two years if kept growing strongly. Both kinds of trees give good shade, but the foliage is not particularly ornamental; that of the Rambutan can sometimes be disfigured by attacks of leaf-eating insects. The trees are suitable for screening purposes where there is room, and may then serve two purposes. In smaller gardens they can be kept to a suitable size by pruning. Good, deep soil and regular manuring are essential for vigorous growth.

Mata Kuching (*Euphoria malaiense* or *Nephelium malaiense*)

When well grown this is an attractive tree with a well shaped crown and can reach 20 m in height, but there is a great deal of variation in crown and leaf size. The foliage is rather heavier in appearance than that of Rambutan. A number of varieties have such thin flesh that to many people they are hardly worth eating, but better races occur and should be propagated. The fruits have a thin, brown shell, rather like that of Lychee. Growers sometimes bag the fruits to prevent bats from eating them.

Rukam (*Flacourtia inermis*) and Kerkup (*Flacourtia jangomas*)

These are small trees, most of them being thorny. All have small, round, juicy fruits varying from red to purple-black when ripe. The trees are easy to grow and need manuring twice or three times each year. They are seasonal in fruiting and the fruits of many varieties are very sour and therefore unpleasant to eat raw, but they can be cooked and make an excellent jelly which is equivalent in flavour and quality to the European red currant jelly. The trees will grow to about 7 m high and have a round or oval crown.

Tree Tomato (*Cyphomandra betacea*)

This is a tall shrub or small tree, native of South America, which grows and fruits well on the mountains in Malaysia, but not in the lowlands. It is not really successful at elevations much less than 1000 m, and is at its best at about 1600 or 1700 m. The fruits have a distinctive and pleasant acid flavour, and are borne freely throughout the year. The trees are usually grown from seeds which germinate easily.

Nephelium lappaceum (Rambutan)

Nephelium lappaceum (Rambutan)

Duku family: Langsat (*Lansium domesticum*)

15 PESTS, DISEASES AND WEEDS

Pests, usually insects, do an immense amount of damage to plants, and unless some definite control measures are taken, the flower garden will lack the beauty it should have and the vegetable garden will lack productivity. Diseases, usually caused by fungi, bacteria or viruses, are also serious, so serious in fact that they often cause the death of the plants and can only be dealt with by preventive measures. The average gardener cannot be expected to be an expert in these matters, but he must be observant (or he will never be a good gardener), and he can soon learn to recognize the signs of attack on his plants. The remedial measures required are few in number, and not difficult to carry out thoroughly and regularly. Because of the danger of bringing in any disease, gardeners wishing to import plants or seeds must apply for import permits and health or phytosanitary permits from the Ministry of Agriculture, or any other relevant authority. A number of plants will also be subject to very strict quarantine regulations and some kinds are not allowed into the country at all.

Before we come to deal with remedies, let us first consider the prevention of diseases. The most important thing in this matter is cleanliness. Do not leave rubbish lying about. Rubbish of all kinds is liable to be a hiding place for pests, and possibly a place for their breeding. All garden refuse which is not immediately dug into the ground or burnt should be made into proper compost heaps in which the hot fermentation processes should prevent the breeding of pests. It should be emphasized that only those things should be burnt which cannot be made into compost, such as coarse palm leaves and other woody matter. (If the gardener makes his own burnt earth, old logs of wood, palm trunks and other such refuse may be used in the burning process.) Burning of cut grass, prunings, dead plants and leaves is wasteful; it is hardly possible to make up too much compost. But the compost heap should be made up regularly, and the materials not left lying about.

A special class of rubbish is particularly dangerous, and that is fallen fruit of all kinds, which often contain larvae of fruit flies or other insects. When the adult flies emerge from the fallen fruit they immediately go to young fruit on the trees or vegetable plants and lay their eggs. Therefore, all fallen fruits should be carefully destroyed by burning or burying.

Cleanliness of a more specialized kind is also necessary, and has been mentioned in previous chapters. All pots used for seedlings should be carefully washed; and potting soil should in many cases be sterilized by heat to cleanse it from the presence of harmful fungi and bacteria.

Pesticides

Insecticides and fungicides are used for the destruction of pests and diseases which attack ornamental plants and food plants. In large gardens these chemicals provide the quickest and easiest means of control when large numbers of plants are maintained, but in small gardens or with a few pot plants only, many pests can be controlled effectively by hand-picking, though fungi will need some chemical control.

At the present time there is a variety of chemicals for the control of different pests and diseases and many of these must be used with great caution. They are mentioned here under the chemical name only and when buying proprietary preparations, gardeners must read the notes on the packet as these should always include the names of the chemicals which have been used in the mixture. Some of these chemicals are poisonous to man, animals and beneficial insects such as bees, so that some elementary precautions are necessary in order to make sure that they are not misused or used in error.

All such chemicals for use in the garden should be stored carefully in containers which can be closed tightly, and these should be kept away from any food store. Some of the chemicals will cause tainting of food and if they are in actual contact with food they can be poisonous. Food crops sprayed with some of these substances should not be harvested for two or more days after treatment and the length of time is usually stated in the instructions for the use of the chemical. All chemicals should be stored safely so that children and animals have no access to them, and it is best, if possible, to keep them in a locked cupboard.

Should it be necessary to transfer any chemicals to new containers, these must be clearly and permanently labelled immediately. Empty soft-drink bottles are frequently used for this purpose and if they are left around the house unlabelled, small children especially are liable to pick them up and drink the contents with disastrous results. There have been several reports of deaths due to the accidental drinking of some of these chemicals for some of which there is no antidote, and it is essential, therefore, to follow scrupulously the directions of the manufacturers. Should there be any doubt about the chemical, advice must be sought from the makers, the Ministry of Agriculture, or some other relevant authority. It should be remembered that these modern chemicals are perfectly safe if used in the way recommended by the manufacturers but it is of the utmost importance to follow all precautions strictly and to keep the chemicals out of the reach of children and domestic animals. Containers of any kind which have been used for these chemicals must be washed thoroughly and stored away immediately so that they cannot be used for any other purpose accidentally. Although these statements may sound somewhat frightening, it is most important that gardeners should be aware of the nature of the chemicals available to them at the present time, and that their correct use poses no danger.

Before using any preparation always read the instructions on the container very carefully and follow these strictly with regard to the concentration, volume to be used, and time of application. Never exceed the recommended concentration, otherwise plants can be severely damaged or killed very quickly.

Some chemicals can be mixed with others and very often readymade mixtures are sold commercially which will control a variety of plant ailments. Other chemicals cannot be mixed as the resulting product would damage plants. With any of these mixtures it is most important, therefore, to read the instructions carefully, and if there is any doubt about the use, enquiries should be made from the manufacturer. (Sellers may not always have the necessary knowledge.)

Herbicides need very special care when they are used as they are active at very low concentrations and if spraying equipment is not washed out thoroughly after use the residual herbicide may damage the plants on which the equipment is next used.

Excess chemicals or those already prepared for use should never be kept in unlabelled containers and should never be thrown away into open ditches or storm drains, otherwise plants growing near by may be damaged and animals drinking the water will be poisoned.

After using any of these chemicals the equipment must be thoroughly washed and cleaned and the person who has been using it should wash all exposed areas of skin, especially hands, arms and face. If possible, it is better to keep separate sprayers for herbicides and pesticides.

Empty containers, which can be of metal, plastic or glass, should be washed out, and either burnt or buried, but should never be left where children and domestic animals may reach them.

Careful attention to the time of application of any pesticides is necessary when dealing with vegetable crops because harvesting cannot be done for a short time afterwards until the chemical has become harmless.

Fish are very susceptible to many of these chemicals so that aquaria and ponds should be avoided when spraying is done. Some of the chemicals are harmful to bees and other pollinating insects so that spraying should not be done when the plants are in flower, otherwise there will be a reduced number of fruits and seeds.

Persistent chemicals should not be used when there are others available which are just as effective, but are not persistent. Whenever possible, use non-poisonous preparations.

Spraying must be thorough otherwise some pests will remain and these can become resistant to the chemical used, so that stronger solutions would be necessary, and as this is undesirable, a change to some other chemical should be made.

Insecticides

Destructive insects may be divided into two main groups; the biting insects and the piercing or sucking insects.

Biting insects damage plants in a variety of ways. Leaf eaters such as **caterpillars** and beetles will reduce the amount of leaf surface so that the plant is unable to make sufficient food for good growth. **Boring insects** may destroy growing points or may interrupt the flow of sap in the stem and some **caterpillars** live underneath the bark and if they ring the entire stem, the plant will die slowly. **Fruit flies** attack young and mature fruits and may cause premature fruit fall or rotting of the fruit while still on the plant. Caterpillars and beetles may also destroy flower buds so that no fruit or seeds can be produced. **Weevils** and **borers** often damage seeds which results in poor germination. Beetles and caterpillars sometimes attack roots so that the absorption of nutrients by the plant is reduced and growth becomes slow. Weevils, caterpillars and beetles often damage storage organs such as tubers, corms and bulbs, and when this is severe, growth in the next season will be weak. **Leaf-miners** destroy the internal tissues of the leaves which become disfigured and are unable to manufacture food for the plant, which then becomes weak and very liable to disease.

Piercing and sucking insects drain the sap from a plant with various results. Growth becomes weak and the plant will wilt more easily. Both flower and fruit production will be severely reduced or entirely prevented and young shoots and leaves will be distorted badly. Premature fruit fall and leaf fall will occur and the pest may inject toxins which cause malformation or decay of stems and tissues. Galls on leaves are one of the results of the activities of these insects. The wounds which they make provide an entry point for bacteria and fungi which will cause further damage.

There are, in addition, a number of useful insects and these also will be killed by insecticides. The most important are bees and other pollinators, predators such as ladybirds and lacewing larvae which fed on aphids, and some parasitic insects which destroy caterpillars. It is usually safe for bees to work a crop 48 hours after the insecticide has been applied, but different combinations of these chemicals will vary in their toxicity to bees.

In very small gardens or with a few pot plants only, hand-picking can be effective, but in gardens of any size chemical control is convenient because it gives the surest and most predictable results, although it must be repeated with each pest outbreak.

Chemicals act in different ways and may be grouped as follows.

Repellants

These keep insects away and are usually used for mosquitoes and other medical pests.

Fumigants

In this group the chemicals are used as gases or smokes in enclosed areas such as seed stores.

Stomach Poisons

In order to be effective, these chemicals must be eaten and consequently they are often mixed with baits to encourage insects to eat them, or they can be applied as a spray to the foliage.

Ephemeral Contact Poisons

These are absorbed through the cuticle of the insect and are usually applied as a spray to the foliage of plants.

Residual Poisons

These are persistent chemicals and remain active for a long period of time. They may be applied to the soil or they can be used as a foliar spray.

Systemic Poisons

The chemicals of this group are able to enter the plant body and are then translocated to all parts of the plant. They can be applied as sprays on the soil or on the foliage; as granules on the soil or on the foliage, or with woody plants, they can be injected directly into the vascular system. Sap feeding insects are more easily controlled than by the use of contact insecticides. Beneficial insects are not affected unless they come into direct contact with the insecticide. Some of the chemicals in this group are very poisonous, but others are available which are still effective against pests but are less toxic to man.

Systemic insecticides must persist inside the plant in an active state until the sap is taken in by the insects. These chemicals are absorbed through the leaves, stems and roots of a plant so that complete coverage of the plant surface is not necessary; once inside the plant they are distributed through all of the tissues. Biting insects are controlled also with these chemicals.

Application of Pesticides

Liquid Preparations

Soluble products are made up as concentrated solutions, sometimes mixed with a wetting agent, and are diluted with water when needed. The wetting agent gives a more even spread of the pesticide over the foliage and helps the solution to adhere to the slightly waxy surface of the plants.

Solid products, which may be insoluble in water, are often combined into wettable powders which form a very fine suspension when mixed with water.

Oils or other liquids which do not mix readily with water may have emulsifiers added which prevent separation when water is added. A very fine suspension of droplets is obtained in the water which can be sprayed on to the plants in the usual way.

Dry Preparations

These are sometimes more convenient to use than a spray. The dust is ready for use when bought and dusting appliances are usually lighter and easier to handle than sprayers. The actual chemical is mixed with a carrier powder so that it can be distributed more evenly over the foliage. Dusting should be carried out in calm weather when there is no wind and it is best done when the foliage is wet with dew or rain so that the powder will stick to the plant surface more easily.

Both liquid and dry preparations can be used also as seed dressings and in all cases two applications are necessary to give complete control as the eggs of many insects are unaffected by the chemicals used, so that these will hatch and a second spraying is necessary to kill the new larvae.

Granules

Some pesticides are available in the form of small solid particles which are useful for treating seedling crops. They can be placed to give the maximum protection with the minimum danger of soil pollution. In this form the active chemical is less affected by the soil. Many pesticides are strongly adsorbed in soil and rapidly become ineffective. Granules are useful for treating standing crops, for control of mosquito larvae in pools and streams and for 'spot' treatment of weeds.

Aerosols

Preparations made up in this form are easy to use, very efficient and have great penetrating power.

Smokes and fumigants

For confined and enclosed spaces, some insecticides can be used in this way as they are prepared in a volatile form. They are useful in greenhouses, under tarpaulins, 'tents' of polythene or PVC, for grain or other storage treatment, and for soil treatment. Naphthalene, nicotine and methyl bromide are used in this manner but great care must be exercised and they are not really suitable for the home gardener.

Chemicals

Some of the earliest used insecticides were arsenical compounds, pyrethrum, Derris and nicotine, but at the present time there are many synthetic organic compounds available which fall into three main groups. There are the chlorinated hydrocarbons such as DDT,

and the organophosphorous compounds such as Malathion, both groups having a cumulative effect. DDT has been banned in a number of countries because of its effect on the environment. The third group of chemicals is that of the carbamate insecticides such as Carbaryl.

The action of the chlorinated hydrocarbons is effected by insects walking over or eating a deposit of the chemical applied to plants or any other surface. The organophosphorous compounds act on the nervous system of the insect and although they work rapidly they are not as persistent as the chlorinated hydrocarbons and consequently residues are less of a problem. Many of these compounds are poisonous to man and must be used with great care, and although they are mentioned briefly here it is better for the home gardener to choose safe chemicals which are equally effective.

Chlorinated Hydrocarbons

Because of their persistence, all of the chemicals in this group can easily pass through a food chain and eventually will accumulate in the body fat of vertebrate animals. Under normal conditions this build-up of chemical in the body of an animal will have no effect, but during times of stress such as a shortage of food or water, the reserves of fat are used up and more of the pesticide is released into the blood so that the various life functions are disturbed and the animal may die. Many countries restrict the use of chlorinated hydrocarbons when suitable alternatives are available, because of this long-lasting contamination and the resulting dangers to the environment. Some pests become resistant to these chemicals after some time and other preparations must then be used.

Aldrin

This is used for the control of soil pests and is very persistent but does not taint root crops. It is harmful to fish and wild life and if seeds are treated with this compound they should not afterwards be used for human consumption.

BHC and Gamma BHC (Lindane)

This is benzene hexachloride and is a very strong stomach poison available in powder form or as an emulsion. BHC taints food crops even when very dilute but Gamma BHC causes very little tainting. The chemicals are used for soil and seed treatment and will kill a wide range of insects. They are dangerous to bees and are harmful to fish and livestock. After spraying, the crop should be left for two weeks before harvesting is done. Both chemicals may be used as a contact insecticide, or as a fumigant in enclosed spaces and they are often used in combination with other insecticides.

Dieldrin

This is a persistent chemical which will control most insects and may be used as a contact or as a stomach poison. Seed treated with this compound must not be used for human consumption and is dangerous to birds.

Endrin

A persistent chemical with similar properties to Dieldrin which can be used to control aphids, caterpillars and white ants.

Organophosphorous Insecticides

In this group there are both contact and systemic insecticides and the latter are especially effective against sucking insects. Many of these chemicals are very toxic to mammals and birds but they persist for a relatively short time and quickly break down to become non-toxic.

Systemic Organophosphorous Insecticides

These are absorbed by the plants and are translocated to all of the tissues in sufficient quantities to be lethal to insects feeding upon them. The chemicals can enter the plant by direct absorption through the seeds, roots, stems, leaves and fruits.

The advantages of using a systemic insecticide are that complete coverage of the plant is not necessary and the chemical is protected within the plant from the effect of weathering. Any new plant growth occurring after application will be protected also because the insecticide will move into these parts as they are formed. There is much less risk of damage to harmless and beneficial organisms.

Systemic insecticides are useful for the control of mealy-bugs, soft scales, leaf hoppers, leaf-miners, leaf-eating insects, mites such as red spider and foliar eelworms. They are a versatile group of compounds, some of which persist for a long time while others remain effective for a short time only. Some will control many kinds of insect but others are more specific and are effective on one or two kinds only. Some of these chemicals have a rapid contact action while others are effective stomach poisons and although some of them are very toxic, others are virtually non-toxic to animals. Dimethoate is one of the most widely used systemic insecticides.

Malathion

This is now one of the most widely used contact insecticides as it controls a great variety of insects. It persists for a short time only and in mammals is rapidly broken down in the liver.

Some ornamentals and plants of the Cucumber family may be damaged by this chemical. It is harmful to bees and fish, and crops which have been sprayed with it should not be harvested for at least four days afterwards.

Carbamates

These chemicals act in a similar manner to the organophosphorous insecticides. Although they control a wide variety of insects, some of them are very specific. The most widely used is Carbaryl which controls many pests of vegetables and fruits. Carbamates are harmful to bees and fish, and crops should not be harvested for at least one week after they have been sprayed with these chemicals.

Miscellaneous Compounds

Lead arsenate

This stomach insecticide does not harm plants when used on its own but may cause some damage if mixed with other chemicals. It is a white powder which is mixed with water in the proportion of 30 g to 4 ½ litres of water. As the powder is insoluble it will sink to the bottom of the container unless stirred frequently and if used in a sprayer the mixture must be agitated constantly. When the spray is applied to foliage it dries as a white film over the surface of the leaves and will remain for some time, but after a period of heavy rainfall, spraying must be repeated. The film of lead arsenate is eaten by any insects attacking the leaves and they are thus killed, though at some loss to the plant. For this reason the lead arsenate is not a complete protection, and it is not effective for the treatment of small seedlings where pests such as beetles are abundant; the seedlings may be eaten completely before all the beetles are killed after eating the lead arsenate. This chemical should not be used on Beans, Brinjals, and other vegetables or fruits which are to be eaten. It must not be used on the same leaves as a spray containing soap or scorching will result, and it may cause damage if mixed with other chemicals.

Lead arsenate is useful principally against attacks by leaf-eating beetles, grasshoppers, caterpillars and other larvae and if persistently applied, all the pests in the neighbourhood will be killed so that the damage to the plants will be greatly reduced. However, the chemical is poisonous to mammals, fish and bees and crops sprayed with it should not be harvested for six weeks after treatment.

Boric acid

Widely used against cockroaches and is very effective.

Natural Organic Compounds

These do not appear to produce resistance in insect pests and are much safer to use.

Derris (Rotenone or Tuba Root)

A compound obtained from the roots of a wild leguminous plant, *Derris elliptica*, found in Malaysia, but it can be obtained also from the roots of some other legumes. It has been used by Malays as a fish poison for a very long time but its use as an insecticide was discovered much later. The fresh roots are sometimes available in the market and about ½ kg of these will yield enough juice to make about 9 litres of solution. The roots should be pounded thoroughly until a milky juice is obtained which can be mixed with the required amount of water and the resulting solution can be used immediately.

The liquid should always be freshly prepared and acts as a contact poison to almost all insects except scale insects which have a protective waxy coat. It will also act as a deterrent, keeping insects away, for which reason it is excellent for seedlings, especially those of some vegetables which are particularly liable to attack by beetles. The effect does not last long and for seedlings, daily spraying may be necessary especially in wet weather, but in other cases, when pests are under good control, a weekly spraying may be sufficient, particularly during dry weather. If mixed with an oil emulsion it can be used to control mealy bugs and scale insects.

Commercial preparations are available now in powder or liquid form and should be used according to the manufacturers' directions. This is one of the safest insecticides for general use. It is, of course, poisonous to fish and should not be sprayed near aquaria or ponds, and it is toxic to pigs. Fruit and vegetables can be harvested one day after spraying.

Nicotine

This was used originally as a tobacco infusion spray and is still good for control of aphids on many plants. It is a non-persistent contact insecticide which can also be used as a fumigant in greenhouses and poultry houses. Vegetables and fruits should not be harvested for two days after spraying. Nicotine is harmful to bees, fish and wild birds. Many commercial preparations are available at the present time and the sprays should be made up according to the instructions on the packet.

A preparation can be made at home by soaking cigarette and cigar ends or uncured tobacco waste in water for 24 hours, or the preparation can be boiled and allowed to cool. The tobacco must be squeezed afterwards to express all the juice and about ¼ kg of tobacco should give sufficient extract for 18 litres of spray. Some soap should be added to the solution so that it spreads and sticks more efficiently on the leaves. If a little kerosene emulsion is added then the spray is very effective against scales and mealy bugs. Nicotine breaks down within 48 hours and so is safe to use on vegetables or fruit which can be eaten after this time.

Pyrethrins

These are contact insecticides obtained from the flowers of some species of Chrysanthemum, and they break down in sunlight. They are among the oldest of the insecticides and are still used a great deal in commercial mixtures because they are safe for all mammals.

Organic Oils

These are derived by distillation from petroleum and other mineral oils and from coal tar. Their action is very strong and they are mostly used when plants are dormant. They are dangerous to fish and some of them cause irritation of the skin, eyes, nose and mouth unless proper care is taken when they are used.

Kerosene Emulsion

This can be made quite easily but some care is necessary. You will need 2¼ litres of water, 4½ litres of kerosene and 250 g of soap. The soap, cut into slices, is dissolved in the water which should be heated to boiling. Remove the liquid from the fire and mix the kerosene with it carefully, using a garden syringe. Mixing must be very thorough and must be done while the liquid is very hot. When cold, one part of this mixture is diluted with nine parts of water in order to make the spray. The latter should be white, rather like milk in appearance and there should be no free oil on the surface. If there is any free oil present it will damage the leaves of any plants. Kerosene emulsion is used especially to control scale insects which have a waxy covering that is resistant to water-based sprays. The emulsion can be used on its own, or some Derris or nicotine can be added to make it more effective.

Kinds of Pests

Caterpillars

Caterpillars of innumerable kinds attack almost all kinds of plants. Fortunately, the damage in many cases is not serious but it makes the plant look untidy and its appearance is only restored after new leaves have been

produced. Young leaves are especially liable to attack (for example, in Lagerstroemia and *Cassia fistula*) and also, in some cases, the flower buds are severely damaged as in most Ixoras. Crinums and Caladiums are very often infested by caterpillars in large numbers, which can destroy all of the leaves within one day. Consequently, it is essential to keep a constant watch so that the early stages of the attack may be detected. When the plants are grown singly any damage by young caterpillars will be noticed immediately, but if plants are grown in mixed groups then the initial damage can be missed very easily. Young caterpillars are often in groups, but many are eaten by birds so that eventually only a few remain, but if these become large, as for example the hawkmoth caterpillars, then a single larva is able to eat a whole Caladium leaf within half a day.

Despite their size, it is remarkably difficult to see these caterpillars, especially if the plants are given a cursory glance only. If only a few leaves or a few large caterpillars are concerned, hand-picking is the quickest and easiest method; but if the attack is extensive, spraying with nicotine or Derris is desirable. Some caterpillars roll up the leaves on which they are feeding, or fasten two leaves together and so are protected from the full effects of spraying. In such cases spraying must be very thorough, or if a wetting agent is mixed with the solution this will make it more effective, and, when possible, hand-picking should be done in addition. Hibiscus leaves and banana leaves are often attacked by these leaf-rolling caterpillars. Waterlilies are sometimes troubled with these caterpillars but hand-picking is really the only remedy as spraying with Derris is toxic to fish.

A serious pest of Ixoras is a small green caterpillar which occurs in considerable numbers and feeds on the flower buds and young leaves. The larvae protect themselves by accumulating a mass of dead blackened buds, together with their own excreta, held together with threads of their own making, and this makes the plant look unpleasant. No flowers will open and the dense arrangement of the buds makes it very difficult to detect the presence of these caterpillars, so that the first indication is the shrivelling of many of the younger buds. When well established, these caterpillars can be controlled only by regular spraying or hand-picking. The only effective remedy, where this pest is troublesome, is to spray all young flower buds every few days with a suitable insecticide mixed with a wetting agent and this will deter the moth from laying its eggs, as well as kill any caterpillars before they have time to accumulate the protective mass of dead material.

Stem-borers

These are caterpillars which live inside the twigs or small branches or under the bark of shrubs and trees. Their presence is often not noticed until the branch withers or breaks off. When an attack is suspected a watch should be kept for the holes in the stem from which the insect expels its excreta. A wire can be inserted into the holes to kill the insect, but it is better to spray the stem with an insecticide and try to make sure that some of it enters the holes. This will be easier if a wetting agent is mixed with the solution.

Leaf-miners

Leaf-miners are small larvae which destroy the inner tissues of the leaf leaving the epidermis untouched. Affected leaves show irregular whitish lines resembling meandering pathways, and if the attack is severe the leaves will drop from the plant very quickly. Normal sprays have practically no effect because this insect is protected inside the leaf tissues. A systemic insecticide will give good control.

Beetles

Beetles are probably the worst of all garden

pests. The adult insects not only eat the leaves of a large number of plants, often at the seedling stage when they are very vulnerable, but also the larvae or grubs of many beetles are almost equally destructive. The commonest leaf-eating beetles hide underground during the day and emerge at about dusk when they fly to their food plants. This means that they are never seen during the day but the damage which they have done to the leaves becomes clearly visible then. If only a small number of plants is concerned, the best method is to take a torch and go out an hour or so after dusk and catch the beetles by hand. This is easily done and if continued every evening for one week the number of beetles will be much reduced and the time needed each evening will be very much less.

When a large number of plants is involved, spraying is the easiest method of control. Lead arsenate, Derris or a systemic insecticide are satisfactory, but the first, although effective, leaves a white residue on the foliage which may not be desirable for ornamental plants, and the second acts as a deterrent if sprayed on in the evening, though the effect does not last very long. The systemic insecticide will give the most effective and long-lasting protection as it will move into all new leaves and flowers as they develop and spraying need be done at monthly intervals only. The other two insecticides mentioned would need to be renewed at weekly intervals or more often in wet weather.

Cannas are especially prone to attack by beetles which eat the flowers as well as the leaves and if they have been mulched with grass clippings this provides an ideal hiding place for the beetles during the day. The coloured-leafed Acalyphas can be badly damaged by beetles and if not sprayed the leaves can be reduced to a network of veins only so that the appearance of the plant is totally ruined.

Seedlings of vegetables are often damaged badly by beetles and spraying with a systemic insecticide would give sufficient control until the little plants have grown larger and stronger. All vegetable seedlings should be examined in the morning and evening for evidence of attack because a small amount of damage to a seedling could kill it whereas it would not be serious on a grown plant.

Several kinds of beetles and their larvae attack orchids. There is a little black weevil which bores into the buds of Arachnis, Vanda and Phalaenopsis and lays its eggs there. Another large yellow beetle lays its eggs on the flowers of the same group of orchids and when the larvae hatch out they devour the buds and open flowers and simultaneously cover themselves with a slimy protective coating. Spathoglottis is also troubled by a beetle which lays its eggs at the base of young leaves which are damaged so much by the larvae that they show large holes when they expand. Regular spraying with Derris or a systemic insecticide will usually keep the beetles away so that they do not lay their eggs on the plants. A lapse in spraying for a few weeks will result in the reappearance of the beetles so it is always wise to take preventative measures.

Grasshoppers

Grasshoppers are voracious creatures that eat many kinds of leaves and spoil the appearance of many garden plants, including young palms. If they are watched for a short time one will be astonished at the speed with which they can devour a leaf. Spraying with Malathion will give good control but these insects appear to be more of a problem in some parts of the country than in others.

Thrips

Thrips are tiny insects but do much damage, mostly to flowers, and sometimes also to young leaves. An adult Thrips insect is a slender black creature, smaller than the tiniest ant, and only just big enough to be seen with the naked eye. It can fly and lays its eggs on the flower buds or young leaves and it is the young insects which hatch that do most of the damage. They are very tiny and greenish in colour so that they are difficult to see without a lens. Usually they hide inside flower buds or in the folds of leaves so that they are difficult to reach with sprays, but the addition of a wetting agent will help considerably in this respect.

Though Thrips may be found in many kinds of flowers, both wild and cultivated, it is fortunate that they only do serious damage in a few cases. The most important for the gardener is with the orchids of the Vanda and Arachnis group because their fleshy flowers seem particularly liable to severe attack. The petals are damaged in the bud and have brown marks on them when the flowers open. As Thrips can fly it is impossible to prevent a continual influx of them from the many other kinds of flowers which they inhabit and it is therefore essential that spraying is done regularly.

Fortunately Derris, which keeps beetles away, will also deal with Thrips and if infestation is serious, spraying twice a week is recommended until the insects are under control, after which once a week should be sufficient. In the case of orchids that are seasonal in flowering, it is only necessary to spray for Thrips control when the flower buds appear. In such cases nicotine or some other insecticide may, if desired, be substituted for Derris; but in the case of orchids which flower continuously, a spray which will not damage or disfigure the open flowers must be used and Derris is quite safe in this respect. Malathion can be used but care must be taken as it will cause distortion in some plants at some concentrations.

Thrips sometimes cause damage to the very young leaves of plants, as for instance in the case of the Sword bean. The leaves then do not expand properly and have brown marks on them; they become yellowish and have a somewhat shrivelled appearance so that it is quite obvious they are not healthy. Spraying with nicotine, Derris or Malathion is the remedy.

Snails and Slugs

Snails and slugs are not insects but do a great deal of damage to plants of all ages and so are considered here. As far as possible, do not have hiding places for snails near the seedling or flower beds, and it should be mentioned here that a rockery provides many suitable places where these pests can hide. The most effective remedy is metaldehyde which is mixed with bran or other material and is available in the form of pellets which can be placed in small heaps around the plants. Regular application of this remedy is necessary until the snail and slug population is reduced and

the dead creatures can be collected each day and buried somewhere in the garden. In a large garden with a good fence an excellent method of control is to keep one or two ducks and if these are given some food every day they will not touch the plants but will clear the garden of slugs and snails.

Scale Insects

Scale insects are very abundant and of many kinds. Fortunately most of them are kept in check by parasites, although they do sometimes pose a serious problem. They exude a sugary secretion upon which ants feed and in many cases the scales are brought by ants to the young parts of plants upon which they feed. Each scale insect, once it becomes adult, remains fixed to the plant, sucking food from the area it covers. Scales may be round or long and most are flattened although some may be hemispherical as in the case of the common large scale found frequently on Hibiscus. They are usually brown and as a rule appear first on the young twigs which in serious attacks can be completely covered with scales.

They are easy to recognize and spraying with kerosene emulsion or some other oil emulsion is the remedy. The addition of nicotine or Derris extract to the emulsion makes a more effective spray and may be necessary to give the best control. A systemic insecticide will be effective also. Sometimes scales attack smooth, fleshy leaves like those of some orchids (especially Cattleyas), and in such cases wiping the leaves with a rag soaked in the emulsion is a good method of dealing with them. A small brown scale often attacks the leaves of Maidenhair ferns but these will not tolerate kerosene emulsion and soap solution can be used instead. However, the best remedy for these plants is to cut off and destroy all of the affected leaflets as soon as they are seen.

Aphids or Greenfly

Aphids or greenfly are also sucking insects and are the carriers of some virus diseases. They are, fortunately, not such serious garden pests as scale insects in Malaysia and the best treatment is usually a nicotine spray, kerosene emulsion or a systemic insecticide.

Mealy-bugs

Mealy-bugs are really a kind of soft scale insect and are often brought by ants. The most common kind is covered with a soft, white wax substance which makes the insects look like a small fungus. The treatment is the same as for scale insects, but oil emulsions alone are usually ineffective and need to be reinforced with one of the contact poisons, or a systemic insecticide may be used. Malathion also gives effective control but the spray must be combined with a wetting agent.

Mealy-bugs attack many kinds of plants, especially shrubs, and will be found on the young twigs or leaves. Sometimes the sticky substance which they exude becomes infected with a black fungus called a sooty mould, and this forms a black film over the surface of the plant. Although this black film is only superficial, it may cause some damage to the leaves by suffocation as it prevents sunlight from reaching them and the plants are unable to manufacture food efficiently. Once the insects are destroyed, the fungus will disappear.

Mites

Mites are tiny, sucking pests which can cause a great deal of damage to plants. They are usually found on the lower surface of leaves and often cause a very characteristic curling of the leaf blade. Many garden plants are attacked by these pests. One of the commonest is red spider which often appears on plants that are a little weak in growth, and especially if these have been grown in hot, dry conditions with little or no air movement around them. The best remedy for mite attack is finely powdered sulphur applied with a blower in the early morning when the leaves are wet with dew. Spraying with a systemic insecticide is also successful in the control of mites.

Leaf-hoppers

These are another group of sucking insects which are often abundant on trees with a flush of new leaves, or on young, fast-growing vegetables. When their attack is serious, they cause the leaves to be deformed and spotty in appearance. The best remedies are Derris, nicotine or a systemic insecticide.

Besides the direct damage that they cause, sucking insects can also affect plants in another way because they pass virus disease from one plant to another, much as a mosquito passes the malaria parasite from one human being to another. It is most important, therefore, that sucking insects are controlled efficiently on both garden and crop plants.

Fruit Flies

These are a serious group of pests. They attack fruits of all kinds, including those which are used as vegetables, such as Brinjals, Cucumbers, and Beans, as well as Citrus, Mango, Starfruit and others which are used as dessert fruits. The flies lay their eggs in the young fruits, sometimes only a day or two after the flower has fallen. The eggs then hatch and the grubs live inside the fruit, from which they eventually emerge as adult flies and disperse to re-infest other fruits.

As the grubs are, from the outset, entirely inside the fruits, no spraying will affect them.

Spraying with Derris, nicotine or Malathion will have some effect in deterring the flies from coming to the plants to lay eggs. One effective measure is to tie a paper bag around each young fruit as soon as the flower has fallen. In practice, a piece of newspaper rolled into the form of a cylinder is sufficient protection. One end of this is tied around the base of the fruit and the opposite end is left open so that the young fruit does not become overheated, as it would if it were totally enclosed. In addition, all fallen fruit which may be infested with flies should be gathered and destroyed. Many gardeners do not do this, so that it is difficult to control these flies effectively. There are also many fruits of wild plants which offer an alternative breeding place for these insects so that the population is maintained.

Attacks of a similar kind are sometimes troublesome in the flower garden. Some insects lay their eggs on the flower bud, and the larvae eat part of the interior of the bud, causing it to fall prematurely, or causing so much damage that the flower is seriously disfigured. Hibiscus flowers are often attacked in this way and Sword bean and Bauhinia flowers are often damaged so badly the flower buds fall before they open. The best remedy is to spray regularly with nicotine, Derris, Malathion or a systemic insecticide.

These are some of the more common pests which are liable to trouble the home gardener. It should be remembered always that prevention is better than cure.

Diseases Caused by Fungi, Bacteria and Viruses

Fungi and bacteria obtain their food from living or dead bodies of plants and animals. They are, in fact, the agents of decay, and as such serve a useful purpose in our compost heaps and in the soil, reducing rubbish to a condition in which it can be taken up again by the roots of plants and rebuilt into living substances. If fungi and bacteria did nothing but decompose dead plants and animals, they would be no trouble; but unfortunately some of them have acquired the habit of attacking living plants. By various means they enter the body of the plant, through the roots, stems or leaves, and when they have penetrated the outer tissues they attack and kill the living cells, causing the gradual or sudden death of part or the whole of the plant.

Many such fungi cause only local damage, and though they may disfigure plants to some extent, their attack is not serious and need not worry the gardener because the plants can resist these attacks to some extent. Many spots

healthy ones transplanted to sterilized soil of good, open texture, and given sufficient light and air.

Fungicides

Chemicals of several kinds are available for the control of diseases caused by fungi and bacteria. Only those which are suitable for the home gardener will be mentioned here and these should be made up very carefully, according to the directions of the manufacturer.

Copper Fungicides

The most well known of these is the mixture of copper sulphate and lime, commonly called 'Bordeaux Mixture'. This will not cure disease but will prevent it from developing, because the fungus spores are killed as they germinate. Various improved preparations are obtainable now and are easy to apply. Copper preparations should not be put into iron or tin containers and should be made up in plastic, earthenware, glass or copper vessels.

Sulphur and Lime Sulphur

These also are controls and not cures for a disease. Sulphur can be dusted directly on to the plant surface or it can be made into a suspension in water, using a wetting agent.

Lime sulphur is available as a liquid but the directions for use must be read carefully because some plants are damaged by sulphur in this form.

Sulphur is effective against mildew but will cause some tainting of fruit.

Other Fungicides

Thiram, Maneb and Zineb are all good general fungicides for the garden and can be used on practically all plants.

Captan is another kind of organic fungicide

which is very effective as a foliage spray or as a seed dressing.

Systemic fungicides are available and one of the most common is Benomyl which will control a wide range of fungi.

There are many commercial preparations available containing one or more of these fungicides, often in combination with an insecticide, and all are efficient.

Weeds

Weeds are plants which grow where they are not wanted and if not kept under control they will compete with the ornamental plants or vegetables for the nutrients and water in the soil. They grow, flower and fruit very rapidly so that they spread very quickly and can soon smother other plants.

In a small garden weeds can be controlled easily by hoeing the ground regularly, or they can be removed by hand. It is important to keep beds of seedlings free from weeds also. Weeds can harbour pests and diseases and will provide hiding places for slugs and snails which is another reason for removing them.

In large gardens they may be controlled by hoeing, but if they are too persistent it may be necessary to use chemicals called herbicides. These are especially useful for keeping gravel paths, paved paths or patios free from weeds whenever necessary. These chemicals must be used carefully because of the risk of damage to the ornamental or food plants near by. There are two kinds of herbicides; those which kill all plants indiscriminately, and those which are described as selective, and will kill certain plants only. A few of those more suitable for ordinary garden purposes are mentioned here.

Sodium Chlorate is a general weed-killer which will destroy all plants and can spread through the soil so its use must be carefully controlled. It is inflammable and best avoided in small gardens, especially as the treated ground cannot be used for planting for several months. It can be used for clearing paths and roadsides where no other planting is done near by.

Selective herbicides

Generally speaking, these chemicals tend to kill off weeds but at the same time leave crop plants unharmed. There are a number of different chemicals available and they act, to a varying extent, on a number of different weeds, some of them being fairly specific. Of these, **2,4-D** is one of the most well known and is a hormone-like preparation which can be absorbed by roots and shoots and moves rapidly through each plant. Complete cover-

age of the plant surface is therefore not necessary. When making up the spray the manufacturers' instructions must be followed strictly in order to avoid damage to ornamental or crop plants. While 2,4-D is used mainly for killing broad-leafed weeds, it is not effective against all weed species. Grass weeds can be controlled with Dalapon which moves quickly through the plants and kills them.

Simazine can be used for non-selective weed control and it may be used alone or mixed with other herbicides when necessary. It is less toxic to mammals than some other herbicides.

Children and domestic animals should be kept away from any water in ditches or drains which may have been contaminated with these chemicals.

In small gardens, especially, it is better to remove weeds by hand or by hoeing, after which they can be raked together and put on the compost heap.

The home gardener will have no need to keep all of the chemicals mentioned, but there are three or four which can be kept as stock remedies and will take up very little storage space. Proprietary mixtures should be bought and these are marketed under a variety of trade names, but in all cases, the name of the active chemicals should be printed on the container; many of the mixtures contain a combination of an insecticide and a fungicide. A **copper compound, powdered sulphur** and **Benomyl** or **Zineb** would be useful as general fungicides. Either **Derris, Pyrethrin, Malathion, Carbaryl** or a compound containing **dimethoate** would be good insecticides, together with a preparation containing metaldehyde for slug and snail control. A small combination of these should be sufficient for all general purposes in a garden of any size and are fairly safe, provided they are used according to the directions, and that all precautions are taken as mentioned previously.

PLANTS FOR VARIOUS PURPOSES

INTRODUCTION

The following are suggestions of plants which are suitable for growing in a number of different situations. In addition, there are lists of plants with bold or variegated foliage, and suggestions for species to be grown in tropical highlands. Finally there is a list of plants named in the book which are also used as house plants in temperate countries.

It should be remembered that the plants listed in each section are those which are most commonly available and there are others which could be used in similar situations with equally good effect.

Plants recommended for one situation should be tried in others because many of them can be maintained in a wider variety of growing conditions than is sometimes expected. For instance, tree species which are usually too large for normal use as pot plants, can be grown as bonsai. Plants requiring full sun to develop flowers and good leaf colour, will tolerate some shade though growth will be weaker, leaf colour not as strong and flowers may not develop. Such plants will still be attractive and although they will not reach their full potential, they are useful as decoration but may need to be replaced at intervals. Additionally, many tropical species are grown now, very commonly, as house plants in temperate countries, and these, very often, must contend with much drier air, a wider range of temperature and less intense light. Under these conditions, they are somewhat slower in growth and remain smaller for a longer time, though the kind of management which they receive will affect both their size and their rate of growth.

The plants suggested in these lists should grow satisfactorily in most soils provided the ground has been prepared as recommended before planting, and that watering and fertilizer application are carried out regularly afterwards.

ARRANGEMENT OF LISTS

Trees
- Size: large, medium and small
- For shelter belts
- For deciduous effect
- For shade
- For short screens
- For formal effect

Climbers
- For fences, trellises and house walls
- For pergolas and arches
- For growing on trunks of trees
- For growing into tree crowns
- For covering walls and rocks

Ground cover plants
Plants for steep banks
- In shade and sun

Hedge plants
- Formal, informal and mixed

Plants needing full sun
Plants needing shade
Lawn grasses
Plants for dry conditions
Plants for wet conditions
Aquatic plants
Plants for large pots and jars
Plants for very small spaces
Plants with bold foliage
Plants with coloured or variegated foliage
Plants for coastal areas
Plants for towns
Plants for highland gardens
Tropical house and summer garden
Plants for temperate countries

Trees

"Large, medium and small" are sizes which refer to well-grown specimens of trees when they are fully grown. The size of a tree will be affected by the soil and the growing conditions, and the different species will show considerable differences in rate of growth.

Large (20 – 30 metres)

Bertholettia
Casuarina equisetifolia
Dacrydium
Dyera
Enterolobium
Eugenia grandis
Ficus benjamina
Mangifera
Peltophorum
Samanea
Terminalia

Medium (10 – 17 metres)

Araucaria
Calophyllum
Cassia
Casuarina nobilis
Casuarina rumphiana
Cupressus
Dillenia indica
Erythrina
Eugenia spps.
Ficus religiosa
Ficus roxburghii
Garcinia
Juniperus
Mesua
Mimusops
Nephelium
Pinus
Pithecellobium
Polyalthia
Salix
Sterculia
Tamarindus

Small (3 – 7 metres)

Averrhoa
Baeckia
Bauhinia
Cassia spps.
Crescentia
Gustavia
Jacaranda
Salix
Thevetia

Shelter Belts

Casuarina equisetifolia
Eugenia grandis
Fagraea fragrans
Melaleuca leucadendron
Millettia atropurpurea
Podocarpus rumphii
Pterocarpus indicus

Deciduous effect

Ceiba pentandra
Cratoxylon formosum
Dyera costulata
Enterolobium cyclocarpus
Erythrina
Ficus bengalensis
Gliricidia
Melia
Peltophorum
Plumeria
Pterocarpus
Samanea
Sterculia parvifolia
Swietenia
Terminalia catappa

Shade

Andira inermis
Baccaurea motleyana
Calophyllum
Enterolobium cyclocarpus
Eugenia aquea (Syzygium aqueum)

Ficus benjamina
Ficus microcarpa
Melia indica
Peltophorum
Samanea

Short screens

Acacia spps.
Bixa
Cerbera
Cinnamomum
Crescentia
Dillenia indica
Erythrina variegata var. orientalis
Ficus roxburghii
Gardenia carinata
Hibiscus tiliaceus
Honckenya
Kopsia
Mimusops
Polyalthia longifolia
Sterculia parvifolia
Thevetia

Formal effect

Some of these species will produce a formal effect while they are still young, but this effect will be lost when they are full grown. However it is possible to prolong this stage for some time by judicious pruning.

Calophyllum (while young)
Casuarina nobilis
Durio zibethinus (while young)
Dyera costulata
Fagraea fragrans (while young)
Gnetum gnemon
Juniperus
Mesua ferrea
Podocarpus rumphii

Climbers

Fences, trellises and house walls

Antigonon
Calonyction
Cardiospermum
Ipomoea
Jasminum
Mina
Pergularia
Porana
Quisqualis
Stigmaphyllon
Tristellateia

Pergola and arches

Antigonon
Argyreia
Bauhinia kockiana
Beaumontia

Bougainvillea (some varieties)
Congea
Dioscorea
Jasminum
Macfadyena unguis-cati
Mucuna
Odontadenia
Petraea
Porana
Quisqualis
Saritaea magnifica
Stenochlaena
Stephanotis
Strongylodon
Strophanthus gratus
Thunbergia grandiflora
Thunbergia laurifolia
Thunbergia mysorensis
Tristellateia

Trunks of trees

Drynaria
Epipremnum
Monstera
Philodendron
Polypodium
Scindapus
Syngonium

Growing into tree crowns

Allamanda
Bougainvillea
Congea
Mucuna
Petraea
Strophanthus gratus

Covering walls and rocks

In full sun
Ficus pumila
Lantana montevidensis
Vernonia elliptica
Wedelia triloba

In shade
Epipremnum
Philodendron
Scindapus
Syngonium

Ground cover plants

These plants are very useful since they are both ornamental and functional: while being decorative, they also help to keep down weeds. When combined suitably with other taller growing plants, they produce a very pleasant effect.

Alternanthera
Cuphea hyssopifolia
Hemigraphis alternata

Lantana montevidensis
Lochnera
Ophiopogon
Pachyrhizus (while flowering)
Phyllanthus myrtifolius
Portulaca
Rhoeo
Setcreasia
Wedelia triloba
Zebrina

Plants for steep banks

In full sun
Congea
Dillenia suffruticosa
Lantana montevidensis
Phyllanthus myrtifolius
Wedelia triloba

In shade
Ferns (many kinds)
Monstera
Philodendron
Selaginella
Caladium

Hedge plants

A single species may be used to make a formal or informal hedge but, in addition, several different kinds can be grown together to form a "tapestry" hedge.

Formal Hedge (single species)
Acalypha siamea
Bamboo (dwarf)
Cordia
Ehretia
Ixora
Ligustrum
Malpighia
Murraya paniculata
Streblus
Triphasia
Podocarpus polystachyus

Informal Hedge (single species)
Acalypha wilkesiana & cvs.
Allamanda
Barleria
Bixa
Bougainvillea
Exoecaria
Gardenia
Hibiscus mutabilis
Hibiscus rosa sinensis
Ixora
Lantana
Murraya paniculata
Pittosporum tobira
Polyscias
Sanchezia nobilis
Strobilanthes hemigraphis
Tecomaria capensis

Mixed Hedge
Acalypha siamea
Acalypha wilkesiana & cvs.
Allamanda
Ehretia
Hibiscus rosa sinensis
Ixora
Lagerstroemia indica
Malpighia
Polyscias
Pseuderanthemum
Sanchezia nobilis
Tecoma stans
Thunbergia

Plants needing full sun

In general, all plants with variegated leaves need as much light as possible in order to develop their full colour. Plants with normal leaves will flower best in full sun but will tolerate a certain amount of shade though they will then produce longer, more slender stems and less flowers.

Acacia
Acalypha
Acrostichum
Agave
Antigonon
Barleria
Bauhinia
Bellamcanda
Blechnum
Bougainvillea
Brunfelsia
Callistemon
Canna
Casuarina
Chrysalidocarpus
Cinnamomum
Coleus
Crossandra
Cyrtostachys
Duranta
Eugenia grandis (Syzygium grande)
Ficus
Gardenia
Helianthus
Heliconia psittacorum
Hemigraphis alternata
Hibiscus
Ipomoea
Ixora
Jacaranda
Jasminum
Kopsia
Lagerstroemia
Livistonia
Lochnera
Millettia
Osbeckia
Orchids (some)
Orthosiphon
Peltophorum

Podocarpus
Polyscias
Plumbago
Quisqualis
Russelia
Salvia
Strophanthus
Tabernaemontana
Tamarindus
Terminalia
Thevetia
Tristellateia
Vitex
Zephyranthes

Plants needing full shade

Almost all of these plants require light shade, dappled shade or shade for the greater part of the day in order to make proper growth.

Adiantum
Alocasia
Anthurium
Asplenium
Begonia
Caladium
Dieffenbachia
Episcia
Fittonia
Maranta
Monstera
Orchids (some)
Pellionia
Peperomia
Philodendron
Pilea
Randia
Saintpaulia
Sinningia
Tacca
Tradescantia
Xanthosoma
Zebrina

Lawn grasses

Axonopus affinis
Axonopus compressus
Chrysopogon ariculatus
Cynodon dactylon
Digitaria didactyla
Eremochloa ophiuroides
Paspalum conjugatum
Stenotaphrum secundatum
Zoysia japonica
Zoysia matrella
Zoysia tenuifolia

Plants for dry conditions

These plants are suitable for sun rockeries or for soil which dries out quickly. Some can be grown as pot plants indoors but they need full sunlight and must not be overwatered.

Adenium
Agave
Aloe
Casuarina
Cereus
Cuphea hyssopifolia
Cuphea ignea
Cuphea miniata
Euphorbia antiquorum & cvs.
Euphorbia milii
Euphorbia spps.
Euphorbia tirucalli
Haemanthus
Hippeastrum
Ixora (dwarf)
Jatropha
Juniperus (creeping)
Kalanchoe
Lantana
Mammillaria
Mesembryanthemum
Opuntia
Pedilanthus
Pereskia
Phyllanthus
Pithecellobium dulce
Portulaca
Sansevieria
Stapelia
Terminalia catappa
Yucca
Zinnia angustifolia

Plants for wet conditions

These plants will grow in soil which is wet for most of the time or they will grow in shallow water, but they will not survive for very long if they are not allowed to dry out completely.

Acorus
Athyrium esculentum
Ceratopteris
Colocasia esculenta
Cyathea
Cyperus spps.
Monochoria
Sagittaria
Salix
Saraca
Scirpus
Typha

Aquatic plants

Aponogeton
Azolla
Blyxa
Cabomba
Ceratopteris
Echinodorus
Eichornea
Hydrilla
Hygrophila

Lemna
Limnocharis
Limnophila
Ludwigia
Marsilea
Monochoria
Myriophyllum
Nelumbo
Nymphaea
Pistia
Sagittaria
Salvinia
Typha
Utricularia
Vallisneria

Plants for large pots and jars

Adenium
Aglaia
Alpinia sanderana
Adiantum peruvianum
Bougainvillea (some)
Brunfelsia
Cereus
Citrus (some)
Chrysalidocarpus
Cordyline
Cyrtostachys
Dracaena
Epiphyllum
Euodia
Euphorbia
Ficus benjamina
Ficus elastica
Galphimia
Heliconia (some)
Ixora (dwarf)
Juniperus
Lagerstroemia indica
Livistonia
Mango (some cultivars)
Monstera
Muehlenbeckia
Murraya
Philodendron
Ptychosperma
Rhapis
Rhododendron (Azalea)

Plants for very small spaces

Many of the plants included here are naturally small but others, which can grow to a large size when fully mature, can be kept to a small size by suitable management. The best way to achieve this is by planting them in small pots so that the roots are restricted in growth and the plants are thus not allowed to develop to their full grown size. These plants can be placed on window sills or shelves and other such small places inside a room but the choice of plant will depend on the amount of light which is available in the chosen position.

Adiantum cuneatum
Adiantum tenerum
Asplenium nidus (while small)
Begonia
Caladium humboldtii
Calathea
Capsicum annuum & cvs.
Cattleya
Coleus
Cordyline (small)
Cotyledon
Cryptanthus
Crassula argentea
Cyperus alternifolius cv. gracilis
Davallia
Dracaena (some)
Echeveria
Epipremnum (while small)
Episcia
Impatiens
Ficus benjamina (while small)
Fittonia
Haemanthus
Haworthia
Maranta
Mammillaria
Moss (various kinds)
Nephrolepis (while small)
Ophiopogon
Oplismenus
Opuntia
Pellaea
Pellionia
Peperomia
Pereskia aculeata (while small)
Pilea
Portulaca
Pteris
Rebutia
Saintpaulia
Sinningia
Syngonium (while small)
Tradescantia
Zebrina

Plants with bold foliage

Anthurium macrolobum
Artocarpus altilis
Asplenium nidus
Caryota
Cocos
Colocasia gigantea
Cyathea
Jatropha curcas
Jatropha multifida
Licuala
Livistonia
Monstera
Musa
Philodendron (some)
Pometia (while young)
Schefflera
Solanum macranthum
Tectona grandis

Xanthosoma violaceum

Plants with coloured or variegated foliage

Acalypha wilkesiana & cvs.
Agave americana
Aglaonema
Alpinia sanderae
Alternanthera
Amaranthus tricolor
Ananas
Anthurium cristallinum
Begonia
Caladium
Carex
Chlorophytum
Cissus
Coleus
Cordyline
Cryptanthus
Dianella
Dieffenbachia
Dracaena
Duranta
Epipremnum
Episcia
Erythrina variegata cv. Orientalis
Euphorbia pulcherrima
Excoecaria
Ficus elasticus cvs.
Ficus pumila
Ficus sagittata
Fittonia
Gynura
Hemigraphis
Hibiscus rosa sinensis cv. cooperi
Iresine
Maranta
Ophiopogon
Pandanus
Pellionia
Peperomia
Philodendron
Phragmites
Pilea
Piper
Rhoeo
Sansevieria
Stenotaphrum
Syngonium
Talinium
Tradescantia
Zebrina

Plants for coastal areas

In these places the plants must be able to withstand a great deal of wind together with the salt spray which the wind carries in from the sea. Also there is a considerable amount of reflected heat and light from the surface of the sea and from large expanses of sandy beaches so that growing conditions are not ideal, and the number of plants which can be grown is considerably reduced. However, there are a number of wild species found in these areas which are adapted to the situation and some of these, especially some of the shrubs and small trees, could be used with good effect in a garden on the coast.

Anacardium
Arfeuillea
Casuarina
Cerbera
Cocos
Crinum asiaticum
Eugenia fragrans
Hibiscus tiliaceus
Melaleuca leucadendron
Pandanus
Podocarpus polystachus
Pongamia
Pterocarpus
Rhodomyrtus
Terminalia catappa
Tristellateia
Zoysia matrella

Plants for towns

For street and roadside planting in towns, it is necessary to use species which will be tolerant of traffic fumes and which can survive in reasonable condition despite a certain amount of neglect. Such plants are also often subject to a great deal of damage by inconsiderate pedestrians.

Acalypha wilkesiana & cvs.
Chrysalidocarpus
Cycas rumphii
Dracaena (some)
Duranta
Euphorbia (cactus type)
Ficus (some)
Gliricidia
Lantana
Millettia
Muntingia
Pandanus
Peltophorum
Pithecellobium dulce
Roystonea
Samanea
Sansevieria
Swietenia
Vernonia
Vitex
Wedelia

Plants for highland gardens

The seeds of many hardy and half-hardy annuals from temperate countries can often be found on sale in shops in the lowlands. This is not appropriate for many of these plants will in fact grow better and will produce more attractive flowers if grown in the highlands because of the slightly lower tempera-

ture. Many of the long established ornamentals in the highlands, such as Fuchsia and Pelargonium, will make weak growth only in the lowlands and will not flower at all. In fact, most of the wild plants in the highlands will behave in a similar manner when grown in the lowlands. However, a number of the wild trees and ferns, as well as many of the smaller herbaceous plants in the highlands will make admirable ornamentals for gardens at that elevation.

The list of plants for highland gardening is rather long, but not all of the species are described in the text because the main emphasis of the book is on lowland gardening. For further information, the reader should consult the natural history section of the public library.

Many of the ornamental plants from the lowlands should be tried also at different elevations in the highlands and it is quite possible that there could be some unexpectedly satisfactory results.

Trees
Agathis
Canarium
Caryota
Casuarina (some)
Cupressus
Cyphomandra
Dacrydium
Elaeocarpus
Engelhardtia
Eucalyptus citriodorus
Eucalyptus sp.
Fagraea (mountain species)
Juniperus
Leptospermum
Lithosperma
Litsea
Pinus
Quercus
Ravenala
Sauraulia
Schima
Symingtonia
Thea
Weinmannia

Shrubs
Acalypha
Acalypha wilkesiana & cvs.
Allamanda
Baeckia
Blastus
Bougainvillea
Cassia laevigata
Cestrum
Citrus
Datura
Dissochaeta
Euohorbia pulcherrima
Fuchsia
Hibiscus mutabilis

Hibiscus rosa sinensis
Medinella
Melastoma
Pandorea
Pyrostegia
Rhododendron
Rosa
Rubus
Sambucus javanica
Schefflera
Thunbergia mysorensis
Tibouchina semidecandra

Ferns
Abacopteris
Adiantum
Aglaomorpha
Angiopteris
Asplenium
Cyathea
Davallia
Dipteris
Drynaria rigidula
Lophogramma
Lycopodium
Merinthosorus
Mosses
Nephrolepis
Photinopoteris
Selaginella
Sphenomeris

Herbaceous plants
Agapanthus
Ageratum
Aeschynanthus
Alcea rosea
Alpinia
Anthurium andreanum
Artemisia
Arundina
Begonia
Brassica
Browallia
Calonyction
Cattleya
Chirita
Chrysanthemum
Coleus
Crinum
Cymbidium ensifolium
Cyperus papyrus
Dahlia
Dahlia imperialis
Dianella
Dianthus
Didymocarpus
Gladiolus
Globba
Godetia
Hemerocallis
Hymenatherum
Hymenocallis
Impatiens
Ipomoea learii

Iresine
Jacobinia
Joinvillea
Malvaviscus
Miscanthus
Musa (some)
Mussaenda mutabilis
Nepenthes
Nymphaea
Olearia
Passiflora edulis
Passiflora vitifolia
Pelargonium x Hortorum
Pennisetum clandestinum
Renanthera
Richardia
Ruta graveolens
Salvia splendens
Sechium
Spathoglottis
Streptocarpus
Tagetes
Tithonia
Tradescantia
Tropaeolum
Trichosanthes
Viola
Zingiber

Tropical plants for house and summer garden cultivation in temperate countries

In temperate countries plants which are bought from nurseries or garden centres are often planted in a potting mixture containing a high proportion of peat which holds water for a long time. It is very easy, therefore, to overwater, so that the roots will begin to die and rot. However this situation can be avoided by repotting the plant, using one of the soil based potting mixtures available commercially. The plants will be a little slow in recovering but will soon grow satisfactorily so that they will appear much happier and will be longer lasting. Watering and fertilizer application must be adjusted to suit the new potting mixture.

Many tropical fruits are available now in temperate countries and the seeds of these will often germinate readily if they are planted immediately, but they will not stand drying for any length of time. The seedlings make interesting house plants but will eventually become too large for the pot and for a small room. One exception is Citrus, the seeds of which germinate very well and the resulting plants can be kept for a long time in a small room where they will flower, provided they receive sufficient light. Seeds of mango, lychee and avocado will germinate easily and make interesting foliage plants for some time but they will eventually become too large and must be discarded. Coconuts can be germinated also but they need a very large pot and germination is slow.

Acalypha hispida
Acalypha wilkesiana & cvs.
Adiantum cuneatum
Adiantum tenerum
Aechmea
Agapanthus
Ageratum
Aglaonema commutatum & cvs.
Allamanda cathartica
Allamanda violacea
Aloe
Alternanthera ficoidea & cvs.
Ananas comosus cv. variegatus
Asparagus densiflorus & cvs.
Asparagus setaceus & cvs.
Asplenium
Anthurium andreanum
Anthurium cristallinum
Aster (annual)
Aster, perennial (Michaelmas Daisy)
Begonia species and hybrids
Beloperone guttata
Bougainvillea
Brunfelsia pauciflora cv. exima
Caladium x hortulanum
Caladium humboldtii
Calathea lancifolia
Calathea lindeniana
Calathea makoyana
Calathea ornata
Calathea wiotii
Calathea zebrina
Canna
Carex morrowii
Celosia
Chlorophytum
Citrus
Chrysanthemum
Codiaeum variegatum
Coleus x hybridus
Cordyline terminalis
Coreopsis drummondii
Cosmos
Crossandra
Cryptanthus
Cyperus alternifolius
Cyperus alternifolius cv. gracilis
Dahlia
Davallia
Dianthus chinensis
Dieffenbachia picta & cvs.
Dracaena deremensis
Dracaena fragrans
Dracaena godseffiana
Dracaena marginata
Dracaena reflexa
Dracaena sanderiana
Episcia cupreata
Episcia reptans
Epiphyllum
Euphorbia cotinifolia
Euphorbia pulcherrima
Euphorbia (cactus-like form)
Epipremnum aureum

Ficus benjamina
Ficus deltoidea
Ficus elastica & cvs.
Ficus lyrata
Ficus pumila & cv.
Fittonia verschaffeltii & cvs.
Gardenia jasminoides
Gerbera
Gladiolus
Gynura aurantica
Haworthia
Hemigraphis alternata
Hibiscus rosa sinensis
Hibiscus rosa sinensis cv. cooperi
Hippeastrum
Hydrangea
Impatiens balsamina
Impatiens oncidiodes
Impatiens wallerana
Iresine herbstii & cvs.
Ixora chinensis
Ixora coccinea
Kalanchoe marmorata
Kalanchoe pinnata
Kalanchoe tomentosa
Kalanchoe tubiflora
Kochia scoparia
Lantana camara
Maranta erythrophylla
Maranta kerchoviana
Maranta leuconeura
Mirabilis
Monstera deliciosa
Monstera epipremnoides
Muehlenbeckia platyclados
Neoregelia biserrata & cvs.
Neoregelia carolinae
Neoregelia cordifolia & cvs.
Neoregelia spectabilis
Nidularium
Nerium oleander
Oplismenus hirtellus variegatus
Opuntia
Pandanus sanderae
Pandanus veitchii
Pellionia daveauana
Pellionia pulchra
Peperomia argyrea
Peperomia caperata
Peperomia hederaefolia
Peperomia magnolifolia
Peperomia obtusifolia
Peperomia scandens
Pellaea rotundifolia
Petunia
Philodendron bipinnatifidum
Philodendron domesticum
Philodendron erubescens
Philodendron scandens var. oxycardium
Philodendron selloum
Philodendron squamiferum
Phlox drummondii
Platycerium
Plumbago auriculata
Pilea cadieri

Pilea involucrata
Pilea microphylla
Pilea nummularifolia
Polyscias balfouriana
Polyscias ficifolia
Polyscias fruticosa
Polyscias guilfoylei
Pseuderanthemum atropurpureum
Pseuderanthemum reticulatum
Rhoeo spathacea
Ricinus communis

Rosa
Rudbeckia purpurea
Saintpaulia
Salvia splendens
Sansevieria cylindrica
Sansevieria trifasciata & cvs.
Schefflera
Selaginella
Setcreasia
Sinningia
Streptocarpus

Spathiphyllum
Stephanotis floribunda
Syngonium podophyllum & cvs.
Tagetes
Tradescantia albiflora
Tradescantia x andersoniana
Tradescantia blossfeldiana
Verbena tenera
Viola
Zantedeschia
Zebrina pendula

GLOSSARY

Annual: A plant which completes its whole lifecycle from seed germination to flowering and fruiting within one growing season, usually assumed to be one year, though many plants need less time than this and can complete the whole cycle in three to nine months. The seeds either germinate as soon as they are planted or they can remain dormant for periods varying from a few weeks to a few years.

Bed: A small, sharply defined cultivated area in which a single plant or a small group of plants are grown.

Binomial: The Latin name given to each plant and made up of a generic name followed by a specific adjective. With many cultivated plants there may be a number of forms or varieties within one species and a second adjective may be added to the name in order to distinguish these.

Border: A cultivated area which is usually large, often elongated, and arranged to be viewed from one side, two sides, or all around. The outline and size can be varied to suit the space available and the individual design of any particular garden.

Bulb: An underground plant storage organ made up of fleshy leaf-bases which remains dormant while growing conditions are poor.

Capital: The top of a short column or pillar made of brick, stone or concrete, and often flat, so that a potted plant can be placed on it.

Conservatory: A kind of greenhouse, often ornamental in design, with many glass sides and a roof which may be of glass or some opaque waterproof material. It is usually attached to a house from which it may be entered conveniently, and is usually heated during the colder months of the year.

Corm: An enlarged stem of various shape and size, usually fairly short and in a vertical position. It may be situated just at the soil surface or at varying depths below this.

Culm: The hollow stems of grasses, but the term is sometimes used for the short stems of other herbaceous plants, especially if they are hollow also.

Cultivar: A variety or race of one species of plant which has arisen under cultivation and sufficiently distinct to be given a name.

Double flower: One which has stamens or pistils, or both, converted into extra petals.

Gall: A large, usually hard, rounded structure which develops on leaves as a result of the activities of an insect.

Generic: An adjective derived from "genus".

Genus: A clearly defined group of plants which are more or less related. It may contain more than one species.

Greenhouse: An individual building with glass sides and roof which may or may not be heated, and used in temperate countries for growing plants which need protection from low temperatures or from too much rain.

Herbaceous plant: One with no persistent stem above ground and producing annual stems from a perennial.

Hothouse: A heated greenhouse used in cool countries for growing tropical plants.

House plant: Small- or medium-sized plants which are grown in various kinds of containers for decoration inside houses, offices or public buildings.

Humus: The organic content of the soil derived from decaying plant or animal remains.

Hybrid: The offspring derived from crossing two different species of plants or two different forms within one species.

Inflorescence: The single or branched stem carrying one or more flowers. There are many different kinds of inflorescences.

Introduced species: A plant brought into a country from some other part of the world.

Leaf scorch: Browning of the leaves as a result of poor growing conditions or a sudden change in growing conditions.

Loggia: A covered avenue or walk formed by a number of arches, with one or more sides open to the air.

Marcot: A form of air-layering in which branches are induced to form roots while still attached to the parent plant. They are then cut off and planted in the soil in the usual way.

Mulch: A layer of compost or dried plant material or some other kind of cover which is spread over the surface of the soil to prevent it from drying out too quickly.

Opposite leaves: Two leaves borne at one point on a stem but on opposite sides of it.

Overpotting: Transplanting from a small pot to a very much larger one so that a plant will tend to make vigorous vegetative growth with little or no flower development. Many plants flower much better when the roots are restricted.

Peltate: A term referring to a leaf in which the stalk is attached to the centre of the under-surface instead of to its edge.

Perennial: A plant which persists for many years producing flowers and fruits each year.

Pollarding: A method of tree pruning which is usually carried out every two or three years. All branches are cut back to a definite level and a large number of new shoots will develop afterwards from the cut ends.

Rootstock: A persistent woody structure which is found at or just below ground level and from which new shoots arise.

Rose: A removable, perforated flat-topped cap which can be fitted over the end of the spout on a watering-can. The distribution of the water will be affected by the number and size of the holes in the cap.

Scandent: Climbing or scrambling.

Seedsmen: Vendors of garden or crop plant seeds.

Mealy bugs 360
Methamidopos 251
Methyl bromide 355
Methylated spirit 42
Miniature gardens 11, 276, 301
  containers for 305
  fertilizers 277
  in pots 305
  plants for 306, 307
  position 305
Miscellaneous compounds 356
Mist sprays 6
Mites 361
Moonfish 291
Mowers 26
Mulch 34
Muriate of potash 39

N
Names of plants 7
Naphthalene 355
Natural organic compounds 357
Nicotine 355, 357
Nitro-chalk 39
Nitrogen 31, 34, 37, 38
Nursery 11
  siting 22

O
Orchids 248
  climbing 253
  epiphytic 256
  jewel 249
  slipper 253
  terrestrial 249
Orchid breeding 248
  flower structure 249
  export 248
  houses 258
  hybridization 248
Organic manures 35
  oils 357
Organophosphorus insecticides 356
    systemic kinds 356

P
Paintbrush 42
Palms 154, 212
  kinds of 189
  planting and siting 188
Paper bags 42
Paths 12, 19
  materials 15
Patios 19, 25
Paving, crazy 19
  materials 19
Peat 40
Perlite 57
Perrenials, herbaceous 3

Pergola 21
Pesticides 26, 352
  aerosols 355
  application 354
  dry preparations 355
  granules 355
  liquid preparations 354
  smokes & fumigants 355
Pests 352, 357
Phytosanitary permits 352
Phosphorus 31, 37, 38
Piercing & sucking insects 354
Planting, formal 15
  informal 15
Plants in air-conditioned rooms 22
    in temperate countries 3
Pollarding 52
Polythene bags 26, 28
Pool establishment 288
  liners, moulded 290
  liners, plastic sheeting 290
Potassium 31, 34, 38, 39
  nitrate 39
Pot plants 55
Pots 26
Potting mixtures 40, 57
Poultry manure 36
Powdered sulphur 365
Prawn dust 36
Prevention of disease 352
Propagation 42
  chamber 46
Pruner 26
Pruning 42, 51
Pyrethrum 355
Pyrethrins 357, 365

Q
Quarantine regulations 352
Quicklime 39

R
Rainfall 2
Rake 26
Rectified spirit 42
Repellants 354
Residual poisons 354
Rock gardens 276
  plants for 280
Rock phosphate 39
Rogor 253
Root cuttings 47
  pruning 52
Root vegetables 322
Rooting hormones 6
  medium 47
Rotation of crops 314
Rotenone 357

S
Saw 26

Scale insects 360
Scissors 42
Seasonal fruits 332
Seaweed 37
Secateurs 26
Seeds 42, 43
  sowing of 44
  storage of 314
Selective herbicide 364
Sevin 251
Shade 4
  rockeries 286
Shrubs 15, 90
  scandent 90
Simazine 365
Slender climbers 90, 137
Slime disease 363
Sludge 37
Slugs 360
Small flowering plants 286, 306
Small gardens 22
  siting of plants 22
  seeds 43
Snails 360
Sodium chlorate 364
  nitrate 39
Softwood cuttings 46
Soil 30
  aeration 4
  mixtures 6
Sowing 44
Soybean cake 36
Species 7
Spices & flavourings 325
Spot-turfing 197
Sprayers 26
Stakes 26
Starchy tubers 315
Stem borers 358
  cuttings 47
Steps 13, 19
Stomach poisons 354
Stone figures 21
String 26
Suckers 50
Sulphate of potash 39
Sulphur 364, 365
Sun, position 4
Superphosphate 39
Surface wash 13
Swimming pool 11
Systemic poisons 354

T
Tanks 287
  drainage 287
  kinds of 287
  size and shape 287
Temperature 3
Tennis courts 12, 14

Terraces 14, 19
Terrarium 302
Thinning 51
Thiram 364
Thrips 253, 359
Tissue culture 52
Tobacco infusion 314
Top dressing 40
Transplanting 44
Trees 14, 154
  kinds of 14
  deciduous 14
  descriptions 157
  growth 14
  planting 156
  pruning 156
  seedlings 45
  siting 155
  staking 156
  young 156
Troughs 11, 25
Tuba root 314, 251, 357
Tubers 50
Turfing 197
2, 4-D 364

U
Urea 39
Urine 34, 36
Urns 27

V
Varieties 7
Vegetables 314
  cultivation 314
  garden siting 22, 314
  pests 314
Vegetative propagation 6, 42, 45
Vermaculite 57
Viruses 361, 362

W
Walls 18
  informal 19
  materials for 19
Water depth 290
  plants 291
  pumps 290
Watering can 26
Weeds 352, 364
Weevils 354
Wheelbarrow 26
Window-boxes 11
Wire 26
Wood ashes 34
Woody climbers 90, 132
Worms 202

Z
Zineb 364, 365

COMMON NAME INDEX

A

African evergreen 221
    lily 60
      marigolds 42, 46
      oil palm 191
      tulip tree 50, 185
      violet 47, 83
Air plant 236
Aluminium plant 240
Amazon lily 73, 233
     sword plant 293
     water lily 299
Anatto 94, 145
Angel's trumpets 50, 121
Angelwing begonia 228
Angled loofah 320
Angsana 3, 46, 51, 52, 181
Apple 49
Arborvitae 187
Artichoke 50
Aroids 213
Arrowroot family 224
Arrowhead 297, 307
    vine 221
Arum 213
    lily 213, 222
Asam gelugor 347
    jawa 185
Asparagus 62
    fern 63, 137, 227
Aster 63
Australian blue conch 199
Avocado pear 332, 333

B

Baby rubber plant 239
Bachang 345
Balloon flower 82
    vine 137
Balsam 63
Bamboo 51, 187
    orchid 249
    palm 193
Banana 51, 237, 333, 335
Barberton daisy 74
Baru 173
Basil 326
Basket grass 237
Bat lily 243
Batai laut 177
Batchelor's buttons 74
Bawang 323
Bayam 324
Bead tree 176
Beans 44, 317
Beef plant 78
Beefsteak begonia 229
    plant 236
Belimbing 336
    asam 336
    manis 336

Bengkuang 316
Bermuda grass 199
Betel palm 189
Biji selasih 326
Binjai 345
Bitter cucumber 321
    gourd 321
Bird's nest fern 208
Black-eyed Susan 83, 286
Bladderwort 299
Blanket flower 73
Bleeding heart 138
Blue hibiscus 110
Blue pea 138
Blue plumbago 82
Blue taro 222
Blushing bromeliad 224
Boat lily 241
Bone bush 106, 284
Bo tree 169
Boston fern 210
Bottle-brush tree 161
Bottle gourd 320
Brazil nut 161, 336
Breadfruit 47, 336, 337
Bridal creeper 136
Brinjal 319
Bromeliad 222
Buah mentega 348
    perah 168
    susu 135, 348
Buddha's belly bamboo 227
Buffalo grass 201
Bullock's heart 333
Bulrush 299
Bungor 173
Burning bush 236
Burro's tail 243
Bush violet 66
Buttercup tree 2, 165
Butterfly bush 66, 94
    ginger 245
Busy Lizzie 306

C

Cabbage 42, 323
    lettuce 323
Cacti 48, 280, 281
Cajeput 176
Calabash tree 165
Calico plant 61
Calla lily 222
Candlestick cassia 97
Cape blue waterlily 296
    honeysuckle 86
Carambola 336
Cardinal's guard 78
Caricature plant 233
Carpet grass 200
Carrot 315, 322
Cashew nut 345

Castor oil plant 124
Cat's tails 90
    whiskers 74, 79
Cauliflower 315, 323
Cayenne cherry 344
Celery 326
    cabbage 323
Cekur 245
Cempaka 177
Cenderai 172
Centipede grass 201
    plant 115, 236
Ceylon iron-wood 176
Chalice vine 124
Chandelier plant 236
Changeable Rose 149
Chayote 322
Chempedak 337
Chermai belanda 344
Cherry tomato 320
Chiku 5, 337
Chilli 5, 325
    padi 326
China berry 176
Chinese cabbage 36, 323
    chives 328
    juniper 17
    lettuce 323
    lychee 349
    mustard 323
    privet 146
    radish 322
Chives 328
Choy sam 323
    sim 323
Cigar flower 70
Cinnamon 49, 164
Climbing begonia 231
    orchids 253
    spinach 324
Clover 202
Cluster bean 319
Cockscomb 67
Coconut 189, 340
Coffee 3
Coleus 328
Common lime 338
Conifer 17
Coral berry 222
    plant 83, 111
    tree 168
Corallita 137
Coriander 326
Cowpeas 37
Crape myrtle 114
Creeping Charlie 240
    fig 133, 233
    juniper 285
Crepe ginger 69, 245
Cress 323
Croton 54, 98, 149, 231

Crown of thorns 284
Cucor atap 160
Cucumber 5, 320
Custard apple 333
Cypress 165

D

Dadap 2, 46, 168
Dahlberg daisy 78
Damar minyak 157
Day lily 77
Daun kesom 325
Derum 165
Devil's backbone 236
    ivy 217
Dolichos bean 318
Donkey's tail 243
Dove orchid 252
Drap d'or 79
Drumsticks 329
Drunken sailors 136
Duckweed 294
Duku 341
Dumb canes 216
Durian 5, 332, 341, 347
    belanda 333
Dwarf bamboo 144
    umbrella plant 71, 232

E

Eel grass 299
Egyptian lotus 296
Elephant bush 240
Elephant's ears 132, 214
Epiphytic ferns 310
    orchids 256

F

Fairy moss 292
False heather 70
Fan palms 212
Ferns 204
Fiddle-leaved fig 233
Fig 342
Fingernail plant 224
Fire bush 236
Firecracker flower 70
    fern 210
Fish-tail palm 189
Flame of the forest 2, 5, 165
Flame nettle 68
    violet 73
    tree 5
Floss flower 60
Flowering inch plant 244
Four-angled bean 317
Four o'clock 79
Foxtail orchids 262
Frangipanni 2, 5, 48, 119
French bean 317
    marigolds 79

Friendship plant 240

G

Gajus 345
Garlic 328
Gelam 176
Getah gerip merah 133
Ginger 51, 245, 311, 329
    family 244
    lily 75
Golden dewdrop 103
    pothos 217
    rod 3, 85
Gourds 320
Granadilla 348
Grapefruit 340
Greater yam 316
Green ripple peperomia 239
Gros Michel 335
Guava 47, 332, 344

H

Halia 245, 329
Hare's foot fern 209
Heart-leaf philodendron 220
Henna 114
Hog plum 345, 347
Hollyhocks 77
Honeysuckle 133
Honolulu creeper 137
Hop tree 160
Hujan-hujan 168

I

Ice plant 284
Icicle plant 284
Ilang-ilang 161
Inch plant 231
Indian borage 231
    kale 222
    laburnum 163
    lotus 296
    mango 345
    spinach 324
India-rubber plant 169
Iron cross begonia 229
Italian lime 340
Ivy-leaf peperomia 239

J

Jackfruit 337
Jack bean 317
Jade plant 232
    vine 136
Jagung 319
Jambu 344
    air 344
    air rhio 344
    bol 344
    chili 344
    hijau 344
    laut 169
    mawar 344
    melaka 344
    merah 344

Jambul merak 173
Japanese canna 75
    cherry 177
    lawngrass 200
    poinsettia 80
    sedge grass 67
Jasmine 131
Java apple 344
    lily 69
Javanese elder 124
Jelutong 168
Jenaris 177
Jerusalem artichoke 317
Jessamine 98
Jiring 180
Johar 163
Joseph's coat 61
Juniper 173

K

Kacang bendi 319
    botor 317
    buncis 317
    kara 318
    panjang 317
    parang 317
    parang putih 318
    perut ayam 317
    sablangah 318
    s'rinding 318
Kai choy 323
    lan 323
Kaki 348
Kale 323
Kangkung 324
Kandis 347
Kantan 245, 329
Kasai 181
Kassod tree 163
Kayu manis 164
Kechupu 347
Kedondong 347
Keladi 5, 50, 213, 316
    betawi 316
    china 316
Kelapa 189, 340
    sawit 191
Kemuning 115, 151
Kemunting 124, 184
Kenanga 161
Kerkup 350
Ketapang 187
Ketola sagi 320
    sanding 320
    ular 321
Ketumbar 326
Kinta weed 249
Kiora payung 171
Korean lawngrass 200
    velvet grass 200
Kuchai 328
Kundangan 345
Kundor 321
Kunyit 245, 329
Kwini 345

L

Labu air 320
Lace fern 210
Ladies' fingers 319
Lady of the night 98
Langkuas 245
Languas 329
Langsat 341
Leek 315
Lemon 340
    grass 329
Leopard flower 66
Lesser yam 316
Lettuce 323
Life plant 236
Lilyturf 237
Lima bean 318
Limau asam 338
    betawi 340
    kesturi 338
    manis 340
    nipis 338
Lime 333
    berry 148
Liverwort 310
Lobak 322
Lobster claw 75
Lokus 173
Long bean 5, 37, 317
Love grass 201

M

Mabolo 348
Madras thorn 180
Mahogany 185
Maidenhair fern 205, 206, 286
Maize 44, 319
Malay apple 344
Mango 333, 345
Mangosteen 5, 332, 347
Manila palm 194
Marigolds 79
Marquesa 348
Marvel of Peru 79
Mascarene grass 200
Mata kuching 349
Mempari 181
Mempat 165
Mempisang 181
Mempoyan 181
Meninjau 172
Mexican sunflower 86
Michaelmas daisy 3, 51, 63
Mickey Mouse plant 118
Milkbrush 106
Mint 328
Mistletoe fig 233
Mock lime 91
Money plant 217
Moon flower 18, 139
    orchids 263
Morning glory 131, 139
Morning-noon-and-night 94
Mother-in-law's tongue 241
Moth orchid 263

Mundu 347
Mung beans 37
Musk lime 338
Mustard 323

N

Nangka 337
Nasturtium 87
Net leaf 233
New Guinea creeper 135
Nona kapri 333
    sri kaya 333
Nibong 192
Nim tree 176

O

Oleander 2, 30, 116
Onion 323
Orange 340
Orange jasmine 115
Ornamental chilli 67
Oyster plant 241

P

Pagoda flower 98
Pak choy 323
Palm 42, 212
Panama hat plant 213
Panax 119, 146
Panda plant 236
Papaya 5, 333, 347
Paprika 326
Parsley 328
Passion flower 136
    fruit 333, 348
Peacock flower 2, 5, 94
    plant 225
Pear 49
Peepul 169
Pek chye 323
Penaga 176
    laut 161
Pen-wiper plant 236
Pepperface 239
Peradun 166
Persian lilac 172, 176
    shield 243
Persimmon 348
Physic nut 236
Pigeon orchid 3, 265
Pineapple 5, 62, 222, 333, 349
    family 222
Pinang 192
    raja 191
Pinetree 180
Pisang embun 335
    mas 335
    rajah 335
    rajah udang 335
    rastali 335
Plum 49
Poinciana 5, 6, 51, 165
Poinsettia 106
Pokok getah 172
Pomelo 340

Pong pong 164
Potato 315
    tree 2, 124, 184
Powder puff 94
Prayer plant 226, 227
Prickly pear 237, 280, 282
Pride of Barbados 5
    India 103, 173
Pulai 161
Pulasan 349
Pumpkin 322
Puncture vine 86
Purple heart 243
Purple passion fruit 136
    velvet plant 75, 234

R
Radiator plant 239
Radish 322
Railway creeper 139
Rain tree 168
Rainbow vine 239
Rajah kayu 163
Rambai 349
Rambutan 5, 332, 349
Rangoon creeper 136
Red cat's tail 90
    ginger 61
    ivy 77, 235
    leaf philodendron 220
    lily 77
    pentas 81
    sentul 341
Reed mace 299
Rice 297
Roses 82
Rose apple 344
    of Sharon 110
    myrtle 124, 184
    periwinkle 87
Roselle 325
Royal jasmine 140
    palm 193
Ru 164
Rubber family 42, 280, 283
    tree 172
Rukam 350
Rumenia 345

S
Saga 157
Sage 83
Saint Augustine grass 201
Satin pellionia 239
    wood 115
Sawi 323
Scorpion orchid 255, 256
Screw pine 118, 237
Sea almond 187
    hibiscus 173
Sealing wax palm 191, 212
Sendudok 115, 311
Sentang 176
Sentul 184, 341
Serai 329
Serangoon grass 199
Serdang 192
Shell ginger 245
Shrimp plant 65
Siglap grass 200
Silver back 181
    vine 221
Simpoh air 166
Singapore rhododendron 115
Slipper flower 80, 284
    orchid 252, 287
Smooth loofah 321
Snake gourd 321
Song of India 103
Soursop 333
Spade-leaf philodendron 220
Spider lily 78
    plant 67, 231
Spiderwort 244
Spinach 315
    mustard 323
Stag's horn fern 211
Star begonia 229
    cactus 234
    fruit 336
Starfish flower 285
Step-ladder plant 245
Stonecrop family 282
Stonewort 293
Strawflower 75
String-bush 144
Succulents 280
Sugar apple 333
    palm 189

Sukun 337
Sunflower 75
Surinam cherry 104, 344
    purslane 324
Susun kelapa 125
Sweet pepper 326
    potatoes 5, 46, 50, 315
Sweetsop 333
Swiss cheese plant 217
Sword bean 317
Sword fern 210

T
Talipot 191
Tamarind 185
Tampoi 349
Tanjung 177
Tapioca 114, 315
Taro 316
Tartogo 112, 236
Teak tree 187
Tembusu 49, 52, 169
Tempui 349
Terung 319
Thuja 17
Tickseed 68
Tipor 166
Timun 320
    belanda 348
Toa chye 323
Tomatoes 320
Tonkin creeper 140
Torch lily 245
Trailing begonia 231
    watermelon begonia 239
Traveller's palm 193
Tree fern 209
    of sadness 116
    tomato 350
True yam 5
Trumpet tree 185
Turmeric 245, 329

U
Ubi atas 316
    kayu 114, 315
    kekedek 315
    nasi 316
    torak 316
Umbrella plant 70, 232
    tree 241

Urn plant 222

V
Variegated ginger 61
Velvet bean 318
Vervain 87
Violet 87

W
Wandering Jew 244
Waringin 169, 307
Wart plant 234
Water apple 344
    convolvulus 324
    cress 324
    hyacinth 294
    lettuce 297
    lily 296
    melon 322
    milfoil 296
    poppy 294
    snowflake 297
    wistaria 294
Watermelon peperomia 239
Wax gourd 321
Weeping fig 169
    willow 142, 184
West Indian cherry 50, 177
    locust 173
White mugwort 62
White scorpion orchid 256
Wishbone flower 86
Witches' tongue 98

Y
Yam 51, 139, 316
    bean 316
Yautia 222, 316
Yellow bells 125
    flame tree 177
    lotus 296
    oleander 125
    passion fruit 348
    sentul 341
    stemmed palm 212
    waterlily 296

Z
Zebra plant 62, 224, 226
Zephyr lily 87

BOTANICAL NAME INDEX

A

Abelmoschus esculentus 319
Acacia 51
    auriculaeformis 157
    cincinnata 157
    mangium 157
    richii 157
Acalypha 145, 148
    hispida 90
    siamea 145, 309
    siamensis 146
    wilkesiana & cvs. 90,
    148
Achras zapota 337
Acrostichum aureum 205
Adenanthera pavonina 157
Adenium coetaneum 281
Adiantum 205, 307
    cuneatum 206
    macrophyllum 208
    peruvianum 206
    polyphyllum 208
    raddianum 206
    tenerum 206
      var. Farleyense 206
      var. Glory of Moor-
      drecht 206
    trapeziforme 208
Aechmea fasciata 222
    fulgens 222
    cv. discolor 222
Aerides lawrenceae 265
    odoratum 265
Afgekia 132
Agapanthus orientalis 60
Agathis alba 157
Ageratum conyzoides 60
Agave 280, 281
    americana 281
    angustifolia 281
    sisalana 281
Aglaia odorata 91
Aglaonema commutatum &
    cvs. 213
    pictum 214
Alcea rosea 77
Allamanda 2, 148
    cathartica 128, 132
      var. Hendersonii
      128, 132
    schottii 128, 148
    violacea 128, 148
Allium sativum 328
    schoenoprasum 328
    sp. 323
    tuberosum 328
Alocasia macrorrhiza 214
Aloe 227, 280, 306
Alpinia 61, 227, 245
    mutica 245
    purpurata 61

sanderae 61
Alstonia 160
Alternanthera 61, 227
    dentata cv. rubiginosa 61
    ficoidea & cvs. 61, 227
Amaranthus 37
    hybridus 324
Amherstia nobilis 160
Anacardiaceae 345
Anacardium occidentale 345
Ananas comosus cv. variegatus
    62, 222, 349
Andira inermis 160
Anemopaegma chamberlaynii
    133
Angelonia salicariifolia 62
Annona muricata 333
    reticulata 333
    squamosa 333
Anoectochilus 249
Anthurium 213, 214, 287
    andreanum 214
    cristallium 214
    macrolobum 215
Antigonon leptopus 137
Aphelandra squarrosa 62
Apium graveolens 326
Aponogeton 292
Arachnis flos-aeris 255
    var. gracilis 256
    var. insignis 256
    "Giant" 256
    hookeriana 256
    var. luteola 256
    hybrids 256
    Ishbel 256
    "Maggie Oei" 256
    maingayi 256
    moschifera 255
    "Red ribbon" 256
    "Yellow ribbon" 256
Aranda City of Singapore 261
    Deborah 261
    Hilda Galistan 261
    Tyersall 261
Aranthera "James Storei" 256
    "Mohamed Haniff" 256
Araucaria 160
    bidwillii 160
    columnaris 160
    cunninghamii 160
    heinsteinii 160
Areca catechu 189
Arenga pinnata 189
Arfeuillia arborescens 160
Argyreia nervosa 132
Aristolochia 137
    gigas var. sturtevantii 137
    tagala 137
Arrabidea magnifica 128, 133
    rotundata 133

Artemisia lactiflora 62
Artocarpus altilis 337
    champeden 337
    heterophyllus 337
Arundina bambusaefolia 249
    graminifolia 249
    speciosa 249
Ascocenda 262
Ascocentrum 262
Asconopsis 262
Asparagus densiflorus 62, 227
    cv. "Myeri" 227
    cv. myersii 62, 227
    cv. "Myers" 62
    cv. "Sprengeri" 63, 227
    plumosus 63, 137
    setaceus 63, 137, 227
Asplenium 208
    caudatum 208
    nidus 208, 307
Aster 63
Asystasia chelonoides 63
    coromandeliana 63
    gangetica 63
Averrhoa bilimbi 336
    carambola 336
Axonopus affinis 201
    compressus 200
Azalea indica 121
Azolla pinnata 292

B

Baccaurea griffithii 349
    motleyana 349
Baeckia frutescens 160
Bambusa ventricosa 227
Baphia nitida 91
Barleria 46, 149, 309
    cristata 91, 94
    lupulina 91
    prionitis 94
Basella alba 324
Bauhinia 132, 309
    acuminata 94
    bidentata 132
    blakeana 161
    kockiana 132
    monandra 161
    purpurea 161
    tomentosa 94
Beaumontia jerdoniana 133
    multiflora 21, 133
    murtonii 133
Begonia vii, 19, 44, 47, 228,
    286, 306, 307, 311
    coccinea 65, 228
    corallina 65
    x erythrophylla 229
    heracleifolia 229
    maculata 65, 228
    masoniana 229

rex 47, 228
    x rex-cultorum 229
    hybrids 229
    x semperflorens-cultorum
    65, 228
Belamcanda chinensis 66
Beloperone guttata 65
Benincasa hispida 321
Bertholettia excelsa 161, 336
Bignonia chamberlaynii 133
    magnifica 128, 133
    rotundata 133
    unguis-cati 133
    venusta 133
Bixa 51, 145
    orellana 94
Blechnum 209
Blyxa 292
Bouea macrophylla 345
    microphylla 345
Bougainvillea 5, 17, 46, 51,
    128, 145, 146, 149, 311
    x Buttiana 129
    glabra 2, 5, 128, 129
      var. formosa 128
      var. magnifica 128,
      149
      var. "Mrs Palmer" 129
      var. sanderiana 145,
      146
    "Golden Glow" 129
    "Louis Wathen" 129
    "Mrs Butt" 5, 128,
    129, 149
    "Mrs Mc Lean" 6,
    129, 149
    peruviana 129
    "Rosa Catalina" 7, 129
    spectabilis 5, 128,
    129, 149
      var. laterita 129
      var. thomasii 129
Brassica juncea 323
    oleracea 323
    alboglabra group 323
    parachinensis 323
    rapa chinensis group 323
Bromeliaceae 222
Browallia elata 66
    speciosa 66
Brownea ariza 161
    grandiceps 161
Brunfelsia 54, 309
    americana 94
    eximia 94
    pauciflora cv. eximia 94
Bryophyllum 47, 282
Buddleia 66

C

Cabomba caroliniana 292

Cactaceae 281
Caesalpinia pulcherrima 2, 51,
94
Caladium 50, 215, 287
x hortulanum 216
humboldtii 216
picturatum 216
Calanthe veratrifolia 252
vestita 252
Calathea 224, 307
insignis 225
lancifolia 225
lindeniana 225
makoyana 225
ornata 225
cv. roseo-lineata 225
picturata 225
cv. argentea 225
cv. vandenheckei
225
wiottii 225
zebrina 226
Calliandra haematocephala 95
surinamensis 95
Callisia elegans 231
Callistemon 161
Calonyction aculeatum 139
Calophyllum inophyllum 161
Calopogonium 37
Camoensia maxima 133
Cananga odorata 161
Canavalia ensiformis 318
gladiata 318
Canna 6, 15, 43, 51, 66
Capsicum annuum 67, 325
var. grossum 326
frutescens 326
Cardiospermum haliacacabum
137
Carex morrowii 67
Carica papaya 347
Carissa carandas 95
Carludovica 213
Caryota mitis 189
Cassia 2
alata 97
auriculata 97
biflora 2, 97
didymocarpas 97
fistula 48, 163
fruticosa 97
grandis 164
javanica 48, 164
laevigata 97
mutijuga 163
nodosa 164
renigera 164
siamea 163
spectabilis 163
Casuarina 45, 142
equisetifolia 164
nobilis 164
rumphiina 164
sumatrana 164
Catharanthus roseus 87
Catimbium muticum 245

Cattleya ashtoni 273
bowringiana 273
mantinii 273
hardyana 273
intermedia 273
Celosia cristata & cvs. 46, 67
Centrosema 37
Cephalocereus 280
Ceratobium 268
Ceratopteris thalictroides 292
Cerbera odollam 164
Cereus 48, 280, 282, 306
Cestrum aurantiacum 98
elegans 98
nocturnum 18, 98
Chara 293
Chlorophytum comosum & cvs.
67, 231
Chonemorpha fragrans 21, 133
Chrysalidocarpus lutescens
189, 212
Chrysanthemum 67
Chrysopogon aciculatus 201
Cinnamomum iners 164
Cissus discolor 231
Citrullus lanatus 322
Citrus 98, 309, 337
aurantifolia 338
limon 340
madurensis 338
maxima 340
sinensis 340
x paradisi 340
Clappertonia ficifolia 110
Clematis 137
Cleome speciosa 74
Clerodendron 2
calamitosum 98
fallax 98
fragrans 98
macrosiphon 98
nutans 98, 287
paniculatum 98
philippinum 98
splendens 133
speciosissimum 98
thomsonae 133, 138
ugandense 98
Clitorea ternatea 138
Clusiaceae 347
Cobaea scandens 138
Cochlospermum religiosum 2,
165
Cocos nucifera 189, 340
Codiaeum variegatum & cvs.
98, 231
Coelogyne asperata 269
dayana 269
kingii 269
mayeriana 269
pandurata 269
rochusseni 269
speciosa 269
Coleus amboinicus 231, 328
x hybridus 68, 231
Colocasia 216

esculenta & cvs. 316
Congea tomentosa 129
velutina 129
Cordia 144
Cordyline 99, 231
terminalis & cvs. 99
Coreopsis 19, 286
basalis 68
perennial 68
tinctoria 68
Coriandrum sativum 326
Corypha umbraculifera 191
Cosmos bipinatus 69
var. "Klondyke" 69
Costus 245
elegans 245
malortieanus 245
speciosus 69, 245
zebrinus 245
Cotyledon 280, 306
Crassula 47, 280, 306
argentea 232
Crassulaceae 282
Cratoxylon formosum 165
Crescentia cujete 165
Crinum 3
amabile 69
asiaticum 70
jagus 69
Crossandra infundibuliformis 70
Cryptanthus zonatus 224
cv. zebrinus 224
Cryptocoryne 293
Cucumis sativus 320
Cucurbita spps 322
Cuphea hyssopifolia 70, 285
ignea 70, 286
miniata 286
x purpurea 70
Cupressus macrocarpa 165, 309
Curcuma 245
domestica 329
Cyamopsis tetragonolobus 319
Cyathea 209
Cycas circinalis 232
rumphii 232
Cymbidium 271
ensifolium 272
finlaysonianum 272
pubescens 272
Cymbopogon citratus 329
Cynodon dactylon 199
Cyperus 293
alternifolius 70, 232
cv. gracilis 71, 232
papyrus 293
Cyphomandra betacea 350
Cyrtostachys renda 191, 212

D
Dacrydium 165
Dahlia 3, 50, 71
Daucus carota 322
Davallia denticulata 209, 307
fejeensis 209
Delonix regia 5, 165

Dendrobium aggregatum 267
anosmum 265
antennatum 268
"Bali" 269
"Caesar" 268
"Champagne" 268
chrysanthum 267
chrysotoxum 267
"Constance" 268
crumenatum 265
dalhousianum 267
discolor 268
farmeri 265, 267
fimbriatum 267
goldii 269
"Helen Park" 269
lasianthera 268
leporinum 268
lineale 268
"Louisae" 269
"Louis Bleriot" 269
moschatum 267
nobile 267
"Pauline" 268, 269
phalaenopsis 267,
268, 269
pierardii 267
"Pompadour" 268, 269
"Rose-Marie" 269
schulleri 268
stratiotes 268
superbiens 269
superbum 265, 267
var. huttonii 265
taurinum 268
thyrsiflorum 267
undulatum 268
veratrifolium 268
"Wilhem Stuber" 269
Derris elliptica 357
Desmodium 202
Dianella ensifolia & cvs. 71
Dianthus chinensis & cvs. 71
Dieffenbachia x bausei 216
maculata 216
cv. Rudolph Roehrs 216
Digitaria didactyla 199
Dillenia indica 166
suffruticosa 166
Dioscorea alata 139, 316
bulbifera 139, 316
esculenta 316
Diospyros discolor 348
kaki 348
Dissotis plumosa 71
Dolichos lablab 318
Dracaena 47, 102, 233, 307
cincta 103
concinna 103
deremensis 102
cv. Bauseii 102
cv. Warneckii 102
fragrans 102
var. lindenii 102
var. Massangeana 102
var. Victoria 102

godseffiana 103
goldieana 103
marginata 103
reflexa 102, 103
sanderiana 103
surculosa 103
Drimiopsis saundersiae 72
Drynaria quercifolia 209
Duranta 2, 51, 149
plumierii 103,
repens 103
Durio zibethinus 341
Dyera costulata 168
Dyssodia tenuiloba 78

E
Echeveria 306
Echinacea purpurea 83
Echinodorus 293, 307
brevipedicellatus 294
cordifolius 294
Ehretia 148
Eichornia crassipes 294
Elaeis guineensis 191
Elateriospermum tapos 168
Encephalartos 233
Encyclia cochleata 273
Enterolobium cyclocarpum 168
saman 168
Epidendrum cochleatum 273
hybrids 273
radicans 273
stamfordianum 273
Epipremnum aureum 217
cv. "Marble Queen"
217
falcifolia 217
giganteum 217
pinnatum 217
Episcia 72, 286
cupreata 72
reptans 72
Eranthemum nervosum 104
pulchellum 104
wattii 73
Eremochloa ophiuroides 201
Erythrina indica 2, 46, 168
variegata 168
Euanthe sanderana 261
Eucharis grandiflora 73, 233
Eugenia 49, 309
grandis 169
javanica 344
michelii 104, 344
uniflora 104, 344
Euodia 106
Euphorbia 280, 306
antiquorum 48, 104, 283
cotinifolia 106, 283
lactea 283
var. splendens 284
milii 284
neriifolia 233, 283
polyacantha 283
pulcherrima 106
tirucalli 106, 284

Euphorbiaceae 283
Euphoria malaiense 349
Eurycles amboinensis 73
Evodia sp. 106
Excoecaria bicolor 149

F
Fagraea fragrans 169
Ficus 309, 342
auriculata 171
benjamina 169, 233, 307
deltoidea 107, 233
elastica 169, 233
lyrata 233
microcarpa 169
pumila 133, 233
religiosa 169
roxburghii 171, 342
Filicium decipiens 171
Fittonia verschaffeltii 233
Flacourtia inermis 350
jangomas 350
Fortunella 309
Fushcia 107

G
Gaillardia 73
Galphimia glauca 2, 73, 309
Garcinia atroviridis 347
mangostana 347
Gardenia 2, 146, 309
carinata 171
jasminoides 2, 107
var. fortuniana 107
Gerbera jamesonii 74
Gladiolus 50, 74
Gliricidia sepium 46, 172
Globba 245
Gloriosa 50
rothschildiana 139
superba 139
virescens 139
Gloxinia 44, 85, 287
Gnetum gnemon 172
Gomphrena globosa 74
Grammatophyllum scriptum 271
speciosum 271
Graptophyllum pictum 233
Grewia tomentosa 172
Gustavia superba 172
Gynandropsis speciosa 74
Gynura aurantiaca 75, 234
Guttiferae 347

H
Haemanthus 286
Haemaria 249
Haworthia 234, 306
linifolia 234
margaritifera 234
reinwardtii 234
subfasciata 234
Hedychium 245
coronarium 75
Helianthus angustifolius 75
annuus 75

perennial 75
tuberosus 317
Helichrysum bracteatum 75
Heliconia 51
humilis 75
pendula 75
psittacorum 75
sp. 77
striata 234
Hemerocallis fulva 77
Hemigraphis alternata 77,
107, 235
colorata 235
repanda 235
Hevea braziliensis 172
Hibiscus 2, 46, 49, 54, 142, 311
mutabilis 110, 149
rosa-sinensis 107, 235
var. cooperi 235
sabdariffa 325
schizopetalus 110
syriacus 110
tiliaceus 173
Hippeastrum 51, 77, 286
Holmskioldia sanguinea 129
Homalocladium platycladum
115, 236
Homalomena rubra 217
wallisii 217
Honckenya ficifolia 110
Hydrangea macrophylla 77
Hydrilla verticillata 294
Hydrocleys nymphoides 294
Hygrophila difformis 294
Hymenaea courbaril 173
Hymenatherum 78, 286
Hymenocallis littoralis 18, 78

I
Impatiens balsamina 63
oncidiodes 63
wallerana & cvs. 63
Ipomoea 311
alba 139
aquatica 324
batatus 315
bona-nox 139
cairica 139
carnea 131
digitata 139
horsfalliae 139
learii 139
pulchella 139
Iresine herbstii 78, 236
Ixora 2, 17, 46, 50, 51, 54, 287
chinensis 111
coccinea 7, 111, 149
finlaysoniana 110
javanica 7, 111, 149
"Sunkist" 7, 285

J
Jacaranda 51, 173
ficifolia 173
obtusifolia 173
Jacobinia coccinea 78

Jacquemontia pentantha 139
Jasminum 131
rex 140
sambac 140
Jatropha 51, 54
betoni caefolia 112
curcas 236
gossypifolia 111
multifida 111
pandurifolia 111
podagrica 112, 236, 284
Juniperus 173
Justicia betonicaefolia 112
brandegeana 65

K
Kaempferia galanga 245
Kagawara 263
Kalanchoe 47, 280, 282, 306
blossfeldiana 283
daigremontiana 236, 282
marmorata 236
orgyalis 236
pinnata 236, 282
tomentosa 236
tubiflora 236, 282
Kochia scoparia 236
Kopsia 149
fruticosa 112
singaporensis 112

L
Lablab niger 318
Lactuca sativa 323
Laelio-cattleya 273
Lagenaria siceraria 320
Lagerstroemia 45, 309
floribunda 173
flos-reginae 173
indica 114
speciosa 173
Languas galanga 329
Lansium domesticum 341
Lantana 2, 114, 146, 149, 286
camara 79, 114
montevidensis 79, 114
sellowiana 79, 114, 286
Lawsonia inermis 114
Lemna 294
Libocedrus 146
Licuala 192
grandis 192, 212
Ligustrum sinense 146
Limnocharis flava 295
Limnophila indica 295
Litchi chinensis 349
Livistona chinensis 192, 212
rotundifolia 192, 212
Lochnera rosea 87
Lonicera 133
Ludwigia natans 295
repens 295
Luffa angulata 320
cylindrica 321
Lycopersicon esculentum 320

M

Macfadyena unguis-cati 133
Macodes 249
Malpighia coccigera 148, 309
Malvaviscus arboreus 114
Mammillaria 280, 306
Mangifera caesia 345
    foetida 345
    indica 345
    odorata 345
Manihot 114
    dulcis 115
    esculenta 315
Manilkara zapota 337
Marantaceae 224
Maranta 226, 307
    arundinacea cv. variegata 226
    leuconeura var. erythro-neura 227
      var. kerchoviana 227
      var. leuconeura 226
      var. massangeana 226
Marsilea crenata 295
Melaleuca leucadendron 176
Melampodium cinereum 46, 79
Melastoma 115
    malabathricum 115
    mutica 115
Melia 309
    azederach 176
    excelsa 176
    indica 176
Mentha spicata 328
Mesembryanthemum 284
Mesua ferrea 176
Michelia 309
    alba 177
    champaca 177
    figo 115
Millettia atropurpurea 177
Mimusops elengi 177, 309
Mina lobata 140
Mirabilis jalapa 79
Mokara 263
Momordica charantia 321
Monochoria 295
    elata 296
    hastata 295
    vaginalis 295
Monstera deliciosa 217
    epipremnoides 219
    leichtlinii 219
Moringa oleifera 329
Mucuna bennettii 21, 135
    pruriens var. utilis 318
Muehlenbeckia 236
    platyclados 115
Muntingia calabura 50, 177, 309
Murraya paniculata 115, 151, 309
Musa 237, 335
Mussaenda erythrophylla 131
    glabra 131
    philippica "Aurorae" 115

Myriophyllum 296

N

Napoleona 116
Nasturtium officinale 324
Nautilocalyx lynchii 237
Nelumbo lutea 296
    nucifera 296
Neoregelia carolinae 224
    spectabilis 224
Nephelium lappaceum 349
    malaiense 349
    mutabile 349
Nephrolepis biserrata 210, 307
    cv. furcans 210
    cordifolia 210
    cv. duffii 210
    exaltata 210
    cv. Bostonensis 210
Neptunia oleracea 296
Nerium indicum 2, 116
    odorum 116
    oleander 116
Nicolaia 245
    speciosa 329
Notocactus 280
Nyctanthes arbor-tristis 116
Nymphaea capensis 296, 297
    lotus 296, 297
    mexicana 296, 297
    pygmaea 297
    zanzibarensis 297
Nymphoides indica 297

O

Ochna serrulata 118
Ocimum basilicum 326
    canum 326
Odontadenia grandiflora 21, 43, 135
Oncidium 273
    cebolatta 274
    flexuosum 273, 274
    x "Golden Shower" 273
    haematochilum 274
    hybrids 273
    kramerianum 274
    lanceanum 274
    luridum 274
    sphacelatum 273
    splendidum 274
    varicosum 274
Oncosperma tigillarium 192
Ophiopogon intermedius 237
Oplismenus hirtellus 237
Opuntia 48, 237, 280, 282, 306
Orthosiphon aristatus 79
    stamineus 79
Oryza sativa 297
Osbeckia 71
Oxalidaceae 336
Oxalis corymbosa 79

P

Pachyrhizus tuberosus 316
Pachystachys coccinea 78

lutea 79
Pandanus 118, 237, 309
    dubius 118
    pacificus 118
    pygmaeus 118
    sanderi 118
    veitchii 118
Pandorea jasminoides 135
    ricasoliana 135
Paphiopedilum barbatum 252
    bellatulum 252
    callosum 252
    exul 252
    glaucophyllum 252
    lowii 252
    "Milmanii" 252
    niveum 252, 287
    philippinense 252
    praestans 252
Paraphalaenopsis denevei 264
Paspalum conjugatum 201
Passiflora edulis 136, 348
    laurifolia 135, 348
    quadrangularis 136, 348
    vitifolia 136
Pedilanthus tithymaloides 80, 284
Pellaea rotundifolia 210
Pellionia daveauana 239
    pulchra 239
    repens 239
Peltophorum pterocarpum 177
Pentas bussei 81
    carnea 80
    coccinea 81
    lanceolata 80
Peperomia 47, 239
    argyreia 239
    caperata 239
    griseoargentea 239
    hederifolia 239
    magnoliifolia & cvs. 239
    obtusifolia 239
    sandersii 239
    scandens & cvs. 239
    serpens 239
Pereskia 280
    aculeata 136, 239, 282
    bleo 282
Pergularia odoratissima 140
Peristeria 252
Peristrophe 81
Persea americana 333
Petraea rugosa 3, 118
    volubilis 131
Petroselinum crispum 328
Petunia 44
    x hybrida 81
Phaeomeria 245
    speciosa 329
Phaius 252
Phalaenopsis amabilis 263, 264
    amboinensis 263
    cochlearis 263
    cornu-cervi 263
    denevei 264

    fuscata 263
    gigantea 263
    grandiflora 263
    hybrids 264
    lueddemanniana 263
    lindenii 263
    mariae 263
    sanderana 263
    schillerana 263
    stuartiana 263
    sumatrana 263
    violacea 263, 264
Phaleria blumei 118
Phaseolus lunatus 318
    vulgaris 317
Philodendron 48, 219
    bipinnatifidum 220
    domesticum 220
    erubescens 220
    hastatum 220
    scandens var. oxycardium 220
    selloum 220
    squamiferum 221
Phlox drummondii 82
Phyllanthus myrtifolius 119, 286, 309
Phymatodes scolopendria 211
Pilea cadieri 240
    involucrata 240
    microphylla 240, 287, 307
    nummularifolia 240
Pinanga 192, 212
Pinus 309
    caribbaea 180
    merkusii 180
Piper porphyrophyllum 240
    sarmentosa 240
Pistia stratiotes 297
Pitcairnia angustifolia 224
Pithecellobium 309
    dulce 180
    jiringa 180
Pittosporum tobira 151
Platycerium coronarium 211
Platycodon grandiflorus 82
Pleomele reflexa 103
Plumbago auriculata 51, 82
    capensis 82
    indica 82
    rosea 82
Plumeria 2, 48
    obtusa 119
    rubra 119
Podocarpus 309
    macrophyllus 180
    polystachyus 180
    rumphii 181
Podranaea ricasoliana 135
Polyalthia longifolia 181
Polygonum 325
Polypodium scolopendria 211
Polyscias 119, 146, 240, 309
    balfouriana 119
    filicifolia 119

fruticosa 119
guilfoylei 119
Pometia pinnata 181
Pongamia pinnata 181
Porana paniculata 136
Portlandia grandiflora 121
Portulaca 285, 286
Portulacaria afra 240
Pritchardia 212
Pseuderanthemum 241
atropurpureum 121, 241
reticulatum 82, 121, 241
Psidium guajava 344
Psophocarpus tetragonolobus 317
Pteris cretica 211
ensiformis 211, 307
Pterocarpus indicus 3, 46, 181
Ptychosperma macarthuri 192, 212
Pueraria 37
Pyrostegia venusta 133

Q
Quisqualis indica 136

R
Randia macrantha 17, 50, 121
Raphanus sativus 322
var. longipinnatus 322
Raphidophora pinnata 217
Ravenala madagascariensis 193
Rebutia 280, 306
Reevesia thyrsoidea 181
Renanstylis 262
Renanthera coccinea 256
hybrids 256
inschootiana 256
matutina 256
monachica 256
storei 256
Rhapis excelsa 193, 212
Rhodamnia trinerva 181
Rhododendron indicum 121
Rhodomyrtus tomentosa 124, 184
Rhoeo spathacea 241
Rhynchospora aurea 293
Rhynchostylis 262
Rhynco vanda 262
Ricinus communis 124
Rosa 82
Roupellia grata 131
Roystonea regia 193
Rudbeckia 286
hirta 83, 286
laciniata 83
purpurea 83
Ruellia ciliosa 83
Russellia 19
equisetiformis 83
juncea 83
sarmentosa 83

S
Sagittaria 297, 307

montevidensis 298
Saintpaulia 287
ionantha 47, 83, 306
Salix 309
sp. 184
tetrasperma 184
Salvia coccinea 85
farinacea 85
splendens 83
Salvinia cucullata 298
Samanea saman 168
Sambucus 124
Sanchezia nobilis 151
Sandoricum koetjape 184
Sansevieria cylindrica 241, 285
trifasciata 47, 241, 285
cv. hahnii & other cvs. 241
Sapindaceae 349
Saraca declinata 184
indica 184
thaipingensis 184
Saritaea magnifica 128, 133
Schefflera 241
Scindapsus aureus 217
pictus 221
Sechium edule 322
Sedum morganianum 243
Selaginella 211, 287, 307
wildenovii 211
Setcreasea pallida 243
purpurea 243
Sinningia speciosa & cvs. 44, 85, 287
Solandra longiflora 124
Solanum macranthum 2, 124, 184
melongena 319
Solidago brachystachys 85
virgaurea 85
Spathiphyllum 221
Spathodea campanulata 185
Spathoglottis aurea 251
"Dwarf legion" 251
kimballiana 251
"Parsonsii" 251
plicata 250, 251
"Primrose" 251
"Singapore Giant" 251
tomentosa 251
Sphenomeris chinensis 211
Spondias pinnata 347
Stapelia 280, 285, 306
Staurochilus fasciata 256
Stenochlaens palustris 211
Stenolobium stans 125
Stenotaphrum secundatum 201
Stephanotis 136
Sterculia parvifolia 185
Stigmaphyllon ciliatum 140
lancifolium 140
Streblus 146
Strobilanthes dyerianus 243
Strongylodon macrobotrys 136
Strophanthus gratus 131
Swietenia macrophylla 185

Syngonium podophyllum & cvs. 221
Synnema triflorum 294
Syzygium aqueum 344
grandis 169
jambos 344
malaccense 344
samarangense 344

T
Tabebuia 185
Tabernaemontana 125
Tacca 243
Tagetes erecta 79
patula 79
Talinum triangulare & cv. 244, 324
Tamarindus indicus 185, 309
Tecoma stans 125, 309
Tecomaria capensis 86, 132, 151
Tectona grandis 187
Telosma cordata 140
Terminalia catappa 187
Thevetia 51, 125, 309
Thuja orientalis 17, 187
Thunbergia 2, 21, 125, 136
affinis 125, 151
coccinea 137
erecta 125
grandiflora 136
kirkii 125
laurifolia 136
mysorensis 136
Thysalonaena maxima 125
Tithonia 126
rotundifolia 86
Torenia fournieri 86
Tradescantia blossfeldiana 244
flamineus 244
virginiana 244
Trapa bicornis 298
Tribulus terrestris 86
Trichoglottis fasciata 256
Tricosanthes anguina 321
Triphasia 148
Tristellateia australasiae 140
Tropaeolum majus 87
Turnera ulmifolia 87
Typha angustifolia 299

U
Utricularia flexuosa 299

V
Vallisneria spiralis 299
Vanda "Amy" 255
coerulea 260
dearei 260
denisoniana 260
"Diana" 255
"E.M.E Dinger" 261
hookeriana 6, 7, 254
hybrids 254
hybrid terete 255
insignis 260

"Josephine van Brero" 261
lamellata 261
luzonica 261
"Marguerite Maron" 261
"Miss Joaquim" 6, 7, 254
white form 255
Rothschildiana 261
sanderana 261
semi-terete 261
suavis 261
sumatrana 261
"Tan Chay Yan" 261
teres 6, 254, 260
tricolor 260
tricuspidata 255
Vanda-Arachnis hybrids 261
Verbena tenera 19, 87
Veitchia merrillii 194
Vernonia elliptica 132
Victoria amazonica 299
regia 299
Vigna 37
unguiculata 317
Vinca rosea 87
Violet hederacea 87
Vitex negundo 126

W
Wedelia triloba 87
Wrightia religiosa 128, 309
Wormia suffruticosa 166

X
Xanthosoma 222
lindenii 222
sagittifolium 316
violaceum 222, 316

Y
Yucca 285

Z
Zamia 244
Zantedeschia aethiopica 222
elliotiana 222
Zea mays 319
Zebrina pendula 244
cv. purpusii 244
cv. quadricolor 244
Zephyranthes 3, 17, 51, 286
cardinalis 87
Zingiberaceae 244
Zingiber officinalis 329
spectabile 245
Zinnia angustifolia 88
elegans 88
linearis 88, 286, 306
Ziziphus 309
Zoysia "Emerald" 200
hybrids 200
japonica 200
matrella 200
tenuifolia 200